WORKING AMERICANS

1880–2011

Volume XII:
Our History Through Music

WORKING AMERICANS

1880–2011

Volume XII:
Our History Through Music

By Scott Derks

A Universal Reference Book

Grey House
Publishing

PUBLISHER:	Leslie Mackenzie
EDITORIAL DIRECTOR:	Laura Mars
ASSOCIATE EDITOR:	Diana Delgado
PRODUCTION MANAGER:	Kristen Thatcher
MARKETING DIRECTOR:	Jessica Moody
AUTHOR:	Scott Derks
CONTRIBUTORS:	Jael Bridgemahon, Jimmy Copening, Lucia Derks, Suzi Kirby, Robert Long, Michael Marturana, J'Vontea Perminter, Jim Reindollar
COPYEDITOR:	Elaine Alibrandi
COMPOSITION:	NPC Inc.

Grey House Publishing, Inc.
4919 Route 22
Amenia, NY 12501
518.789.8700 FAX 845.373.6390
www.greyhouse.com
e-mail: books@greyhouse.com

Publisher's Cataloging-In-Publication Data

Derks, Scott.
  Working Americans 1880-2011 / by Scott Derks.

  v. : ill. ; cm.

Title varies.
"A universal reference book."
Includes bibliographical references and indexes.
Contents: v. 1. The working class—v.2. The middle class—v.3. The upper class—v.4. Their children.—v.5. At war.—v.6. Women at work—v.7. Social movements—v.8. Immigrants—v.9. Revolutionary war to civil war—v.10. Sports & Recreation.—v.11. Inventors & Entrepreneurs.—v.12. Our History Through Music.
  ISBN: 1-891482-81-5 (v.1)
  ISBN: 1-891482-72-6 (v.2)
  ISBN: 1-930956-38-X (v.3)
  ISBN: 1-930956-35-5 (v.4)
  ISBN: 1-59327-024-1 (v.5)
  ISBN: 1-59237-063-Z (v.6)
  ISBN: 1-59237-101-9 (v.7)
  ISBN: 978-1-59237-197-6 (v.8)
  ISBN: 978-1-59237-101-3 (v.9)
  ISBN: 1-59237-441-7 (v. 10)
  ISBN: 1-59237-565-3 (v. 11)
  ISBN: 978-1-59237-762-6 (v. 12)

1. Working class—United States—History. 2. Labor—United States—History. 3. Occupation—United States—History. 4. Social classes—United States—History. 5. Immigrants—Employment—United States—History. 6. United States—Economic conditions. 7. Music—United States—History. 1. Title.

HD 8066 .D47 2000
305.5/0973/0904

DEDICATION

To my musical friends Will Zimmer, Tom Berry and Bobby Long, thanks for your help and friendship.

TABLE OF CONTENTS

1930 – 1939 INTRODUCTION

1940 – 1949 INTRODUCTION

1970 – 1979 INTRODUCTION

1980 – 1989 INTRODUCTION

1990 – 1999 INTRODUCTION

PREFACE

This book is the twelfth in a series examining the social and economic lives of working Americans. In this volume, the focus is on music and musicians whose skill and creativity bring so much joy. Without their willingness to practice countless hours each day, their excitement in exploring new sounds and technology, their creativity not always with monetary reward, the world would be a much poorer place. Their stories range from a self-trained clarinetist in John Philip Sousa's Marching Band to the wild world of funk master George Clinton. This volume explores the role emerging technology played in the popularity of crooners, Broadway musicals and the demise of records, as well as life as a "Dead head" following the Grateful Dead from event to event. Along the way we encounter a rock critic turned promoter who represented one of Britain's premier acts, an opera singer who mesmerized the royalty of Europe, a small-town barbershop quartet, a fledgling band who spent a summer playing at Myrtle Beach, South Carolina, and a master guitar maker with dozens of playing awards to his credit. In all, there are 36 stories about making music, learning to perform and the joys of a perfect set.

In this volume of the *Working Americans* series, a variety of musical occupations are explored, ranging from copyright attorney to opera singer, guitar maker to disc jockey, traveling musician to promoter. For most, the love of music began in childhood and blossomed continuously as they grew older—whether they were amateurs or professional performers. Luck occasionally helped them gain notice and opportunity, but only dedication to their craft and talent allowed them to succeed. Some became rich through music; some simply enjoyed their lives more fully. As in previous volumes, all the profiles are modeled on real people and events, with details added based on statistics, the popularity of an idea, or writings of the time. Unlike most previous volumes, the need to identify well known performers by name overrode the historical pattern of these books using no factual names. Therefore, the majority of the individuals profiled in this volume include their real names. They are:

Amy Beach (1898), Arthur Farwell (1909), Geraldine Farrar (1916), Zo Elliott (1918), Florence Mills (1927), Russ Columbo (1934), Mary Lou Williams (1939), Charlie Christian (1942), Helen Jones (1945), Martin Block (1949), Carol Lawrence (1957), Gil Evans (1958), Johnny Bragg (1959), Estelle Axton (1964), Reid Miles (1966), Danny Goldberg (1976), Lalo Guerrero (1979), George Clinton (1983), Soni Sonefeld (1995) and Wayne Henderson (2011).

Otherwise, every effort has been made to profile accurately the individual's expertise, as well as home and work experiences. To ensure that the profiles reflect the mood of each decade and the feelings of the subjects, letters, biographies, interviews, high school annuals, and magazine articles were consulted and used. In some cases, the people profiled represent national trends and feelings, but mostly they represent themselves. Ultimately, it is the working Americans and their activities—along with their investment, spending decisions, passions and jobs—that shape the society and economy of the United States.

The first three volumes of *Working Americans: 1880-1999* explore the economic lives and loves of working-class, middle-class and upper-class Americans through the eyes and wallets of more than 100 families. Employing pictures, stories, statistics and advertisements of the period, these intimate profiles study their jobs, wages, family life, expenditures and hobbies throughout the decades. Although separated by levels of wealth, each volume also captures the struggles and joys of a shifting American economy and the transformation they brought to communities and families in the workplace, regardless of economic status. The fourth volume, *Their Children*, builds upon the social and economic issues explored previously by examining the lives of children across the entire spectrum of economic status. Issues addressed include parents, child labor, education, peer pressure, food, fads and fun. *Volume V: Americans at War* explores the life-changing elements of war and discusses how enlisted personnel, officers and civilians handle the stress, exhilaration, boredom and brutality of America's various wars, conflicts and incursions. *Volume VI: Women at Work* celebrates the contributions of women, chronicling both their progress and roadblocks along the way, and highlighting the critical role of women in the front lines of change.

Working Americans VII: Social Movements explores the various ways American men and women feel called upon to challenge accepted conventions, whether the issue is cigarette smoking in 1901 or the construction of a massive hydroelectric dam in 1956. *Working Americans VIII: Immigrants* examines the lives of first- and second-generation immigrants with a focus on their journey to America, their search for identity and their emotions experienced in the new land. *Working Americans IX: The Revolutionary War to the Civil War* steps back in time to chronicle the lives of 36 families from the 1770s to the 1860s, detailing their troubles and triumphs, whether they were farmers, postal clerks, whiskey merchants, lawyers or cabinetmakers. *Working Americans X: Sports and Recreation* tackles the diverse and ever-changing world of competitive sports in America from the viewpoint of the professional, the amateur and the spectator. Along the way, we meet Olympic swimmers, basketball players who rarely play, boxers with extraordinary stamina, weightlifters of unbelievable determination and weekend athletes thrilled by the opportunity to be in the open air.

Working *Americans XI* focuses on the inventors and entrepreneurs whose willingness to take risks transformed America. This romp through time unveils the efforts needed to invent zippers, vacuum cleaners and FM radio. Entrepreneurs establish insurance companies, launch restaurant chains and seed companies with varying degrees of success.

Each of these 12 volumes—embracing the lives of families throughout American history—strives to tell a simple story of struggling, hoping and enduring. And if I've learned anything in the last 13 years of writing these books, it is that the American spirit lives on, maintains its free will, and endeavors to meet the challenges of the day. This spirit is alive and well, and still lives in America.

Scott Derks

INTRODUCTION

Working Americans 1880-2011 Volume XII: Our History Through Music is the 12th volume in the *Working Americans* series. Like its predecessors, this work profiles the lives of Americans – how they lived, how they worked, how they thought – decade by decade. The earliest volumes focus on economic status or social issues. More recent volumes focus on a specific group of Americans – athletes in *Volume X* and entrepreneurs in *Volume XI*. This volume highlights American music and musicians – from classical performers to rock star groupies, from production crews to impresarios. *Our History Through Music* depicts the soundtrack of America – from Appalachia to the Big Apple, from the phonograph to iTunes.

Arranged in 12 chapters, this newest *Working Americans* includes three **Profiles** per chapter for a total of 36. Each profile offers personal insight using *Life at Home, Life at Work* and *Life in the Community* categories. These personal topics are followed by historical and economic data of the time. **Historical Snapshots** chronicle major milestones. **Lists of Popular Songs, Quotes of Famous Musicians**, and **Timelines** of music-related events, i.e. *Development of the Clarinet,* and the *Creation of the Victor Phonograph Company* appear throughout. A variety of **News Features** puts the subject's life and work in context of the day. These common elements, as well as specialized data, such as **Selected Prices**, in currency of the time, punctuate each chapter and act as statistical comparisons between decades. The 36 individuals profiled in this volume represent all regions of the country, and a wide variety of ages and ethnic backgrounds.

In *Volume XII: Our History Through Music*, you will:

- March with clarinet player Albert Gustoff in John Philip Sousa's Band.
- Go behind the scenes with diva Geraldine Farrar.
- Read of the rivalry between crooners Russ Columbo and Bing Crosby.
- Learn how the Lindbergh kidnapping created the disc jockey.
- Join the Prisonaires behind bars by day and on stage outside by night.
- Get in the mood with Blue Note Records designer Reid Miles.
- Build guitars with master Wayne Henderson.

All twelve volumes, regardless of economic status, time period, or specific focus, offer a unique, almost uncanny, look at those Americans whose talents, desires, motivations, struggles, and values shaped – and continue to shape – this nation. Without exception, the 401 individuals profiled in the twelve volumes of this *Working Americans* series are working toward their version of the American dream.

Like its companion volumes, *Working Americans 1880-2011 Volume XII: Our History Through Music* is a compilation of original research (personal diaries and family histories) plus printed material (government statistics, commercial advertisements, and news features). The text, in easy-to-read bulleted format, is supported with hundreds of graphics, such as photos, advertisements, pages from printed material, letters, and documents.

All twelve *Working Americans* volumes are "point in time" books, designed to illustrate the reality of that particular time. Some Americans portrayed in this 12th volume went on to realize fame and fortune, while others did not. What they all did, however, is help America find her voice, and many of their stories and struggles march on.

Praise for earlier volumes –

" . . . *by arranging the people chronologically rather than alphabetically, users can see how industry changed over time and how ideas and inventions built upon each other. . . .an outstanding overview of the unique inventions and entrepreneurial efforts . . . This work is highly recommended for school libraries from middle school through high school as well as college libraries from community college through graduate school. It should also be found in public libraries of every size.*

American Reference Books Annual

"*this volume engages and informs, contributing significantly and meaningfully to the historiography of the working class in America...a compelling and well-organized contribution for those interested in social history and the complexities of working Americans.*"

Library Journal

"*these interesting, unique compilations of economic and social facts, figures, and graphs...support multiple research needs [and] will engage and enlighten patrons in high school, public, and academic library collections.*"

Booklist

"*[the author] adds to the genre of social history known as 'history from the bottom up' ...Recommended for all colleges and university library collections.*"

Choice

"*the volume succeeds at presenting various cultural, regional, economic and age-related points of view... [it is] visually appealing [and] certainly a worthwhile purchase...*"

Feminist Collections

ACKNOWLEDGEMENTS

Writing this even dozen volume of the *Working Americans* series has been enormous fun. Music is inherently entwined in the human soul—at once as individual as a snowflake and as familiar as an old pair of boots that fit like a glove. Once again, it took a tribe of talented folks to make this volume possible. Thanks go to writers/researchers Jimmy Copening, Michael Marturana, Jim Reindollar, as well as contributors Robert Long, Suzi Kirby, Laura Mars, Lucia Derks and J'Vontea Perminter. Photography help came from Will Zimmer, technical tips from Tom Berry and Bill Johnson, and editing from Elaine "Brandy" Alibrandi (who wore out YouTube listening to the songs mentioned in the book). As always, support was abundant from Grey House Publishing and the library staffs of Blue Ridge Regional Library, Wake Forest University, and Saluda, North Carolina.

1880–1899

The last two decades of the nineteenth century danced in the reflected glow of the Gilded Age, when the wealth of a tiny percentage of Americans knew no bounds. It was a time of vast, accumulated wealth and an abundance of emerging technology—all racing to keep up with the restless spirit of the American people. The wealth propelled the founding of the New York Metropolitan Opera in 1883, and the restless spirit discovered its voice in the emerging popularity of ragtime music. The rapid expansion of railroads opened up the nation to new industries, new markets, and the formation of monopolistic trusts that catapulted a handful of corporations into positions of unprecedented power and wealth. This expanding technology also triggered the movement of workers from farm to factory, the rapid expansion of wage labor, and the explosive growth of cities. Farmers, merchants and small-town artisans found themselves increasingly dependent on regional and national market forces. The shift in the concentrations of power was unprecedented in American history. At the same time, professionally trained workers were reshaping America's economy alongside business managers or entrepreneurs eager to capture their piece of the American pie. It was an economy on a roll with few rudders or regulations. In this environment, the popular song industry known as Tin Pan Alley both prospered and dramatically influenced the taste and direction of American music.

Across America the economy—along with its work force—was running away from the land. Before the Civil War, the United States was overwhelmingly an agricultural nation. By the end of the century, non-agricultural occupations employed nearly two-thirds of the workers. As important, two of every three Americans came to rely on wages instead of self-employment as farmers or artisans. At the same time, industrial growth began to center around cities, where wealth accumulated for a few who understood how to harness and use railroads, create new consumer markets, and manage a ready supply of cheap, trainable labor. Jobs offering steady wages and the promise of a better life for workers' children drew people from the farms into the cities, which grew at twice the rate of the nation as a whole. A modern, industrially based work force emerged from the traditional farmlands, led by men skilled at managing others and the complicated flow of materials required to keep a factory operating. This led to an increasing demand for attorneys, The new cities of America were home to great wealth and poverty—both produced by the massive migrations and influx of immigrants willing to work at any price. It was a time symbolized by Andrew Carnegie's steel mills, John D. Rockefeller's organization of the Standard Oil monopoly, and the manufacture of Alexander Graham Bell's wonderful invention, the telephone. By 1894, the United States had become the world's leading industrial power, producing more than England, France, and Germany—its three largest competitors—combined. For much of this period, the nation's industrial energy focused on the need for railroads requiring large quantities of labor, iron, steel, stone, and lumber. In 1883, nine-tenths of the nation's entire production of steel went into rails. The most important invention of the period—in an era of tremendous change and innovation—may have been the Bessemer converter, which transformed pig iron into steel at a relatively low cost, increasing steel output 10 times from 1877 to 1892.

The greatest economic event during the last two decades of the nineteenth century was the great wave of immigration that swept America. It is believed to be the largest worldwide population movement in human history, bringing more than 10 million people to the United States to fill the expanding need for workers. In the 1880s alone, 5.25 million immigrants arrived, more than in the first six decades of the nineteenth century. This wave was dominated by Irish, German, and English workers. Scandinavia, Italy, and China sent scores of eager workers, normally men, to fill the expanding labor needs of the United States. To attract this much-needed labor force, railroad and steamship companies advertised throughout Europe and China the glories of American life. To an economically depressed world, it was a welcome call.

The national wealth in 1890 was $65 billion; nearly $40 billion was invested in land and buildings, $9 billion in railroads, and $4 billion in manufacturing and mining. By 1890, 25 percent of the world's output of coal was mined in the United States. Annual production of crude petroleum went from 500,000 barrels in 1860 to 63.6 million in 1900. This was more than the wealth of Great Britain, Russia, and Germany put together.

Despite all the signs of economic growth and prosperity, America's late-nineteenth-century economy was profoundly unstable. Industrial expansion was undercut by a depression from 1882 to 1885, followed in 1893 by a five-year-long economic collapse that devastated rural and urban communities across America. As a result, job security for workers just climbing onto the industrial stage was often fleeting. Few wage-earners found full-time work for the entire year. The unevenness in the economy was caused both by the level of change underway and irresponsible speculation, but more generally to the stubborn adherence of the federal government to a highly inflexible gold standard as the basis of value for currency.

Between the very wealthy and the very poor emerged a new middle stratum, whose appearance was one of the distinctive features of late-nineteenth-century America. The new middle class fueled the purchase of one million light bulbs a year by 1890, even though the first electric light was only 11 years old. It was the middle class also that flocked to buy Royal Baking Powder, (which was easier to use and faster than yeast) and supported the emergence and spread of department stores that were sprouting up across the nation.

1891 PROFILE

Joshua Hamilton was enamored with the idea of being part of a barbershop quartet, with its unaccompanied four-part harmonies and ringing chords.

Life at Home

- When Joshua Hamilton turned 35 years old, he discovered a new love that haunted him day and night.
- Married with four children—all girls—Joshua found himself humming to himself late in the afternoon as he considered ways to satisfy his new obsession.
- His wife thought his request was crazy, but supported his need to be away every Tuesday night and many a Sunday afternoon.
- But she still could not understand how or why being a member of a barbershop quartet had captured his soul.
- Joshua had sung in the church choir most of his life—his baritone voice prized by every preacher who had traveled through Cincinnati, Ohio—but without explanation, he insisted that being a member of a barbershop quartet was different.
- Born in 1856, prior to the war that divided and devastated the nation, Joshua grew up the son of a merchant whose every expectation was that his biblically named son would follow in his footsteps.
- Not that he objected—Joshua was good at math, found peace in the often meticulous process of stocking shelves, and loved to flirt with the girls who came into the store to buy candy and cloth.
- In fact, he met his future wife in the store and assisted her in the buying of whale-bone corsets and other unmentionables that ladies seemed to require.

Joshua Hamilton joined a barbershop quartet at age 35, bringing new meaning to his life.

Joshua courted his future wife around her family's piano, his rich voice drowning out other suitors.

- As was the custom at all stores, no prices were shown on the merchandise, which allowed him to offer her great deals that made her feel special.
- He courted her around her father's piano, where his rich singing voice set him apart from other suitors; during Sunday night family "sings" around the piano, he was always the star.
- Nearly half the homes in middle-class Cincinnati housed pianos for family song sessions; when friends gathered, group singing was often planned and expected.
- Thomas Edison's phonograph machine, invented a decade earlier, was still not in wide distribution, so live music dominated.
- The Hamilton clan had moved to Ohio from Pennsylvania in the 1840s to escape the onslaught of German and Welsh immigrants arriving from Europe.
- Grandpa Hamilton concluded Pennsylvania was just getting too crowded and it was time to move; he established a new store in the countryside outside Cincinnati and watched in amazement as America's population explosion commenced to crowd around him once again.
- By the 1870s, the Cincinnati store was practically within the city and no longer stocked with steel plows or harnesses for a brace of oxen.
- Times had changed: For every farmer moving to the area, there were 20 men looking for factory jobs, which paid steadily and required less risk.
- But supplies for horses and mules still dominated one corner of the store despite the epizootic of 1872, when four million horses—nearly one-fourth of the nation's stock—died of the disease, bringing the nation to a virtual standstill for three months before the winter weather killed the mosquitoes that transmitted the virus.
- The outbreak was blamed on unrestricted immigrant microbes; similarly, the Panic of 1873 was blamed on an excessive supply of unskilled labor, which had run amuck in the economy.
- In 1882, a $0.50 head tax was imposed on any immigrant entering the country by water, but it did little to slow down the flood of immigrants seeking opportunity in America.
- Most arrived saying they planned to return to their native land once they had made a fortune; one quarter did return, and many more crossed back and forth on an annual basis.
- Immigrants also arrived in Cincinnati as children, wards of the New York Children's Aid Society, whose "orphan trains" annually moved thousands of abandoned and orphaned children from East Coast cities to new homes in the West.

Grandpa Hamilton stocked his Cincinnati store with horse and mule supplies.

- Joshua was four when he first witnessed the spectacle of dozens of children—many of whom couldn't speak English—lined up at the railroad depot station.
- Couples desiring a child would then pick one or two children from the group and take them home for adoption.
- The rest would be loaded onto trains and taken to the next city where they would be picked over by the next set of adults.
- In all, 90,000 children found shelter in this manner—sometimes purely as unpaid labor, sometimes as members of the family.
- The New York Children's Aid Society was the source of Joshua's best friend Wayne, who became the town mortician and a fellow member of the barbershop quartet.
- Wayne was born Gert Derkondoeff, but his new adoptive family didn't think it sounded American enough; they told him at breakfast on his third day in Ohio that he was to call himself Wayne and that was that.
- Wayne's new father was a conductor on the railroad who often returned home after weeks away with wonderful tales of colorful Indians, smelly stockyards in Chicago, and famous people who had ridden on his train.

Abandoned and orphaned children rode America's Orphan Train from coast to coast, with hopes of adoption at every stop.

- During the summers, Wayne's family went to the cool atmosphere of a lakeside resort and Joshua was often invited to go along; Wayne's father would join them every other weekend.
- One night, when the boys were 14 or 15, the evening's entertainment was a barbershop quartet known for its sweet harmonies.
- The boys were mesmerized by what they heard and practiced for weeks without achieving a satisfactory sound.
- When school began in the fall, the experience was set aside.

Life at Work

- With Joshua Hamilton's newfound interest in barbershop quartet singing came a renewed excitement about the store.
- For the first time in years, Joshua took great pleasure in constructing the elaborate chromolithographed W. A. Burpee Seed display, arranging the Merrick's Six Cord Soft Finish Spool Cotton display cabinet, and selling nickel packs of firecrackers to the neighborhood boys.
- Joshua was having fun again.
- The cooperation, the teamwork, the harmonizing sound and the applause all pleased him.
- And just ahead was an opportunity to demonstrate their skills at a fundraiser for the children's school; each of his four girls was sewing a new dress for the big event.

Joshua's singing brought him renewed enthusiasm for working in the family store, and he took great pride in creating elaborate product displays.

Joshua's daughters wore new dresses for their school fundraiser, which starred their father's barbershop quartet.

- Admission was priced at the popular sum of five cents.
- Since 1883, when the Treasury Department issued a five cent coin composed of one part nickel and three parts copper, merchants had been competing for the coin bearing the American Indian profile.
- In Joshua's establishment, customers ordered "a nickel's worth" of cheese; a handful of crackers pulled from the cracker barrel cost a nickel, as did a draft beer down the street.
- Even the "dime" novels sold for a nickel.
- Dr. Will Zimmer, the tenor in Joshua's partnership group, often joked that he would be happy to receive a nickel for his medical services: "It would be more than I'm receiving now."
- The fourth member of the quartet, R. H. Long, came from a long line of theater people and often took the initiative to obtain singing dates and promote the events.
- Barbershop music, with its close, unaccompanied four-part harmonies and ringing chords, was believed to be a uniquely American tradition.
- Joshua believed it had evolved from numerous musical styles featuring uncomplicated melodies that could be harmonized with a variety of four-part chords when sung *a cappella*.
- Barbershop harmony's four voice parts required a tenor, lead, baritone and bass to be effective; the melody was sung by the lead voice while the first tenor harmonized in a lighter voice above it.
- The bass sang the roots and fifth of the chord, while the baritone filled in the chord sometimes below the lead, sometimes above it.
- It was a glorious way to spend an evening with friends—especially when the harmonies were solid and produced the fifth ring.
- The defining characteristic of the barbershop style for Joshua was the ringing chord—also called the angel's voice or the fifth voice.
- Barbershop arrangements stressed chords and chord progressions that favored "ringing" at the expense of suspended and diminished chords.
- Wayne talked about the physical impact on him personally: "a tingling of the spine, the raising of the hairs on the back of the neck, the spontaneous arrival of gooseflesh on the forearm."
- Will often described the effect as an addiction, a great big chord that gets people "hooked."
- Achieving the effect produced in Joshua the emotional impact of rapture.

Business in Cincinnati's downtown grew, as railroads carried people and products in and out of the city.

Life in the Community: Cincinnati, Ohio

- Chartered as a village in 1803, Cincinnati acquired significant growth in 1811 with the introduction of steam navigation on the Ohio River.
- Thanks to the Ohio River, opportunities abounded: hotels, restaurants, and taverns opened to meet the needs of settlers traveling westward; steamboats were manufactured and repaired in the city; and farmers brought their fresh-grown crops to the city for transport down the Ohio and Mississippi rivers to New Orleans, Louisiana, one of Ohio's major markets.
- At the same time, the availability of the Miami and Erie Canal reduced the cost of traveling from western Ohio to Cincinnati, allowing the city to develop into an important meatpacking center.
- Farmers brought their livestock—especially pigs—to the city, where they were slaughtered, processed, and sold to Western settlers or shipped to various markets.
- This earned the city a tag as the "Porkopolis" of the United States.
- The first mass migration of Germans in 1830 and then the Irish a decade later swelled Cincinnati's population to close to 50,000 people.
- With the introduction of lager beer in the 1830s, German brewers became the predominant force in the industry, and the number of breweries in the city increased from eight in 1840 to 36 in 1860.
- William Holmes McGuffey first published his *Eclectic Reader* for school children in Cincinnati in 1836, and eventually 122 million copies were sold.
- Harriet Beecher Stowe—the author of *Uncle Tom's Cabin*—called Cincinnati home for 18 years, while the city itself was a hotbed of abolitionist activity located directly across the Ohio River from Kentucky, a slaveholding state.
- Abolitionists taking part in the Underground Railroad began to secretly smuggle runaway slaves across the Ohio River to potential freedom in Ohio.
- Many in the city opposed the abolitionists, fearing that if slavery ended, they would face competition from the freed African-Americans.
- With the outbreak of the Civil War, George B. McClellan, a prominent Cincinnati resident and the commander of Ohio's State Militia, selected a site near the city for the recruitment and training of 50,000 union soldiers.
- By the 1880s, Cincinnati boasted a population of 300,000 and the honor of being the largest city in Ohio.
- During this period, Cincinnati's major cultural institutions also began to take shape, including the art museum and art academy, the conservatory of music, the public library, the zoo, and Cincinnati Music Hall.
- In response to the decline of riverboat trade in the 1870s, the city built its own Southern rail line—the only Ohio city to make such a move—at a cost of $20 million.
- By 1890, more than 15 railroads connected Cincinnati's industry to other parts of the United States: iron production, meat packing, cloth production and woodworking.
- Cincinnati's industries employed 103,325 people in 1887, and produced more than $200 million in goods.

HISTORICAL SNAPSHOT
1891

- George A. Hormel & Co. introduced the packaged food Spam
- Painter Paul Gauguin arrived in Papeete, Tahiti
- The penalty kick was introduced into soccer
- The International Brotherhood of Electrical Workers was organized
- New Scotland Yard became the headquarters of the London Metropolitan Police
- Eugène Dubois discovered *Homo erectus* fossils in the Dutch colony of Java
- Bicycle designer Charles Duryea, 29, and his toolmaker brother James designed a gasoline engine capable of powering a road vehicle
- Edouard Michelin obtained a patent for a "removable" bicycle tire that could be repaired quickly in the event of puncture
- The Jarvis winch, patented by Glasgow-born Scottish shipmaster John C. B. Jarvis, enabled ships to be manned by far fewer men and permitted the development of the windjammer
- Rice University and Stanford were chartered
- John T. Smith patented corkboard using a process of heat and pressure to combine waste cork together for insulation
- American Express issued the first traveler's checks
- Commercial bromine was produced electrolytically by Herbert H. Dow's Midland Chemical Company in Michigan
- Bacteriologist Anna Williams obtained her M.D. from the Women's Medical College of New York and accepted a position in the newly created diagnostic laboratory of the city's Health Department, the first such lab in America
- Chicago's Provident Hospital became the first interracial hospital in America
- The lapidary encyclical "Of New Things" by Pope Leo XIII declared that employers have the moral duty as members of the possessing class to improve the "terrible conditions of the new and often violent process of industrialization"
- Educator William Rainey Harper agreed to become president of the new University of Chicago with funding from merchant Marshall Field and oilman John D. Rockefeller
- Irene Coit became the first woman admitted to Yale University
- The electric self-starter for automobiles was patented
- The first full-service advertising agency was opened in New York by George Batten
- The Automatic Electric Company was founded to promote a dial telephone patented by Kansas City undertaker Almon B. Strowger, who was convinced that "central" was diverting his incoming calls to a rival embalmer
- Important books included *Tess of the d'Urbervilles* by Thomas Hardy; *The Light That Failed* by Rudyard Kipling; *The Picture of Dorian Gray* by Oscar Wilde, and *Tales of Soldiers and Civilians* by Ambrose Bierce

Selected Prices

Bicycle Costume	$7.50
Candy, One Box	$0.06
Corset	$1.25
Harness, Double Buggy	$25.00
Horse Muzzle	$2.50
Shoes, Button	$1.50
Suspenders	$0.05
Ticket, Buffalo Bill's Wild West Show	$0.50
Top Coat	$10.00
Typewriter	$25.00

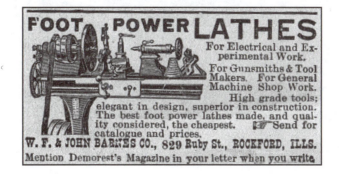

"Editor's Drawer," *Harper's New Monthly Magazine*, **May 1886:**
A Western correspondent sends the following:

I recently listened to a debate in one of the school lyceums of this city upon the momentous question of "woman suffrage."

The debater upon the "anti-women" side was doubtless engaged in his first effort, and this fact, together with a slight impediment of speech and a most original series of arguments, combined to produce one of the funniest and most unanswerable speeches I've ever heard. Here it is, almost in full:

"Ladies and gentlemen, the first thing to find out is w-w-what man was m-made for, and what w-w-woman was made for. God created Adam first, and put him in the Garden of Eden. T-then he made Eve, and p-put her there, too. If he hadn't created Eve, there never would have been all the s-s-sin there is now in this w-world. If He hadn't made Eve, she never would have p-p-picked the apple and eaten it. N-n-no she never would have picked it and g-given it to Adam to eat. Paul in his epistles said woman should k-k-keep still. And besides, ladies and gentlemen, women couldn't fill the offices. I d-d-defy you to p-point to a woman in this city or c-country that could be sheriff. Would a woman turn out in the dead of night to track and arrest a m-m-murderer? I say n-no! Ten to one she would elope w-w-with him!" And amid thunders of applause and laughter, the gallant defender of men's rights triumphantly took his seat.

A student of "Squire" Farley, a distinguished lawyer of Groton Massachusetts, says to the Squire one day, "I cannot understand how circumstantial evidence can be stronger than positive testimony."

"I will illustrate it," said the Squire. "My milkman brings a can of milk, and says, 'Squire, I know that this is pure milk, for I have milked it from the cow, washed the can thoroughly, strained it into the can, and nobody else has handled it.' Now when I take the stopper from the can, out leaps a bullfrog. Surely the frog is stronger evidence than the man."

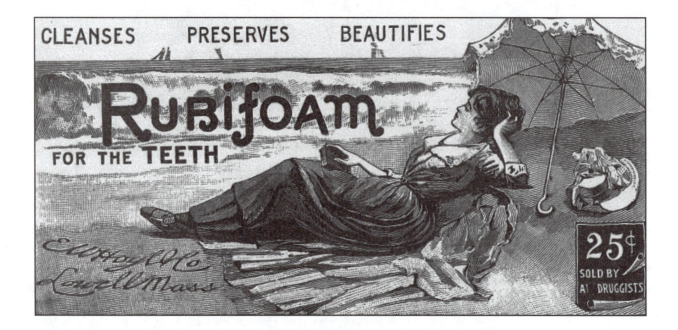

"Editor's Study," *Harper's New monthly Magazine,* **May 1886:**

Mr. Robert Louis Stevenson, in his new romance, *The Strange Case of Dr. Jekyll and Mr. Hyde*, follows the lines explored by Mr. Edward Bellamy in this romance of Miss Ludington's sister. But the Patent Office abounds in simultaneously invented machinery, and, at any rate, Mr. Stevenson may claim an improvement upon the apparatus of Mr. Bellamy. The American writer supposed several selves in each human being, capable of meeting one another in a different state of existence. Mr. Stevenson immensely simplifies the supposition by reducing the selves to the number two—a moral self and an unmoral self. The moral self of Dr. Jekyll, who, by the use of a certain drug, liberated Mr. Hyde, his unmoral self or evil principle, went about wreaking all his bad passions without the inconvenience of substantial remorse; all he had to do was take the infusion of that potent salt and become Dr. Jekyll again. The trouble in the end was that Mr. Hyde, from being at first smaller and feebler than Dr. Jekyll, outgrew him and formed the habit of coming forth without the use of the salt. Dr. Jekyll was obliged to kill them both.

The romancer cannot often be taken very seriously, we suppose. He seems commonly to be working out a puzzle, and at last we have produced an intellectual toy; but Mr. Stevenson, who is inevitably a charming and sympathetic writer, and whom we first knew as the author of certain poems of deep meaning and sincerity, does something more than this in his romance. He not only fascinates, he impresses upon the reader the fact that if we indulge the evil in us, it outgrows the good. The lesson is not quite new, and in enforcing it he becomes dangerously near the verge of allegory, for it is one of the hard conditions of romance that his personages starting with a *parti pris* can rarely be characters with a living growth, but are apt to be types, limited to the expression of one principle, simple, elemental, lacking the God-given complexity of motive which we find in all the human beings we know.

"Ta-ra-ra-boom-dee-ay,"
attributed to Henry Sayers, 1891:

I'm not extraordinarily shy,
And when a nice young man is nigh,
For his heart I have a try,
And faint away with tearful cry!

When the good young man in haste,
Will support me 'round the waist,
I don't come to while thus embraced,
Till of my lips he steals a taste!

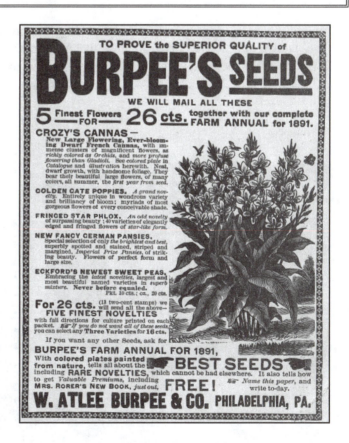

"Washington," *The Youth's Companion*, February 19, 1891:

Ninety-one years have rolled away since the death of George Washington. During that long period, many brilliant reputations have shone upon us for a while, only to fade away and collapse into oblivion. His name retains all its interest for us, and probably more people have been particularly occupied of late with his career, its relics and its records than ever before.

At the great sale of Washington mementos, held a few weeks ago in Philadelphia, the prices paid even for trifling objects once possessed by the great man and his family were extraordinary.

A legal document related to the execution of his will, which his hand had never touched, brought $50, and an autographed letter $85.

A list of his slaves, written and signed by his own hand, brought $440. Two of his memorandum books brought $800. His family Bible was sold for $760, and books from his library, containing his signature or that of his wife, commanded prices varying from $60 to $150 each.

Pieces of piano music, which had been played by Miss Custis, brought considerable sums, and a dinner invitation was sold for $18.

The sale attracted universal attention, and everyone lamented that the whole collection had not been bought by Congress and deposited at Mount Vernon, where it could have been seen by every pilgrim to that sacred site.

There is a special reason for this vivid survival of his celebrity, apart from his services to this country; it is his singularly interesting career.

From his boyhood to the last week of his life, he was a prolific writer. As soon as he could write well enough, he kept a book into which he copied anything that pleased or impressed him in his reading, and carefully entered his early cipherings and surveys in a book that is preserved to the present day.

Popular Barbershop Quartet Songs

- "Down by the Old Mill Stream"
- "Down Our Way"
- "Honey/Li'l Lize Medley"
- "Let Me Call You Sweetheart"
- "Mister Jefferson Lord, Play That Barbershop Chord" (referenced above)
- "My Wild Irish Rose"
- "Shine on Me"
- "The Story of the Rose" ("Heart of My Heart")
- "Sweet Adeline"
- "Sweet and Lovely"
- "Sweet, Sweet Roses of Morn"
- "Wait 'Til the Sun Shines, Nellie"
- "You Tell Me Your Dream (I'll Tell You Mine)"
- "From the First Hello"
- "Goodbye, My Coney Island Baby"

1898 Profile

Child prodigy Amy Marcy Cheney Beach embraced musical composition at an early age and produced more than 300 works to become one of the most widely performed composers of large-scale art music of her generation.

Life at Home

- Amy Marcy Cheney Beach crushed the widely held belief that the female brain had not evolved enough to handle the complexity of a multipart symphony.
- Born in 1867 in West Henniker, New Hampshire, Amy began to make music before she could speak.
- At the age of one year, she could accurately hum 40 tunes, most of them in the key in which she first heard them.
- At age two, she could improvise a perfectly correct alto to her mother's soprano and demanded—often loudly—a steady flow of singing and songs from the adults around her.
- Amy's mother, determined that her daughter should grow up as a normal child, restricted Amy's use of the piano—she made practicing a special treat—a "top drawer event" always to be desired.
- At the same time, middle-class Victorian girls were consistently taught to be modest, not take undue pride in their accomplishments, and never be boastful.
- Amy was taught that her musical talent was a gift from God, preserving her modesty while suggesting the magnitude of the gift.
- Influenced by Horace Bushnell's child-rearing book *Christian Nature*, Amy's mother Clara believed indulgence of any kind corrupted a child, and that by withholding the sensuous medium of music, she was teaching discipline.

Child prodigy Amy Beach wrote, at 29 years old, the first symphony by an American woman to be performed by the country's leading orchestra – the Boston Symphony.

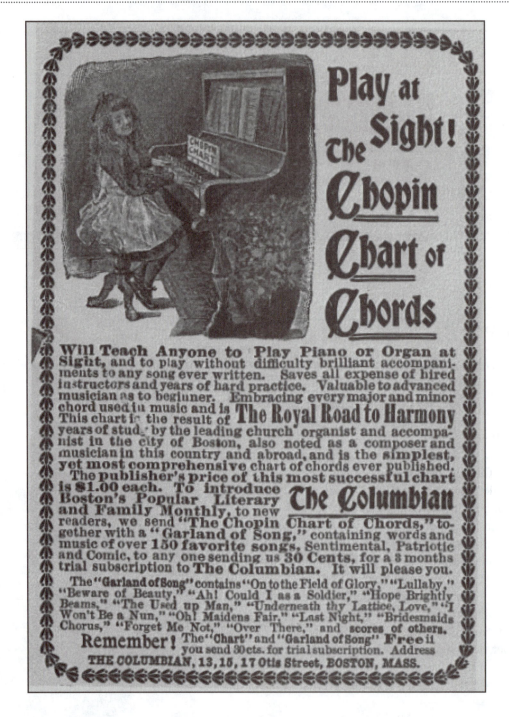

- The first piece Amy played on the piano at age four was a Strauss waltz she had learned simply by listening to her mother play.
- Later, to punish misbehavior, Amy's mother played the piano in minor keys, knowing it would make her sensitive daughter sad.
- Amy's first composition—a waltz—was created when she was four while visiting her grandfather in the country; because no piano was available, she wrote the music in her head.
- By the time she was five, she had devised a color association system for the major modes that designated the mood produced by the major keys: E was yellow, G was red.
- When she was six, her mother finally agreed to provide her formal piano lessons; by the time she was seven, she started giving public recitals, playing works by Handel, Beethoven, Chopin, and her own pieces.
- But Amy chafed under the restrictions customarily imposed on Victorian girls.

Amy resented that young boys were given trousers and groomed to become men of good character, while young girls were taught to be submissive.

- Until the age of five or six, most children, boys and girls alike, were treated with little gender differentiation; both sexes wore long dresses and were taught to be compliant and submissive.
- But when boys turned six they were "breeched" and given trousers with the expectation that strong wills as children would make boys manly men of good character.
- Girls continued to be dressed in restrictive clothing and taught to be submissive.
- The intense and emotional Amy resented the continuous restrictions.
- In 1875, the Beach family moved to Boston, where they were advised to enter their talented eight-year-old into a European conservatory.
- Some musical teachers even proposed that she be booked on a music performance tour across the Eastern seaboard.
- Her parents declined the opportunity but continued her education, despite the dangers espoused by nineteenth-century physicians that girls should not divert too much energy toward intellectual pursuits lest they harm their health and make them prone to disease.
- Boston, a city that considered itself the Athens of America, was filled with musical opportunities for a prodigy eager to fulfill her potential.
- Although most of Amy's lessons were taken in her home, she was permitted to attend concerts.
- Eventually, she moved on to private lessons by Carl Baermann, a pupil of Franz Liszt and a former professor of music at the Munich Conservatory.
- By 1883, at age 16, she made her piano debut; "No words can tell the pleasure I felt performing with the band instrumentalists…. I can only compare my sensations with that of the driver who holds in his hands the reins that perfectly control a glorious, spirited pair of horses. One must live through such an experience to properly appreciate it."
- Amy played Chopin's *Rondo in E-flat* and Moscheles's *G-minor Concerto*.
- Nine Boston newspapers and the *New York Tribune* covered the event; the *Boston Gazette* said "her natural gifts and her innate artistic intelligence were made apparent in the very first phrases she played."
- At her solo debut with the Boston Symphony Orchestra in 1885, she earned glowing reviews for her performance of Chopin's *F-minor Concerto*.
- During the next year, as she began to fully explore life as a music composer, she exhibited an extraordinary memory for musical sounds, and often composed without the aid of a piano or even a pencil and paper.
- Yet she was not eligible for serious study of composition.
- Most of the leading music conservatories still barred women from the composition classes because it was generally believed women's brains were less highly evolved than men's and less capable of responding to the intricate training.
- So Amy started a multiyear process of self-education focusing on the major composers in history while making a name for herself as a concert pianist.
- At 18, Amy married a man 24 years her senior—older than her father.

- At age 42, her husband was a surgeon at Massachusetts General Hospital and taught surgery at Harvard Medical School.
- Dr. Henry Beach was a man of his age: he believed that the man should support his wife.
- He demanded that Amy limit her concert performances to one or two a year and donate all the fees she earned giving concerts to charity.
- Dr. Beach wanted Amy to devote her time to composition, in which he believed she had an important gift, and even though she reveled in the intensity of live performances, she agreed.
- In addition, Amy halted her private piano lessons with Baermann and, at the urging of her husband, did not hire a composition teacher in an effort to keep her style pure: women were assumed to be too impressionable to retain control of their own creativity when coached.

Life at Work

- The marriage of Amy Beach changed her musical focus from performances to composition at the insistence of her new husband.
- The child prodigy, whose life had been dominated by her mother, now had to find her musical destiny as the bride of an influential doctor more than two decades her senior.
- Blessed with the good fortune to compose without a concern for money, Amy retreated to the solitude of her music room, where her discipline was self-imposed and well practiced.
- "Very few people would be willing to work so hard. It may be that it kept for me my individuality; at any rate, I enjoyed it immensely."
- To prepare properly for a career as a composer, she collected dozens and dozens of composition books and created a workbook that detailed the works of others.
- There, she copied and memorized whole scores of symphonies until she knew perfectly just how they were made.
- She described it as "...like a medical student's dissection. I began to know instrumentation on paper."
- She learned to recognize each voice in the orchestra as intimately as she knew the voices of her own family; once she learned a score, she would write it out from memory and then go to the concert hall in order to compare her work with that played by the orchestra.
- "I learned whole movements from symphonies by heart."
- She also improved her critical thinking by writing reviews of orchestral and chamber performances she attended.
- And she composed her own works.
- Her first major success was the *Mass in E-flat major*, which was performed in 1892 by the Handel and Haydn Society, a 75-minute work for solo quartet, chorus, organ, and orchestra.
- Since the Renaissance, composers had engaged the Mass as a way to demonstrate their skills through the production of a "masterpiece."
- As recently as 1865, John Knowles Paine of Boston had created his first large-scale work using the Mass.
- The well-received performance of the Mass moved Amy into the rank of America's foremost composers.
- It was a long, intricate process.
- Amy had written the vocal and choral parts as early as 1887 and completed the orchestral score in 1889.

- The Boston Commonwealth heralded the production as "one of the chief musical events of the season" and an important celebration of women's achievement in music.
- The public was intrigued by the novelty of such a large work by a woman, especially one as young as Amy, whose diminutive size made her look even younger.
- When Antonin Dvořák, the new director of the National Conservatory of Music in New York, stated that women's intellectual inferiority would prevent them from being trained as professional composers, Amy fought back.
- She wrote Dvořák a letter detailing the 153 works composed by women from 1675 to 1885, including 55 serious operas, six cantatas, and 53 comic operas.
- In her newly acquired status as America's leading woman composer, Amy went on to explain the reason for the small number of female composers: "Music is the superlative expression of life experience, and woman, by the very nature of her position, is denied many of the experiences that color life."

Amy composed the dedication for the Women's Building at the World's Columbian Exhibit in Chicago, which brought together female composers, performers and teachers.

- Her work and her words triggered several commissions, including a piece for the dedication the Women's Building at the World's Columbian Exposition to be held in Chicago in 1893.
- Theodore Thomas, head of the Exposition's Bureau of Music, promised to prove to an international crowd in the millions that art music had risen to the pinnacle of the Darwinian evolutionary ladder in America.
- The Columbian Exposition brought together for the first time female composers, performers, teachers and representatives of the emerging music club movement in a showcase of talent.
- The Exposition was also a celebration of America's coming of age as a world power and an opportunity to lay claim to the cultural achievements of a young nation so often dismissed by the European élite.
- Amy's commissioned work was entitled *Festival Jubilate* built on the theme of Psalm 100, "Oh, be joyful in the Lord, all ye lands"; it was completed in six weeks.
- Presented at the Exposition following a robust critique on the limitations currently placed on women, Amy's work opened her to a wider audience and attracted several newspaper features extolling her work and potential.
- Next came a symphony, despite the shadows cast by Beethoven.
- As in the past, she mastered composition problems including orchestration without assistance.
- In 1894, Amy began work on her *Gaelic Symphony in E-minor*; its premiere on October 30, 1896, was given by the Boston Symphony Orchestra.
- Headlines celebrated the work as the first symphony by an American woman, stressing her gender but ignoring any nationalist implications of her composition.
- Fixated on the gender of the composer, one critic commented that the work "has not the slightest trace of effeminacy, but is distinctly entirely masculine in every effect."
- Following the Boston Symphony's first performance of the piece in 1897, a reviewer from the *Brooklyn Eagle* praised its "strong writing" as "manful."
- A review in the suffragette publication *Women's Journal* stressed the intellectual and scientific aspects of the work, praising "technical skills in orchestration, and that rare inner sense of tone-color and picturesqueness belonging only to the sensitive musician."
- Finally, a woman had written a symphony and one of the country's leading orchestras had given its premiere—an American-trained woman at that.

- No critic declared it as an American piece even though it fit the contemporary definition of a nationalist work, as it drew on the music of an ethnic group in the United States—the Irish.
- Four of the symphony's themes are traditional Irish-Gaelic melodies, hence, the designation "Gaelic."
- In choosing Irish music, Amy tapped into a rich heritage that had been part of the American musical mainstream for at least a century, and by the 1890s, was assimilated into the new genre called popular music.
- Amy believed that the older the tunes, the more authentic, and found her source for the symphony in a collection published in 1841 by a folk-song collector in Dublin.
- A lively fiddle tune appeared as the closing theme of the first movement, orchestrated to recall the chanter and drone of the bagpipe.
- The first and second themes, however, were Amy's own, borrowed from her turbulent sea song, "Dark is the Night," op. 11 no. 1.
- The monothematic second movement had as its theme a Gaelic love song, first presented as an oboe solo, next by the full woodwind choir, and repeated by strings.
- As her talents grew, so did her wealth.
- With the royalties from the sale of her song "Ecstasy," Amy purchased five acres of country property in New Hampshire.
- But it was Boston that nurtured her career.
- During the city's long history, it had developed a legacy in literature, art and music.
- By 1898, Amy, who signed all her music "Mrs. H. H. A. Beach," had become the youngest member of the Boston composers' group, the "Second New England School" alongside composers John Knowles Paine, Arthur Foote, George Chadwick, Edward MacDowell, George Whiting, and Horatio Parker.
- When Second New England School composer George Chadwick wrote to congratulate Amy on her symphony, he remarked, "I always feel a thrill of pride myself whenever I hear a fine work by any of us, and as such you will have to be counted in, whether you will or not—one of the boys."

Life in The Community: Boston, Massachusetts

- Boston, the capital of and largest city in Massachusetts, was one of the oldest cities in the United States.
- The largest city in New England, Boston had long been regarded as the unofficial "Capital of New England" for its economic and cultural impact on the entire New England region.
- During the late eighteenth century, Boston was the location of several major events during the American Revolution, including the Boston Massacre and the Boston Tea Party.
- Through land reclamation and municipal annexation, Boston has expanded beyond the peninsula and, after American independence, became a major shipping port and manufacturing center, and claimed several firsts, including America's first public school, Boston Latin School (1635); America's first public park, the Boston Common (1634); and the first subway system in the United States (1897).

Faneuil Hall, "The Cradle of Liberty", Boston, Mass.

- With numerous colleges and universities within the city and surrounding area, Boston became a center of higher education and medicine.
- A dense network of railroads facilitated the region's industry and commerce, and from the mid- to late nineteenth century, Boston flourished culturally.
- It became renowned for its rarefied literary culture and lavish artistic patronage, as well as a center of the abolitionist movement.
- In the 1820s, the city's ethnic composition changed dramatically with the first wave of European immigrants, especially Irish immigrants.
- By 1850, about 35,000 Irish lived in Boston; during the latter half of the nineteenth century, the city saw increasing numbers of Irish, Germans, Lebanese, Syrians, French Canadians, and Russian and Polish Jews settle in the city.
- By the end of the nineteenth century, Boston's core neighborhoods had become enclaves of ethnically distinct immigrants—Italians inhabited the North End, Irish dominated South Boston and Charlestown, and Russian Jews lived in the West End.
- Irish and Italian immigrants brought with them Roman Catholicism.
- Following the Great Fire of 1872, Boston was rebuilt with more parks, grander roads, and elaborate plans for transforming the mud flats of the Back Bay with elegant homes.
- At the same time, Boston's musical community was expanding at Harvard, where John Knowles Paine was appointed the first professor of music.
- Boston also boasted a plethora of touring musicians including numerous women of accomplishment, both American and German trained.
- Meanwhile, construction was underway on Boston's Symphony Hall, an acoustical marvel that was regarded as one of the world's great concert halls.
- Unlike most American concert halls, which tended to favor a wider, fan-shaped configuration, Symphony Hall was built along European lines—deep, narrow and high.

HISTORICAL SNAPSHOT
1898

- New York City annexed land from surrounding counties, creating the City of Greater New York composed of five boroughs: Manhattan, Brooklyn, Queens, The Bronx, and Staten Island
- Emile Zola published *J'Accuse*, a letter accusing the French government of anti-Semitism
- The electric car belonging to Henry Lindfield of England hit a tree, becoming the world's first fatality from an automobile accident on a public highway
- The USS *Maine* exploded and sank in Havana Harbor, Cuba, killing 266 men—the event that led to the United States declaring war on Spain
- Robert Allison of Port Carbon, Pennsylvania, became the first person to buy an American-built automobile when he bought a Winton automobile that had been advertised in *Scientific American*
- Wild West Show entertainer Annie Oakley wrote President William McKinley offering the government "the services of a company of 50 'lady sharpshooters' who would provide their own arms and ammunition should war break out with Spain"
- Photographs of the Shroud of Turin revealed that the image appeared to be a photographic negative
- The 1898 Boston Beaneaters won their second straight National League baseball pennant—their eighth overall
- The Trans-Mississippi Exposition World's Fair opened in Omaha, Nebraska
- During the Spanish-American War, the United States captured Guam, making it the first U.S. overseas territory, and then annexed the Hawaiian Islands
- Joshua Slocum completed a three-year solo circumnavigation of the world
- Caleb Bradham named his soft drink "Pepsi-Cola"
- Ojibwe tribesmen defeated U.S. Government troops in northern Minnesota in the Battle of Sugar Point
- The Phi Mu Alpha Sinfonia Fraternity was founded at the New England Conservatory of Music in Boston
- A two-day blizzard known as the Portland Gale piled snow in Boston, Massachusetts, and severely impacted the Massachusetts fishing industry
- Marie and Pierre Curie announced the discovery of a substance they called radium
- As a result of the merger of several small oil companies, John D. Rockefeller's Standard Oil Company gained control of 84 percent of United States oil and most American pipelines

Selected Prices

Child's Suit	$2.00
China, 130 Pieces	$30.00
Flour, Half Barrel	$2.50
Folding Bed	$15.00
Fountain Pen	$3.50
Hair Curler	$1.00
Music Box	$2.50
Parasol, Satin	$3.90
Piano Lessons, 24	$8.00
Woman's Bicycle Costume	$7.50

The Yorkville Enquirer (South Carolina), November 7, 1897:

A new disease, contagious and fatal, says a New York dispatch of Sunday, has reached that port, causing much alarm among the health authorities at quarantine. The disease is imported from Japan, where it is known as "Beri-Beri." The *H. P. Cann* arrived off quarantine yesterday, 170 days out of Iliola, and reported that two deaths from the disease had occurred en route. Both were buried at sea. When the ship arrived in Norfolk, Virginia, the first mate and seven men were stricken with Beri-Beri, were put ashore and sent to the hospital. The disease is unknown here. The authorities were at a loss how to handle it should other ships follow with the disease on board. *Cann* is laden with sugar and tea, and makes the third vessel which has reached this port in the last four weeks in which deaths from the disease have been reported. The disease is said to resemble the yellow fever somewhat, but it is more fatal. The *Cann* will be detained at quarantine and thoroughly disinfected, while stringent measures will be adopted to cope with the disease from other vessels arriving from fever-stricken Japanese ports.

"Women in the World of Music, Her Influence, Indirect Rather Than Active, Is Yet Appreciable," *The New York Times*, July 22, 1894:

Mr. L. C. Elson, in a recent lecture, discussed the influence of women on music. Why is there no George Eliot of music? Mr. Elson admitted that there were no great women composers, but he dwelt on the indirect influence of women upon music, illustrated by the fact that many compositions owe their origin to the power of woman exerted upon this or that composer. It was not until the Middle Ages that women achieved any prominence in music. Among the first and most notable women composers was Anne Boleyn, who, just before she was beheaded, composed the words and music to that pathetic dirge, "Oh Death, Rock Me to Sleep." In reviewing the history of music, it was noted that in the intellectual period of music, the influence of women was slight. The period of the emotional marks the dawn of the musical sense of woman. Bach, one of the pioneers of this school, owed much to his first wife's artistic inspiration. Mozart and Weber were greatly assisted in the vocal value of their works by their wives, who are vocalists....

Another, more striking example of the musical sense in woman is that of Wagner's first wife, Monica Planer, a most talented woman, who would doubtless have been famous had she never met Wagner. He rewarded her self-sacrifice by treating her shamefully. He worshiped (next to himself) his second wife, daughter of Franz Liszt, and upon the birth of their son, Siegfried, Wagner composed the exquisite Siegfried Idyll.

Among the women composers who have attained some reputation are Miss Chaminade of Paris; Miss Augusta Holmes, the Irish musician in Paris; Mrs. Beach (Miss Cheney), the head of the American list; Miss Lang; Miss Sparmann, the author of the very able philosophical treatise on music; and last of all Clara Schumann. None of these, however, would be classed as "great composers." In spite of the absence of feminine genius in musical composition, it is only just to acknowledge the influence of women upon our great composers and to recognize the fact that the old-fashioned notion that women should be slaves of men in at least one instance prevented a woman from becoming a great composer. Mr. Elson accounts for the lack of women composers by the fact that they are too anxious to please and are "too susceptible to influences...." The next century is likely to produce great musical composers among women as well as great novelists, teachers, and artists.

Recorded Popular Songs: 1898

- "At A Georgia Camp Meeting"
(words/music: Kerry Mills), Sousa's Band on Berliner Gramophone, Dan W. Quinn on Columbia Records

- "The Battle Cry Of Freedom"
(words/music: George Frederick Root), John Terrell on Berliner Gramophone

- "Believe Me, If All Those Endearing Young Charms"
(words: Thomas Moore, music: Trad.), J. W. Myers on Berliner Gramophone

- "Break The News To Mother"
(words/music: Charles K. Harris), George J. Gaskin on Edison Records

- "Chin, Chin, Chinaman"
(words: Harry Greenbank, music: Sidney Jones), James T. Powers on Berliner Gramophone

- "Happy Days In Dixie"
(music: Kerry Mills), Arthur Collins on Edison Records

- "A Hot Time In The Old Town"
(words: Joseph Hayden, music: Theodore A. Metz), Sousa's Band on Berliner Gramophone, Len Spencer with banjo, Vess L. Ossman on Columbia Records, Roger Harding on Edison Records

- "I'se Gwine Back To Dixie"
(words/music: C. A. White), Edison Male Quartette on Edison Records

- "Just Before The Battle, Mother"
(words/music: George Frederick Root), Frank C. Stanley on Edison Records

- "Mister Johnson Don't Get Gay"
(words/music: Dave Reed Jr.), Press Eldridge on Edison Records

- "My Old Kentucky Home, Good Night"
(words/music: Stephen Collins Foster), Diamond Four on Berliner Gramophone, Edison Male Quartette on Edison Records

- "Rocked In The Cradle Of The Deep"
(words: Mrs. Emma Hart Willard, music: Joseph Phillip Knight), William Hooley on Edison Records

- "She Was Bred In Old Kentucky"
(words: Harry Braisted, music: Stanley Carter), Albert C. Campbell on Edison Records

- "Stars And Stripes Forever"
(music: John Philip Sousa), Sousa's Band on Berliner Gramophone

- "Sweet Rosie O'Grady"
(words/music: Maude Nugent), Steve Porter on Berliner Gramophone

- "When Johnny Comes Marching Home"
(words/music: Louis Lambert), Frank C. Stanley on Edison Records

- "Yankee Doodle"
(Trad.), Frank C. Stanley on Edison Records

"Wonders of Patient Teaching, How Helen Keller, Without Sight or Hearing, Learned to Speak," *The New York Times*, December 29, 1891:

The Volta Bureau of Washington has prepared a souvenir of the first summer meeting of the American Association to Promote the Teaching of Speech to the Deaf. The book deals solely with the case of Helen Adams Keller, the wonderful child who at the age of 11 years has learned to speak and to write, although she is blind and deaf.

The child's progress was the subject of an essay at the last meeting of the Association by Sarah Fuller, Principal of the Horace Mann School for the Deaf of Boston. The child was possessed of all the faculties and senses of a healthy child, so far as was known, until after recovery from a serious illness at the age of 18 months she was found to have lost her hearing and sight. In 1887, she was placed under the supervision of Miss A. M. Sullivan, who had been educated at the Perkins Institute for the Blind in Boston. Under this instruction, Helen developed with astonishing rapidity the genius which has since commanded the admiration of those interested in instructing the deaf.

In 1888, Helen paid a visit to the Horace Mann School. The interest that she then manifested in the children and in the course of instruction suggested to Miss Fuller that she could be taught to speak. It was nearly two years later, however, before any effort was made in this direction. Learning at that time that a deaf and blind child had acquired speech, Helen became anxious to learn to speak, and Miss Fuller was quite ready to undertake to teach her.

Miss Fuller's essay describes how she gave the child her first lesson. It was evidently a task requiring much patience, for Helen was obliged to learn how to use her organs of speech by feeling her teacher's mouth and throat and determining by the same means the position of the tongue and teeth. She proved an apt pupil, and in a little while she was able to pronounce the vowels and give utterance also to some of the consonants.

Having gone through this preliminary drill, the teacher shaped her lips with a vowel "A" and, with the child's fingers as guides, she slowly closed her lips and pronounced the word "arm." Without hesitation, Miss Fuller says, the child arranged her tongue, repeated the sound, and was delighted to know that she had pronounced a word.

Her next attempt at pronunciation was with the words "Mama," and Papa," which she tried to speak before going to the teacher. The best she can do with these words was "mum-mum" and "pup-pup." The teacher commended her efforts, and in order to illustrate to her how the word should be correctly pronounced, she drew her finger along the back of the child's hand to show the relative height of the two syllables, the child's other hand in the meantime resting in the teacher's lips. After a few repetitions, the words "Mama" and "Papa" came with almost musical sweetness from her lips.

There were nine lessons after this in which the child proved an ideal pupil, following every correction with the utmost care, and seeming never to forget anything told her. At the close of her lessons, she used speech fluently.

INSTRUCTION BOOK FREE WITH EACH CLARIONET.

ALWAYS STATE KEY AND PITCH WANTED.

1899 Profile

Albert Gustoff was 31 when he was hired to play clarinet for John Philip Sousa's band. Having worked for seven band leaders in 13 years, he couldn't imagine a better job.

Life at Home

- With the recent addition of the song "Stars and Stripes Forever" to the repertoire of John Philip Sousa's band, 31-year-old clarinetist Albert Gustoff got goose bumps just from the opening notes.
- He almost wept with joy the first time he witnessed the crowd's reaction to the marching tune; he was convinced that his boss, "The King of March" had captured the essence of America's spirit—energy, strength and beauty.
- Born in California to a serial entrepreneur, Albert learned early that homelessness was often only one bad decision away.
- Several of the relocations were highly opportunistic—coming in the middle of the night with less than 10 minutes to pack.
- In fact, one of his father's elaborate schemes was responsible for Albert's interest in music, and specifically the clarinet.
- To promote a saloon he was helping to open, Albert's father, Smiley Gustoff, had formed a small band to play out front and attract attention.
- When several of the band members failed to show, six-year-old Albert was presented a clarinet and pressed into service.
- The little boy was barely able to coax a coherent note from the instrument, but he loved the attention it garnered and enjoyed the way it felt in his hands.
- With sufficient begging and a promise to carry his father's beer bucket back to the boarding house, Albert got lessons from a semi-talented, occasionally sober musician from back East whose reasons for heading West involved a married woman, her powerful husband, shots fired in the darkness and a posse hunting for him in three states.

Albert Gustoff worked for seven band leaders before being hired to play clarinet in John Philip Sousa's marching band.

- In California, he liked to keep a low profile.
- Originally from Pennsylvania, Albert's father moved West during the 1849 Gold Rush.
- Gold turned out to be difficult to find and backbreaking to recover, so Smiley Gustoff began selling wheelbarrows to miners—a most profitable business that required minimal sweat.
- Wheelbarrows were owned by the successful and unsuccessful alike; an optimistic newcomer could be sold two.
- Albert's mother left her second husband to follow Smiley into Texas in 1867 where the defeated and defiant Southerners were migrating to start a new life.
- Smiley was there to sell them land he didn't actually own, along with farm equipment they couldn't actually use.
- Like many of Smiley's entrepreneurial adventures, the Texas land business had a short life once the sheriff began informing the newcomers they were farming on someone else's land.
- Albert was born in 1868 at midnight; he was the only sober person in the motel room that night.
- Albert quickly came to find comfort in the sounds of dance hall music pounded out on the piano below; if there was dancing underway, he knew where to find his mother.

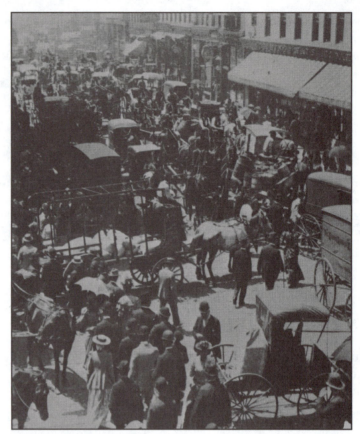

Albert's father moved west during the Gold Rush, selling wheelbarrows to miners.

- Albert's school met only when a teacher was available, but money could be made day or night by a clever child able to play five instruments for tips.
- Despite the adulation that came from playing a peppy tune on the trumpet or piano, Albert never forgot the joy of blowing through a clarinet.
- But it was not until he visited St. Louis in the early 1890s that he fully understood that there are various types of clarinets, including octave, sopranino, soprano, alto, tenor, baritone, and bass.

Life at Work

- Albert Gustoff had just completed a long night of entertaining the party crowd in one of St. Louis's more high-class dance halls when he was approached by a sober man in a black suit.
- He would have looked like trouble if his enthusiasm had not glowed on his face.
- The man was a talent scout for John Philip Sousa, the legendary leader of the Marine Corps Band.
- "Mr. Sousa wants you to try out for his touring band," the man said. "He thinks you may be the B-flat clarinetist he has been seeking."
- Albert was stunned.
- The John Philip Sousa Band, established in 1892, was a living symbol of America's emerging power in the world.

- The band toured across the United States and Europe to heavy applause and packed audiences; its musicians represented the cream of the world's musical crop, hailing from outstanding schools such as the Paris Conservatory and the Leipzig Conservatory, and from previous employment with the Boston Symphony Orchestra, the New York City Ballet Orchestra, and the Grand Opera House in London.
- What an honor for a ragamuffin musician with no foreign training of any kind!
- To be viewed as a clarinetist was a particular honor; thanks to Sousa and Patrick Gilmore, the clarinet had been raised to a high level of appreciation—a woodwind of special skills.
- The clarinet's introduction in American musical culture was largely through military bands; over 80 British regiments serving America between 1755 and 1783 had their own band comprising an assortment of instruments including clarinets, oboes, bassoons, horns and trumpets.
- By the late nineteenth century, approximately 18,000 amateur and professional concert bands had spread throughout the United States with varying qualities.
- One of the most successful and influential American bandleaders was Patrick Gilmore, who first organized his own military band in 1859.
- By 1875, Gilmore had organized a military band in New York made up of the finest musicians available that toured across the United States performing concerts, dramatically popularizing military music.
- Aspiring musician and violinist John Philip Sousa was but one of many inspired by the concerts.
- Unlike most American bandleaders at the time, Gilmore used a large woodwind section to balance the sound of the brass instruments.
- Five years later, the 26-year-old Sousa, who had served two tours with the U.S. Marine Corps Band as an apprentice musician and had been playing the violin professionally and composing for several years, accepted leadership of the Marine Band.
- He grew a robust black beard to give his appearance more authority.
- In 1891, Sousa led the Marine Band on a concert tour lasting five weeks—the first tour in the band's history; it included eight to nine concerts a week and traveled through 12 states.
- It was an exhausting experience.

Before directing his own band, John Philip Sousa led the U.S. Marine Corps band on their first tour through 12 states.

- Shortly thereafter, Sousa left the Marine Corps to direct his own band and Albert was given an opportunity of a lifetime.
- For Sousa, it was a chance to earn $6,000 a year plus 20 percent of the new band's profits after 12 years of service to the Marine Corps Band; for Albert, it was an opportunity to play music with some of the finest instrumentalists in the world.
- A teacher in St. Louis had alerted Sousa of a raw talent he needed to hire.
- Albert was ready, and by 1899 he was an occasional soloist.
- His fellow clarinetists hailed from Italy, France and Spain, and they were demanding.
- Sometimes Albert's lack of formal training showed, which only increased his anxiety of not being foreign trained.
- One frustrating day was spent trying to make a permanent "record" of the band's powerful but subtle sound.
- For a band known for its "marching music," the John Philip Sousa Band rarely marched in a row playing music.

- Most concerts were staged affairs in grand halls before a seated audience.
- The concerts always started on time—precisely on time—often opening with the William Tell Overture played so smoothly and with such subtlety it sounded like the work of a great symphony orchestra.
- This would be followed by El Capitan, and The High School Cadets—all to thunderous applause—before Albert stepped to the front of the stage to play "Bride of the Waves," written by his fellow band mate Herbert L. Clarke.
- When Clarke played the solo, his sweet, crystal tones brought stout women to tears; Albert was always intimidated on the concerts when the solo was assigned to himself.

For a band known for marching music, the John Philip Sousa band rarely marched as they played.

Life in the Community: St. Louis, Missouri

- St. Louis, Missouri, was the nation's fourth-largest city when Albert Gustoff was discovered.
- Located at the confluence of the Mississippi and Missouri rivers, St. Louis was dubbed the "Gateway City" for the thousands of settlers who passed through on their way West.
- The city was also a melting pot for dozens of musical ideas and movements, including the blues and ragtime.
- St. Louis served as the center for ragtime music, a syncopated sound symbolized by musician Scott Joplin's famous song "Maple Leaf Rag."
- This ragtime piano tradition, plus a wealth of raucous clubs throughout the city, also led to the birth of the blues.
- The dynamic flow of people through the city allowed for various styles to combine, meshing the folk music traditions of the river community with the highly formalized classical sounds from the big cities.

St. Louis bridge and levee.

- The rough nature of the city also contributed songs to the lexicon of American music; "Frankie and Johnny" depicted the murder of 17-year-old Allen Britt by 22-year-old St. Louis dancer Frankie Baker on Targee Street; the song "Stagger Lee" described a December 1895 shootout between "Stack" Lee Shelton and William "Billy" Lyons in a saloon on 11th and Morgan streets.
- St. Louis was also a budding center of innovation.
- The first "horseless carriages" appeared on the streets of St. Louis in 1893 after a few entrepreneurs formed several automobile companies.
- Some companies lasted only long enough to produce a handful of cars, while others lasted for years and manufactured thousands.

HISTORICAL SNAPSHOT
1899

- Opel Motors opened for business
- The Philippine-American War began as hostilities erupted in Manila
- The Spanish-American War formally ended with a peace treaty between the United States and Spain
- Voting machines were approved by the U.S. Congress for use in federal elections
- Mount Rainier National Park was established in Washington State
- Felix Hoffmann patented aspirin and Bayer registered the drug as a trademark
- At Sing Sing, Martha M. Place became the first woman executed in an electric chair
- Students at the University of California, Berkeley, stole the Stanford Axe from Stanford University "yell leaders," thus establishing the Axe as a symbol of the rivalry between the schools
- The First Hague Peace Conference was opened in The Hague by Willem de Beaufort, Minister of Foreign Affairs of The Netherlands
- Three Denver, Colorado, newspapers published a story (later proving to be a fabrication) that the Chinese government under the Guangxu Emperor was going to demolish the Great Wall of China
- The paper clip was patented by Norwegian Johan Vaaler
- Mile-a-Minute Murphy earned his famous nickname after he rode a bicycle for one mile in under a minute on Long Island
- America's first juvenile court was established in Chicago
- The White Star Line's transatlantic ocean liner RMS *Oceanic* sailed on its maiden voyage
- The Second Boer War erupted in South Africa between the United Kingdom and the Boers of the Transvaal and Orange Free State
- The Alpha Sigma Tau Sorority was founded in Ypsilanti, Michigan
- The Bronx Zoo opened in New York City
- A large standing stone at Stonehenge near Salisbury, England, fell
- David Hilbert created the modern concept of geometry with the publication of his book *Grundlagen der Geometrie*
- Gold was discovered in Nome, Alaska

Selected Prices

Buggy	$59.75
Camera, Delmar Folding	$3.75
Coffee, One Pound	$0.30
Cooking Stove	$4.85
Fertilizer, 100 Pounds	$2.00
Handkerchiefs, Dozen	$3.00
Ice Box	$27.50
Song Sheet	$0.30
Vaudeville Show	$0.25
Water Closet	$19.75

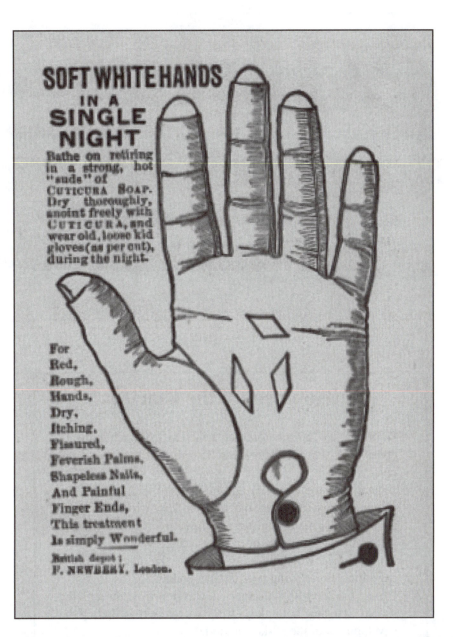

Development of the Clarinet

- During the late 1600s, before the clarinet existed, the chalumeau, considered the first true reed instrument, was used by musicians.
- Johann Christoph Denner and his son Jacob improved the chalumeau by inventing the speaker key, which gave the instrument a greater register and Johann Christoph Denner recognition as the inventor of the clarinet.
- Unlike other woodwind instruments, the clarinet has a cylindrical bore giving it its distinct sound.
- During the late 1700s, the clarinet was improved through the shape of the tone holes; keys were also altered, including the development of the 13-keyed model.
- In the mid-1800s, the fingering system developed by Theobald Boehm for the flute was adapted to the clarinet by Hyacinthe Klose and Auguste Buffet.
- Wolfgang Amadeus Mozart, Johannes Brahms, Carl Maria von Weber and Hector Berlioz all wrote music for the clarinet.
- The cylindrical bore is primarily responsible for the clarinet's distinctive timbre, which varies among its three main registers, known as the chalumeau, clarino, and altissimo; the tone quality can vary greatly with the musician, the music, the instrument, the mouthpiece, and the reed.
- Clarinets have the largest pitch range of common woodwinds, thanks to the intricate key organization.

John Philip Sousa Quotations

America can well expect to develop a goodly amount of composers, for she has a goodly number of people.

American teachers have one indisputable advantage over foreign ones; they understand the American temperament and can judge its unevenness, its lights and its shadows.

Any composer who is gloriously conscious that he is a composer must believe that he receives his inspiration from a source higher than himself.

Anybody can write music of a sort. But touching the public heart is quite another thing.

Composers are the only people who can hear good music above bad sounds.

From childhood I was passionately fond of music and wanted to be a musician. I have no recollection of any real desire ever to be anything else.

Governmental aid is a drawback rather than an assistance, as, although it may facilitate in the routine of artistic production, it is an impediment to the development of true artistic genius.

Grand opera is the most powerful of stage appeals, and that almost entirely through the beauty of music.

I can almost always write music; at any hour of the 24, if I put pencil to paper, music comes.

I firmly believe that we have more latent musical talent in America than there is in any other country. But to dig it out, there must be good music throughout the land—a lot of it.

Everyone must hear it, and such a process takes time.

I have always believed that 98 percent of a student's progress is due to his own efforts, and 2 percent to his teacher.

I still feel the impulse to give young writers a hearing, and I believe I have played more unpublished compositions than any other band leader in the country.

I think that the quality of all bands is steadily improving, and it is a pleasant thought to me that perhaps the efforts of Sousa's Band have quickened that interest and improved that quality.

Jazz will endure just as long people hear it through their feet instead of their brains.

No nation as young as America can be expected to become immediately a power in the arts.

"Sweet Tooters," *Elyria Democrat* (Ohio), December 19, 1889:

The Marine band this is smallest national band in the world, yet one the most deservedly famous. Until 1878, the band was composed of 76 pieces, but Secretary of the Navy Hon. Richard Thompson reduced the number to 38, and it so remains until this day. At the Paris Exposition of 1888, a prize was competed for by nine national bands, in the presence of 30,000 spectators. It was one of the grandest musical carnivals in the history of civilization. In the Austrian band, there were 70 pieces, the Prussian, 87; Bavarian, 52; Baden, 54; Belgian, 59; Holland, 56; French, 62; Spanish, 64, and Russian, 71. The prize was awarded to the Bavarian Band. The British and American national bands did not compete. The above facts were communicated to me by Mr. John Philip Sousa, the leader of the Marine Band. He added: "The German national band is now composed of 47 pieces; the Austrian has from 70 to 90; and the British band has 60 to 75 pieces. You can see, therefore, that the Marine Band of only 38 pieces is comparatively a small band; what we lack numerically we tried make up in quality. When it comes to supplying volume of harmony, we managed to make ourselves heard."

Yes, and during the recent conclave of Sir Knights Templar in this city, the people of Washington were led to look with greater pride than ever upon the Marine Band, for by contrast with the celebrated bands of other cities, the Marine Band demonstrated its great superiority. Accustomed as we were to hear the great orchestra, for it is such, our people have come to take it as a matter of course that the Marine Band shall always play well, but the recent parade participated in by 20,000 plumed Knights and about 100 bands from every city in the nation awakened local pride and stirred enthusiasm to fevered heat. When the red-coated musicians, with their unpretentious leader, marched by, steadily, carefully, methodically, as one great organ fingered by a master, it seemed as though the very air was filled with the "sound of a great Amen," and that the lost chord had been found. Mr. Sousa, on the following evening, said: "Yes, the band played well, never better, in fact; I am proud of them. In fact, we are all proud of each other; we are really a band of brothers now, in the sense that there's an esprit du corps such as was never before developed in the band. Every man is proud of his own part, does it well and conscientiously, and all together are proud of their work and perfectly confident so that we do not falter nor question whether we are doing well or not."

1899 News Feature

"The Vaudeville Theater," Edwin Milton Royle, *Scribner's Magazine*, **October 1899:**

The Vaudeville Theater is an American invention. There is nothing like it anywhere else in the world. It is neither the Café Chantant, the English music-hall, nor the German garden. What has been called by a variety of names, but has remained always and everywhere pretty much the same—reeky with smoke, damp with libations, gay with the informalities of the half world—is now doing business with us under the patronage of the Royal American family.

Having expurgated and rehabilitated the tawdry thing, the American invites in the family and neighbors, hands over to them beautiful theaters, lavishly decorated and appointed, nails up everywhere church and army regulations, and in the exuberance of his gayety passes around ice water. He hasn't painted out the French name, but that is because he has been, as usual, in a hurry. Fourteen years ago, this may have been a dream in a Yankee's brain; now it is part of us. The strictly professional world has been looking for the balloon to come down, for the fad to die out, for the impossible thing to stop, but year after year these theaters increase and multiply, till now they flourish the country over.

Sometimes the vaudeville theater is an individual and independent enterprise; more often it belongs to a circuit. The patronage, expenses, and receipts are enormous. One circuit will speak for all. It has a theater in New York, one in Philadelphia, one in Boston, and one in Providence, and they give no Sunday performances; and yet these four theaters entertain over 5,000,000 people every year, give employment to 350 attachés and to 3,500 actors. Four thousand people pass in and out of each one of these theaters daily. Ten thousand dollars are distributed each week in salaries to the actors and $3,500 to the attachés. Take one theater, for example, the house in Boston. It is open year-round and costs $7,000 a week to keep it up, while its patrons will average 25,000 every week. On a holiday it will play to from ten to twelve thousand people. How is it possible?

A holiday to an American is a serious affair, so the doors of the theater are open and the performance begins when most people are eating breakfast; 9:30 a.m. is not too soon for the man who pursues pleasure with the same intensity he puts into business. There are no reserved seats, so one must come first to be first served. One may go in at 9:30 a.m. and stay until 10:30 at night. If he leaves his seat, though, the nearest standing socialist drops into it and he must wait for a vacancy in order to sit down again.

Not over two percent of an audience remains longer than to see the performance through once, but there are people who secrete campaign rations about them, and camp there from 9:30 a.m. to 10:30 p.m., thereby surviving all of the acts twice and most of them four or five times. The management calculates to sell out the house two and a half times on ordinary days and four times on holidays, and it is this system that makes such enormous receipts possible. Of course, I have taken the circuit which is representative of the vaudeville idea at its best, but it is not alone in its standards for success, and what I've said about the houses in New York, Boston, and Philadelphia applies more or less, of course, to all the principal cities of the country, and in a less degree, of course, to the houses in the smaller cities...

So far as the vaudeville theaters are concerned, one might as well ask for censorship of a "family magazine." It would be a work of supererogation. The local manager of every vaudeville house is its censor, and he lives up to his position laboriously and, I may say, religiously. The bill changes usually from week to week. It is the solemn duty of this austere personage to sit through the first performance of every week and let no guilty word or look escape. This is precautionary only.

"You are to distinctly understand," say the first words of the contract of a certain circuit, "that the management conducts this house upon a high plane of respectability and moral cleanliness."

But long before the performer has entered the dressing room, he has been made acquainted with the following pledge which everywhere adorns the walls:

Notice To Performer

You are hereby warned that your act must be free from all vulgarity and suggestiveness in words, action and costume, while playing in any of Mr._____'s houses and all vulgar, double meaning and profane words and songs must be cut out of your act before the first performance. If you are in doubt as to what is right or wrong, submit it to the resident manager at rehearsal.

Such words as Liar, Slob, Son of a Gun, Devil, Sucker, Damn and all other words unfit for the ears of ladies and children, also any references to questionable streets, resorts, localities, and bar-rooms are prohibited under fine of instant discharge.

And this is not merely a literary effort on the part of the management; it is obligatory and final. When we have about accepted as conclusive the time-honored theory that "You must give the public what it wants," and that it wants bilge-water in champagne glasses, we are confronted with the vaudeville theater, no longer an experiment, but a comprehensive fact….

The character of the entertainment is always the same. There is a sameness even about its infinite variety. No act or "turn" consumes much over 30 minutes. Everyone's taste is consulted, and if one objects to the perilous feats of the acrobats or juggling, he can read his programme or shut his eyes for a few moments and he will be compensated by some sweet bell ringing or a sentimental or a comic song, graceful or grotesque dancing, a one-act farce, trained animals, legerdemain, impersonations, clay modeling, for the biograph pictures, or the stories of the comic monologuist. The most serious thing about the programme is its seriousness is barred, with some melancholy results….

So far as the character of the entertainment goes, vaudeville has the "open door." Whatever or whoever can interest an audience for 30 minutes or less, and has passed quarantine, is welcome. The conditions of the regular theaters are not encouraging to progress. To produce a play or launch a star requires capital from $10,000 upward. There is no welcome and no encouragement. The door is shut and locked. And even with capital, the conditions are all unfavorable to proof. But if you can sing or dance or amuse people in any way; if you think you could write a one-act play, the vaudeville theater will give you a chance to prove it. One day of every week is devoted to these trials. If at this trial you interest a man who is looking for good material, he will put you in the bill for one performance, and give you a chance at an audience, which is much better. The result of this open door attitude is a very interesting innovation in vaudeville which is more or less recent, but seems destined to last—the incursion of the dramatic artist in vaudeville.

1900–1909

The first decade of the twentieth century was marked by dramatic innovation and keen-eyed energy as America's men and women competed to invent a better automobile, mass market soft drinks or configure the right land deal that would propel them into the millionaires' mansions so frequently described by the press. In this environment the first Broadway musical, George M. Cohan, *Little Johnny Jones*, took root and the energetic Ziegfeld Follies got a stylish leg up on the competition.

At the same time, the number of inventions and changes spawned by the expanded use of electricity was nothing short of revolutionary. Factories converted to the new energy force, staying open longer. A bottle-making machine patented in 1903 virtually eliminated the hand-blowing of glass bottles; another innovation mechanized the production of window glass. A rotating kiln manufactured in 1899 supplied large quantities of cheap, standardized cement, just in time for a nation ready to leave behind the bicycle fad and fall madly in love with the automobile. Thanks to this spirit of innovation and experimentation, the United States led the world in productivity, exceeding the vast empires of France and Britain combined.

In the eyes of the world, America was the land of opportunity. It was also a time for reflection on America's past spearheaded by Arthur Farwell's fascination on native American music—America's musical roots—popularized through the Wa-Wan Press. Millions of immigrants flooded to the United States, often finding work in the new factories of the New World—many managed by the men who came two generations before from countries like England or Germany or Wales. When Theodore Roosevelt proudly proclaimed in 1902, "The typical American is accumulating money more rapidly than any other man on earth," he described accurately both the joy of newcomers and the prosperity of the emerging middle class. Elevated by their education, profession, inventiveness, or capital, the managerial class found numerous opportunities to flourish in the rapidly changing world of a new economy.

At the beginning of the century, the 1900 U.S. population, comprising 45 states, stood at 76 million, an increase of 21 percent since 1890; 10.6 million residents were foreign-born and more were coming every day. The number of immigrants in the first decade of the twentieth century was double the number for the previous decade, exceeding one million annually in four of the 10 years, the highest level in U.S. history. Business and industry were convinced that unrestricted immigration was the fuel that drove the growth of American industry. Labor was equally certain that the influx of foreigners continually undermined the economic status of native workers and kept wages low.

The change in productivity and consumerism came with a price: the character of American life. Manufacturing plants drew people from the country into the cities. The traditional farm patterns were disrupted by the lure of urban life. Ministers complained that lifelong churchgoers who moved to the city often found less time and fewer social pressures to attend worship regularly. Between 1900 and 1920, urban population increased by 80 percent compared to just over 12 percent for rural areas. During the same time, the non-farming work force went from 783,000 to 2.2 million. Unlike farmers, these workers drew a regular paycheck, and spent it.

With this movement of people, technology, and ideas, nationalism took on a new meaning in America. Railroad expansion in the middle of the nineteenth century had made it possible to move goods quickly and efficiently throughout the country. As a result, commerce, which had been based largely on local production of goods for local consumption, found new markets. Ambitious merchants expanded their businesses by appealing to broader markets.

In 1900, America claimed 58 businesses with more than one retail outlet called "chain stores"; by 1910, that number had more than tripled, and by 1920, the total had risen to 808. The number of clothing chains alone rose from seven to 125 during the period. Department stores such as R.H. Macy in New York and Marshall Field's in Chicago offered vast arrays of merchandise along with free services and the opportunity to "shop" without purchasing. Ready-made clothing drove down prices, but also promoted fashion booms that reduced the class distinctions of dress. In rural America the mail order catalogs of Sears, Roebuck and Company reached deep into the pocket of the common man and made dreaming and consuming more feasible.

All was not well, however. A brew of labor struggles, political unrest, and tragic factory accidents demonstrated the excesses of industrial capitalism so worshipped in the Gilded Age. The labor reform movements of the 1880s and 1890s culminated in the newly formed American Federation of Labor as the chief labor advocate. By 1904, 18 years after it was founded, the AFL claimed 1.676 million of 2.07 million total union members nationwide. The reforms of the labor movement called for an eight-hour workday, child-labor regulation, and cooperatives of owners and workers. The progressive bent of the times also focused attention on factory safety, tainted food and drugs, political corruption, and unchecked economic monopolies. At the same time, progress was not being made by all. For black Americans, many of the gains of reconstruction were being wiped away by regressive Jim Crow laws, particularly in the South. Cherished voting privileges were being systematically taken away. When President Roosevelt asked renowned black educator Booker T. Washington to dine at the White House, the invitation sparked deadly riots. Although less visible, the systematic repression of the Chinese was well under way on the West Coast.

The decade ushered in the opening of the first movie theater, located in Pittsburgh, in 1905. Vaudeville prospered, traveling circuses seemed to be everywhere, and America was crazy for any type of contest, whether it was "cure baby" judging or hootchy-kootchy dancing. The decade marked the first baseball World Series, Scholastic Aptitude Tests, and Albert Einstein's new theories concerning the cosmos. At the same time, the Brownie Box camera from Eastman Kodak made photography available to the masses.

1903 PROFILE

Floyd Morioka was astonished that he had been offered a job as choirmaster and dumbfounded that its veteran members were so bad. Clearly the church music renaissance that was sweeping the nation had missed this corner of America.

Life at Home

- Twenty-two years old and eager to fulfill his destiny as a Methodist choirmaster, Floyd Morioka had grown up in San Francisco, the product of a Japanese father and an American mother.
- Both had been raised in the Methodist Church and were delighted when Floyd wanted to play the violin and be a choir member; they were told repeatedly that their son had the voice of an angel.
- Even as a child, Floyd was thrilled by the power of a marching band, the trill of a circus flute or the rhythms of a street dance.
- His first teacher was a choir member who insisted that he learn how to read music—no matter how gifted he might be at plucking songs out of the air.
- His second-generation father insisted that his Japanese be as effortless as his English.
- "There was this battle at home about whether we were going to speak Japanese or English," said Floyd. "Me and my friends felt far more American than Japanese."
- Both the Japanese and American communities shunned Floyd at times; interracial mixing was the biggest fear of both.
- Social scientists were convinced the Japanese were too different culturally to mix well with Americans.
- Prior to the 1880s, relatively few Japanese had immigrated to America, unlike the Chinese who had arrived in large numbers to work on the railroads.

Floyd Morioka fulfilled his dream at age 22, when he became choirmaster at Spokane Methodist Church.

- When the Japanese arrived, they were assumed to be Chinese—an attitude the Japanese deeply resented.
- Japan had only opened its borders recently—with the encouragement of a fleet of American gunboats in 1853.
- Afterwards, the Japanese embarked a dramatic—and highly successful—program of technological reform.
- Within 50 years, Japan had begun to develop a modern bureaucracy and navy, defeated China in two wars, and was now competing with European nations for trade.
- As Japanese emigration to Hawaii and America became more common, American citizens and Japanese immigrants developed a delicate shadow dance of mutual need and avoidance.
- Although barred from obtaining American citizenship, many Japanese came to the West Coast of the United States initially to fill the jobs once held by the Chinese laborers, who were no longer welcome.
- Japanese immigrants first arrived in eastern Washington during the late 1800s, mostly as railroad workers and mine laborers.
- Having struggled mightily to modernize, industrialize, and meet the expectations of the West, many Japanese resented the racial prejudice and unequal treatment they encountered as an affront to both themselves and the honor of their nation.

Chinese nursery girls were often mistaken for Japanese.

- America—especially the West Coast—was awash in protest over "the Yellow Peril" and the potential problems that continued Asian immigration might cause.
- California, although heavily dependent upon Chinese and Japanese agricultural workers, was actively discussing ways to limit immigration—even though the numbers were small.
- The total number of Japanese immigrants in 1903 was 19,000 (including those moving to Hawaii), compared to 814,000 from Europe.
- The average Japanese immigrants brought $35.00 with them to start a new life; the best jobs—at sawmills—paid $1.75 to $2.75 per day, and restaurant laborers made $30 to $70 per month.

- As Japan rose to power in Asia, Americans became increasingly concerned about the threat of the "Yellow Peril" as a challenge to the "Anglo-Saxon, Christian" way of life.
- Many went back to Japan when the work ran out, yet a significant number stayed and settled in Spokane.
- In 1903, the population of Issei (Japanese immigrants) and Nisei (first-generation Japanese-Americans) reached about 1,000, most living in a crowded downtown block in Spokane called Japanese Alley.
- Nationwide, approximately 110,000 Japanese lived in the United States, mostly on the West Coast; approximately 150,000 Japanese had emigrated to Hawaii, then a U.S. territory.

Immigrants from Europe still outnumbered those from Japan at the turn of the century.

Life at Work

- When Floyd Morioka arrived, the Spokane Methodist Church boasted 400 members, largely a congregation of Issei and Nisei Japanese people.
- The previous choir leader had lasted only 18 months, unable to cope with the rigors of railway work during the week to support his love of church music on Sunday.
- In addition, he was considered "too Japanese" by the Nisei and "too American" by the Issei.
- They didn't like the hymns he selected, and they didn't like the way they sounded.
- At one point, the choir had organized itself around their alliances to the choir master, not their voices.
- When Floyd arrived, the choir had received little leadership in months, and turmoil abounded.
- Everyone seemed mad at everyone and skeptical that this mixed-race, 22-year-old could bring them together.
- The choir battles were beginning to impact the rest of the church.
- Plans of forming Americanization classes for young Japanese brides, that would emphasize Christian living and loyalty to America, were now controversial.
- Church attendance was off and everyone blamed someone else.
- In addition, the choir was just plain bad.
- Surely 14 people who had been singing in a church choir Sunday after Sunday for years had to know more than this group demonstrated.
- In order to learn an anthem, it was necessary to take each part and bang it on the piano over and over again.
- Anthems which they had learned by rote the previous year had to be taught over again because they had forgotten everything but the melody and the words.
- One choir member said she knew every time the notes went up she was supposed to go up and when the notes went down she went down.
- "Wide-open notes, especially the ones without little stems, are held much longer than the black-faced ones," she said.
- The previous director of the choir had taught the singers to imitate him in tone, rhythm, and time.
- When the choir sang anthems with contrapuntal music, he brought them in at the right spot by a wave of the hand so that they didn't have to think.
- It wasn't that the choir lacked energy: they were energetic, cooperative to a fault, and eager to get better.
- Two members could play the piano, but made no connection between that and singing in the choir.
- More disturbing, the music committee was satisfied with the choir and grateful that someone was willing to donate his time and lead the singing so regularly.
- It was Floyd's job to convince the choir that they would enjoy their work more if they knew what they were doing.

- That would require special classes one night a week in addition to the Thursday night choir practice.
- He had his work cut out for him.
- Floyd knew that every choir had its own personality, taking turns at being quirky, delightful, cantankerous, wise and downright mean.
- And among choir members, there are long-nurtured likes, loves, resentments and memories that often resurfaced at the most inappropriate times.
- Floyd was shocked that the smallest and quietest member of the choir was the first to accept his call for additional practice to gain a deeper understanding of church music.
- The man, who often struggled to express himself in English, delivered a passionate endorsement of Floyd's plan to improve the choir via a three-month crash course in music.
- In conclusion, the man said, "I want to be better."
- The rest of the choir fell in line immediately, including three women whose husbands only marginally supported their being away from the house one night a week.

- The first night, Floyd made sure everybody had fun as each choir member identified every note in the familiar hymns, "A Mighty Fortress," and "Onward, Christian Soldiers."
- Within an hour's time, the choir was able to recognize scale-wise progressions and jumps of thirds and fourths.
- Learning rhythm and time was a little more difficult, but much more fun.
- The mathematical basis of time was explained, and choir members divided groups of notes into measures on the blackboard.
- After they had divided and measured the notes, each choir member was required to clap the time to teach it to other members.
- The second week, Floyd taught them how to beat time in 3/4 and 4/4.
- As the group would sing various hymns, one member would lead the group by beating the time.
- Within 15 minutes, the choir became extremely time conscious; at the same time, they were having fun.
- On the second night, Floyd moved to anthems.
- First, they got the notes and then clapped out the rhythm and time elements to each section of the anthem.
- No accompaniment was used; choir members tried sight reading the music.
- Later in the evening, he divided the group into quartets.
- For each singing quartet, there was a monitoring quartet who corrected the errors in notes, time and rhythm.
- To make it more interesting, the sopranos monitored the basses, the altos the tenors, the tenors the sopranos, the basses the altos.
- By this method, they not only learned their own parts, but the other parts as well.
- The third and fourth weeks were spent in a complete review of the first two lessons.
- Since the sopranos were the poorest of that particular choir, Floyd inverted parts: sopranos sang alto, tenor, and, on occasion, bass notes.
- At the end of the fourth night, the sopranos had gotten to the point where they were no longer dependent on the piano to lead them and could sing independently.
- In the meantime, five new members had joined the group.
- The new members had always wanted to join the choir, but were afraid they could not carry a tune in a bucket.
- The choir taught them how to carry tunes; no bucket was necessary.
- For his next lesson, Floyd began working toward the psychological approach—the striving for a "ringing head tone."
- Using the music of "Caro Mio Ben," the choir began to understand when the tone slipped from the right spot in the head, and they could tell when their partners lost the head tone.
- The choir was beginning to understand the "psychological feel" of the head tone.
- More important, the congregation was beginning to sense "a whole new choir" was in their midst.
- Within weeks, the choir decided as a group to attend evening services of a fellow church and observe what the choir was doing right or wrong.
- An excited, energized, all-Japanese choir gathered at the church with Floyd to report that the neighboring church's choir "sang in its throat and had little variety in tonal quality."
- They observed that the organ was always "a fraction ahead of the choir," and as such, "the hymns got consistently slower and slower"; the soloist, they reported, "had a beautiful head tone and his voice sang all over the church" but the "choir was ragged on its entrances and did not know when to come in."
- "In other words," as one member said, "they sound like we used to."
- Still ahead for Floyd was diction, proper breathing, and the more advanced works of Bach, Handel, and Mozart.

The railroad lured settlers to Spokane from as far away as Finland and Germany.

Life in the Community: Spokane, Washington

- Located in eastern Washington, Spokane originally was known as "Spokane Falls," was settled in 1871 and officially incorporated as a city in 1881.
- The city's name was drawn from the Native American tribe known as the Spokane, which means "Children of the Sun" in Salish.
- Completion of the Northern Pacific Railway in 1881 brought major settlement to the Spokane area, with the population increasing from 1,000 residents at incorporation to 19,922 in 1890.
- The railroad lured settlers from as far away as Finland, Germany, and England, and as close as Minnesota and the Dakotas.
- Spokane's growth was transformed by the Great Fire of 1889, which destroyed the city's downtown commercial district.
- Technical problems with a pump station resulted in no water pressure in the city when the fire started; even dynamiting buildings in the path of the inferno did not slow its progress.
- In the fire's aftermath, 32 blocks of Spokane's downtown were destroyed.
- The rebuilding process allowed for department stores to bloom and catalogue sales to take root in that developing city.
- Thanks to innovation, cheaper manufacture of plate glass in the mid-1890s had unleashed larger, stronger, cleaner display windows in department stores.
- Shopping was promoted as more of a social function; some stores even adopted the custom of calling female customers "ladies."
- Simultaneously, department stores were offering a kind of social equality at an affordable price.
- The demands of producing thousands of Civil War uniforms 40 years earlier had resulted in a new understanding of mass production of clothing—including the concepts of incremental sizing—which department stores used to expand factory-made, ready-to-wear clothing for men and women.
- At the same time, the availability of catalogs from faraway cities created competition on prices and informed consumers of the newest trends.
- The 1900 Sears, Roebuck catalogue made no mention of automobiles or automobile accessories; the mail order book did have 67 pages devoted to buggies, harnesses, saddles and horse blankets.
- Within a few years, automobiles made their presence known.
- Bestsellers for the year included books on fortune telling, palm reading, dream books, and after-dinner toasts.

(Offer expires December 31, 1908)

The best paid jobs in Spokane were in the lumber industry.

HISTORICAL SNAPSHOT
1903

- The first west-east transatlantic radio broadcast was made from the United States to England
- The Oxnard Strike of 1903 became the first time in U.S. history that a labor union was formed from members of different races, Mexican and Japanese in the agricultural fields of California
- Morris and Rose Mitchom introduced the first teddy bear in America
- El Yunque National Forest in Puerto Rico became part of the United States National Forest System as the Luquillo Forest Reserve
- Cuba leased Guantanamo Bay to the United States "in perpetuity"
- In New York City, the Martha Washington Hotel, the first hotel exclusively for women, opened
- The Hay-Herran Treaty, granting the United States the right to build the Panama Canal, was ratified by the U.S. Senate over the objections of Colombian Senate
- Dr. Ernst Pfenning of Chicago became the first owner of a Ford Model A
- The first stock car event was held at the Milwaukee Mile
- The wreck of the Old 97 engine at Stillhouse Trestle near Danville, Virginia, which killed nine people, inspired a ballad
- The first modern World Series pitted the National League's Pittsburgh against Boston of the American League
- Orville Wright flew an aircraft with a petrol engine at Kitty Hawk, North Carolina, in the first documented, successful, controlled, powered, heavier-than-air flight
- A fire at the Iroquois Theater in Chicago killed 600
- The Lincoln-Lee Legion was established to promote the Temperance Movement and signing of alcohol abstinence pledges by children
- The first box of Crayola crayons was made and sold for $0.05, containing eight colors; brown, red, orange, yellow, green, blue, violet and black

Selected Prices

Alarm Clock $2.50
Automobile, Graham Roadster $850.00
Baseball Calendar $0.30
Bookcase $18.25
Buggy $59.75
Camera $3.75
Corset $2.25
Light Bulb $1.50
Motorcycle $200.00
Tombstone $29.00

The entire range of human experience is present in a church choir, including, but not restricted to, jealousy, revenge, horror, pride, incompetence (the tenors have never been on the right note in the entire history of church choirs, and the basses have never been on the right page), wrath, lust and existential despair.
—Connie Willis, *The Winds of Marble Arch*

Editorial, *The Providence Journal*, May 10, 1903:

The day is coming when practically every household will have a telephone, just as it has other modern facilities. This may seem a broad statement, but no one can read the figures of the last few years without seeing how general the use of the instrument is getting to be.

"Prediction of inventor Thomas A. Edison," *The New York Times*, July 31, 1903:

Next year I will wager I can take a car of my own design, fitted with my motor and battery, and go to Chicago and return in less time, and with more pleasure, than any machine in existence. There will be no breakdowns, no explosion of gas or gasoline, and the trip will be made at an even 25 miles an hour.

Women should not be part of a choir; they belong to the ranks of the laity. Separate women's choirs, too, are totally forbidden, except for serious reasons and with permission of the bishop.

—Roman Catholic Sacred Congregation for Liturgy, Decree 22, November 1907

"The Most Wonderful Body of Water in the World Discovered in the State of Washington," *The New York Times*, November 2, 1902:

In the state of Washington, situated about 20 miles from the city of Spokane, there is a wonderful body of water that is known to the white people as Medical Lake, and to the Indians for years past as the Scookum Limechin Chuck, or Strong Medicine Water, which was said by them to come from the Sahaia Tyee, or Great Spirit, a pool that he had created to cure the Indians of all the ills that human flesh is heir to. This beautiful little lake is situated in the midst of a fine grazing and agricultural country, flanked by majestic mountain ranges, and lies like a medallion nestled in the midst of groves of stately pine trees. It is about a mile and a half long by a mile in width, and a more beautiful or wildly romantic spot cannot be found in the world, its natural surroundings being grand beyond description. Its shores are gently sloping, arising to no great height above the water's edge, the lake lying like a silver sheen at one's feet. This pretty little lake was first prominently called to the notice of the white settlers of that portion of the country about 30 years ago through the yearly pilgrimage of the Indians, who came from many miles on every side to bathe in and drink of its wonderful waters. While encamped about its shore they perform strange religious rites, singing and dancing and beating on their huge drums, whose thunder roll could be heard for miles reverberating through the canyons and hills, calling all Indians who might be within reach of their drums to join in the strange celebration and ceremonies, which oftentimes continue for days. It has only been within recent years that it was safe for white settlers to enter that portion of the state where the lake is situated, for the famous old Indian, Chief Joseph, one of the most renowned Indian warriors the West has ever known, sent out word that he would scalp any white man who dared to invade this (to the Indians) sacred ground or to bathe in or drink of the waters of the lake. After his subjugation, the country quickly settled up and the lake became immediately famous among the white settlers on account of its wonderful medicinal healing and curative properties. The lake is known to have been the rendezvous of the sick and afflicted Indians as far back as 1807, some of them being known to come from as far south as lower California, a distance of nearly 1,300 miles. One reason why such long pilgrimages were made was because of the fame the salts had achieved from the fact that the Indians had for years been taking away with them a powder discovered in the bottoms of the cooking utilities or dishes that they boiled the water of the lake in. These salts were carried to those whose infirmities made a personal visit to the lake impossible.

"A Civil Rights Case: Negro, Excluded From Spokane Restaurant, Loses Suit for Damages," *The New York Times*, December 2, 1900:

The jury in the suit of Emmet L. Holmes against the Washington Water Power Company returned a verdict this morning in favor of the defendant. Holmes was not served at a restaurant owned by the company because he is colored. He demanded $5,000 in damages.

It is claimed that by this decision, colored men can be excluded from any restaurant or saloon.

"Sparks From the Wire," *Atlanta Constitution*, March 14, 1902:

Capt. F. H. Smith, a well-known Englishman, who has arrived at Seattle, Washington, from Japan, declares the war between that country and Russia is soon to come. "Trouble over the Russian occupation of Manchuria is the cause of the trouble," said Capt. Smith, "and the Japanese are spoiling for a chance to whip someone. They are making all preparations for the scrap graph that must come very soon."

"Brave Little Japs, Many of Those Who Come to New York Are Bitterly Poor," *The Boston Sunday Globe*, June 7, 1903:

I make no defense for the ambition that causes one to cross thousands and thousands of miles of land and water to come to a strange and alien country for the pitiful employment of domestic service in the foreigner's household. There are not many Americans who would do this. Still, there is something admirable in the spirit behind it, which, after all, is superior to the pride scorning such employment. Many of the Japanese who come to New York are bitterly poor. It is an old delusion that the average student here is sent by the generous Japanese government. On the contrary, many of the young Japanese men in New York have come on their own account to satisfy their native curiosity and thirst for more knowledge of the great and fascinating West. How many of these youths arrive utterly penniless and friendless! But having reached the land of desire, they must at once "study the country." For this, time and money are required: the former they have; the latter they must obtain at once in order to exist. And so they go to work—the easiest work to obtain. They make excellent butlers, valets and cooks. They are both clean and dignified, excellent traits in a servant.

It is told of the Marquis Ito that, when a youth, he wandered about the streets of London, penniless, ragged and hungry, a starving alien in a strange land. No employment was too low for that one whose eager and ambitious mind was to point out to the civilized world a new sun of astonishing brightness arisen in the East.

That the Japanese merchants and men of means appreciate the real spirit which has brought their poorer countrymen to New York is shown by the really beautiful benevolence of these men. Many of them are private benefactors on a most unexpected scale, as is shown in the case of three tea merchants who have imported to this country a number of Japanese youths and are personally paying for their education and living. Besides this, the number of their protégés among the clerks and artisans is astounding.

1905 PROFILE

After 15-year old Monty Mandell got kicked out of his house for skipping school, he decided that the perfect job would be playing the piano and not having a boss to tell him what to do.

Life at Home

- At age 15, Monty Mandell became a journeyman piano player, which he defined as someone who was "willing to go somewhere today, to play somewhere tonight, so they can eat tomorrow."
- His musical preference was the emerging sound of ragtime—dance music for a nation ready to strut its stuff.
- Besides, by 1900, ragtime had leapt up and grabbed the public's attention by the throat; any musician who could capture the unique syncopation of ragtime was guaranteed a steady job.
- After his move to New Orleans, Monty landed two: the nighttime gig involved piano playing in an upscale cathouse near downtown New Orleans, while by day he recorded the most popular ragtime songs for a player piano company.
- Some nights Monty could earn from $75 to $100 in tips if the patrons liked his work; special tips were often paid by the customer after he selected both a prostitute and a piano player to accompany the adventure.
- Born at home in his parents' bed in 1884, Monty was christened Nicholas Mullikin Munguia, but changed his name after being thrown out of his father's house for skipping school to play piano in a low-rent whorehouse that got raided.
- Monty's boss had thought that her in-kind services would be sufficient to keep the police away; she was wrong and Monty was among those arrested.
- His explanation to his parents was viciously interrupted by a fist to the mouth.

Monty Mandell hit the road as a journeyman piano player at 15, always looking for his next job and his next meal.

- Monty had brought shame upon the family, his father succinctly exclaimed—no further explanation was necessary.
- According to his father, Monty's biggest transgression was not skipping school or working in a house of ill repute; it wasn't even his arrest—no, his biggest sin was devoting his time to ragtime music.
- "We come to America for opportunity and you take this gift and turn it into ragtime? It is not even music."
- That was five years earlier, when Monty's name was Nicholas like his father and his father's father.
- Monty was not about to turn loose of ragtime.
- He considered ragtime a purely original, all-American musical genre made unique by its driving syncopated, or "ragged," rhythm.
- And Monty was on the ground floor of its invention.
- Begun as dance music in the red-light districts of American cities such as St. Louis, ragtime was also suited to being published as popular sheet music, allowing for widespread distribution.
- Ragtime was preceded by its close relative, the cakewalk.
- In 1895, black entertainer Ernest Hogan published two of the earliest sheet music rags, one of which ("All Coons Look Alike to Me") eventually sold a million copies.
- He was the first to put on paper the kind of rhythm that was being played by non-reading musicians.
- In 1899, Scott Joplin's "Maple Leaf Rag" was published, demonstrating the depth and sophistication of ragtime.
- Monty found that playing The "Maple Leaf Rag" heavily influenced how he laid down melody lines, harmonic progressions and metric patterns.
- Monty started his career as an "earman" capable of learning music by listening, until he realized that the best musicians knew how to read written notes and considered an earman to be an untutored "faker."

Monty brought shame to his family, playing ragtime in houses of ill repute.

Life at Work

- Monty Mandell loved the unfailing cheerfulness of ragtime.
- Born toward the end the economic Panic of 1893, which lasted more than five years, ragtime was associated with good times and festivals.
- Monty was convinced that the popularity of ragtime had spread so quickly because so many people first heard its distinctive beat while soaking in the excitement of "World Fairs" in cities such as Chicago, Omaha, Buffalo, and St. Louis.
- Ragtime's blending of West African and European musical elements gave audiences a taste of the familiar beside the exotic.
- It could be instantly recognized anywhere in the world because of its rhythm.
- Whereas syncopation—the accenting of the normally weak beat—was sparingly employed in classical music, in ragtime a musician used both a syncopated and unsyncopated beat at the same time.
- In its simplest form, the rhythm of ragtime consists of a steady beat in the left hand and a syncopated beat in the right; in this way, the left-hand plays a 2/4 rhythm while the right-hand plays a piece in the same rhythm, but accents every third beat.
- Monty's black musician friends insisted that this approach was pure Africa; Monty just knew it was fun to play.
- One goal was to create the distinctive percussion sound of the banjo using a piano.

- To play the best ragtime music well required a sophisticated touch on the piano; most audiences, however, just wanted it to be happy, loud and upbeat.
- To make ragtime accessible to the average piano player, the sheet music sold in thousands of music stores nationwide was simpler and required less dexterity.
- On the other hand, the pieces Monty was hired to play for the player piano company were complex, nuanced and often brutally hard.
- But the hard work was worth it; when done right, the perforated paper rolls that propelled the player piano were almost magical—and brought music into the homes of all people—whether they had musical talent or not.
- One brand of player piano, the Pianola, was advertised using full-page color ads to sell the $250 musical device to homeowners.
- In addition, huge sums were spent producing piano rolls, with each company creating specifications—making them incompatible with others.
- By 1903, the Aeolian Company had more than 9,000 roll titles in its catalogue, adding 200 titles per month.
- Many companies' catalogues ran to thousands of rolls, mainly of light, religious or classical music.
- The position and length of the perforation determined the note played on the piano; when a perforation passed over one of the 65 holes, the note sounded.
- Piano rolls were in continuous mass production starting from around 1896.
- Monty was particularly adept at converting non-ragtime pieces of music into ragtime by changing the time values of melody notes, a style known as "ragging."
- Ragtime pieces came in a number of different styles and appeared under several different descriptive names.

Monty worked hard to master complex pieces for player pianos.

Life in the Community: New Orleans, Louisiana

- New Orleans was undergoing dramatic social change at the turn of the twentieth century.
- Long applauded as one of the most racially open cities in America, where blacks and whites and Creoles mixed freely in public places, by 1905, the Crescent City was being swept up in the same Jim Crow laws being passed throughout the South.
- Whereas in 1897, 97 percent of black men were eligible to vote, by 1901, the number had fallen to 1 percent.
- Black children were removed from the schools they had traditionally attended and athletes such as boxers and cyclists were no longer allowed to cross racial barriers to compete.
- Despite the city's good times and musical traditions casually constructed in a multicultural environment, New Orleans by 1905 was a segregated city.
- This shift in the racial climate of New Orleans also opened up job opportunities for white musicians like Monty Mandell.
- Positions in high-class cathouses that were once given to black musicians increasingly went to whites, whose presence was less controversial.
- Monty arrived in the Crescent city in 1898 only months after the United States declared war on Spain; fevered patriotism was everywhere.
- Brass bands vied with one another to create the most impressive sendoff of troops headed for battle in Cuba.
- New Orleans was alive with music: jazz, blues and ragtime could be heard beside waltzes, spirituals, polkas and mazurkas.
- There was music in the streets, at tea dances, in Audubon Park where people picnicked, and at balloon ascensions.
- The park featured sports fields and picnic facilities along the Mississippi River.
- In 1898, the Audubon Golf Course opened within the park, followed by the Audubon Zoo.
- At the same time, New Orleans was officially establishing its red-light district known as Storyville, a carefully defined area where prostitution, or "sporting matters," was permitted.
- Storyville was named for Alderman Sydney Story, a respectable businessman who was aiming to control the lewd activity, not allow it, and was appalled when the district came to be named for him.
- Approximately 2,000 prostitutes worked in the district, averaging about $70 per week.
- The 40 largest parlor houses brought in an average of $350,000 in alcohol weekly, which was sold at a 400 percent profit.
- Overall, the district generated $15 million a year in business that was then spent on a range of items including clothing, rent, perfume and police protection.

HISTORICAL SNAPSHOT
1905

- Rotary International was founded by four men in Chicago
- The Supreme Court invalidated New York's eight-hour workday law
- Las Vegas, Nevada, was founded with the auction of 110 acres
- The electromagnetic seismograph, chemical fire extinguisher, Vicks VapoRub (marketed as Vicks Magic Croup Salve), Palmolive Soap, Spiegel mail-order catalogue, and the National Audubon Society all made their first appearance
- Albert Einstein published four papers in which he formulated the theory of special relativity and explained the photoelectric effect by quantization
- Kappa Delta Rho was founded in Old Painter Hall at Middlebury College in Vermont
- Pledging to cover all phases of show business, *Variety* was first published
- A treaty mediated by President Theodore Roosevelt was signed by Japan and Russia; the latter ceded the island of Sakhalin and port and rail rights in Manchuria to Japan
- Oklahoma and New Mexico were admitted to the Union
- The French psychologist Alfred Binet invented intelligence tests
- Sigmund Freud sparked controversy with the publication of *Three Essays on the Theory of Sexuality*
- The Intercollegiate Athletic Association of the United States was founded and became the NCAA
- Frances Willard became the first woman honored in National Statuary Hall
- A. G. MacDonald drove the first auto to exceed 100 mph at Daytona Beach, Florida
- The engine in the new Ariel car was air-cooled in winter and water-cooled in summer
- A four-cylinder Cadillac debuted, with three-speed planetary transmission
- The Winton Motor Company acquired Cleveland Cap Screw Company, which became the Electric Welding Company
- The play *The Scarlet Pimpernel* opened at the New Theatre in London and began a run of 122 performances
- The Wright Brothers' third airplane (*Wright Flyer III*) stayed in the air for 39 minutes with Wilbur piloting the first flight lasting over half an hour
- A bomb that killed Frank Steunenberg, ex-governor of Idaho, resulted in a highly publicized trial against leaders of the Western Federation of Miners
- The ninth annual Boston Marathon was won by Fred Lorz of New York in 2:38:25.4
- *Huckleberry Finn* and *Tom Sawyer* were banned from the Brooklyn Public Library for setting a "bad example"
- The Niagara Movement was founded by W. E. B. Dubois

Selected Prices

Adding Machine $10.00
Baking Powder, Pound..$0.10
Drug, Worm Syrup, for Children $0.18
Handkerchief, Men's, White Linen..........................$0.50
Iron Stove..$19.50
Piano, Steinway $800.00
Rocking Chair, Leather...$9.75
Rolltop Desk 37.50
Stockings, Women's..$0.25
Tooth Cleanser, Tube $0.25

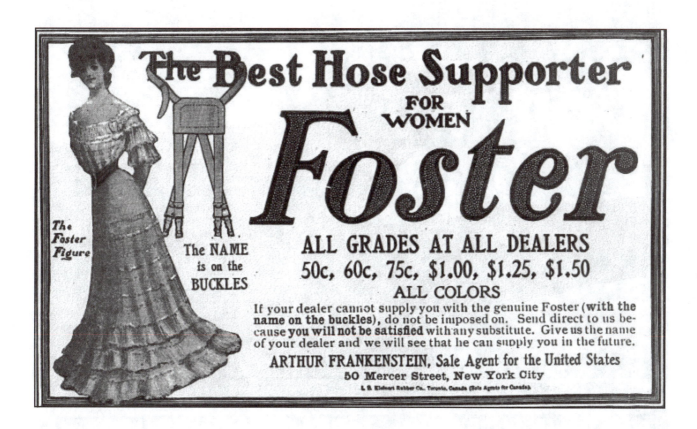

Ragtime is syncopation gone mad in its victims, and, in my opinion, can be treated successfully only like the dog with rabies, with a dose of lead. Whether it is simply a passing phase of our decadent art culture or an infectious disease which has come to stay, time alone can tell.

—Editor, *Etude Magazine*, 1903

"The Development of Motor Traffic," *Scientific American*, April 8, 1905:

Some interesting remarks were made by Mr. C. S. Rolls in the course of a paper on "The Development of Motor Traffic." After describing older types of vehicles, Mr. Rolls said that it was not until 1894 that the development became rapid. In the Paris-Bordeaux race in 1895, a speed of 15 miles an hour was obtained, while in the Paris-Madrid race of last year, the rate was nearly 70, and now a maximum speed of 100 miles has been reached. After the passage of the Light Locomotive Act, 1896, the manufacture of motor cars in Great Britain had shown remarkable growth. There are now at least 130 makers, but the trade did not yet equal that of France, where the industry employed 200,000 men, and last year's exports amounted to $5 million. England, however, produced more cars for heavy traffic. Last year, 6,133 light vehicles were imported, as against 3,747 in 1904, and the value of cars and parts imported during the year amounted to nearly $10 million. He anticipated that the time was approaching when a trustworthy car to carry three persons at a rate of 20 to 25 mph could be purchased at about $500-$750.

Copyright, 1905, by U. Co., N. Y.
"ME AND JACK."

"The Great Premier Diamond," *Scientific American*, April 8, 1905:

Quite a stir was made a couple of months ago by the announcement that a huge diamond, three times as large as any before discovered, had been unearthed in the Premier Mine, near Pretoria, South Africa. This precious jewel has since been brought to London, carrying, on the way, an insurance of $1.25 million. The first report that the stone was as large as a tumbler, and was worth three or four million dollars, has proved to be no exaggeration. The mammoth gem measures approximately 4 x 2 ½ x 1 1/4 and weighs 3,032 carats, or 1.7 pounds troy, equivalent to about one pound and six ounces avoirdupois. The stone is almost perfectly pure; a few grains are present, and it contains some flaws or cleavage planes, but fortunately they are so disposed that they can be cut away without appreciably reducing the size of the cut gem. Dr. G. A. F. Molengraaff describes the diamond as a single crystal having no twinning planes or lamellae. It is perfectly transparent, and looks like a piece of pure ice. He said, "It is certainly the purest of all very big stones known." Its structure shows that the stone was originally much larger. This is proved by the four flat cleavage planes, which have the regular octahedral position. Only a small portion of the natural surface of the stone remains, and the fragments broken must each have been very large.

"Celestial Cooks," *The Saturday Evening Post*, March 31, 1906:

We humbly submit that the United States should open a small backdoor in the stiff wall which shuts out the Chinese laborer. We hasten to explain why. There are at present 1,647,301 families, more or less, in this most prosperous land who cannot corral the "hired girl" (of tradition) by love, money or physical force. But we would not suggest that one job, even that of a domestic servant, be taken from the hands of true Americans (be they Swede, Irish, Italian, Greek or Hottentot). Nevertheless, some remedy is due the distressed American housewife, who, with money in hand, sits all day in the employment bureau and is spurned by "American" labor. Therefore, let the government admit in bond, to be kept in storage in some central spot, a couple of hundred thousand meek Celestials. Then, whenever the American housewife shall have duly advertised in vain for "help," let her have the right to apply to the nearest judge for an order of the court permitting her to extract from the said place of storage no more than one domestic servant—the employer to pay the maximum current wage and to make affidavit yearly that due efforts are being made to secure an American substitute for the coolie laborer. Whenever an American female shall apply for the Chinaman's job, the court can order that the Celestial be returned to the central depot.

Recorded Popular Songs: 1905

- "A Woman Is Only a Woman But a Good Cigar Is a Smoke"
  (words: Harry B. Smith, music: Victor Herbert)
- "And the World Goes on Just The Same"
  (words: Jean Lenox, music: Harry O. Sutton)
- "Bunker Hill"
  (words: Sam Erlich, music: Albert Von Tilzer)
- "Can't You See That I'm Lonely?"
  (words: Felix Feist, music: Harry Armstrong)
- "Daddy's Little Girl"
  (words: Edward Madden, music: Theodore F. Morse)
- "Everybody Works But Father"
  (words/music: Jean Havez)
- "Forty-Five Minutes From Broadway"
  (words/music: George M. Cohan, from the musical of the same name)
- "How'd You Like To Spoon With Me?"
  (words: Edward Laska, music: Jerome Kern)
- "I Love a Lassie"
  (words: Harry Lauder and George Grafton, music: Harry Lauder)
- "I Want What I Want When I Want It"
  (words: Henry Blossom, music: Victor Herbert)
- "If A Girl Like You Loved a Boy Like Me"
  (words/music: Will D. Cobb, music: Gus Edwards)
- "In My Merry Oldsmobile"
  (words: Vincent P. Bryan, music: Gus Edwards)
- "In the Shade of the Old Apple Tree"
  (words: Harry H. Williams, music: Egbert Van Alstyne)
- "It Ain't All Honey and It Ain't All Jam"
  (words/music: Fred Murray and George Everard)
- "Jolly Pickaninnies"
  (music: Ernst Rueffe)
- "Just a Little Rocking Chair and You"
  (words: Bert Fitzgibbon and Jack Drislane, music: Theodore F. Morse)
- "Little Girl, You'll Do"
  (words: Benjamin Hapgood Burt, music: Alfred Solman)
- "My Gal Sal"
  (words/music: Paul Dresser)
- "Automobile Honeymoon"
  (words: William Jerome, music: Jean Schwartz)
- "Ramblin' Sam"
  (words: Harry H. Williams, music: Jean Schwartz)
- "Tammany"
  (words: Vincent P. Bryan, music: Gus Edwards)
- "The Umpire Is a Most Unhappy Man"
  (words: Will M. Hough and Frank R. Adams, music: Joseph E. Howard)

"Lyceum Theater," *The Boston Daily Globe*, October 17, 1897:

Fred Rider's Moulin Rouge extravaganza company will appear at the Lyceum Theater this week in a sensational program. A burlesque satire, entitled *A Hot Box*, will be the spectacular feature of the show, in which the 30 members of the company will be introduced in musical and comedy diversions.

In the vaudeville will appear Harris and Walters, comedy sketch artists; the Blackberry sisters; an entertaining novelty in "rag time" coon imitations; Gordon and Lick, musical comedians; Jack and Jennie Bernard, in a lively sketch; Urline sisters; burlesque stars and duelists; and Cooper and Stewart, in funny parodies and sayings.

Among other novelties will be seen the "Golf Girls" in a review of the famous pastime, "Frolic of the Shepherds," the Plerot Quartet, a dancing novelty in the "Moulin Rouge Bal Champetre.

ADVERTISEMENT: If You Love Music You Should Own a Cecilian, *Marion Daily Star (Ohio)*, April 24, 1904:

Music is desirable under all circumstances. If there are guests to entertain, an impromptu dance suggested, or a college "sing," the Cecilian will be found a never-ready accompanist. Perhaps you prefer a concert with a Paderewski, or a Hofmann, or would you like to run over the airs you heard at last night's opera. With the Cecilian, every taste can be gratified, whether calls for grand or light opera, ragtime favorites, old-fashioned melodies, or accompaniments for solo or chorus singing, violin or "cello." Come in anytime and have us play the Cecilian for you. Perry & Hale, Grand Opera House Block, Marion, Ohio

1909 PROFILE

Despite the scorn of his fellow musicians, Arthur Farwell used the musical rhythms of native Americans to compose "American" music, earning himself the title of being an "Indianist."

Life at Home

- When publishers rejected Arthur Farwell's concept of using Native American musical rhythms to create "American" music, he founded the Wa-Wan Press in 1901 to promote the importance of exploring folk music in search of America's musical roots.
- For the past eight years he had run the operation from his house, doing nearly everything by himself.
- Arthur was born in 1872 in St. Paul, Minnesota, to well-educated New England transplants; his father prospered in the hardware business.
- This provided the family with servants, tutors and luxuries such as electricity.
- Arthur studied the violin as a boy and displayed enormous prowess.
- His educated mother encouraged his interests and wrote several progressive articles on child rearing for the Chicago-based *Christian Union Magazine*.
- At home, she reveled in the opportunity to stage musicals featuring Arthur, his sister Sidney, and children of their neighbors.
- As a teen, Arthur also developed his handyman skills with excessive tinkering, created his own camera and fashioned a dark room, built a recording telegraph and visited Indian camps along the shores of Lake Superior.
- There he witnessed Sioux Indians perform sun dances and drank in the impressive speeches made by the old Indian priests.

Arthur Farwell used the rhythms of Native American music to compose what he called American music.

- Hunting expeditions into the North Woods were led by Indian guides, and trips to the Winter Ice Carnival in St. Paul included visits to a Sioux Indian village.
- Arthur and his sister Sidney attended the Baldwin Seminary in St. Paul, designed for the children of "upper-class families."
- An advertisement for the school in 1888 highlighted its "Thorough preparation for our best eastern colleges" and "full courses in the classics, German, French, music, elocution, and drawing."
- During the summer prior to college, Arthur worked at a music camp, cutting trails by day and playing music by night.
- The artistic challenge and camaraderie were exhilarating.
- As an engineering student at the Massachusetts Institute of Technology, Arthur realized his vocation while attending a presentation by the Boston Symphony.
- "The concert opened a whole new world for me, and I decided on the spot to become a composer," he recalled. "The heavenly Shubert spread through my nerves like liquid fire…the mysteries of nature, of life, of creation were revealed to me. Like Tiresias of old, the heavens being open to me, I became blind to the things of earth. I was lost and I was saved."

Once Arthur heard the Boston Symphony, he decided to become a composer, and the old music hall became his shrine.

- After that, "the shrine for me was the old music hall…there, weekly was the vivifying Grail unveiled."
- In his spare time, Arthur continued with photography, lexical tinkering and inventing, and received a patent for a toy puzzle in 1890.

- To earn money at school, he created astrological charts for his classmates for their amusement.
- After completing his degree in 1893, he studied for a time with composer George Chadwick in Boston, a member of the Second New England School, but rebelled against his teacher's academic drift.
- At the same time, the panic of 1893 was taking a toll on the family.
- His father had sold the highly successful hardware business at the right time and invested in a foundry at the wrong time; it failed during the worst depression in recent history.
- When he returned to St. Paul, the big house and servants were gone.
- The financial independence of the family had disappeared; the Panic would linger until 1897.
- Changes were also underway in the measurement of time, thanks to the ubiquitous needs of the railway system.
- Time no longer conformed to the natural rhythms of the seasons but to the mechanical pace of the pocket watch and the factory whistle, or the railroad station clock.
- Until then, towns and cities had used the sun directly overhead to set the public clocks; since every town was geographically different, every town had a different established time.
- Sacramento, California, for example, was three minutes and 56 seconds later than San Francisco, creating havoc for a nation now addicted to railroads and their schedules.
- After decades of discussion and considerable rancor, an association of businesses and scientists, without benefit of federal law, had established standardized time in 1883.
- A decade later, their Standard Railway Time had replaced a panoply of local times and standard time zones; as the *Indianapolis Daily Sentinel* noted, "The sun is no longer to boss the job. Fifty-five million people must now eat, sleep and work, as well as travel, by railroad time."
- In St. Paul and later in Boston, Arthur began to compose in earnest, completing dozens of pages while making progress on learning to play the piano, which he practiced for two hours a day.
- Writing proved difficult and torturous.
- "How I long for the time when I can take up the beautiful clean paper and put notes down as I am writing now, knowing just how they will sound. At present, I cannot do anything. Everything I attempt disgusts me for I butcher it so."
- To make ends meet, he worked in a bookstore, gave music lessons, and sold a few of his songs "to grudging publishers for five dollars each."
- In July 1897, he sailed for Germany, where he studied with German composer Engelbert Humperdinck, best known for his opera, *Hänsel und Gretel*, before returning to the States, teaching briefly at Cornell University, and eventually settling in Newton Centre, near Boston.

Life at Work

- Arthur Farwell discovered his musical calling in Bartlett's old Cornhill bookshop in Boston.
- There, a clerk found him a copy of Alice Fletcher's *Indian Story and Song*, which he studied carefully.
- The book brought back memories of Minnesota and his encounters with the Indian village on Lake Superior.
- He was taken by the spiritual life of the Indians and their reverence shown in ceremonies and songs to the Great Spirit.
- His truest revelation took place when he actually sang the songs of the Native Americans and took the time to create the rhythms exactly as described in the book.
- The melodies took on new meaning; even primitive songs, he realized, could be a distinct and concentrated musical idea.
- "Here was congenial poetic material, the substance of art, in inexhaustible quantity, and the spur of twin-born melodies with it, to set it moving in a musical direction. Nothing was more natural than to take advantage of the situation."
- Arthur set to work on a number of sketches based on the melodies and legends in the book, retaining the Indian themes while developing the scores around them.

Arthur worked on Native American melodies and legends he read about, forging a distinctive personal voice from America's roots.

- In doing so, he forged a distinctive personal voice by looking to the roots of America at a time when most classically trained musicians rejected anything American, let alone Indian.
- After finishing a number of musical sketches, Arthur tried them out before an audience during a morning lecture at Cornell; he received such interest, he was asked to play them again the same afternoon at the house of one of the professors.
- The time had come for Arthur to take up the cause of native music full time.
- Even though Arthur's musical education was rooted in German Romanticism, and his early composition training in the classicism of the Second New England School, he became convinced that native voices should be heard.
- Recent studies in ethnology and folklore were yielding information about various American Indian cultures.
- In 1880, Theodore Baker transcribed songs from a number of tribes and published them two years later in a German-language dissertation for his doctorate from the University of Leipzig.
- Edward MacDowell borrowed themes from Baker's work when composing his Second Indian Suite for orchestra in 1894.
- Further impetus came with the arrival, in 1892, of Antonín Dvořák to teach in New York City.
- He exhorted American composers to stop imitating European models, and to turn instead to indigenous sources.
- Composer Frederick Burton transcribed several melodies which he later turned into art songs.
- But it was left to Arthur, as founder of the Wa-Wan Press, a not-for-profit music publishing venture based in Newton, Massachusetts, to champion the movement.
- Convinced that the future of American art music rested in folk traditions, Arthur realized that America must first throw off the overbearing German influence that closed so many musical doors.
- "Since our national musical education, both public and private, is almost wholly German, we inevitably, and unwittingly, see everything through German glasses. The result of this today is that the German quality in music, dominating our whole musical life, has made it almost impossible for any other quality to gain recognition," Arthur wrote.
- In 1903, he said in the Wa-Wan Press, "We demand an impossibility of the American composer. We ask you not to shock us by being un-German, but at the same time, to give us American music."
- The Wa-Wan Press was simply the first step in the movement to help change the musical scene in America within a decade.
- That meant publishing the music of contemporary American composers, many working in an experimental vein, while weathering the criticism of traditionalists.
- Arthur started without capital or backing from a small office supported by his own composition sales and lecture fees.
- The intent was to showcase American talent and "expose interesting or worthwhile work done with American folk material as a basis."
- "Salability had nothing to do with the matter whatsoever" when selecting music, he wrote.

- To advance the cause of this "new music," Arthur published beautifully designed and engraved vocal and instrumental compositions supported by program notes and essays eight times annually for the first five years, and then increased to monthly editions in 1906.
- His critics fired back that "no great music has ever been written by people living under a republican form of government."
- Reginald de Koven, a composer of operettas, held that Indians were a dying race who had no influence on America, and that the Negro melodies were from "imported exotics" and not American music at all.
- Gustav Mahler was equally unsympathetic: "It seems to me that the popular music of America is not American at all, but that which the American Negro, transplanted to American soil, has chosen to adopt."
- To tell his "Indianist" story, Arthur composed extensively and traveled widely throughout the United States lecturing about the "American story."

Arthur's arrangements of tribal melodies responded to the spirit of Native American music, rather than its context.

- Many trips were planned around where a paying audience could be found to support the shoestring operation.
- Then, to bring even greater notice to his cause, Arthur formed National Wa-Wan Societies across the nation and encouraged established professional singers to perform the new American pieces.
- Some were concerned that representing the new works would harm their reputation.
- Slowed by a breakdown and financial problems, Arthur believed the time had come for others to carry the torch of ethnic music.
- Arthur's own arrangements of tribal melodies, while colored by European harmonic practices, boldly departed from the literal context of Native American music and responded, instead, to its spirit.
- One of the young composers to join Farwell's movement was Henry Franklin Belknap Gilbert, who composed several songs based on the music of Native Americans and African-Americans.
- In addition, he collaborated with Edward Curtis to transcribe the wax cylinder recordings of Indian music collected during Curtis's work, *The North American Indian.*

Life in the Community: St. Paul, Minnesota

- Located on the north bank of the Mississippi River, St. Paul, Minnesota's economy and nicknames have been dictated by water.
- The city's defining physical characteristic, the connecting Mississippi and Minnesota rivers, was carved into the region during the last ice age.
- Serving as the last accessible point to unload boats coming upriver, St. Paul was dubbed "The Last City of the East."
- Founded near historic Native American settlements as a trading and transportation center, the city rose to prominence after it was named the capital of the Minnesota Territory in 1849.
- The settlement originally was referred to as "Pig's Eye" when Pierre "Pig's Eye" Parrant established a popular tavern.
- After Father Lucien Galtier, the first Catholic pastor of the region, established the Log Chapel of Saint Paul, he made it known that the settlement was now to be called by that name.
- Together with its twin city Minneapolis, St. Paul grew into the largest urban area in the state.
- By 1858, when Minnesota was admitted to the Union, more than 1,000 steamboats were in service at St. Paul, making the city a gateway for settlers to the Minnesota frontier, or Dakota Territory.
- By the turn of the twentieth century, St. Paul and Minneapolis were the center of commerce.
- New buildings were being constructed as America began seeing itself as a modern nation and even a world power in light of the Spanish-American War, which earned the United States possession of foreign lands.
- In the early 1900s, the average American earned $12.79 per 59-hour week; America was starkly divided between its rich and poor.
- In 1907, just 8 percent of the country's homes were wired for electricity; one architect claimed the electrical lighting cost reckless, while legions of workers were convinced it was too dangerous to have in one's house.
- The impact of mass-market magazines was growing; in 1885, four monthly magazines with circulations of 100,000 or more cost at least $0.35 a copy.
- By 1905, there were 20 mass-market magazines that cost $0.10 to $0.15 each, with a combined circulation of 5.5 million; most were supported by full-page or half-page advertisements peddling beer, talcum powder, salad dressing, or photography film.

St. Paul, with its twin city Minneapolis, grew into the largest urban area in Minnesota.

Manage Your Home by Telephone

Then any servant, any member of the family will be in sound of your voice at any time of the day or night.

You save steps—you save time—by using

Western-Electric Inter-phones

Simply pushing the proper button on the little switch-board rings and connects you with the desired party.

Inter-phones require no operator. They will last a lifetime, and cost less than one cent a week per station to maintain.

Inter-phones are made only by the Western Electric Company. This is assurance of highest quality. They can be installed complete, including labor and all material, at a cost ranging from $6 to $30 per station, depending upon the type of equipment selected.

This telephone is the desk type. The wall type combines both telephone and switch-board. All types are neat, compact and beautifully finished.

Write our nearest house for Booklet No. 8266 containing complete information. No home is complete without an Inter-phone System.

The Western Electric Company Furnishes Equipment for Every Electrical Need

WESTERN ELECTRIC COMPANY

New York,	Chicago,	*Manufacturers of*	Saint Louis,	San Francisco,
Philadelphia,	Indianapolis,	*the 5,000,000*	Kansas City,	Los Angeles,
Boston,	Cincinnati,	*"Bell" Telephones*	Denver,	Seattle,
Pittsburg,	Minneapolis.		Dallas,	Salt Lake City.
Atlanta.			Omaha.	London

Montreal   Toronto   Winnipeg   Vancouver   Antwerp

Berlin   Paris   Johannesburg   Sydney   Tokyo

HISTORICAL SNAPSHOT
1909

- The National Association for the Advancement of Colored People (NAACP) was formed with the memory of the Springfield, Illinois, race riots still fresh
- The first subway car with side doors went into service in New York City
- America's Great White Fleet returned to its base in Virginia, following its triumphant circumnavigation of the globe
- The University of Minnesota became the first U.S. university to establish a school of nursing
- Federal legislation was approved prohibiting the use of opium
- Professional baseball ruled that players who jumped contracts would be suspended for five years
- Gustav Mahler conducted the New York Philharmonic for the first time
- Joan of Arc was declared a saint by the Catholic Church
- "Shine On, Harvest Moon" by Ada Jones and Billy Murray was one of the year's top songs
- The 13th Boston Marathon was won by Henri Renaud of New Hampshire in 2:53:36.8
- Glenn Curtiss sold the first U.S. commercial airplane
- The Payne-Aldrich Tariff Act abolished the import duty on hides to help the U.S. shoe industry, but maintained high duties on iron and steel and raised duties on silk and cotton goods
- The Sixteenth Amendment to the U.S. Constitution providing for the taxation of incomes was submitted to the 46 states for ratification
- Moved by the words of 19-year-old Clara Lemlich, the 20,000 members of the Ladies' Waist Makers' Union voted to strike for better working conditions and resulted in New York's wealthiest women joining the picket line
- Texas Gulf Sulphur Company was incorporated to compete with Herman Frasch's Union Sulphur Company in exploiting deposits found in the Gulf of Mexico (see 1895)
- The distress signal, SOS, was used by an American ship, *Arapahoe*, off Cape Hatteras, North Carolina, for the first time
- The U.S. Mint issued the first Lincoln head pennies
- Colored moving pictures were demonstrated at Madison Square Garden, New York City
- Leo Baekeland of Yonkers, New York, patented the first thermosetting plastic, which he called Bakelite
- Wilbur Wright flew from Governors Island up the Hudson to Grant's Tomb and back in 33 minutes, marking the first successful flight ever seen in New York; his flying machine was equipped with a red canoe for emergency water landings

Selected Prices

Camera, Kodak	$50.00
Children's Woolen Hosiery, Pair	$0.25
Corn Whiskey, Gallon	$2.65
Horse Bit	$0.50
Ice Box	$16.50
Magic Lantern, 12 Colored Slides	$4.98
Men's Cuffs, Pair	$0.25
Petticoat	$1.39
Player Piano	$700.00
Snake Fight Ticket	$2.00

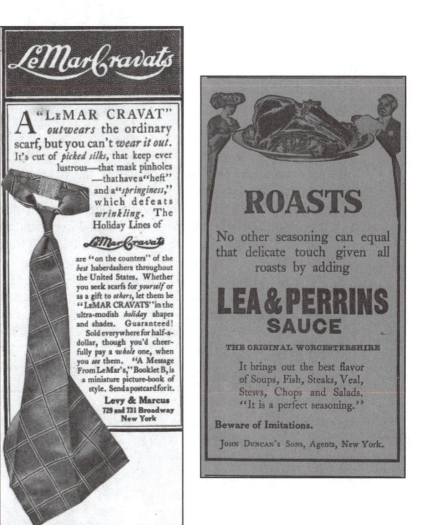

"Arthur Farwell's 'Object of the Movement'," *Wa-Wan Press*, 1901:

The Wa-Wan Press, at Newton Centre, Massachusetts, is an enterprise organized and directly conducted by composers, in the interest of the best American compositions. It aims to promote by publication and public hearings, the most progressive, characteristic, and serious works of American composers, known or unknown, and to present compositions based on the melodies and folklore of the American Indians.

God has not been preparing the English-speaking and Teutonic peoples for a thousand years for nothing but vain and idle self-contemplation and self-admiration. No! He has made us the master organizers of the world to establish a system where chaos reigns. He has given us the spirit of progress to overwhelm the forces of reaction throughout the earth. He has made us adept in government that we may administer government among savage and senile peoples. Were it not for such a force as this, the world would relapse into barbarism and night. And of all our race, He has marked the American people as His chosen nation to finally lead in the regeneration of the world. This is the divine mission of America, and it holds for us all the profit, all the glory, all the happiness possible to man. We are trustees of the world's progress, guardians of its righteous peace. The judgment of the Master is upon us: "Ye have been faithful over a few things; I will make you ruler over many things."

—U.S. Senator Albert J. Beveridge of Indiana, January 9, 1900

"An American Indian Composer," Natalie Curtis, *Harper's Magazine*, September 1903:

"What has Pahana (the Hopi word for American) come for, how long is she going to stay, what are in all those boxes?" My hostess was peppered with questions by the group of curious Hopi Indians who had gathered to witness my arrival in their village after a two-day drive across the Arizona wilderness of beauty known as the "Painted Desert."

What was in those boxes? Ah, thereby hung the tale! They held the purpose of my visit to the Indian Reservation: a phonograph. Many have said truly that the songs of the Negro and the American Indian contain a wealth of musical material for the composer. But I sought the Indian songs solely that I might reverently record and preserve what I could of an art that is now fast passing beneath the influence of the Moody and Sankey hymn tunes and patriotic songs taught to the Indians in the government schools.

Before coming West, I had the vague idea that all Indian music was a monotonous, barbaric chanting without form, with no beginning and no end. I shared, too, in the ignorance regarding the Indian that makes us class all tribes together as a race of savage people in the same primitive grade of development. Not until I saw with my own eyes the vast differences even in tribes who are close neighbors could I realize the absolute truth of the authoritative statement that there are as great differences between the tribes of North American Indians as there are between Norwegians and Spaniards among Europeans.

Certainly no people could be more unalike than the peace-loving Hopis and their warlike neighbors, the Navajos. And yet, their reservations lie side-by-side in the desert and tablelands of northeastern Arizona. The Hopis are commonly known as "Moquis," a word of their own language, signifying "death." It is thought that it was derisively applied to them by the Navajos, for they call themselves the Hopis which means "quiet" or "good people." It was to escape the ravages of the Ute and Apache that the agricultural Hopis fled to the very summit of the rocky plateaus that rise 600 feet abrupt and sheer from the level sands. On inaccessible craggy heights, they built their villages, seven in number, of which Oraibi is the largest and most characteristic….

The scarcity of water can hardly be conceived by those who have not been there. Every drop used in Oraibi has to be brought for a distance of two miles, one-half of which is up the steep trail, and carried all that long way in heavy earthen jars on the backs of toiling women.

And so the Hopi prays for rain. His ceremonial dances are all for rain; it is a great need, the great want, the one cry I have heard since I had come West much of these village dwelling Indians, and I expected to see in them a higher grade of culture than that of the nomad Navajos or the Indians of southern Arizona. But I was not prepared to find people with such definite art forms, such elaborately detailed ceremonials, such crystallized traditions, beliefs, and customs.

Their music astounded me. I felt that I had come in search of gold and had found diamonds. The Hopis' every act of life seems to be a ceremonial rite, containing a symbol, a poetic significance known only to those outsiders who have dwelt in the Hopi land and are deeply versed in Hopi lore. "We have songs for everything," my little Hopi neighbor explained when I caught her singing as she combed her baby's hair. "We have songs for dancing, songs for planting, songs for grinding corn, for putting the babies to sleep, even for combing the baby's hair." She laughed as she continued the refrain which my visit had interrupted.

These songs for different purposes are different in character. They are all definite in form, with forceful, graceful, or poetic words. The Katcina dance songs consist of an introduction of vowel syllables, then the song itself, almost interspersed with vowel refrains, and lastly a sort of coda, again with vowel sounds.

And the Hopi sing. Theirs is no crooning over a campfire, no monotonous chanting, no nasal droning. The men have fine, clear voices, and the women sing softly with a "breathy" tone, the quality of which sounds often just a little sharp in pitch. The gentle lullabies, the pretty, graceful basket-songs of the women, and the melodies to which they grind their corn are different from the rugged, rhythmic Katcina songs as are the cliffs of the mesa from the blooms in the fields below.

There are three great elements in music: rhythm, melody, harmony. The rhythmic quality of the Hopi Katcina songs is, in its intensity and variety of syncopation, unlike anything I ever heard. And it must be heard to be realized, for to me the Hopis sense of rhythm seems far to surpass ours. In Japanese music, also, I had found a wonderful variety of rhythm. Here again, the rhythmic forms seem more complex and interesting than ours. But the Japanese have no harmony, and their melodies are monotonous, so that they rely chiefly on the ever-changing rhythm for variety and musical effect. Not so the Hopi. Though he, too, lacks harmony, his melodies are rich and full of beauty. And so Japan, with its written language and advanced civilization, is still behind our American Village Indian in the art of music. Indeed, it is a question whether in their free use of unusual intervals, the Hopi do not surpass in melodic variety not only the Japanese, but the Europeans as well. Rhythm and melody are essential in any music, no matter how crude; but harmony, being a later development, is naturally absent in primitive forms of music. For this reason, though we may compare them, we cannot place Japanese and Hopi music on the same plane with our own. Our system of polyphony and harmony with its instrumentation, its combination of choral and instrumental effects, and its wealth of tone color, is a world of which the Hopi who sings always in unison, does not dream. He has but one really musical instrument, the flute, and marks the rhythm of his songs with the rattle, the drum, and the crude scraping of wooden sticks.

We are used to consider Americans musical people, and it was impossible to say whether they will ever create anything like the symphonies of Beethoven and the operas of Wagner, yet the music I see before me has overturned forever my attitude towards her musical creation.

1909 NEWS FEATURE

"The World's Music After Five Decades," Oscar G. Sonneck, director of the music division, Library of Congress, Washington, *The New York Times*, December 12, 1909:

You desire my view on the difference then and now in the art of music. Here it is:

In opera we are just as much a colony of Europe as we were 50 years ago. Opera is still mainly a showman's business and not yet an integral part of our daily musical life. Opera is not less of an exotic hothouse plant now than it was in 1850 or 1750. The problem's only sensible solution: good opera and good English is as little appreciated by managers and guarantors and patrons as 50 years ago.

Music as an essential factor of national culture is not recognized now officially by our people very much more than it was 50 years ago. Hence, the cause of federal, state, municipal encouragement of the art for economic, artistic, and educational reasons in the interests of the people has not greatly been advanced. Rank commercialism in music still outweighs a little the more businesslike professional attitude of art for art's sake, which incidentally means art for the people's sake.

Musical trash is published and consumed in vastly greater quantities than 50 years ago; in fact, the craze for adulterated musical food products has more than kept its pace with the growth and standardization of the population, which, on the other hand, of course, automatically created a much larger demand for and supply of good music, whether light or heavy.

You see, I began with the Lamento, now for the Triomfo. Fifty years ago, American-born musicians worthy of the name were few and far between. Today, they number many, many thousands, and the European invasion has been reduced to almost normal proportions. Then the musicians were without organization: now they, too, have their unions, and, on the whole, their good deeds outnumber their sins. .

Fifty years ago, our musical industries were in their infancy: today they contribute a remarkable share to the country's business. Fifty years ago, musical criticism reflected the still provincial atmosphere of our musical life: today we have some, though not enough, critics who deserve the name and who are fully as capable as their best European colleagues. Fifty years ago, music schools were extremely few; today, we number them by the hundreds, unfortunately, still including numerous musical bucket shops.

In those days the importance of public school music was just dawning on the authorities; now the matter is beyond the controversial stage, and the chaotic conditions of method are rapidly being settled by experts far beyond Lowell Mason's attainments. Fifty years ago, music had no place in the curriculum of our colleges; today, colleges without a musical department are rapidly being forced into the minority. We have even succeeded in forcing credit for music on professors who consider the proper interpretation of a Beethoven sonata less of an intellectual accomplishment than that recitation of a "mensa rotunda est."

Fifty years ago, we had no musical libraries; today, European librarians are beginning to view our competition with concern. Fifty years ago, our church music was floundering about in an erratic course; today, in spite of partly secular byproducts, it is the field of music in which we are most efficient, and this is largely due to the now splendid equipment of the American organist and choirmaster. (N. B.—not included in this praise are bank clerks, chemists, grocers, etc., who make music on Sundays.)

Fifty years ago, American songbirds were to be found in the woods only; today, they are invading European opera houses, etc., by the dozen, with a reasonable prospect of being re-imported to America sooner or later with a maximum import duty borne by the American public. Fifty years ago, our orchestras, with two or three exceptions, were still in the provincial scratch variety; today, we have at least a dozen that range from good to excellent, and though they are far too few for a country like ours, and most of them lead a somewhat precarious existence, yet we have them.

Fifty years ago, the American composer was practically an unknown species; today, we possess a score of composers who hold their own against their European brethren, geniuses, of course, being hors de concours. Fifty years ago, America practically did not exist for encyclopedias of music; today, American institutions and musicians figure noticeably in Grove, Riemann, etc.

It would seem, then, that in music, too, "the world has been remade in 50 years." I have been dealing only with American conditions! Now I'm perfectly willing to admit that ours is God's own country, but I do not believe that therefore all of the other countries still or already belong to the devil and hence should be disregarded.

In music, at least, Europe is not yet an old dog without teeth. If we were limping behind times 50 years ago and now have caught up with European countries in many respects, that surely does not have the substitution of the pars pro toto….

I suppose that your special number aims at overwhelming proof that the progress of mankind has been unprecedented and revolutionary during the last 50 years. If progress means a timely adaptation to changing conditions, then conditions must change so absolutely within a given period that the results will change "the whole face of the world," as you put it.

In music, we have witnessed no such progress, because music moves very much as it did 50 years ago. Some channels of expression and opportunity have become wider, some deeper, some erring, some shallower, and the whole network is perhaps more complicated, but on the whole the differences for external, not internal, are vital.

Indeed, not even the pianola and kindred musical instruments have revolutionized music, except in the advertisements of manufacturers. We use the same tonal system in the same instruments as 50 years ago. The human hand still has five fingers, and the human voice is still the same, though our virtuosos have changed….

By this I mean many so-called novelties are by Chopin, without having been composed by him, which is rather fortunate for Chopin's reputation. Similarly, we're still being fed on Wagner, Liszt, Brahms and Verde. There is apparently no limit to the supply of blotting paper used by them.

We have had great composers during the last 50 years, but they have not revolutionized the vital principles nor even the forms of music. With all this genius, with all his inventions and discoveries of musical details, Richard Strauss has not opened an aesthetically new era in music. Whether or not Claude Debussy is doing this remains to be seen, but even he, unless he be merely a meteor, fell from the clouds.

And here I am at last! I believe too firmly in the phylogenic method of observation, as against the photographic method of computing aesthetic results for quantity, volume, surface and externals to be any assistance to you in proving your point. The 50 years from 1600 to 1650 were revolutionary in your sense; those from 1850 to 1900 were not. Thus, while faces have changed during the last 50 years, the face of the musical world has not, and most assuredly in music, the world has not been remade within 50, even though that be true, which I doubt, in all other respects.

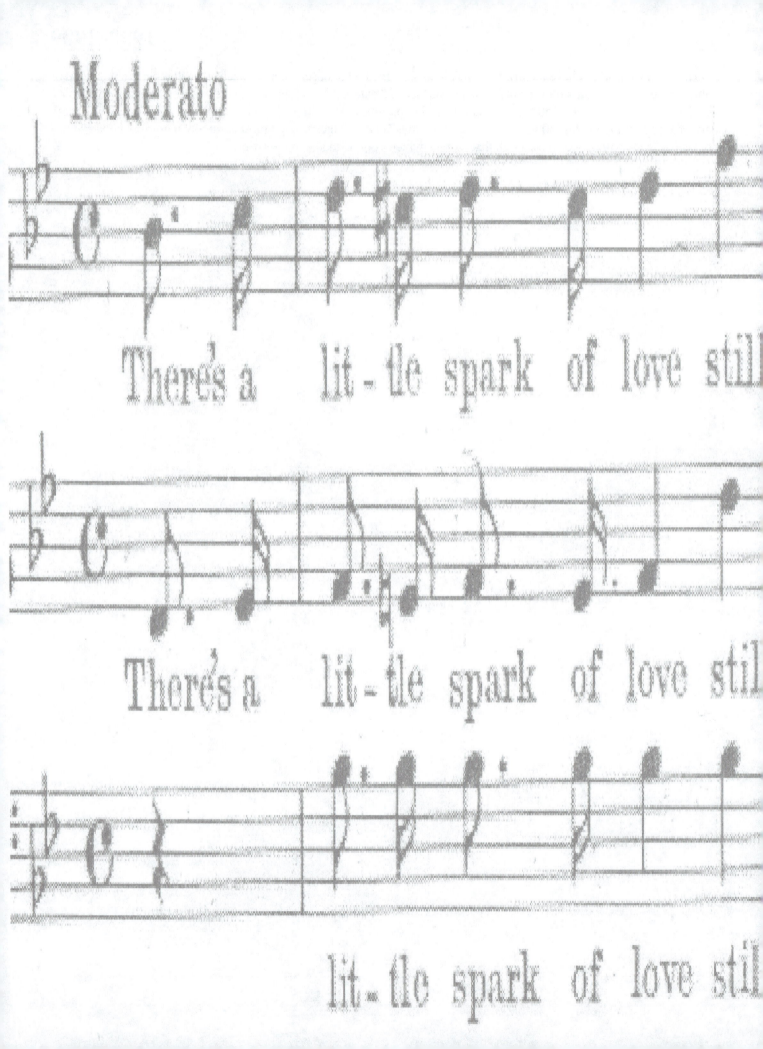

Moderato

There's a   lit - tle spark of love still

There's a   lit - tle spark of love still

lit - tle spark of love still

1910–1919

America was booming during the second decade of the century, and economic excitement was in the air as exemplified by the new dance sensation—the tango. Anything seemed possible to those who had any resources to explore the possibilities. America's upper class now enjoyed the world's finest transportation—by train and automobile—and spent considerable time discovering new forms of entertainment. Opera continued to grow in popularity, and church music expanded its reach and sophistication. At the same time, an emerging middle class was showing that it was capable of carrying a greater load of managerial decisions, freeing factory owners and stockholders to travel, experiment, and study ways to cure the ills of the poor. Millions of dollars were poured into libraries, parks and literacy classes designed to uplift the immigrant masses flooding to American shores. America was prospering and the country's elite were reevaluating America's role as an emerging world power which no longer had to look to Britain for approval.

During the decade, motorized tractors changed the lives of farmers, while electricity extended the day of urban dwellers. Powered trolley cars, vacuum cleaners, hair dryers, and electric ranges moved onto the modern scene. Wireless communications bridged San Francisco to New York and New York to Paris; in 1915, the Bell system alone operated six million telephones, which were considered essential in most middle class homes as the decade drew to a close. While the sale of pianos hit a new high, more than two billion copies of sheet music were sold as ragtime neared its peak; of course, the patriotic spirit ignited by America's entry into World War I resulted in dozens of rousing or romantic songs that could be loudly sung while marching, drinking or celebrating. Thousands of Bibles were placed in hotel bedrooms by the Gideon Organization of Christian Commercial Travelers, reflecting both the emerging role of the traveling "drummer" or salesman and the evangelical nature of the Progressive Movement.

Immigration continued at a pace of one million annually in the first four years of the decade. Between 1910 and 1913, some 11 million immigrants—an all-time record—entered the United States. The wages of unskilled workers fell, but the number of jobs increased dramatically. Manufacturing employment rose by 3.3 million, or close to six percent in a year during the period. At the same time, earnings of skilled workers rose substantially and resulted in a backlash focused on protecting American workers' jobs. As a result, a series of anti-immigration laws was passed, culminating in 1917 with permanent bars to the free flow of immigrants into the United States. From the beginning of World War I until 1919, the number of new immigrants fell sharply while the war effort was demanding more and more workers. As a result, wages for low-skilled work rose rapidly, forcing the managerial class—often represented by the middle class—to find new and more streamlined ways to get the jobs done—often by employing less labor or more technology.

In the midst of these dynamics, the Progressive Movement, largely a product of the rising middle class, began to shape the decade, raising questions about work safety, the rights of individuals, the need for clean air and fewer work hours. It was a people's movement that grasped the immediate impact of linking the media to its cause. The results were significant and widespread. South Carolina prohibited the employment of children under 12 in mines, factories, and textile mills; Delaware began to frame employer's liability laws; the direct election of U.S. Senators was approved; and nationwide communities argued loudly over the right and ability of women to vote and the need and lawfulness of alcohol consumption.

Yet in the midst of blazing prosperity, the nation was changing too rapidly for many—demographically, economically, and morally. Divorce was on the rise. One in 12 marriages ended in divorce in 1911, compared with one in 85 only six years earlier. The discovery of a quick treatment for syphilis was hailed as both a miracle and an enticement to sin. As the technology and sophistication of silent movies improved yearly, the Missouri Christian Endeavor Society tried to ban films that included any kissing. At the same time, the rapidly expanding economy, largely without government regulation, began producing marked inequities of wealth—affluence for the few and hardship for the many. The average salary of $750 a year was rising, but nor fast enough for many.

But one of the biggest stories was America's unabashed love affair with the automobile. By 1916, the Model T cost less than half its 1908 price, and nearly everyone dreamed of owning a car. Movies were also maturing during the period, growing rapidly as an essential entertainment for the poor. Some 25 percent of the population, including many newly arrived immigrants, went weekly to the nickelodeon to marvel at the exploits of Charlie Chaplin, Mary Pickford, and Douglas Fairbanks, Sr.—each drawing big salaries in the silent days of movies.

The second half of the decade was marked by the Great War, later to be known as the First World War. Worldwide, it cost more than nine million lives and swept away four empires—the German, the Austro-Hungarian, the Russian, and the Ottoman—and with them the traditional aristocratic style of leadership in Europe. It bled the treasuries of Europe dry and brought the United States forward as the richest country in the world.

When the war broke our in Europe, American exports were required to support the Allied war effort, driving the well-oiled American industrial engine into high gear. Then, when America's intervention in 1917 required the drafting of two million men, women were given their first taste of economic independence. Millions stepped forward to produce the materials needed by a nation. As a result, when the men came back from Europe, America was a changed place for both the well-traveled soldier and the newly trained female worker. Each had acquired an expanded view of the world. Yet women possessed full suffrage in only Wyoming, Colorado, Utah, and Idaho.

The war forced Americans to confront one more important transformation. The United States had become a full participant in the world economy; tariffs on imported goods were reduced and exports reached all-time highs in 1919, further stimulating the American economy.

1913 PROFILE

Sarah Washington grew up surrounded by the sounds of her mother singing "the old songs"—spirituals comprising new words for old tunes that spoke to the past and present equally well.

Life at Home

- Sarah Washington was born into the desperately impoverished community of Denmark, South Carolina, in 1897.
- She only learned she was poor after visiting at age nine her rich cousins in Sumter, South Carolina.
- Sarah was astonished that her cousin owned three dresses, two pairs of shoes and could draw water from a pump inside the kitchen.
- While on the same trip, she saw a building that actually had electricity and would light up at night.
- More important, she became aware of the good things in her life.
- Sarah was delighted to learn how much fun her church was in Denmark compared to her cousin's.
- The people in Sumter were too dignified to sing and clap and dance; in Denmark, she was swept away by the magical singing of a praise meeting.
- Sarah decided right then she liked best a God who permitted his worshipers to make a loud, joyful noise.
- Besides, there was no reason that the devil should have all the best tunes.
- She didn't care that her cousin called them "slave ways"; spiritual singing was meant to be fun.
- Daily her mother breathed modern life into the old spirituals.

Sarah Washington grew up singing new life into traditional spiritual music.

- If the water turned sour, that dilemma joined the song being sung; when the rain arrived in sheets, that, too, was added; and if the cotton crop was excellent, that also came alive in song.
- In this way, a spiritual tune was always under construction in Sarah's house.
- Spirituals and spiritual singing arrived in North America with the first African slaves, who were snatched from their homeland and deposited— still possessing all their former customs, habits and desires—on the isolated plantations of the South.
- Over time, the African rhythms blended with English words and evolved into songs drenched in pain, hoping for freedom and filled with double meanings.
- Many spirituals were used to communicate escape plans or safe routes, or simple displeasure with the slave owner.
- Spirituals themselves came to the attention of the general public in the 1860s after they were described in popular publications such as *The Atlantic Monthly* and collected into a book, *Slave Songs for the United States*, in 1867.
- Fourteen years later, the Fisk Jubilee Singers, of Fisk College in Nashville, Tennessee, began to spread the magic of spiritual music through their tours nationwide, establishing spirituals in the national consciousness.
- In addition to raising enough funds to keep the college open, the Fisk Jubilee Singers popularized the "Negro spiritual" genre and made it part of the American popular culture.
- Historically, spirituals constituted a living folk art with no authors, no composers, no lyricists, nothing written down, no fixed or authoritative text; everything belonged to the community.
- Writer W. E. B. Du Bois called spirituals "sorrow songs," which was "the music of an unhappy people, of the children of disappointment; they tell of death and suffering and unvoiced longing toward a truer world."
- Spirituals were improvisational.
- Usually a lead singer sang one line and the others would repeat it or reply with a familiar chorus in an antiphony.

Only after visiting a city did Sarah realize that she was poor.

City life was dazzling to a country girl.

- Anyone could add new verses, and the best of those survived through a kind of musical natural selection; when singing spirituals, there was no separation between artist and audience, no distinction between creator and performer.
- The religious music of African-Americans also included the ring shout, the song sermon, the Jubilee, and the Gospel song.
- The ring shout survived because it did not violate the Protestant prohibitions against dancing and drumming, since the song is "danced" with the whole body, including hands, feet, and hips.
- The most common spirituals employed the call-and-response pattern that Sarah's mother had perfected, but the songs most familiar to white audiences—"Nobody Knows the Trouble I've Seen," "Go Down Moses," and "Swing Low, Sweet Chariot"—represented a mixture of European and African music.
- Many of the songs make strong biblical allusions, especially popular Old Testament stories that included conquest and personal achievement.
- "He delivered David from de lion's den/Jonah from de belly of de whale/and de Hebrew children from de fiery furnace/why not everything, man?"
- An early custom of the rural Black church included "lining out" the song, whereby the preacher read the words before the congregation sang them.
- Over time, in the churches where hymn books were few and literacy low, the congregation learned the words by heart.
- Musically, this folk style of singing allowed everyone to sing the tune in unison without concern for harmony.
- Sarah learned all the standard spirituals from the neighborhood ladies: "Deep River," Nobody Knows the Trouble I've Seen," "Little David Play Yo Harp," and "Shout All Over God's Heab'n."
- Then she created her own spiritual songs—most dwelling on the woes she encountered using the familiar biblical allusions, carefully crafted during the days of slavery.
- "Then Moses said to Israel/when they stood upon the shore/"Your enemy you see today/you will never see no more"/old Pharoah and his host/got lost in the Red Sea."

Sarah's schoolmates rarely saw her in school more than 60 days in any school year.

Life at Work

- As one of 11 children, Sarah Washington didn't have to be told when the crops were poor and money tight.
- Between planting season, deer season, sickness of her younger brothers and sisters and demands that she help at home, Sarah rarely attended school more than 60 days a year.
- Now that she was turning 16 and was ready to leave school, she knew that her future included marriage, babies and more farm work.
- But she wanted to sing spirituals.
- Thanks to the recent creation of a school in her community called Voorhees, she had an opportunity and a plan.
- The financially struggling Voorhees, created in the image of Booker T. Washington, was founded on the principles of self-help.

- What if, Sarah asked herself, she could form a touring spiritual singing group similar to the Fisk Jubilee Singers that would support the college and herself?
- She had organized the youth choir church, an all girls' choir school, and spent most of her days dreaming up new words for old songs.
- Why not, indeed?
- Voorhees was envisioned and created by Elizabeth Evelyn Wright, who was 23 when she came to Bamberg County.
- A native of Georgia, Wright had found her inspiration while studying at Booker T. Washington's famed Tuskegee Institute.
- Tuskegee gave her a mission in life: being "the same type of woman as Mr. Washington was of a man."
- Knowing the importance of education, she moved to South Carolina to start the first of several schools in the rural areas.
- She survived threats, attacks and arson.
- Her first attempt at creating a school for blacks ended in a blazing fire.
- Her second attempt ended when an arsonist, opposed to secondary education for African-Americans, burned all the lumber purchased for a new building.
- Then, when she negotiated the purchase of property with existing buildings, all the buildings on the land were torched.
- Still convinced that education was the path to black prosperity, Wright moved her vision to Denmark, eight miles from the new county seat of Bamberg.
- There, she founded Denmark Industrial School in 1897, modeling it after Tuskegee with the aid of a leading white state senator and a recommendation letter from Booker T. Washington.
- New Jersey philanthropist Ralph Voorhees and his wife donated $5,000 to buy the land and build the first building, allowing the school to open in 1902.
- It was the only high school and industrial school for blacks in the area and soon was named Voorhees Industrial School for its primary benefactors.
- At the same time, black urban intellectuals were beginning to bemoan the potential loss of spiritual singing, predicting that, as the literacy increased throughout the South, the old ways would be lost.
- The crushing oppression of Jim Crow laws, designed to strip African-Americans of most of their rights, was having the opposite impact.
- Rural blacks were suffering more and singing more, not less.
- By 1913, the racial crackdown had strengthened the one institution white society couldn't touch—the Black church, especially the rural Black church, where black preachers, black deacons and black women in huge hats held sway one day a week.
- Sarah understood that essential to the celebration of life was the singing of spirituals and gospel songs, many of which contained verses with double meanings similar to the coded messages of slave days.
- Sarah proposed to the leaders of Voorhees that a touring choir be formed among its students and faculty, and that the first gathering of the Voorhees Jubilee Voices take place in Columbia, South Carolina, the state capital, where a large paying audience was available.

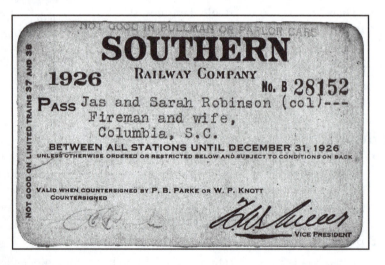

- The goal was $100, enough to prove her ability.
- Within days, the college was buzzing about the little girl who wanted to duplicate the success of the Fisk Jubilee Singers; many were mad that one so young had gained the initiative.
- Within a week, she had talked her uncle into driving her in the horse and buggy 45 miles to Columbia, where three Baptist preachers agreed to help launch the Voorhees Jubilee Voices—provided their choir could sing, also.
- Two more choirs were added later in the week, and suddenly Sarah was in charge of the biggest songfest—featuring 120 singers—in years.
- Several attempts were made to push her aside by the more experienced men, but she didn't budge.
- Instead, she focused on building a bigger network and leading a newly created Voorhees Jubilee Voices, agreeing on a repertoire in which words would actually be sung.
- A fellow choir member loaned her some shoes for the long walks.
- A former teacher got her a travel pass that allowed her to ride the train to Columbia; it carried the teacher's name, address, and racial designation "col" for colored.
- Three weeks before the event, she actually talked the state newspaper into writing a story about a "Negro spiritual gathering"—a feat the black Baptist ministers claimed to be impossible.
- Three days before the event, Sarah took a horse and buggy to Columbia, along with her supplies, convinced she would need the time to decorate the church.
- But two days were consumed in simply getting there, when rain washed out roads and frightened her horse.
- She slept in the buggy one night in the pouring rain, since no other accommodations were available and she knew no one.
- Wet, cold and insecure, Sarah arrived in Columbia on the morning of the big event to find the ministers energized, the choirs prepared, and more than 500 tickets sold at $0.25 each.
- First, she broke into tears and then into song.
- And the entire gathering joined with "Go Down, Moses."
- The event itself was a dream; the choirs and choir leaders got along, the audience was engaged, and the music heavenly.
- Scheduled to last two hours, it lasted three.
- No one wanted the music to stop.

Life in the Community: Denmark, South Carolina

- Denmark, South Carolina, was a flourishing community of approximately 750 people, evenly divided between whites and blacks.
- The farming community was originally known as Graham, named after the Z. G. Graham family who sold 17 acres to the Charleston- Hamburg Railroad in 1837 for a rail siding named Graham's Turnout.
- By 1913, three railway companies crisscrossed the town and its name had been changed to Denmark for a family who were major railway promoters.
- Cotton dominated the fields of South Carolina in 1913; its value was greater than all other South Carolina agricultural products combined.
- Cotton production in the Palmetto State grew from 224,000 bales in 1870 to nearly one million in 1913.
- At the same time, rice production fell dramatically in the coastal regions of the state, as mechanized farming in the Southwestern states proved a competitive advantage.
- Bright leaf tobacco, introduced into the state in the 1890s, was increasing in its production, thanks to a boom in tobacco usage with the introduction of machine-made cigarettes.
- But between the Civil War and World War I, farmers' lives were most affected by the expansion of South Carolina railroad system; nearly every town in the state was connected by rail.
- The time and energy required to get supplies in and crops out was dramatically decreased.
- Road improvements began in 1895 after the state legislature permitted counties to use convict labor to do the work; by 1913, the state had more than 20,000 automobiles.

- The biggest economic change overall was the growth of textile manufacturing, which employed cheap white labor, eager to leave the vagaries of agricultural life.
- Public education, for blacks and whites, remained a low priority; in the rural areas, the typical school operated for only a few months a year.
- In 1907, the legislature allocated $8.00 per white enrollee annually and $1.57 per black pupil.
- The same year, state-supported high schools for whites were created; no high schools were funded for blacks.
- In 1911, the state's first elementary rural school superintendent reported, "The Negro schoolhouses are miserable beyond description...most of the teachers are absolutely untrained."

Often, boys who were old enough to work dropped out of school.

Three railroads operated in the town (originally named Graham), which was renamed Denmark for a family of major railroad promoters.

HISTORICAL SNAPSHOT
1913

- Delta Sigma Theta Sorority was founded on the campus of Howard University
- A rebuilt Grand Central Terminal in New York City opened as the world's largest train station
- The Sixteenth Amendment to the Constitution was ratified, authorizing the federal government to impose and collect income taxes
- The Armory Show opened in New York City, featuring cutting-edge artwork that both excited and repelled critics
- Woodrow Wilson succeeded William Howard Taft to become the 28th President of the United States
- The U.S. Department of Commerce and U.S. Department of Labor were established by splitting the duties of the 10-year-old Department of Commerce and Labor
- The first U.S. law regulating the shooting of migratory birds was passed
- In the First Battle of Bud Dajo, American troops decisively defeated Moro rebels in the Philippines
- The Seventeenth Amendment to the Constitution was passed, providing for the direct election of senators
- The Woolworth Building opened in New York City
- Mary Phagan was raped and strangled on the premises of the National Pencil Factory in Atlanta; Jewish supervisor Leo Frank was tried and convicted for the highly sensationalized crime
- Swedish engineer Gideon Sundback of Hoboken patented an all-purpose zipper
- The Paul Émile Chabas painting *September Morn* created a national sensation concerning nudity and censorship
- New York Governor William Sulzer approved the charter for the Rockefeller Foundation, which began operations with a $100 million donation from John D. Rockefeller
- The Arab Congress of 1913 opened, during which Arab nationalists met to discuss desired reforms under the Ottoman Empire
- The fiftieth anniversary commemoration of the Battle of Gettysburg drew thousands of Civil War veterans and their families to Gettysburg, Pennsylvania
- Stainless steel was invented by Harry Brearley in Sheffield, England
- President Woodrow Wilson triggered the explosion of the Gamboa Dike, ending construction on the Panama Canal
- The Lincoln Highway, the first automobile road across the United States, was dedicated
- Ford Motor Company introduced the first moving assembly line, reducing chassis assembly time from 12 and a half hours to two hours, 40 minutes
- The first crossword puzzle was published in the *New York World*
- The Federal Reserve was created
- The Anti-Defamation League was founded
- The Camel cigarette brand was introduced by R. J. Reynolds in the United States, the first packaged cigarette

Selected Prices

Baby Walker	$2.75
Cake Turner	$0.02
Egg Incubator and Brooder	$10.00
Inlaid Linoleum, per Yard	$2.35
Phonograph Record	$0.65
Piano, Steinway Baby Grand	$2,000.00
Toilet Paper, Six Rolls	$0.27
Trunk	$16.95
Tuition, Harvard University, per Year	$150.00
Umbrella	$2.74

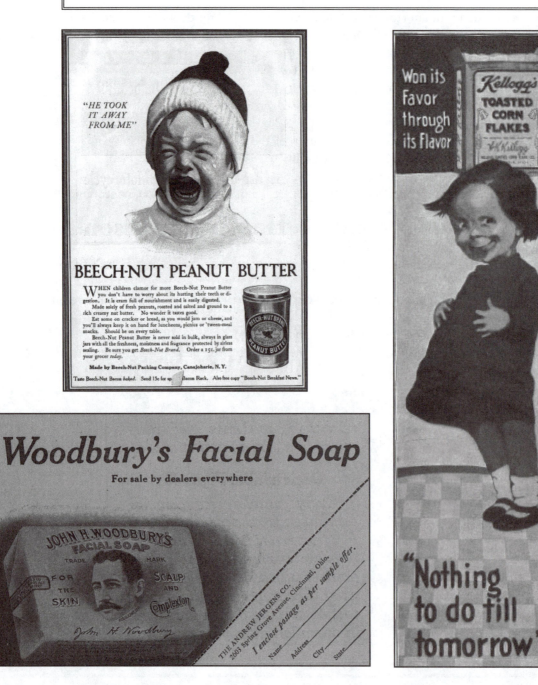

"The Ring Shout," H. G. Spaulding, *The Continental Monthly*, 1863:

At the "praise meetings" on the plantations, one of the elders usually presides. Passages of Scripture are quoted from memory, and the hymns, which constitute the principal feature of the meeting, are deaconed off as at church. After the praise meeting is over, there usually follows the most singular and impressive performance of the "shout" or religious dance of the Negroes. Three or four, standing still, clapping their hands and beating time with her feet, commence singing in unison one of the peculiar shout melodies, while the others walk around in a ring, in single file, joining also in the song. Soon, those in the ring leave off their singing, the others keeping it up for a while with increased vigor, and strike into the shout step, observing most accurate time with the music. This step is sometimes halfway between a shuffle and a dance, as difficult for an uninitiated person to describe as to imitate. At the end of each stanza of the song, the dancers stop short with a slight stamp on the last note, and then, putting the other foot forward, proceed through the next verse. They will often dance to the same song for 20 or 30 minutes, once or twice perhaps, varying the monotony of their movement by walking for a little while and joining in the singing. The physical exertion, which is really very great, as the dance calls into play nearly every muscle in the body, seems never to weary them in the least, and they frequently keep up a shout for hours, resting only for brief intervals between the different songs. Yet in trying to imitate them, I was completely tired out in a very short time. The children are the best dancers, and are allowed by their parents to have a shout at anytime, though with the adults the shout always follows a religious meeting, and none that church members are expected to join.

Booker T. Washington Quotations:

The plantation songs known as "spirituals" are the spontaneous outburst of intense religious fervor.... They breathe a childlike faith in a personal Father, and glow with the hope that the children of bondage will ultimately pass out of the wilderness of slavery into the land of freedom. In singing of a deliverance which they believed would surely come, with bodies swaying, with the enthusiasm born of a common experience and of a common hope, they lost sight for the moment of the auction block, of the separation of mother and child, of sister and brother. There is in the plantation songs the pathos and the beauty that appeals to a wide range of tastes, and their harmony makes abiding impressions upon persons of the highest culture. The music of these songs goes to the heart because it comes from the heart.

No race can prosper till it learns that there is as much dignity in tilling a field as in writing a poem.

Nothing ever comes to one that is worth having except as a result of hard work.

One man cannot hold another man down in the ditch without remaining down in the ditch with him.

Success in life is founded upon attention to the small things rather than to the large things, to the everyday things nearest to us rather than to the things that are remote and uncommon.

Success is to be measured not so much by the position that one has reached in life as by the obstacles which he has overcome.

The individual who can do something that the world wants done will, in the end, make his way regardless of his race.

There are two ways of exerting one's strength: one is pushing down, the other is pulling up.

Imagery in Plantation-Based Spirituals:

Satan = slave owner
King Jesus = slave benefactor
Babylon = winter
Hell = traveling farther south
Jordan (River) = first steps to freedom
Israelites = enslaved African-Americans
Egyptians = slaveholders
Canaan = land of freedom
Heaven = Canada or points north
Home = Africa

Spiritual: "Changed My Name"

I tol' Jesus it would be all right
If He changed mah name

Jesus tol' me I would have to live humble
If He changed mah name

Jesus tol' me that the world would be 'gainst me
If He changed mah name

But I tol' Jesus it would be all right
If He changed mah name

Spiritual: "Going to Set Down and Rest Awhile"

Going to set down and rest awhile
When my good Lord calls me.

Sister Mary went to heaven
And she went there to stay
And she didn't go to come back no more.

She sang a song that the angels couldn't sing
"Hosanna, carry on."

Little children, don't you moan,
When my good Lord calls me.
O, Zion!
When my good Lord calls me.

"Get Songs That Really Help People" Says Mr. Alexander, *Fort Wayne Weekly Sentinel*, December 14, 1910:

Go to Princess rink any evening during the services of the Chapman-Alexander evangelistic campaign in Ft. Wayne, and you will come away with a better comprehension why Charles M. Alexander has come to be known as one of the very foremost directors of gospel the world has ever known.

Mr. Alexander doesn't merely sing—he preaches while he sings and while he is directing the choir or the audience in the rendition of the swinging hymns that carry a personal message. True, his preaching is by methods quite apart from those one usually sees in the pulpit, but it's preaching, nevertheless. No other man does this sort of thing quite as Dr. Chapman does it. From the outset, he takes his audiences completely into his confidence.

Perhaps Mr. Alexander's most striking characteristic is his ability to make people readily see and carry home the gospel message, which he says is in every song that is really worthwhile. The whole force of this tremendous enthusiasm is thrown into his work, and a listless or indifferent spirit in the audience is completely incomprehensible when Mr. Alexander is interpolating between the verses of the hymns and his running fire original interpretation....

"I began to look around to see how it could help the most men in the best way, and I decided that my work lay in helping them by song. I found out that a hymn set to music is like a sermon on wheels, and soon became more and more firmly convinced of the power of a gospel hymn to reach and save people," he said.

"Where you get your hymns?"

"From the wide world. Here, there and everywhere. From all sorts of people in all kinds of places. The man who sets out to make a collection of gospel songs never knows when he might find a treasure. I can tell you stories enough to fill columns about the origins of some of the songs that have been sung in this mission. I received through the mail the music of "What Will You Do With Jesus?" And it has become a great invitational song that Mrs. Asher uses with such power. Then I shall never forget how "Don't Stop Praying" had its birth. I also received it through the post; the sender told me it had been refused by two music publishers. I was so struck with it that I asked the writer to call and see me. She came, and told me that she had a very great trouble. She prayed for help, but help did not seem to be coming. Still she kept praying, and one morning at breakfast she opened a letter that lifted the whole trouble from her. She was so convinced her faith been justified, and so inspired by that belief, that before she got up from the table she wrote the words and music to "Don't Stop Praying" almost exactly as they stand today."

Victrola

1916 PROFILE

Soprano opera singer Geraldine Farrar, the daughter of a professional baseball player, became a reigning figure of the New York metropolitan opera with her glorious voice and physical attractiveness.

Life at Home

- Opera singer Geraldine Farrar's clothes, food, travels and every word she spoke were chronicled in the New York press.
- They invariably discussed her beauty, acting ability and the intimate timbre of her singing voice.
- She was paid a salary second only to that of tenor Enrico Caruso.
- She insisted she was not a singer but a singing actor.
- Among her fans was a large following of young women, who were nicknamed "Gerry-flappers."
- Born in Melrose, Massachusetts, in 1882, Geraldine began studying music at the tender age of three with her mother; both her parents sang in the church choir.
- When Geraldine decided that she liked the black "devilish" piano keys best and refused to play the white "angel" keys, her mother bribed her with a tricycle to play "regular."
- A lover of animals as a child, she dressed the family cats, dogs, alligators, rabbits, bullfinch and robin in elaborate costumes.
- Then, at 10 years old, her dramatic side emerged after a classmate and occasional suitor tragically drowned while ice skating; for six weeks, Geraldine acted the widow: she dressed in black, eschewed all gaiety, and went to school with a black fringed handkerchief to wipe her weepy eyes.
- She made her public singing debut at 12, portraying the legendary soprano Jenny Lind at a springtime carnival.

Geraldine Farrar was a reigning soprano opera singer with the New York Metropolitan Opera.

- When her moment arrived, the prima donna in Geraldine insisted on first singing an aria from *Faust*—even though she knew no Italian—before breaking into "Home, Sweet Home," the song she was scheduled to sing.
- As a teen, her temper was so sharp and moods so dark, she took to wearing black-and-white checked stockings when she wanted to be left alone.
- After studying in Boston, she moved to New York to work with American soprano Emma Thursby and was given a successful audition with the Metropolitan Opera.
- Geraldine's mother encouraged her to turn down the offer until she was more fully prepared.

Geraldine started studying music at age 3, and made her public singing debut at age 12.

- To gain sufficient funds for Geraldine to study in Germany, her father sold his hardware store and the family borrowed $30,000 from a Boston benefactor—all of which was repaid within two years of returning to America.
- The family sailed to Europe on a cattle boat.
- While in Paris, Geraldine went to Reutlinger, a famous fashion photographer, and demanded professional rates.
- When Reutlinger objected that she was unknown, Geraldine replied, "But I am going to be famous."
- Her first professional opera performance abroad in 1901 was as Marguerite in *Faust*, where she sang her role in Italian while the rest of the cast performed in German.
- Nineteen-year-old Geraldine created such a sensation at the Berlin Hofoper with her debut, she remained with the company for four years; many German opera lovers were captivated by a songbird who was neither fat nor 40, while others condemned the very idea of an American singing Italian in the great German Royal Hall.
- She became a pupil of Lilli Lehmann and appeared in the title roles of Ambroise Thomas's *Mignon* and Jules Massenet's *Manon*, as well as Juliette in Gounod's *Roméo et Juliette*.
- In 1903, when the Kaiser invited her to perform at the Palace, she accepted the opportunity, but refused to wear black or lavender as dictated by the Court.
- Nor would she agree to wear long gloves.
- The Kaiser relented and she performed.
- Her admirers in Berlin included Crown Prince Wilhelm of Germany, igniting a storm of German press concerning a possible relationship.
- Before she ended her stay in Europe, Geraldine performed in Italy with Enrico Caruso, where she was nearly struck dumb by the power and clarity of his voice.

Her family sailed to Europe on a cattle boat so Geraldine could study in Germany.

Life at Work

- After years away from the U.S., Geraldine Farrar made her debut in *Roméo et Juliette* on November 26, 1906—at the New York Metropolitan Opera, the place she had always dreamed of performing.
- Personally recruited by Metropolitan Opera general manager Heinrich Conried, Geraldine returned to glorious reviews and quickly became a reigning figure in the New York Opera.
- The press described her clothing, her moods, her every word; she was truly a star.
- She appeared in the first Met performance of Giacomo Puccini's *Madama Butterfly* in 1907, a role she would dominate for the next decade.
- To prepare, she "slaved with ardor and enthusiasm" to master the style, gestures and mannerisms of a Japanese woman, with the help of a Japanese actress.
- To meet all her ambitions and offers, Geraldine performed in New York, Paris, and Berlin that year; she was continually afraid that her voice would disappear or her energy would give out.
- At one point in January 1908, Geraldine performed four times in six days, bouncing from *Faust* to *Butterfly* to *Pagliacci*.
- Fatigue took its toll, and during her third season at the Met, she fought with Italian conductor Arturo Toscanini over nearly everything; the estrangement was complete after the opening performance of *Madama Butterfly* when "we both lost our manners and tempers in a high-handed fashion."
- The press helped fan the flames with dozens of stories about the artistic dispute—frequently quoting anonymous sources.
- Geraldine was prepared to flee New York, but then, Toscanini made warm overtures and became an important musical impresario for the star.
- Geraldine had a seven-year love affair with Toscanini which ended after she issued an ultimatum to leave his wife and children and marry her.
- This resulted in Toscanini's abrupt resignation as principal conductor of the Metropolitan Opera in 1915.
- Geraldine created the title roles in Pietro Mascagni's *Amica* (Monte Carlo, 1905), Umberto Giordano's *Madame Sans-Gêne* (New York, 1915), as well as the Goosegirl in Engelbert Humperdinck's *Die Königskinder* (New York, 1910)
- In 1914, Caruso and Geraldine were together for a performance of *Carmen* which would become one of her career triumphs.

The press described Geraldine as a true star, from her clothing to her moods.

- One seasoned New York critic gushed, "She was indeed a vision of loveliness, never aristocratic, yet never vulgar, a seductive, languorous, passionate Carmen of the romantic gypsy blood. It was full of imagination and delicate touches of art. And above all, it was beautifully sung."
- During her career, she recorded extensively for the Victor Talking Machine Company and was often featured prominently in that firm's advertisements.
- She also shocked many of her fans by agreeing to appear in silent movies, which were filmed between opera seasons.
- The silent movies included a 1915 adaptation of Georges Bizet's opera *Carmen*.
- On the moving picture screen it was her acting, not her voice that counted.
- While most bel canto singers sacrificed dramatic action to tonal perfection, Geraldine was more interested in the emotional than in the purely lyrical aspects of her roles.
- Her marriage to cinema actor Lou Tellegen on February 8, 1916, was celebrated in the press and closely chronicled as it fell apart.

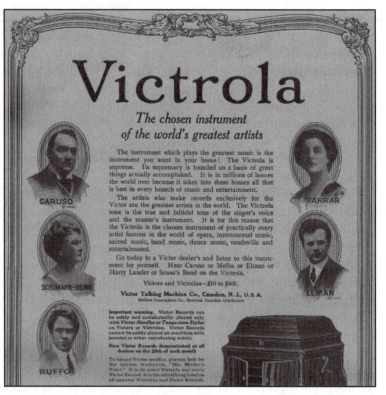

Geraldine recorded extensively for the Victor Talking Machine Company, and was often featured in their advertisements.

Life in the Community: New York City

- With a population of 4.6 million, New York was emerging as one of the world's great seaports in 1916.
- The war in Europe had also transformed the city into the world's money center—a designation that had been affixed to London.
- In 1888, group of prominent, super wealthy businessmen formed a new organization expressly for opera.
- The completion of the Metropolitan Opera House three years later brought stability to the New York music scene.
- Located between Thirty-ninth and Fortieth streets on the West Side, and taking up the entire block to Seventh Avenue, the Metropolitan Opera House opened on October 22, 1883, with Henry E. Abbey as manager.

The Metropolitan Opera House, New York City.

- Being too large in size for ordinary theatre, the house was devoted almost exclusively to grand opera.
- It was also the scene of many great gatherings on patriotic occasions, of many public balls, and of concerts, as well as several fairs.
- Its interior was destroyed by fire in September 1892, but was rebuilt the following year.
- Metropolitan Opera orchestra seats sold for $5.00; a one-sided 78 rpm recording with Enrico Caruso singing "Celeste Aida" cost $3.00.
- Opera lovers would attend live performances multiple times to become thoroughly familiar with its sounds and nuances.
- Operas, which were performed in Italian, tended to lose money, while German-language operas were moneymakers.
- The competition was Oscar Hammerstein's opera company, whose booked talent and facilities were first class.
- German immigrant Oscar Hammerstein was an inventor whose cigar-producing machines earned him a fortune, which supported his writing, plays and theaters.
- In 1889, he opened his first theater, the Harlem Opera House on 125th Street, featuring operas sung in German.
- New York's music infrastructure also included Carnegie Hall, completed in 1891, and marked by an appearance by the famed Russian composer Pyotr Ilyich Tchaikovsky.
- In 1892, Antonín Dvořák became Director of the National Conservatory of Music where he promoted Native and African American folk music.
- New York's position as a center for European classical music was established early, thanks to the New York Philharmonic, formed in 1842.
- In the opening decades of the twentieth century, New York City's music scene spawned and supported Tin Pan Alley, Broadway theaters, Yiddish theater, vaudeville, ragtime, operetta, jazz, the music of the Gullah people, and the Impressionist and Post-Romantic music of European composers.

Historical Snapshot
1916

- The Royal Army Medical Corps' first successful blood transfusion used blood that had been stored and cooled
- Impressionist painter Monet painted his *Water Lilies* series
- For the first time, German zeppelins were used in the World War I bombing of Paris
- The art movement called Dadaism emerged
- The Baltimore Symphony Orchestra presented its first concert
- Mexican Revolutionary Pancho Villa led 500 Mexican raiders in an attack against Columbus, New Mexico, killing 12 U.S. soldiers; the U.S. military responded with 12,000 soldiers
- The light switch was invented by William J. Newton and Morris Goldberg
- *The Saturday Evening Post* published its first cover with a Norman Rockwell painting: *Boy with Baby Carriage*
- President Woodrow Wilson signed a bill incorporating the Boy Scouts of America
- More than one million World War I soldiers died during the Battle of the Somme, including 60,000 casualties for the British Commonwealth on the first day
- In Seattle, Washington, William Boeing incorporated Pacific Aero Products, later renamed Boeing
- President Wilson signed legislation creating the National Park Service
- D. W. Griffith's film *Intolerance: Love's Struggle Through the Ages* was released
- Margaret Sanger opened the first U.S. birth control clinic, which was raided nine days later by the police, after which she served 30 days in prison
- The first 40-hour work week officially began in the Endicott-Johnson factories of western New York
- Republican Jeannette Rankin of Montana became the first woman elected to the U.S. House of Representatives, four years before American women obtained the right to vote
- The White Star Liner *HMHS Britannic*, sister ship of the *RMS Olympic* and the legendary *RMS Titanic*, sank in the Mediterranean Sea after hitting a mine
- Oxycodone, a narcotic painkiller closely related to codeine, was first synthesized in Germany
- The Summer Olympic Games in Berlin, Germany, were cancelled because of World War I
- Ernst Rüdin published his initial results on the genetics of schizophrenia

Miss Jeannette Rankin

Selected Prices

Automobile, Hudson	$1,675.00
Farmland, per Acre	$20.00
Gin, Fifth	$2.15
Hair Curlers	$0.25
Opera Ticket	$1.00
Phonograph Record	$0.65
Phonograph	$65.95
Shampoo	$0.33
Theater Ticket	$2.75
Travelers' Checks	$0.50

BEAUTY IS AN ASSET CULTIVATE IT

Nature displays her loveliest expressions in form and color as in all things else, not by chance but, inevitably, when the conditions she requires are present. Keep your skin clean, not by the insufficient soap and water method, but **hygienically clean** by the regular use of a good cold cream, and Nature will give it a satisfying beauty it has not known before.

Daggett & Ramsdell's PERFECT COLD CREAM
"The Kind That Keeps"

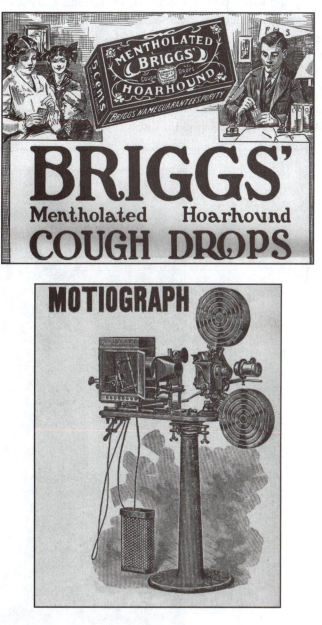

Review by Richard Aldrich, *The New York Times*, November 27, 1906:

Miss Farrar comes back to her native land as one of the American singers who have made name and fame for themselves abroad. It is not always easy to establish the same success in this country, and it may be that all she does will not meet with quite so unqualified acceptance as it has abroad. But she went far upon that road in what she accomplished last evening. She made a most agreeable impression in her impersonation of Juliette, for she is full of excellent instincts, making for the best things as a lyric actress. She has a charming personality, a graceful and winning one, and her stage presence is alluring and with much of the girlishness of Juliette.

It has been said that by the time an actress has learned the art of denoting the passion and the ecstatic emotion of Juliette, she could rarely still be in possession of the juvenile charm that the part needs. But Miss Farrar has it, and has at the same time skill and resource in stagecraft. She is a singer of remarkable gifts. Her voice is a full and rich soprano, lyric in its nature and flexibility, yet rather darkly colored and with not a little of the dramatic quality and with a power of dramatic nuance that she uses in the main skillfully. Her singing is generally free and spontaneous in delivery, well phrased and well enunciated, yet she is not a wholly finished vocalist, and there were matters in her singing that could not meet with entire approbation, as in the duet in the fourth act, where she sang with a certain constraint.

There will be more interesting and more important music of the exhibition of her artistic powers before the season is much further advanced, but there was ample cause in her Juliette of last evening for the high expectations that have been raised for her in the musical public of New York.

From the review by Henry Krehbiel, *The New York Tribune*, November 26, 1906:

Miss Farrar was most graciously received, and was then permitted with kind encouragement to win her way to popular approval. She won that approval, and she won more: She achieved her place among those whom a Metropolitan audience recognizes as in the foremost of the world's operatic artists. She appeared as a beautiful vision; youthful, charming in face, figure, movement and attitude. She sang with a voice of exquisite quality in the middle register, and one that was vibrant with feeling almost always. She acted like one whose instincts for the stage were full and eager, but also like one who, not needing to learn what to do, had neglected to learn that it is possible to do too much. Had she been one-half less consciously demonstrative, whenever she stepped out of the dramatic picture, one-half less sweeping in her movements and gestures when she was in the picture, she would have been twice as admirable to her compatriots who were rejoicing in her success, and twice as convincing to those who were sitting in judgment upon an artist for whom the trumps of acclaim have been so loudly sounded that their din will make calm listening difficult for some time to come. But she has won a welcome that must have emphatic expression. The few crudities in her vocalization are pushed into notice by the very excellence of her merits. Red and warm blood flows in her voice and pulses in harmony with the emotions of the play. She is eloquently truthful in declamation, and correct taste dictates her choice of nuance and vocal color. It is only when she forces her upper tones that sensuous charm leaves her voice in a measure and one deplores the departure all the more because the voice is of a carrying power that makes strenuousness unnecessary.

"Wilson the Political Weather Vane," *The Melting Pot*, May 1916:

President Wilson was in favor of a single presidential term. Now he is against it.

President Wilson was in favor of the Garrison Continental Army plan. Now he is against it.

President Wilson was opposed to increasing the Navy. Now he demands that the Navy be made the largest in the world.

Preston Wilson was opposed to young men spending time in military training. Now he demands that 400,000 be trained.

President Wilson was opposed to a Tariff Commission. Now he demands a Tariff Commission.

President Wilson was in favor of free Panama Canal tolls. After his election, he compelled the Democratic majority to repeal the free tolls law….

President Wilson was for women's suffrage in New Jersey and against women's suffrage in Washington.

President Wilson was opposed to preparedness as late as last year. Now he is preaching preparedness fervently….

To us, it seems that President Wilson has no fixed principles or convictions upon any subject under the sun, and that he is consistent only in advocating anything that promises to promote his re-election in his personal ambitions.

—From the *Los Angeles Examiner*

"The Holy Inquisition in Power in Boston," *The Melting Pot*, October 1916:

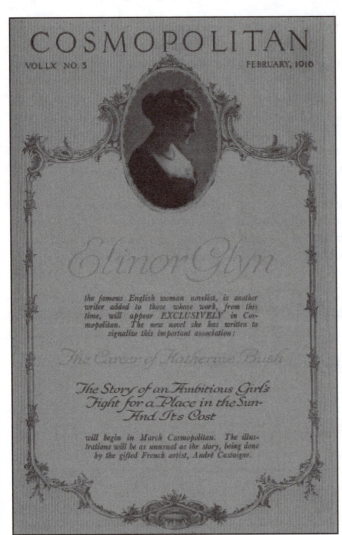

The Holy Inquisition is now in power in the Roman Catholic city of Boston.

The haters of free speech, with help of a judge of their stripe on the bench, have defied the supposedly constitutional rights of an American citizen and sentenced to prison the young student and a newspaperman for giving a papal sneak a leaflet on birth control.

The following account, taken from *The Masses*, tells the story:

Van Kleck Allison, 22 years, a former Columbia student and newspaperman, was sentenced to three years in the penitentiary in Boston on July 20, for having given a lying plainclothes man a leaflet on birth control.

The officer told Allison that he was a married man in poor circumstances, and that his wife was giving birth to another child. He could not afford more children and asked for methods.

Allison was sentenced on four counts. Three were on the leaflet given to the officer, and one was for publishing an article on birth control by Dr. W. J. Robinson and Allison's newsmagazine, *The Flame*.

The trial was horrible. The district attorney said that women present in the courtroom ought to blush for their womanhood. Judge Murray had the verdict ready right after district attorney concluded. Judge Murray said birth control was a blow to the foundations of Divine Law.

Appeal has been taken. The fight is on.

"Why Should You Be Punished for Not Living in New York?,"
Pictorial Review, January 1918:

A blow has been struck at every magazine reader in America. After July 1, 1918, you will pay more for every magazine and newspaper you wish to read. And this because you do not happen to live within 150 miles of the place of publication. You who live in Texas or California will have to pay one price. You who live in Idaho or Colorado will have to pay another, while, all of you who live in Illinois or Tennessee will have to pay still another price. Why? Because the War Revenue Bill recently passed by Congress contains a clause compelling magazines and newspapers being mailed on the zone system after July 1, 1918. Think how you in California, Washington, and Texas will feel when you have to pay something like $2.20 for this magazine that has cost you only $1.50. And while you are paying $2.20, subscribers within 150 miles from New York to still be paying only $1.50.

The zone system had already been defeated in the United States Senate. It was tacked onto the War Revenue Bill against the wishes of the majority of the conferees. It had no place there. It was not needed there. It was reported by the newspapers that the only reason it was there was due to political manipulation. Strong pressure was brought to bear. Delay in passing the War Revenue Bill would have hampered the government in its war program.

The members of the conference were powerless. They did not wish to prevent the War Revenue Bill from passing, so they had to yield. This is how this unjustified imposition on magazine readers came to be included in the War Revenue Bill where did not belong.

"*Carmen* Again Today at Palace," *The Racine Journal News* (Wisconsin), May 22, 1916:

Today is the second and last showing of that great photo dramatization of the greatest play, *Carmen*, which attracted such tremendous crowds Sunday at the Palace Theater. This is the only real picturization of *Carmen*, and the fact that so renowned an artiste as Geraldine Farrar appears in the leading role made so many anxious to see it that the limited seating capacity of the Palace was inadequate to accommodate half the crowds who came Sunday. The special music arranged for this great picture is charming, and the management of the Palace is to be highly commended for bringing to Racine such a magnificent attraction in both the picture and music.

Several scenes in this picture are so startling that it fairly brings the audience to their feet. The fight scene in the cigarette factory between Carmen and Anita King is the most realistic ever staged, and in fact is real in one instance when Miss Farrar is dangerously wounded in the terrific fight during which Miss King accidentally cut her with the dagger, and Miss Farrar was confined to a hospital for two months following the taking of this picture.

Geraldine Farrar is the highest-salaried female opera star, having received $5,000 for a single performance. Her favorite role is that of Carmen. The string of pearls which Miss Farrar wears in this picture was given to her by Kaiser Wilhelm of Germany. She is a favorite of the nobility, has appeared at the Royal Opera House in Berlin, and has also appeared before all the crowned heads of Europe. It was rumored that she was engaged to the Crown Prince, who is now leading the terrific assault on Verdun. It was only after he was exiled to the Royal Palace in Potsdam that he gave up the vivacious queen of the opera.

Moderato

There's a lit-tle spark of love still burn-ing, and yearn-ing down in my

There's a lit-tle spark of love still burn-ing, and yearn-ing down in my

lit-tle spark of love still burn-ing, and yearn-ing down in my

1918 PROFILE

Alonzo "Zo" Elliott made musical history from his dorm room at Yale in 1913, where he composed one of the most successful songs of World War I.

Life at Home

- Alonzo "Zo" Elliott wrote "There's a Long, Long Trail A-Winding" as a lark and a last-minute entry for a fraternity skit.
- The song ended up earning $3 million in sheet music sales.
- By 1918, Zo's song was on the lips of millions of soldiers eager to leave the fighting in France behind and dream while singing: "I forget that you're not with me yet/When I think I see you smile."
- The future musician was born in Manchester, New Hampshire, of Puritan stock; Zo's father was a banker and his mother a graduate of the Boston Conservatory of Music.
- She provided Zo with his first music lessons, yet never pushed him to be a musician.
- "Although my musical mother had what was virtually a professional training, she did not try to persuade my father that music was the only profession for a man," Zo said.
- Zo was educated at St. Paul's School in Concord, New Hampshire; Phillips Academy in Andover, Massachusetts; and Yale University.
- While at Yale, in the years before the start of World War I in Europe, Zo met Stoddard King, who was to become his co-writer of "There's a Long, Long Trail A-Winding."
- Stoddard King was born in Spokane, Washington, and had gained Zo's respect because he was obliged to work his way through college.
- Zo and King were both members of the fraternity Zeta Psi, and both became interested in the dramatic productions of the fraternity.

Zo Elliott (right) grew up a privileged child, whose path led him to Yale University and musical history.

- Their first collaboration was in 1911 when they both worked on John Gay's *Beggar's Opera*.
- By the spring 1913 semester, Zo and King wanted desperately to be sent as delegates to a Zeta Psi smoker in Boston.
- Delegates to the smoker were to have their expenses paid, and were excused from classes.
- But to be elected for the honor, they had to prove themselves entertainers by preparing an act to entertain their fraternity brothers.
- One morning, Zo was in Connecticut Hall at college, reading Baron Segur's report of Napoleon's retreat from Moscow, when he went to the piano and spontaneously improvised the chorus of "There's a Long, Long Trail A-Winding."
- When Stoddard King arrived a few minutes later, Zo confided, "I have a song with a 'sticky' harmony."
- Sticky harmony was college slang for a tune to which a tenor part, usually starting a third above, could be added.
- The melody appealed to King immediately, and almost as quickly as Zo had composed the tune, the two men came out with the words.
- Traditionally, the words to songs were written first, followed by the melody, but not always.
- In the case of Gilbert and Sullivan, Sullivan usually wrote the melodies first; Gilbert then mortised the words and song together.
- King had a similar gift, and took the melody in a different direction.
- When composing his tune, Zo was picturing Napoleon at the end of his tragic trail to Moscow; King saw the trail as leading to home and romance.
- The next week, when the two men were scheduled to perform their song at the Zeta Psi banquet in Boston, Zo took a painful fall while ascending the steps of the stage.
- The results, in the midst of the college festivities, were jeers, cheers and calls to "do it again."

- Zo and Stoddard King were so flustered after the hubbub they had raised that all they could do was sing the chorus.
- Then, to their great surprise, the tune captured everyone's imagination, and one of the fraternity boys demanded the words so they could heartily sing along.
- It was a huge hit that night.
- But New York's music publishers failed to share Zeta Psi's enthusiasm for the song; Zo and King submitted the song to practically every sheet music publisher in New York with no luck.

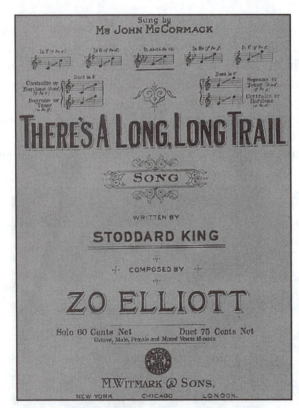

Written as a lark for a fraternity skit, Elliott's There's a Long, Long Trail A-Winding, *became one of the most successful songs of World War I.*

Into the land of my dreams,
Where the nightingales are singing
And a white moon beams.
There's a long, long night of waiting
Until my dreams all come true;
Till the day when I'll be going down
That long, long trail with you.
All night long I hear you calling,
Calling sweet and low;
Seem to hear your footsteps falling,
Ev'rywhere I go.
Tho' the road between us stretches
Many a weary mile,
I forget that you're not with me yet
When I think I see you smile.
There's a long, long trail a-winding.

Life at Work

- After graduation from Yale, Alonzo "Zo" Elliott entered Trinity College in Cambridge, England, where he went shopping at a music store for a piano.
- "In trying the instruments, I played the song," Zo recalled. "The proprietor was a tune scout for a London publisher, and he sent for his chief to come to Cambridge to hear it."
- Claude Yearsley, representing West and Company, liked what he heard and the song was published in December 1913.
- Sales were slow until the outbreak of World War I in Europe, when British soldier boys came pouring into France to fight Germans in "the war to end all wars."
- Several Canadian soldiers saw the gorgeous song sheet cover of a trail leading down a mountain valley, read the words, and were homesick; this song had perfectly captured the emotional loneliness of being away from home with no assurances of ever returning.
- After it became the rage in every London music hall, a New York house took a gamble on it.
- And sales exploded.
- In all, more than five million song sheets featuring "There's a Long, Long Trail A-Winding" were sold, earning $3 million.
- Sheet music, costing from $0.25 to $0.60 per song, was a big business despite the emerging competition of phonograph machines.
- Millions of families entertained themselves by gathering around the piano after dinner to sing.
- Following the American Civil War, more than 25,000 new pianos were sold annually in the U.S., and by 1887, over 500,000 youths were studying piano.
- As a result, the demand for sheet music grew rapidly, and more and more publishers entered the market.
- As the twentieth century began, New York was emerging as the center of popular music publishing, as well as an important center for the musical and performing arts.
- Song composers were hired under contracts that gave the publisher exclusive rights to popular composers' works.
- The market was surveyed to determine what style of song was selling best, and then the composers were directed to compose in that style.
- Before publication, songs were tested with both performers and listeners to determine which song would be published and which would go into the trash bin; music was becoming an industry more than an art.
- Once a song was published, song pluggers— performers who worked in music shops playing the latest releases—were hired and performers were persuaded to play the new songs in their acts to give the music exposure to the public.
- And Zo's music passed the popularity test— led by the English Tommies who had entered the Great War three years before the United States.
- In Oklahoma's Fort Sill, thousands of raw recruits began to swelter to it.
- In Massachusetts' Fort Devens, thousands more shivered to it.
- The song was a favorite of President Woodrow Wilson to sing after dinner in the White house.
- Camp Gordon's men shaved to it, groomed horses to it, and built roads to it.
- They sang it whether they wanted to or not.

- The government's morale-boosters made it compulsory for soldiers to sing.
- By the time America entered the war in 1917, the American song first published in England united the Tommies who had ploughed through Flanders' mud with the doughboys who marched through the black night into the Argonne.
- Soldiers who were herded aboard transports and troop trains, recruits who dug straddle ditches and loaded ammunition, had one song which helped more than any other to see them through the war.
- By then, the words had changed to "There's a long, long trail that's winding/Into no man's land in France/Where shrapnel shells are bursting/And where we must advance./There'll be lots of drills and hiking/Before our dreams come true/But someday we'll show the Kaiser/What machine-gun boys can do. WOW."

Artifacts

Graphic Patriotism
America's participation in the war was brief; its fleeting impact on pop culture is best captured in recruiting posters and a famous song

- It was a war made for singing.
- Irving Berlin supplied, "Oh, How I Hate to Get Up in the Morning" as an expression of soldier grumpiness; Geoffrey O'Hara created "K_K_K_Katy" to capture spontaneity; George M. Cohen fashioned the rallying cry of the soldier with "Over There," a song written by Cohen as he traveled from Long Island to Manhattan the morning after Wilson's war address.
- And in leaky barracks, smoky cafés and on endless marches, "There's a Long, Long Trail A-Winding" was sung rowdily and nostalgically.
- Tenor Enrico Caruso sang it in Liberty Loan drives; Elsie Janis sang it in France from the back of a truck.
- The first U.S. troops to land in England marched in review to it before Ambassador Page and Admiral Sims.
- British soldiers sang it when they were lined up on deck waiting to be taken off the torpedoed troop ship *Tyndarius*.
- They even sang it after the Armistice when they marched across the bridge into Cologne.

Life in the Community: New York, New York

- Already a major manufacturing hub, once the war in Europe got underway, New York became the world's financial center, replacing both London and France.
- After America officially joined the war in Europe, the city of New York quickly focused on "women power," which one government brochure called "One of the Increasingly Valuable and Undeveloped Assets of our Country."
- By December 1917, women filled the office chairs of thousands of newly minted American soldier
- New Yorkers, for whom "time is money," fell in love with the pageantry displayed in the dozens of war parades staged at the city's very center.
- New Yorkers even accepted a mayoral curfew decree that shortened the night by closing restaurants, bars and theaters by 1 a.m.
- After the start of the Great War, German-Americans were sometimes accused of being too sympathetic to the German Empire.
- Former president Theodore Roosevelt denounced "hyphenated Americanism," insisting that dual loyalties were impossible in wartime.
- Nationwide, about 1 percent of the 480,000 enemy aliens of German birth were imprisoned in 1917-1918.

The Ladies Band was one of the many results of the focus on women after America joined the war.

- Charges included spying for Germany or endorsing the German war effort.
- Thousands of Germans in New York City were compelled to buy War Bonds to show their loyalty.
- In fear of sabotage, the Red Cross barred individuals with German last names from joining.
- In Collinsville, Illinois, German-born Robert Prager was dragged from jail as a suspected spy and lynched; in Minnesota, a minister was tarred and feathered when he was overheard praying in German with a dying woman.
- Orchestras replaced music by the German composer Wagner with that by the French composer Berlioz.
- German-named streets were renamed; Germania Avenue was renamed Pershing Avenue; Berlin, Michigan, changed its name to Marne, Michigan (honoring those who fought in the Battle of Marne).
- Nebraska banned instruction in any language except English.
- In response, German-Americans often "Americanized" their names: Schmidt became Smith, while Müller evolved into Miller.
- Total war casualties were estimated at 10 million dead, 21 million wounded, and 7.7 million missing or imprisoned.

Former President Theodore Roosevelt insisted that dual loyalties were impossible in wartime.

HISTORICAL SNAPSHOT
1918

- Woodrow Wilson delivered his "Fourteen Points" speech, which called for the creation of the League of Nations
- The SS *Tuscania* was torpedoed off the Irish coast, the first ship carrying American troops to Europe to be torpedoed and sunk
- Popular movies included *The Kaiser, the Beast of Berlin; A Dog's Life* starring Charlie Chaplin; and *Hearts of the World*, directed by D. W. Griffith
- The last captive Carolina parakeet, a parrot native to North America, died at the Cincinnati Zoo, resulting in the extinction of the species
- Excavations began in Babylonia directed by Leonard Woolley
- Congress established time zones and approved daylight saving time
- Booth Tarkington's novel *The Magnificent Ambersons* captured the Pulitzer Prize for literature; Carl Sandburg was awarded the Poetry Prize for *Corn Huskers*
- Dr. Karl Muck, music director of the Boston Symphony Orchestra, was arrested under the Alien Enemies Act and imprisoned for the duration of World War I
- Manfred Von Richthofen (The Red Baron), World War I's most successful fighter pilot, died in combat at Morlancourt Ridge near the Somme River
- General Motors acquired the Chevrolet Motor Company of Delaware
- The United States Post Office Department began regular airmail service between New York City, Philadelphia and Washington, D.C.
- The Spanish Flu became a worldwide pandemic, killing 30 million people in the six months
- The Boston Red Sox defeated the Chicago Cubs for the 1918 World Series baseball championship
- In the Argonne Forest in France, U.S. Corporal Alvin C. York almost single-handedly killed 25 German soldiers and captured 132
- In the last major naval engagement of World War I, British battleship HMS *Britannia* was sunk by German submarine *U-50* off Trafalgar
- World War I ended on November 11, when Germany signed an armistice agreement with the Allies in Marshal Foch's railroad car in Compiègne Forest in France
- President Woodrow Wilson traveled by ship to the Paris Peace Conference, becoming the first United States president to travel to any foreign country while holding office

R.M.S. *Aquitania*
Dimensions:—
Length, 901 ft.
Breadth, 97 ft.
Tonnage, 47,000

Selected Prices

Automobile, Franklin Runabout $1,900.00
Boy's Suit.. $2.95
Electric Radiator $5.75
Luden's Cough Drops $0.05
Man's Nightshirt $1.15
Mousetrap $0.02
Rum, Bacardi, Fifth $3.20
Theater Ticket, including War Tax $2.20
Woman's Hose, Artificial Silk $0.35
Wrigley's Chewing Gum, 25 Packs $0.73

There's a Long, Long Trail A-Winding

Nights are growing very lonely,
Days are very long;
I'm a-growing weary only
List'ning for your song.
Old remembrances are thronging
Through my memory
Till it seems the world is full of dreams
Just to call you back to me.

Chorus:
There's a long, long trail a-winding
Into the land of my dreams,
Where the nightingales are singing
And a white moon beams.
There's a long, long night of waiting
Until my dreams all come true;
Till the day when I'll be going down
That long, long trail with you.

All night long I hear you calling,
Calling sweet and low;
Seem to hear your footsteps falling,
Ev'rywhere I go.
Tho' the road between us stretches
Many a weary mile,
I forget that you're not with me yet
When I think I see you smile.

Chorus:
There's a long, long trail a-winding
Into the land of my dreams,
Where the nightingales are singing
And a white moon beams.
There's a long, long night of waiting
Until my dreams all come true;
Till the day when I'll be going down
That long, long trail with you.

> The (Tin Pan) Alley's strident songs and nervous dance tunes, its blurbs and ballads and banalities, are as evanescent as the encircling smoke in which they are ground out in accordance with constantly changing recipes. In one essential, however, there is no change, for this frankly commercial pursuit involves a ceaseless and eager following of the taste of the crowd—the indiscriminate and undiscriminating crowd—an inseparable part of the American scene.
>
> —William Fisher, *One Hundred and Fifty Years of Music Publishing in the United States*

Recorded Popular Songs from WWI Era: 1914-1918

- By the Beautiful Sea
- Keep the Home-Fires Burning (Till the Boys Come Home)
- Missouri Waltz (Hush-a-Bye, Ma Baby)
- The Aba Daba Honeymoon
- When You Wore a Tulip and I Wore a Big Red Rose
- Are You From Dixie? (Cause I's From Dixie, Too!)
- Battle in the Sky
- I Didn't Raise My Boy to Be a Soldier
- Nola (A Silhouette for the Piano)
- Pack Up Your Troubles in Your Old Kit-Bag and Smile, Smile, Smile
- Thank God for a Garden
- When the Lusitania Went Down
- If You Were the Only Girl in the World
- Mother's Good Night Song
- The Hero of the European War
- Me and My Gal
- Good-bye Broadway, Hello France!
- Hail! Hail! The Gang's All Here (What the Deuce Do We Care?)
- Time for Ev'ry Boy to Be a Soldier
- Over There
- The Battle Song of Liberty
- I'm Always Chasing Rainbows
- In Flanders Fields the Poppies Grow
- Keep the Trench Fires Going for the Boys Out There
- Oh! How I Hate to Get Up in the Morning
- Over The Sea, Boys
- Rock-a-Bye Your Baby With a Dixie Melody
- Somebody Stole My Gal
- Yanks With the Tanks (Will Go Through the German Ranks)
- Till We Meet Again
- We Don't Want the Bacon (What We Want Is a Piece of the Rhine)
- When Pershing's Men Go Marching Into Picardy

"Our Responsibility in the War," *The Christian Herald*, April 7, 1915:

To a very large portion of the American people, the fact is becoming increasingly apparent that, while we are acclaimed by the whole world as neutrals, we are in reality one of the principal participants in the European strife. By our shipments of weapons and ammunition we are assisting materially in keeping up the slaughter. How we can logistically claim to be a peace-loving and humane nation, and still supply the means of destroying thousands of human lives, is a problem which the American people must ultimately square with their own conscience….

Almost from the beginning of hostilities, our war materiel-producing plants have been coining money, at the cost in human lives, at a tremendous rate. From September 1 to December 31, 1914, exports of war materiel totaled $49,466,092, being an increase over the same months in the proceeding year of $37,751,255. The September increase was slightly over a million, the increase of October was $6,973,964, the November increase was $12,554,957, the December increase was $17,209,495. The figures for January and February of the current year are not available, but it is known they maintain the rising ratio.

In its issue of March 4, *The New York World* gives an amazing description of the martial activities of the plants in the industrial communities of Western Pennsylvania, eastern Ohio and West Virginia, known collectively as the "Pittsburg district." No sooner had the war begun than these plants sprang into sudden activity, working double and triple shifts and continually increasing their workforce until it is estimated that not less than 150,000 men are now employed in turning out war orders….

There was a bill before the late Congress, providing for an arms embargo, but it came to nothing for the reason given by U.S. Sen. Moses E. Clapp (Minnesota) in a letter to one of his correspondents, which he said: "The spectacle of the United States sending shiploads of food and clothing to the orphaned and widowed people of Europe, and at the same time sending shiploads of guns and ammunition to make more widows and orphans, is one of those grotesque contrasts we sometimes find." And he added: "There is so much money invested in the making and the sale of arms and war munitions that we have simply been powerless to get anywhere with the bill."

"Celebrating Yale," *The Youth's Companion*, **November 16, 1916:**

The great Bowl at Yale was the scene last month of one of the most elaborate and impressive pageants ever staged—although as a spectacle some persons prefer the Harvard-Yale game to be played in the same place next week. The pageant was in celebration of the 200th anniversary of Yale's moving from Saybrook to New Haven. About 7,000 persons took part in the episodes that pictured important events in the history of Yale and Connecticut, and nearly 70,000 spectators looked on. The 200th anniversary that Yale is celebrating covers a long period, for the New Haven colony began to think of having a college as early as 1644, when it began contributing to the support of Harvard. It had no name until 1718, when the first building erected for use in New Haven was named for its benefactor, Elihu Yale, a native of Boston, who gained his fortune in India.

"New York City in War Time," Arthur Hepburn, *Vanity Fair*, **December 1917:**

New York in war time has revealed herself in her true light. She has shown an adaptability to strange and trying conditions which has surprised even those who knew her best.

Already the greatest manufacturing center in the world, our coming into the war made New York the money center, the distributing center, the very hub of the universe as far as resources were concerned. London and Paris sank to the level of mere distributing points.... If the Kaiser is a bad sleeper, and he ought to be, he must be haunted in the mid-hours of the night by visions of the skyscrapers of lower Manhattan Island, for they symbolize the staying power which he should dread most of all.

"New York's Fourth," *The Outlook*, July 12, 1916:

Six years ago, Mayor Gaynor decided to give the people of New York a "safe and sane fourth." To replace the accustomed joys of burned fingers, blazing homes, and ruined eyes, he devised a series of popular and interesting entertainments.

This year, the mayor's "Independence Day Committee" has grown to permanent strength, and it arranged an elaborate programme for the day which would make accessible to every citizen a steady performance as varied as a three-ring circus from morning till night. It districted the city so as to provide "block celebrations" for 20 geographical units, each of which included band concerts, dancing, patriotic addresses, and the "movies." In 200 public schools, Independence Day exercises were held from 10:30 to noon, while song rallies took place out of doors in places ranging from the Bronx to Staten Island.

The day started with a flag-raising at the Old Block House in Central Park at 5:30 in the morning, followed by a band concert in the Park at eight o'clock, with speeches and songs. At 10 in Union Square, there were songs again from workingmen, most of them cloak and suit makers, now on strike. The Declaration of Independence was being read when two of the strikers came late into the range of the speakers' voices. As they listened, they were evidently puzzled at the words they heard; one turned to the other and asked if it was a manifesto from the Mexican workers to their American brethren. "No," said his companion. "I think it is an Irish revolutionary document of some kind…."

The small boy, although forbidden explosives, was happy all day with athletic competitions arranged throughout the city by the mayor's Independence Day Committee. In 36 public parks youngsters ran races, jumped both broad and high, put the shot, dashed gaily for 40, 50, for 60 yards. Swimming contests were won and lost, and grown folks strove with children in potato races and obstacle runs. In Chinatown, Wing Lee won the one-lap race for boys up to 110 pounds, while his brother, Non Lee, took second place in the 60-yard dash. In Washington Square, little Italian girls drilled and danced the morning away.

In the evening, 15,000 people went up to the stadium at City College for an elaborate programme of music, oratory, and tableaux. Madame Gadski sang the "The Star-Spangled Banner," while the audience applauded equally "Paul Revere's Ride" and the "Child Labor" pageant. That night, all of Thirty-ninth St. between Fifth and Sixth Ave. was turned into a dancing floor for the girls and their friends of the Vacation Association. A huge screen was hung on one side of the street, and those who would not dance could watch the pictures thrown there until midnight.

The fist that figs "The Punch".

The American Army of Occupation celebrating the Fourth of July, 1919, in Coblenz, Germany.

With the Allies on the Rhine

1919 News Feature

"With the Allies on the Rhine," Charles Victor, *Leslie's Weekly*, November 18, 1919:

I wonder how many people thought, when we went into war, that any part of the American army would be stationed for 10 years on the banks of the Rhine? Very few, I am sure. And not many more, probably, have a very clear idea of the nature of this "occupation." Officially, of course, the occupation has just one purpose: to enforce the provisions of the treaty of peace. With a hostile army in his country at all times ready for action, it is safely expected that the defeated enemy will be rather particular about "paying up" promptly. But, as a matter of fact, the army is not, strictly speaking, a hostile one, and its military duties are destined to be largely perfunctory. Unofficially, however, its presence in the country is bound to have a considerable influence, and incidentally to bring about consequences that were neither foreseen nor intended by those who decreed the occupation.

These effects, to some extent apparently today, after 12 months, are bound to vary greatly in different zones, according to the temperaments of the nations involved, and according to the policies of their authorities. I had just had an excellent opportunity of observing these differences at close range.

The policy of the British is perfectly clear from the moment you arrive in Cologne. Aside from the primary purpose of occupation, their objects are frankly commercial. As soon as the bars of the blockade were let down, the British government considered that it was its particular duty to help British businessmen into Germany as fast as it was physically possible. There is not the slightest attempt to hide this purpose. The corporal in charge of the passport control of the railroad makes you "show cause" before he allows you to enter town. If your job is anything but "business," you are shoved aside, for Cologne is too crowded to accommodate mere pleasure seekers, journalists, and such-like. In the office at the town major, where every visitor must go to be "billeted," advertisements of German agents, acting as go-betweens, are posted up; large signs elsewhere indicate the way to the official purveyor of commercial information. The result is that Cologne is a seething maelstrom of business, a metropolis such as it never was before, and the Rhine bridges are groaning under the burden of goods passing not only from west to east, but from east to west.

The British, in short, appeared to have called it a war, and to have settled down to reaping the fruits of peace.

Not so the French. The French are busy at Mayence making the Germans understand that they—the French—are the victors. They have old scores to settle, and they propose to settle them here and now. Their purpose is not commercial, but political, as their protection of the "Rhine Republic" of Dr. Dorten indicates. In the English and American zones, harmless Army newspapers are published, recording the doings and diversities of the boys; in the French zone there appears a handsome illustrated weekly, in German and French, recording the latest achievements of the separatist, and "stimulating French interest in Rhinish affairs." While the British in Cologne examine the passports of foreigners, letting the Germans pass without control, a ferocious-looking Algerian in Coblenz scrutinizes every native that attempts to pass the gate, and a German woman crossing her street without a passport is liable to arrest and fine. A strict censorship continues to be exercised on all written or printed material passing in or out of the French zone, and no German papers containing political articles are permitted to circulate. The political isolation of this region from the rest of Germany is complete.

The American policy is less easy to define. Strictly speaking, we have no policy at all, except to fulfill our engagements with our allies, irksome as they may be. Our "watch on the Rhine" is a purely military action, carried out strictly in conformity with the rules of war, with a minimum amount of discomfort to the natives and no material advantage to ourselves. In the early days of the armistice, when Cologne and Mayence were centers of illicit trading with the enemy, when one truckload of goods after another was smuggled across the "neutral zone," and when unscrupulous officers are said to have grown rich on bribes, Uncle Sam stood guard over the morals of his men so that not a single case of such nefarious dealings could be held against them. The Germans, who abetted this practice for their own benefit, now say that every French officer is a "schieber" (profiteer), but are obliged to admit that the Americans are proof against all temptation.

This and other unsuspected qualities have greatly heightened the natives' respect for Americans, and this respect is largely responsible for the good relationship between victor and vanquished in our zone. Much has been written of the alleged friendship between Americans and Germans, and many sinister whispers have contrasted it with the experiences of our boys in France. There should be nothing surprising about this, if we consider, first, the temperamental difference between the French and the American character; second, the difference in the boys' attitude toward the two people. I have asked many of them about it on the spot, and all of them admitted frankly they don't like the French. They do not, on the other hand, profess that they like the Germans. They do say that they are clean, well behaved on the whole, even deferential, and they do not overcharge. The last is perhaps not so much of a virtue when one considers that the American authorities have absolute power to punish cheating as well as thievery, and we are exercising that whenever the occasion arises.

The Germans' deference is not, I should say, the grand preconceived scheme of wheedling the Americans and setting them against their allies that it has been made out to be. It is, rather, a traditional respect for authority, especially when it presents itself in uniform. One must not forget that the revolution has hardly touched this side of the Rhine. But it must also be admitted that a large section of the German people feels itself related to the America that is the home of their brothers, sons and cousins. These people profess to see in us the virtues which they ascribe to themselves, and they like us as sincerely as they hate the French. They frankly admire our boys, those tall, heroic-looking chaps are courteous ad chivalrous, even to their enemies. The American boy, for his part, is too big-hearted to vent his anger or show his disdain of the beaten foe. He is, if anything, given to brag a little to his own brother-in-arms. He is not afraid of his equal, but he does not hit a fellow when he's down.

This, I believe, is the simplest explanation of what has boomed up some writers into something approaching a scandal.

What puzzles me more is the attitude of the Germans to the English. They seem to like them, and they say so, all "hymns of hate" and "starvation blockade" protests to the contrary notwithstanding. In Cologne, they have come to like their easygoing ways, their sportsmanlike behavior—even their arrogance, which some admit is like their own. Through fraternization, which the English authorities permit, they have come to know them better even than the Americans, and it is a common sight to see Tommy Atkins go fishing with a German lad, or taking his beer in the open, with the fraulein or the whole family of his billet.

In the American zone, fraternization is still strictly forbidden, but the boys that are billeted with private families find it mighty hard to live up to the rule. Some of them have gotten to feel very much at home, while the great majority is aching to get back to America. There are always some who hate to leave when the moment of parting arrives. Every troop train pulling out of the Coblenz leaves a bunch of weeping Gretchens standing at the platform.

If Americans can't fraternize, the French won't. The hatred between French and German is obviously becoming worse as the days go by. One evidently can't blame the French. One look at the north of France would pull up the average German civilian who grumbles at the treatment being meted out to him. But the pride of the Frenchman is too much for Fritz, and as a consequence, the court-martials have their hands full. Whether he fights for a place on the train, or disputes the superior right of Gaston to the affections of his girl, the "Boche" gets the worst of it every time. The people of Rhinish Germany dread the months to come.

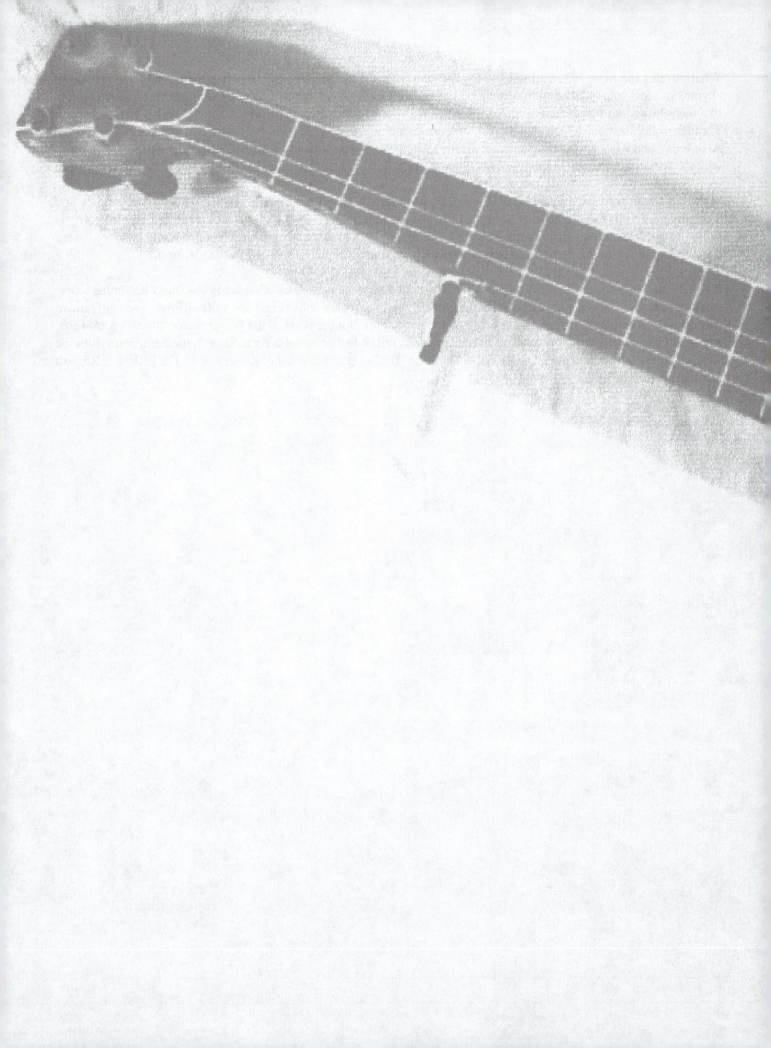

1920–1929

America was booming during the second decade of the century, and economic excitement was in the air. No invention better defined this desire than the radio. By mid-decade, the radio was a "must have" device for every family blessed with electricity. Songwriters' income from sheet music sales declined dramatically. Piano sales slowed as families gathered together around the radio instead, to be entertained and hear music ranging from jazz to old-time country once foreign to their region.

The years following the Great War were marked by a new nationalism symbolized by frenzied consumerism. By 1920, urban Americans had begun to define themselves—for their neighbors and for the world—in terms of what they consumed. The car was becoming universal—at least in its appeal. At the dawn of the century, only 4,192 automobiles were registered nationwide; in 1920, the number of cars had reached 1.9 million. Simultaneously, aggressive new advertising methods began appearing, designed to fuel the new consumer needs of the buying public. And buy, it did. From 1921 to 1929, Americans bought and America boomed. With expanded wages and buying power came increased leisure time for recreation, travel, or even self-improvement. And the advertising reinforced the idea that the conveniences and status symbols of the wealthy were attainable to everyone. The well-to-do and the wage earner began to look a lot more alike.

Following the Great War, America enjoyed a period of great expansion and expectation. The attitude of many Americans was expressed in President Calvin Coolidge's famous remark, "The chief business of the American people is business." The role of the federal government remained small during the period and federal expenditures actually declined following the war effort. Harry Donaldson's song "How Ya Gonna Keep 'Em Down on the Farm after They've Seen Paree?" described another basic shift in American society. The 1920 census reported that more than 50 percent of the population—54 million people—lived in urban areas. The move to the cities was the result of changed expectations, increased industrialization, and the migration of millions of Southern blacks to the urban North.

The availability of electricity expanded the universe of goods that could be manufactured and sold. The expanded use of radios, electric lights, telephones, and powered vacuum cleaners was possible for the first time, and they quickly became essential household items. Construction boomed as—for the first time—half of all Americans now lived in urban areas. Industry, too, benefited from the wider use of electric power. At the turn of the century, electricity ran only five percent of all machinery, and by 1925, 73 percent. Large-scale electric power also made possible electrolytic processes in the rapidly developing heavy chemical industry. With increasing sophistication came higher costs; wages for skilled workers continued to rise during the 1920s, putting further distance between the blue-collar worker and the emerging middle class.

Following the war years, women who had worked men's jobs in the late teens usually remained in the work force, although at lower wages. Women, now allowed to vote nationally, were also encouraged to consider college and options other than marriage. Average family earnings increased slightly during the first half of the period, while prices and hours worked actually declined. The 48-hour week became standard, providing more leisure time. At least 40 million people went to the movies each week, and college football became a national obsession.

Unlike previous decades, national prosperity was not fueled by the cheap labor of new immigrants, but by increased factory efficiencies, innovation, and more sophisticated methods of managing time and materials. Starting in the 'teens, the flow of new immigrants began to slow, culminating in the restrictive immigration legislation of 1924 when new workers from Europe were reduced to a trickle. The efforts were largely designed to protect the wages of American workers—many of whom were only one generation from their native land. As a result, wages for unskilled labor remained stable; union membership declined and strikes, on average, decreased. American exports more than doubled during the decade and heavy imports of European goods virtually halted, a reversal of the Progressive Movement's flirtation with free trade.

These national shifts were not without powerful resistance. A bill was proposed in Utah to imprison any woman who wore her skirt higher than three inches above the ankle. Cigarette consumption reached 43 billion annually, despite smoking being illegal in 14 states and the threat of expulsion from college if caught with a cigarette. A film code limiting sexual material in silent films was created to prevent "loose" morals, and the membership of the KKK expanded to repress Catholics, Jews, open immigration, make-up on women, and the prospect of unrelenting change.

The decade ushered in Trojan contraceptives, the Pitney Bowes postage meter, the Baby Ruth candy bar, Wise potato chips, Drano, self-winding watches, State Farm Mutual auto insurance, Kleenex, and the Macy's Thanksgiving Day Parade down Central Park West in New York. Despite a growing middle class, the share of disposable income going to the top five percent of the population continued to increase. Fifty percent of the people, by one estimate, still lived in poverty. Coal and textile workers, Southern farmers, unorganized labor, single women, the elderly, and most blacks were excluded from the economic giddiness of the period.

In 1929, America appeared to be in an era of unending prosperity. U.S. goods and services reached all-time highs. Industrial production rose 50 percent during the decade as the concepts of mass production were refined and broadly applied. The sale of electrical appliances from radios to refrigerators skyrocketed. Consumers were able to purchase newly produced goods through the extended use of credit. Debt accumulated. By 1930, personal debt had increased to one third of personal wealth. The nightmare on Wall Street in October 1929 brought an end to the economic festivities, setting the stage for a more proactive government and an increasingly cautious worker.

1925 PROFILE

Born in 1887 in Chicago, Illinois, Leo Kunstadt had grown up with the evolving technology of talking machines.

Life at Home

- Sales of Victor phonographs had been declining for two years and Leo Kunstadt was ready for the next big change and a new challenge.
- For 22 years, he and his father had been on the leading edge of phonograph talking machine sales.
- Now, Victor Records had announced revolutionary plans to upgrade their discs even more.
- Leo's best customers were buzzing with excitement; with all the technological changes underway, this was a great time to be alive.
- Thomas Edison had first developed the phonograph in 1877, 10 years before Leo was born, during a cavalcade era of innovations in the communications industry that included the telegraph, the typewriter, and the telephone.
- As conceived by Edison, the phonograph translated the air vibrations created by the human voice into minute indentations on a sheet of tinfoil placed over a metallic cylinder, which could then reproduce the sounds.
- Edison believed that its best commercial benefit was for office dictation.
- Others said that the possibilities were endless: songs, sermons, speeches, orchestras and poetry could all be recorded.
- The first financially successful use of sound recording was "penny in the slot" machines that played music on command.
- As a result, dozens of phonograph machines were invented under a variety of different names to bring recorded music into the home.
- Leo could hear it in no other way.

Enamoured with talking machines, Leo Kunstadt made sure his hardware store carried the latest recording technology by the Victor Company.

- He was enthralled by the phonograph, played on wax cylinders, the first time his father played a marching tune in his hardware store in downtown Chicago.
- Leo was mesmerized, despite the hissing sounds and chorus of pops and burps.
- The phonograph cylinder dominated the recorded sound market when Leo was a child; the scratchy sound and high-pitched tones could be ignored for the sake of hearing music in your home when you wanted it.
- It was simply magical to have music on demand, even if one critic described the cylinder's sound as resembling a "partially educated parrot with a sore throat and a cold."
- These problems were in part solved by the development of the phonograph record, a flat disc with an inscribed, modulated spiral groove, which brought sound recordings to a new level of quality.

Having music in your home whenever you wanted it was worth the scratchy sounds of early recordings.

- Eventually, records dominated the field.
- As early as 1888, lateral-cut disc records invented by Emile Berliner were marketed under the Berliner Gramophone label.
- Eldridge R. Johnson improved the fidelity so Johnson's and Berliner's separate companies merged to form the Victor Talking Machine Company, whose disc record would dominate the market.
- Early disc recordings were produced in a variety of speeds ranging from 60 to 130 revolutions per minute, and a variety of sizes, from five to seven to 12 inches.
- By 1894, Emile Berliner's United States Gramophone Company was selling single-sided seven-inch discs with an advertised standard speed of "about 70 rpm" (revolutions per minute).
- Soon, 78 rpm became the standard for the phonograph industry, because it was the speed created by one of the early hand-cranked machines.
- To improve the quality of the records played on the Talking Machines, Victor pioneered new manufacturing processes and then launched an ambitious project to sign exclusive contracts with the most prestigious singers of the day.
- Often, these artists demanded fees higher than the company could hope to make up from the sale of its records.
- Johnson calculated that he would get his money's worth through the promotion of the Victor brand name.
- These new "celebrity" recordings bore red labels, and were marketed as "Red Seal" records.
- As intended, the public assumed that Victor Records must be superior to cylinder records.
- In Chicago, Leo's father followed the changes carefully and considered the Victor Record recording made of opera singer Enrico Caruso a masterpiece.
- He used Caruso's voice to demonstrate his Victor phonographs for sale; he believed that Caruso's rich, powerful, low tenor voice highlighted the best range of audio fidelity.
- To compete, Thomas Edison introduced the Amberol cylinder in 1909, with a maximum playing time of four and a half minutes (at 160 rpm) to be in turn superseded by the Blue Amberol Record, whose playing surface was made of celluloid.
- Because of technological limitations, early recordings failed to pick up the high end and low end of the musical range and featured voices no better than violins.
- Therefore, despite an obsession within the industry to prevent "the lower classes" from polluting the instrument, "vaudeville trash" was easily recorded and sold extremely well.
- Leo kept some of the racier recordings behind the counter for special customers.
- Industry spokesmen liked to rhapsodize about the various ways the talking machine could serve as an "active agent in the spread of civilization," but Leo knew from experience that most households needed a little vaudeville to mix with their opera.
- Leo figured that the need to create an "oasis of calm" within the home with only highbrow music was clearly conceived by someone with no children or at least two housekeepers.

- He figured the manufacturers could talk "highbrow" while he made a living helping regular customers every day.
- Several advertisements depicted the great recording stars as specially selected "after-dinner guests personally invited to entertain you."
- Another read, "Measured by every standard, what could be more valuable, more concretely useful, as well as delightfully entertaining than the Victrola? Second only to the actual physical needs of the body is the imperative hunger of the mind and spirit for the essential "foods"—music, literature, inspiration, education, comfort and laughter. The Victrola is the tireless servant, bringing to them at any place, any time, the greatest art and entertainment of the whole world."

Life at Work

- Leo Kunstadt had been made co-owner of Kunstadt Hardware with his father only a year earlier.
- Now was the time to demonstrate all he had learned.
- For two decades, Kunstadt Hardware had been following a national trend in shifting from general to specialty products.
- The phonograph display in the big picture window never failed to attract attention, and now that Victor was planning a recording revolution, Leo wanted to take full advantage of the opportunity.
- He was even willing to shift the store's second window from a radio cabinet montage to all phonographs and phonograph records; his children had agreed that their fox terrier could pretend to be the Victor logo dog Nipper listening to "his master's voice."
- *The Voice*, a publication issued by the Victor Company, included instructions, pictures and scale drawings of display windows that produced high sales because they told a story.
- Leo remembered how excited he was when Victor added a spring-loaded motor to its talking machines to ensure a constant turntable speed, and when high-class cabinets were introduced, allowing the phonograph to become an honored piece of furniture.
- That allowed middle class families to embrace the idea of a "musical library" and move away from the accusation that phonograph players were simply "soulless machines."
- But more needed to be done.
- Since the introduction of talking machines, large orchestras had been at a disadvantage in acoustical recordings; musicians had to gather as closely as possible around the recording horn and some percussion instruments could not be heard on the recordings.
- So in 1924, under pressure from the industry, Victor had agreed to shift from the acoustical, or mechanical, method of recording sound to the new microphone-based electrical system developed by Western Electric.
- Victor decided to name its version of the improved fidelity recording process "Orthophonic" and sold a line of new designs of phonographs to play these improved records, called "Orthophonic Victrolas."
- The highest-quality models of Orthophonic Victrolas had a six-foot-long horn coiled inside the cabinet featuring audio fidelity unmatched by most home electric phonographs until some 30 years later.
- With a large advertising campaign, Victor introduced its Orthophonic records on "Victor Day," November 2, 1925.

After the war, America was alive with music.

- Kunstadt Hardware was flooded with customers eager to hear the new sound recordings.
- Leo believed Victor was the best in the business at advertising in a way that drove customers into his store.
- He heartily agreed with the assessment of Talking Machine World that "instead of losing time and waiting for the people to become acquainted with the charms of the talking machine in the ordinary way, the creative forces have accomplished in 10 years what would have taken half a century."
- Thanks to the quality of the advertisements in upscale magazines, even the most sophisticated customers wanted the pleasure of the phonograph machine.
- Victor also provided customer financing; by the mid-1920s, 90 percent of phonographs—ranging in price from $15 to $250—were bought on credit over time.
- The purchase of phonographs totaled 15 percent of all consumer debt; automobiles represented 50 percent.
- Leo often went to the Victrola purchaser's house personally to collect his or her monthly payment so he could then demonstrate a generous handful of the newest records.
- A family only needed one talking machine, but to fully use their asset, they needed to keep up with the newest musical trends.
- Leo had also gotten the idea to loan a phonograph player to the neighborhood school under a Victor-sponsored program to put "a great army of music educators" in the classroom, who owe it to "yourself to foster a love of music."
- During World War I, inventory had been tight with more than five million records on back order in 1919.
- Then came the prosperous times of 1921 and 1922 when Leo—and in fact the entire industry—sold a record number of machines and records, despite the new competition posed by radio.
- In fact, the entire industry was exploding with new companies and new ideas.
- It seemed the nation was alive with music.
- Thousands of soldiers returning from the war were so enamored with the military-style large choral singing, they organized group singing in their factories, neighborhoods and villages.
- Schoolchildren were encouraged to enter music memory contests which necessitated proud parents to invest in a talking machine and records "for the children's sake."
- A 1924 survey of 36 American cities determined that 59 percent of households owned a hand-cranked or electric phonograph.
- Radio set sales were in their infancy, but growing exponentially, following their commercial introduction in 1922.
- Initially, radio stations were created to support radio sales; "We broadcast primarily so that those who purchase RCA radios may have something to feed those receiving instruments," said David Sarnoff, vice president of Radio Corporation of America.

Schoolchildren were encouraged to play instruments, sing, and enter music contests – which were easier to win if there was a talking machine at home.

Life in the Community: Chicago, Illinois

- Chicago was developed to be a city that understood business.
- Starting in the 1830s, entrepreneurs saw the potential of Chicago, Illinois, as a transportation hub and engaged in land speculation to obtain the choicest lots; by 1840, the boomtown had a population of over 4,000.
- To open the surrounding farmlands to trade, the Cook County commissioners built roads south and west, which enabled hundreds of wagons per day of farm produce to be shipped East through the Great Lakes.
- By the 1850s, the construction of railroads made Chicago a major hub; over 30 lines entered the city.
- Factories were created, including the Harvester Factory, which was opened in 1847 by Cyrus Hall McCormick.
- Chicago became a processing center for natural resource commodities extracted in the West.
- The Wisconsin forests supported the millwork and lumber businesses; the Illinois hinterland provided the wheat, and hundreds of thousands of hogs and cattle were shipped to Chicago for slaughter.
- In 1883, the standardized system of North American Time Zones was adopted by the general time convention of railway managers in Chicago, giving the continent a uniform system for telling time.
- Chicago's role as the transportation hub of the U.S., with its road, rail and water connections, positioned the city to become home to several national retailers offering catalog shopping, including giants Montgomery Ward and Sears, Roebuck and Company.

Chicago's surrounding farmlands prospered by the building of roads for wagons and the laying of tracks for trains.

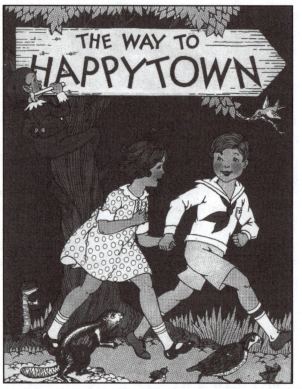

Chicago was a thriving, happy community.

- This growth allowed Chicago to surpass St. Louis and Cincinnati as the major city in the Midwest.
- Most of the newcomers were Irish Catholic and German immigrants and their descendants.
- In 1871, the city burned in the Great Chicago Fire.
- In the fire 300 people died, 18,000 buildings were destroyed and nearly 100,000 of the city's 300,000 residents were left homeless.
- The building boom that followed saved the city's status as the transportation and trade hub of the Midwest.
- Between 1870 and 1900, Chicago grew from a city of 299,000 residents to nearly 1.7 million.
- After the turn of the twentieth century, immigrants from Eastern and Southern Europe, including Poles, Lithuanians, Ukrainians, Hungarians, Czechs, Slovaks, Greeks, and Italians, and Jews from throughout Eastern Europe, flocked to the city.
- Then, after 1914, the First World War cut off immigration from Europe.
- After the war's end, federal immigration legislation in 1924 restricted populations from Eastern and Southern Europe.
- As the First World War cut off immigration, tens of thousands of African Americans came north in the Great Migration out of the rural South.
- In 1919, the Chicago Race Riots erupted in what became known as "Red Summer," when other major cities also suffered mass racial violence based on competition for jobs and housing as the country tried to absorb veterans in the postwar years.
- By 1920, a third of Chicago's 2.7 million residents were foreign-born; more than a million were Catholic, and another 125,000 were Jewish.
- Professional football had come to Chicago in 1923 amid criticism that the sport might tarnish the reputation of the collegiate sport, where the game was played for the thrill of battle rather than for money.
- Harold "Red" Grange, from Wheaton, Illinois, a football hero at the University of Illinois in the early part of the decade, signed with the Bears for their final two games of the 1925 season.

HISTORICAL SNAPSHOT
1925

- Benito Mussolini announced he was taking dictatorial power over Italy
- Nellie Tayloe Ross became the first female governor of Wyoming, and 15 days later, Ma Ferguson became the first female governor of Texas
- *The New Yorker* magazine published its first issue
- Art Gillham recorded for Columbia Records, the first Western Electric master to be commercially released
- Calvin Coolidge was the first U.S. president to have his inauguration broadcast on radio
- Tennessee Governor Austin Peay signed the Butler Act, prohibiting the teaching of evolution in the state's public schools; teacher John Scopes was convicted of teaching Charles Darwin's Theory of Evolution and fined $100
- Radio station WOWO in Ft. Wayne, Indiana, began broadcasting
- F. Scott Fitzgerald published *The Great Gatsby*
- The Chrysler Corporation was founded by Walter Percy Chrysler
- Charles Francis Jenkins achieved the first synchronized transmission of pictures and sound, which he called radiovision
- Adolf Hitler published his personal manifesto, *Mein Kampf*
- The Ku Klux Klan demonstrated its popularity by holding a parade in Washington, DC; 40,000 male and female members of the Klan marched down Pennsylvania Avenue
- The country variety show *WSM Barn Dance*, later renamed *The Grand Ole Opry*, made its radio debut
- The Great Sphinx of Giza was unearthed
- The Thompson submachine gun sold for $175 in the 1925 Sears, Roebuck and Company mail order catalog

Selected Prices

Apartment, Chicago, Five Rooms.............................$70.00
Bathing Suit, Men's $5.00
Carpet Sweeper..$5.00
Crib $17.50
Handkerchiefs, Dozen......................................$1.80
Hotel Room, New York, per Day $3.00
Poker Set, 100 Chips.......................................$6.25
Radio...$39.95
Talking Machine, Victrola 405, Walnut Case, Electric ...$290.00
Typewriter, Remington $60.00

7 million drinks a day

New Simplified Lawnmower

$18.00 direct from factory

Cutters gather grass and shear it off evenly. No ridges are left in the lawn.

MONTAMOWER

NO GEARS—NO LONG BLADES

The Pen of Accomplishment

Waterman's Ideal Fountain Pen

"The Daddy of Them All"

SPECIAL With flexible Gold Filled lip band $7.50

Other Waterman's from $2.50 to $30.00 in barrel sizes and point tempers to fit the hand and preference of individual owners.

Every age in pen-ownership has its appropriate

Waterman's Ideal Pen

The sturdy pen of school day utility, dependable aid to neatness and accuracy.

The appreciated companion of office and campus hours—a pen selected to keep pace with growing hands and more exacting employment.

Finally, the insignia of success—the handsome gold mounted pen of the man of affairs, dignified as his treasured time piece and as efficiently ready for instant call.

Pride of possession goes with every Waterman's Pen that's sold.

Selection and Service at Best Dealers Everywhere

L.E. Waterman Company

Pen illustrated ½ actual size.

191 Broadway, New York
Chicago   Boston   San Francisco   Montreal

The complete keyboard makes writing easier

"Scientist Says Moving Pictures by Radio Certain," *Oakland Tribune* (California), November 21, 1924:

In a little while, if all goes well, it may be as easy to "see-in" film plays at home as it is today to "listen-in" to broadcast plays and concerts.

The citizen in his easy chair will adjust his tuner, much as he does now, but, instead of a voice coming out of space, figures will move to and fro across the screen in his darkened room.

This will be the natural sequel to the great step forward in the development of television towards the possibility of broadcasting cinematograph plays, which is claimed by two British inventors.

Hitherto, the transmission of photographs to a distance by wire or wireless has been a matter of minutes, but W. S. Stephenson, the managing director of the General Radio Company, and G. W. Walton, one of his colleagues, now state that they have discovered a "light-sensitive device" which will permit this to be done almost instantly.

"In fact, in the near future," said W. S. Stephenson to me yesterday, "we hope to have instruments actually working which would be capable of transmitting pictures at the same speed as that now necessary to "maintain persistence of vision in cinematography, 18 pictures per second."

The chief difficulty in the past was the slow-action selenium, the element most generally used to convert light into electrical current which can be sent over wires or by wireless.

Messers. Stephenson and Walton, who already hold patents covering apparatus devised for the transmission of pictures, claim that their "light-sensitive device" takes the place of selenium.

Stephenson showed a small photograph with a parallel line effect reminiscent of fine-screen halftone reproduction.

"This photograph," he declared "was transmitted by our method in 20 seconds. It is only a question of speeding up the apparatus to the time necessary for persistence of vision."

"Victor Co. Produces a New Record, Officials Say Invention for Phonograph Will Revolutionize the Industry," *The New York Times*, **August 14, 1925:**

The Victor Talking Machine Company announced yesterday that it will soon place on the market an improved music-producing instrument which "will revolutionize the entire industry."

This statement came less than 24 hours after the announcement of the Brunswick-Balollender of the Panatrome substitute for the phonograph, which has been developed by the Radio Corporation of America, the General Electric Company, the Westinghouse Electric Company, and the Brunswick Company.

Both the Victor and the Brunswick companies say that there is no reason for scrapping the existing instruments. The new records which they are issuing can be played on the existing phonographs and Victrolas. They are said to be an improvement over the old records when played on the ordinary machines, but it is asserted that the new reproducing instruments are needed to bring our their full values.

E. K. McEwan, secretary of the Victor Talking Machine Company, described the new Victor invention as "a knockout." He said it would be placed on the market very soon.

E. R. Fenimore Johnson, president of Victor Co., said that he was not ready to describe the invention in detail, but he called it "the ultimate sound reproduction." He said that it gave complete mechanical reproduction for the entire range of audible sound.

The New Brunswick machine, called the Panatrome, is equipped with vacuum tube amplifiers and disc resonators run either by batteries or by connection with an electrical system. The new Victor machine, it was said, is non-electrical.

While both inventions are intended as an answer to the competition of radio, which has cut heavily into the music reproduction businesses, both are indebted to radio. The Brunswick instrument is almost a byproduct of radio. Many of its features are adapted from inventions and developments resulting from radio research. It is asserted that the Brunswick instrument makes it possible to put eight or nine times as much music on a 12-inch record as at present, or, in other words, to make a 12-inch record that will play 40 or 45 minutes. This development, however, is so far only in the laboratory stage. Practical difficulties, it was said, would make it a year or two before 45-minute records can be marketed.

Victor officials declined to say whether the new product would make possible records which could play a great length of time without change.

Discussing the statement that the New Brunswick music reproduced partly on principle that used in the talking film, Dr. Lee De Forest, inventor of the Phonofilm, said yesterday his patents were not in any way infringed.

"I welcome this invention. I believe it will save the phonograph. I am very fond of the phonograph, I haven't played mine for months, simply because I am tired of changing the records every few minutes. If they are successful in getting out a record which will play for half an hour without interruption, it will certainly be a remarkable achievement which the public would greatly appreciate."

Advertisement for Eagle brand Graphophone, 1899:

Possession of a Graphophone makes it possible, at modest cost, to keep up-to-date with the latest operatic and musical comedy successes, with concert singers of the highest renown, to hear the voice of a noted comedian reciting some of his sidesplitting monologues. The Graphophone is to the ear what the camera is to the eye; superior, in fact to a camera because it is Simple and Instantaneous, recording and reproducing on the spot, with utmost fidelity anything it is allowed to hear.

Timeline of the Victor Phonograph Company

1900

Eldridge Johnson purchased the Berliner Gramophone Company after Berliner lost a legal battle over rights to manufacture flat-disc gramophones; Johnson formed the Consolidated Talking Machine Company.

1901

Johnson reorganized Consolidated Talking Machine and called the new venture The Victor Talking Machine Company.

Victor $3, Type A, Type B, Type C, Monarch, and Monarch Deluxe models were introduced.

Victor sold 7,570 phonographs during the year.

1902

Victor introduced the "Rigid Arm" tone arm concept, which allowed the arm to pivot independently from the horn.

Victor Monarch Jr., Monarch Special, Type P, Royal, Victor II, Victor III and Victor IV models were introduced.

1903

Victor introduced Type D, Type Z, Victor I models.

Initial sketches of an internal horn phonograph design appeared, eventually leading to production of the Victrola.

1904

Victor introduced the deluxe gold-trimmed Victor VI model, selling for $100.

A tapering tone arm debuted on certain models.

1905

Victor sold 65,591 phonographs during the year.

1906

The pneumatic-powered Victor Auxetophone, introduced in May, sold for $500.

The Victrola, the first internal horn phonograph, was introduced and became an instant success.

1907

Victor began transitioning manufacture of Victrola cabinets to its Camden plant.

The "domed lid" was introduced on the Victrola.

1908

Victor sold a record 107,000 phonographs.

1909
Victor introduced the first tabletop internal horn phonograph, the Victrola XII, which sold for $125, and the economy

Monarch Jr. external horn phonograph, priced at $10.00.

Victor sales plummeted over 50 percent during the year due to the economic downturn.

1910
Victor focused design and production efforts on the internal horn phonograph and away from the external horn models.

1911
Victor introduced the Victrola IX, the first truly low-cost internal horn tabletop model, selling for $50.

Internal horn Victrola sales exceeded those of the external horn Victor phonographs for the first time.

Victor sales were at a record 125,000 for the year.

1912
Victor sales nearly doubled from the previous year, passing 252,000.

1913
Victor introduced the automatic brake feature on many models.

The Victor XXV "Schoolhouse" model was introduced.

1914
Victor introduced brown mahogany as a finish option.

1915
The elegant Victrola XVIII was introduced, selling for $300 in basic mahogany.

1917
Victor reached an all-time production high of 573,000 phonographs during the year.

1918
Wartime inflation resulted in a series of price increases for all Victor products.

Victor production partially converted to rifle components and biplane wings; phonograph production dropped over 40 percent from the previous year.

1919
Victor production converted back to phonographs, with annual production rising to 474,000 units.

Additional price increases were implemented due to inflation.

1920
Annual sales of Victor phonographs topped 560,000, the second-best year ever.

1921

Intense competition reduced sales by 30 percent for the year.

Victor offered its first "suitcase portable" model, the Victrola No. 50.

1922

Victor introduced a low-priced line of "flat-top" consoles, selling for $100, that were immediately successful.

New phonograph competitors and the rise of radio sales increased to five percent.

1923

Victor launched a series of upper-medium-priced consoles; total Victor production levels remained stagnant at around 400,000 units per year.

1924

Victor sales continued to slide during the year, deteriorating to a low point during the usually busy Christmas season.

Radios were now the dominant Christmas entertainment gift.

1925

Victor licensed the electric recording process.

During the summer, Victor launched a "half-price" sale to unload its stock of old-style Victrolas in anticipation of the Orthophonic debut.

Four new Orthophonic Victrolas were introduced on November 2; the products were highly successful, since the fidelity and volume were many times greater than the earlier Victrolas, and costs ranged from $85 to $275.

Victor offered its first radio/phono combination console, the Alhambra I, selling for $350.00.

Victor sales dropped nearly 40 percent to an annual rate of 262,000 units.

1927 PROFILE

The voice of blues singer Florence Mills was described as being "bell-like" with "bird-like tones," characteristics that made her one of the prominent entertainers of the 1920s.

Life at Home

- Known as the "Queen of Happiness," Florence Mills, born Florence Winfrey, captivated the public with her enchanting song "I'm a Little Blackbird Looking for a Bluebird," and her stage performances in *Shuffle Along*.
- The song was created by Tin Pan Alley songwriter George W. Meyer, who also wrote the music for the songs "For Me And My Gal," "If You Were the Only Girl in the World" and "Where Did Robinson Crusoe Go With Friday on Saturday Night?"
- When Florence died at age 31, more than 150,000 people came to her funeral; kings sent flowers, Americans—black and white—mourned, and Harlem came to a standstill.
- The youngest of three daughters of John and Nellie Winfrey, Florence was born into extreme poverty on January 25, 1895.
- Both her parents were born in slavery in Amherst County, Virginia, and worked in the tobacco industry.
- When tobacco farming tanked, the family moved from Lynchburg, Virginia, to Washington, DC, where her father worked as a day laborer and her mother took in laundry.
- Both parents were illiterate.
- Florence grew up in the streets of Goat Alley, Washington, DC's infamous slum, where she demonstrated natural gifts as a singer and dancer which brought her to the attention of an international audience.

Blues singer Florence Mills was one of the most prominent entertainers of the 1920s, before her untimely death at age 31.

- At age five, she won prizes for cakewalking and buck dancing, and was awarded a bracelet by the wife of the British ambassador for entertaining her international guests from the diplomatic corps.
- By age seven, Florence was a regular performer in theaters and private homes, and rapidly developed a name for herself on the vaudeville and burlesque circuits.
- Some of her earliest roles were as a "pickaninny" or "pick" in white vaudeville, then as a sister act on the black popular entertainment circuit.
- It was a tough life for a small child, playing small venues all over the country, putting in endless hours rehearsing, and traveling.
- The high point of her childhood was her appearance in the road company production of Bert Williams and George Walker's *Sons of Ham*, in which she sang "Miss Hannah from Savannah."

Florence's parents were born into slavery and the tobacco industry.

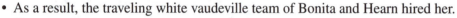

- As a result, the traveling white vaudeville team of Bonita and Hearn hired her.
- Florence then moved to New York with her mother and sisters, and by age 14 had organized a traveling song-and-dance act with her sisters known as the Mills Sisters.
- From then on, Florence Mills was the name she used instead of Florence Winfrey.
- Florence was innovative: skilled in all varieties of jazz and tap dance, she was especially renowned for her "acrobatic" and "eccentric" dancing, some of which she learned from her husband U.S. "Slow Kid" Thompson, the originator of "slow motion dancing" and one of the earliest practitioners of Russian dancing or "legomania."
- Her lessons in tap came from her close personal friend Bill "Bojangles" Robinson when she was living in Chicago in 1916-1917.
- At the same time, new opportunities were developing for the artistic black community—long a victim of humiliating discrimination and Jim Crow laws.
- White promoter Otto Heinemann and his company OKeh Records were struggling to get established; Heinemann was willing to try anything when he asked Cincinnati's young black singer Mamie Smith to cut a record.
- For the premiere recording, Smith sang "That Thing Called Love" and "You Can't Keep a Good Man Down," backed by the house orchestra—to keep the record from sounding "too colored."
- This was quickly followed by the recording of "Crazy Blues" and "It's Right Here for You (If You Don't Come Get It, 'Taint No Fault of Mine)," this time accompanied by a five-piece black band known as the Jazz Hounds.
- The result was impressive and possibly the first actual blues recording by a black artist with black accompaniment.
- Within a month, 75,000 copies of "Crazy Blues" had been sold in Harlem record shops; in only seven months, national sales topped one million copies.
- Mamie Smith and her band were pure gold; everything they recorded sold immediately.
- Smith made more than $100,000 in recording royalties alone; in addition, she was making between $1,000 and $1,500 a week in the large theaters in New York and Chicago.
- As a result, record companies scrambled to sign new blues singers; Columbia Records even bragged that it had "more colored artists under exclusive contract than any company today."
- Black Swan Records, produced for Pace Phonograph Company of New York, advertised itself as the "only genuine colored record. Others are only passing for colored."

Life at Work

- Florence Mills's big break came in 1921 with *Shuffle Along*, the off-Broadway hit show that introduced syncopated song and dance to White America.
- Florence luxuriated in the music and lyrics by black songwriters Noble Sissle and Eubie Blake.
- When the show opened in New York, it was an immediate hit.
- Writer Langston Hughes believed *Shuffle Along* initiated the Harlem Renaissance and inaugurated the decade when "the Negro was in vogue."
- Florence's uninhibited singing and dancing stunned the audiences.
- She was paid $125 per week.
- "We were afraid people would think it was a freak show and it wouldn't appeal to white people," said Eubie Blake. "Others thought that if it was a colored show, it might be dirty."
- Sissle and Blake first joined forces as members of the World War I "Hell Fighters" Jazz Band of the 369th Infantry led by James Reese Europe.
- They transformed an old sketch named "The Mayor of Jimtown" into a lively musical featuring hit songs such as "I'm Just Wild About Harry" and "Love Will Find A Way," combined with energetic dancing.

The off-Broadway hit Shuffle Along *introduced syncopated song and dance to white America.*

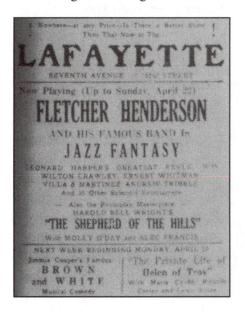

- After *Shuffle Along*, Lew Leslie, a white promoter, hired Florence to appear in a revue at the Plantation Club that featured Florence and a wide range of black talent including visiting performers such as Paul Robeson.
- The show—which charged a $3 admission—introduced white audiences to the ebullient, fast-paced rhythms of black music.
- Edith Wilson and the Jazz Hounds served as Florence's house orchestra.
- Florence was paid $200 per week.
- In 1922, the nightclub act was converted into a Broadway show called *The Plantation Revue*, and Florence was positioned to become one of the first black female performers to break into the racially restricted show business establishment.
- She was paid $500 per week, for no fewer than 35 weeks a year.
- Civil rights crusader Bert Williams believed that Florence would accomplish more than he had: "This is once where the pint is better than the quart."
- Florence did it all: she sang blues, "hot jazz" and ballads, plus she danced, acted, and was an accomplished comedian and mime.
- Luminaries such as Jelly Roll Morton, James P. Johnson and Willie "The Lion" Smith helped dub her "The Queen of Jazz."

- Composer Irving Berlin said that if he could find a white woman who could sing like Florence, he would be inspired to write a hit a week.
- Writer James Weldon Johnson wrote, "The upper range of her voice was full of bubbling, bell-like, bird-like tones. It was a rather magical thing Florence Mills used to do with that small voice in her favorite song, 'I'm a Little Blackbird Looking for a Bluebird,' and she did it with such exquisite poignancy as always to raise a lump in your throat."
- But that did not change the fact that the set where she performed was fashioned like a pre-Civil War southern plantation featuring a large watermelon slice, whose seeds were electric lights, and a bandanna-coifed black woman flipping pancakes.
- Nonetheless, Florence brought the house down with the naughty song, "I've Got What It Takes But It Breaks My Heart to Give It Away"; Edith Wilson performed her showstopper in the same revue: "He May Be Your Man, But He Comes to See Me Sometimes."
- Florence was reported to be the "highest-salaried colored actress on the American stage."
- The Great White Way was not solely white anymore.
- On opening night for the second, 1922-1923 season, the audience included Charlie Chaplin, Irving Berlin and Irene Bordoni.
- One of the new songs added to the second season, "Aggravatin' Pappa," became a radio hit—by Sophie Tucker; by the end of the year, a dozen female singers had recorded Florence's new song.
- When Sir Charles B. Cochran began looking for attractions for the London stage, he invited the Plantation Company to the Pavilion in the spring of 1923, despite a newspaper headline reading, "Nigger Problem Brought to London."
- The show that Cochran devised was called *Dover Street to Dixie*; it was staged with an all-English cast in the first half and featured Florence and the Plantation cast in the second half.
- It proved so successful that issues of race were soon forgotten.
- The Prince of Wales was said to have seen the show numerous times; Florence became so popular that she was to London what Josephine Baker was to Paris.
- Composer Duke Ellington wrote a musical portrait for Florence called "Black Beauty"; she was featured in *Vogue* and *Vanity Fair* and photographed by Bassano and Edward Steichen.
- In 1923, upon her return to New York, Florence received an invitation to appear in the Greenwich Village Follies annual production—the first time a black woman was offered a part in the major white production.
- She was also offered a contract to join the Ziegfeld Follies but turned it down.
- She elected to stay with Lew Leslie to create a rival show with an all-black cast.
- She felt she could best serve her race by providing a venue for an entire company of actors and singers; "If in any way I have done anything to lift the profession, I am unconscious of it, and it was done only for love of my art and for my people."
- Florence enjoyed a triumphant return.
- Her popularity knew no bounds—she was now an international star.
- Florence and her husband bought a new house—a five-story brownstone in the middle of Harlem—and furnished it with carpets imported from China and a music box that played records without rewinding.

Florence and her husband filled their new house with fine and expensive furnishings.

- *Dover Street to Dixie*, which had thrilled in London, became *Dixie to Broadway* when it opened in New York on October 29, 1924, with a brand-new slate of songs.
- Advertisements proclaimed Florence to be "The World's Greatest Colored Entertainer: The Sensation of Two Continents."
- One critic said, "The vital force of the revue proceeds from the personality of Miss Mills."
- In 1926, when Leslie produced *Blackbirds*, Florence had achieved her goal of creating a major all-black revue with the opening of this show at the Alhambra Theatre in Harlem.
- The show then moved to London's Pavilion Theatre and enjoyed 276 performances.
- Exhausted from so many successive performances, Florence went to Germany to rest, but her condition did not improve.
- In 1927, she returned to New York to a royal welcome and decided to have an appendectomy she had put off for too long.
- On October 24, 1927, she entered the hospital for the operation.
- One week later, on November 1, 1927, Mills died.
- She believed that every white person pleased by her performance was a friend won for the race.
- Florence Mills's funeral brought over 150,000 people out onto the streets—the largest such gathering in Harlem's history.

Life in the Community: Harlem, New York

- Harlem was defined by a series of boom-and-bust cycles, with significant ethnic shifts accompanying each one.
- Black residents began to arrive en masse in 1904, the year the Great Migration began by Southern blacks fleeing poverty, few opportunities and aggressive enforcement of discriminatory Jim Crow laws.
- In the 1920s, the neighborhood was the locus of the "Harlem Renaissance," an outpouring of artistic and professional works without precedent in the American black community.

Manhattan Field and the Harlem River.

- Harlem earned a reputation as the Mecca for jazz and blues.
- Venues like the Cotton Club and the Apollo Theater made stars out of entertainers such as Duke Ellington, Cab Calloway, Ella Fitzgerald, James Brown, Michael Jackson, and D'Angelo and Lauryn Hill.
- Harlem began life as a haven for European immigrants and citizens of European descent.
- Initially attracted by its fertile soil and location, Dutch settlers founded Harlem in 1658.
- Governor Peter Stuyvesant named the town Nieuw Haarlem after a city in Holland—British immigrants renamed it Harlem.
- Harlem's economy in the early days was based on agriculture until the railroad and Manhattan street system brought industry to the area.
- A housing boom in the 1890s produced an overabundance of houses, and by 1903, builders opened their doors to tenants of all colors and races.
- Entrepreneur Philip Payton and his company, the Afro-American Realty Company, actively recruited black families and almost single-handedly ignited the migration of blacks from their previous New York neighborhoods, the Tenderloin, San Juan Hill and Hell's Kitchen.
- The move by black residents to northern Manhattan was partially driven by fears of anti-black riots that had occurred in the Tenderloin in 1900 and in San Juan Hill in 1905.
- By 1910, Harlem had a population of around 500,000, of whom 50,000 were African-American and 75,000 were native-born whites; the rest were immigrants from Ireland, Germany, Hungary, Russia, England, Italy and Scandinavia.
- During World War I, expanding industries recruited black laborers to fill new jobs.
- By 1920, central Harlem was 32.43 percent black; between 1920 and 1930, 118,792 white people left the neighborhood and 87,417 blacks arrived.

School band in Harlem.

HISTORICAL SNAPSHOT
1927

- The first transatlantic telephone call was made from New York City to London
- The U.S. Federal Radio Commission began to regulate the use of radio frequencies
- In New York City, the Roxy Theater was opened by Samuel Roxy Rothafel
- The first armored car robbery was committed by the Flatheads Gang near Pittsburgh, Pennsylvania
- The Great Mississippi Flood of 1927 affected 700,000 people in the greatest natural disaster in U.S. history
- Philo Farnsworth transmitted the first experimental electronic television pictures
- *To The Lighthouse* was completed by Virginia Woolf
- The Academy of Motion Picture Arts and Sciences was founded
- Saudi Arabia became independent of the United Kingdom under the Treaty of Jedda

- Charles Lindbergh completed the first solo non-stop transatlantic flight from New York to Paris in the single-seat, single-engine monoplane *Spirit of St. Louis*
- Mount Rushmore was dedicated with promises of national funding for the carving
- The Columbia Phonographic Broadcasting System, later known as CBS, was formed and went on the air with 47 radio stations
- A treaty signed at the League of Nations Slavery Convention abolished all types of slavery
- *The Jazz Singer*, a movie with sound, ushered in "talkies" in the United States
- Leon Trotsky was expelled from the Soviet Communist Party, leaving Joseph Stalin with undisputed control of the Soviet Union
- The Holland Tunnel opened to traffic as the first Hudson River vehicular tunnel linking New Jersey to New York City
- After 19 years of Ford Model T production, the Ford Motor Company unveiled the Ford Model A, available in four colors, with a self-starter
- The musical play *Show Boat*, based on Edna Ferber's novel, opened on Broadway—one of 268 plays on Broadway
- Harold Stephen Black invented the feedback amplifier
- Sears, Roebuck and Co. distributed 15 million catalogues to American homes
- Arthur H. Compton won the Nobel prize in physics for his discovery of wavelength change in diffused x-rays
- The Voluntary Committee of Lawyers was founded to bring about the repeal of Prohibition in the U.S.
- Hit songs included "Ol' Man River," "Can't Help Loving Dat Man," "I'm Looking Over a Four Leaf Clover," "The Best Things In Life Are Free" and "Me And My Shadow"
- The world population reached two billion

Selected Prices

Bath Salts, Jar $1.50
Bathtub...$29.95
Cigarette Case..$11.72
Dress, Crepe...$49.50
House Paint, Gallon $2.15
Incense and Burner $1.00
Iron..$4.45
Oil Heater $4.95
Refrigerator, Ice Capacity 100 Pounds $56.95
Toilet..$6.95

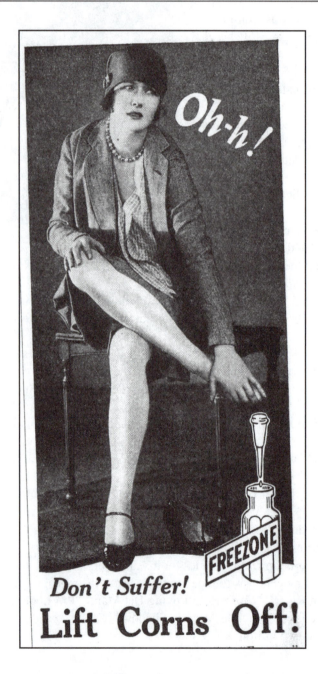

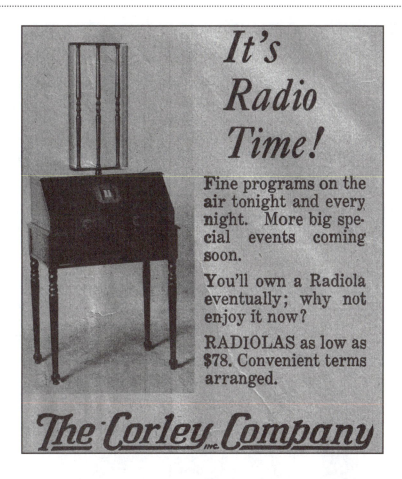

It's Radio Time!

Fine programs on the air tonight and every night. More big special events coming soon.

You'll own a Radiola eventually; why not enjoy it now?

RADIOLAS as low as $78. Convenient terms arranged.

The Corley Company INC.

THE PATRICIAN GOLD BAND REED SUITE, No. A-100—*created by* A. L. RANDALL COMPANY

A NEW and delightful American Period in furniture is now established. Randall Gold Band Reed and Fibre Furniture has achieved new beauty, cheer, and comfort for every room in the home. An infinite variety in design and covering affords selection to harmonize with every decorative scheme and architectural style, even to the pure colonial. In suites, davenport beds, or single pieces, Randall Gold Band Reed and Fibre Furniture strikes a new note of charming grace in the home, the club or the hotel.

See it at the better stores or write for our book, "The New American Period in Furniture."

A. L. RANDALL COMPANY, Chicago, Illinois

RANDALL Reed&Fibre Furniture

TRADE MARK

THE ONLY FURNITURE
TRADE-MARKED WITH THE
GOLD BAND OF QUALITY
Copyright 1923, by A. L. Randall Company

Florence Mills's description of her own dancing:

"I never know what I'm going to do. Perhaps I'm the black Eva Tanguay: I don't know. And I don't care. I just go crazy when the music starts and I like to give the audience all it craves. I make up the dances to the songs beforehand, but then something happens, like one of the orchestra talking to me, and I answer back and watch the audience without appearing to do so. It's great fun. Something different at every performance. It keeps me fresh. Once in New York, I fell down, literally. Did the split. The audience thought I was hurt. I heard some sympathetic expressions. So I got up and started to limp comically. It got a burst of applause. Then I winked and that got another hand. So the producer ran backstage and asked me to keep it in. I did for several nights, but other things happened and I forgot. I never remember just what to do. I'm the despair of stage managers who want a player to act in a groove. No groove for me. The stage isn't large enough for me at times. But it is during the midnight performances that I let out the most. We all do. Not that we overstep the conventions, you understand. But it's just the feeling that it's after hours, I suppose. And we whoop it up."

"Colored Singing," *Variety*, 1923:

Colored singing and playing artists are riding to fame and fortune with the current popular demand for "blues" disc recordings, and because of the recognized fact that only a Negro can do justice to the native indigo ditties, such artists are in great demand.

Mamie Smith is generally credited with having started the demand on the Okeh Records. Not only do these discs enjoy wide sales among the colored race, but they caught on with the Caucasians. As a result, practically every record-making firm, from the Victor down, has augmented its catalog with special "blues" recordings by colored artists.

As a result of this "blues" boom and demand, various colored publishers are prospering. Perry Bradford and the Clarence Williams Music Company are among the representative Negro music men cleaning up from the mechanical royalties with the sheet music angle negligible and almost incidental. No attention to professional plug-in is made; these publishers are concentrating on the disc artists.

"Paul Robeson on the English Stage," Marie Seton, 1958:

Something happened in Drury Lane Theatre on the night when *Show Boat* opened there in April 1928. Leaving their five-month-old Pauli in the care of Essie's mother, Mrs. Goode, the Robesons had sailed again for England for Paul to appear as Joe the Riverman in Jerome Kern's musical of Edna Ferber's Book. Robeson sang "Ol' Man River" and everything else in *Show Boat* was forgotten by both audience and critic. His was the voice of a man speaking in the midst of a puppet-show. The audience did not realize that what moved them was the fusion point where real experience is transmitted into art.

As the weeks passed and more and more people went to see *Show Boat*, the impact of Robeson was like a chain reaction. The first to "discover" him were the smart Mayfair set who went in search of the latest sensations and inaugurated new fashions, but soon the country people who came to London for the "season" were telling their friends to go to Drury Lane. Then, the elderly, frowsty people who go to matinees began talking about Robeson's voice. Soon, the "intelligentsia" of Bloomsbury and Chelsea, who seldom deigned to go to musical comedies, were discussing him. At last, young people from Chapham and Tooting could be heard talking about him from the tops of buses on the Underground. Like many other Londoners, I went to see *Show Boat* shortly after it opened. I remembered Robeson's name from reviews I had read of *Emperor Jones*, but I not seen the O'Neill play.

When the curtain rose, *Show Boat* began to unfold according to the traditional mechanics of romantic musical plays. Only the setting was different—a steamboat plying the Mississippi River. Jerome Kern's musical was pleasant and tuneful; but 24 hours after leaving the theatre, the romance based on Edna Ferber's story faded in one's memory. It was surprising that there seemed to be no dramatic buildup to the entrance of this new star, Paul Robeson.

The scene shifted from the ship's steamboat to the wharf. Suddenly, one realized that Joe the Riverman was Robeson, the silent figure endlessly toting bales of cotton across the stage—a black man with grayed hair moving about like a walk-on, an extra—in life, the man who is overlooked because his role is to work and serve. Suddenly, Joe the Riverman filled the whole theatre with his presence. Robeson began to speak in song. He sang about the flowing Mississippi, and the pain of the black man whose life is like the eternal river rolling towards the open vastness of the ocean:

> "Tote that barge and lift that bale,
> You get a little drunk
> And you lands in jail.
> I gets weary and sick of trying,
> I'm scared of livin' and feared of dyin'...."

> The expression on Robeson's face was not that of an actor.
> "I'm scared of livin' and feared of dyin'...."
> The pathos of Robeson's voice called up images of slaves and
> overseers with whips. How had a man with such a history risen?

The creation of jazz by black artists gave this country a language that it was searching for, and gave it a rhythmic identity, and so it makes perfect sense that the composers would use this inventive language and rhythm for the theater.

—George C. Wolfe, director

"The Turn of the Tide, What's Going On in the World," *McCall's*, April 1928:

Under the masterly direction of Prince Otto von Bismarck and Count Helmuth von Moltke, the greatest military machine ever devised by man sprang into being during the '60s and '70s of the last century. In order to make this machine yet more potent, a doctrine of "blood and iron" was proclaimed. The State—social, political, and industrial—was molded into a compact organization for its successful enlargement by means of war, and Denmark, Austria and France successively succumbed to its irresistible force.

Bismarck, in his wisdom, halted to allow his Fatherland to consolidate and become accustomed to the sudden change from a kingdom to an empire. What might have happened had Bismarck lived and held his power no man may say, but the direction of German affairs fell into less capable hands and disaster came. The deed was done and the consequences were to follow.

While in Germany war had become glorified, the balance of Europe was terrified by this new menace to peace. Fear led the Great Powers, in self-protection, to form an iron circle around the dreaded borders of this great military state.

Through the bitterness of defeat in the Great War came salvation, not alone for the German people, but, perhaps, for Europe as well. Today, the tide has turned in the nation formerly the protagonist of ruthless and relentless war, and has become an earnest advocate of disarmament and peace. Germany has gone so far as to announce her intention to accept the optional clause in the World Court making obligatory peaceful settlements of international disputes of judicial character. In Geneva, the voice of Germany constantly is raised on behalf of every measure having for its purpose conciliation as opposed to war. The terms of reproach heretofore leveled at her by opponents are now used against other nations less yielding in the cause of disarmament and compulsory arbitration.

It may be of interest for Americans to know that the wartime ambassador from Germany to the United States—Count von Bernstorff—is one of the foremost leaders in the movement for general disarmament and the abolition of war. Together with the German Minister for Foreign Affairs—Gustafson Stressemann—he has represented Germany at the League of Nations' conferences and has gone further than almost any delegate in his demands for measures to secure the peace of Europe.

Those, from long habit, still critical of Germany see in her a sinister purpose. It is said that she is restrained by the Versailles Treaty from having a large army and navy, and that she is actuated not so much by a change of heart as by a change in circumstance. But it may well be that the German people are awakened to the truth that peace has more possibilities for their welfare than war, and if they lead as fervently in the direction of peace as they formerly did for war, the ultimate result will not alone be of advantage to Germany, but to all of Europe as well.

There is a tremendous urge among the small nations of Europe against war. This feeling has never been so strong as now. The fear of another catastrophe like that of 1914-1918 hangs over them. This dread is one of the most marked results of the Great War. It is a shadow that can never be wholly lifted during the lives of this generation.

While the forebears of the American people came almost wholly from Europe, it is difficult for us to think in terms of Europeans. From the dawn of history until now, the fear of aggressive wars has haunted them. From the tribal raids of the misty past all through the ages, we find the same story. Civilization has hewn its way with the sword. The cost, the misery, and the mental anguish are beyond computation. And in our day of supposed enlightenment came the greatest holocaust of all. The madness of it is just beginning to make an impression sufficiently strong to give the world hope.

1928 NEWS FEATURE

"The Debut of Yehudi Menuhin, The Musical Event of the Month," Deems Taylor,
McCall's Magazine, **April 1928:**

Every once in a while, some community produces a boy or girl, anywhere from seven to 12 years old, who plays the piano or violin with what seems uncanny skill. The youthful marvel gives concerts before crowded houses, his or her parents make a good deal of money, and the local press predicts the second Kreisler or Hoffmann—and the music critics yawn. For the critics have learned that, while a child may develop technical skills at an early age, the unfortunate prodigy pays, as a rule, for his precocious development by ceasing development at all after about his fifteenth year; the great artists, like oak trees, seldom grow as fast as weeds.

However, the proverbial exception to this rule appeared earlier this winter—the child prodigy whose gifts are so extraordinary that one is justified in believing that his career, far from being at its zenith, has just begun, and that 15 years hence, he will be one of the world's great violinists. On the twenty-fifth of last November, a 10-year-old youngster named Yehudi Menuhin appeared in Carnegie Hall as a soloist with the New York Symphony Orchestra under Fritz Busch. His playing of the Beethoven *Violin Concerto* not only received thunderous acclaim, but elicited such praise from the music critics as has not been matched, for enthusiasm, since the reviews of Jascha Heifetz's American debut.

After such a reception, it was inevitable he would make a second New York appearance. This took the form of a recital in Carnegie Hall on the twelfth of last December. The house was completely sold out one week in advance, with 300 seats sold on the stage. The audience that assembled to hear him was probably the most brilliant as well as the largest ever seen in Carnegie Hall. Over 500 people were turned away, and the police reserves had to be called out to handle the crowd and pounce upon nearly 100 overzealous music-lovers who attempted to get in through the fire escapes, cellar, and roof of the hall.

This second appearance was a success even more emphatic than his debut had been. What New York thought of young Menuhin may be inferred from the fact that, before noon the following day, his parents had received a dozen requests for his appearance at private musicales, the aggregate of the fees offered amounting to $65,000.

The quality that makes the boy such a phenomenon is not, as in the case of most prodigies, his technique, so much as his qualities of real musicianship—qualities that are generally associated only with mature artists.

At his debut he played, as I said, the Beethoven *Concerto*. His recital program comprised Tartini's hideously difficult Devil's Trill Sonata, the Bach Chaconne, Mozart's Seventh Concerto in D. major, the Chausson *Poème*, and Wieniawski's *Souveir of Moscou*. Of these, the Tartini sonata and the Wieniawski piece alone are chiefly useful for technical display. The others all demand interpretive gifts of an exceedingly high order.

Yet it is in just such numbers as the Beethoven *Concerto* and the Bach *Chaconne* that, as most of his critics agree, the boy is at his best. In brilliant passage work and cadenzas, where one would expect a prodigy to shine, he is good, but not extraordinary. But in his flawless rhythm, beautiful tone, and maturity of style, he is, even now, an artist to be taken seriously.

In appearance, he is diminutive, towheaded, and rather plump. On the platform, he wears a white blouse, black knickerbockers, and rolled socks. He was born in New York, in 1918, of Palestinian Jewish parents, and he was taken to San Francisco at the age of nine months. His first—and with one exception, his only—teacher was Louis Persinger, head of the San Francisco Chamber Music Society and leader of the Persinger String Quartet.

He began studying the violin at six, and made his first public appearance at eight, with the San Francisco Orchestra. A little over a year ago, he gave a single concert in the Manhattan Opera House, New York, in order to raise funds to go abroad. He lived in Paris last year, studying with George Enesco, the famous Romanian virtuoso. While there, he gave two concerts with the Lamoureux Orchestra whose members gave him a gold plaque in token of their admiration. He plays a three-quarter-size Grancino violin, valued at about $10,000. He practices every day, goes to school (he is a brilliant mathematician), and studies musical theory.

Luckily, he is in wise hands. The glittering offers of the day following his New York recital were all refused by his father, who is taking him back to San Francisco for three more years of study under Mr. Persinger. During this time, he will make only two public appearances. The world at large will not hear from him again until 1931. What it will hear, when that time comes, is fascinating to conjecture.

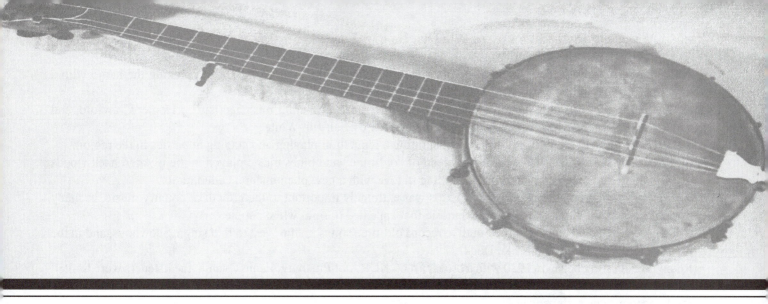

1929 PROFILE

The career of banjo picker-singer Dock Boggs was shaped by the rough landscape of Virginia's coal country and the newly emerging entertainment medium known as radio.

Life at Home

- When Moran Lee Boggs was born in West Norton, Virginia, in February 1898, radio was in its infancy; by 1927, when he recorded his first record, no home was complete without one.
- Named for a local physician, Dock grew up in the same region of Virginia as the Stanley Brothers and the Carter family—all known for their deep country roots and hillbilly music.
- His father was a mountain farmer, a blacksmith and singer, who encouraged his children's musical interests.
- The youngest of 10 children, Dock was one of many siblings who could sing and play the banjo.
- Some of his earliest music lessons came from an African-American guitarist named "Go Lightning," whom Dock would follow up and down the railroad tracks between Norton and Dorchester.
- Dock would also sneak over at night to the African-American camps in Dorchester, where he watched string bands playing at dances and parties.
- Dock started working in the coal mines when he was 12 years old and continued his musical education playing the banjo with the black miners.

Dock Boggs worked in the coal mines by day and played the banjo by night.

- Although he initially learned the claw-hammer style of playing the banjo, Dock began picking the banjo with a three-finger style similar to the way a guitarist picks a guitar.
- He learned to play "Hustlin' Gambler" during this time from an itinerant musician named Homer Crawford, and added "Turkey in the Straw" to his repertoire, thanks to musician Jim White.
- By 1918, coal miner Dock Boggs had begun building a reputation playing and singing at parties in the region.
- Over time, he was widely influenced by a blend of "old-time" and blues music played in the isolated back woods of Virginia, while much of the nation was falling in love with a new phenomenon called radio.
- Radio's increasing popularity during the 1920s was extremely important to the growth of country music, as many stations gave airtime to live and recorded music that appealed to rural white people.
- Big city record labels flocked to the South to record old-time songs, to the West to find singing cowboys, and in the process, to discover musicians like Dock.
- Radio broadcasting began in 1920 with a broadcast by KDKA of Pittsburg, Pennsylvania; the listeners were limited to the few who had built their own receivers.
- Public response was immediate.
- Manufacturers were overwhelmed by the demand for receivers, as customers stood in line to complete order forms for radios after dealers had sold out.
- In 1922, WSM, a radio station based in Georgia, was the first to broadcast folk songs to its audience.
- Crystal radios were among the first radios to be used and manufactured.
- They used a piece of lead galena crystal and a cat whisker to find the radio signal.
- Magazines encouraged young boys to make their own radios, and included step-by-step instructions for the crystal radio.
- Supplies could be purchased for as little as $6.00.
- Prior to 1920, most Americans couldn't even fathom the idea of voices and music coming over the air into their homes.
- But the availability of free over-the-air music and information fueled tremendous growth, with sales of in-home radio sets growing from 5,000 units in 1920 to more than 2.5 million units in 1924.
- By the time aviator Charles Lindbergh made his historic transatlantic flight in 1927, some six million radio sets were in use.
- Surveys indicated that an average of five people listened to each set, making a potential market of 30 million people.
- In 1926, the first national radio network—dubbed the National Broadcasting Company (NBC)—was created.
- The Rose Bowl football game of 1927 was heard coast to coast, thanks to NBC.
- Encouraged by the radio response, in 1923, 55-year-old Georgia fiddler John Carson recorded two Southern rural songs, starting the march of "hillbilly" or "country" music.
- The term "hillbilly" was introduced in 1924 by "Uncle" Dave Macon's *Hill Billie Blues*.
- In 1924, Chicago's radio station WLS, which stood for "World's Largest Store" began broadcasting a barn dance that could be heard throughout the Midwest.
- This was followed the next year by Nashville's first radio station, WSM, which started a barn dance of its own that would eventually be called the *Grand Ole Opry*.
- Old-time "hillbilly" music was an amalgamation of styles, rather than a monolithic style.
- Its origins incorporated Scottish reels, Irish jigs, square dances, British ballads, and religious hymns of church and camp meetings.
- It was a mongrel mix as unique as America itself.

By the time Charles Lindbergh flew across the Atlantic, home radio sales grew to 6 million.

- Across America, families by the millions gathered around their radios for night-time entertainment—mesmerized by the sounds magically coming from the box.
- That meant money was to be made, setting off a mad scramble for listeners; chaos reigned.
- Without radio wave regulations, programs overlapped as stations arbitrarily changed their broadcasting ban to gain an advantage.
- Listeners of one program were frequently interrupted by a competing program.
- Initially, the government viewed radio as a public service, not a commercial enterprise, setting off additional battles with advertisers.
- Eventually, government intervention was demanded to end the free-for-all, resulting in the Federal Radio Commission in 1926 and the Radio Act of 1927.

Life at Work

- Dock Boggs's big moment came when the Brunswick Label held a mass audition in western Virginia, searching for hidden talent.
- Old-time music was hot, and the record companies were willing to go into the isolated corners of Appalachia to find unique voices and sounds.
- Auditions were held at the Norton Hotel, where Dock used a borrowed banjo and a bracer of whiskey to display his talents.
- Dock's style personified the folk strain of country music; strong, personal, cruel and tinged with the blues.
- A hard life working in the coal mines of western Virginia was reflected in his tone.
- Out of the dozens who tried out, two were selected: Dock Boggs and the Dykes Magic City Trio.
- The Carter family participated in the audition but was not selected.
- The reward for winning the audition was a recording session in New York City.
- Boggs made his first trip out of the mountains, accompanied by his banjo.
- Dressed in his trademark dark suit, necktie and polished shoes, Dock cut eight sides, featuring a raw, bluesy mountain voice and five-string banjo.
- Brunswick wanted more, but Dock decided that his remuneration was worth eight sides—no more.
- The path for mountain-style music had been smoothed by banjoist Charlie Poole of the North Carolina Ramblers, who recorded "Don't Let Your Deal Go Down" in 1925 and the "White House Blues" in 1926.

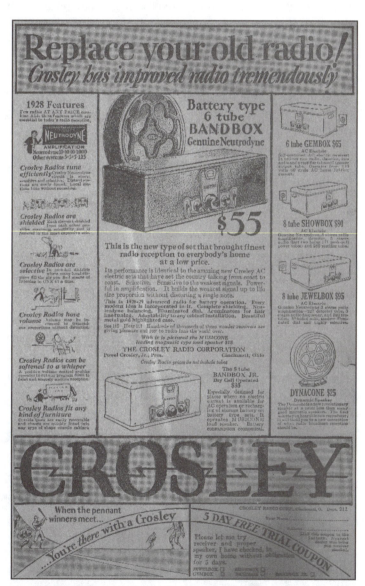

The growing popularity of radios increased the need for broadcast talent.

- "Uncle" Dave Macon, one of the bestselling artists of the twenties, had recorded "Keep My Skillet Good And Greasy," "Chewing Gum," and "Sail Away Ladies."
- They used the banjo as more than a mere rhythmic device, but Dock Boggs was perhaps the first white banjoist to play the instrument like a blues guitar.
- During his sessions in 1927, he recorded six plantation blues numbers and "Sugar Baby," a rockabilly tune.
- His records sold moderately well and he returned to southwestern Virginia, where he played at parties and mining camps.
- In 1928, he had added numerous gospel and religious songs to his repertoire, thanks to his brother-in-law, a holiness preacher and singer.
- He also began making enough money singing and playing the banjo so that he could quit working in the mine and focus exclusively on music.
- He bought a new banjo and formed a band called Dock Boggs and His Cumberland Entertainers.
- At times he was making three to four hundred dollars a week.
- Until the late 1920s, hillbilly artists were comedians as much as musicians, mixing a repertoire of both songs and skits.
- The Skillet Lickers were probably instrumental in creating the charisma of the country musician, as opposed to the image of the hillbilly clown.
- But Dock's success was tempered by problems at home.
- His religious neighbors equated the life of a traveling musician with a life of sin; his wife Sara despised secular music and objected to her husband earning a living by playing music.
- Besides, the mining camps where Dock and his band played were often violent, and Dock did not always escape the drunken brawls unscathed.
- Finally, he returned to the studio in 1929, this time for Lonesome Ace Records in Chicago.
- But the stock market crash ushered the tiny recording company into bankruptcy, dried up the party income, and put Dock back into the coal mines.

Dock's hometown of Norton, Virginia was rural and isolated, and often visited by touring minstrel shows.

- Automaker Henry Ford invested heavily in promoting country music in the 1920s, terrified by what he saw as the urban decadence of couples jazz dancing.
- In response, he organized fiddling contests and promoted square dances across the country to encourage what he saw as the older, more wholesome forms of entertainment.
- Much of country music of the 1920s could be rowdy and bawdy, too.
- The B side of one of the first country music records, by Fiddlin' John Carson, had the barnyard double-entendre lyric, "The old hen cackled, and the rooster's going to crow."
- Country music was cleaned up as radio became the major medium for promoting country music performers and advertisers, such as Crazy Water Crystals, insisted on sanitized lyrics.

Life in the Community: Norton, Virginia

- Norton, Virginia, located in the Appalachian Mountains, was one of the commonwealth's smallest towns in one of its poorest regions.
- One of the last parts of the state to be settled by Europeans, its settlers were most often English, Germans, and the Scots-Irish who engaged in subsistence farming on the rocky hillsides.
- During the American Revolution, residents from southwest Virginia were among those who participated in the Battle of King's Mountain, and during the Civil War, southwest Virginia was deeply divided between sentiment for the Union and the Confederacy.
- The Appalachian Mountains defined the people and were often blamed for isolating its residents from the rest of the commonwealth.
- However, they fostered the region's unique language and musical styles.
- Researchers could still find remnants of seventeenth-century Elizabethan speech in the 1920s, despite the intrusion of big coal into the region.
- Prior to the Civil War, the coal counties in southwestern Virginia were unable to ship their product to market.
- After 1865, Northern financiers supported the extension of Virginia railroads into the timber-rich and coal-rich mountains.
- By World War I, the Norfolk and Western Railroad had built a rail line capable of moving the coal to the east; the Pocahontas Mine became a major supplier of coal for the Navy.
- By that time, the musical traditions of Appalachia were well established—including the role of the banjo and the fiddle.
- Originally, the American banjo was developed from an instrument the Africans played which they called banzas, banjars, banias, and bangoes.

High society warmed up to the banjo, with leading universities creating banjo orchestras, playing everything from classical to ragtime.

- Africans, brought to the new world in bondage and not allowed to play drums, started making their banjars from calabash gourds.
- To Americans, the banjo was an oddity and was denied respectability; it was considered a musical outcast, lowlier than the fiddle, which many "righteous people" knew was from the devil.
- By the 1840s, a fifth string was added called the short thumb string or bass string.
- Touring minstrel shows, with white musicians in black-face, popularized the banjo, along with circus acts.
- Soon for mountain folks, the fiddle and the banjo were linked in performances and became paired.
- During the Civil War, thousands of banjo players from both North and South joined the army.
- As a result, the instrument found its greatest growth as these banjo players taught others to play during the long days of boredom between battles.
- Banjos and fiddles also moved West with the largest migration ever after the close of the war.
- Most of the men who became cowboys were from the South, due to Reconstruction and a lack of jobs.
- At the same time, the popularity of the banjo grew with the expansion of minstrel shows.
- The most popular minstrel troupes—Christy's Minstrels, Buckley's Serenaders, The Congo Melodists and the Virginia Minstrels—remained on Broadway in New York and other big Eastern cities, where they reigned for 50 years.
- Lesser known minstrel troupes traveled to small towns and territories to make a living.
- As early as the 1850s, players stepped away from the banjo-stroke style of playing, which employed the back of the fingernails, and adopted the thumb-and-fingers technique, just as the guitar was played.
- Noted musician Frank Converse perfected this style and introduced it in his 1865 banjo instruction book.
- Together with another instruction book published in 1868 by previously noted minstrel banjoist James Buckley, the finger-picking style was taught and developed.
- Around 1880, Henry Dobson became the first to manufacture banjos with frets, which increased the accuracy of the notes when playing up the neck.
- As the banjo started to become more sophisticated, it moved into high society and more ladies started to play.
- In the 1880s and 1890s, entertainment was often found in a social club organized around a common interest such as poetry, railroads, rowing, bicycling, theater or science.
- Countless banjo clubs were formed all over the country and in the leading universities and colleges, all of which had their own banjo orchestras.
- The socially elite thought it fashionable to play banjo in these orchestras, with the music ranging from classical to marches to waltzes to rags.

HISTORICAL SNAPSHOT
1929

- William Faulkner published *The Sound and the Fury*, Ernest Hemingway published *A Farewell to Arms* and John Steinbeck wrote *Cup of Gold*
- Edward Doisy isolated the female sex hormone estrogen in pure form
- Alexander Fleming successfully treated a skin infection with penicillin
- Radio premieres included *The Hour of Charm*, *Blackstone Plantation*, *Amos 'n' Andy*, and *The Rise of the Goldbergs*
- Hit songs included "Tiptoe Through the Tulips," "Singin' in the Rain," "Honeysuckle Rose," "Happy Days Are Here Again," "Ain't Misbehavin'" and "Stardust"
- Despite Prohibition, approximately 32,000 speakeasies existed in New York City
- After the stock market crash, New York Mayor Jimmy Walker urged movie houses to show cheerful movies
- Nationwide, the number of movie theaters equipped with sound facilities increased from 1,300 and 9,000
- A Baltimore survey discovered rickets in 30 percent of the city's children
- New York Yankees baseball star Babe Ruth hit his 500th home run
- RCA Victor recorded the first 33⅓ rpm LP—Victor Salon Suite No. 1, arranged and directed by Nathaniel Shilkret
- Dunlop Rubber Company produced foam rubber
- Broadway openings included *The Showgirl*, *Hot Chocolates*, *Street Singer* and *Death Takes a Holiday*
- CBS was founded by 27-year-old William S. Paley
- The Museum of Modern of Art was founded in New York City
- Plans for the Empire State Building included mooring masts for giant zeppelins
- Louis Armstrong recorded his hit song "When You're Smiling"
- Federated Department Stores, Conoco, the Oscar Meyer wiener trademark and auto sunroofs all made their first appearance
- Following the stock market crash, U.S. unemployment rose from 700,000 to 3.1 million people

Selected Prices

Airplane, Single Engine $2,000.00
Automobile, Willys-Knight $1,450.00
Bathing Suit $8.50
Phonograph $290.00
Pocket Watch $63.50
Radio, Crosley 50 .... $14.50
Stationery, 24 Sheets and Envelopes $0.50
Suntan Lotion $2.50
Train, Chicago to Yellowstone, Round Trip $56.50
Traveling Bag $10.50

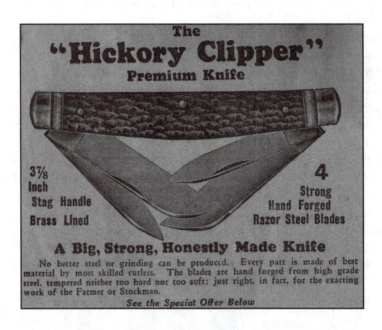

Red *and* Green Lights on Every Highway

Traffic signals flash in every town and city. And every start and stop grinds off rubber.

Hood tires are built to meet these modern conditions. To give more satisfactory mileage, comfort and safety... even with the higher speeds, smaller wheels, four-wheel brakes and the quicker starts and stops of present-day motoring.

Made by
HOOD RUBBER CO.
Watertown, Mass.

*Hood tires are worth more
because they give more*

Look for the Hood Arrow

Fifteen years is the average period of probation, and during that time the inventor, the promoter and the investor, who see a great future, generally lose their shirts.... This is why the wise capitalist keeps out of exploiting new inventions and comes in only when the public is ready for mass demand.
> —Owen D. Young, the General Electric Company executive who coordinated General Electric's purchase of American Marconi, and its transformation into the Radio Corporation of America

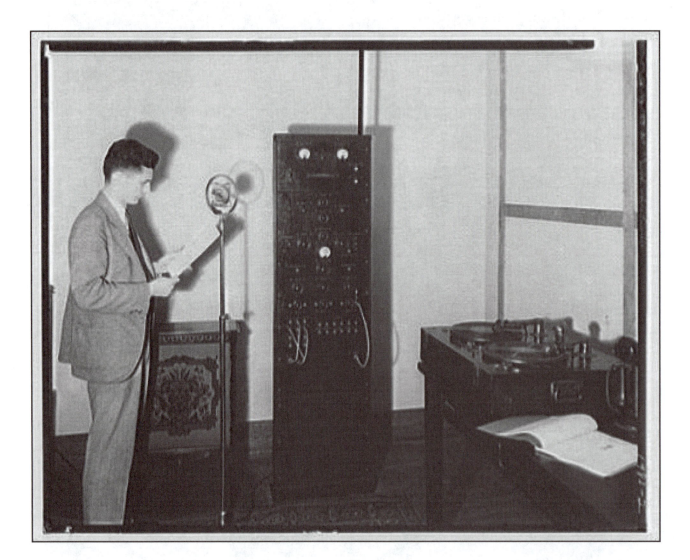

"Behind the Scenes at a Broadcast Studio," *Science and Invention*, **June 1930:**

The days of radio programs which consisted of two or three performers and an announcer, who did almost everything but operate the transmitter, are gone forever. In the place of these somewhat scanty programs have come ornate presentations consisting of a large orchestra, chorus, and several featured singers. To accommodate such grandiose entertainment, the whole technique of broadcasting, from continuity writing to studio construction, has necessarily been changed....

Floodlighting plays no little part in the attempt to create an atmosphere about the players. The cast and orchestra are so arranged that the correct volume of sound is picked up without any extraneous noises. To further this end, several microphones are placed at strategic points. New directional microphones—mounted on a platform and operated by a studio technician, have recently been installed in the New York studios for the National Broadcasting Company. These microphones have been used in programs such as *The Westinghouse Salute*, where the effect of distant voices has been desired. Presiding over the broadcast programs is the program director, whose job it is to see that the precious moments are utilized to the fullest degree. The announcer usually stands at the switchboard to make the incidental announcements which come during and after the broadcast. He is the one largely responsible for the program signing "on" and "off" at the right time.

In most studios, acoustic effects are made by using a belted trench. These curtains are adjusted so that the correct amount of sound reflection or extortion is obtained. It is the incorrect adjustment of these drapes which causes the hollow sound which sometimes comes through the ether. In the new Chicago studios of NBC, there has been a wall constructed of specially designed units, which may be adjusted to regulate the quality of the sound reflected by the wall. In the picture above, "A" is the control room of the broadcasting studio, "B" is the observation corridor, "C" is the organ loft, "D" is the monitoring room, "E" are the floodlights, "F" is the projection room, "G" and "H" are for the orchestra and chorus, "J" is the audience, "K" is the organ room, "L" are the pylons and "M" is director of the orchestra and program. The directional microphones may be seen mounted on the platforms.

The scene in a broadcast studio is usually one of great informality. At times, the musical director places himself outside the range of microphones and tells his individual players his opinion of their work—good or bad—as it may seem to him. The actors and singers of any radio drama do not hesitate to express their opinion of one another, but always being certain that they are far removed from the tyrannic "mike." Sometimes the program director, with script in hand, moves toward the players and urges them to speed up the scene, for he knows only too well how the time flies.

The new Chicago studios for the National Broadcasting Company, located in the huge merchandise mart of the Marshall Field & Co., typify the latest design in modern broadcasting technique. The set of studios occupies the entire two top floors of this new Chicago's skyscraper in the "Loop."

"Mountaineers Wed Before Microphone," *The New York Times*, July 10, 1930:

A Kentucky Mountain wedding was staged last night in the studios of WABC, 485 Madison Avenue, when Albert Crockett, 23, one of the six Crockett Mountaineers of Kentucky whose daily program of "hillbilly" songs is heard over the Columbia network, was married to Miss Josephine Phillips, 22, also from Kentucky.

It was described by the Columbia Broadcasting System as the first international marriage on the air, and on the shortwave hook-up, the wedding vows of the couple as they stood with the minister before the microphone, and the music suitable to the genuine mountaineer wedding, including "Pop Goes the Weasel," were carried to New Zealand and parts of South America. The word "obey" was omitted from the ceremony.

The ceremony went on the air at seven o'clock. "The bride certainly looks sweet," said Don Carney, announcer, as the couple stepped to the microphone and faced the Rev. Warner S. Alexander, pastor of Hyde Park Christian Church, Brooklyn. This was a cue for the Crockett family to start playing "Haste to the Wedding," on the fiddle and guitar, and with "bones" accompaniment.

The mouth organ was missing from the musical ensemble, for the bridegroom is the mouth organ player. He took part in the aired program, however, making the calls for square dances, such as "balance all" and "get your partner and promenade home," immediately after the ceremony....

While the newlyweds were showered with rice, the fiddlers played "Turkey in the Straw" and "Little Brown Jug." After the mountaineer tune "The Fun's All Over," the bridal party went to a restaurant for a wedding dinner.

Young Crockett and his bride became engaged four months ago. He said at the ceremony they would spend their honeymoon "going around New York and New Jersey" between the daily programs at the WABC studio.

The Crockett Mountaineers have been appearing on the air in New York for three months.

"Year's Radio Sales Put at $650,550,000," *The New York Times*, January 13, 1929:

Radio sales in 1928 amounted to $650,550,000, against $425,600,000 in 1927. All records for the total cost and number of sets sold and the growth of the listening public were exceeded, according to Radio Retailing, which made public yesterday the statistics of its annual survey of the radio industry in this country.

The listening public was said to have increased this year in America to about 35,000,000 persons against an estimated 26,000,000 in 1927 and 75,000 in 1922. Sets of all types in use this year were said to have reached 9,000,000 in number, as compared to 7,500,000 in 1927 and 60,000 in 1922.

An itemized account of the survey, the report said, shows that 2,550,000 factory-built sets, including consoles and built-in receivers, were sold for a total of $306,000,000 in 1928, against 1,350,000 sets sold for $168,750,000 in 1927 and 100,000 sold for $5,000,000 in 1922. Radio-phonograph combinations sold last year totaled 81,000, and the outlay for them was $38,000,000.

1930–1939

Few Americans—including the very rich—escaped the devastating impact of America's longest and most severe depression in the nation's history. Banks failed, railways became insolvent, unemployment factories closed and the upper class moved out of the biggest houses in town. Economic paralysis gripped the nation. Promising businesses and new inventions stagnated for lack of capital and customers. By 1932, one in four Americans was jobless. One in every four farms was sold for taxes. Five thousand banks closed their doors, wiping out the lifetime savings of millions of Americans—rich and poor.

As the stock market sank into the doldrums, Americans turned to Big Band music to get a lift. This musical stage included a wide variety of songs generated by the relatively talking movies and the boom in Broadway musicals, including *Porgy and Bess*. As the decade came to a close, jazz, evolved into swing music. Bread lines became common sights. The unemployed wandered from city to city seeking work, only to discover the pervasive nature of the economic collapse. In some circles the American Depression was viewed as the fulfillment of Marxist prophecy—the inevitable demise of capitalism.

But dancing to energetic music could not chase away the bad times. Backed by New Deal promises and a focus on the "forgotten man," Franklin D. Roosevelt produced a swirl of government programs designed to lift the country out of its paralytic gloom. Roosevelt's early social experiments were characterized by relief, recovery, and reform. Believing that the expansion of the United States economy was temporarily over, Roosevelt paid attention to better distribution of resources and planned production. The Civilian Conservation Corps (CCC), for example, put 250,000 jobless young men to work in the forests for $1.00 a day. By 1935, government deficit spending was spurring economic change. By 1937, total manufacturing output exceeded that of 1929; unfortunately, prices and wages rose too quickly and the economy dipped again in 1937, driven by inflation fears and restrictions on bank lending.

Nonetheless, many roads, bridges, public buildings, dams, and trees became part of the landscape thanks to federally employed workers. The Federal Music Project, for example, employed 15,000 musicians during the period, giving 225,000 performances to millions of Americans. Despite progress, 10 million workers were still unemployed in 1938 and farm prices lagged behind manufacturing progress. Full recovery would not occur until the United States mobilized for World War II.

While the nation suffered from economic blows, the West was being whipped by nature. Gigantic billowing clouds of dust up to 10,000 feet high swept across the parched Western Plains throughout the 1930s. Sometimes the blows came with lightning and booming thunder, but often they were described as being "eerily slight, blackening everything in their path." All human activity halted. Planes were grounded. Buses and trains stalled, unable to race clouds that could move at speeds of more than 100 miles per hour. On the morning of May 9, 1934, the wind began to blow up the topsoil of Montana and Wyoming, and soon some 350 million tons were sweeping eastward. By late afternoon, 12 million tons had been deposited in Chicago. By noon the next day, Buffalo, New York, was dark with dust. Even the Atlantic Ocean was no barrier. Ships 300 miles out to sea found dust on their decks. During the remainder of 1935, there were more than 40 dust storms that reduced visibility to less than one mile. There were 68 more storms in 1936, 72 in 1937, and 61 in 1938. On the High Plains, 10,000 houses were simply abandoned, and nine million acres of farm turned back to nature. Banks offered mortgaged properties for as little as $25 for 160 acres and found no takers. The people of the 1930s excelled in escape. Radio matured as a mass medium, creating stars such as Jack Benny, Bob Hope, and Fibber McGee and Molly. For a time it seemed that every child was copying the catch phrase of radio's Walter Winchell, "Good evening, Mr. and Mrs. America, and all the ships at sea," or pretending to be Jack Benny when shouting, "Now, cut that out!" Soap operas captured large followings and sales of magazines like *Screen* and *True Story* skyrocketed. Each edition of True Confessions sold 7.5 million copies. Nationwide, movie theaters prospered as 90 million Americans attended the "talkies" every week, finding comfort in the uplifting excitement of movies and movie stars. Big bands made swing the king of the decade, while jazz came into its own. And the social experiment known as Prohibition died in December 1933, when the Twenty-first Amendment swept away the restrictions against alcohol ushered in more than a decade earlier.

Attendance at professional athletic events declined during the decade, but softball became more popular than ever and golf began its drive to become a national passion as private courses went public. Millions listened to boxing on radio, especially the exploits of the "Brown Bomber," Joe Louis. As average people coped with the difficult times, they married later, had fewer children, and divorced less. Extended families often lived under one roof; opportunities for women and minorities were particularly limited. Survival, not affluence, was often the practical goal of the family. A disillusioned nation, which had worshipped the power of business, looked instead toward a more caring government during the decade, United Airlines hired its first airline stewardess to allay passengers' fears of flying. The circulation of Reader's Digest climbed from 250,000 to eight million before the decade ended and Esquire, the first magazine for men, was launched. The early days of the decade gave birth to Hostess Twinkies, Bird's Eye frozen vegetables, windshield wipers, photoflash bulbs, and pinball machines. By the time the Depression and the 1930s drew to a close, Zippo lighters, Frito's corn chips, talking books for the blind, beer in cans, and the Richter scale for measuring earthquakes had all been introduced. Despite the ever-increasing role of the automobile in the mid-1930s, Americans still spent $1,000 a day on buggy whips.

1931 NEWS FEATURE

"The Art of Singing for the Radio," George H. Eckhardt, *The Etude*, October 1931:

Time was when the operatic and concert stage were the goal of the vocal aspirant, but today the broadcasting studio has largely supplanted those two ends of the endeavor, and it is probable that in the not very distant future, the radio will offer about the only practical outlook for the vocal artist. Naturally, this latter statement is made with some reservation, but facts must be faced. Aside from church work, the vocalist must look more and more to the radio field for engagements.

It is deplorable, but nonetheless true, that practically nothing worthwhile has been written or said regarding the technic of broadcasting in the microphone. There are singing teachers and vocal coaches without number, each with methods of his or her own, some good, some harmless, and some of the others downright vicious. Yet it's been all a matter of art; one opinion has been as good as another, it seems, but nothing has been definite.

In the matter of radio, however, definite engineering and scientific facts are encountered. The artist meets a cold mass of electrical wires, all assembled according to definitely worked out plans. It is no longer a matter of opinion. It's a matter of fact.

The one device in the radio world, which the artist meets, is the microphone, the instrument into which he sings. This creates no need of going into the baffling details of the construction of the microphone or the engineering side of the broadcasting; but it's absolutely necessary that the artist master the "technic of using the microphone."

From the very start, the artist must realize the microphone is a heartless, cold-blooded instrument, looking not unlike the back of an alarm clock, with definite limitations. The violin becomes part of the player, responds to his emotions, and becomes a living thing, but the microphone always remains a mass of wire and metal; it never becomes a part of the artist. This must be always borne in mind. The microphone will not compromise with the artist, so the artist must compromise with it. When this is fully right realized, a fair part of the battle is won.

Might it not be well, therefore, to look to the reasons behind the undeniable fact that some very remarkable voices are failures over the radio, while some voices that are well below the average in the concert hall have proved outstanding on the air?

Consciously or otherwise, the successful radio star understands the technic of their microphone; she realizes the instrument is unyielding and hints to its whims, as it were.

As before stated, an engineering description of the microphone would lead only to confusion in the reader's mind; it is a matter rather for the student of engineering and for the vocal student. It must be stated, however, that the microphone transfers sound waves into electronical waves. The voice passes from one medium to another. In the concert hall, sound waves of the voice of the artist reach the ears of the audience. In radio, the sound waves of the voice enter, or strike, the microphone, are transferred into electrical waves, or carried over land wires to the broadcasting station proper, where electrical waves are in turn transferred into radio waves and sent to the air. These radio waves are again picked up by the instrument of the listener and transferred back into sound waves. Naturally, much can happen between the sound waves that leave the throat to the singer in the broadcast studio and the sound waves that reach the ears of the audience, probably hundreds of miles away. A beautiful voice in the broadcasting studio may be anything but beautiful when it issues from the loudspeaker in the home in the suburbs, while an otherwise commonplace voice may sound beautiful as it entertains the family comfortably seated around its radio set.

While before the microphone, the artist must never forget the instrument has a definite capacity. It can handle just so much sound, and if more is forced into it there is "crowding," a phenomenon that causes unpleasant reception. When singing in the concert hall, the artist can give full vent to her emotions, and the audience takes, or receives, as it were, any volume, no matter how great. But the microphone, now in use in many broadcasting stations, can take care of just so much sound, so much volume…. Emotions must be expressed through tone color more than through tone volume.

So important is this matter of "volume" that in the broadcasting of large orchestras, a musician is often stationed beside the control-room man, and from a score he tells the operator when to expect loud passages so he may anticipate them. The average artist, however, cannot expect such elaborate attention to details. Some studios have tried placing a small galvanometer, a dial instrument showing the "load" on the microphone, right before the singer, but this has proved too disturbing to the artist….

Naturally, the singer will wonder how to control the voice, for volume is necessary to vocal expression. The voice must be raised and lowered in power; otherwise the offering will be most colorless.

There are various "tricks" that must be learned in order to minimize the limitations of the instrument. In the first place, the artist must learn the volume limitations of the microphone as compared to her particular voice, and the control-room man will help in this. She must keep always in the power limitation of the microphone.

In coming to a forte passage, the head should be slightly turned from the microphone, so that a part of the waves will not strike the instrument and therefore will not crowd it. This is a trick that can be easily learned and which will be found to mean much towards the success of a program by eliminating unpleasant qualities.

Again, the singer should always keep the microphone on a level with the voice itself, since the best effects are thus obtained. There is a definite engineering reason why the voice registers better when the sound waves strike the instrument on a horizontal line. Since all microphones are now adjustable by means of a screw arrangement, retaining this condition is a very simple matter.

The artist should maintain a constant distance from the microphone and not move forward and backward, which will cause a change in the level of the voice. To be sure, the artist may move backwards on a higher forte note, instead of turning the head.

The effect is the same, but this is dangerous, since control by moving away from and nearer to the microphone is not so reliable and requires great skill. Facial expression and gestures mean nothing whatsoever over the radio; therefore, one must train oneself to sing at a microphone, not thinking of an audience.

1934 PROFILE

The "Romeo of Song" Russ Columbo had established himself, along with Bing Crosby, as a crooner positioned to become one of America's versatile talents when he was shot by his best friend.

Life at Home

- Throughout his singing and movie career, Russ Columbo insisted he was not a blues singer, a crooner, or a straight baritone, but a unique talent with a sound all his own.
- "You see," he told a reporter in 1931, "I've been singing for quite a while now. Also, I studied voice and have a musical background. Therefore, whatever I have done comes naturally."
- Born in Camden, New Jersey, on January 14, 1908, to Italian immigrants Nicola Columbo, a stonemason and his wife Giulia, Ruggiero Eugenio di Rodolpho Columbo was the couple's twelfth child.
- The name Russ came from a childhood friend that was unable to properly say Ruggiero, and it eventually stuck.
- Russ was considered a child prodigy, mastering the violin by age five despite frequent moves in the early years, with stops in Philadelphia and San Francisco, before winding up in Los Angeles when Russ was eight.
- Siblings suspected that the constant moving of the large family gave Russ the best tutelage of the violin.
- The family paid $15 for his student violin, but eventually saved up $45 to purchase a standard violin for him to continue learning.
- Russ was very popular; his humble family life, his good looks, and musical talent made him a favorite among a diverse high school crowd.

Russ Columbo was a popular crooner, along with rival Bing Crosby, before being accidentally shot and killed at age 26.

- He played first violin in the school orchestra and was noticed because he would smile while playing.
- In 1925 at age 17, he quit high school to tour as part of an orchestra, and also became involved in the motion picture industry.
- He played his violin on the set of films to provide atmosphere.
- As a child, Russ had been fascinated by the growing popularity of motion pictures.
- When he was 10, Russ saw the moving picture *The Bond* starring Charlie Chaplin, which recast his music ambitions to include movies.
- Chaplin, who was already earning $10,000 a week, was cinema's first great talents, writing, directing, producing, and acting in his films, which featured wild comedic scenes blended with pathos and social commentary.
- Nearby Hollywood had become a factory of the fantastic with hundreds of major motion pictures being made by celebrities who preferred the warmer southern California climate to New York.
- In 1924, Hollywood had put up a sign comprising 50-foot-high letters to say "Hollywoodland" atop Mt. Lee; the sign had 4,000 20-watt light bulbs.
- The cost was $21,000 with the intention that sign would remain for only 18 months; for thousands, it became a symbol of lost and found dreams.

After seeing a Charlie Chaplin film, Russ added movies to his music ambitions.

Rudolf Valentino, who died at age 31, gave actress Pola Negri an opal ring, who gave it to Russ; Valentino was told the ring was cursed.

- By the early 1920s, music scores were written for the silent pictures, which previously had local orchestras performing their own music to accompany the films.
- The orchestra would now play charts written specifically to set moods that the filmmaker intended.
- Russ fell in love for the first time on the set of a movie with actress Pola Negri, who would be the first of many celebrity romances in his life.
- The two would reunite on another film in 1932, where she presented Russ with an opal ring.
- She told him that the ring once belonged to the late actor and sex symbol Rudolf Valentino who had died at age 31.
- When Valentino had purchased the ring, he was told that it was cursed, carrying with it a disastrous history.
- Negri said she presented it to Russ as "from one Valentino to another."
- Despite his sex symbol status, Russ lived with his parents and kept only a few close friends, though he did begin dating actress Carole Lombard.
- Russ's best friend was photographer Lansing Brown.
- One day, while visiting Brown's modest home, Russ was looking at a collection of antique dueling pistols when a shot suddenly discharged, ricocheted off the wall and caught Russ in the left eye.
- Believing Russ to be dead, Brown called the police, who discovered that Russ was still alive.
- He was rushed into surgery, but died later that night.

- Universal Studios makeup artist Jack Pierce, best known for his work on Boris Karloff in the movies *Frankenstein* and *The Mummy*, was charged with making Russ presentable for funeral viewing.
- Pallbearers included Zeppo Marx and singing rival Bing Crosby.
- His siblings went out of their way to keep his death a secret from their mother, who was in the hospital with a heart ailment, by sending postcards, playing records of old radio shows and carefully editing the newspapers she read to keep up the illusion that he was still alive.
- After Carole Lombard's death, rumors arose of her ghost being seen coming down the stairs of her house in a red dress (her attire the night Russ died and what she was to wear for their dinner engagement), and looking happily at a young man waiting for her.
- Naturally, when the man was described, he fit the description of Russ Columbo.

Life at Work

- In 1928, Russ Columbo began singing in a new vocal style that came to be known as "crooning."
- Before the perfection of the microphone, singers needed to be loud to be heard in the back of a night club or concert hall, but with the amplification provided by the microphone, the vocalist could be softer, more subtle and more intimate.
- The microphone made this style possible by converting acoustic energy into electric energy while retaining its sound wave characteristics.
- Sound waves are inherently short-lived, and unless boosted—or amplified—sink below the limits of audibility.
- Since 1876, microphones had been used as a telephone voice transmitter, but it was not until the 1920s that the broadcasting microphone was created.
- Singing softly and seductively was a style that suited Russ well, even if the form was not universally praised.
- Crooning was mocked because it involved a man sounding sensitive and overly romantic.
- Al Bowly and Gene Austin were the pioneers in the crooning technique, but it was Rudy Vallee who made the style famous in 1928.
- Women in particular loved the new singing technique that the handsome young men were employing, and it became popular on radio and later as movies incorporated sound; the crooner made an ideal voice for the cinema.
- Vallee quickly became a popular singer and actor.
- Bing Crosby was making an impact in both art forms, and Russ was soon joining their ranks.
- While the women loved it, the men generally were not too thrilled about it.
- Cardinal O'Connell of Boston publicly denounced the new style.
- In 1931, a song was recorded called *Crosby, Columbo, and Vallee* calling upon men to fight these "public enemies" who epitomized the crooner's style.
- *The New York Times* considered the style corruptive and said it needed to go.

CBS rushed to sign acts, including Bing Crosby, to meet the demand of radio listeners.

- Russ hated the term and did not consider himself a crooner; he even took lessons in opera singing to try to shake the moniker.
- Race was also a factor; the jazzy background accompaniment to many of the tunes also brought protests about the impact that people of color were having on white musicians.
- There were also concerns about the influence of cannabis, or marijuana use; Crosby was introduced to smoking it from jazz trumpeter Louis Armstrong and was an outspoken advocate of the legalization of marijuana.
- Other singing techniques such as scat and boo-boo-booing were considered lame by critics, but they caught the attention of musicians and singers who found the approach inventive and which allowed artists to explore music.
- In addition, while the orchestra was usually the star, with the vocal refrain merely an afterthought, singers began literally to take center stage.
- Singers, once positioned off to the side while the band leader held center stage, became stars.
- In addition to singing, acting and playing the violin, Russ also tried his hand at songwriting, helping to pen the tunes "Prisoner of Love" and "You Call It Madness (But I Call It Love)."
- At the same time, the Victor Company was experimenting with a new sound called "high fidelity" on a few recordings, but initial high fidelity recordings were a disaster, being referred to as loud and "blasty."
- Victor quickly shelved the process of "hi-fi" when dealers complained.
- During the early years of the Great Depression, lack of work gave new meaning to the Horace Greeley phrase "Go west, young man," but Russ would be told differently.
- Songwriter Con Conrad heard him performing one night and encouraged Columbo to move east to New York City and try his hand at radio, just as Bing Crosby had recently done with great success.

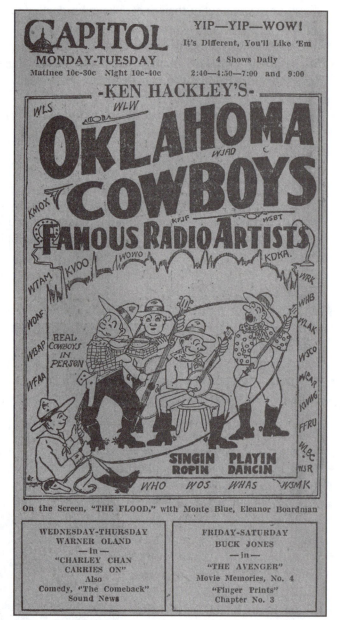

- Russ was initially turned down at the first office he tried, but NBC took him on for their less-than-desirable Tuesday 11:30 p.m. slot.
- He was so successful on radio, sponsors Maxwell House and later Listerine paid Russ $2,500-$3,000 per week.
- Radio advertising had become big business; more than 22 million American homes had a radio, up from 12 million four years earlier.
- By 1934, Bing Crosby boasted some of the top recordings and was on his way to bigger things in movies when the public relations men concocted a fake rivalry between him and Russ.
- Their phony story was aided by the fact that Crosby was a CBS radio personality, and Russ occupied a similar time slot on NBC.
- Known as the "Battle of the Baritones" the war was short-lived, with the media declaration, "Bing is King."

- Some critics thought Russ was more hype than talent, his good looks rather than his abilities accounting for his attention from the ladies.
- The Conrad PR machine didn't care and dubbed Russ, "The Romeo of Radio" and the "Valentino of Song."
- Conrad even created the rumor of a romance between Russ and former Miss Universe Dorothy Dell.
- The duo rapidly became a popular celebrity couple making headlines; Dell was prepared to have them go through with a marriage, even if it was just for show.
- When the story had run its course and female fans began to think that their "Romeo" had become wed, Conrad created a break-up that kept Russ in the news and brought back the female fans.
- There would be other "romances," but Columbo soon tired of it and parted with Conrad in 1932.
- Shortly thereafter, he left NBC and began touring the country with his own orchestra.
- He would move back to Los Angeles and give Hollywood another try.
- Critics felt he was raw as an actor, but had unlimited potential in need of a little training.
- Days before his death, Russ returned to the recording studio for the first time in two years, leaving fans with one more hint of what he could have become.

Life in the Community: Camden, New Jersey

- On the banks of the Delaware River in northern New Jersey lies Camden.
- In 1830, Camden ferries were important for travel between Philadelphia and New York City.
- Originally a suburb of Philadelphia, it soon began to hold its own as a manufacturing city.
- From 1901-1929, it was home to the Victor Talking Machine Company and its successor, RCA Victor.
- RCA Victor was the world's largest manufacturer of phonographs and the records to be played on the machine; RCA had 23 of its 25 factories in Camden.
- It was home to one of the first commercial recording studios in the United States.
- At Camden's peak, RCA employed 10,000 workers, and the New York Shipbuilding Company employed 40,000.
- In 1933, Camden hosted the first drive-in movie, the brainchild of Camden native Richard M. Hollingshead, Jr.
- A sales manager at his father's auto parts store, Hollingshead began experimenting with finding a wider theater seat more comfortable for larger people, mostly with his mother in mind.
- The first drive-in offered 500 slots with a 40x50-foot screen; the debut movie was *Wife Beware*.
- The advertising slogan was "The whole family is welcome, regardless of how noisy the children are"; the cost was $0.25 per person and $0.25 per car, with a maximum charge of $1.
- Camden was also the headquarters of Campbell's Soup.

HISTORICAL SNAPSHOT
1934

- On an island off the coast of San Francisco, Alcatraz prison was opened
- Germany, under Nazi control, passed the Law for the Prevention of Hereditary Diseased Offspring
- The comic *Flash Gordon* was published
- Fuji Photo Film was established in Japan
- Gangster John Dillinger, "Public Enemy No. 1" escaped from a prison in Crown Point, Indiana, using a wooden pistol; he would later be gunned down outside the Biograph Theater in Chicago

- Published books included *Tender is the Night* by F. Scott Fitzgerald, *Murder on the Orient Express* by Agatha Christie, *The Postman Always Rings Twice* by James M. Cain, and *Fer-De-Lance* by Rex Stout, the last of which marked the debut of Stout's corpulent sleuth Nero Wolfe
- On top of Mt. Washington in New Hampshire, the strongest wind in the world—231 mph—was recorded
- Dr. R. K. Wilson claimed that he photographed a monster in Loch Ness, Scotland
- The cartoon character Donald Duck debuted in *Silly Symphonies*
- Bank robbers Clyde Barrow and Bonnie Parker were killed in Louisiana, following an intensive hunt for them after they had shot two young highway patrolmen
- The U.S. unemployment rate was 24.9 percent
- Cinemagoers saw *Cleopatra*, *It Happened One Night*, *The Thin Man*, and *The Man Who Knew Too Much*
- The first All-American Soap Box Derby was held in Dayton, Ohio
- Adolf Hitler become chancellor of Germany, with 90 percent approval
- Bruno Richard Hauptmann was arrested in connection with the Lindbergh kidnapping
- The Quality Network, a co-op radio network, was reorganized as the Mutual Broadcasting Network
- New music on the 78 rpm discs included "Autumn in New York," "Blue Moon," "For All We Know," "I Get a Kick Out of You," "You and the Night" and the Music," and "Winter Wonderland"
- Off the coast of New Jersey, 134 people died in a fire aboard the passenger liner *Morro Castle*
- Metro-Goldwyn-Mayer purchased the rights to *The Wonderful Wizard of Oz* from the estate of L. Frank Baum for $40,000

Selected Prices

Buck Rogers Pocket Watch	$0.75
Buster Brown Hose Supporter	$0.24
Canoe	$68.00
Eggs, Dozen	$0.38
Electric Washer	$79.85
Girdle	$1.74
Ice Box	$18.75
Kraft Marshmallows, Box of 200	$0.65
Microphone	$1.00
Portable Typewriter	$49.50

LICENSED by RCA and HAZELTINE
All Electric

Improve your kitchen with HIGH-POWER PERFECTION

"He's Thrilling Girls, This Russ Columbo," *Sandusky Star Journal* (Ohio), October 17, 1931:

Russ Columbo came out of the west very reluctantly.

When a man is only 23 and is packing the cinema folk into his own nightclub, and when the same movie maestros are dangling contacts in front of the patrician nose, there is considerable trepidation involved in a decision to toss this aside and go to New York to crash the gates of broadcasting.

But friends finally persuaded Columbo that only the biggest time was good enough for his voice. So we said goodbye to the Club Pyramid, his band, his friends, the movies and thousands of women admirers who had petitioned him to remain in their ecstatic midst.

Now there are a lot of excellent singers in New York who are getting gray waiting for their chance in broadcasting. Some of them are almost as tall and dark and handsome as Russ Columbo.

However, after a few anxious days trying to identify himself as a Pacific Coast celebrity who really had something to sell, he was permitted to sidle up to an NBC microphone and warble "Body and Soul."

And already, scented stationery and daintily inscribed requests for photos are tumbling into the cubbyhole for the Columbo mail.

It is an exciting chapter in the life and times of a once-poor Italian-American boy who was christened Ruggiero. Columbo is his real name, incidentally.

He was born in San Francisco in 1908, began practicing on the violin at seven and got his first orchestra job at 17, in a Los Angeles high school.

Part of his money went to help support the family, and the rest went for violin lessons under a capable teacher. In an emergency one night, he doubled for the orchestra's vocalist and kept on singing ever after.

He sang leading roles in a number of talkies, but only as a sideline.

He organized his own bright spot, The Club Pyramid, composed of a few seductive tunes, wrote a few lyrics, led his orchestra, sang winningly to the cash customers and grinned happily over the gate receipts.

Con Conrad, New York songwriter, was the one who really induced Columbo to try for radio fame. Columbo now is grateful.

"About my style of singing," said Russ. "I have a lot of trouble defining it. I'm not a crooner, or a blues singer, or a straight baritone. I've tried to make my phrasing different, and I take a lot of liberty with the music.

"One of the things they seem to like best is the voice obbligato on repeat choruses, very much as I used to do them on the violin.

"I like to lead an orchestra and try to work at different effects. I'm also composing a little. I write late at night mostly; I get some of my best ideas after I've gone to bed."

"Mae West Film at Granada Saturday," *West Seattle Herald*, December 12, 1934:

In *Belle of the Nineties*, showing four days starting Tuesday, Mae West traumatizes the strident days when men gambled with hearts, paid off with aces and fought for fun. She is cast as Ruby Carter, the center of a whirlpool of action that brings her down the river from a St. Louis burlesque show to one of the most famous gaming houses in the South. John Mack Brown and Roger Pryer support her, with Duke Ellington and his orchestra also featured. Russ Columbo, June Knight and Roger Pryor will share the bill in *Wake Up and Dream*, a gay comedy romance with music. "The Flying Mouse," Walt Disney's *Silly Symphonies*, will be a third sensation.

"Gleams From Film Capital, Burlington," *Daily Times News* (North Carolina), December 27, 1934:

Children will take over the household of many Hollywood couples. Although too young to clamor for toys, three children of the Bing Crosbys will blink their delight at an immense lighted Christmas tree. Gene Markey and Joan Bennett have prepared a gay party for their two young daughters. There'll be a reunion at the home of Will Rogers. Will, Jr., has come home from Stanford, Jimmy from Pomona College and Mary from the East where she is working with a stock company.

Contrary to expectations, Mary Pickford and Douglas Fairbanks will exchange the season's greetings at Pickfair. Fairbanks rushed home from New York but if it augered reconciliation, neither will tell.

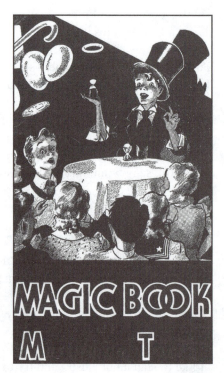

Happy in ignorance of what awaits her, Mrs. Nicholas Columbo proudly exhibited a cablegram simulating Christmas greetings from her son, Russ Columbo, popular crooner who was killed accidentally early last fall.

"With love, from Russ" the message read, and the mother was unaware that her other children were still practicing the merciful hoax they carried out since Russ died. She believes he is in Europe, too busy making a motion picture to return for the holidays. Physicians say she may have recovered sufficiently from a heart attack to be told of his death within a week or so.

*"You Call It Madness
(But I Call It Love)"*

(By Con Conrad, Gladys DuBois,
Russ Columbo, Paul Gregory)

I can't forget the night I met you,
That's all I'm dreaming of.
Now you call it madness,
But I call it love.

You made a promise to be faithful
By all the stars above.
And now you call it madness,
But I call it love.

My heart is beating,
It keeps repeating for you constantly.
You're all I'm needing
And so I'm pleading,
Please come back to me.

You made a plaything out of romance,
What were you thinking of?
Now you call it madness,
But I call it love.

"Rudy Vallee," *Radio Album*, Spring 1935:

Wistful, boyish, sophomoric Rudy Vallee crooned his way with a gay heigh-ho into Mrs. and Miss America's hearts back in 1928. No Gallup polls accounted for the whys of his whirlwind success, but as Whistler had his mother, Morgan her piano, so Rudy had a nasal twang that makes him the number one vagabond lover. Perhaps astrologists saw it in the stars, but in Island Pond, Vermont, on July 28, 1901, when Herbert Prior Vallee first graced the village druggist's nursery, no one predicted any spotlights for him. Young Herbert might still be delivering aspirin and jerking sodas if he hadn't heard Rudy Wiedoeft. Promptly, he borrowed a never-to-be-returned saxophone, inveigled a correspondence course out of Wiedoeft and for his teacher's and publicity's sakes changed Herbert to Rudy. Saxing his way into the University of Maine hall of incurable musicians, he put the "Stein Song" and S.A.E.'s "Violet" on the top of the campus hit parade. Leaving those careless hours and happy days, Rudy took up the baton at Yale, where his Connecticut Yankees roused slumbering Eli. Some Londoners heard about the boys and asked them over. For two years the gang stopped at the Savoy with nightly visits of the Prince of Wales, their best publicity. Again Rudy yenned for the New Haven quads in the Whiffenproof songs at Morey's and returned to a B.A. in romantic languages. Sunk in academic oblivion, he was down to his last pawn ticket when the Heigh-Ho Club put him on the air. He wowed the matinee listeners. In a fervor, Fleishman's yeast rose to snatch him up. This was Rudy's hour. Opening his eyes to new talent, he unearthed, among others, McCarthy, Bob Burns, Alice Faye, and Burns and Allen. As a maestro master of ceremonies, only he could think of using the many-wived, Hamlet-minded Barrymore as his stooge. Only Rudy could take it when, to his surprise, the great lover gets the last laugh. Women will always adore Rudy; men will always hate him.

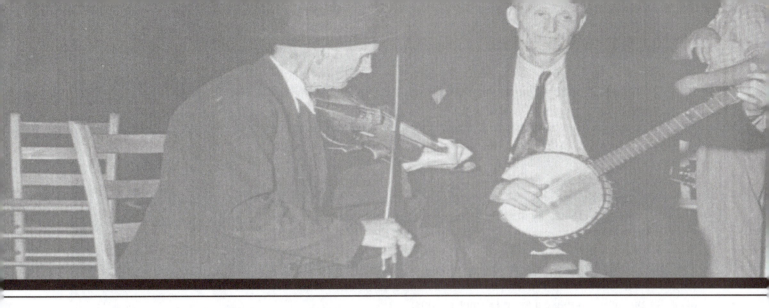

1936 PROFILE

When he applied for a job with the Works Progress Administration, Mark Strahorn was unemployed, the father of three small children and the husband of an invalid wife; playing music full time was his secret—unspoken—dream.

Life at Home

- The textile mill where Mark Strahorn worked in Winston-Salem, North Carolina, had closed abruptly two years and two months earlier.
- When he was working, Mark's family lived financially from week to week; once he lost his job, they lived minute to minute.
- The only income possible in a community littered with unemployed textile workers was with his fiddle as a member of a band known as the Empty Road.
- The Works Progress Administration was to be his salvation in tough times.
- Mark was a Great War baby, conceived the night before his father shipped out to France, only to return with severely burnt lungs, a terrible temper and a thirst for alcohol.
- Mark stayed in school through the sixth grade before taking a job beside his cousin and uncles in the gray cloth mill run by the money men in Chicago.
- The mill had run three shifts during the late 1920s as the price of cotton fell and demand grew for the cotton products it produced.
- Mark was informed that his services were no longer needed, along with 631 other workers, by a small note taped to a locked door.
- Alcohol did not cure the pain of losing his livelihood.
- One-third of the nation was unemployed, and everyone Mark knew was in the same dilemma.

Mark Strahorn (center), unemployed father of three, played his fiddle in a band called Empty Road.

- The only road back, President Franklin Roosevelt believed, was public works jobs funded by the government such as building roads, laying out parks, constructing bridges and creating art.
- Paying the unemployed a wage for work reinforced the idea that everyone was working together to end the economic crisis—which helped remove the social stigma of being on relief.
- The pay also stimulated both the individual self-worth of Americans and the national economy.
- The largest agency created by the Emergency Relief Appropriations Act was the Works Progress Administration, commonly called the WPA, headed by Harry Hopkins.
- The high-energy Hopkins was described as having "a mind like a razor, a tongue like a skinning knife, a temper like Tartar and a sufficient vocabulary of parlor profanity to make a mule skinner jealous."
- Even in a town populated by go-getters, the 42-year-old Hopkins stood out.
- The United States had mobilized 4.7 million soldiers, sailors, and marines to fight in World War I; Hopkins was determined to employ a similar number— four million jobless men and women—as rapidly as possible to fight the Depression.
- The WPA hired more than three million people in its first year.
- Its mission was broad: to build one million miles of highway, nearly 100,000 bridges, and buildings as diverse as The Dock Street Theatre in Charleston, South Carolina, and Timberline Lodge on the slopes of Oregon's Mount Hood.

Mrs. Strahorn.

- Often, local political bosses determined who got the jobs; some jobs came only after political donations, while others were meted out fairly.
- Critics abounded; workers' advocates criticized the creation of federal work gangs, while conservatives lodged complaints about the "undeserving poor."
- The president's wife, Eleanor, pushed Hopkins to establish projects for thousands of artists, musicians, actors and writers.
- To those who complained, Hopkins replied, "Hell, they've got to eat just like other people."
- Hopkins believed that the Federal Project Number One, the collective name for a group of arts projects under the WPA, was an opportunity to rediscover and redefine American culture.

Harry Hopkins, right, head of the Works Progress Administration.

- Mark had applied for construction work, but the search was on for touring musicians who were willing to entertain.
- Mark preferred rubbing a fiddle to moving rock any day, especially in the heat of the Southern sun.

- His uncle had nurtured his musical talent by buying him a youth's fiddle from a Sears, Roebuck catalog, and within six months, Mark could play by ear every tune in the songbook.
- At age nine, he was asked to play with a local mountain music band that entertained at area churches.
- When he was 12, he had enough experience playing rural dance halls to predict which "good ol' boys" were going to pick a fight before the night was over.
- He married at 16, was a father at 17, and unemployed at 28.
- Only a few years earlier, after nearly three decades of quality economic growth, including seven years of unprecedented prosperity in the 1920s, the American mood had been bright.
- In the glow of annually increasing abundance, few workers fully appreciated that America was standing on the doorstep of the Great Depression.

Life at Work

- The American music scene was alive with possibilities and variety when Mark Strahorn was hired by the Federal Music Project in 1935.
- Jazz was gaining momentum, thanks to the talent of Count Basie, Duke Ellington, and Louis Armstrong.
- Ragtime was evolving into swing as Big Bands led by popular entertainers such as Artie Shaw ignited a dance craze, and the ubiquity of radio permitted every home to be a concert hall.
- At the same time, talking pictures had eliminated the need for 22,000 theater musicians essential to the silent movie experience, while the emerging quality of phonographic records suppressed the public's desire for live performances.
- Even the New Jersey Funeral Directors Association promoted the cost-effective use of radio instead of live musicians.
- In 1933, when Mark lost his textile job, 12,000 of the 15,000 members of the American Federation of Musicians in New York City were out of work.

America was on the brink of the Great Depression.

- Across the nation, symphony orchestras were closing their doors at an alarming rate, while musicians like Mark who played popular music found that the "tip jar" was nearly empty at the end of an evening.
- Russian-born conductor and violinist Nikolai Sokoloff was selected to head the Federal Music Project in 1935 after 15 years of directing the Cleveland Symphony.
- His extensive musical background was in the European Masters such as Mozart Bach, Beethoven and Brahms; early on, he decided to give Americans a diet of classical music in order to improve their musical taste.
- "Swing music," he said, "is like comparing the funny papers to the work of a painter."
- At first, Sokoloff attempted to pay higher wages to musicians who could read music and had classical training, but advocates of "popular music" eventually convinced him that all performing musicians who had been on the relief roles should make $23.86 a week.
- Musicians' pay was nearly double the average WPA wage of $52 a month.
- Eager to promote "quality music," Sokoloff's Federal Music Project sponsored concerts in symphony halls and county parks—anywhere he could lift the musical IQ of Americans.
- In all, its 15,000 musicians gave 225,000 performances, including free concerts at New York's Central Park.
- Millions of Americans flocked to the concerts and brought their children.

- Mark performed in his first concert in Raleigh, North Carolina, followed by Richmond, Virginia, and Washington, DC; no audience was too small, no event too unlikely.
- Initially, he was instructed to play the fiddle in a more cultured manner.
- Mark quickly learned that the difference in playing the violin was more than style: the goal of violin music was beauty and power, while the goal of fiddling was danceability.
- Violin music was often harder to play than it sounded and left little room for improvisational riffs.
- But the biggest difference was that violin music made people sit still and the fiddle made them dance.
- Mark worked hard to make the transition from fiddle to "fancy" music; the showdown came seven months into his job traveling from school to school playing "proper" music.
- The band arrived playing mountain music in a bus one late afternoon, knowing that, for the rest of the evening, they were expected to be an orchestra and play selections from three European composers.
- Only this time, a large crowd that had gathered in the parking lot heard the informal jam session.
- So that evening after the first movement of Bach was completed and the sweet sounds of the violin had died away, a tall, thin man in overalls rose from his seat and said, "Not to be ungrateful, but we were wanting some more bus music."

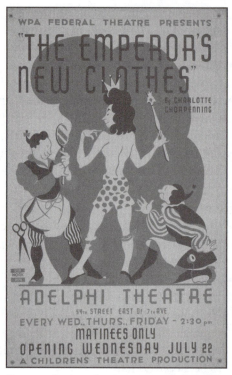

Poster of a production sponsored by the WPA.

- After that, every concert opened with "quality music" and ended with a hoedown, energetically driven by Mark's fiddling.
- The WPA aggressively advertised the music project and charged $0.25-$0.50 per person when there was any cost at all; in the first nine months of 1936, 32 million Americans attended Federal Music Project performances.
- While the emphasis was on "quality music," meaning classical, over time the project embraced Texas fiddlers, Ohio jug bands, and Appalachian banjo pickers.
- American composers such as George Gershwin, Victor Herbert and John Philip Sousa were given wide exposure to avoid accusations of being un-American; Broadway-style music, epitomized by Jerome Kern, Oscar Hammerstein and Irving Berlin, began to appear more regularly.

Many protested cutbacks in Federal Project Number One – which employed musicians and artists.

- The Federal Project Number One also celebrated the talent of artists, actors and writers, and resulted in hundreds of public murals, books about each of the 48 states, and thousands of photographs depicting the everyday life of Americans.
- President Roosevelt was determined to use any means of "disposing of surplus workers" during the deep economic downturn.
- He considered work relief, unemployment insurance, and old age pensions as part of a comprehensive package and pathway to sustainable economic stability.
- Mark's favorite concert was in July 1936 when his band, the Mountain Minstrels, performed country music in Burlington, North Carolina.
- The day was hot, the crowd was temperamental, and Mark's skills were nothing short of magical.
- Taking the lead instrumental in the second song, he drove the crowd into a frenzy as the other musicians hustled to catch up.
- It wasn't classical that day, but it was fun.
- During the last four months of 1936, Mark performed at dozens of school concerts across North Carolina and Virginia.

The Moravian church in Winston-Salem, North Carolina.

- After one week of touring schools, he told his wife, "I didn't know there were that many kids in the entire world."
- As a result, children came to him eager to learn how to play an instrument, and many telling their parents about what they had heard and why it stirred their souls.
- Electricity was just reaching many of the rural areas of North Carolina, bringing light to the night and radio music to the family for the first time.
- Thanks to the variety of sounds coming from the radio, musical tastes of working Americans grew more sophisticated, and a rural farm family could stay informed about world events.
- In the fall of 1936, Mark had a decision to make.
- Despite new signs of a second Depression, the textile mills were reopening in Winston-Salem; music or the mills was his choice.
- Cutbacks in the Federal Project Number One told Mark he should return to textiles.
- The totally alive feeling it had for the last 18 months told him he should stay in the music business.

Life in the Community: Winston-Salem, North Carolina

- Winston and Salem grew up together as separate towns.
- Salem, North Carolina, was born first in 1753, when Bishop August Gottlieb Spangenberg, on behalf of the Moravian Church, established a settlement site on 99,000 acres in the three forks of Muddy Creek.
- He called this area "die Wachau" or Wachovia after the ancestral Austrian estate of benefactor Count Nikolaus Ludwig von Zinzendorf.
- The later name of Salem, from the Hebrew word *shalom* for "peace," was chosen by the Moravians' now late patron, Count Zinzendorf.
- Salem was a typical Moravian settlement with the public buildings of the congregation grouped around a central square, which included the church, a Brethren's House and a Sisters' House for the unmarried members of the congregation, which owned all the property in town.
- Winston was not founded until 1849, and was named after a local hero of the Revolutionary War, Joseph Winston.
- It thrived as an industrial town, producing tobacco products, furniture and textiles, and in 1913, the towns were officially joined with a hyphen as "Winston-Salem."
- By 1935, the R. J. Reynolds Tobacco Company dominated the economic heartbeat of the two towns; more than half of Winston-Salem's workers were employed either for Reynolds or in the Hanes textile factories.
- Founded in 1874, R. J. Reynolds was known for its innovative branded products as Prince Phillip chewing tobacco in 1907 and Camel cigarettes in 1913.
- The Reynolds company imported so much French cigarette paper and Turkish tobacco for Camel cigarettes that Winston-Salem was designated as an official port of entry for the United States.
- Despite being 200 miles inland, Winston-Salem was the eighth-largest port of entry in the U.S. by 1916.
- In 1917, the company bought 84 acres of property in Winston-Salem and built 180 houses that it sold at cost to workers to form a development called "Reynoldstown."
- In 1929, the 21-story Reynolds Building—the tallest building in the U.S. south of Baltimore, Maryland—was completed in Winston-Salem.
- The Wesley Hanes's Shamrock Hosiery Mills in Winston-Salem began making men's socks in 1901.
- Later renamed Hanesbrands, the company was responsible for textile innovations such as two-piece men's underwear in 1902 and women's nylon hosiery in 1938.
- In 1934, Malcolm Purcell McLean formed McLean Trucking Company.
- The firm benefited from the strong tobacco and textile industries headquartered in Winston-Salem.

HISTORICAL SNAPSHOT
1936

- The first building to be completely covered in glass was built in Toledo, Ohio, for the Owens-Illinois Glass Company
- *The Green Hornet* radio show debuted
- John Maynard Keynes's book *The General Theory of Employment, Interest and Money* was published
- Radium E became the first radioactive element to be made synthetically
- The first superhero to wear a skin-tight costume and a mask, *The Phantom*, made his appearance in U.S. newspapers
- Construction of Hoover Dam was completed
- In violation of the Treaty of Versailles, Nazi Germany reoccupied the Rhineland
- Bruno Richard Hauptmann, convicted of kidnapping and killing Charles Lindbergh III, was executed in New Jersey
- The 1936–1939 Arab revolt in Palestine against the British government and in opposition to Jewish immigration began
- *Peter and the Wolf*, a Russian fairy tale of Sergei Prokofiev's composition, debuted at the Nezlobin Theater in Moscow
- The Santa Fe Railroad inaugurated the all-Pullman *Super Chief* passenger train between Chicago, Illinois, and Los Angeles, California
- Margaret Mitchell's novel *Gone with the Wind* was published
- German Max Schmeling knocked out American Joe Louis in the twelfth round of their heavyweight boxing match at Yankee Stadium in New York City
- The 1936 Summer Olympics opened in Berlin, Germany, and marked the first live television coverage of a sports event in world history
- African-American athlete Jesse Owens won the 100-meter dash at the Berlin Olympics; Hitler refused to shake his hand, believing him to be of an inferior race
- The sculpture of Thomas Jefferson's head at Mount Rushmore was dedicated
- H. R. Ekins, reporter for the *New York World-Telegram*, won a race to travel around the world on commercial airline flights, beating out Dorothy Kilgallen of the *New York Journal* and Leo Kieran of the *New York Times*; the flight took 18 and a half days
- In the U.S. presidential election, Franklin D. Roosevelt was reelected to a second term in a landslide victory over Alf Landon
- The first edition of *LIFE Magazine* was published
- The Abraham Lincoln Brigade sailed from New York City on its way to fight in the Spanish Civil War
- Radio station WQXR was founded in New York City
- Polaroid sunglasses and Ambré Solaire sunblock were both marketed for the first time

Selected Prices

Antifreeze, Gallon	$1.00
Baby Carriage	$12.98
Electric Coffee Mill	$9.75
Flashlight	$0.55
Fountain Pen	$1.00
Garden Tractor	$242.00
Lawn Mower, Power	$69.50
Motor Yacht	$26,300
Seat Covers, Sedan	$5.85
Sofa and Chair	$66.85

"First Woman Inventor in U.S. Is Attractive Beulah Henry," *GRIT*, April 18, 1937:

Speak of inventors, and most folks will conjure up a picture of test tubes, electrical whatnots, littered rooms, soiled smocks, and men or women with a far-off look in their eyes.

Quite the opposite of this picture, however, is blonde Beulah Louise Henry, the "Lady Edison" of inventors, who has received patents for 52 inventions in the last 15 years. Her "laboratory" is a modern hotel room. She is vivacious, cultured, and attractive. She is an artist of considerable ability and, feminine-like, very proud of her cooking.

The secret of her inventive ability, Miss Henry says, is spiritual. Inventions just come to her out of the air, "finished and in color, just like a picture." She had no mechanical training to prepare for the life of an inventor. But at the age of nine, ideas for improvements began coming to her almost like visions. When these visions come, she goes to her mechanic and describes them, and they go to work. Sometimes she has to work as long as four years on one invention before it is perfect.

Miss Henry's newest invention is an office equipment device which she asserts will save time, money, and trouble for the employer and worker. It is called a "protograph" and is an attachment which can be adjusted to any standard typewriter and make from one to four copies, all-in-one writing, without the use of carbon paper. Additional copies are made by the use of typewriter ribbons which are fed from side to side automatically, as the original ribbon. The protograph may be released from operating position by pressing a button.

Among her other inventions for parasols, toys, bathing slippers with high heels, football valves, water bottle stoppers, many mechanical devices which hardly seem possible for a woman to have devised, and the "Radio Rose."

The last is a life-size, lifelike doll, dainty and attractive, with a seven-tube radio concealed in its body.

Fiddling was popular in the mountains.

"Thousands in One Music Class: Piano Instruction Is Latest Form of Radio Activities,"
The Raleigh Times, **April 11, 1931:**

Fifty thousand piano pupils in one class! Impossible? No, indeed, for the radio has stepped from its role as entertainer and turned instructor. Last week Dr. Sigmund Spaeth stepped before the microphone at 11:30 in the morning and informed listeners on the WEAF network that learning to play the piano was not the long, weary task that we had been led to believe in our youth, but really quite simple if you wanted to try it. Then he proceeded to prove his point by showing the few chords that are necessary to provide a satisfactory accompaniment for many well-known songs.

On Tuesday—on the WJZ network, 3 p.m.—Osbourne McConathy demonstrated the ease with which a simple melody may be played on the piano. And in doing this, he proved two things: that it is not hard for the allegedly unmusical to learn to play, and that the radio can be effective as a medium for teaching, even in the case of such an ephemeral subject as music.

And this last point is highly important; it may answer many questions skeptics have been asking for several years. Radio, you know, has been something of a black sheep in certain circles, especially among musicians. Many unkind things have been said about it, chiefly to the effect that it's been freezing American people into passive listeners, making them content to sit back and listen (or talk) while others do their playing and singing for them. It is one of the evils of the machine age, some said, for it stifles all desire to learn to do things for ourselves.

Who will play the piano in the future if we don't have to do it in order to hear music? they asked. And it has required pretty stout-hearted enthusiasts to keep courage, under the fire of such comments, not to admit that the doubters were probably right.

"My Struggle to Escape the Cotton Mill, 1930," Anonymous, from autobiographies written by Southern summer school students in 1930:

After mother and father were married, they lived on a homestead in Alabama. The house was built of logs with one large room. The cooking was done in iron pots. Some little distance from the yard to the north was built the crib, in which to keep feed of different kinds. Here were horse and corn stalls, for then we kept a cow and father had to keep a horse to plow his little farm and to pull the buggy, for it was miles to where anyone lived and too far to walk….

"Hard times" forced my father to rent this little house and move elsewhere to run the farm for someone who had capital to farm on a large scale. This was the beginning of the end, for we moved from place to place until the home was finally sold. Then I was old enough to start school, but we lived too far from a school and I was too small to go alone, so all the schooling I had till I was eight years old was a few months when my aunt taught me. All this time, the family was growing larger, there being six children. The 1907 Panic hit the country. We moved to a town in Alabama, to the cotton mills, and father, my sister, and I went to work. I wasn't quite 15 years old. In a short time, another brother was born.

My sister and I were sent to the spinning room to learn to spin. My sister made better progress than I, but the bosses being harsh and I being timid, I was half scared to death all the time and could not learn the work. This kept up about three months. My father was making $1.00 per day and my sister and I were making $0.50 each per day. Then it was decided we had served our apprenticeship and should go on as "sides." I was given two sides of spinning and was paid $0.11 per side, making my daily pay $0.22, and I was living in terror all the time, in fear of the boss. When father found out I would no longer get $0.50 per day, he told me to stay home. In the meantime, my sister had been taken to the weave room to fill "batteries," making $0.70 per day. After some red tape, I was allowed to go to work in the weave room, and for nearly two years, my sister and I worked for $0.70 per day. It took very little skill to keep this job going, and there being no harsh bosses over me, I was fairly happy there until father began to insist that my sister and I become weavers. I hated the cotton mill and I swore I would not stay in it all my life. My sister did not mind so much, tried, and became a good weaver.

After quite a struggle on my part to keep from learning to be a weaver, I gave it a thorough trial and found I could not learn weaving very easily, and being very anxious to earn more money, I began to think of how I could find better-paying work. Then I was allowed to go to the spooler and warper rooms, where I worked at different times in both rooms making $1.25 per day and finally getting $9.00 per week.

The long hours and nervous state in which I worked had caused me to have much less strength than I would have had otherwise, and it was all I could do to keep the work up with the other worker who was required on the job and a boy to roll the bores workers. Then one day we were told that the boy could not help us anymore and I quit. My father had left the mill by this time because he had been too ready to talk to anyone he saw about conditions in the mill. With no one working in the mill but me, the company notified us to move, and when I quit, we were not living on company property.

The same day I quit the cotton mill, I went to an overall factory to get work and succeeded. While talking with the owner of the business, he told me that some of his employees make $10 per week, and I thought, if there was even a remote chance of me making that much money, it was a wonderful opportunity for me, so I went to work the next day. I worked for four days that week and made $2.40 on piecework. I had worked 11 hours in the mill, but here I only worked nine hours and conditions were so different. A very nice, kind, patient young woman was my instructor and the superintendent was never harsh spoken. This was a union factory, and I advanced so well that in a short time I was making as much as I had made after working years in the cotton mill. However, the things that the cotton mill life did to me have just now, after many years, begun to leave me.

1939 PROFILE

Serving as the pianist, arranger and musical inspiration for the band Clouds of Joy, Mary Lou Williams could be summed by the title to one of her records: "The Lady Who Swings the Band."

Life at Home

- Jazz pianist Mary Lou Williams was fittingly described by one critic as "the swingingest female alive."
- In partnership with Andy Kirk, Mary Lou also was a pioneer of the smooth simplicity and extended solo riffs that came to be known as Kansas City jazz.
- Born Mary Elfreida Scruggs in 1910, Mary Lou was one of 11 children who moved to Pittsburgh when she was five or six years old.
- Mary Lou, who sat on her mother's lap as the latter played the organ, began playing the piano for money at neighbors' houses when she was seven, sometimes earning $20 to $30 a day with her skills.
- In the fifth grade, she displayed her ability to produce an unaided perfect pitch when she substituted for a mislaid pitch pipe.
- When Mary Lou was 10 years old, the fabulously rich Mellon family paid her $100 to play piano for a party and brought her to the event in a chauffer-driven limousine.
- And when she was 11, Mary, who occasionally sat in with the Earl Hines Band, was asked at the last minute to substitute for the regular pianist on a touring show, *Hits and Bits*.
- Since there was no written score, a member of the cast hummed all the tunes for her on the day of the performance; she performed flawlessly.
- For the next two summers, she traveled with the show and returned to Pittsburgh in the fall for school.
- The travel schedule, especially trips to Harlem, brought her into contact with popular groups like McKinney's Cotton Pickers and Duke Ellington's Washingtonians.
- She played with both bands and proved that she could do more than simply keep up.

Mary Lou Williams was a jazz pianist with fans all along the East Coast – including Louis Armstrong – by the time she was 13 years old.

- By the time she turned 13, she was a veteran musician with fans all along the East Coast.
- One of those fans was future husband and saxophonist John Williams, whose combo joined *Hits and Bits* in 1924.
- When Seymour and Jeanette, a top vaudeville team on the Orpheum circuit, proposed that John Williams could join their circuit, he insisted on taking Mary Lou along.
- "Cut her hair and put pants on her!" shouted Seymour in response. "We cannot have a girl in the outfit."
- After she played the piano, Seymour changed his mind and she stayed with the act until it broke up a year later.
- Another major salute to her talent came that same year when she was only 15.
- One morning at 3 a.m., when she was jamming with McKinney's Cotton Pickers at Harlem's Rhythm Club, Louis Armstrong entered the room, paused to listen, then "Louis picked me up and kissed me."
- John and Mary Lou were married in 1926 when she turned 16.
- Together they toured the South with her own small band until John joined Clouds of Joy in 1928.
- A year later they moved to Kansas City for a steady job at the Pla-Mor, one the city's top ballrooms; for the next seven years they worked out of Kansas City, Missouri.
- "Kaycee was really jumping," Mary Lou said. "So many great bands have sprung up there or moved in from over the river. It attracted musicians from all over the South and Southwest."

Louis Armstrong at the piano.

Life at Work

- Kansas City was a wide-open town, firmly under the control of political boss Tom Pendergast, who ignored the national Prohibition against alcohol sales, while promoting gambling and other vice in the city.
- "Naturally, work was plentiful for musicians," Mary Lou Williams said.
- Talented musicians flocked to the town—where the music never went to bed—to play in after-hours jam sessions with established musicians like Herschel Evans, Coleman Hawkins and Lester ("Prez") Young.
- "We didn't have closing hours in those spots," Mary Lou said. "We'd play all morning and half through the day if we wished, and, in fact, we often did. The music was so good we seldom got to bed before midday."
- By the 1930s, Kansas City jazz was recognized as a unique sound with its preference for a 4/4 beat that made it more relaxed and fluid.
- New York had developed its own swinging jazz sound, Chicago was recognized as a center for jazz, and the crossroads community of Kansas City owned its own distinctive sound.
- Extended soloing fueled by a culture whose goal was to "say something" with one's instrument also marked Kansas City jazz as distinctive.
- At times, one "song" could be performed for several hours, with the best musicians often soloing for dozens of choruses at a time.
- Constructed around a 12-bar blues structure, rather than the eight-bar jazz standard, the style left room for elaborate riffing by individuals or pairs.
- And since the big bands in Kansas City also played by memory, composing collectively rather than sight-reading, the KC style was often looser and more spontaneous.
- It was a sound that suited Mary Lou's musical skills.
- Critics wrote of Mary Lou, "If you shut your eyes, you would bet she was a man."

Clouds of Joy's success was a direct result of the songs that Mary Lou wrote and arranged for them.

- *Time* magazine said she played "the solid, unpretentious, flesh-&-bone kind of jazz piano that is expected from such vigorous Negro masters as James P. Johnson."
- For a decade, Andy Kirk's Clouds of Joy and Mary Lou were inseparable.
- She wrote most of its arrangements, and many of them such as "Roll 'Em" and "Froggy Bottom" quickly became classics among jazz players.
- One week she got down 15 scores and, all told, she provided the Clouds of Joy with 200 arrangements, including "Walkin' and Swingin'," "Twinklin'," "Cloudy'," and "Little Joe from Chicago."
- During a recording trip to Chicago, Mary Lou recorded "Drag 'Em" and "Night Life" as piano solos.
- The records sold briskly, lifting Mary Lou to national prominence.
- Soon afterwards, she also began playing solo gigs and working as a freelance arranger for Earl Hines, Benny Goodman, and Tommy Dorsey.
- Mary Lou and the Clouds of Joy also scored another hit with "Until The Real Thing Comes Along,"—an exceptional achievement in the midst of a national Depression—thanks to the development of jukeboxes.
- Suddenly, their sound was coming from every bar; when they played live, thousands of music lovers had to be turned away.
- At times they would perform "Real Thing" half a dozen times per show because the demand was so great.
- But the lugubrious ballad was a departure from KC swing, and the critics made sure the musicians knew it.
- In 1937, she produced *In the Groove*, a collaboration with Dick Wilson, and Benny Goodman asked Mary Lou to write a blues number for his band.
- The result was "Roll 'Em," a boogie-woogie piece based on the blues, which followed her successful "Camel Hop," Goodman's theme song for his radio show sponsored by Camel cigarettes.
- Goodman wanted Mary Lou to write for him exclusively, but she refused, preferring to freelance.
- She was accustomed to making her own path.

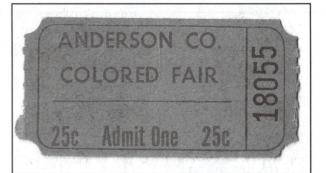

Wherever they played, tickets to see Clouds of Joy always sold out.

Life in the Community: Kansas City, Missouri

- Kansas City, Missouri, which straddles the border between Missouri and Kansas at the confluence of the Kansas and Missouri rivers, was incorporated in 1850 with a population of 1,500.
- Throughout the 1840s, the population of the Town of Kansas swelled as it increasingly became a vital starting point on the Oregon, Santa Fe, and California trails for settlers heading West; rail travel came to Kansas in 1847.
- The first newspaper and telegraph service were established in the Town of Kansas in 1851.
- In 1889, with a population of around 130,000, the town adopted a new charter and changed its name to Kansas City as it became the second-busiest train center in the country, trailing only Chicago.
- The Kansas City Stockyards became second only to Chicago's in size, and the city itself was identified with its famous Kansas City steak.
- The Pendergast era, under Democrat big city bosses James Pendergast and Tom Pendergast from 1890 to 1940, ushered in a colorful and influential era for the city.

Mildred Bailey was one of the first successful non-Black jazz singer in Kansas City.

- During this period, the Pendergasts declared that national Prohibition was meaningless in Kansas City, and the Kansas City boulevard and park system was developed.
- American aviator Charles Lindbergh helped lure the newly created Transcontinental & Western Airline—later TWA—to locate its corporate headquarters in Kansas City because of its central location, making Kansas City a hub of national aviation.
- During the later part of the Golden Age of Aviation—the 1930s and 1940s—TWA was known as "The Airline Run by Flyers."
- When Prohibition finally was repealed in 1933 by means of the Twenty-first Amendment, little changed in Kansas City.
- The first Kansas City band to achieve a national reputation was the Coon-Sanders Original Nighthawk Orchestra, a white group which broadcast nationally in the 1920s.
- Kansas City was a national crossroads resulting in a mix of cultures; transcontinental trips by plane or train often required a stop in the city.

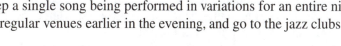

The Chesterfield Club was one of many popular jazz clubs in Kansas City.

- Jazz musicians associated with the style were born in other places but got caught up in the friendly musical competition among performers that could keep a single song being performed in variations for an entire night.
- Members of the Big Bands would perform at regular venues earlier in the evening, and go to the jazz clubs later to jam for the rest of the night.
- Clubs were scattered throughout city, but the most fertile area was the inner city neighborhood of 18th Street and Vine.
- Among the clubs were the Amos 'n' Andy, Boulevard Lounge, Cherry Blossom, Chesterfield Club, Chocolate Bar, Dante's Inferno, Elk's Rest, Hawaiian Gardens, Hell's Kitchen, the Hi Hat, the Hey Hey, Lone Star, Old Kentucky Bar-B-Que, Paseo Ballroom, Pla-Mor Ballroom, Reno Club, Spinning Wheel, Street's Blue Room, Subway and Sunset.

HISTORICAL SNAPSHOT
1939

- The Hewlett-Packard Company was founded
- Amelia Earhart was officially declared dead two years after her disappearance while attempting to fly around the world
- *Naturwissenschaften* published evidence that nuclear fission had been achieved by Otto Hahn
- Adolf Hitler ordered Plan Z, a five-year naval expansion effort intended to create a huge German fleet capable of crushing the Royal Navy by 1944
- Hitler prophesied that if "Jewish financers" started a war against Germany, the result would be the "annihilation of the Jewish race in Europe"
- The Golden Gate International Exposition opened in San Francisco, and the 1939 World's Fair opened in New York City
- Sit-down strikes were outlawed by the Supreme Court
- In Bombay, Mohandas Gandhi began a fast protesting against British rule in India
- Students at Harvard University demonstrated the new tradition of swallowing goldfish to reporters
- British Prime Minister Neville Chamberlain gave a speech in Birmingham, stating that Britain will oppose any effort at world domination on the part of Germany
- African-American singer Marian Anderson performed before 75,000 people at the Lincoln Memorial in Washington, DC, after having been denied the use of both Constitution Hall by the Daughters of the American Revolution, and of a public high school by the federally controlled District of Columbia
- John Steinbeck's novel *The Grapes of Wrath* was published
- Billie Holiday recorded "Strange Fruit," the first anti-lynching song
- *Batman*, created by Bob Kane, made his first comic book appearance
- Major League Baseball's Lou Gehrig ended his 2,130 consecutive games played streak after developing amyotrophic lateral sclerosis (ALS)
- Pan-American Airways begins transatlantic mail service with the inaugural flight of its *Yankee Clipper* from Port Washington, New York
- The *St. Louis*, a ship carrying 907 Jewish refugees, was denied permission to land in Florida after already having been turned away from Cuba, and was forced to return to Europe, where many of its passengers later died in Nazi death camps during the Holocaust
- The National Baseball Hall of Fame and Museum was officially dedicated in Cooperstown, New York
- The 1st World Science Fiction Convention opened in New York City
- The sculpture of Theodore Roosevelt's head was dedicated at Mount Rushmore
- Albert Einstein wrote to President Franklin Roosevelt about developing the atomic bomb using uranium, leading to the creation of the Manhattan Project
- MGM's classic musical film *The Wizard of Oz*, based on L. Frank Baum's novel, and starring Judy Garland as Dorothy, premiered
- As World War II began in Europe with Germany's attack on Poland, the United States declared its neutrality
- Gerald J. Cox, speaking at an American Water Works Association meeting, publicly proposed the fluoridation of public water supplies in the U.S.
- Nylon stockings went on sale for the first time
- *Hedda Hopper's Hollywood* premiered on radio with Hollywood gossip columnist Hedda Hopper as host
- La Guardia Airport opened for business in New York City
- General Motors introduced the Hydra-Matic drive, the first mass-produced, fully automatic transmission, as an option in 1940 model year Oldsmobiles

Selected Prices

Camera, Kodak	$20.00
Coca-Cola	$0.25
Home Movie, 16 mm	$8.75
Movie Camera	$49.50
Movie Ticket	$0.25
Nylons	$1.95
Pocket Telescope	$1.00
Seat Covers, Sedan	$5.85
Toothpaste	$0.25
Wall Clock	$6.98

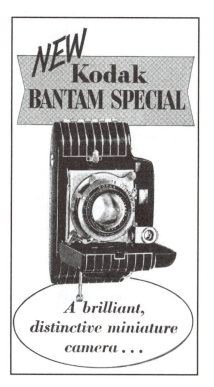

NEW Kodak **BANTAM SPECIAL**

A brilliant, distinctive miniature camera . . .

SWEET and LOW

YOU CAN COMPARE a bowl of Kellogg's Corn Flakes to a lullaby. These crisp, delicious flakes are an excellent sleep-inducer these warm evenings. They're satisfying and easily digested. Result — you sleep sweetly and arise cheerfully.

Try a bowl of Kellogg's after that late party. They're sold every place where you can buy food.

Nothing takes the place of
Kellogg's
CORN FLAKES

Catch it! WITH *Contax*

The Candid Camera of Unlimited Scope

QUICK as a flash, and under the most trying conditions, Contax will enable you to take such pictures as you never took before!—Candid, true-to-life photos full of character and human interest, fast-action, sport-shots, portraits, close-ups of birds, etc.—Any picture, anywhere, any time—indoors or out, in daylight or ordinary artificial light.

Zeiss Lenses and automatic range-finder-focusing produce needle-sharp negatives with all the detail and tone values that make a picture "sing."

ZEISS IKON. Contax is now available in two models, Contax I (black) and a new Contax II (Chromium), which at slightly higher price offers new features and advantages. At leading dealers.

Write for Literature
CARL ZEISS, Inc., Dept. C
485 Fifth Ave., New York
726 So. Hill St., Los Angeles

"The New York World's Fair Music Festival," Olin Downes,
Etude Music Magazine, May 1939:

A visitor from Cape Town, South Africa, who was taken for a preview through the New York World's Fair grounds, was heard to exclaim in a kind of neo-Mayfair accent, "My word, one couldn't begin to see all this in a lifetime." The reason for this, doubtless, is that highly experienced and energetic men behind the huge project realized that Canadians who will visit the World's Fair would be presented with an enormous variety of appeals—high-brow, low-brow, broad-brow and narrow-brow—something representative of everything under the sun, for everyone under the sun.

One might say that the same dimensions and characteristics apply to the music programs arranged and still being arranged for the World's Fair. In fact, these dimensions are so extensive that, even though I have been surrounded with them since the beginning, I'm still bewildered by their size. They've long since left the boundaries of the Fair itself.

This reminds me of the story of a colored man named Esau, who worked upon the campus of a little Southern college in a town invisible upon the map. At the time of the Chicago Fair, he was enraptured by the posters in the railroad station so as to take his savings to venture upon the long trip. Practically none of the colored folks had ever been more than three miles from town. When he left, every worker from the neighboring plantations was at the station to see him off. He was gone a month. Colored picture postcards of the Fair thrilled his friends. When he came back, an anxious and excited crowd was on hand to greet him. The president of the college asked the traveler what he liked best at the Fair. Esau scratched his head, meditated, and then said, "Well, Massa Boss, you see when I got to Chicago I just got so busy I never did get time to get to the fairgrounds."

As a matter of fact, the plans for the music of the Fair, as now outlined, will very properly be devoted to concerts and operas in New York City itself. About one-half of the celebrations will be upon Manhattan Island and one-half at the fairgrounds. As projected, the first six months of the fair season (May 1 to November 1) will include so many important occasions that one can confidently predict that it will be the most significant musical festival the world has ever known....

We have given a suggestion as to the participation of some foreign governments. It may be interesting to know that several countries overseas recognize the importance of music as a glorified expression of national ideals, and therefore these countries have arranged to engage great American symphony orchestras to play the music of their famous composers at a distinguished series of concerts given under the auspices of these countries. The plans are so far-reaching that I can give here only a sketch. Two performances of the New York Philharmonic Symphony Orchestra are certain, and six to 10 are possible. Poland has engaged this great orchestra for a Polish program Monday third; and Roumania has engaged it for May 5. Roumania has also engaged the Philadelphia Orchestra from May 14 to 16, to be conducted by the eminent Roumanian composer George Enesco. Czechoslovakia, Brazil, Switzerland, Finland, Argentina, and other nations are now negotiating for similar engagements with American orchestras. Practically all of the leading American orchestras have been invited to come to the Fair, and many have accepted.

MUSIC FURNISHED BY THE ORIGINAL TUXEDO JAZZ BAND

There was usually something worth hearing in town in those days, even if Pittsburgh was not one of the jazz centers. One Saturday night I went to the theater on Frenchtown Avenue where all the Negro shows were booked. But I hardly noticed any part of the show; my attention was focused on a lady pianist who worked there. She sat cross-legged on the piano, cigarette in her mouth, writing music with her right hand while accompanying the show with a swinging left! Impressed, I told myself, "Mary, you'll do that one day." And I did, traveling with Andy Kirk's band in the 1930s on one-nighters.

—Mary Lou Williams

Recorded Popular Songs: 1939

- "Over the Rainbow"
  (Judy Garland)

- "God Bless America"
  (Kate Smith)

- "Three Little Fishies"
  (Kay Kyser)

- "When the Saints Go Marching In"
  (Louis Armstrong)

- "Moonlight Serenade"
  (Glenn Miller)

- "Beer Barrel Polka"
  (Will Glahe)

- "Sunrise Serenade"
  (Glenn Miller)

- "Says My Heart"
  (Red Norvo)

- "Little Brown Jug"
  (Glenn Miller)

- "South of the Border (Down Mexico
  Way)" (Shep Fields)

- "Jeepers Creepers"
  (Al Donohue)

- "If I Didn't Care"
  (Ink Spots)

- "Wishing (Will Make It So)"
  (Glenn Miller)

- "And the Angels Sing"
  (Benny Goodman)

- "Deep Purple"
  (Larry Clinton)

- "Heaven Can Wait"
  (Glen Gray)

- "They Say"
  (Artie Shaw)

- "Stairway to the Stars"
  (Glenn Miller)

- "Scatter-Brain"
  (Frankie Masters)

- "At the Woodchopper's Ball"
  (Woody Herman)

"Mary Lou Williams With Andy Kirk Band," *Cumberland Evening Times* (Maryland), July 13, 1937:

Mary Lou Williams is featured with Andy Kirk's Orchestra Thursday evening at Crystal Park. She is known as "America's Sweetheart of the ivories," and the most talked about "swing" pianist in the orchestral world. She's the girl that swings the band. She makes the piano speak in a language to which every dance responds…an unusual personality…she's America's foremost femme stylist of the piano.

Mary Lou Williams is the gal that makes all of Benny Goodman, Lou Armstrong, and Bob Crosby's special swing numbers.

1940–1949

The dramatic, all-encompassing nature of World War II dominated the lives and economies of Americans. Despite a nation suddenly consumed by the national war effort, a wide variety of musical styles still flourished, thanks to the now-ubiquitous influence of radio and the creation of a mass market. All-female bands were formed, and the down-to-earth hominess of Rodgers and Hammerstein's Broadway play *Oklahoma!* in 1943 resulted a major hit, magnified by the creation of the first cast recordings of the musical's entire song repertoire. People from every social stratum either signed up for the military or went to work supplying the military machine. Even children, eager to do their share, collected scrap metal and helped plant the victory gardens that symbolized America's willingness to do anything to defeat the "bullies." In addition, large amounts of money and food were sent abroad as Americans observed meatless Tuesdays, gas rationing and other shortages to help the starving children of Europe.

Businesses worked on partnerships with the government; strikes were reduced, but key New Deal labor concessions were expanded, including a 40-hour week and time and a half for overtime. As manufacturing demands increased, the labor pool shrank, and wages and union membership rose. Unemployment, which stood as high as 14 percent in 1940, all but disappeared. By 1944, the U.S. was producing twice the total war output of the Axis powers combined. The wartime demand for production workers rose more rapidly than for skilled workers, reducing the wage gap between the two to the lowest level in the twentieth century.

From 1940 to 1945, the gross national product more than doubled, from $100 billion to $211 billion, despite rationing and the unavailability of many consumer goods such as cars, gasoline, and washing machines. Interest rates remained low, and the upward pressure on prices remained high, yet from 1943 to the end of the war, the cost of living rose less than 1.5 percent. Following the war, as controls were removed, inflation peaked in 1948; union demands for high wages accelerated. Between 1945 and 1952, confident Americans—and their growing families—increased consumer credit by 800 percent.

To fight inflation, government agencies regulated wages, prices, and the kinds of jobs people could take. The Office of Price Administration was entrusted with the complicated task of setting price ceilings for almost all consumer goods and distributing ration books for items in short supply. The Selective Service and the War Manpower Commission largely determined who would serve in the military, whose work was vital to the war effort, and when a worker could transfer from one job to another. When the war ended and regulations were lifted, workers demanded higher wages; the relations between labor and management became strained. Massive strikes and inflation followed in the closing days of the decade and many consumer goods were easier to find on the black market than on the store shelves until America retooled for a peacetime economy. The decade saw the flowering of composer Irving Berlin, the development of bebop, and the stirrings of rock 'n' roll. By 1948 the long-playing record was introduced, and the following year, *Billboard* substituted the phrase "rhythm and blues," for "race records."

The decade of the 1940s made America a world power and Americans more worldly. Millions served overseas; millions more listened to broadcasts concerning the war in London, Rome, and Tokyo. Newsreels brought the war home to moviegoers, who numbered in the millions. The war effort also redistributed the population and the demand for labor; the Pacific Coast gained wealth and power, and the South was able to supply its people with much-needed war jobs and provide blacks with opportunities previously closed to them. Women entered the work force in unprecedented numbers, reaching 18 million. The net cash income of the American farmer soared 400 percent.

But the Second World War exacted a price. Those who experienced combat entered a nightmarish world. Both sides possessed far greater firepower than ever before, and within those units actually fighting the enemy, the incidence of death was high, sometimes one in three. In all, the United States lost 405,000 men and women to combat deaths; many suffered in the war's final year, when the American army spearheaded the assault against Germany and Japan. The cost in dollars was $350 billion. But the cost was not only in American lives. Following Germany's unconditional surrender on May 4, 1945, Japan continued fighting. To prevent the loss of thousands of American lives defeating the Japanese, President Truman dropped atomic bombs on the Japanese cities of Hiroshima and Nagasaki, ending the war and ushering in the threat of "the bomb" as a key element of the Cold War during the 1950s and 1960s.

Throughout the war, soldiers from all corners of the nation fought side by side and refined nationalism and what it meant to America through this government-imposed mixing process. This newfound identity of American GIs was further cemented by the vivid descriptions of war correspondent Ernie Pyle, who spent a considerable time talking and living with the average soldier to present a "worm's eye view" of war. Yet, despite the closeness many men and women developed toward their fellow soldiers, spawning a wider view of the world, discrimination continued. African-American servicemen were excluded from the Marines, the Coast Guard, and the Army Corps. The regular army accepted blacks into the military—700,000 in all—only on a segregated basis. Only in the closing years of the decade would President Harry Truman lead the way toward a more integrated America by integrating the military. Sports attendance in the 1940s soared beyond the record levels of the 1920s; in football the T-formation moved in prominence; Joe DiMaggio, Ted Williams, and Stan Musial dominated baseball before and after the war, and Jackie Robinson became the first black in organized baseball. In 1946, Dr. Benjamin Spock's work, *Common Sense Baby and Child Care*, was published to guide newcomers in the booming business of raising babies. The decade also discovered the joys of fully air-conditioned stores for the first time, cellophane wrap, Morton salt, Daylight Saving Time, Dannon yogurt, Everglades National Park, the Cannes Film Festival, Michelin radial tires, Dial soap, and Nikon 35 mm film.

1942 PROFILE

As a key figure in the development of bebop and cool jazz, Charlie Christian perfected the single-string technique combined with amplification, and helped bring the guitar out of the rhythm section and into the forefront of the band as a solo instrument—all before he was 25 years old.

Life at Home

- The man who transformed the role of the guitar, Charlie Christian, grew up surrounded by music and musical instruments; as a pre-teen he danced and played in a quartet with his father and brothers.
- Born on July 29, 1916, in Bonham, Texas, Charles Henry Christian was the son of Clarence James and Willie Mae Booker Christian.
- Charlie's father played a wide variety of instruments and enjoyed a diverse musical palette; his mother was a musician and singer who played background music at the local silent movie houses.
- They taught their three sons to play a variety of instruments and popular songs of the day.
- When Charlie was a baby, his father would place small stringed instruments next to the child and let him explore the sonority.
- In the fall of 1918, when Charlie was two, his father was struck blind from fever and moved the family to Oklahoma City to find work.
- As the child grew, so would the size of the instruments; he sampled the trumpet and the tenor saxophone, and played stringed instruments he made from a cigar box.
- Charlie attended Douglass Elementary School at Oklahoma City, where the music instructor, Miss Zelia Breaux, taught the children music appreciation, including the classics, and offered personal instruction.

Charlie Christian's technique with the guitar brought it out of the rhythm section and into the spotlight.

- By the time Charlie was a teenager, he was already proficient on the guitar, and used those skills as a street performer, or busker, playing music with his brothers for cash or clothing in the better neighborhoods of Oklahoma City.
- In 1936, Christian played shows in Dallas during the Texas Centennial and purchased his first electric guitar, a Gibson, in 1937 when he was 20.
- Beginning in the late 1800s, Orville Gibson built mandolins and guitars with a carved top design before he incorporated Gibson Mandolin and Guitar Co., Ltd in Kalamazoo, Michigan, in 1902.
- After years of success as a mandolin and "F Hole" archtop guitar manufacturer, in 1937 Gibson Guitars introduced their first electric guitar, the ES-150.
- Charlie's skills would transform how the guitar was viewed at the same time Louis Armstrong was demonstrating to young blacks that they could achieve financial, if not racial, equality through jazz.
- Duke Ellington was making his mark on a national radio broadcast originating from New York City; jazz was beginning to break down some racial barriers.
- Charlie also learned from his father the passion of baseball life, when the Negro Leagues offered a chance at financial freedom and racial pride.
- But it was local trumpeter James Simpson and guitarist Ralph "Bigfoot Chuck" Hamilton who boosted Charlie's career when they secretly taught him three popular songs: "Rose Room," "Tea For Two," and "Sweet Georgia Brown."
- When he was ready, Charlie wrangled an invitation to one of the many after-hours jam sessions along "Deep Deuce," Northeast Second Street in Oklahoma City, where his older brother Edward was already a regular.
- "Let Charles play one," they told Edward.
- Edward was reluctant, but when Charlie played all three new songs on the guitar that resulted in two encores, Deep Deuce was in an uproar.
- Charlie then coolly dismissed himself from the jam session; his mother knew about his success before he got home.
- From then on the young guitarist immersed himself in jazz, marijuana, and wearing fine clothes, like his hero Louis Armstrong.

Charlie's learned to love baseball from his father.

Life at Work

- By the time he turned 21, Charlie Christian and his guitar established a regional following in Oklahoma City.
- Heralded for his unique single-note soloing style, he jammed with many of the big-name performers traveling through Oklahoma City, including Teddy Wilson and Art Tatum, and toured with Alphonso Trent and his orchestra.
- It was Mary Lou Williams, pianist for Andy Kirk and His Clouds of Joy, who told New York record producer John Hammond about Charlie.
- She pronounced him the "greatest electric-guitar player" she'd ever heard and was instrumental in persuading Hammond to give Charlie an audition.
- Hammond was so blown away by what he heard, he orchestrated a surprise audition of Charlie with bandleader Benny Goodman, one of the biggest names in the business.
- Goodman was one of the few white bandleaders willing to hire black musicians for his live band presentations.
- Goodman had already made a musical statement when he hired Teddy Wilson on piano in 1935, and Lionel Hampton on vibraphone in 1936.
- At the time as the audition, Goodman was trying to buy out Floyd Smith's contract from Andy Kirk, but hired Charlie instead.
- Initially, the meeting between the young, shy Charlie and the famous bandleader did not go well, so Hammond arranged for Charlie to sit in with the Goodman band that night without consulting Goodman.
- Displeased at the surprise, Goodman called for "Rose Room," a tune he assumed that Christian would be unfamiliar with.
- Charlie had been reared on the tune, and when he came in with his solo, it was unlike anything Goodman had heard before.
- That version of "Rose Room" that night lasted 40 minutes—including some 20 distinctive solos from Charlie.
- As a member of the Goodman sextet, Charlie went from making $2.50 a night to making $150 a week, and joined talents as renowned as Lionel Hampton, Fletcher Henderson, Artie Bernstein, and Nick Fatool.
- In December 1939, *Downbeat Magazine* headlined the story "Guitar Men, Wake Up and Pluck! Wired for Sound, Let Them Hear You Play."
- Charlie was determined that the guitar would be a frontline band instrument like a saxophone or trumpet; in February 1940, Charlie Christian dominated the jazz and swing guitar polls and was elected to the Metronome All-Stars.
- By the spring of 1940, Goodman had reorganized his band to bring together Charlie Christian, Count Basie, Duke Ellington, Cootie Williams, Georgie Auld, and later, drummer Dave Tough.
- This all-star band reigned over the jazz polls in 1941, and brought another election for Christian to the Metronome All-Stars.
- Charlie's distinctive solos—which helped move the electric guitar into the forefront—were heavily influenced by horn players such as Lester Young and Herschel Evans, whose sounds had been influencing the frontline of jazz.

Benny Goodman was one of the few white bandleaders willing to hire black musicians.

- In addition, after his electric guitar was featured on recordings from 1939 to 1941, country and western music moved quickly to elevate the role of the guitar.
- Charlie wanted his guitar to sound like a tenor saxophone and helped to usher in a style later known as "bop" or "bebop."
- His use of tension and release, a technique present on "Stompin' at the Savoy," and his use of eighth-note passages, triplets and arpeggio all made a contribution to the sounds of early 1942.
- Many of these sounds were shared, cultivated and matured as a regular in the early-morning jam sessions at Minton's Playhouse in Harlem with Charlie Parker, Thelonious Monk, Dizzy Gillespie, and Kenny Clarke.
- Unfortunately, Charlie's brilliant career was cut short by tuberculosis.

The guitar was becoming a popular addition to many musical groups.

- Following several short hospital stays, Charlie was admitted to Seaview, a sanitarium on Staten Island in New York City.
- He was reported to be making progress, and *Downbeat Magazine* reported in February 1942 that he and Cootie Williams were starting a band.
- Charlie died March 2, 1942, at 25 years old.
- "Solo Flight," the Goodman hit featuring Charlie Christian, made the top of Billboard's Harlem Hit Parade in 1943.

Life in the Community: Oklahoma City, Oklahoma

- Oklahoma was born amidst the Native American relocation to the Oklahoma Territory in the 1820s, when the United States Government forced the Five Civilized Tribes to endure a difficult resettlement into the lands of Oklahoma.
- Much of the western lands of Oklahoma, were part of the "Unassigned Lands," including what is now Oklahoma City.
- These areas were settled by a variety of white pioneers in the late 1800s.
- Often settling on the land without permission, these pioneers were referred to as "Boomers," and eventually created enough pressure that the U.S. Government opted to hold a series of land runs for settlers to claim the land.

Oklahoma City skyline.

- On April 22, 1889, an estimated 50,000 settlers gathered at the boundaries; some, called "Sooners," snuck across early to claim some of the prime spots of land.
- Oklahoma City was immediately popular to the settlers as an estimated 10,000 people claimed land there.
- By 1900, the population in the Oklahoma City area had more than doubled, and out of those early tent cities, a metropolis was being born.
- Oklahoma became the forty-sixth state of the Union on November 16, 1907.
- As a result of oil speculation, Oklahoma grew exponentially in its early years, and by 1910 the capital of Oklahoma was moved to Oklahoma City as its population surpassed 60,000.
- Oklahoma City's various oil fields not only brought people to the city, but they also brought fresh ideas, giving rise to a vibrant music culture.
- Oklahoma City became a meeting place of different people for the blending of the songs and dance music of the American Indians, Anglo-Celtic ballads from the upland South, country blues from the Mississippi Delta, black and white spirituals from the lowland South, European immigrant music from Italy, Germany, and Czechoslovakia, polka music from the upper Midwest, and Mexican mariachi from the Rio Grande Valley.
- This cultural confluence of different genres of American music encouraged cross-cultural innovation and became the perfect breeding ground for the formulation of jazz styles.
- Deep Deuce, or Northeast Second Street, was the core for Oklahoma City jazz, harboring institutions such as the Aldridge Theater, Ruby's Grill, Richardson's Shoe Shine Parlor, and Rushing's Café—all of which catered to jazz musicians and enthusiasts.
- Uptown ballrooms, such as the Ritz, were also important outlets.
- In addition, in the 1920s and 1930s, numerous bands including the Jolly Harmony Boys, Pails of Rhythm, and Ideal Jazz Orchestra worked out of Oklahoma City.

"Boomers" who settled in Oklahoma without permission were often ejected by soldiers.

- This musical gumbo city produced many notable jazz artists, including Jimmy Rushing, Henry Bridges, Charlie Christian, and Don Cherry.
- Appropriately, jazz has been called "America's classical music," and was nurtured in many sections of the United States.
- Originally inspired by ragtime and folk songs, early jazz artists drew their musical inspiration from country dances, field hollers, work songs, and the blues.
- Oklahoma musicians were instrumental in the creation of the so-called "Kansas City" style of jazz, a bluesy dance music contrasting with the Dixieland ragtime of New Orleans, or the sounds dominating Chicago or New York.

HISTORICAL SNAPSHOT
1942

- The United States and The Philippines fought the Battle of Bataan as Manila was captured by Japanese forces and General Douglas MacArthur was forced to flee
- A German air-raid on Liverpool, England, destroyed the home of William Patrick Hitler, Adolf Hitler's nephew, who emigrated to the U.S. and joined the navy to fight against his uncle
- Japan declared war on The Netherlands and invaded The Netherlands East Indies
- The Americans made *Sikorsky R-4*, the first mass-produced helicopter during World War II
- Actress Carole Lombard and her mother were among those killed in a plane crash near Las Vegas, Nevada, while returning from a tour to promote the sale of War Bonds
- Nazis at the Wannsee conference in Berlin decided that the "final solution to the Jewish problem" was relocation and extermination

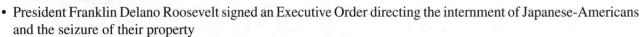

- President Franklin Delano Roosevelt signed an Executive Order directing the internment of Japanese-Americans and the seizure of their property
- Daylight saving time went into effect in the U.S.
- *The Voice of America* began broadcasting
- *How Green Was My Valley* won best picture at the 14th Academy Awards ceremony
- The Nazi German extermination camp Bełżec opened in occupied Poland; between March and December 1942, at least 434,508 people were killed
- The FCC required TV stations to cut airplay from 15 hours to four hours a week during the war
- Tokyo was bombed by B-25 Mitchells commanded by Lieutenant Colonel James Doolittle
- The Battle of the Coral Sea, which ended in an Allied victory, was the first battle in naval history in which two enemy fleets fought without seeing each other
- Aaron Copland's *Lincoln Portrait* was performed for the first time by the Cincinnati Symphony Orchestra
- The first African-American seamen were taken into the U.S. Navy
- At the Battle of Midway, the Japanese naval advance in the Pacific was slowed
- On her thirteenth birthday, Anne Frank made the first entry in her new diary
- Walt Disney's animated film *Bambi* premiered
- Mohandas Gandhi was arrested in Bombay by British forces
- A Japanese floatplane dropped incendiary devices at Mount Emily, near Brookings, Oregon, in the first of two "Lookout Air Raids," the first bombing of the continental United States
- Award-winning composer and Hollywood songwriter Ralph Rainger ("Thanks for the Memory") was among 12 people killed in the midair collision between an American Airlines DC-3 airliner and a U.S. Army bomber
- In the naval Battle of Guadalcanal, the U.S. Navy suffered heavy losses, but retained control of Guadalcanal
- The movie *Casablanca* premiered at the Hollywood Theater in New York City
- Gasoline rationing began in the U.S.
- DDT was first used as a pesticide

Selected Prices

Ashtray	$8.50
Automobile, De Soto	$2,200.00
Barbell	$8.95
Electric Food Liquidizer	$35.00
Guitar	$8.45
Home Permanent Kit	$1.40
Mattress	$54.50
Radio Phonograph	$199.95
Record Cabinet	$13.50
Trombone	$12.50

Light as A Fiddle

It's the New SOPRANI AMPLIPHONIC *Midget* GRAND

This new Soprani Ampliphonic "Midget Grand" is actually smaller, and much lighter, than most 12 bass accordions. Yet it has 34 treble and 90 bass keys, giving complete range, the most beautiful tone, and positively amazing volume!

This reduction in size and weight, made possible by Soprani's patented Ampliphonic reed block, triples the fun and the ease of playing for recreation, enjoyment, profit. Ideal for boys and girls, men and women. See, try this new Soprani "Midget Grand" at your dealer's, or write for illustrated description and complete details. No obligation. Send coupon now.

TO SALUTE YOUR ACTIVE DUTY

TO GO EVERYWHERE WITH YOUR NEW FALL SUIT

TO BE GAY COMPANIONS FOR AFTER-FIVE FUN

VAGABOND No. 8

OUR CLASSIC COLLECTION OF THE NEW

RED CROSS SHOES

They're designed for the new times . . . your new life. For walking and working and playing . . . for keeping your spirits high and your step young. Come in, choose your complete fall shoe wardrobe from our collection of trim, tailored, classic Red Cross Shoes. Every perfect-fitting pair an amazing value.

America's unchallenged shoe value

$6.95

Globman's

"WE MADE A GREAT DISCOVERY"

Say the "Hopkins Twins!"

HOLLYWOOD'S FAMOUS HOPKINS TWINS

—winners of sixteen National and four World swimming records—Stars of San Francisco's "Aquacade"—and now starring in "Faster Follies of 1941" which is touring the United States and Canada.

TWINS don't always agree—but for once we're unanimous—that Baby Ruth helps give us that quick pick-up in pep we need in the strenuous, energy-draining sport of competitive swimming. Wholesome, delicious Curtiss

CURTISS CANDY
Baby Ruth

"As a Matter of Record," Jeff Davis, *San Antonio Light*, November 5, 1939:

Probably one of the most talked of new talent finds of the year will be a young Oklahoman named Charlie Christian, whose work on the electric guitar is nothing short of inspired.

Christian is to be heard in Benny Goodman's Sextette, which includes Christian, Goodman, Arthur Bernstein, Fletcher Henderson, Nick Fatool and Lionel Hampton. It is a brilliant aggregation. Christian sounds like a tenor sax in single-string work, and like an entire band on his chords. They debut with "Flying Home," and "Rose Room." It is a Columbia Record.

"Pearl Harbor Ended Her Musical Cruises," Jobyna Carpenter, *Reminisce*, January/February 2002:

In 1941, I needed a summer job to earn money for my last year in music at the University of Washington. So when a friend, Helen Hart, asked my sister Yvonne and me to join her on a cruise from Seattle to Nome, Alaska, we accepted. What an opportunity!

As musicians aboard the *SS Baranof*, Helen played piano, Yvonne the trumpet; I played sax and clarinet.

It turned out we made several trips that year, and I never got home in time to sign up for school. That ended my college career, but after December 7, many careers were interrupted.

Our first trip that summer was quite an event. We left Seattle about 4 p.m. and played our first dinner program.

Afterward, we were served dinner. We could order anything on the menu, and the food was delicious.

The evening dance started after dinner, and we performed from 8 p.m. to midnight. For dancing, we played peppy songs like "Five Foot Two," "It Had To Be You," "Under A Blanket of Blue" and "Four Leaf Clover."

The next day we had played three lunch programs, but by dinner, Yvonne and I became very seasick. Helen, who never got seasick, played piano for the people who showed up at dinner.

During the five days it took to get to Dutch Harbor in the Aleutian Islands, the crew gave sis and me food they thought would make us feel better—crackers, apples, coffee—but nothing helped. After we were docked in Dutch Harbor for a few days, we got our "sea legs" and never got sick again.

There was only one other lady on the crew, the nurse, so we had lots of invites to go ashore with nice-looking fellows, crew members and passengers. Helen ended up marrying the ship's barber!

When we arrived at Nome, there were no docks to tie up to and the water was very rough. It was a fun experience when we were finally allowed ashore. The crew had us sit on a bale of hay, then hoisted us and the bale into the air, and swung us onto a tug boat that was tied alongside.

We were in Nome for several days, so we took our instruments ashore and played for the people there.

The most interesting and exciting cruise was also our last. It was December, and while at sea on December 7, we were playing a lunch program when the ship's radio operator came in to listen.

Since he was always kidding with us, we thought he was joking when he said that the Japanese attacked Pearl Harbor.

He became very serious, though, and said that Captain Ramsauer was going to announce the attack to the passengers after lunch. After the captain's announcement, he ordered everyone to take part in a fire drill.

The next day, the ship was docked at the nearest inlet. We were given brushes and buckets of black paint and told to help paint the ship's windows so no light would show through.

That also ended our music. We would not be playing again because the sound of the music carried over the water, and submarines had been sighted in those waters.

"Dave Rose Arranged His Way to Film, Radio Fame," Robert Bagar, *Movie-Radio Guide*, October 10, 1942:

Dave Rose was tinkling away at a piano for all he was worth with a band in Chicago some years ago. A saxophone player, during an intermission, complained that he had lost his part. The musicians all looked high and low, but it was no use; it was gone.

The leader of the outfit asked Rose to try to fill in the missing lines for the despairing saxophonist. He did. And so well that from that moment he became the band's arranger. He got a reputation for the unusual color effects of his orchestrations, and soon his work was much in demand.

He went with Ted Fio-Rito's Orchestra as pianist and arranger, remaining with the group for a year. After that he became a staff pianist at NBC's Chicago station. It was Roy Shield who shifted him to the position of staff arranger.

In 1938, Rose gave up his Chicago job to accept what he thought was an offer to write and arrange music for Hollywood films. However, when he got to the film capital, he discovered that he had been the victim of a hoax. There was no job. Making the best of a bad bargain, he decided to remain in Hollywood and look around for something to do. But in practically no time at all, as his fortune decreed, he was making arrangements for the well-known singing stars of filmland Dorothy Lamour, Jeanette McDonald, Martha Raye, Don Ameche and others.

Subsequently, he was appointed music director of the Los Angeles radio station, a post that provided him with complete artistic freedom, and that was the real beginning of his batonistic career, which is currently being sustained through his directorship of the Ginny Simms-Philip Morris *Johnny Presents* show over NBC Tuesday.

Rose was born in London, but he came to this country with his parents when he was four. He spent his early years in and around Chicago and obtained his musical education at the Chicago Musical College. While a student there, he composed three tone-poems, "Ensenada Escapade," "Shadows," and "Swing Etude," all three of which were premiered by the Chicago Symphony Orchestra.

Dave Rose is a teacher of student pilots for the U.S. Army, a job that takes four days each week, being an exceptional flyer. He composes, arranges until all hours of the morning. He hopes to write the great American symphony someday.

1945 PROFILE

Trombonist Helen Elizabeth Jones was a diminutive star in the all-girl traveling band, The International Sweethearts of Rhythm, which was formed to raise money for their impoverished Mississippi school.

Life at Home

- Helen Elizabeth Jones was born in Meridian, Mississippi, in 1923 and initially placed in a white orphanage.
- She was removed when it became obvious that Helen was of mixed racial parentage and was no longer eligible to be in a white institution in the Jim Crow South.
- At three, she was adopted by Lawrence Clifton Jones, the founder of the Piney Wood Country Life School, and his wife Grace Morris Allen Jones.
- From then on her history became deeply entwined in the development of the school and the activities her adoptive father, Lawrence Jones.
- The oldest of four children, Lawrence Jones was born in St. Joseph, Missouri, in 1882, and was 44 when he rescued Helen.
- His father was a hotel porter and his mother an industrious and practical homemaker and seamstress.
- Spurred by his parents' dreams of self-improvement, Lawrence Jones became the first Negro graduate from the University of Iowa in 1907.

Helen Jones played trombone in The International Sweethearts of Rhythm.

- His wife, Grace Morris Allen Jones, grew up in Burlington, Iowa, and studied at the Chicago Conservatory of Music.
- The couple met at a missionary society function during Jones's junior year, and they married in 1912.
- Piney Woods Country Life School had begun three years earlier with Jones teaching one student sitting on a log underneath a cedar tree.
- Formerly occupied by sheep, snakes and weeds, the school was fully operational by New Year's Day 1910.
- A prominent local African-American farmer donated the shed, 40 acres of land, and added $50 in cash—at a time when a hammer cost $0.66.
- Students cleared the grounds and made the necessary repairs and improvements to the building.
- By the close of the first full school year, Jones had secured the services of five teachers, enrolled 85 students, and laid the foundation for the first school building.

Laurence Jones adopted Helen when she was three years old.

- For the school year 1912-1913, the Piney Woods' income was $3,269 against expenses of $3,617, leaving the school $348 in debt.
- At that time, the average annual income for black teachers was $311 per year.
- The State of Mississippi paid an average of $10.60 per year to educate each white child, while paying $2.26 per black child.
- In 1913, Piney Woods Country Life School officially received its charter from the State of Mississippi.
- Its mission, according to the charter of incorporation, was to establish, develop and maintain a country life school in which to train "the head, heart and hands of boys and girls for a life of Christianity, character and service."
- To meet the needs of all families, Piney Woods School allowed children with no financial means to work at the school to earn the $12 monthly tuition.
- Everyone enrolled at Piney Woods worked to support the institution through home economics endeavors or industrial arts, farming or forestry.
- Jones agreed with Booker T. Washington's decree that "no race can prosper until it learns there is as much dignity in tilling a field as in writing a poem."
- After the sudden death of her adoptive mother in 1929, six-year-old Helen became part of the general student population of the school.
- Since the 1920s, Dr. Jones had been sending choral groups on tour—following a model established by Fisk University—to bring in money and give the musicians a wider view of the world.
- Helen got her first exposure to the music world in the mid-1930s when she toured with the school's Cotton Blossom Sisters, performing plantation songs like "Old Black Joe" and "Carry Me Back to Old Virginny."
- To increase the school's fundraising, in 1937 Dr. Jones decided to form an all-girl swing band composed of students; the Swing Era had pulled big band jazz into the forefront of American music again.
- The best female musicians were chosen from the concert and marching bands to perform for the International Sweethearts of Rhythm.
- Dr. Jones chose to use "international" because many of the girls were of mixed parentage, and he thought it reflected a global vision; the students included American blacks, Native Americans, Mexicans, Chinese and Puerto Ricans.
- The 15-piece band took to the road during the 1938-1939 school year, first touring their home state to attract other musically inclined students to Piney Woods.

- Most of the students who traditionally entered the school had never played a musical instrument, could not read music, had never seen an orchestra or performed in public.
- Seventeen-year-old Helen played the trombone and traveled extensively through Tennessee, Alabama, Louisiana, Arkansas and Texas in a specially designed semi-trailer equipped with Pullman beds, laboratory facilities, a kitchenette, and closets for each performer.
- In the segregated South, where few black motels existed, such facilities were essential to the survival of the troupe.

Most young children discovered music in school.

- The International Sweethearts of Rhythm shows were so successful that professional musicians asked to join the band.

Life at Work

- Helen Jones and the International Sweethearts of Rhythm were originally led by Consuela Carter, who graduated from Piney Woods in 1927 and remained with the institution for 15 years.
- Under Carter's direction, Helen and the other girls—all between the ages of 14 and 19—began to climb toward national recognition.
- The dance music combined African rhythms, Indian war dancing and the charm of the Orient.
- Indicative of the band's rise in popularity, in September 1940 they played nine engagements in 11 days, including dates in Alexandria, Emporia, Petersburg and Martinsville, Virginia.
- By December 1940, they were ranked 11th in the Number One Fan poll held by the black-owned *Chicago Defender* newspaper.

The International Sweethearts of Rhythm early in their career.

- On and off the bandstand, chaperone Rae Lee Jones demanded that the girls exude professionalism and refinement; contact with the audience was limited to protect their reputations and virtue.
- Renowned trumpet player Jean Starr was the first of many established performers to express an interest in joining the Sweethearts.

- In early 1941, negotiations were underway for Helen and the International Sweethearts of Rhythm to film two movie shorts in Hollywood.
- Daniel Gary, a Washington, DC, agent with business savvy and vision, was hired to handle bookings.
- Rated as one of the nation's best draws by January 1941, the Sweethearts had broken box office records at both Cincinnati's Cotton Club and DC's Howard Theatre.
- The original Sweethearts had proven that they could survive the arduous touring, and working together without bickering, petty jealousies and hostilities against one another.
- The young women who had entered Piney Woods with the simple aspiration to acquire a basic education and the skills for just bookkeeping or stenography were competing with Count Basie and Duke Ellington in the popularity polls.
- But trouble was brewing.
- In the beginning, it was proposed that the Sweethearts would tour only during the summer months, returning to classes in the fall.
- However, as their popularity grew, they were soon touring year round and traveling extensively without the benefit of school.
- Helen and each of the Sweethearts were allotted only $2.00 a week in wages and $0.50 a day for traveling expenses, while they earned thousands of dollars for the school's coffers.

The International Sweethearts of Rhythm changed their look as their popularity increased.

- Then, when several seniors were told they would not receive their high school diplomas because they had missed too many classes, the girls began to openly question the motives of the administration concerning their personal academic development.
- Also, strong disagreement between chaperone Rae Lee Jones and founder Dr. Lawrence Jones over operational procedures bubbled to the surface.
- In April 1941, the 17 attractive and talented young women, including the school founder's adopted daughter Helen Jones, broke their affiliation with the Piney Woods Country Life School.
- The school attempted to have the orchestra arrested for stealing the school bus, but failed.
- The group fled to Washington, DC, where booking agent Daniel Gary secured the option on a house at 908 S. Quinn Street in Arlington, Virginia, as their headquarters.
- After three months of grueling rehearsals under new music director Eddie Durham, the Sweethearts made their professional debut at the Howard Theatre in Washington, DC, in late August 1941.
- Two weeks later, they headlined an all-female review at New York's famous Apollo Theater, where they received rave reviews.
- By 1944, the Sweethearts were ranked by *DownBeat Magazine* as the number one all-girl orchestra in the nation.
- When World War II ended a year later, the State Department was bombarded by requests for the Sweethearts by GIs who remained in Germany with the U.S. occupation forces.
- So on July 15, 1945, Helen Jones and the band, attired in their USO uniforms, sailed for Europe to entertain the troops; during the previous four years, 4,500 entertainers had participated in USO Camp Shows scattered across the war fronts of the world.
- The Sweethearts' tour lasted six months, entertaining primarily the third Army and the seventh Army, where they performed their unique sound in venues large and small and on radio.
- And they always left the men dancing in the aisles.

Wartime Entertainers

- The United States entered World War II only months after the International Sweethearts of Rhythm broke with the Piney Woods Country Life School and turned professional.
- Despite being well established, touring was difficult.
- The creation of all-female ensembles was seen by some detractors as novelty acts to be admired more for their looks than for their musical ability.
- At the same time, male musicians defined jazz as essentially a male activity and thought that girl bands like the International Sweethearts of Rhythm lacked the power and drive to blow hot jazz.
- Plus, hotel accommodations for racially diverse groups such as the Sweethearts were virtually out of the question in most of the nation.

Many male jazz musicians did not take female bands seriously.

- On one occasion in El Paso, Texas, Jewish saxophone player Roz Cron was arrested and held overnight in jail for being a member of a racially integrated group.
- On such occasions, the white girls pretended to be racially mixed, claiming that their fathers were white and their mothers were black, as this arrangement would seem more acceptable.
- White trumpeter and bassist Toby Butler related that these experiences helped her mature emotionally, providing her with a greater understanding of the black experience.
- Responding to the needs of a nation at war, in September 1942, 38-year-old Glenn Miller disbanded his popular and successful swing orchestra to enlist in the Army.
- Miller, like nearly every other patriotic American, felt obliged to lend as much support to the war effort as possible.
- He would turn his music toward a wartime ideal that would affect millions of young people nationwide.
- However, not all musicians shared Miller's zeal to serve America in its hour of need.
- Some sought to avoid the draft by hatching schemes which ranged from drug use to professing homosexuality—often with mixed results.
- In 1943, just as young Frank Sinatra's star was ascending, he was declared ineligible for military service and the activities of his fervent female fans were scandalizing the nation.
- The swooning young women displayed their passion for Sinatra by tossing their undergarments onto the stage when Frank performed.
- Labeled a 4-F slacker by enlisted men, Sinatra was hated by GIs irate with his draft status.
- At the New York Paramount Theater, where Sinatra was performing, sailors yelled from the audience, "Hey, wop, why aren't you in uniform?"
- In response to his own personal experiences with intolerance, Sinatra became an early crusader for racial equality, often speaking and performing at high schools where racial incidents had occurred.

Female musicians often worked harder than their male counterparts.

HISTORICAL SNAPSHOT
1945

- The evacuation of Auschwitz concentration camp opened the eyes of the world to the Holocaust
- Franklin D. Roosevelt was inaugurated to an unprecedented fourth term as president of the United States
- Eddie Slovik was executed by firing squad for desertion, the first American soldier since the American Civil War to be executed for this offense
- President Roosevelt and British Prime Minister Winston Churchill met with Soviet leader Joseph Stalin at the Yalta Conference
- About 30,000 U.S. Marines landed on Iwo Jima where a group of Marines were photographed raising the American flag by Joe Rosenthal
- Jewish Dutch diarist Anne Frank died of typhus in the Bergen-Belsen concentration camp
- American B-29 bombers attacked Tokyo, Japan, with incendiary bombs, killing 100,000 citizens
- The 17th Academy Awards ceremony was broadcast via radio for the first time; Best Picture was awarded to *Going My Way*
- Cartoon character Sylvester the cat debuted in *Life with Feathers*
- Adolf Hitler, along with his new wife Eva Braun, committed suicide
- Hamburg Radio announced that Hitler had died in battle, "fighting up to his last breath against Bolshevism"
- President Roosevelt died suddenly at Warm Springs, Georgia; Vice President Harry S. Truman became the 33rd President, serving until 1953
- Rodgers and Hammerstein's *Carousel*, a musical play based on Ferenc Molnár's *Liliom*, opened on Broadway and became their second long-running stage classic
- The Western Allies rejected any offer of surrender by Germany other than unconditional on all fronts
- Ezra Pound, poet and author, was arrested by American soldiers in Italy for treason
- A Japanese balloon bomb killed five children and a woman near Bly, Oregon, when it exploded as they dragged it from the woods; they were the only people killed by an enemy attack on the American mainland during World War II
- Trinity Test, the first of an atomic bomb, required about six kilograms of plutonium, succeeded in unleashing an explosion equivalent to that of 19 kilotons of TNT
- Winston Churchill resigned as the United Kingdom's Prime Minister after his Conservative Party was soundly defeated by the Labour Party in the 1945 general election
- A United States B-29 Superfortress, the *Enola Gay*, dropped an atomic bomb, codenamed "Little Boy," on Hiroshima, Japan
- The Zionist World Congress approached the British Government to discuss the founding of the country of Israel
- Arthur C. Clarke promoted the idea of a communications satellite in a *Wireless World* magazine article
- At Gimbels Department Store in New York City, the first ballpoint pens went on sale at $12.50 each
- John H. Johnson published the first issue of the magazine *Ebony*
- The Nag Hammadi scriptures were discovered
- The Berklee College of Music was founded in Boston, Massachusetts
- At the Mayo Clinic, streptomycin was first used to treat tuberculosis
- Percy Spencer accidentally discovered that microwaves can heat food, leading to the invention of the microwave oven
- The herbicide 2,4-D was introduced

Selected Prices

Deep Freezer	$225.00
Fountain Pen	$15.00
Harmonica	$1.79
Hotel Chesterfield, New York, per Day	$2.50
Ouija Board	$2.00
Pressure Cooker	$10.50
Records, Four 12"	$4.72
Silk Stockings	$0.98
Trumpet	$135.00
Whiskey, Seagram's, Fifth	$2.70

Popular Board Games for All Ages

AN INVENTOR LOOKS INTO THE FUTURE

WAR ENDS

Now IS THE TIME INVENTORS SHOULD PREPARE TO CASH IN!

Many times IN THE PAST, big manufacturers have hesitated to buy a worthwhile patent because it might mean re-tooling and a new set-up of their entire plants. TODAY, those same manufacturers have scrapped their expensive dies, their intricate machines to convert to war work. TOMORROW, they'll be receptive as never before to devices which will *save them time, save them money and save them labor.* Far-sighted inventors are right now preparing for a vast patent-buying era by having their patent applications prepared and prosecuted NOW. These times offer an absolutely unique opportunity for YOU MEN WITH IDEAS.

Send today for FREE BOOKS

Plainly written books which tell you, step by step, how to safeguard your invention, how to sell it. With books we also send important "Evidence of Invention" form.

44 YEARS' EXPERIENCE HELPING MEN LIKE YOU!

No matter how good your invention may be, its commercial value depends upon the careful preparation of the patent covering it. This strong firm of Registered Patent Attorneys has helped and wisely advised individual inventors for almost half a century. WE CAN HELP YOU!

SEND COUPON NOW!

VICTOR J. EVANS & Co.

Registered Patent Attorneys
640-L Merlin Building,
Washington, D. C.

Please rush books and "Evidence of Invention" form, without cost or obligation.

Name_____

Address_____

City and State_____

all our friends

something new has been added...

it's BEAR CREEK *Gardens*

BEAR CREEK GARDENS is Harry and David in the flower business. How come? Well, you see, our Bear Creek Country is also one of Mother Nature's favorite bulb-'n-flower growing districts. And lots of folks have asked if we couldn't do as nice things for their gardens as our Royal Riviera Pears * do for their tables.

So . . . *starting next January we'll be able to offer you*—
Bulbs that will grow the biggest, by-goshest Begonias you ever dreamed of . . . The most gorgeous, gladdest Gladiolus you ever laid eyes on . . . The dandiest dilly-Dahlias that grow. And America's 1st-prize-winning Roses, too. Don't plant other flowers too close. They'll turn green with envy! . . . and we'll have *lots* of other wonderful bulbs and seeds . . . striking handwoven hanging baskets . . . a strawberry barrel . . . and garden gadgets.

Even if you don't know a petunia from a baked potato, we'll have things YOU can grow to handsome-up your home or garden! Every one fully guaranteed and backed by our reputation for shipping only the finest.

Best of all YOU'LL GET THE VERY FINEST BULBS 'N BUSHES AT THE BEST BARGAIN PRICES YOU EVER SAW. HONEST!

Sound good? Then just fill in the reverse side of this card and send it scootin' back to us (we pay postage). In January — we'll send you our brand new baby — the Bear Creek Gardens catalog.

Then, when you've had time to make your selections, there'll be plenty of time to order your flowers that bloom in the spring, Tra-la

Harry and David at Bear Creek Gardens Medford, Oregon

For FREE Catalog fill out postpaid card on other...

On our troopship bound for Europe in April 1945, the only place where I and a few other guys could play our "hillbilly" music was the latrine. The toilet was a long trough through which sea water was pumped. Crude wooden seats were fastened to the top. So while we sat on those seats pickin' and grinnin', water trickled between us like a babbling brook.

—David Massey, Raleigh, North Carolina

"Here Comes the Band!" *The Etude*, August 1945:

The days when troops went into combat with the roll of guns and the blare of trumpets are gone. They do not advertise their approach with music, now. Every bandsman must undergo basic military field training. When the steel begins to fly, the bandsmen are called into action just as any other G.I. Joes….

Music is a powerful morale factor in the life of G.I. Joe at the fighting front. Realizing this, the Army trains its bands to follow the troops to the combat zone, so that battle-weary men may be entertained by music which runs the gamut from boogie-woogie to symphonic concerts.

The first duty of the bandsman is to be a good soldier, and at Camp Lee's Army Service Forces Training Center, the 326th and in 328 ASF bands receive battle conditioning training no less rugged than Quartermaster troops who drive trucks, work in laundry units, or in any of the other specialized Quartermaster fields.

The obstacle courses, hiking, rifle marksmanship, and long hours of drilling are no strangers to Camp Lee bandsmen. But in addition to these basic duties, they play for retreat parades and other army functions, maintain a regular schedule of concerts, and are called upon for such diversified tasks as presenting their talent to boost the sale of War Bonds.

Recently, the band spent two weeks in A.P. Hill Military Reservation, near Fredericksburg, Virginia, where they learned to operate in the field under simulated battle conditions. They took forced marches, learned how to solve compass and combat problems, lived in "pup" tents, ate from mess gear, wore gas masks, steel helmets, and carried automatic pistols at all times. The regular schedule was supplemented by two open-air Sunday concerts for the trainees, and two concerts for soldiers confined at the Reservation's Station Hospital.

"Novel Orchestra Will Play for Dance of Moose," *Muscatine Journal and News-Tribune*, (Iowa) April 4, 1945:

Rated as one of the greatest box office attractions in the nature of dance bands, the International Sweethearts of Rhythm, an all-girl orchestra, will provide music for a dance to be held in Muscatine Lodge Number 388, Loyal Order of Moose, Thursday night.

The orchestra includes 16 versatile and talented musicians, plus the director, Anna Mae Winburn, who fronts and sings, and Evelyn McGee, vocalist.

The orchestra is made up of Negro, American Indian, Chinese and Mexican nationalities, and was first organized as a unit to play popular music at the Piney Woods School in Piney Woods, Mississippi. The band was so outstanding, the girls decided to go professional, and they jumped to national fame within a year.

The girls have already traveled through 38 states of the nation as a proving ground for their rhythmical wares, and have been called the "Greatest Musical Novelty of the Century" by many who have heard them.

The International Sweethearts of Rhythm played before a crowd of 10,000 in an "swing battle" at the largest annual Negro festival in the nation last year, and it was proved the girls could put out music equal to their musical brothers in open competition.

One of the chief reasons contributing to the success of this girl orchestra is the girls lived together harmoniously at the school for several years before the band was formed.

The dance is only for members of the Moose, their wives or sweethearts, and admission is by presentation of a paid-up membership card.

1945 NEWS FEATURE

"The Music of the North American Indians," Anna Heuermann Hamilton
The Etude, July 1945:

In the early days in America, Indian music was not considered music by the white man, but rather a haphazard noise used in a haphazard way. Then, in 1794, James Hewitt, English violinist, immigrant (whose birth and death years coincide with those of Beethoven), wrote an opera on Indian themes. That opera was called *Tammany*. It was a surprise to learn that Tammany was name of a friendly chief of the Delaware tribe. The Library of Congress contains the libretto of that opera, but the score has been lost.

Nothing more is recorded about Indian music until, in 1880, a young New Yorker named Theodore Baker was studying in Germany. For the thesis required for his Ph.D., he had a brilliant idea: Why not investigate this noise the Indians make, and try to discover whether it is really haphazard or whether there are principles underlying it? So he approached the Seneca of his native state, was adopted into the tribe, and was given every opportunity for investigation. The result was the thesis written in German: "Concerning the Music of North American Wild Men."

It seems that Dr. Baker did not pursue the subject further, being content with having opened it up; he left it to others to carry on.

The Peabody Museum of American Archaeology and Etymology is connected with Harvard University. Miss Alice C. Fletcher became interested in the work of the museum, and for a number of years carried on investigations among several tribes of Indians. In the beginning, her studies were not connected with music. But while among the Indians, she suffered a severe attack of rheumatism which eventually lamed her for life. While she lay on her bed week after week, anxious Indians came every day to sing to her. She was fascinated by the music, and on recovery began recording it, first by ear and then by the aid of a phonograph. Her paper on Indian music at the Anthropological Congress in Chicago in 1893 inaugurated a work that is enriching the music of the world.

Inspired by Miss Fletcher's revelations, Miss Francis Densmore, pianist and lecturer on musical subjects, turned her attention to Indian music and made a lifetime study of it. Her work was done for the Bureau of American Ethnology of the Smithsonian Institution. Her original records are in the National Archives. The number of records that have been transcribed into musical notations is 2,632; there are many more that still await transcribing. The Smithsonian has published a number of Miss Densmore's books, illustrated with such recordings.

Miss Densmore relates that once, after a record of a song had been made by an old woman, the woman desired to hear the result. As the record was being played, she asked: "How did the phonograph learn that song so quickly? It is a hard song."

In one respect, the music reminds us of the ancient Irish music: It is coextensive with the life of the people. Every public ceremony and every important event in the life of the people have their own peculiar song, such as fasting and prayer, setting of traps, hunting, courtship, playing of games, facing death.

Some of the music has beauty of a peculiarly affecting kind; much of the music arouses wonder and admiration. Some songs have no words, vocables being used, but that does not prevent their being understood by the Indians. There is plural singing in two or three octaves—each singer using his or her natural range. Men and women with good voices lead the singing.

Songs are the property of clans, societies, individuals. In ceremonial songs, accuracy is absolutely indispensable. Such songs are appeals to the Creator, and the path must be straight or the songs will not reach their goal, and evil will result. So, when a mistake is made, the singers will stop at once; either the song or the whole ceremony is repeated, or a rite of penance is enacted. Then the ceremony may proceed.

Women compose the lullabies. But the Indian braves have not a high regard for the women's singing. When asked about the lullabies, the men said: "Yes, the women have a noise to make children sleep, but that is not music."

The instruments are drums of various sizes and structure; whistles of bone, wood or pottery, some producing two or more tones; Pandean pipes; notched sticks rasped together; rattles of cords or bones; and flutes.

On the whole, the music gives the impression of being in the minor mode, but when examined, much of it proves to be in the major. Rhythms vary greatly, and much mixed rhythm is used. We are familiar with all of this. But the Indians have one practice that is quite foreign to us; in some of their music, not only the rhythm but the time of song and accompaniment differ. It seems as if each, the singer and the player, proceed on its way regardless of the other. The song may have 96 quarter-notes in a minute, and the accompaniment 120 quarter-notes in the same time. Reduced to its lowest terms, this means that the singer produces four beats while the accompaniment produces five and one-quarter beats. This is not accidental, for in making a number of recordings several days apart of the same song, the result will always be the same. This is an accomplishment not yet acquired by white musicians.

1949 PROFILE

Martin Block, in a novel proposal, suggested to his boss at WNEW that phonograph records rather than live music be played between the bulletins of the Lindbergh baby kidnapping trial, accompanied by Martin's commentary.

Life at Home

- For Martin Block, the trial of the century was also the opportunity of a lifetime.
- Bruno Richard Hauptmann was on trial for the kidnapping and murder of Charles A. Lindbergh's infant son, and New York radio station WNEW was the only station inside the courthouse.
- Unfortunately, the on-site reporter and engineer were not set up to carry minute-by-minute coverage of the six-week-long trial, despite extraordinarily high interest nationwide.
- If WNEW switched its broadcasting schedule to feature an orchestral remote, it might lose its logistical advantage and miss a chance to broadcast the latest kidnapping news.
- So in January 1935, Martin proposed to his boss that phonograph records be played between the bulletins, accompanied by Martin's commentary.
- Playing records was something that respectable radio stations hardly ever did; WNEW prided itself on broadcasting live music.
- After all, why would listeners turn on the radio if they could play the record itself?
- Besides, many of the nation's top performing artists refused to allow their records to be played on radio, fearing reduced sales.

Martin Block became the first disc jockey by playing records, rather than live music, between news of the Lindbergh kidnapping trial.

- After the part-time, $25-per-week broadcaster gained approval, Martin faced another hurdle: WNEW didn't own any records.
- So he trotted out to the nearest Liberty Record Shop and bought five of them, all by Clyde McCoy, and quickly demonstrated that records—played by a knowledgeable disc jockey—were the future of radio.
- Martin's intimate, personalized approach attracted thousands of listeners to the broadcast—especially housewives—who now had a friend to talk to them as they washed the dishes or completed their sewing.
- The world's first radio disc jockey was Ray Newby, of Stockton, California.

Respectable radio stations prided themselves on broadcasting live music.

- In 1909, at 16 years of age, Newby began regularly playing records on a small spark transmitter while a student at Herrold College of Engineering and Wireless, located in San Jose, California, under the authority of radio pioneer Charles "Doc" Herrold.
- He played popular records, mainly Caruso records from various operas, because they were very good music but also loud enough to overcome the primitive equipment.
- By 1910, regular radio broadcasting had started to use "live" as well as pre-recorded sound; programming typically included comedy, drama, news, music, and sports reporting.
- Martin Block was born February 3, 1903, in Los Angeles, California, and began his career in sales as a youngster, peddling razor blades and potato peelers off a sound truck on Broadway.
- At age 13, he became an office boy at General Electric.
- By the early 1930s, Martin got his first radio job with a small outfit in Tijuana and then worked his way up to Los Angeles.
- There, in 1932, Al Jarvis of KFWB, was building a reputation with a radio-record show called *The World's Biggest Make-Believe Ballroom*.
- Jarvis would play several records in a row by the same artist while painting a picture for his listeners of this music wafting over a sparkling dance floor.
- Three years later and now working in New York, Martin envisioned a WNEW show on the same model, even after the sales staff balked, claiming no sponsor would buy time for a program of pre-recorded music.
- So Martin found his own sponsor: the makers of Retardo pills, a harmless if useless weight loss gimmick that sold for $1 a box.
- "Ladies," Martin would purr into the microphone, "be fair to your husband by taking the reducing pill."
- A week later, Martin and WNEW claimed Retardo had received 3,750 responses, and soon enough there was little doubt the show was a hit.
- The term "disc jockey" was created to describe Martin's style and New York housewives had a friend.
- Within a few years, *The World's Biggest Make-Believe Ballroom* commanded a remarkable 25 percent of the radio audience.

Life at Work

- Radio broadcaster Martin Block's success with the New York-based *Make Believe Ballroom* was propelled by his casual style—similar to that used by President Franklin Roosevelt in his fireside chats—and his ability to make every listener believe he was talking to him or her personally.
- During the broadcasts, he even appeared to chat with the band members, even though the sounds was entirely encased in shellac.
- One sponsor, who doubted that people would actually tune in to the radio program to hear the same records that could be played at home, tested Martin's appeal by offering refrigerators at a deep discount in the middle of a major snowstorm—but only if listeners came immediately to the store.
- One hundred nine customers showed up right away in the midst of the storm and the sponsor was sold; soon Martin possessed a waiting list of advertisers.
- Martin's daily broadcasts featured jazz, but varied widely in tone from day to day; he maintained control of the play list and rarely was restricted from making any comments he chose on the air.
- Pre-recorded music and big personalities had joined forces to create a new era in radio.
- *The World's Biggest Make-Believe Ballroom* gained so much popularity that it went into national syndication in 1940, and by the end of World War II, Martin Block was making $22,000 a week.
- That same year, Martin hosted what was billed as a "$20,000 Jam Session" featuring both Dorsey brothers, Count Basie, Harry James, and Gene Krupa.
- Martin and *The Make-Believe Ballroom* made the cover of *Billboard* magazine in April 1942.
- When Spike Jones and his City Slickers returned from entertaining the troops in 1944 and no New York hotel rooms were available for the night, his first call was to Martin.
- Within minutes of Martin's broadcast concerning Spike Jones's dilemma, WNEW was flooded with listener calls offering to accommodate Jones and his band.
- By 1947, Martin hosted two daily editions of *The Make-Believe Ballroom:* one in the late morning and another around dinnertime.
- But commercial radio was fighting formidable trends in the 1940s.
- The National Association of Broadcasters had created Broadcast Music Inc., or BMI, to break the monopoly held by the American Society of Composers, Authors and Publishers (ASCAP), which required station owners to pay 2.5 percent of the revenues for blanket permission to use music copyrighted by its members.
- When ASCAP attempted to raise its fees, station owners decided to go their own way both to save money and to open the airwaves to songwriters who were not part of ASCAP.
- Almost overnight, more music was available to station owners who were willing to build relationships with small-label record promoters and record shop owners.
- In 1942, the American Federation of Musicians called a strike and ordered its members to refuse to make anymore records; they were determined to prevent recording from putting musicians and live bands out of business.

- For nearly a year, no new recordings were available.
- For the prior 30 years, radio had consisted almost entirely of live performances.
- Since the early days of radio, music producers had demanded royalties for any records played on the air, providing an incentive to radio station owners to play live music or the classics.
- In addition, radio technology was still evolving, which did not allow quality transmission of records.
- Even the Department of Commerce got into the act; applicants for radio licenses were told that those who used live music would be favored over stations that played records.
- Only in 1940 did the federal agency relax the rules that required an announcement every half-hour if the music was not live.
- But Martin's style quickly converted listeners and enticed commentator Walter Winchell to coin the term "disc jockey" as a description of Martin.
- The term "disc jockey" appeared in print in *Variety* in 1941.
- In addition to his radio personality work, Martin claimed credit for two famous advertising slogans for his sponsors: "ABC-Always Buy Chesterfield" for Liggett & Myers and "LSMFT"-Lucky Strike Means Fine Tobacco" for Lucky Strike.
- In August 1946, KFWB announced that Martin was moving West to take his *Ballroom* show there.
- Almost a year of headlines later, in June 1947, he moved West but not to glory.
- People in Los Angeles considered him an arrogant, know-it-all New Yorker and tuned him out by the millions.
- By the fall of 1948, he was ready to return to New York to take advantage of the new television opportunities, but found his fit back at radio station WNEW.
- In 1949, in addition to his twice-daily show, he also did a weekly international version of *The Make-Believe Ballroom* for Voice of America.
- When Block heard that Voice of America would begin broadcasting a popular music program, he volunteered to host the show without pay.

Newscasters at CBS.

Life in the Community: New York City

- New York emerged from the war as the leading city of the world, with Wall Street at the helm of America's ascendancy.
- America's largest city began the transition away from industrial toward a service economy; the ports converted to container ships, reducing the power of longshoremen.
- Large corporations moved their headquarters to the suburbs, but the city saw enormous growth in services, especially finance, education, medicine, tourism, communications and law.
- The late 1940s was also a transition period for radio.
- Already a new invention called television was crowding the entertainment market.
- Jack Benny, Bing Crosby, Johnny Carson, the Lone Ranger, and Superman had all vacated their radio shows and taken their skills to the tiny home screen.
- And with the big stars went the major advertisers for cars, cigarettes and household products.
- Many radio stations were losing money; commercial advertising spots sold for $1.00, or "a dollar a holler."
- Futuristic writers were predicting that television would do to radio what radio had done to sheet music, home pianos and vaudeville.
- Plus, the lineup of network programs was stale; 108 programs had been on a decade or more: 12 programs recorded their birth at the very beginning of radio networking in the early 1920s.

Television was gaining popularity.

- Television had been in development since the 1920s, but the Great Depression, World War II and skepticism concerning pictures that flew through the air had prevented it from catching on.
- On the plus side, Americans were fleeing to the suburbs, where their life revolved around the car and often the car radio.
- Families may never gather around the living room radio again, but drive time could become the new gold mine.
- Chevrolet offered the first car radio in 1922; the Westinghouse Radio Sedan was a $200 option that included an antenna that covered the car's entire room.
- The first built-in car radio arrived in 1934, and the first pushbutton radio selector followed in 1939.
- By 1946, 40 percent of American cars were equipped with a radio.
- Also, radios themselves were shrinking in size and becoming more portable—about the size of a small, overnight bag.
- Omaha radio station owner Todd Storz realized radio listeners enjoyed hearing the same song played over and over, and thus, the emergence of the top 40.
- Few understood how America's teenagers had heard the message of freedom and rebellion as a personal invitation.
- Radio's new identity emphasized fast, fun, and frenetic; DJs competed with one another to accomplish the stunt everyone would be talking about tomorrow.
- New competitors might copy the music you were playing, but they couldn't copy your antics.
- Personality paid good money.
- By the late 1940s, DJs were becoming well-known personalities, including Mike Wallace, Hugh Downs, Arthur Godfrey in Washington and Soupy Sales in Cleveland.

Radio sponsors manufactured pins and other advertising items.

HISTORICAL SNAPSHOT
1949

- President Harry S. Truman unveiled the Fair Deal
- KDKA-TV became the first local, on-air television station in the United States
- The first VW Type 1 arrived in the U.S., a 1948 model brought to New York by Dutch businessman Ben Pon
- *Death of a Salesman* by Arthur Miller opened on Broadway and ran for 742 performances
- Ezra Pound was awarded the first Bollingen Prize in poetry by the Bollingen Foundation and Yale University
- World heavyweight boxing champion Joe Louis retired
- The B-50 Superfortress *Lucky Lady II* under Captain James Gallagher completed the first non-stop around-the-world airplane flight
- Giuseppe Verdi's opera *Aida*, conducted by legendary conductor Arturo Toscanini, was telecast by NBC
- Fred Hoyle coined the term *Big Bang* during a BBC Third Programme radio broadcast
- The North Atlantic Treaty was signed in Washington, DC, creating the NATO defense alliance
- Rodgers and Hammerstein's *South Pacific* opened on Broadway; the score's biggest hit was the song "Some Enchanted Evening"
- The Soviet Union lifted its Blockade of Berlin
- Celebrities including Helen Keller, Dorothy Parker, Danny Kaye, Fredric March, John Garfield, Paul Muni and Edward G. Robinson were named in an FBI report as Communist Party members
- George Orwell's book *1984* was published
- Albert II, a rhesus monkey, became the first primate to enter space, on U.S. Hermes project V-2 rocket *Blossom IVB*, but was killed on impact at return
- Glenn Dunnaway won the inaugural NASCAR race at Charlotte Speedway, a .75-mile oval in Charlotte, North Carolina, but was disqualified due to illegal springs
- The first television Western, *Hopalong Cassidy*, aired on NBC
- The last six surviving veterans of the American Civil War met in Indianapolis
- The Vatican announced that bones uncovered in its subterranean catacombs could be the apostle Peter
- This was the first year in which no African-American was reported lynched in the U.S.
- Joseph Stalin launched a savage attack on Soviet Jews, accusing them of being pro-Western and antisocialist

Gold-Digger for Uncle Sam

HEDY LAMARR is after your money! She's sold millions of dollars' worth of war bonds, and is still going strong. That's why she says proudly, "I'm just a plain gold-digger for Uncle Sam"

BUY AND BUY is the theme of bond-selling quartet above (l. to r.): Bing Crosby, Hedy Lamarr, Jimmy Cagney, Kay Kyser. Hedy sold $4,500,-000 worth of bonds in one show. Below: Bing and Jimmy do a bond routine

Selected Prices

Adding Machine	$120.00
Antacid, Tums	$0.10
Baby's Car Seat	$1.98
Clock Radio	$36.95
Dinette Set, Five-Piece	$89.95
Gin, Fifth	$3.12
Hairdryer	$9.95
Mink Coat	$1,650.00
Movie Ticket	$1.00
Tattoo	$0.25

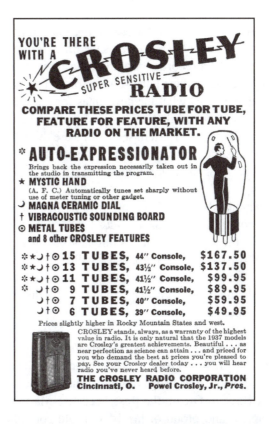

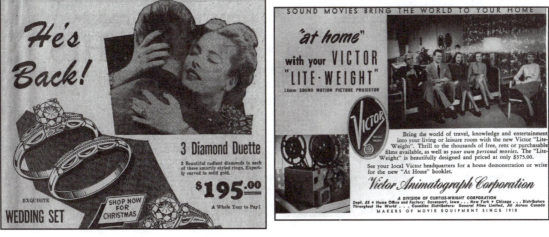

"In New York," George Tucker, *Frederick Post* (Maryland), October 31, 1941:

I wonder how many burnt puddings Martin Block is responsible for every day, how many forgotten roasts? He is one of the curious phenomena of our times. He has lent a new rhythm to dishwashing and floor sweeping and brought a gossip columnist's philosophy to wives, mothers, and sweethearts all over the metropolitan area. Martin Block is the housewife's friend.

When he steps to a mike in the studios of WNEW each morning at 10 and puts his *Make-Believe Ballroom* on the air, he gives a lift to the little woman who is cleaning the carpet. At night, in their bridge games, the girls say, "Did you hear what Martin had to say this morning? He was out late again last night. He had a headache. But, after only two capsules of Red Dog Pain Killer, he felt fine." That's the girls. That's the housewife. They hang on every word he says, and because they do, it will mean that his income will soar to $100,000 a year.

Martin Block is a trim, mustached young man in his upper thirties who talks a couple of hours to the public every morning over WNEW. He buys the time from the station, and resells it to the clients. He emcees his *Make-Believe Ballroom*, a recorded program, during which he adlibs and gossips to his listeners with the familiarity of a confidant. He is their father-confessor and a town-crier. He tells them which nightclubs he visited, who's going to have a baby, what the new tunes for the week will be. Last summer, he returned after a brief absence with the announcement that he suffered a slight heart attack—a "flutter," I think he called it—and wives and sweethearts all over the Eastern seaboard were thrown into a mild panic.... "Martin had a heart attack...." "Martin had a heart attack...." It was a kind of horrified rhythm as the news beat up and down the suburban streets and dominated bridge table talk for days.

How to explain Mr. Block? Simply this: he had an idea and he sold it. During the Depression he was beating across the country selling razor blades for a living. He got to New York and put what he called his *Make-Believe Ballroom* on the air, and began his unrehearsed small talk between recordings to the listening housewives. They eat it up. Wives who miss a broadcast will telephone their friends to inquire, "What did Martin have to say this morning?" Frequently, he brings his pals into the studio—orchestra leaders, dancers, composers. He tells you what they do, how they look, what they like and dislike. The women absorb like sponges.

As a result, there are now *Make-Believe Ballrooms* in every section of the country. It has proved a crowd-pleaser. It has added a little stardust to the gold dust. The housewives have a theme song now. "I Guess I'll Have to Dream the Rest," because Martin wrote it. He's cocky, dapper, and proud of his 14-year-old son who's a cadet at Culver Military Academy.

The one thing calculated to make him madder than a wet hen is the infrequent occasion when he puts an untested record on the air and it turns out to have smutty or double-entendre lyrics. He stops the turntable, makes public apologies to his listeners and cracks the record before the open mike.

That's Martin Block.

"Disc Jockey Wins American Favor Abroad," *Portsmouth Times* (Ohio), November 3, 1949:

American popular music served up by a disc jockey is helping this country win the world's goodwill.

The Voice of America, the State Department's foreign broadcaster, is beaming a half-hour program of U.S. jazz once a week to Europe, the Far East and Latin America.

Presiding over this unique show is Martin Block, pioneer platter turner who volunteered for the job.

Block calls it *International Make-Believe Ballroom*. He mixes varied portions of jazz with his usual easygoing informal chatter about bands and singers and tunes. Once he went backstage at *South Pacific* and interviewed the stars as a lead-in for recorded songs from their musical.

The worldwide reaction has amazed Voice of America officials, even though they tried out the idea in the hope that it would build up their general listening audience for all Voice programs.

"Disc Riders Don't Work for Peanuts," *Oakland Tribune*, **May 28, 1947:**

Let us consider for a moment the disc jockey, a man who announces the name of the next record. One of the most original disc jockeys and by all accounts the most successful is Martin Block, who has been earning a reputed $400,000 a year at this task, which seems like quite a lot considering the duties involved. Last year, Block announced that he would soon start a one-hour program over the Mutual Broadcasting System which would boost its earnings to around $1 million year.

Paul Whiteman, who has been leading bands almost as long as the white man has been in this country, will turn disc jockey on a full-hour afternoon show over the American Broadcasting Company on June 30. His five-day-a-week show has been sold to four sponsors and the take (if Whiteman brings on all the sponsors for the full year, which is not altogether certain) will amount to $3 million.

About the time you don't like a record, Mama's just beginning to learn to hum it. About the time you can't stand it, Mama's beginning to learn the words. About the time you're ready to shoot yourself if you hear it one more time, it's hitting the Top 10.
— Radio station manager Bud Armstrong's instructions to disc jockeys, 1950.

Recorded Popular Songs: 1949

- "(Ghost) Riders in the Sky" (Vaughn Monroe)

- "Mule Train" (Frankie Laine)

- "'A' You're Adorable (the Alphabet Song)" (Perry Como)

- "You're Breaking My Heart" (Vic Damone)

- "I've Got a Lovely Bunch of Coconuts" (Freddy Martin)

- "Some Enchanted Evening" (Perry Como)

- "A Little Bird Told Me" (Evelyn Knight)

- "Cruisin' Down the River" (Russ Morgan)

- "Baby, It's Cold Outside" (Dinah Shore and Buddy Clark)

- "That Lucky Old Sun" (Frankie Laine)

- "Rudolph the Red-Nosed Reindeer" (Gene Autry)

- "Forever and Ever" (Russ Morgan)

- "Bamboo" (Vaughn Monroe)

- "My Darling, My Darling" (Jo Stafford and Gordon MacRae)

- "Dear Hearts and Gentle People" (Dinah Shore)

- "Powder Your Face With Sunshine" (Evelyn Knight)

- "For You My Love" (Larry Darnell)

- "She Wore a Yellow Ribbon" (Eddie "Piano" Miller)

- "Beans and Corn Bread" (Louis Jordan and his Tympany Five)

- "Slippin' Around" (Margaret Whiting and Jimmy Wakely)

- "I've Got My Love to Keep Me Warm" (Les Brown)

- "Buttons and Bows" (Dinah Shore)

- "The Huckle-Buck" (Paul Williams and His Hucklebuckers)

- "All She Wants to Do Is Rock" (Wynonie Harris)

- "Someday (You'll Want Me to Want You)" (The Mills Brothers)

1950–1959

As the 1950s began, the average American enjoyed an income 15 times greater than that of the average foreigner. Optimism and opportunity were everywhere. The vast majority of families considered themselves middle class; many were enjoying the benefits of health insurance for the first time. Air travel for the upper class was common, and the world was their oyster. America was manufacturing half of the world's products, 57 percent of the steel, 43 percent of the electricity, and 62 percent of the oil. The economies of Europe and Asia lay in. ruins, while America's industrial and agricultural structure was untouched and well-oiled to supply the needs of a war-weary world.

America's music reflected this newfound prosperity and sense of place. Jazz became cool, symphony orchestras bloomed in major cities, and by the mid-1950s, songs by Elvis Presley, Fats Domino, and Little Richard were broadcast into homes, car radios and jukeboxes across America. At the same time, television was altering the definition of "celebrity." In addition, the war years' high employment and optimism spurred the longest sustained period of peacetime prosperity in the nation's history. A decade of full employment and pent-up desire produced demands for all types of consumer goods. Businesses of all sizes prospered. Rapidly swelling families, new suburban homes, televisions, and most of all, big, powerful, shiny automobiles symbolized the hopes of the era. During the 1950s, an average of seven million cars and trucks were sold annually. By 1952, two-thirds of all families owned a television set; home freezers and high-fidelity stereo phonographs were considered necessities. Specialized markets developed to meet the demand of consumers such as amateur photographers, pet lovers, and backpackers. At the same time, shopping malls, supermarkets, and credit cards emerged as important economic forces.

Veterans, using the GI Bill of Rights, flung open the doors of colleges nationwide, attending in record numbers. Inflation was the only pressing economic issue, fueled in large part by the Korean War (in which 54,000 American lives were lost) and the federal expenditures for Cold War defense. As the decade opened, federal spending represented 15.6 percent of the nation's gross national product. Thanks largely to the Cold War, by 1957, defense consumed half of the federal government's $165 billion budget.

This economic prosperity also ushered in conservative politics and social conformity. Tidy lawns, bedrooms that were "neat and trim," and suburban homes that were "proper" were certainly "in" throughout the decade as Americans adjusted to the postwar years. Properly buttoned-down attitudes concerning sexual mores brought stern undergarments for women like bonded girdles and stiff, pointed, or padded bras to confine the body. The

planned community of Levittown, New York, mandated that grass be cut at least once a week and laundry washed on specific days. A virtual revival of Victorian respectability and domesticity reigned; divorce rates and female college attendance fell while birth rates and the sale of Bibles rose. Corporate America promoted the benefits of respectable men in gray flannel suits whose wives remained at home to tend house and raise children. Suburban life included ladies' club memberships, chauffeuring children to piano and ballet classes, and lots of a newly marketed product known as tranquilizers, whose sales were astounding.

The average wage earner benefited more from the booming industrial system than at any time in American history. The 40-hour work week became standard in manufacturing. In offices many workers were becoming accustomed to a 35-hour week. Health benefits for workers became more common and paid vacations were standard in most industries. In 1950, 25 percent of American wives worked outside the home; by the end of the decade the number had risen to 40 percent. Communications technology, expanding roads, inexpensive airline tickets, and a spirit of unboundedness meant that people and commerce were no longer prisoners of distance. Unfortunately, up to one-third of the population lived below the government's poverty level, largely overlooked in the midst of prosperity.

The Civil Rights movement was propelled by two momentous events in the 1950s. The first was a decree on May 17, 1954, by the U.S. Supreme Court which ruled that "in the field of public education the doctrine of 'separate but equal' has no place. Separate educational facilities are inherently unequal." The message was electric but the pace was slow. Few schools would be integrated for another decade. The second event established the place of the Civil Rights movement. On December 1, 1955, African-American activist Rosa Parks declined to vacate the White-only front section of the Montgomery, Alabama, bus, leading to her arrest and a citywide bus boycott by blacks. Their spokesman became Martin Luther King, Jr., the 26-year-old pastor of the Dexter Avenue Baptist Church. The year-long boycott was the first step toward the passage of the Civil Rights Act of 1964.

America's youths were enchanted by the TV adventures of *Leave It to Beaver*, westerns, and *Father Knows Best*, allowing them to accumulate more time watching television during the week (at least 27 hours) than attending school. TV dinners were invented; pink ties and felt skirts with sequined poodle appliqués were worn; Elvis Presley was worshipped and the new phenomena of *Playboy* and Mickey Spillane fiction were created, only to be read behind closed doors. The ever-glowing eye of television killed the "March of Time" newsreels after 16 years at the movies. Sexual jargon such as "first base" and "home run" entered the language. Learned-When-Sleeping machines appeared, along with Smokey the Bear, Sony tape recorders, adjustable shower heads, *Mad Comics*, newspaper vending machines, Levi's faded blue denims, pocket-size transistor radios, and transparent plastic bags for clothing. Ultimately, the real stars of the era were the Salk and Sabin vaccines, which vanquished the siege of polio.

1951 NEWS FEATURE

"The Grass Roots of Opera in America, Colleges and Universities Set the Pace in Creating Opera Centers Throughout the U.S.," H. W. Hinesheimer, *The Etude*, December 1951:

It was only yesterday—or was it the day before?—when it was a commonly accepted fact, never doubted and scarcely questioned by anyone, that this country would never give a hoot about opera. Opera—why, it was always considered an Un-American Activity. Foreign singers, conductors and managers presenting foreign works in foreign languages (although for domestic dollars) to an audience which stepped out of their Rolls Royce just before the first intermission, displayed their ermine capes, jewels and queen-like necklines and left as soon as the lights dimmed for the beginning of the last act. Opera, many a wise man told me when I first came here, full of enthusiasm after years of operatic adventures in Europe and expecting the same experiences over here, opera will never catch on in America. Unless it has a horse or at least soap to its name, it won't go. Forget it.

But this is a strange and wonderful country. The unexpected happens all the time, and when it happens, it happens big. Having saturated its musical air with the creation of some 150 symphony orchestras within the short period of one human generation—something unheard of in musical history—America is now beginning to open its door to opera. Strangely enough—it's the backdoor that admits the merry procession of unexpected guests: singers, stage managers, conductors, composers, colorful costumes, whirling dancers, the wonderful make-believe world of opera that has nothing like it in all the world of arts.

It's a spectacle, scarcely to believe and unique again, as have been so many facets of American cultural progress, in the annals of musical history, something that, in its freshness, spontaneity and scope, could only happen here. Professors, economists and scholars have bemoaned and are still bemoaning the lack of operatic activity in America. Here's the world's richest country, they point out—and look what we have: Two big professional companies, the Metropolitan and San Francisco, both drawing from the same roster of international stars, a few smaller ones, a few traveling companies of questionable artistic competence—no Stadttheater, no state support here—nothing. Compare this with impoverished countries like Austria and Germany or almost any European country and their flourishing operatic life, many independent opera houses, public support, regular seasons of eight or even 10 months.

All this, of course, is true. America, that just began to build its first roads through the wilderness and organize a continent of staggering dimensions, when Europe was already dotted with opera houses, has never caught up with the intricate organization of operatic life that is part of 300 years of European history, a firm and established heritage of its greater past, carried on into its smaller present.

But look what is happening now. Cities or states do not pay lavish subsidies to American operatic groups. Yet they are spreading rapidly all over the country. There are at present more than 200 different organizations producing opera in America. Most of them did not exist only a few years ago….

The driving force behind it is the university. One can almost say that the American university is now taking the place of the archbishops and princes that supported opera in its European beginnings. That is exactly what is happening here. The opera departments of such diversified places as Drake University in Des Moines, Indiana University in Bloomington, Minnesota in Minneapolis, University of Washington in Seattle, Louisiana State in Baton Rouge, University of Southern California in Los Angeles, University of Colorado at Denver—to mention just a few that come to mind—have taken over active leadership in a new, modern, aggressive, and very American approach toward opera. The response is tremendous. Denver, for example, produced, last summer, Menotti's difficult opera *The Consul*, complete with singers, scenery and orchestra. The success with the students and townspeople was so outspoken, a whole series of additional performances had to be scheduled. The theaters of the University of Minnesota, which, only recently, added opera to its repertory, report of similar striking and most unexpected response. Drake in Des Moines, after they gave their first college performance of *The Consul*, wired the composer to say this was "the most important and most exciting event in the history of the University."

Many of these operatic centers—and that is what they swiftly grow into—started out simply as part of the school activities. In Urbana, for instance, the school of music had no opera department until 1947. The students themselves approached the faculty with a request to add operatic activities to the curriculum. The Opera Workshop at the University of Illinois now presents regularly at least one complete opera at the University of Illinois Theater, usually on four consecutive nights....

Just as active as are the universities in living up to the demands of this new, sweeping movement are the workshops that have developed everywhere during the past few years. I have seen many of them, and believe with all my heart in their mission and eventual success. Take Cincinnati, for instance, where the Music Drama Guild, for several years already, is presenting a most unusual fare—contemporary works as well as off-the-beaten-path classical operas—with continued and ever-increasing success. They have rapidly become a set feature in the cultural life of their town—and if such sustained, ambitious and well-patronized activities are not the closest to a successful, decentralized operatic life along the lines of the European Stadttheater that can be expected, I'd like to know what is. The fact that this group, to whom it is all a labor of love and certainly not a business, have done so successfully what they have done, has perhaps greater significance for the musical presence and future of America than still another lavishly endowed *Fledermaus* or even *Don Carlo* at the Metropolitan Opera.

1957 PROFILE

When Carol Lawrence starred as Maria in the groundbreaking Broadway musical *West Side Story*, the play simultaneously elevated her visibility on the American stage and announced itself as a new breed of drama: a hybrid of opera, musical theater and ballet, with a contemporary urban edge.

Life at Home

- In its first iteration, the play was called *Romeo and Juliet*, a tale of star-crossed lovers by William Shakespeare.
- Three hundred and fifty years later, the tale had been reframed as a New York-based gang rivalry between Jews and Catholics to be called *East Side Story*.
- But when this American musical finally arrived on the Broadway stage in 1957, the story pitted Puerto Rican immigrants against native-born Americans.
- Carol Lawrence was cast in the center of the love and violence as Maria in the *West Side Story*.
- Born Carolina Maria Laraia on September 5, 1932, actress/singer Carol Lawrence grew up in Melrose Park, Illinois, near Chicago where her father was village clerk.
- Carol was born to dance; by the age of 12, her tap class lessons were dominated by professionals already working in the Chicago theaters.
- At age 13, she lied about her age to get a theater work permit.
- As a teenager, Carol was active in local theatrical productions and was selected to appear in a number of television productions created in Chicago.

Carol Lawrence broke new ground with her performance as Maria in West Side Story.

- At her strict Italian father's suggestion, she also changed her last name to Lawrence from Laraia.
- "Laraia is really beautiful in Italian" Carol said, "but the poor TV announcers nearly went mad trying to get their tongues around it."
- Carol entered Northwestern University, but after her freshman year persuaded her parents that her future was on New York's Broadway stage.
- So the three of them—mother, father and daughter—journeyed to New York City to visit Broadway; "They must have decided it was no worse than Chicago. Anyway, they let me stay, though they've always been a little nervous about the whole thing."
- Carol supported herself with a chorus job here, a small feature part there, a few television spots—anything that would keep the dream alive.
- Her first Broadway play was in the chorus line of a show called *Borsch Capades*, for which she was paid $25 a week.
- When New York slowed down in the summertime, she gained singing and dancing experience doing summer stock that demanded a different show each week, from *Guys and Dolls* to *Oklahoma!* to *Anything Goes*.
- Still, her mother lamented that she had not taken a secretarial course, and her father wanted to know whether she was supporting herself as a "streetwalker."

Young Carol tapped her way to Broadway.

- She also fell in love with a puppet-master named Cosmo Allegretti, 11 years her senior, who worked on an experimental TV program called *Captain Kangaroo* that featured grown people singing children's songs and acting crazy in a gentle manner.
- They married in 1956 and settled into an apartment near Gramercy Park, where she helped Cosmo create puppets and repair lost eyes and whiskers whenever necessary.
- Then one day, she heard talk of a new musical set in the slums of the city's West Side; the Juliet part sounded beautiful.
- Carol decided she wanted the role more than anything in the world.
- *West Side Story* featured a script by Arthur Laurents, music by Leonard Bernstein, lyrics by Stephen Sondheim, and choreography by Jerome Robbins.
- "So I marched to the first informal audition with my heart in my mouth, and praise be, they asked me to come back."
- After the second audition, they asked her to come back again to work on a real stage, "and I began to dream."
- Her third tryout was on the stage of the 46th St. Theater; "Leonard Bernstein, the composer, was sitting out front, and I was afraid he'd know right away that I hadn't much voice training."
- Carol had taken voice lessons, but primarily considered herself to be a dancer.
- Bernstein loved her voice because it wasn't "schooled."
- "We had to look for charm rather than perfection, because the audience might not believe in our "Juliet" if she sang like a full-blown opera star," the legendary composer said.
- She was asked back for one additional audition when someone beyond the light asked her for her age.

"I'm Earning $1200 More a Year— as Secretary to a Hollywood Director Thanks to SPEEDWRITING Shorthand"

Writes former clerk-typist Judith L. Adkins of Santa Monica, Cal.

SHORTHAND IN 6 WEEKS

Speedwriting

Famous ABC Shorthand ®

NO SYMBOLS — USES ABC's

Why spend months mastering a symbol shorthand when in ONLY 6 WEEKS you can be taking 120 words per minute with SPEEDWRITING — the shorthand that uses the ABC's!

Over 350,000 men and

Carol's mother thought she should be at secretarial school.

- "I was afraid to answer for a second," Carol said. "I knew the girl was supposed to be 17, and I was 23."
- That's when the show's author, Arthur Laurents, shouted "She's exactly seventeen" and the issue was dropped.
- Laurents already knew that he wanted Carol in the role of Maria and "wouldn't have cared whether she was 70."
- Carol was then asked back for one more audition.
- "That time I thought I'd really made a good impression, but then they asked me to take my hair down. I had a hair-do that I'd spent two hours on, and when it all fell in ruins, I was sure I'd look like a real mess."
- It was exactly the look that Jerome Robbins was seeking.
- Set in New York City in the mid-1950s, *West Side Story* explored the rivalry between the Jets and the Sharks, two teenage street gangs of different ethnic backgrounds.
- The members of the Sharks from Puerto Rico were taunted by the Jets, a white working-class group.
- The young protagonist, Tony, one of the Jets, fell in love with Maria, the sister of Bernardo, the leader of the Sharks.
- The dark theme, sophisticated music, extended dance scenes, and focus on social problems marked a turning point in American musical theater.
- Bernstein's score for the musical included "Something's Coming," "Maria," "America," "Somewhere," "Tonight," "Jet Song," "I Feel Pretty," "A Boy Like That," "One Hand, One Heart," "Gee, Officer Krupke," and "Cool."

Life at Work

- *West Side Story* began the birthing process in 1949, when Jerome Robbins approached Leonard Bernstein and Arthur Laurents about collaborating on a contemporary musical adaptation of Romeo and Juliet.
- He proposed that the plot focus on the conflict between an Italian American Roman Catholic family and a Jewish family living on the Lower East Side of Manhattan during the Easter-Passover season.
- Eager to write his first musical, Laurents immediately agreed.
- Bernstein wanted to present the material in operatic form, but Robbins and Laurents resisted the suggestion.
- Laurents wrote a first draft he called *East Side Story*, but the three men went their separate ways and the piece was shelved for almost five years.

Leonard Bernstein loved Carol's voice and cast her as Maria in West Side Story.

- When it was resurrected, the atmosphere surrounding *West Side Story* had been transformed by recent headlines detailing the brutal murder of two young teenagers in a Hell's Kitchen park by gang members.
- Even then, the creative team was told that *West Side Story* was an impossible project; no one was going to be able to sing augmented fourths, as with "Ma-ri-a."
- Besides, who wanted to see a show in which the first-act curtain comes down on two dead bodies lying on the stage?
- And then they had the tough task of casting because the characters had to be able not only to sing but dance, act and be taken for teenagers.
- Numerous producers had turned down the show, deeming it too dark and depressing, when Sondheim convinced his friend Hal Prince to read the script.
- He liked it enough to fly to New York to hear the score; Prince recalled, "Sondheim and Bernstein sat at the piano playing through the music, and soon I was singing along with them."
- At rehearsal, Carol was confronted with newspaper stories describing the violent gang murders posted on the bulletin board along with the words, "This is your life."

- In rehearsal, the director told the two rival gangs they were not allowed to eat together or socialize, and demanded that the actors address each other using only their character's names.
- He wanted to cultivate the tension and endemic hatred into every line of the play.
- After all, this musical was taking a daring step—its plot concerned a serious subject in which two characters died in the first act.
- The intensity of the atmosphere helped foster friendship between Carol and Chita Rivera, who played Anita, the sister she had always wanted.
- "That was a new experience for me; it's almost impossible for women in the theater to form friendships because we're all competing for the same roles."
- In *West Side Story*, Maria worked in a bridal shop with Anita, the girlfriend of Maria's brother, Bernardo.
- Although the musical was painted with an urban-tinted score accented by surly street attitudes, slanguage and snapping fingers, language posed a problem.
- Cursing was uncommon in the theater at the time, and slang expressions were avoided for fear of dating the work.
- Ultimately, a new language was invented that sounded like real street talk but actually wasn't: "Cut the frabba-jabba," for example.
- As rapidly as her singing career was cresting, so too was her marriage crashing; fame came at a price.
- Her husband's equally successful career as a puppeteer on a popular TV program begin to appear pale compared to that of a Broadway actress starring in the most talked-about musical of the year.
- Despite being the voice behind Mr. Moose, Grandfather Clock, and the Bunny Rabbit, her husband was called Mr. Lawrence at public functions, and he fully understood that they got the finest table at a classy restaurant because of her fame, not his.

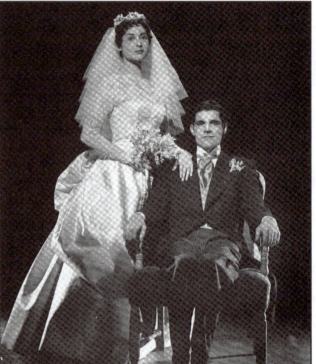

Carol's marriage couldn't survive her fame.

Life in the Community: New York City

- Throughout the 1950s, Broadway musicals were a major part of American popular culture evidenced by the number of hit records created each year from the newest stage musicals.
- Public demand, a booming economy and abundant creative talent kept Broadway fresh because it refused to stand still.
- As the Civil War came to a close, New York City slowly became the center of theatrical activity in America.
- By the mid-1880s, Union Square on 14th Street and Broadway became a gathering spot for producers to assemble touring companies, managers to book tours, and actors and singers to acquire new material.
- Soon a handful of theaters congregated around Union Square and Broadway began to develop its reputation.
- By the turn of the twentieth century, the theater district stretched from West 37th Street along Broadway to 40th Street, culminating at the Metropolitan Opera House.
- About the same time, a half-block on West 28th Street between Broadway and Sixth Avenue, began to hold tremendous sway over the burgeoning entertainment industry.

- This was the home of Tin Pan Alley, where an ever-changing collection of songwriters had gathered to support the booming song sheet industry.
- And the two learned to live in creative synergy.
- The theater district provided the publishers with a natural outlet for their material.
- By 1910, at least two billion copies of song sheets were purchased annually by the American music-loving public.
- The pioneer architect within the theater district was Prussian immigrant, inventor of cigar machines and successful businessman, Oscar Hammerstein, grandfather of the famous lyricist.
- He developed several parcels of land from 43rd Street to 45th Street on the east side of Broadway, which became the anchor of the theater district.

Songwriters in Tin Pan Alley: Gene Buck, Victor Herbert, John Philip Sousa, Harry B. Smith, Jerome Kern, Irving Berlin, George W. Meyer, Irving Bibo, and Otto Harbach.

- In 1899, he opened the Victoria Theater on the corner of 42nd and Seventh Avenue.
- By 1904, the city's new subway system was delivering thousands of theatergoers nightly, each eager for the Broadway experience, even though most of the theaters were not actually on Broadway itself.
- By 1910, there were 34 theaters north of or near 42nd Street, all focused on the tourist dollar and the opportunity to have their production advertised as "Direct from New York," which was understood nationwide to represent the gold standard in entertainment.
- There, the beautiful sets and girls of Ziegfeld Follies unashamedly sold the American dream, comedienne Fanny Brice spoofed the grand pretensions of middle-class art, and Will Rogers and W.C. Fields built their reputations.
- The outbreak of World War I spawned hundreds of patriotic songs and dozens of Broadway plays symbolizing America's devotion to its fighting men.
- During the 1920s, when the nation officially went dry thanks to prohibition, Broadway stayed wet.
- Following an evening at the theater, after the curtain went up at 8:45 most evenings, patrons completed their Broadway experience at a speakeasy or supper club nearby.
- By the late 1920s, 20 new theaters were constructed and as many as 264 plays and musicals were performed.
- The play, *Shuffle Along*, for example, introduced a variety of new dance styles, pioneered by America's finest emerging black talent.
- Broadway theaters prided themselves that, despite the showiness outside, the greatest glamour was inside where the gold gilt and dramatic décor might feature Victorian, art deco, or glitz galore.
- The 1930s arrived with a thunderous bang; tourists stopped traveling, producers shut down shows, and ushers had no one to usher.
- An estimated 25,000 theater people, the majority in New York, were displaced by the effects of the Great Depression.
- In some theaters, prices were dropped to a $0.25 minimum, with $1.00 being the top price.
- Actors and producers experimented with repertory productions to keep as many working as often as possible, and to keep as many productions active as they could.
- The 1929-1930 season produced 233 productions, whereas the 1930-1931 season was reduced to 187 productions; new productions on Broadway dipped to 98 shows in 1939.
- Yet this period featured the work of Eugene O'Neill's *Ah, Wilderness!*, Ethel Merman, who opened in George and Ira Gershwin's *Girl Crazy*, and plays by Moss Hart such as *Once in a Lifetime, Merrily We Roll Along, You Can't Take It With You*, and *The Man Who Came to Dinner*.

- Comedy of the 1940s was rich with farces including *George Washington Slept Here*, a collaboration between George Kaufman and Moss Hart, and Irving Berlin's, *This Is the Army*.
- *On the Town* marked the Broadway debut of composer Leonard Bernstein and choreographer Jerome Robbins; songs included "New York, New York (It's a Helluva Town)."
- Then, breakout hit *Oklahoma!* spawned the first-ever original cast album to be released; the songs "People Will Say We're in Love," "Oh, What a Beautiful Mornin'" topped the charts.
- As the decade came to an end, Cole Porter's "Kiss Me, Kate" debuted; Carol Channing starred in *Gentlemen Prefer Blondes*, and *South Pacific* by Rodgers and Hammerstein won a Pulitzer Prize.
- The 1950s opened with the hit show *Guys and Dolls*, whose songs included "If I Were a Bell" and "Luck, Be a Lady," and the show *The King and I* starring Yul Brynner.
- By 1955, *Damn Yankees* became the second big hit for the songwriting team of Richard Adler and Jerry Ross, and the press began to call the era the Golden Age of Broadway.
- Monster hit *My Fair Lady* opened on Broadway and launched the careers of Julie Andrews and Rex Harrison.
- In 1957, all of Broadway's talk was devoted to *West Side Story*, and *The Music Man*, which won the Tony for Best Musical.

HISTORICAL SNAPSHOT
1957

- Italian conductor Arturo Toscanini suffered a stroke and died
- The San Francisco and Los Angeles stock exchanges merged to form the Pacific Coast Stock Exchange
- Hamilton Watch Company introduced the first electric watch
- After 69 years, the last issue of *Collier's Weekly Magazine* was published
- Elvis Presley appeared on *The Ed Sullivan Show* for the third and final time; he was only shown from the waist up because his hip gyrations were considered too suggestive
- Wham-O Company produced the first Frisbee
- Dwight D. Eisenhower was inaugurated for a second term as president of the United States
- Dr. Seuss' *The Cat in the Hat* was published
- Rodgers and Hammerstein's *Cinderella*, the team's only musical written especially for television, was telecast live and in color by CBS, starring Julie Andrews in the title role
- IBM sold the first compiler for the FORTRAN scientific programming language
- Allen Ginsberg's poem "Howl" was seized by U.S. Customs officials on the grounds of obscenity
- Brooklyn Dodgers owner Walter O'Malley moved the team from Brooklyn, New York, to Los Angeles, California
- John Lennon and Paul McCartney met for the first time as teenagers at Woolton Fete, three years before forming the Beatles
- Elvis Presley's *Loving You* opened in theaters
- Marine Major John Glenn flew an F8U supersonic jet from California to New York in three hours, 23 minutes and eight seconds, setting a new transcontinental speed record
- *American Bandstand*, a local dance show produced by WFIL-TV in Philadelphia, joined the ABC Television Network
- Senator Strom Thurmond (D-SC) set the record for the longest filibuster with his 24-hour, 18-minute speech railing against a Civil Rights bill
- The Academy Award-winning movie *The Three Faces of Eve* was released
- President Eisenhower sent federal troops to Arkansas to provide safe passage into Central High School for the Little Rock Nine, a group of African-American students
- The Soviet Union launched *Sputnik 1*, the first artificial satellite to orbit Earth
- The comedy sitcom "Leave It to Beaver" premiered on television
- Toyota begin exporting vehicles to the U.S., beginning with the Toyota Crown and the Toyota Land Cruiser
- *The Bridge on the River Kwai* was released and won the Academy Award for Best Picture
- The CBS afternoon anthology series *Seven Lively Arts* presented Tchaikovsky's ballet *The Nutcracker* on U.S. television for the first time, although heavily abridged
- Mao Zedong admitted that 800,000 "class enemies" had been summarily liquidated between 1949 and 1954

Selected Prices

Bedroom Set, Walnut	$645.00
Coffee Maker, Percolator	$16.88
Lipstick, Cashmere Bouquet	$0.49
Mattress, Serta	$79.50
Nylons	$1.00
Paneling, 70 Panels	$47.00
Refrigerator	$259.00
Typewriter, Smith-Corona, Electric	$209.35
Vacuum Cleaner, Eureka	$69.95
Watch, Bulova	$59.50

"*West Side Story* Review," Walter Kerr, *New York Herald Tribune*, September 27, 1957:

The radioactive fallout from *West Side Story* must still be descending on Broadway this morning. Director, choreographer, and idea-man Jerome Robbins has put together, and then blasted apart, the most savage, restless, electrifying dance patterns we've been exposed to in a dozen seasons...the show rides with a catastrophic roar over the spider-web fire-escapes, the shadowed trestles, and the plain dirt battlegrounds of a big city feud...there is fresh excitement in the next debacle, and the next. When a gang leader advises his cohorts to play it "Cool," the intolerable tension between an effort at control and the instinctive drives of these potential killers is stingingly graphic. When the knives come out, and bodies begin to fly wildly through space under buttermilk clouds, the sheer visual excitement is breathtaking.... Mr. Bernstein has permitted himself a few moments of graceful, lingering melody: in a yearning "Maria," in the hushed falling line of "Tonight," in the wistful declaration of "I Have a Love." But for the most part, he has served the needs of the onstage threshing machine.... When hero Larry Kert is stomping out the visionary insistence of "Something's Coming," both music and tumultuous story are given their due. Otherwise, it's the danced narrative that takes urgent precedence....

"Only Three Hits on Broadway," *Long Beach Press-Telegram*, November 7, 1957:

A lackluster theater season is breaking up Broadway's box-office traffic jam.

Last year, shows had to wait on the road or delay production because all available Broadway theaters were taken.

This year, the number of plots and near flops is taking care of the theater shortage. A United Press tally shows that, of the 32 legitimate theaters along Broadway, nine are dark and awaiting tenants. This is one gauge of the new season's quality, for its axiomatic that a rousing theater season leads to a shortage of theaters.

There have been 18 openings so far this season, and eight of the newcomers have been closed or posted closing notices. Of the 10 survivors, only three are doing quality business: *West Side Story, Look Back in Anger*, and *Jamaica*.

Richard Maney, the Broadway booster, believes the new season is because our established playwrights aren't writing.

"It all begins with the writer," he said. "When he doesn't write anything, nobody works." Maney points out that our top playwrights—Tennessee Williams, Arthur Miller, Lillian Hellman—do not have incoming plays this season.

In order to become a hit, a Broadway show must make money. More and more, they have greater amounts to make up. *West Side Story* cost about $225,000 to bring in. The show is able to net about $15,000 a week when the theater is grossing a capacity of $60,400. It may make money after December 23, when the top prize for a ticket is hiked from $7.05 to $8.05.

The Backstage Story, Carol Lawrence, 1990:

Over quite a long period, I auditioned 13 times for the role of Maria in what they finally called *West Side Story*. Even then, 13 auditions was a lot, and today, Actors Equity would not permit it. But I was working in other shows and I can be patient. Besides, maybe people were right; maybe *West Side Story* would never happen.

When I was called back for the thirteenth time, Larry Kert was there to audition for the role of Tony. We had read for the roles together before, but this time I had asked if we could take the scenes home and memorize them. Jerry Robbins had agreed. But instead of asking us to sing a few songs, Jerry told Larry to go backstage and wait there. Then he said "You," pointing to me but calling me, "Maria."
"See that scaffolding up there over the stage?" he said. "Look around, find out how to get up there. Then stay there, out of sight."
It was an unusual request, but I would have found a way to get up there even if I had to grow wings. Instead, I found a narrow metal ladder leading to who knows where, and up I went.

Jerry called Larry on stage and told him to find me and take it from there. Up where I was, I began to feel as if I really was Maria, watching Tony search for me, but afraid to call out for fear of alerting my family. And Larry/Tony was genuinely desperate to find me. By the time he saw me and climbed up to where I was, the two of us were almost breathless. We did the balcony scene from there.
When we came down, Jerry said, "You've both got the parts" and then went on to other things. He was like that.

I burst into tears of relief. The producer, Hal Prince, said "No, really—you're Maria!" And I cried for pure joy.

JAZZ

1958 PROFILE

Gil Evans and jazz legend Miles Davis teamed up around their love of sound to change music, creating albums such as *The Birth of Cool* and *Miles Ahead*.

Life at Home

- Miles Davis described Gil Evans as "the greatest musician in the world," even while Gil was invisible to most of the music establishment.
- Gil Evans's mother Julia was 45 years old and on her third of five husbands when Gil was born in Canada in 1912.
- His father, a doctor and a committed gambler, died penniless a few months after Gil's birth, leaving his wife and child without support.
- As a child, Gil traveled extensively with his mother as she moved from one job to another, from one end of the North American continent to another, and from boardinghouse to boardinghouse.
- When he was four or five, they lived in Florida, where his mother ran a hotel near Lake Worth; alligators abounded, as did rattlesnakes and wild horses.
- One of the rooms was rented by counterfeiters to manufacture phony money.
- From Florida they moved to Nelson, British Columbia, and then back to the United States, making stops in Spokane, Seattle, and Odessa, Washington.
- His mother then worked as a housekeeper and cook in the lumber camps of Oregon, Montana, and Idaho.
- She was up at 3 a.m. to start breakfast for the crew and was rarely home before 6 p.m.
- Gil, whose friends called him Buster, essentially raised himself in the midst of miners and lumberjacks.

Gil Evans teamed up with jazz legend Miles Davis, who called Evans "the greatest musician in the world."

- He learned to be flexible and resourceful…and tough.
- By the time he was 10 years old, he had settled in Stockton, California, where his musical influences were a Victrola, a few records and "hillbilly" music, which held little interest.
- By 1922, Julia was married to a miner when Gil, whose full name was Ian Ernest Gilmore Green, took his stepfather's last name to become Gil Evans.
- In 1927, 15-year-old Gil bought his first Louis Armstrong record, *No One Else But You*, and traveled to San Francisco to see Duke Ellington play at the Orpheum; these events set a new direction in his life.
- Gil plunged headlong into music, immersing himself in Red Nichols and His Five Pennies, the Wolverines, Fletcher Henderson, McKinney's Cotton Pickers, and, of course, Armstrong and Ellington.
- Gil was blessed with a remarkable ear and a lifelong fascination with sound.
- With his back turned, he could identify the make of a passing car from the sound of its motor.
- In a similar fashion, Gil taught himself—with no formal training—to pick out the notes from every record he played; he could transcribe a song straight from a live radio broadcast.
- By 1933, Gil was the leader of an orchestra performing the latest dance hits, jazz dance music, and the sound of the Casa Loma Orchestra, which was regularly heard on a coast-to-coast radio broadcast.
- They predominantly played one-night stands at country clubs and fraternity houses around Stockton; the musicians each earned between $2.00 and $5.00 a night.
- In 1934, they were hired to play at Lake Tahoe in the summer—their first steady, out-of-town gig; the pay was $12 a week plus room and board.
- "We got our meals, which consisted of creamed turkey necks and turkey wings every night. And we slept up in this sort of an attic room above the ballroom. Most of us put our beds up in the rafters, because of the rats."
- This led to a steady five-nights-a-week job at the Stockton Dreamland Ballroom, where each musician was paid $25.
- On off days, members took a music lesson in the afternoon and then gathered to hear the latest jazz offered at the Palomar Ballroom in Los Angeles, featuring Jimmy and Tommy Dorsey, the Casa Loma Orchestra, and the biggest attraction of the day—Benny Goodman.
- Benny Goodman effectively launched the swing era from the Palomar starting in 1935, promulgating a sound that would change the face of pop music.
- Gil and his orchestra enthusiastically grabbed a hold of swing music and achieved success, only to have Goodman hire away the band's best musicians.
- Gil's goal was perfection, and his standards were high when it came to music; when it came to finances, promotion, bookings, he was very casual.
- This laissez-faire approach caused the band to lose numerous bookings and earn less, causing dissent.

Despite the availability of music lessons, Evans was self taught, and had a remarkable ear.

Life at Work

- The assent of swing music reflected America's love of bigness, while still enjoying "hot" sounds.
- After all, now that Prohibition had ended, jazz could emerge from the shadows of the speakeasy and dance to the rhythms of a nation desperately tired of the Depression.
- By 1938, Gil Evans had linked up with Claude Thornhill— pianist, arranger and composer—in a union of true respect.
- Gil was impressed with Thornhill's writing, while Thornhill was taken by Gil's distinctive arrangements and orchestrations.
- The collaboration would set the stage for Gil's extensive work with Miles Davis.
- Thornhill, who enjoyed backing from his friend Glenn Miller, landed a major East Coast assignment at the Glen Island Casino, on the northern shore of Long Island Sound, and considered the most prominent and popular dance hall on the East Coast.

Miles Davis.

- Thornhill's light, "cloudlike" swing band sound was achieved using an unorthodox mixture of instruments: as many as six clarinets, several French horns and three trumpets for rhythm.
- Gil arrived in 1941 as an arranger, providing him a musical workshop to experiment freely with new musical ideas.
- This partnership lasted—off and on—until 1948, during which time Gil's modest apartment behind a New York City Chinese laundry became a meeting place for musicians looking to develop new musical styles outside of the dominant bebop beat of the day.
- Those present included the leading bebop performer Charlie Parker himself.
- The unique sound created by Gil Evans and Claude Thornhill, whose moods and colorings thrilled live dance audiences, quickly became caught up in two wars: World War II and the American Society of Composers, Authors and Publishers (ASCAP) war over publishing rights.
- A 1941 ban against ASCAP was imposed by the radio networks during a financial dispute over royalties.
- Unable to agree on key fee schedules by which songwriters and publishers would be paid for performing rights on copyrighted material controlled by the ASCAP network, the radio networks boycotted ASCAP.
- For 10 months, ASCAP-affiliated musicians received no radio airplay at all, and bands performing at dances were prevented from performing ASCAP material on their live radio broadcasts.
- Some bands had to replace virtually all their music, including major hits the public had come to love and demand during live performances.
- In 1942, another dispute arose between the major record companies and the American Federation of Musicians (AFM).
- This time, the issue was the AFM's demands for the establishment of a trust fund for aiding unemployed musicians, to be financed by the record companies.
- The dispute would last for two years, retarding recording and music during this time.
- The union struggle to win compensation for its members also meant musicians failed to have their newest music recorded during the strike.
- Also, because singers were not part of the American Federation of Musicians, record companies turned away from Big Bands to fill the public's need for records.
- The strike, the shift to vocal talent, and the military draft hastened the demise of Big Bands.
- But a war-imposed 20 percent entertainment tax—on top of state and federal taxes—which incorporated any music played for dancing, caused musical promoters and entrepreneurs to seek out instrumental groups willing to play small locations unsuitable for dancing.
- That way, they could avoid the tax and still provide quality entertainment.

- In many venues, particularly in Harlem, a premium was placed on performances where virtuoso work was prized—spawning bebop musician Charlie Parker.
- In 1945, when Gil returned from military service—mostly as a musician—his reputation as an orchestrator gained him immediate entry into the new music scene at 52nd Street.
- The military experience had mixed blacks and whites together, and it was impossible to separate them once the war ended—especially if they were musicians.
- Fifty-second Street became a center for the "new"—innovation, talent and technique were highly prized.
- Marx Roach said, "Gil was always interested in the improvisational things we were doing. He was really fascinated with the lines of what Charlie Parker played."

Unlike the Jim Crow south, blacks and whites mixed together as soldiers during WW II and as musicians after the war.

- Those melodic lines—more than the rhythmic innovations of bebop—were central to Gil's musical education.
- When Claude Thornhill reformed his orchestra after the war in April 1946, the days of the Big Bands were over.
- And jazz was not yet considered serious music; the art form needed a figurehead in the same way that Pablo Picasso symbolized modern art.
- Miles Davis, the mysterious, trumpet-playing Prince of Darkness, filled that role with the help of Gil Evans.
- Handsome and debonair, Davis dressed well, drove exotic sports cars, and enjoyed the company of glamorous women.
- On the bandstand, he did not engage in idle stageside chatter; rather, he cultivated the image of a brooding, darkly romantic figure intent on perfection.
- He was also the musician who led the charge to shift the sound of jazz from bebop to cool, from chord-based to scale-based modal improvisation, and from acoustic instrumentation to electric.
- *Miles Ahead*, released in 1957, was the first album following *Birth of the Cool* that Davis recorded with Gil Evans, with whom he would go on to release albums such as *Porgy and Bess* and *Sketches of Spain*.
- Gil combined the 10 pieces that made up the album in a kind of suite, each following the preceding one without interruption.
- The album was also designed to showcase Davis, so he was the only soloist on *Miles Ahead*; Davis had disappeared from the jazz scene for six years while he wrestled with a heroin addiction.
- The album was pronounced a "quiet masterpiece."
- The musical, commercial and critical success of *Miles Ahead* helped make future Miles Davis and Gil Evans ventures possible.
- Columbia Records bestowed on them further artistic control at that period—the Samuel Goldwyn film adaptation of the George Gershwin/DuBose Heyward/Ira Gershwin opera *Porgy and Bess*, in production and set for release in June 1959.
- The pair then teamed up on *Porgy and Bess* in 1958 based on the book by DuBose Heyward and George Gershwin's opera *Porgy and Bess*.
- The album was recorded in four sessions on July 22, July 29, August 4, and August 18, 1958, at Columbia's 30th Street Studio in New York City.
- The standard was three recording sessions—to control costs—but Gil's style demanded more time.
- Within the structure of the album, Gil and Davis expressed their dissatisfaction with bebop and its increasingly complex chord changes.

- Five years earlier, pianist George Russell published his *Lydian Chromatic Concept of Tonal Organization*, which offered an alternative to the practice of improvisation based on chords.
- He proposed abandoning the traditional major and minor key relationships of classical music and developed a new formulation using scales or a series of scales for improvisations.
- *Porgy and Bess* gave both men more room for experimentation with Russell's concept and with third stream playing.
- The collaboration became one of Davis's bestselling albums.
- In early 1958, Miles Davis and his sextet began experimenting with this approach.

Porgy and Bess brought prosperity to both Miles and Evans.

- Instead of soloing in the straight, conventional, melodic way, Davis's new style of improvisation featured rapid mode and scale changes played against sparse chord changes.
- The album brought prosperity to both artists.

Life in the Community: New York City

- In New York City, 52nd Street between Fifth Avenue and Seventh Avenue was convenient to musicians playing on Broadway and the "legitimate" nightclubs, and was also the site of a CBS studio.
- Musicians who played for others in the early evening played for themselves on 52nd Street.
- In its heyday from 1930 through the 1950s, 52nd Street hosted such jazz legends as Charlie Parker, Billie Holiday, Miles Davis, Louis Prima, Dizzy Gillespie, Art Tatum, Thelonious Monk, Fats Waller, Harry Gibson, Marian McPartland, Nat Jaffe, and many more.
- After Minton's Playhouse in uptown Harlem, 52nd Street was the second most important place for bebop.
- A tune called "52nd Street Theme" by Thelonious Monk became a bebop anthem and jazz standard.
- Virtually every jazz great of the era performed at clubs such as The Onyx, The Downbeat, The Three Deuces, The Yacht Club, Jimmy Ryan's, and The Famous Door.
- Jazz disc jockey Symphony Sid frequently did live broadcasts from the street, marking 52nd Street as the place to be across the country.

The CBS studio on 52nd Street in NYC was in the heart of the theater and nightclub scenes.

HISTORICAL SNAPSHOT
1958

- *Sputnik 1*, launched on October 4, 1957, fell to Earth from its orbit and was burned up
- Fourteen-year-old Bobby Fischer won the United States Chess Championship
- Anne de Vries released the fourth and final volume of *Journey Through the Night*
- Baseball player Roy Campanella was involved in an automobile accident that ended his career and left him paralyzed
- The first successful American satellite, *Explorer 1*, was launched into orbit
- Ruth Carol Taylor became the first African-American woman hired as a flight attendant; her career with Mohawk Airlines lasted only six months, due to another discriminatory barrier—the airline's ban on married flight attendants
- Pope Pius XII declared Saint Clare the patron saint of television
- The peace symbol was designed by Gerald Holtom and commissioned by the Campaign for Nuclear Disarmament to protest the Atomic Weapons Research Establishment
- The USS *Wisconsin* was decommissioned, leaving the United States Navy without an active battleship for the first time since 1896
- A U.S. B-47 bomber accidentally dropped an atomic bomb on Mars Bluff, South Carolina, but no nuclear fission occurred
- The U.S. Army inducted Elvis Presley, transforming the "King of Rock 'n' Roll" into U.S. Private #53310761
- Unemployment in Detroit reached 20 percent, marking the height of the Recession of 1958 in the U.S.
- Van Cliburn won the Tchaikovsky International Competition for pianists in Moscow
- Actor-singer and civil rights activist Paul Robeson, whose passport had been reinstated, sang in a pair of sold-out one-man recitals at Carnegie Hall, after which he was rarely seen in public in the U.S. again
- The bodies of unidentified soldiers killed during World War II and the Korean War were buried at the Tomb of the Unknowns in Arlington National Cemetery
- The first International House of Pancakes (IHOP) opened in Toluca Lake, California
- Congress formally created the National Aeronautics and Space Administration (NASA)
- The nuclear-powered submarine USS *Nautilus* became the first vessel to cross the North Pole under water
- Vladimir Nabokov's controversial novel *Lolita* was published in the United States
- *Have Gun, Will Travel* debuted on radio
- The conservative John Birch Society was founded in the U.S. by Robert Welch, a retired candy manufacturer
- Total passengers carried by air exceeded total passengers carried by sea in transatlantic service for first time in U.S. history
- During the International Geophysical Year, Earth's magnetosphere was discovered

Selected Prices

Automobile, Cadillac	$13,075
Cat Food, Three Cans	$0.39
Cough Syrup	$0.49
Eyelash Curler	$1.00
Grill	$79.95
Hamburger, Burger King	$0.37
Ironing Table	$13.95
Lawn Sprinkler	$16.95
Milk, Quart	$0.60
Sofa Bed	$69.99

air-wick

NEW! air-wick spray NATURAL

NEW! air-wick spray FLORAL

air-wick New! Improved!

kills indoor odors

Now! a new world of *Musical Magic*

New enchantment for family leisure hours with

THE *Orga·sonic* by BALDWIN

The new spinet organ that anyone can play

As modest in price as in the space it requires

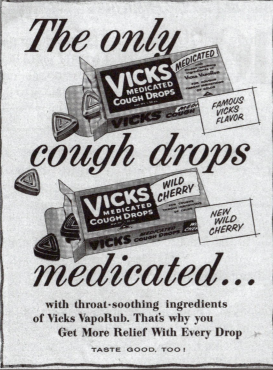

The only

VICKS MEDICATED Cough Drops

FAMOUS VICKS FLAVOR

cough drops

VICKS MEDICATED Cough Drops WILD CHERRY

NEW WILD CHERRY

medicated...

with throat-soothing ingredients of Vicks VapoRub. That's why you **Get More Relief With Every Drop**

TASTE GOOD, TOO!

Comments by Gil Evans to Nat Hentoff, *DownBeat Magazine*, 1957:

At first, the sound of the band was almost a reduction to inactivity of music, the stillness. Everything—melody, harmony, rhythm—was moving at a minimum speed. The melody was very slow, static; the rhythm was nothing much faster than quarter notes and a minimum of syncopation. Everything was lowered to create a sound; nothing was to be used to distract from that sound.

But once this stationary effect, this sound, was created, it was ready to have other things added to it. The sound itself can only hold interest for a certain length of time. Then you have to make certain changes within that sound; you have to make personal use of harmonies rather than work within the traditional ones; there has to be more movement in the melody, more dynamics, more syncopation, speeding up of the rhythms. For me, I had to make these changes, these additions, to sustain my interest in the band, and I started to as soon as I joined. I began to add from my background in jazz, and that's where the jazz influence began to be intensified.

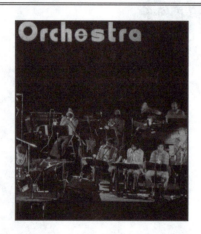

"Trumpeter Red Rodney discussing Claude Thornhill's Big Band Orchestra in 1947-8," Larry Hicock, *Castles of Sound, The Story of Gil Evans*, 2002:

I didn't know anything about Gil Evans. I didn't know him or know of him. When I got there and played, my first impression was, "Good God, this is gorgeous." And I didn't play first trumpet. I was the jazz player; I was the soloist in the band, and, you know, when you're playing the harmony part, it's just that—it's a harmony part. But yet Gil had a knack for writing so that even the second and third trumpets had beautiful melody to them. That band, musically, was a sensational orchestra; it was a gorgeous, gorgeous orchestra—primarily because of Gil.

"Coltrane May Quit Davis, Form Quartet," *Oakland Tribune*, June 14, 1959:

John Coltrane is considering leaving the Miles Davis sextet to form his own quartet.

"There's nothing definite yet," he said the other evening at the Black Cock, where the Davis combo today starts the last week of his engagement. Coltrane has informed Miles of this; should the parting come, it will be amicable. Davis understands Coltrane's viewpoint and will not stand in his way….

Coltrane, who has played with Dizzy Gillespie and Thelonious Monk, has been with Davis since 1955 except for a couple of brief instances when Trane headed a quartet. In the last year or so, he's come to be regarded as one of the most exciting and influential tenor saxophonists in jazz, a factor that figures in his thinking.

"Old Time Jazz Musicians Tops With New Generation," Eugene Gilbert, President of the Gilbert Youth Research Company, *Oelwein Daily Register* (Iowa), November 18, 1959:

The Old Masters of American jazz are still the favorites of American teenagers.

We asked more than 600 youngsters to pick their favorite jazz musicians, and this is the musical group they put together:

On the trumpet, Louis Armstrong; clarinet, Benny Goodman; trombone, JJ Johnson; tenor sax, Stan Getz; alto sax, Paul Desmond, baritone sax, Gerry Mulligan; bass, Ray Brown; at the piano Erroll Garner; and at the drums, Gene Krupa.

In earlier surveys, teenagers named Ricky Nelson and Connie Francis as their favorite vocalists, Marlon Brando and Debbie Reynolds as their favorite stars.

There is every evidence that teenagers know their jazz and their jazz musicians.

There's a tendency to associate teenagers with rock 'n' roll when it comes to music, but rock 'n' roll is actually decreasing in popularity.

Careful examination of the top hits on 20 records chosen each week by teenagers discloses very few that are true rock 'n' roll. Most are jazz.

There is also evidence of a growing-up process in the normal young person's musical taste. Rock 'n' roll appeals primarily to the pre-teenagers and young teenagers. At about 14 or 15, he suddenly becomes enthusiastic about jazz.

Jazz, the musical heartbeat of America, seemed to decline in popularity in the years after World War II. But today it has climbed to a new popularity.

In the last year, jazz concerts have grown tremendously all over the country. In major cities, these concerts are sellouts or had an attendance beyond the promoters' optimistic predictions. Most of attendance comprised college and high school students.

In our poll, we found many teenagers who could identify a jazz musician on a new record simply by his technique, just as they can identify a baseball player by his batting stance.

The most surprising thing about the poll was the popularity of the older musicians. In the trumpet voting, for example, the modern great, Miles Davis, was in the fourth spot.

RCA Victor High Fidelity records and
new RCA Victor High Fidelity
"Victrola" Phonographs *double the realism of recorded music!*

When Gil wrote the arrangement of "I Loves You, Porgy," he only wrote a scale for me. No chords...gives you a lot more freedom and space to hear things...there will be fewer chords but infinite possibilities as to what to do with them. Classical composers have been writing this way for years, but jazz musicians seldom have.

—Miles Davis to Nat Hentoff, *The Jazz Review,* 1958

1959 PROFILE

Born in 1926, Johnny Bragg grew up a self-described wild child who became a rock 'n' roll pioneer, discovered while in prison for crimes he did not commit.

Life at Home

- Singer-songwriter Johnny Bragg's mother Maybelle died in childbirth.
- The baby she left behind in 1926 was blind, black and poor in segregated Nashville, Tennessee, and needed constant care.
- It was not a propitious beginning for the rock and roll pioneer discovered while in prison serving 594 years for rapes he did not commit.
- Johnny's father, Wade, was a railway man who worked 12 hours a day, six days a week; he earned $6 weekly for his 72 hours of labor.
- Unable to care for the motherless flock, Wade Bragg farmed out Johnny and his three siblings to the children's grandmother and later their uncle, who was a minister and a lover of gospel music.
- At an early age Johnny learned to sing songs that reflected his life: "My Blue Heaven," and "What You Goin' to Do When the Rent Come 'Round?"
- The three boys, who saw their father only on Sundays, shared one room and one bed.
- The economic boom of the 1920s had largely ignored the poor and working class of America; black families in North Nashville typically earned $15 to $25 a month, a large percentage of which went to pay rent to white landlords for the two-bedroom frame houses without indoor plumbing.
- At the age of six, Johnny inexplicably regained his sight, was able to enter school and immediately discovered he had no interest in an education.
- That year, 1,800 children entered the first grade; only 52 students received high school diplomas 12 years later.
- Johnny was a wild kid who relished fighting chickens for sport; when he was 14, he served a month's confinement for riding in a stolen car.

Rock and roll pioneer Johnny Bragg discovered his musical calling while in prison.

- His life changed forever in 1943 when he caught his girlfriend, Jenny, having sex with his best friend.
- The naked girl angrily attacked Johnny and later, in order to explain her bruises, she accused Johnny of raping her.
- Her mother phoned the police, who beat Johnny until he signed a confession.
- While he was in his jail cell, the police paraded a dozen rape victims in front of Johnny—six of whom claimed that the 16-year-old had raped them.
- Even after Johnny's former girlfriend retracted her story and told the truth, Johnny was still tried for the other crimes and given six 99-year sentences; he was then sent to the notorious Tennessee State Penitentiary.
- On his seventeenth birthday, Johnny Bragg became one of 1,400 inmates; his sentence was for 594 years.
- At the Tennessee State Prison, he was assigned to making prison clothes.
- Early on, when the prison authorities thought he was not working quickly enough, the guards tied him to a ring suspended from the ceiling and beat him unconscious with their leather belts.
- Prison was also where he became reacquainted with the gospel music of his youth.
- When Bragg heard a group of prisoners singing spirituals, he did not understand why they could not be as disciplined as the groups he had heard in church.
- He had a natural ear for harmony and quickly moved into the role of lead tenor.
- And he began to write songs, even though he could barely read and write.
- "I'd pick up an old piece of paper off the ground. If the song had the word 'heart' in it, all I would put in it was maybe a T or an H. If there was a girl I'd put G. I wrote a lot of songs that way."
- He formed the Prisonaires vocal group with Ed Thurman, tenor (who had killed the man who had killed his dog), William Stewart, baritone (charged with bludgeoning a white man to death, even though someone else had confessed to the killing), Marcell Sanders, bass (who stabbed the man who stabbed his girlfriend), and John Drue Jr., tenor (serving time for car theft).
- Their first performances were serenading prisoners before their state-sponsored execution in the electric chair.
- After the singing and the disturbing sight of a man's death by electrocution, Johnny would stay behind to loosen the straps on the condemned and clean up the mess.
- By the late 1940s, World War II was over and the culture of America was changing, dancing to the beat of soldiers returning from war.
- Approximately 55 percent of American homes had indoor plumbing; the minimum wage was $0.43 an hour, the average teacher was paid $1,400 year, and the life expectancy of an American male was 60.8 years.

Bragg formed the Prisonaires vocal group with other prisoners.

- At the beginning of the decade, Big Bands had dominated popular music, especially those led by Glenn Miller, Tommy Dorsey, Duke Ellington, and Benny Goodman.
- Bing Crosby's smooth voice made him extremely popular, vying with Frank Sinatra, Dinah Shore, Kate Smith, and Perry Como for the public's attention.
- By the end of the decade, bebop and rhythm and blues were merging with distinctly black sounds, epitomized by Charlie Parker, Dizzy Gillespie, while Thelonious Monk, Billie Holiday, Ella Fitzgerald, and Woody Herman forged new avenues in blues and jazz.
- Radio was the lifeline for Americans in the 1940s, providing news, music and entertainment; programming included soap operas, quiz shows, children's hours, mystery stories, fine drama, and sports.
- Within the Tennessee State Prison, the radios, all of which were owned or controlled by the guards, blared blues, gospel, country-western, and some pop music all day long.
- Nashville stars would sometimes perform at the prison and, when Johnny met Hank Williams, he asked, "Do you ever sing songs written by other people?" "Depends," said Williams, "Are you one of those other people?"
- Johnny sang Williams a song which Williams bought for $5.
- Johnny always insisted that the song eventually became "Your Cheatin' Heart," a country standard.

Life at Work

- Johnny Bragg's music career outside the walls of the Tennessee State Penitentiary began with the election corner of Frank Clement—a politician whose style was a cross between the Rev. Billy Graham and President "Give 'em Hell" Harry Truman.
- Interested in being Tennessee's governor since he was 16, Clement became the nation's youngest governor at age 32 in 1953.
- To please his wife, Clement transformed the Governor's mansion into a showcase for music makers and music lovers; to please himself, he tackled the thorny issues of prison reform.
- Johnny Bragg and the Prisonaires were the benefactors of both.
- In an unprecedented move, the Prisonaires were allowed to perform under armed guard at churches and civic functions, and then on local radio.
- For their first performance at the Governor's mansion, a 1929 Georgian brick estate boasting 22 rooms, the prisoners were driven and escorted by the warden's petite wife when the assigned prison guard failed to show up on time.

Tennessee Governor Frank Clement.

- They wore suits fashioned by Johnny in the prison laundry, were allowed to enter through the front door of the Governor's mansion, were introduced personally by the governor by name, and then sang for an élite group of guests that included future president Texas Senator Lyndon Johnson and U.S. Senator Albert Gore of Tennessee.
- The evening was a grand success, and within weeks the Prisonaires became regulars on local white radio stations, at churches and services organizations.
- "The Prisonaires represent the hopes of tomorrow rather than the mistakes of yesterday," Governor Clement announced the same week the men performed briefly on radio Station WSM, home of the Grand Ole Opry, a musical institution since 1926.
- Their next big break came when Johnny was walking across the courtyard to his duties in the laundry with habitual housebreaker and thief, Robert Riley.
- As the rain beat down, Johnny said, "Here we are just walking in the rain and wondering what the girls are doing." Riley said, "That's a song."
- Within a few minutes, Johnny had composed two verses and was convinced it was a hit: "Just walkin' in the rain, gettin' soakin' wet, torturin' my heart, tryin' to forget."
- Unable to read and write, he asked Riley to write it down in exchange for a writing credit.
- When the group recorded their first record for Sam Phillips of Sun Records, "Just Walkin' in the Rain" was on the A side—the song most likely to become popular.
- Johnny heard his song for the first time on WSOK, one of two stations that gave them their start.

When performing for the Governor, the Prisonaires wore prison-made suits.

- "We was coming in from dinner. Some of the guys were already in their cells. I passed Ed's headbolter desk where a radio was playing. I get within earshot and I keep moving closer to a familiar sound. The radio's playing 'Just Walkin.' Ed, he walked in behind me and sat at his desk. I said, 'Ed you hear that? That's us.' and he said, 'Yeah, it is. Sounds all right.'"
- By that time, the cellblock came alive with voices yelling with excitement.
- "The guards, they were looking us up and down, but they let it go."
- Soon after its June 1953 release, "Just Walkin'," with its elegant but simple arrangement, made the nation's R&B Top 10 and quickly sold 50,000 copies.
- The record was produced by Sun Studios, the same studio where Elvis Presley, Johnny Cash, and Carl Perkins had their starts.

- According to Johnny, he and Elvis Presley often traded musical ideas.
- The Prisonaires then received national publicity when the country star Roy Acuff presented them with a Gibson guitar.
- Their privileges were such that when bass singer Marcell Sanders was offered parole, he refused, saying that he wanted to stay with the group.
- In August 1953, they recorded a raucous "Softly and Tenderly" with Ike Turner on piano; their third single, the plaintive "A Prisoner's Prayer," was printed with stripes on the label, and their next, "There Is Love in You," was recorded at the penitentiary itself.
- The whole prison caught the magic of performing and writing songs; producer Sam Phillips picked up two songs from white inmates, "Without You" and "Casual Love Affair," that he was to rehearse with Elvis Presley.

The Prisonaires' frequently entertained at the governor's mansion.

- Eventually, Sanders was told that he would have to leave the prison, and tenor John Drue was also given parole.
- Not eligible for parole, Bragg reconstituted the group even though the mood at the prison began to change.
- Other prisoners became resentful of Johnny's freedom to leave the prison to perform, fights were started, and four white inmates threatened to cut out his vocal cords.
- Also, to meet the demands of the new rock 'n' roll era, the Prisonaires began recording more upbeat material and decided to change their name.
- They first chose the name Sunbeams, then switched to the Marigolds to record the song "Rocking Horse," which quickly topped the R&B chart; it was outsold by a cover version for the pop market by the Fontane Sisters.
- Songs originated by black groups but covered by white singers were becoming increasingly common.
- In 1956, Johnnie Ray's record producer, Mitch Miller, rediscovered "Just Walkin' in the Rain" and realized it was perfect for the popular singer nicknamed the "Cry Guy."
- Ray's performing style included rock 'n' roll theatrics, including beating up his piano, writhing on the floor and crying, earning the Oregon-born white singer the nicknames "Mr. Emotion," "The Nabob of Sob," and "The Prince of Wails."
- Ray's fully orchestrated and highly histrionic performance went to No. 2 in the U.S. and topped the U.K. chart.
- The No. 1 American song was Elvis's "Don't Be Cruel."
- Johnny Bragg's songwriting royalties topped $8,700 for the year—the most he ever made—money that was put into a trust fund for him.
- He was even invited to the Broadcast Music Inc. black tie banquet because of the level of radio play that "Just Walkin'" had received.
- The warden did not allow him to attend.

- When Governor Clement asked the Marigolds to perform at an event at the Governor's mansion honoring Elvis Presley, he told them to perform "Jailhouse Rock."
- Presley had a wonderful time harmonizing with the inmates and suggested that they record together, but his manager Colonel Parker did not consider this a good career move.
- In March 1956, the Marigolds went to Nashville to record "Foolish Me" and "Beyond the Clouds," while "Heartbreak Hotel" by Elvis Presley was enjoying an eight-week run at the top of the charts.
- Thanks to the efforts of the Governor, Johnny Bragg was released on parole in January 1959 as one the last acts of Gov. Clements.
- He was 32 years old and had spent 15 years in prison for crimes he almost certainly did not commit.
- It was time to begin again.

The Prisonaires changed their name to The Marigolds, and began recording more upbeat material.

Life in the Community: Nashville, Tennessee

- When Johnny Bragg was growing up, Nashville, Tennessee, was considered to be the "Athens of the South," even though a pattern of racial exclusiveness prevailed in Nashville's schools and public facilities, including restrooms, waiting areas, snack counters, transportation terminals, libraries, theaters, hotels, restaurants, and neighborhoods.
- In 1958, local black leaders founded the Nashville Christian Leadership Conference (NCLC), an affiliate of Martin Luther King, Jr.'s Southern Christian Leadership Conference.
- Early in 1959, the NCLC began a movement to desegregate downtown Nashville.
- The policy of segregation was tested at Harvey's and Cain-Sloan's department stores, where the Reverends Smith and James M. Lawson, Jr.'s students John Lewis, Diane Nash, James Bevel, Marion Barry, and others bought goods and then attempted to desegregate the lunch counters.
- Before the end of 1959, students from Nashville's black colleges, including Fisk University, Tennessee A&I State University, Meharry Medical College,

Segregation was the norm in Nashville, from schools to lunch counters.

and American Baptist Theological Seminary, were being trained to participate in the non-violent protests.
- Opened in 1898, the Tennessee State Prison was located near downtown Nashville, Tennessee.
- The Tennessee Prison contained 800 small cells, each designed to house a single inmate.
- The prison's 800 cells were opened to receive prisoners on February 12, 1898, and that day admitted 1,403 prisoners, creating immediate overcrowding.

- Overcrowding persisted throughout the next century.
- It was the advent of the Grand Ole Opry in 1925, combined with an already thriving publishing industry, that positioned Nashville to become "Music City USA."
- Beginning in the mid-1950s, the Nashville sound turned country music into a multimillion-dollar industry.
- Under the direction of producers such as Chet Atkins, Owen Bradley, and later Billy Sherrill, the sound brought country music to a diverse audience and expanded its appeal.
- The sound borrowed from 1950s pop stylings: a prominent and smooth vocal, backed by a string section and vocal chorus.
- Leading artists in this genre included Patsy Cline, Jim Reeves, and Eddy Arnold.
- The "slip note" piano style of session musician Floyd Cramer was an important component of this style.

The Tennessee Prison.

HISTORICAL SNAPSHOT
1959

- CBS Radio eliminated four soap operas: *Backstage Wife, Our Gal Sunday, The Road of Life*, and *This is Nora Drake*
- Alaska was admitted as the forty-ninth U.S. state; Hawaii became the fiftieth
- The United States recognized the new Cuban government of Fidel Castro
- Motown Records was founded by Berry Gordy, Jr.
- Walt Disney released his sixteenth animated film, *Sleeping Beauty*—Disney's first animated film to be shown in 70 mm and modern six-track stereophonic sound
- A chartered plane transporting musicians Buddy Holly, Ritchie Valens, and The Big Bopper went down in foggy conditions near Clear Lake, Iowa, killing all four occupants on board, including pilot Roger Peterson
- At Cape Canaveral, Florida, the first successful test firing of a Titan intercontinental ballistic missile was accomplished
- The United States launched the *Vanguard II* weather satellite
- Racecar driver Lee Petty won the first Daytona 500
- Recording sessions for the album "Kind of Blue" by Miles Davis began at Columbia's 30th Street Studio in New York City
- The Marx Brothers made their last TV appearance in *The Incredible Jewel Robbery*
- The Barbie doll debuted
- Busch Gardens in Tampa, Florida, was dedicated and opened its gates
- The Dalai Lama fled Tibet and was granted asylum in India
- NASA selected seven military pilots to become the first U.S. astronauts
- The St. Lawrence Seaway linking the North American Great Lakes and the Atlantic Ocean officially opened to shipping
- The USS *George Washington* was launched as the first submarine to carry ballistic missiles
- Charles Ovnand and Dale R. Buis became the first Americans killed in action in Vietnam
- The first skull of *Australopithecus* was discovered by Mary Leakey in the Olduvai Gorge of Tanzania
- The Soviet rocket *Luna 2* became the first manmade object to crash on the moon, and *Luna 3* sent back the first-ever photos of the far side of the moon
- Rod Serling's classic anthology series *The Twilight Zone* premiered on CBS
- MGM's widescreen, multimillion-dollar, Technicolor version of *Ben-Hur*, starring Charlton Heston, was released and won a record 11 Academy Awards
- The Henney Kilowatt went on sale in the United States, becoming the first mass-produced electric car in almost three decades

Selected Prices

Clearasil	$0.59
Cornet	$99.50
Fruit Cocktail	$0.93
Guitar, Washburn	$27.50
Hamburger, Burger King Whopper	$0.37
Hotel Room, Ritz-Carlton, Boston	$9.00
Man's Shirt, Arrow	$5.00
Movie Projector	$89.95
Theatre Ticket, New York	$3.85
Vodka, Smirnoff, Fifth	$5.23

"No Longer Walkin' in the Rain," *Long Beach Independent*, January 2, 1959:

Johnny Bragg, who wrote "Walkin' in the Rain" in prison, walked into the sunshine of freedom Wednesday.

The Negro convict faced almost certain imprisonment for life when he was sentenced to six 99-year terms for rape when he was 17 years old. He spent 16 years in the Tennessee Penitentiary here.

Wednesday, he was paroled. Former Gov. Frank Clement, who had befriended and helped Bragg, commuted his sentence to life just before he left office earlier this month. With time served and good behavior, Bragg became eligible immediately for parole.

The Pardons and Parole Board said Bragg appeared to have been rehabilitated, and that he has a job in his uncle's barbershop in Nashville. He must report regularly to a parole officer for the rest of his life.

Bragg was the last of a prison singing group which he organized to be released. The group, "The Prisonaires," often entertained at parties given by Clement. Bragg wrote and collaborated on a number of popular tunes, but "Walkin' in the Rain" was his biggest hit.

Recorded Popular Songs: 1950s

1950
1. The Fat Man—Fats Domino
2. Please Send Me Someone to Love—Percy Mayfield
3. Teardrops From My Eyes—Ruth Brown
4. Mona Lisa—Nat "King" Cole
5. Tennessee Waltz—Patti Page
6. Long Gone Lonesome Blues—Hank Williams
7. Mardi Gras In New Orleans—Professor Longhair
8. I'm Movin' On—Hank Snow
9. Rollin' Stone—Muddy Waters
10. Double Crossing Blues—Johnny Otis (Little Esther & the Robins)

1951
1. Sixty Minute Man—Dominoes
2. Rocket 88—Jackie Brenston
3. Dust My Broom—Elmore James
4. Cry—Johnnie Ray
5. Too Young—Nat "King" Cole
6. Cold Cold Heart—Hank Williams
7. Glory of Love—Five Keys
8. Three O'Clock Blues—B.B. King
9. Hey Good Lookin'—Hank Williams
10. How High The Moon—Les Paul & Mary Ford

1952
1. Lawdy Miss Clawdy—Lloyd Price
2. Jambalaya (On The Bayou)—Hank Williams
3. Have Mercy Baby—Dominoes
4. One Mint Julep—Clovers
5. Night Train—Jimmy Forrest
6. My Song—Johnny Ace
7. Goin' Home—Fats Domino
8. Moody Mood For Love—King Pleasure
9. Juke—Little Walter
10. Baby, Don't Do It—"5" Royales

1953
1. Money Honey—Drifters featuring Clyde McPhatter
2. Your Cheatin' Heart—Hank Williams
3. Crying In The Chapel—Orioles
4. Gee—Crows
5. Shake a Hand—Faye Adams
6. Honey Hush—Joe Turner
7. Mama, He Treats Your Daughter Mean—Ruth Brown
8. Hound Dog—Willie Mae "Big Mama" Thornton
9. Kaw-Liga—Hank Williams
10. The Things That I Used To Do—Guitar Slim

1954
1. Rock Around The Clock—Bill Haley & His Comets
2. Shake, Rattle and Roll—Joe Turner/Bill Haley & His Comets
3. Earth Angel—Penguins
4. Sh-Boom—Chords
5. That's All Right—Elvis Presley with Scotty and Bill
6. Pledging My Love—Johnny Ace
7. Goodnite Sweetheart Goodnite—Spaniels
8. I've Got a Woman—Ray Charles
9. White Christmas—Drifters featuring Clyde McPhatter
10. Work With Me Annie—Royals/Midnighters

1955
1. Tutti Frutti—Little Richard
2. Maybellene—Chuck Berry
3. Bo Diddley—Bo Diddley
4. Why Do Fools Fall in Love?—Teenagers
5. The Great Pretender—Platters
6. Ain't That a Shame—Fats Domino
7. Folsom Prison Blues—Johnny Cash and the Tennessee Two
8. Speedo—Cadillacs
9. Story Untold—Nutmegs
10. My Babe—Little Walter

1956
1. Hound Dog—Elvis Presley
2. Long Tall Sally—Little Richard
3. Blue Suede Shoes—Carl Perkins/Elvis Presley
4. Don't Be Cruel—Elvis Presley
5. Be-Bop-a-Lula—Gene Vincent & the Bluecaps
6. Roll Over Beethoven—Chuck Berry
7. In the Still of the Night—Five Satins
8. Blueberry Hill—Fats Domino
9. Please, Please, Please—James Brown & the Famous Flames
10. I Walk The Line—Johnny Cash and the Tennessee Two

1957
1. Jailhouse Rock—Elvis Presley
2. Whole Lotta Shakin' Going On—Jerry Lee Lewis
3. That'll Be the Day—Crickets
4. Bye Bye Love—Everly Brothers
5. Great Balls of Fire—Jerry Lee Lewis
6. School Day—Chuck Berry
7. Rock and Roll Music—Chuck Berry
8. Peggy Sue—Buddy Holly
9. Lucille—Little Richard
10. Rocking Pneumonia & the Boogie Woogie Flu—Huey "Piano" Smith & the Clowns

1958
1. Johnny B. Goode—Chuck Berry
2. Summertime Blues—Eddie Cochran
3. Good Golly Miss Molly—Little Richard
4. For Your Precious Love—Jerry Butler & the Impressions
5. Sweet Little Sixteen—Chuck Berry
6. Yakety Yak—Coasters
7. La Bamba—Ritchie Valens
8. Since I Don't Have You—Skyliners
9. Rumble—Link Wray
10. Lonely Teardrops—Jackie Wilson

1959
1. What'd I Say—Ray Charles
2. I Only Have Eyes for You—Flamingos
3. Mack the Knife—Bobby Darin
4. There Goes My Baby—Drifters
5. Shout—Isley Brothers
6. Kansas City—Wilbert Harrison
7. Poison Ivy—Coasters
8. Money—Barrett Strong
9. Love Potion No. 9—Clovers
10. You're So Fine—Falcons

Music Trivia

- Little Richard's song "Tutti Frutti" originally contained the lyrics "Tutti Frutti, good booty," but in 1955, Specialty Records had songwriter Dorothy LaBostrie tame it down to "Tutti Frutti, oh Rudy."
- Ray Charles's 1959 release "What'd I Say" was created on the spot when he ran out of songs during a marathon dance show in Pittsburgh; concerning the sexy vocal bridge that made the song famous, Charles said, "Hell, let's face it, everybody knows about the ummmmh, unnnh. That's how we all got here."
- The rock 'n' roll song "Johnny B. Goode" by Chuck Berry, which was released in 1958, originally contained the words "That little colored boy could play," but was changed to "country boy" so the record could get airtime on the radio.
- Elvis Presley's release of "Hound Dog" in 1956 went through 31 takes at the RCA studios in New York. "I don't care what you say," he told a reporter. "It ain't nasty."
- The title of the Buddy Holly and the Crickets song "That'll Be the Day" came from a recurring line in the John Wayne Western movie *The Searchers*
- Fats Domino's biggest hit "Blueberry Hill," released in 1956, was originally recorded by Gene Autry in 1940.

THE CASH BOX
The Nation's
Rhythm & Blues
TOP TEN

1 CRYING IN THE CHAPEL
The Orioles
(Jubilee 5122)

2 GOOD LOVIN'
The Clovers
(Atlantic 1000)

3 THE CLOCK
Johnny Ace
(Duke 112)

4 SHAKE A HAND
Faye Adams & Joe Morris
(Herald 416)

5 PLEASE DON'T LEAVE ME
Fats Domino
(Imperial 5240)

6 TOO MUCH LOVIN'
The "5" Royales
(Apollo 448)

7 PLEASE LOVE ME
B. B. King
(R.P.M. 386)

8 GET IT
The Royals
(Federal 12133)

9 DON'T DECEIVE ME
Chuck Willis
(Okeh 6985)

10 JUST WALKIN' IN THE RAIN
Prisonaires
(Sun 186)

> Music can name the unnamable and communicate the unknowable.
> —*Leonard Bernstein*

"Cash, An American Man," Bill Miller, 2004:

Johnny Cash returned to Memphis, Tennessee, in 1954 after being discharged from the Air Force. He was squeezing out a living as a door-to-door appliance salesman when he found out through his brother, Roy, about two men who were trying to organize a band. Marshall Grant and Luther Perkins worked in a Memphis auto repair shop. After hours, they picked guitars and sang for friends and coworkers, and Johnny soon joined them. Luther played lead guitar, and Marshall played an upright bass that he had bought used. Johnny knew three cords on his acoustic guitar. None of the three was an accomplished player, but the stark, raw and unadorned sound the three produced on their instruments was the ideal complement to Johnny's strong, clear baritone voice. Johnny hoped the trio would become a gospel group, but Sun Records founder Sam Phillips discouraged that plan. After listening to the group, Phillips told Johnny, Marshall and Luther to come see him again when they had changed their repertoire. And that's exactly what they did.

1960–1969

The 1960s were tumultuous. Following the placid era of the 1950s, the seventh decade of the twentieth century contained tragic assassinations, momentous social movements, remarkable space achievements, and the longest war in American history. Civil Rights leader Martin Luther King, Jr., would deliver his "I have a dream" speech in 1963, the same year President John F. Kennedy was killed. Five years later in 1968, King, along with John Kennedy's influential brother Bobby, would be shot. And violent protests against American involvement in Vietnam would be led and heavily supported by the educated middle class, which had grown and prospered enormously in the American economy.

From 1960 to 1964, the economy expanded; unemployment was low and disposable income for music, vacations, art or simply having fun grew rapidly. Internationally, the power of the United States was immense. Congress gave the young President John F. Kennedy the defense and space-related programs Americans wanted, but few of the welfare programs he proposed. Then, inflation arrived, along with the Vietnam War. Between 1950 and 1965, inflation soared from an annual average of less than two percent (ranging from six percent to 14 percent a year) to a budget-popping average of 9.5 percent. Upper class investors, once content with the consistency and stability of banks, sought better returns in the stock market and real estate.

Music, especially in the form of rock 'n' roll, made its presence felt during the decade, displaying threads reaching back to the blues embodied by Muddy Waters, B.B. King, and Howlin' Wolf. The music of the 1960s branched into several directions. The R&B and Soul scenes were heralded by the Motown record label founded by Berry Gordy Jr., in Detroit and Stax Records in Memphis. This was followed by the British invasion led by the Beatles and the Rolling Stones, but also gave voice to groups such as the Byrds and the Animals. At the same time, the American folk music revival grew into a major movement, pioneered by figures such as Woody Guthrie and Pete Seeger, and represented during the decade by Joan Baez and Bob Dylan or groups like the Mamas & the Papas and Crosby, Stills and Nash. Psychedelic rock then gained a huge following thanks to the Doors, the Grateful Dead, Country Joe and the Fish, and Jefferson Airplane. The Cold War became hotter during conflicts over Cuba and Berlin in the early 1960s. Fears over the international spread of communism led to America's intervention in a foreign conflict that would become a defining event of the decade: Vietnam.

Military involvement in this small Asian country grew from advisory status to full-scale war. By 1968, Vietnam had become a national obsession leading to President Lyndon Johnson's decision not to run for another term and fueling not only debate over our role in Vietnam, but more inflation and division nationally. The antiwar movement grew rapidly. Antiwar marches, which had drawn but a few thousand in 1965, grew in size until millions of marchers filled the streets of New York, San Francisco, and Washington, DC, only a few years later. By spring 1970, students on 448 college campuses made ROTC voluntary or abolished it.

The struggle to bring economic equality to blacks during the period produced massive spending for school integration. By 1963, the peaceful phase of the Civil Rights movement was ending; street violence, assassinations, and bombings defined the period. In 1967, 41 cities experienced major disturbances. At the same time, charismatic labor organizer César Chavez's United Farm Workers led a Civil Rights-style movement for Mexican-Americans, gaining national support which challenged the growers of the West with a five-year agricultural strike.

As a sign of increasing affluence and changing times, American consumers bought 73 percent fewer potatoes and 25 percent more fish, poultry, and meat and 50 percent more citrus products and tomatoes than in 1940. California passed New York as the most populous state. Factory workers earned more than $100 a week, their highest wages in history. From 1960 to 1965, the amount of money spent for prescription drugs to lose weight doubled, while the per capita consumption of processed potato chips rose from 6.3 pounds in 1958 to 14.2 pounds eight years later. In 1960, approximately 40 percent of American adult women had paying jobs; 30 years later, the number would grow to 57.5 percent. Their emergence into the work force would transform marriage, child rearing, and the economy. In 1960, women were also liberated by the FDA's approval of the birth control pill, giving both women and men a degree of control over their bodies that had never existed before. During the decade, anti-establishment sentiments grew: men's hair was longer and wilder, beards and mustaches became popular, women's skirts rose to mid-thigh, and bras were discarded. Hippies advocated alternative lifestyles, drug use, especially marijuana and LSD, increased; the Beatles, the Rolling Stones, Jimi Hendrix, and Janis Joplin became popular music figures; college campuses became major sites for demonstrations against the war and for Civil Rights. The Supreme Court prohibited school prayer, assured legal counsel to the poor, limited censorship of sexual material, and increased the rights of the accused.

Extraordinary space achievements also marked the decade. Ten years after President Kennedy announced he would place a man on the moon, 600 million people around the world watched as Neil Armstrong gingerly lowered his left foot into the soft dust of the moon's surface. In a tumultuous time of division and conflict, the landing was one of America's greatest triumphs and an exhilarating demonstration of American genius. Its cost was $25 billion and set the stage for 10 other men to walk on the surface of the moon during the next three years. The 1960s saw the birth of Enovid 10, the first oral contraceptive (cost $0.55 each), the start of Berry Gordy's Motown Records, felt-tip pens, Diet-Rite cola, Polaroid color film, Weight Watchers, and Automated Teller Machines. It's the decade when lyrics began appearing on record albums, Jackie and Aristotle Onassis reportedly spent $20 million during their first year together, and the Gay Liberation Front participated in the Hiroshima Day March, the first homosexual participation as a separate constituency in a peace march.

1964 PROFILE

Nothing about Estelle Stewart Axton's background in 1958 suggested that she was destined to become the South's premier record producer for black artists.

Life at Home

- Estelle Stewart Axton was white, 40 years of age, a former schoolteacher, and married with two children.
- She was working as a bookkeeper at Union Planters Bank in Memphis, Tennessee, when she agreed to mortgage her house to buy a $2,500 one-track Ampex Recorder.
- Her business partner and brother, Jim Stewart, hardly fit the record producer mold, either.
- He worked in the bond department of a rival bank and played fiddle in several swing bands.
- He found much more pleasure in the latter.
- But together, they created Stax Records, a label that would challenge the supremacy of Motown Records in Detroit.
- Stax was home to Otis Redding, Rufus Thomas, Booker T and the MGs, and Isaac Hayes.
- Estelle was born September 11, 1918, in Middleton, Tennessee, and grew up on a farm.
- She moved to Memphis as a schoolteacher, married Everett Axton, and was working in a bank when, in 1958, her brother Jim Stewart asked for help in developing an independent record label he planned to call Satellite Records.
- He wanted to issue recordings of local country and rockabilly artists.
- All he needed was $2,500 to buy a recording machine, and in exchange, Estelle would be his partner.

Estelle Steward Axton was an unlikely record producer for black artists.

- When Estelle talked to her husband about it, his response was, "No way!"
- But the more she thought about the concept, the more she liked it.
- Eventually, she convinced her husband that they should remortgage their house and, in 1959, she joined Satellite as an equal partner.
- Initially, the brother and sister pair set up shop in an abandoned, rent-free grocery store in a small community 30 miles from Memphis.
- At the time, the newspapers were full of headlines concerning the new *Sputnik*, the Russian satellite that had become first manmade object in space.
- It appeared to represent the future, so they named the company Satellite Productions, which attracted a trademark lawsuit and resulted in a name change to Stax Records, comprising the first two letters in their last names, Stewart and Axton.

Estelle created Stax Records with her fiddle playing brother, who became her business partner.

- The following year, Estelle and Jim discovered the unused Capitol Theatre in a black Memphis neighborhood and turned it into a recording studio and record shop; the cost was $150 a month.
- Once the studio was set up, they opened a record shop next-door in a space that formerly housed the theater's candy counter; Estelle kept her day job at the bank.
- To get inventory for the store, Estelle took orders for records from her coworkers at the bank, then went to Poplar Tunes, the largest record store in town, bought the records for $0.65 and resold them for $1.00.
- Initially, the record store kept the Stax Records studio afloat.
- None of their early records were successful, that is, until popular black disc jockey Rufus Thomas came to the studio to pitch some ideas with his 16-year-old daughter, Carla, in tow.
- That day they previewed "'Cause I Love," written by Rufus Thomas, and convinced Estelle and Jim to record and distribute it.
- Rufus Thomas's most successful recording had been an answer song, created in response to a Big Mama Thornton's "Hound Dog," titled "Bear Cat" and released in 1953; "Hound Dog" would later be successfully covered by a white singer named Elvis Presley.
- About 15,000 copies later, Atlantic Records head Jerry Wexler offered $1,000 for the right to distribute "Cause I Love" nationally—giving the studio some exposure, some cash and its white owners of Stax a sense of the potential of black music.
- Their recording studio itself had acoustical drapes handmade by Estelle, a control room built on the movie theater stage, insulation on the one outside plaster wall to reduce echo, and baffles made with burlap hung from the ceiling.
- The end result was a very live recording environment issuing a reverberation effect similar to that of the concert hall; this would become an important component of what was later known as the Stax Sound.

Life at Work

- Stax Records' big break came when Rufus and Carla Thomas returned to the station with another idea, another song.
- "As soon as Jim and I heard that song, we knew it was a hit. It's funny, when you hear a song, you know if it's got something in it that will sell," Estelle said.
- With the $1,000 they had received from Atlantic Records, Stax Records recorded "Gee Whiz, (Look at His Eyes)" and established itself as a hit-maker.
- Carla Thomas, who commandeered the title of Queen of Memphis Soul, grew up in the projects, in close proximity to Palace Theater on world-famous Beale Street.
- The talented Thomas first became a member of the high school-oriented Teen Town Singers in 1952 at the age of 10.
- Thomas was responsible for not only attending classes and completing her schoolwork, but she also had to attend rehearsals on Wednesdays and Fridays after school and then perform at the radio station on Saturday.
- Somehow she found the time to write "Gee Whiz" when only 16, using a 32-bar AABA pop song structure.
- Sales of "Gee Whiz" began slowly in 1960, but just as Thomas was in the midst of her first year at Tennessee A&I University in Nashville, the success of the single propelled her into the visual spotlight as she performed on *American Bandstand*.

Carla Thomas – Queen of Memphis Soul – and Stax Records both became stars with song Gee Whiz.

- The song provided a launching pad to Thomas's first album, and gave Stax Records national exposure and label recognition; Atlantic also signed on to handle distribution.
- Estelle's next hit arrived courtesy of a neighborhood group, the Mar-Keys, playing "Last Night," an instrumental played by a racially integrated R&B group that included Estelle's son; when the band toured, its members were all white.
- The song was played on WLOK radio before it became a record, generating enormous interest in the Memphis area; however, Jim Stewart was reluctant to take time to cut a record.
- Estelle, known as Lady A, finally got it into the marketplace by pleading, cussing and finally betting $100 it would be a hit; she knew that the kids could "twist" to the record.
- Memphis Radio station WHBQ introduced the record to white audiences and played it over and over before it went national and Estelle collected her $100.
- The neighborhood surrounding Stax Records would adopt the Soulsville moniker and honor performers such as Aretha Franklin, Johnny Ace, and James Alexander of the Mar-Keys.

Stax recorded Last Night *by the Mar-Keys, a neighborhood group that included Estelle's son.*

- Stax sounds were different from its rival Motown in Detroit, whose urban, smooth sounds were more polished.
- "Once you crossed the Mason-Dixon line and got down to Memphis," "Rufus Thomas said, "it was altogether different."
- In 1959, a young black songwriter named Berry Gordon Junior formed Motown for the purpose of aggressively marketing black rock 'n' roll to a white audience.
- Motown turned out hit records in an assembly line fashion—each one technically perfect, efficiently marketed, and designed to have a broad crossover appeal.
- Motown carefully supervised the repertoire of its acts and required them to take classes in diction, stage presence, and choreography.
- As a result, Gordy developed headliner acts such as Diana Ross and the Supremes, the Temptations, and Michael Jackson of the Jackson Five.
- Estelle and Jim's system was less formalized and more prone to an occasional misfire.
- Stax also became one of the most successfully integrated companies in the country—from top management and administration to its artists.
- "We didn't see color," Estelle said, "We saw talent."
- By 1963, Stax was releasing two or three records per month and four or five albums per year; even so, Stewart still worked for the bank.

Songwriter Berry Gordon, Jr. formed Motown Records.

- All the while from her perch at the record store, Estelle led impromptu songwriting sessions on new releases by competitors.
- Every word was parsed by the music crowd as thoroughly was if it were an ancient manuscript.
- The elements of a song's appeal were identified and then analyzed to determine why they worked.
- At the same time, jazz great Phineas Newborn Jr. might drop by and play the piano for hours while David Porter, who worked across the street bagging groceries, was learning the craft of songwriting.
- Saturdays were set aside for musicians, amateur and professional alike, to audition—establishing yet another link to the community.
- Singer Otis Redding got his start at Stax with "These Arms of Mine," recorded at the end of another band's recoding session; Rufus Thomas continued his string of hits with "Walking the Dog," which he wrote while watching an attractive woman dance one night.

Stax Records connected to the community by holding impromptu songwriting sessions and auditions for amateurs and professionals alike.

- In 1963, three albums were issued by Stax: Gus Cannon's "Walk Right In," (also covered by the Rooftop Singers), an artist's anthology titled "Treasured Hits From the South," and Rufus Thomas's "Walking the Dog."
- The bottom line profits of Stax in 1964 were steady but unspectacular, with a majority of its records being sold to black customers through inner-city mom-and-pop record stores.
- Meanwhile, Motown Records was in its ascendancy with the Supremes, Mary Wells, the Miracles, the Temptations, and Stevie Wonder all topping the pop charts.
- In Detroit, Motown based its image around "Hitsville, U.S.A." while Stax was based on being "Soulsville, U.S.A."
- One of Stax's assets was its ability to grow talent.
- When impoverished musician Isaac Hayes began hanging out, Stax's system made room for the talented youngster with the miraculous ear and special knowledge of arrangement.
- And when Hayes combined his talents with Otis Redding's, they became ambassadors to the Memphis Sound.
- Estelle wouldn't have it any other way.

Otis Redding got his start at Stax with These Arms of Mine.

Life in the Community: Memphis, Tennessee

- Majestically perched on a bluff on the eastern bank of the Mississippi River, Memphis had long been a land apart.
- While Tennessee consisted of rolling hills that nurtured country music, Memphis was as flat as the Delta and historically a breeding ground for classic blues, black gospel, and rockabilly.
- The city had long served as a stopping-off point for large numbers of travelers—black and white—mesmerized by the great migration to St. Louis or Chicago.
- Urban by definition, Memphis was still rural in mindset as the 1960s unfolded.
- The city was musically known as both the nurturing ground for the Pentecostal music of the Church of God in Christ and the sophistication of Big Band blues led by BB King.
- Out of this polyglot grew Memphis Soul, defined as stylish, funky, uptown soul music, a sultry style produced at Stax and Hi Records, using melodic unison horn lines, organ, bass, and a driving beat on the drums.
- When Jim Stewart and Estelle Axton converted that old movie theater into a recording studio at the corner of McLemore Avenue and College Street, they gave witness to the level of homegrown talent in the area.
- Their record store became one of the hipper local hangouts, attracting musicians, songwriters, and vocalists, all eager to hear the latest sounds.
- "I think there would have been no Stax Records without the Satellite Record Shop," Booker T. Jones, of Booker T. and the MGs. "Every Saturday I was at the Satellite Record Shop—that's where I went after school; I got to go in there and listen to everything."
- The shop also served as a testing ground for new recordings; Estelle often played recently recorded demo tapes to the record shop patrons.
- Their reactions often determined whether the new record would be changed, dumped or promoted heavily.
- Hi Records was started by three Sun Studio musicians—Ray Harris, Bill Cantrell, and Quentin Claunch—as well as Joe Cuoghi, one of the owners of Poplar ("Pop") Tunes, a local record store.
- Hi Records' early releases were primarily rockabilly.
- Just as the Mar-Keys' "Last Night" helped Stax, the success of Bill Black's Combo changed Hi from a rockabilly label to an instrumental powerhouse during the early 1960s.

Memphis, Tennessee.

HISTORICAL SNAPSHOT
1964

- In the first meeting between leaders of the Roman Catholic and Orthodox churches since the fifteenth century, Pope Paul VI and Patriarch Athenagoras I met in Jerusalem
- In his first State of the Union Address, President Lyndon Johnson declared a "War on Poverty"
- Surgeon General Luther Leonidas Terry reported that smoking may be hazardous to one's health (the first such statement from the U.S. Government)
- Thirteen years after its proposal and nearly two years after its passage by the Senate, the Twenty-fourth Amendment to the Constitution, prohibiting the use of poll taxes in national elections, was ratified
- General Motors introduced the Oldsmobile Vista Cruiser and the Buick Sport Wagon
- The Beatles, having vaulted to the Number 1 spot on the U.S. singles charts for the first time with "I Want to Hold Your Hand," appeared on *The Ed Sullivan Show*, and were seen by an estimated 73 million viewers, launching the mid-1960s "British Invasion" of American popular music

- The Supreme Court ruled that congressional districts must be approximately equal in population
- Muhammad Ali beat Sonny Liston in Miami Beach, Florida, and was crowned the Heavyweight Champion of the World
- Teamsters President Jimmy Hoffa was convicted by a federal jury of tampering with a federal jury in 1962
- In *New York Times Co. v Sullivan*, the Supreme Court ruled that, under the First Amendment, speech criticizing political figures cannot be censored
- The first Ford Mustang rolled off the assembly line at Ford Motor Company
- A Dallas, Texas, jury found Jack Ruby guilty of killing John F. Kennedy assassin Lee Harvey Oswald
- Merv Griffin's game show *Jeopardy!* debuted on NBC
- The Beatles dominated the top five positions in the Billboard Top 40 singles in America: "Can't Buy Me Love," "Twist and Shout," "She Loves You," "I Want to Hold Your Hand," and "Please Please Me"
- Three high school friends in Hoboken, New Jersey, opened the first BLIMPIE restaurant
- The Rolling Stones released their debut album, *The Rolling Stones*
- The New York World's Fair opened to celebrate the 300th anniversary of New Amsterdam being taken over by British forces and renamed New York in 1664
- John George Kemeny and Thomas Eugene Kurtz ran the first computer program written in BASIC (Beginners' All-purpose Symbolic Instruction Code), an easy-to-learn, high-level programming language
- College students marched through Times Square and San Francisco in the first major student demonstration against the Vietnam War
- Three Civil Rights workers—Michael Schwerner, Andrew Goodman, and James Chaney—were murdered near Philadelphia, Mississippi, by local Klansmen, cops, and a sheriff
- President Johnson signed the Civil Rights Act of 1964 into law, legally abolishing racial segregation in the United States
- At the Republican National Convention in San Francisco, presidential nominee Barry Goldwater declared that "extremism in the defense of liberty is no vice," and "moderation in the pursuit of justice is no virtue"
- The Supreme Court ruled that, in accordance with the Civil Rights Act of 1964, establishments providing public accommodations must refrain from racial discrimination
- Cosmic microwave background radiation was discovered
- Dr. Farrington Daniels's book, *Direct Use of the Sun's Energy*, was published by Yale University Press
- The first Moog synthesizer was designed by Robert Moog

Selected Prices

Air Conditioner	$455.00
Beer, Schlitz, Six-Pack	$0.99
Calculator, Remington	$189.50
Camera, Kodak Instamatic	$240.00
Girdle	$11.00
Record Album	$5.98
Refrigerator-Freezer	$300.00
Shoes, Men's Leather	$13.80
Slide Projector	$149.50
Watch, Timex	$9.95

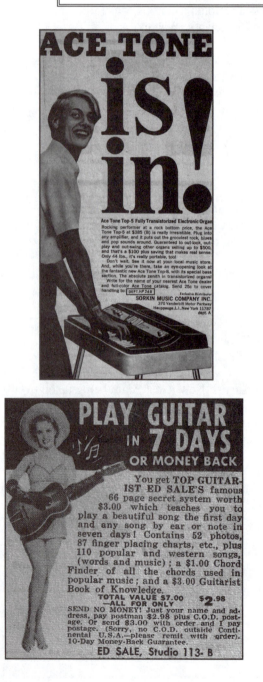

"The Stax Story Part Six, Porter and Hayes Producers," *Hit Parader*, February 1968:

Isaac Hayes and Dave Porter have written about 150 songs together for Stax artists and also produced most of them. So far their most successful collaboration has been with Sam and Dave on songs like "Hold On, I'm Coming" and "Soul Man"; in addition, Isaac plays piano on his own sessions in many of the other Stax sessions.

Isaac was born in 1942 on a farm in Covington, Tennessee, and raised by his grandparents who worked as sharecroppers. His mother died when he was an infant and he never saw his father. When Isaac was seven, the family moved to Memphis. He won several music scholarships, but he couldn't afford to buy an instrument, so he took the vocal training. He had to drop out of school to help support the family, and took singing jobs in local nightclubs where he also taught himself to play piano. Gradually, he worked into full-time gigs and met Dave.

Dave was born in Memphis in 1942, one of nine children. He grew up never knowing what his father looked like. "It was just my mother and a bunch of kids. I ran around barefoot and we were so poor it hurt." He sang in church regularly and wrote a class poem in the sixth grade. He formed a singing group in high school and wrote original songs—"which were really horrible." Then he got a job in a grocery store across from Stax and watched the musicians coming and going. In his spare time he sang in nightclubs and hung out around the Stax studio. "Then I met Isaac. We worked as a duet and wrote 30 straight flops, but we learned a lot."

HP: Who writes the lyrics and who writes the melodies?

Dave: Normally I write the lyrics and Hayes comes up with the melodies.

HP: Do you ever work with Steve Cropper?

Dave: Yes, we do. Steve's a tremendous writer himself. We get together with Steve on arrangements.

Isaac: Sometimes the three of us work together or we work with Steve individually.

HP: Who are the main singers you produce?

Dave: Sam and Dave, Carla Thomas, Johnny Taylor, some of Otis Redding, Mabel John, Rufus Thomas, Jean and the Darlings, a new group we have. We've also been working with some new songwriters, Homer Banks and Alan Jones, and a girl named Betty Crutcher. They're very good.

HP: Do you write songs with particular artists in mind?

Dave: Normally we tailor-make songs for a particular person. We block out all other things so that we can find a trait that the artist can protect the best.

Isaac: If we write something for another Stax artist, we present it to the producer in charge. Maybe we'll give something to Booker T., who produces William Bell.

HP: What's the difference in writing material for Johnny Taylor and Sam and Dave?

Isaac: With Sam and Dave, we have to create excitement in the material. With Johnny, the material has to be more subtle.

Dave: Johnny is selling 100 percent message. He's capable of getting any message over. So we concentrate on that. With Sam and Dave, we concentrate on sound, gimmicks as well as message.

HP: Sam and Dave must do a lot of improvising on your material.

Dave: Not necessarily. When we write a song, we include ad-libs. This keeps the message together. This gives the audience a chance to grasp everything.

Isaac: We'll throw in little phrases they can use on the side. Once they get the song down, they naturally use their own interpretation when they're delivering the tune.

HP: Isaac, you play piano on a lot of things, don't you?

Isaac: Yes. I play piano on all the records Dave and I produce. I'm on quite a few others, too. Wilson Pickett cut "99 1/2" and "634-5789" down here, and I played on those. I'm on Albert King's records. I also play piano and organ with the Monkeys. Booker T. usually plays organ on all the records, but sometimes we switch. Booker's playing is slower and smoother than mine.

HP: Were both of you born in Memphis?

Isaac: I've been in Memphis since I was seven, but I was born a few counties away. I came to Stax three or four times with bands and vocal groups trying to sell records. I played saxophone at the time. I finally got on as a session man. Porter came to me and we worked together in nightclubs as a team. I used to work in a meatpacking plant but I got laid off. I joined a band and decided to stick with it until I made it.

Dave: I was born in Memphis and I've been here all 25 years. I lived in the neighborhood of Stax since its inception. Stax started about five years ago, and I was one of the first artists on the label, with a record that didn't do anything. I sang on a corny R&B thing called "Old Gray Mare." It was one of the first records cut here. Hayes came in on a few sessions, and when we talked, we found many similarities in our thoughts. We decided to try it as a team. Before I came to Stax, I was working across the street in a grocery store pushing carts, and at night I sang in nightclubs.

HP: Describe how your work is different from Holland Dozier at Motown?

Isaac: I really don't know how they work or what the formula is, but it seems to me they do have a formula. We try to make our tunes more natural.

Dave: The truth is, we work with a formula, too. We have a plan. We know what to look for on any tune we write. Before we okay an idea, it must possess the things we're looking for. We count on the rhythm and the naturalness of it, whereas Holland and Dozier, which we admire to the fullest, seem to go more for sound. They have strong lyrics, but they're going for a specific sound. We hope our things sound good, too, but we concentrate on the natural feelings. There might be a mistake here and there, but if it feels good, we leave it in.

Isaac: We regard a mistake as being natural. We put ourselves into the stories we're writing. I also make my music complement the words.

HP: What's your favorite song that you've produced as a team?

Dave: "Hold On, I'm Coming" by Sam and Dave.

Isaac: That's my favorite, too.

"Music: Folk Music Revival," Robert Shelton, folk music critic, *Encyclopedia Yearbook*, 1964:

In 1963, folk music entrenched itself as an established part of the popular music industry of the United States. Attendance at folk concerts reached record proportions; nearly one out of every three pop music discs had some folk flavor, and the term "hootenanny" became a household word.

The current revival of interest in folk music stems from 1957, when the Kingston Trio burst on the scene. There had been earlier waves of popularity in the cities and among collegians in folk music, which is actually the oldest form of music in the world.

The largest previous revival had been during World War II, when such names as Leadbelly, Burl Ives, Josh White, Richard Dyer-Bennet, Woody Guthrie, and Susan Reed dominated the scene. Another spurt occurred in 1950 with the popularity of Pete Seeger and the Weavers in the North and Hank Williams in the South.

But by 1963, the picture had changed considerably. The chief impetus probably came from the American Broadcasting Company's *Hootenanny* television show. The program, which started as a half-hour musical visit to various college campuses during the spring of 1963, received favorable notice from the critics and grew to an hour by autumn.

With as many as 11 million people watching the *Hootenanny* show on Saturday night, the impact of the mass audience was irrefutable. It immediately reflected itself in the establishment of a "hootenanny craze"—touring companies of that name, dozens of records. Besides the rather low-level "folk music" the show—and its offshoots—offered, the craze had its good side effects. It obviously affected the record turnout for Newport Folk Festival of July.

The television show and the Newport Folk Festival represent the two polarities of American folk music. *Hootenanny* has come to represent the most commercial, least probing and most superficial approach to the folk song. The Newport Festival dealt in folk music of integrity, performances that spoke as musical expression as well as social document of a high order. The festival, which has its counterparts in programs at the University of Southern California, Chicago, Cornell and elsewhere, stressed traditional, little-known, authentic singers in performance, workshops and panels. The television show is primarily run for profit, has become embattled with either an outright boycott or indifference by major performers in the field, chiefly because of its overt blacklisting of Pete Seeger as well for its low esthetic concept....

Between these two poles lies American folk song, a commercial product and artistic product. It can be heard in the bright and urbane stylings of Peter, Paul and Mary, the only pop music group ever to have had three discs among the nation's top five simultaneously. It can be heard in the purling, sensuous voice of Joan Baez, singing the ancient ballad of the Anglo-Scots-American tradition. It can be echoed in the angry, passionate poetry of the newest major star of the folk cosmos, Bob Dylan, the songwriter who reflects a growing tension of social protest in his music. It is in the contemporary folk songs of the many followers of Dylan. It is the songs of the Negro integration battler, chanting "We Shall Overcome" in the South.

1966 PROFILE

Artist Reid Miles's innovative use of type, moody photography, and a minimalist color palette helped Blue Note Records establish itself as one of the hippest of all jazz labels.

Life at Home

- Artist Reid Miles, whose 500 jazz album covers for Blue Note Records defined "cool" in the era of Thelonious Monk, often traded away the albums that Blue Note gave him.
- He preferred classical music.
- Yet almost single-handedly, he defined the look of cool jazz: a harmonious blend of modernism with a distinct personality.
- Born in Chicago on July 4, 1927, Reid moved to Long Beach, California, with his mother following the stock market crash and the separation of his parents in 1929.
- After high school, Reid joined the Navy and, following his discharge, moved to Los Angeles to enroll at Chouinard Art Institute.
- By that time, the record industry, once a fledgling in the business world, had grown up dramatically; jazz was America's number two export behind only Hollywood movies.
- It was also the Golden Age of jazz when this distinctly American sound dominated pop music.
- American products all—Duke Ellington, Billie Holiday, Benny Goodman, Tommy Dorsey, Ella Fitzgerald, and Count Basie—were known worldwide as jazz icons and stylistic leaders.
- To take advantage of the rapidly rising popularity of the music, the major record labels emphasized quantity over innovation, and required its stars to record numerous albums each year.
- In 1937, RCA booked Tommy Dorsey and His Orchestra for 22 recording sessions to maximize their earning potential while the band was still popular.
- Smaller bands were ignored and young musicians were expected to conform.
- Into this niche slipped Blue Note Records.
- The tiny record label was founded by Alfred Lion in 1939, who became interested in jazz while living in Germany.

Artist Reid Miles helped Blue Note Records define cool.

- Lion became a lifelong devotee of jazz on December 23, 1938, when he attended a sold-out performance at Carnegie Hall composed of "talented Negro artists from all over the country who have been denied entry to the white world of popular music."
- Many of Lion's earliest recording sessions started at 4:00 in the morning, when musicians got off work from a night gig.
- Then, Lion ignored most of the commercial rules concerning recording—such as the "appropriate" length of a tune—delighting the jazz musicians and attracting additional talent.
- Lion's partner, Francis Wolff, was equally committed to the evolving world of jazz and a talented photographer.
- Wolff's warm, intimate photographs of musicians emphasized the informal, fluid nature of the genre.
- His portraits dominated the cover designs of Blue Note Records.

Alfred Lion, founder of Blue Note Records (left) and partner/photographer Francis Wolff.

- At the same time, the phonograph record itself was evolving.
- Around 1910, 78 rpm records had replaced the phonograph cylinder as the medium for recorded sound.
- The 78 rpm records were issued in both 10" and 12" diameter sizes and were usually sold separately, in brown paper or cardboard sleeves that carried little more than the name of the retail store.
- Beginning in the 1920s, bound collections of empty sleeves made of plain paperboard were sold as "record albums" so customers could store their records.
- Starting in the 1930s, record companies began issuing collections of 78 rpm records by one performer on specially assembled albums.
- In 1938, Columbia Records' Alex Steinweiss invented the concept of album covers and cover art.
- Other record companies followed his lead, and by the late 1940s, record albums routinely featured their own colorful paper covers.

Life at Work

- Reid Miles worked for *Esquire* magazine in the early 1950s before he was hired by Frank Wolff to design album covers for Blue Note Records.
- Although Blue Note had employed talented artists to design its covers, the jazz label still lacked a look.
- Reid changed that—almost immediately.
- One of his first covers featured Thelonious Monk with the word Thelonious split across two lines with a hyphen between the 'o' and 'n' set in dark type; the word Monk was in white against a background of ochre-yellow.
- Then, with the type dominating the design, Reid placed a small Frank Wolff photograph at the corner of the frame to complete the Blue Note look.
- The unexpected, stylized, nonconformist look on the album sleeves coolly echoed the innovation of the music inside; Reid gave Blue Note a look that matched the "Blue Note Sound."

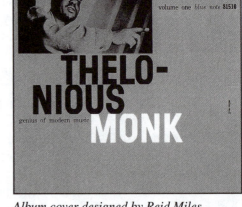
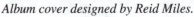

Album cover designed by Reid Miles.

- This unconventional, eclectic design was embraced by Albert Lion, who sought out "the different" and liked Reid's ability to creatively incorporate the moody, mostly black and white photographs of Wolff with innovative cropping, unconventional-type faces, and off-balance designs.
- But Reid was restless, constantly changing, frequently reinventing his look to keep it fresh.

- He specialized in the unexpected—manipulating type, employing unconventional fonts and severe cropping of photographs.
- Few of the covers were full-color; Reid preferred using black and white with only one other color.
- "Typography in the early 1950s was in a renaissance, anyway. It happened especially on album covers because they were not so restrictive as advertising," Reid said.
- Reid enjoyed unrestricted access to Frank Wolff's atmospheric photography and broad discretion concerning the album's final look and feel.
- Fans raved that a Reid Miles sleeve was as recognizable and distinctive as "the trumpet timbre of Miles Davis or the plaintive phrasing of Billie Holiday."
- Reid wasn't particularly interested in jazz, professing to have much more of an interest in classical music, but he didn't hesitate to mirror the atmosphere of a jam session in his artwork.
- "Frank tried to get the artist's real expression…the way he stood. Reid was more avant-garde and more chic, but the two together worked beautifully," according to Albert Lion.
- "Frank always hated it when I cropped one of his photographs of his artist through the forehead," Reid said.
- For a decade, his look wowed and inspired; hired in 1956, Reid exited 10 years later when Blue Note was sold, having grown up and risen to maturity with jazz.

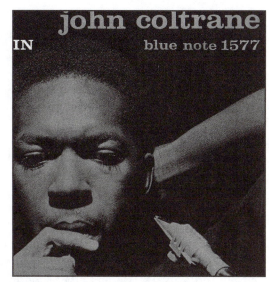

Album cover designed by Reid Miles.

Life in the Community: New York City

- By mid-century, jazz bands around the world took their stylistic cues from the American orchestras harbored in New York City, where innovation and creativity were in no short supply.
- There, jazz lovers could hang out at Gabler's Commodore Music Shop and debate the merits of "hot" jazz or the perfect size of a jazz band.
- New Orleans, Chicago, Kansas City and others all staked a special claim to the development of jazz, but New York City was where big events took place.
- It was at Carnegie Hall in 1914 that James Reese Europe and His Clef Club Orchestra performed his "popular music," syncopated transition from ragtime to jazz.
- By 1923, the Club Alabam in Chicago was home to Fletch Henderson's influential orchestra that deviated from New Orleans style by adding three saxophones and dropping a clarinet.
- This created a true reed section, one of the fundamentals of Big Band jazz.
- By 1934, the Benny Goodman Orchestra broadcasts out of New York were a national sensation, using a formula that emphasized Big Band orchestration while leaving room for instrumentation.
- At the start of World War II, jazz had attained enough momentum and maturity to stage a revolution within itself with the emergence of bebop.
- By the end of the war, eager patrons lined up at New York's Royal Roost on Broadway to hear fully integrated orchestras, whose very compositions served as a catalyst for innovation.
- New York City was also in the center of the musical action in the 1950s as Thelonious Monk developed his pioneering modulations known as "Zombie Music."

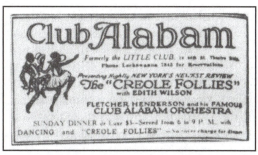

Club Alabam in Chicago hosted jazz that deviated from New Orlean's style.

HISTORICAL SNAPSHOT
1966

- The first Acid Test was conducted at the Fillmore, San Francisco
- President Lyndon Johnson stated that the United States should stay in South Vietnam until Communist aggression there ended; U.S. troop commitment in Vietnam totaled 250,000
- Soviet space probe *Venera 3* crashed on Venus, becoming the first spacecraft to land on another planet
- The Texas Western Miners defeated the Kentucky Wildcats with five African-American starters, ushering in desegregation in athletic recruiting
- An artificial heart was implanted in the chest of Marcel DeRudder in a Houston, Texas, hospital
- Bob Dylan's album, *Blonde on Blonde* was released
- In New York City, Dr. Martin Luther King Jr. made his first public speech on the Vietnam War
- The final episode of *The Dick Van Dyke Show* aired
- Civil Rights activist James Meredith was shot while trying to march across Mississippi
- The Supreme Court ruled in *Miranda v. Arizona* that the police must inform suspects of their rights before questioning
- The National Organization for Women (NOW) was founded in Washington, DC
- Groundbreaking took place for the World Trade Center in New York City; Caesars Palace opened in Las Vegas
- The Beatles released their *Revolver* album; the Doors recorded their self-titled debut LP
- In the People's Republic of China, Mao Zedong began the brutal Cultural Revolution to purge and reorganize China's Communist Party
- The Beatles toured the United States for the last time, ending with a concert at Candlestick Park in San Francisco, California
- *Star Trek* debuted on NBC-TV with its first episode, titled "The Man Trap"
- The Metropolitan Opera House opened at Lincoln Center in New York City with the world premiere of Samuel Barber's opera, *Antony and Cleopatra*
- Bobby Seale and Huey P. Newton established the Black Panther Party
- The Toyota Corolla automobile was introduced
- ABC-TV broadcast a 90-minute television adaptation of the musical *Brigadoon*, starring Robert Goulet, Peter Falk, and Sally Ann Howes
- Grace Slick joined the Jefferson Airplane
- The merger of the AFL-NFL in football was approved by Congress

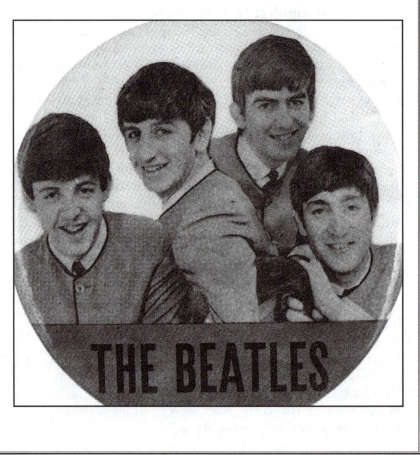

Selected Prices

Drill, Black & Decker $10.99
Film, 35 Millimeter Color Slide $2.49
Food Processor $39.95
Hat, Pillbox $4.97
Pepsi, Six-Pack $0.59
Radio, Portable Transistor $12.95
Socket Set, 57-Piece $56.95
Stereo $499.95
Tape Player, 8-Track $67.95
Ticket, Newport Jazz Festival $6.50

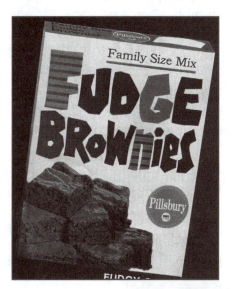

The History of Blue Note Records

1925

Sixteen-year-old Alfred Lion, the future founder of Blue Note Records, was profoundly influenced by a live performance he attended in his native Germany of Sam Woodyard and His Chocolate Dandies.

1930

During his first trip to United States, Lion purchased more than 300 records unavailable in Germany.

1938

To escape the rising tide of Nazism, Lion emigrated to the United States, where he feasted on the variety of music ranging from spirituals to swing to boogie-woogie pianists Albert Ammons and Meade Lux Lewis.

1939

After Lion recorded Ammons and Lewis, 50 discs were produced and soon sold.

1941

Photographer Francis Wolff left Germany and joined Lion.

1942

Blue Note suspended record production in deference to the war effort; Lion was drafted into the Army.

1948

Blue Note started recording emerging talent such as Thelonious Monk, Bud Powell and Fats Navaro.

1951

Blue Note moved from 78 rpms to the 10-inch platform and began using album cover art designed by Paul Bacon, Gil Melle and John Hermansader.

1953

Recording engineer Rudy Van Gelder's attention to audio detail, such as the audibility of the high hat cymbal, began to mold the distinctive Blue Note sound.

1956

Reid Miles began working with Lion and Wolff as Blue Note's graphic designer.

1958

Rising star Andy Warhol designed a Blue Note album cover featuring Kenny Burrell.

1964

Blue Note registered hits with "Song For My Father" by Horace Silver and "The Sidewinder" by Lee Morgan.

1965

Recording giant Liberty purchased Blue Note Records from Alfred Lion and Francis Wolff.

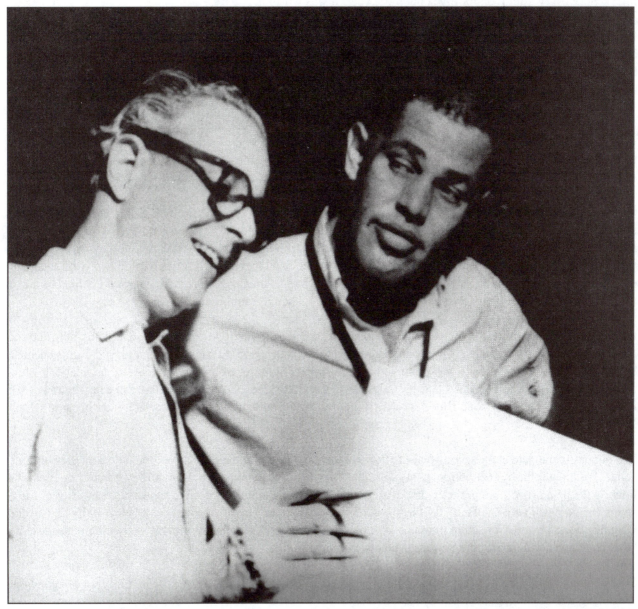

Founder Alfred Lion with a Blue Note artist.

Robert Hamilton Long

I fell in love with playing drums when I saw Ringo Starr and the Beatles on *The Ed Sullivan Show* in February 1964. My parents bought me my first drum set from the Sears Catalog in September 1966. I remember seeing my father drive past our school with the boxes in the back of the station wagon on his way to pick me up after school. I was so excited. The deal was that I would earn enough money to pay $15 a month for 10 months to pay for the $150 drum set. To earn this money, I joined the cleaning crew and swept the halls and classrooms of the high school every afternoon for my sophomore year. It was worth it.

In the spring of 1967, I joined a group of my classmates and started rehearsing. Rollie was the lead singer, Johnny and Chris played guitars, Sandy played bass, and I was the drummer! We rehearsed in the upstairs hallway of my house on Saturday mornings. I played my drums before breakfast, after breakfast, before dinner and after dinner, and my parents never complained, but said, "We love to hear music." They were saints.

The big moment arrived. Our first paid gig. We didn't have a name for the band. A church group invited us to play in the meeting room of the Andrew Jackson Hotel on Main Street. The deal was that we would split the proceeds from the door. The entrance fee was $1.00 per person. Two girls came. We split $1.00 five ways, and we each earned $0.20, which was enough to buy a Coca-Cola from the machine.

Our next gig was to play for a high school sock-hop on Friday night after the football game. Our team lost and the sock-hop wasn't much fun. We still had a great time. But Rollie told us that he didn't have time to rehearse anymore. So we began to rehearse without him, and I began to sing the lead vocals while playing drums. We were getting pretty good at Beatles and Rolling Stones covers, and had enough songs to play two good sets. Our next gig was at a party in the next town over. By then, we had a "manager"! As manager, Scott helped to move the equipment and set up the few lights that we had accumulated, for ambiance.

In the fall of our junior year in high school, we made the decision to mix two bands together. Sandy played bass, Johnny and Chris played guitars, Dobby and Bill played trumpets, my good friend Preston played drums because he was a better drummer, and I was promoted to lead singer, right out front. We were pretty popular for a few months and played at some parties and several times at the Cotton Belt Community Center in a nearby town. We named the band The Claystone Blues and had a repertoire of Southern soul music, which later became Beach Music.

The big day came, late in the school year of 1968, for the local Battle of the Bands. We could do a medley of three songs. We bought flashy bell-bottom pants with matching broad-collared shirts from a local pawn shop. Sandy's father gave us a 50-watt amplifier, which was a huge step up in sound power. We rehearsed a medley of three songs including "I've Been Hurt" by the Tams, "It's Not Unusual" by Tom Jones, and "Hey, Baby" by Bruce Channel, because they were all in the same key. We came in second, which was almost like winning, because no band could ever win against the Scribes, who always came in first.

Summer came and we all drifted apart. When school started again for our senior year in 1968, we talked about rehearsing and playing, but everybody was too busy.

Music, in performance, is a type of sculpture. The air in the performance is sculpted into something.

Personal Essay
Frank Zappa

Music Trivia

- Bob Dylan included the old folk ballad "House of the Rising Sun" on his 1962 debut album detailing the life of a Southern girl trapped in a New Orleans whorehouse; in 1964 Eric Burden of the Animals turned the old song into a new hit when he changed the gender in the lyrics and added an organ solo inspired by jazzman Jimmy Smith's hit "Walk on the Wild Side."
- Wilson Pickett's song "In the Midnight Hour" became a soul classic after it was recorded in Memphis in a style that pushed the second beat while holding back the fourth.
- Only after Paul McCartney changed the words in the song Eleanor Rigby from "blowing his mind in the dark/with a pipe full of clay" to "Picks up the rice in a church where a wedding has been" did he realize the song was about the loneliness of old age.

Cash, An American Man, Bill Miller, 2004:

On a summer night in the 1960s, the Johnny Cash Show was in town for a performance at the local high school gymnasium, just another stop on the long dusty trail for the touring musicians. As townspeople filled the place and the air became electric with anticipation, the troupe realized that the star was missing. Tommy Cash, who was part of the show, walked the halls and checked the classrooms in search his brother. The last place he looked was the boys' locker room. He found Johnny walking slowly and peering deliberately into each of the mesh wire lockers, a rolled $100 bill tucked between his thumb and index finger.

"What are you doing? The show's about start," Tommy said.

"I'm looking for the dirtiest, rattiest tennis shoes I can find," Johnny said. "I figure the boy could use this."

Blue Note Records were very meticulous in every aspect of the production: they used the best vinyl, they paid for rehearsal, and when I asked to be in on the other parts of my album, Alfred Lion gave me every opportunity. A lot of musicians in those days worked very hard to make good music, and once the music was done, they let Albert Lion go with the rest of it. One day I went to Albert and said, "I want to sit down with you and look at the pictures you want to use and pick them together and check the sleeve notes before you print them." He agreed to that, so I had input over a lot of things the other guys didn't bother with. I learnt a lot of things from that, and what I learnt about making a record, I learnt from Albert Lion.

—Horace Silver, Foreword, *Blue Note, The Album Cover Art*, 1991

"Music," *Compton Yearbook Edition*, 1966:

The musicians of the Chicago Symphony and the Minneapolis Symphony Orchestra began the 1965-66 season under new five-year contracts with the orchestra's managing associations. These are the first contracts of such duration with any major American orchestra. During the 1964-65 season, the New York Philharmonic Orchestra was the first symphony orchestra in the United States to work for a full 52 weeks. In August, the Philharmonic drew an audience of 70,000 at the first of a series of free outdoor concerts. This is an attendance record for a musical event in New York City.

The Cleveland Orchestra, under conductor George Szell, was the first U.S. symphony orchestra in six years to tour Russia. In October, at Carnegie Hall in New York City, the Moscow Philharmonic performed in the U.S. for the first time….

There were almost 1,000 community orchestras in the U.S. in 1965. The community orchestras in Fort Wayne, Indiana; Norwalk, Connecticut; Colorado Springs, Colorado; and Huntsville, Alabama reported preseason sellouts for 1964-65 concerts.

The National Foundation on the Arts and the Humanities Act of 1965, signed by Pres. Lyndon B. Johnson in September, provided for the federal support of symphony orchestras. It also authorized funds for commissioning new works.

1968 PROFILE

Marshall Borowitz had begun playing the guitar at age nine, enjoyed private lessons for five years, started a four-piece cover band at 14, abandoned the band at 15, and started a band called One Night Stand at 16.

Life at Home

- When he named his band "One Night Stand," Marshall Borowitz felt delightfully wicked and provocative.
- Every night, when the bar closed down at 3:00 a.m. and the equipment still had to be packed and hauled to the VW bus, the mildly naughty name sounded like the monthly schedule set by his booking agent.
- Getting frisky at the end of an evening with the local groupies was pretty difficult when there was a three-hour drive still ahead.
- Band life on the road, in a word, sucked.
- Marshall was born on July 1, 1947, a product of the postwar years that would come to be ubiquitously called the Baby Boomer generation.
- He grew up the middle of three children, the son of an IBM executive with a mother who loved to play bridge and drink whiskey sours after five o'clock.
- It was simply assumed that he would attend college—he was never asked—and follow the pattern set by his do-gooder sister who knew how to get along.
- Marshall did not always know how to get along.
- During his teenage years, he had thoroughly absorbed the raucous comedy albums of Lenny Bruce and spent many late-night hours listening to Bob Fass on WBAL, where he first heard Arlo Guthrie singing his 15-minute-long antiwar song, "Alice's Restaurant."

Marshall Borowitz started playing guitar at age 9 and formed his own band at age 16.

- The entire universe was exploding with exciting music.
- Bob Dylan's *Blonde on Blonde*, the Jimi Hendrix Experience's *Are You Experienced?*, Cream's *Disraeli Gears*, and the Beatles' *Sgt. Pepper's Lonely Hearts Club Band* had all been released in 1967.
- What was the use of attending college to read seventeenth-century literature when a revolution was underway in the twentieth century?
- The Beatles were the modern Shakespeare; music had become the most comprehensive form of communication thus far invented by humankind.
- The evidence was everywhere: Muddy Waters, Jefferson Airplane, Janis Joplin, Steppenwolf, Country Joe and the Fish, the Who, Otis Redding, and the Rolling Stones.

Marshall was inspired by Arlo Guthrie's anti-war song, Alice's Restaurant.

- Two rock music-inspired magazines chronicled this explosion of creativity: Paul Williams created *Crawdaddy!* in 1966, followed the next year by Jann Wenner's *Rolling Stone*.
- *Rolling Stone* signaled its expansive view of the cultural change underway when it informed its readers that it would be dedicated "not just to the music, but everything it represents."
- Music companies such as Elektra Records recognized the uniqueness of the moment and, for example, gave one employee the title of "company freak" with an assignment to work with super talents like Jim Morrison.
- Marshall became giddy at the sound of Janis Joplin singing "Me and Bobby McGee," and acquired enormous guilty pleasure from listening to the Rascals performing "Good Lovin'," "I've Been Lonely Too Long," and "People Got to Be free."
- It was his older sister—the one he didn't want to be like—who convinced him that he had a good enough singing voice to accompany his masterful guitar work.
- His band, One Night Stand, was a present to himself—his liberation vehicle after his junior year in high school.
- Several musicians in the area were looking for something to do; earning money as a band member appealed to all.
- Before settling on One Night Stand as the band's moniker, they tried out "Slippery When Wet," "Nighttime Itch Cream" and "Better With Beer."
- Each was rejected for a different reason.
- The next stage involved determining what kind of band they wanted to be: rock, blues rock, folk rock, straight R&B?
- The cornucopia of emerging musical trends during his growing-up years made it difficult to isolate a style.
- When he was 10, Marshall saw Buddy Holly and the Crickets playing "It's So Easy" on *American Bandstand*; he was enthralled by the energy radiating from the band.
- The next year, he wanted to be Bobby Darin singing "Mack the Knife" or a member of the R&B Drifters belting out "There Goes My Baby."
- And, like everyone else, he took a shot at Bob Dylan's singer/songwriter approach and discovered how high that hill had become.
- His first band, enthusiastically named the Seagram 7 (even though it only had five members), could predictably begin a dancing frenzy with Lesley Gore's "It's My Party" and any song by Little Richard—especially "Tutti Frutti."'

Life at Work

- When Marshall Borowitz and his band One Night Stand were asked to take a one-month, July summer slot in North Myrtle Beach, South Carolina, in 1968, Marshall couldn't believe his luck.
- The parental heat factory was already spewing out guilt by the globule concerning his inability to commit to college in the fall.
- Not only could he escape Connecticut for the sun and surf of South Carolina for part of the summer, but this fortuitous change of events allowed him to escape the "stink eye" his mother gave him every morning.
- Besides, being a part of the emerging cultural scene was special work.
- Rock music was on the precipice of taking over the world, Marshall believed.
- The musical *Hair* was awakening society to the issues of the day, *Rolling Stone* magazine had become his Bible, and the entire nation, it seemed, had paused to mourn the death—in an airplane crash near Madison, Wisconsin—of Otis Redding, whose greatest hit, "Sittin' on the Dock of the Bay," was recorded three days before his death.

As Hair *encouraged society to be free, Marshall persuaded his Connecticut-based bandmates to accept a one month gig in Myrtle Beach, South Carolina.*

- But Marshall's first struggle was to convince the band.
- The drummer had a girlfriend he couldn't possibly leave for the summer, while the lead singer had agreed to work for his father, an optometrist, grinding glasses and helping to run his office.
- The bass guitarist had been planning to drive out West, but going south of the wide beaches of Ocean Drive sounded good enough for him.
- Eventually they all came around.
- The next challenge was the music.
- Although Marshall had enjoyed the crosscurrents of cultural sound, he was unsure that the band's repertoire was sufficient for a teenage hangout magnet in love with a dance called "The Shag."
- Marshall had seen the six-count, partnered dance featuring defined steps at the Myrtle Beach Pavilion the summer before, but he had failed to master the fancy footwork required.
- The dancers would be listening to songs by the Tams, the Temptations, the Drifters; to please this crowd of well-dressed dancers, they would need to expand their play list.
- Problem number three was money—immediate cash.
- Once they arrived in Myrtle Beach, the gig included room and board and $79 each per week—more than enough incentive to leave Connecticut for the annual bikini invasion of South Carolina.

The annual bikini invasion of Myrtle Beach was added incentive to leave Connecticut.

- But recently, gasoline had gone to $0.37 a gallon, with rumors of topping $0.40 by summer's end, and they still needed to buy replacement speakers and coordinate their clothes so they would look nice.
- Marshall wanted the band to wear color-coordinated shiny shirts during the first and second set and then change into a laidback Hawaii motif for the third and fourth sets.
- Problem number three, however, was solved: Marshall's father said okay to the entire scheme and agreed to front the necessary money—provided it was paid back.

- After two weeks of frantic rehearsing, at least six shouting matches over music selections and two boyfriend-girlfriend breakups, the band was ready.
- Or at least that's what they thought.
- Traditionally, every textile factory in North Carolina, South Carolina, and Virginia closed down the week of July 4, providing its employees with a vacation and time for workers to completely clean and repaint the mill.
- And going on vacation in the Carolinas meant one thing: Myrtle Beach.
- Marshall and his bandmates had never seen so many cars on so few roads; 60 miles outside their destination, cars came to a stop and barely moved.
- The VW bus they drove, which was originally bought in the cooler climate of Connecticut, didn't recognize the word "air-conditioning."
- When they finally arrived at Ocean Drive, they were hot, exhausted, and scheduled to play that night.
- Two members of the band took a nap on the beach and came back so sunburned they could barely walk; Marshall got everything set up and crossed his fingers—not being sure God was answering his prayers these days.
- By the time they opened their first song, 200 rampaging vacationers, eager for excitement, were milling around the dance floor.
- They didn't respond to the first three songs—two by the Young Rascals.
- That's when Marshall hauled out "Tutti-Frutti" and the room began to rock; he followed it with some James Brown.
- The second night was better; the third night was the best.
- That's when he met Penny, whose Southern accent was wider than her bikini bottom.
- It was also the night the drummer climbed off the stage and helped get the dancing going.
- By the end of the week, word was out: One Night Stand was the band to see.
- Their Tams imitations were terrible; their Beach Boys sound was off key, but the mood was just right when they played.
- Marshall became hypersensitive to news in the music world: the opening of the Kaleidoscope Club featuring Canned Heat and the Jefferson Airplane; Country Joe and the Fish's attempts to answer the question, "What does a piano sound like when dropped from a great height?," and the breakup of Buffalo Springfield.
- After two weeks, they had their routine down: play till 2:00 a.m., party till four, sleep till noon, eat cereal, spend time on the beach, spend time with new girlfriends, scrounge up something to eat at an all-you-can-eat restaurant, and be on stage at 8:00 p.m.
- Marshall didn't want the summer to end, even though Penny had returned to Salisbury, North Carolina, and had not yet been replaced.
- He wanted music to be his life, and his mantra was taken straight out of *Rolling Stone* magazine.
- Writer Ralph Gleason wrote in the June 22, 1968, *Rolling Stone*: "At no time in American history has youth possessed the strength it possesses now. Trained by music, linked by music, it has the power for good change the world. That power for good carries the reverse, the power of evil.

The drive down to South Carolina was long and slow.

It didn't take long for One Night Stand's routine to include beach time.

Life in the Community: Myrtle Beach, South Carolina

- Originally inhabited by the Winyah and Waccamaw Indians, Myrtle Beach was first named "Chicora," meaning "the land."
- The Spanish were next to explore the Myrtle Beach area as early as 1514, then with Blackbeard's pirates inhabiting the bays and inlets in the 1700s.
- Indigo plantations were established in the area; but transportation difficulties left most of the beach uninhabited until 1902, when the first railroad was created by the Burroughs and Chapin families.
- The arrival of the railroad in 1902 began the transformation of Myrtle Beach from an isolated agricultural community into a summer beach resort.
- Still a sleepy community when the Great Depression arrived, Myrtle Beach, with its long stretch of white sand beaches, offered wealthy industrialist John T. Woodside the opportunity to purchase some 65,000 acres.
- His construction of a golf course and the magnificent Ocean Forest Hotel inaugurated Myrtle Beach's resort culture.
- Likewise, Horry County officials made full use of New Deal programs to develop infrastructure and service institutions supporting the region.
- World War II further enhanced the development of Myrtle Beach as the region's population swelled with the creation of Myrtle Beach Army Air Force Base.
- Each March since 1951, during Ontario's spring break, Myrtle Beach hosted Canadian-American Days, when tens of thousands of tourists flocked to the area for a week's worth of special events.
- These events, and the construction of dozens of golf courses, expanded the holiday season from four months to seven.
- The area was incorporated as a town in 1938 and became a city in 1957, and the building of beach motels accelerated.
- Its name was derived from the wax myrtle shrub that grows throughout the area.
- In the late 1960s, largely for marketing ease, the communities of Ocean Drive, Cherry Grove, and Windy Hill were combined into North Myrtle Beach.

Beautiful golf courses established Myrtle Beach as a resort town.

HISTORICAL SNAPSHOT
1968

- The Green Bay Packers won *Super Bowl II*
- *Rowan & Martin's Laugh-In* debuted on NBC
- North Korea seized the USS *Pueblo*, claiming the ship violated its territorial waters while spying
- The Tet Offensive began in Vietnam, as Viet Cong forces launched a series of surprise attacks across South Vietnam, reducing American support for the war
- The public execution of a Viet Cong officer named Nguyễn Văn Lém by Nguyễn Ngọc Loan, a South Vietnamese National Police Chief, was photographed by Eddie Adams and distributed worldwide
- The Pennsylvania Railroad and the New York Central Railroad merged to form Penn Central, the largest-ever corporate merger up to that time
- Three black college students were killed during a Civil Rights protest staged at a white-only bowling alley in Orangeburg, South Carolina
- The Florida Education Association (FEA) initiated a mass resignation of teachers to protest state funding of education, the first statewide teachers' strike in the United States
- NET televised the first episode of *Mister Rogers' Neighborhood*
- Ex-teenage singer Frankie Lymon was found dead from a heroin overdose in Harlem
- President Lyndon B. Johnson mandated that all computers purchased by the federal government support the ASCII character encoding
- President Johnson announced that he would not run for re-election after he edged out antiwar candidate Eugene J. McCarthy in the New Hampshire Democratic Primary, a vote which highlighted the deep divisions in the country over Vietnam
- In Vietnam, hundreds of civilians—children, women, and elderly—were raped, sodomized and killed by U.S. soldiers in what became known as the My Lai Massacre
- Congress repealed the requirement for a gold reserve to back U.S. currency
- Folk singer Joan Baez married activist David Harris in New York
- The films *2001: A Space Odyssey* and *Planet of the Apes* were released in theaters
- Martin Luther King, Jr. was shot dead at the Lorraine Motel in Memphis, Tennessee, resulting in riots lasting for several days across the U.S.
- Apollo-Saturn mission 502 (*Apollo 6*) was launched, as the second and last unmanned test-flight of the *Saturn V* launch vehicle
- The rock musical *Hair* opened on Broadway
- The Beatles announced the creation of Apple Records; James Taylor was the first non-British musician they signed on
- The Catonsville Nine entered the Selective Service offices in Catonsville, Maryland, took dozens of selective service draft records, and burned them with napalm as a protest against the Vietnam War
- Radical feminist Valerie Solanas shot Andy Warhol as he entered his studio, wounding him
- The Standard & Poor's 500 Index closed above 100 for the first time
- Presidential candidate Robert F. Kennedy was shot and killed at the Ambassador Hotel in Los Angeles, California, by Sirhan Sirhan
- The soap opera *One Life to Live* premiered on ABC
- Pope Paul VI published the encyclical entitled *Humanae Vitae*, condemning birth control
- Police clashed with antiwar protesters in Chicago, Illinois, outside the 1968 Democratic National Convention, which nominated Hubert Humphrey for president and Edmund Muskie for vice president
- Television crime show *Hawaii 5-0* and *60 Minutes* both debuted on CBS
- Led Zeppelin performed their first live performance, at Surrey University in England
- In Mexico City, black American athletes Tommie Smith and John Carlos raised their arms in a Black Power salute after winning, respectively, the gold and bronze medals in the Olympic men's 200 meter race
- Yale University announced it was going to admit women
- The Beatles released their self-titled album popularly known as The White Album
- The *'68 Comeback Special* marked the concert return of Elvis Presley

Selected Prices

Automobile, Datsun...$2,196.00
Blender...$13.49
Camera, 8 mm..$129.95
Car Battery..$12.88
Dryer..$178.00
Electric Shaver...$13.97
Guitar, Electric...$199.95
Lawn Mower...$79.95
Pepsi, Six 10-Ounce Bottles $0.59
Whiskey, Seagram's, Fifth.......................................$5.79

"Beatles Still Tops in Poll," *San Antonio Light*, February 27, 1969:

The Beatles, Janis Joplin, Donovan, Jim Morrison, and Jimi Hendrix were among the top winners in *Eye Magazine's* first annual nationwide rock 'n' roll poll. Some 6,800 teenagers in 50 states voted in the January issue of *Eye*, a monthly magazine geared to 18 to 20 year olds of both sexes.

Divided into 30 categories from Best Album to Most Exciting New Face, the poll revealed youngsters dig progressive rock (like Cream), but they put down teenybopper bubblegum rock (like the 1910 Fruit Gum Company).

The Beatles walked off with three categories—Album of the Year, Best Group, and Top English Group—and "Hey Jude" by the Beatles won the Best Single and Best Lyrics awards.

The top American group was the Doors.

Tiny Tim took the 1968 Public Nuisance Award, and his album was voted runner-up to The Rolling Stones' *Their Satanic Majesties Request* as Bad-Trip Album of the Year.

Janis Joplin took Best Female Vocalist and also captured "Sexiest Woman in Rock 'n' Roll." Jim Morrison was Sexiest Man and runner-up to Donovan as Top Male Vocalist.

The sleeper in the poll was Frank Zappa, named as 1968 Private Delight ("I don't care what anyone says, I dig it.")

Cream was hailed as the Most Lamented Breakup of the Year and also runner-up as Top English Group.

The King and Queen of Soul were James Brown and Aretha Franklin.

"When Sun Sinks Out of Sight, Beach Gang Comes Alive," Scott Derks,
Rock Hill Evening Herald, June 9, 1969:

OCEAN DRIVE BEACH—When the sun gets sleepy and sinks out of sight, most of to the beach community, like a night hunting cat, stretches and comes alive.

An 18-year-old boy, who seems all laughing eyes and strong, sunburned chin, works at the beach "because it is the only live place in the world." But, at night, he puts away the wooden box he pushes, by day a snow cone dispensary, and swings.

Most of us slide into the black lights and brassy trumpet in the Beach Club, open every night, and get there early or you'll have to wedge in sideways. Illustrated posters hang on the walls and my date's trim, white dress glows in the dim neon. It's a changing crowd. At $6 a couple, few go more than once.

The Drifters and Major Lance and the Footnotes created the din from the den: tangy, damp air and draft beer, the mood.

"Clap your hands," Major Lance shouts; "clap with me and be happy."

It's a gymnasium-sized room, half-filled with chairs and completely filled with people. Many remember the first time they heard "Sitting in the Park" or "Up on the Roof."

Quick beer or two and on down Ocean Boulevard cheek by jowl are the "Pad" and "The Barrel," and I want to check the action. On the walls and tables of each are carved those immortal legacies left by teenagers: "Bill was here" or "Check with Annie" or "This is where it's at" delicately and laboriously inscribed in ball-point ruts.

The Barrel is named for its shape and, like all the others, provides beer and juke music. It doesn't come alive until 11 o'clock, but by 1 a.m., it slowly empties. Parties don't die: they shift back to the beach houses, and out on the Strand, were cool night air from the Atlantic revives those who may have become a little full.

It seems, although certainly not applying to all equally, that action focuses on beer or harder drink, and dancing, loud music and, accompanied by any or all of these, police visits.

If any of the above ingredients gets out of hand, the police have a habit of dropping by. There are, have been, and will be arrests. Friends wander the beach and other houses collecting money to post bond for the miscreant who has had too much of any of the ingredients.

"Let me have a buck, a dime, quarter anything," the offender's buddies will beg of friends and strangers.

The bond will be $40 for being drunk, $100 for disorderly conduct.

But for most, the nights end in the early morning, under large, large moons, stalking the Strand with us.

Wind sprinkles my legs with the rising tide and our footprints are soon washed away. Just as thousands before us.

No more high school. The next trip will be as college folks, and many of us may not go again until we are grown and have our own children. Who knows?

Billboard's Top Songs: 1968

1. "Hey Jude," The Beatles
2. "Love Is Blue ," Paul Mauriat
3. "Honey ," Bobby Goldsboro
4. "(Sittin' on) The Dock of the Bay ," Otis Redding
5. "People Got to Be Free ," Rascals
6. "Sunshine of Your Love ," Cream
7. "This Guy's in Love With You," Herb Alpert
8. "The Good, the Bad and the Ugly ," Hugo Montenegro
9. "Mrs. Robinson ," Simon and Garfunkel
10. "Tighten Up," Archie Bell and The Drells
11. "Harper Valley P.T.A. ," Jeannie C. Riley
12. "Little Green Apples ," O.C. Smith
13. "Mony, Mony," Tommy James and The Shondells
14. "Hello, I Love You ," The Doors
15. "Young Girl ," Gary Puckett and The Union Gap
16. "Cry Like a Baby ," Box Tops
17. "Stoned Soul Picnic ," Fifth Dimension
18. "Grazin' in the Grass ," Hugh Masekela
19. "Midnight Confessions ," The Grass Roots
20. "Dance to the Music," Sly and the Family Stone
21. "The Horse," Cliff Nobles and Co.
22. "I Wish It Would Rain ," Temptations
23. "La-La Means I Love You," Delfonics
24. "Turn Around , Look At Me," Vogues
25. "Judy In Disguise (With Glasses)," John Fred and His Playboy Band
26. "Spooky ," Classics IV
27. "Love Child ," Diana Ross and The Supremes
28. "Angel of the Morning ," Merrilee Rush
29. "Ballad of Bonnie and Clyde ," Georgie Fame
30. "Those Were the Days ," Mary Hopkin
31. "Born to Be Wild ," Steppenwolf
32. "Cowboys to Girls ," Intruders
33. "Simon Says ," 1910 Fruitgum Company
34. "Lady Willpower ," Gary Puckett and The Union Gap
35. "A Beautiful Morning ," Young Rascals

"Music: Sand Symphony, Second Florida Festival Lures Londoners (and J.B. Priestley) to Daytona Beach," Alan Hughes, *The New York Times*, July 14, 1967:

DAYTONA BEACH, FLORIDA—Now add music to the sun, sand and sea that are year-round attractions to this resort city. The second annual Florida International Music Festival began last night with a concert by the London Symphony Orchestra. And from now through August 6, the Peabody Auditorium will be filled with the sights and sounds of concerts and operas.

There are Englishmen, women and children here, for the airlift that brought the 98 orchestral musicians from London carried also 117 wives and children of the players.

Here with the orchestra are Istvan Kertesz, its regular conductor, and Sir Arthur Bliss, composer, conductor, honorary president of the organization and Master the Queen's Musick. Another Englishman of note is here, too: the writer J.B. Priestley. He thinks there might be a book in the Symphony's relation with Daytona Beach.

This afternoon was Sir Arthur's first meeting with the Festival Institute's 83-member student ensemble, whose members are 15 to 50 years old. Sir Arthur, a peppery 76, had just finished greeting the players with a joke, when he discovered a few instrument parts for a piece he was going to rehearse were missing. Instantly, he was sputtering with anger. "I came here to play with students," he said," and by God I will play with all of them."

After a few tense moments, the storm subsided, and Sir Arthur began the rehearsal without the missing parts. Soon, he was all smiles again and was praising the players for their sight reading.

Tomorrow, the pianist Vladimir Ashkenazy will begin his series of master classes for pianists. Szymon Goldman has master classes for violinists, the Iowa String Quartet teaches chamber music, and first-desk players in the London Symphony also give instruction. An opera workshop is being offered under the direction of Robert Hause, and members will participate in midnight "Opera Cabaret" performances, weekends at the Daytona Beach hotel

"Hippie Meccas, Sun-Soaked Beaches Are Top Attractions,"
Columbus Daily Telegraph, July 19, 1967:

Last month, students were today's summer nomads, pouring onto the sun-soaked beaches of the East and West Coast and into the hippie meccas of San Francisco and New York City by the hundreds of thousands.

A year ago, Southern California's beaches were the number one lure on the West Coast for young people who gathered to swim, surf and take the sun.

The big change is that this summer, the main draw is San Francisco's psychedelic resort, Haight-Ashbury. Spokesman for the hippies predicts before the summer is out, half a million people will stop in this "love" district. Worried city officials expect 50,000 to 100,000.

Says Linda Taylor, 23, from Stamford, Connecticut: "I've been to every resort on the East Coast, from Fire Island to Fort Lauderdale. But San Francisco tops them all. There's more to see here. You don't have to just lie in the sun or swim. San Francisco has sophistication."

Mitzy McKenna, a slim young brunette from the Los Angeles area, now making her home in San Francisco, sums it up: "Haight-Ashbury's what's happening."

This summer the hippie district is overshadowing the city's traditional attractions such as its European atmosphere, Golden Gate Park, an exciting cultural scene and Golden Gate Bridge. A bus tours Haight-Ashbury. Weekend traffic jams and police arrests for "mill-ins" are features of the district.

Jazz and rock music critic Ralph Gleason calls it "the second immigration to the West," and says it is a result "of the total environment of the city which has made it the rock capital.

Dozens of rock bands—Jefferson Airplane, the Grateful Dead, Big Brother and the Holding Company, The Sopwith Camel, Country Joe and the Fish, and the Steve Miller Blues Band, to name a few—make the city their home. The Fillmore Auditorium and the Avalon Ballroom regularly host big-name groups from all over the country.

1968 NEWS FEATURE

"Jefferson Airplane, *After Bathing at Baxter's*," Paul Kantner interviews Marty Balin, *Hit Parader*, February 1968:

Our next album will be called *After Bathing at Baxter's*. I wrote about five songs on it. I really can't say which one of our songs is my favorite. They all mean different things to me. "Ballad of You and Me and Pooneil" is one of the things I wrote which will be on the album. There's a lot of Winnie the Pooh in that song. We just put music to it and wrote new words.

It also has a little bit of "Memphis" by Chuck Berry and a little bit of "Spoonful" by Howling Wolf in the music. But I still wouldn't call it blues. To me blues are the classic things like Gary Davis. We sat down and started playing different things, and the ones we liked we put in the song, like Grace doing the hard piano thing. The piano sounds much nicer on the album. The single lost a lot of sound. We're always searching for parts that will fit well. Hopefully, it will all come together. We don't always succeed, naturally.

The songs are very hard to describe. I can't say if it's a better album than *Surrealistic Pillow* because I haven't heard the completed masters. It looks as though it will be better, however.

One of the other songs is called "No Paper Cloud Gives Grass Apples." This song is also subtitled "Martha." It starts off with a finger-picking guitar, which is the root of the song, then it dribbles back to the picking thing. There is also a very far-off voice playing against it. I wrote that with a friend of mine called Irving Estus. He wrote part of the words.

There is another song called "Wild Time," sort of a down up-tempo tune. It's very slow and pulsy rather than what you'd think a wild time is. It has a three-part vocal.

Another song I haven't titled yet might be "Watch Her Ride." It's a love song of sorts. It's difficult for me to put the other songs into words because I didn't write them. Jorma wrote two songs and we're going to take one for the album. Besides Gracie's "Two Heads," she'll have a new one called "Ulysses," which is sort of a social commentary. She used a lot of the text from James Joyce's *Ulysses*. That song has to be worked out. Spencer even wrote a song. I'm not sure we'll use it. Marty wrote a thing called "Young Girl Sunday Blues."

There's another one that's sort of two songs put together. It's called "Saturday Afternoon—Won't You Try." It's a sketch of a song on "Saturday afternoon," referring to the San Francisco Be-In back in January. This goes into "Won't You Try," which is up-tempo.

We did a lot of live recording on location at the Fillmore quite a few months ago. A couple of the tracks on the album will be from that. We might have to overdub some vocals on those tracks. It's nice to get the life of a room, like the Stones' live album, despite all its discrepancies, had a nice feeling.

We were trying to finish the album in four weeks, but we had to boost it to six weeks, and we'll probably need another week to master.

You asked about the fancy out-front bass playing in San Francisco groups.

Our own bassist, Jack Casady, is responsible for a lot of that. Looking back over the groups, I'd say you're right. Most of the bass players use their instruments for more than rhythm. A lot of times we sing with the bass. It's just the bass players. We aren't musically restricted. If someone played bass like that a year or so ago, we'd say it was crummy. It's getting away from accepted rock 'n' roll rhythm. We work everything around each other, so everybody has a chance to speak rhythmically and lyrically. Moby Grape and the Grateful Dead have excellent bass players, too.

The recording people are having trouble working with the new electric bands even though they've been recording rock 'n' roll for years. It's actually a brand-new sound for them. Just the bass playing, for example, is new. It has to be defined. Everybody from San Francisco has had trouble recording—The Grape, Grateful Dead, Big Brother, Quicksilver. Somebody once described it as a "wall of sound" and it is a solid wall. To take things out of that wall, an engineer must know how to record it, which takes time. We're starting to get a nice sound, though.

In the studio everything is intellectual. You have to think about what you're doing. On stage it's strictly emotional. In the studio you have to do an instrumental track and then put a vocal over it. It's all in pieces and it has to be put together.

We're also having a lot of censorship problems. There is probably less censorship in America today and anywhere else, but we still have it. Censorship here, however, isn't very effective anymore. We've learned how to bypass censorship. In might be difficult to understand what the singers are saying, but after a while you can understand them.

Then, in the promotion departments, someone wanted us to work Carol Doda into our "act" at the Fillmore. The Fillmore audience would have laughed at it. That topless junk is for the short-hair freaks. It's really depressing, those topless clubs.

When we come back off the road, we like to have a few days by ourselves, but when we work on songs, we live together. Like for this album, we rented a house in Hollywood to work on all the material. We have lots of arguments. It's more civil debate rather than armed conflict. It gets pretty wild sometimes with all the ideas. We don't have one person who controls everything. Whoever yells the loudest wins.

Our producer, Al Smith, who is an excellent producer, feeds everything we give him into the board. He takes care of the proper balance of the sounds we feed him. We are in full charge of the music. Smith is in charge of the electronics.

It took us about three records before we caught on, because we were a new group and our first records weren't very good productions. We're very fortunate to have Al Smith now. San Francisco was unheard of at the time and our songs were strange compared to what was on the top 40.

We're interested in the sounds of the horns but it's more a day philosophical concept. We'd rather do it with voices and guitar sounds. Nobody in the group really plays the horn. Grace sings some nice horn lines and Jorma plays nice horn lines on his guitar. We're getting more into that now. Most of the horn things I've been hearing are dull imitations of Motown things. They're not using the horns creatively. That's like the sitar, which was just used because it had a funny sound. Mike Bloomfield's band does some nice things with horns, however. The Cream is a good example of a group that doesn't need horns.

I'm not into jazz enough to say anything about it. I had a lot of fun jamming with Dizzy Gillespie, and I like John Coltrane and Charles Lloyd. But for me, jazz as such has been dead for a long time. Only certain elements in jazz get to me. By and large, jazz and a lot of classical music is very dull.

I grew up with Carl Perkins and Fats Domino just like everybody else in our generation. Now, they were great people. We still love that stuff, because Rosemary Clooney, or somebody like that, was singing things that didn't mean anything. That pop music was really irrelevant to anything human. That eventually turned out to be muzak. Restaurant music for people over 40.

Musically, we're just expanding, maturing. We're getting more familiar with ourselves.

1970–1979

The Vietnam War finally came to an end, only to spawn spiraling costs and set off several waves of inflation. The result was an America stripped of its ability to dominate the world economy and a nation on the defensive. The era also gave rise to the video cassette recorder and numerous technical enhancements to music and sound. In 1971, President Richard Nixon was forced to devalue the U.S. dollar against foreign currencies and allow its previously fixed value to "float" according to changing economic conditions. By year's end, the money paid for foreign goods exceeded that spent on U.S. exports for the first time in the century. Two years later, during the "Yom Kippur" War between Israel and its Arab neighbors, Arab oil producers declared an oil embargo on oil shipments to the United States, setting off gas shortages, a dramatic rise in the price of oil, and rationing for the first time in 30 years. The sale of automobiles plummeted, unemployment and inflation nearly doubled, and the buying power of Americans fell dramatically. The economy, handicapped by the devaluation of the dollar and inflation, did not fully recover for more than a decade, while the fast-growing economies of Japan and western Europe, especially West Germany, mounted direct competitive challenges to American manufacturers. The value of imported manufactured goods skyrocketed from 14 percent of U.S. domestic production in 1970 to 40 percent in 1979. The inflationary cycle and recession returned in 1979 to disrupt markets, throw thousands out of work, and prompt massive downsizing of companies—awakening many once-secure workers to the reality of the changing economic market. A symbol of the era was the pending bankruptcy of Chrysler Corporation, whose cars were so outmoded and plants so inefficient they could not compete against Japanese imports. The federal government was forced to extend loan guarantees to the company to prevent bankruptcy and the loss of thousands of jobs.

The appointment of Paul Volcker as the chairman of the Federal Reserve Board late in the decade gave the economy the distasteful medicine it needed. To cope with inflation, Volcker slammed on the economic brakes, restricted the growth of the money supply, and curbed inflation. As a result, he pushed interest rates to nearly 20 percent—their highest level since the Civil War. Almost immediately the sale of automobiles and expensive items stopped.

By mid-decade, disco became the music genre most readily associated with the 1970s. First appearing in dance clubs by the middle of the decade, the style was popularized by the movie *Saturday Night Fever*, released in December 1977, starring John Travolta and featuring the music of the Bee Gees. The soundtrack to *Saturday Night Fever* became the best-selling album of all time. The 1970s also saw the emergence of hard rock, personified by Alice Cooper, Lynyrd Skynyrd, Aerosmith, and Kiss. But it was Don McLean's 1971 song "American Pie," inspired by the death of Buddy Holly, that became one of the most recognizable songs of the rock era.

The decade also was marred by the deep divisions caused by the Vietnam War. For more than 10 years the war had been fought on two fronts: at home and abroad. As a result, U.S. policymakers conducted the war with one eye always focused on national opinion. When it ended, the Vietnam War had been the longest war in American history, having cost $118 billion and resulted in 56,000 dead, 300,000 wounded, and the loss of American prestige abroad. The decade was a time not only of movements, but of moving. In the 1970s, the shift of manufacturing facilities to the South from New England and the Midwest accelerated. The Sunbelt became the new darling of corporate America. By the late 1970s, the South, including Texas, had gained more than a million manufacturing jobs, while the Northeast and the Midwest lost nearly two million. Rural North Carolina had the highest percentage of manufacturing of any state in the nation, along with the lowest blue-collar wages and the lowest unionization rate in the country. The Northeast lost more than traditional manufacturing jobs. Computerization of clerical work also made it possible for big firms such as Merrill Lynch, American Express, and Citibank to shift many of their operations to the South and West.

The largest and most striking of all the social actions of the early 1970s was the women's liberation movement; it fundamentally reshaped American society. Since the late 1950s, a small group of well-placed American women had attempted to convince Congress and the courts to bring about equality between the sexes. By the 1970s, the National Organization for Women (NOW) multiplied in size, the first issue of *Ms. Magazine* sold out in a week, and women began demanding economic equality, the legalization of abortion, and the improvement of women's roles in society. "All authority in our society is being challenged," said a Department of Health, Education, and Welfare report. "Professional athletes challenge owners, journalists challenge editors, consumers challenge manufacturers and young blue-collar workers, who have grown up in an environment in which equality is called for in all institutions, are demanding the same rights and expressing the same values as university graduates." The decade also included the flowering of the National Welfare Rights Organization (NWRO), founded in 1966, which resulted in millions of urban poor demanding additional rights. The environmental movement gained recognition and momentum during the decade starting with the first Earth Day celebration in 1970 and the subsequent passage of the federal Clean Air and Clean Water acts. And the growing opposition to the use of nuclear power peaked after the near calamity at Three Mile Island in Pennsylvania in 1979. As the formal barriers to racial equality came down, racist attitudes became unacceptable and the black middle class began to grow. By 1972, half of all Southern black children sat in integrated classrooms, and about one third of all black families had risen economically into the ranks of the middle class.

The changes recorded for the decade included a doubling in the amount of garbage created per capita from 2.5 pounds in 1920 to five pounds. California created a no-fault divorce law, Massachusetts introduced no-fault insurance, and health food sales reached $3 billion. By mid-decade, the so-called typical nuclear family, with working father, housewife, and two children, represented only seven percent of the population and the family size was falling. The average family size was 3.4 persons compared with 4.3 in 1920.

1972 PROFILE

Even though Melissa Goldberg had grown up happy, she, like many young people in the U.S., felt disenchanted and disgusted by the "Establishment's" hypocrisy, authoritarianism, and focus on capitalism and commercialism.

Life at Home

- Melissa Goldberg first fell under the spell of the Grateful Dead at the Monterey Pop Festival.
- Even though the Grateful Dead were sandwiched between the Who's Pete Townshend's guitar-smashing finale and Jimi Hendrix's electric guitar explosion, the Dead's long, intricate riffs captured Melissa's attention.
- Two months earlier she had abruptly left home and college behind in Madison, Wisconsin, to be part of the 1967 Summer of Love celebration well underway in San Francisco, California.
- Her father, a heart surgeon, and her mother, an English literature professor, had insisted that they knew what was best for their 19-year-old daughter.
- Melissa disagreed.
- She knew in her heart that now was the time to discover the rest of the world.
- She had grown up happy and well cared for in Madison; she even looked forward to the harsh winters when her snow-covered neighborhood felt at peace with itself.
- Then came the Vietnam War and America's invasion of that Asian country.
- Vietnam was but the first of many crimes that she had discovered during her freshman year: the virtual slavery of Negroes in Mississippi, the corruption of the industrial military complex, and the nation's materialistic obsession that robbed poor countries of opportunity.
- Melissa even came to realize that her parents—who had attended her every dance recital and piano performance—were part of the problem.

Melissa Goldberg became a full-fledged Deadhead at the Monterey Pop Festival.

- She had been raised by the enemy.
- Even the cold winters seemed oppressive now.
- To prove her purity, she gave away all her possessions to the Salvation Army while home from college one weekend.
- Her father's response was swift and clear: He took away her car, further proving that America's ruling class was willing to do anything to crush rebellion.
- So initially, she let her parents catch her smoking marijuana.
- They first threatened to take her to the police: "I will not have illegal drugs in my house," her father had shouted as loudly as he could.
- Then they invited a friend for dinner, who turned out to be a psychiatrist intent on "letting her talk."
- She had no interest in discussing her internal hurts with a moldy old friend of her mother; besides her boyfriend was more than willing to share his stash of dope, drive her where she wanted to go, and even give her a place to stay if her parents threw her out of the house.
- The last major fight had been about the boy she was dating.
- They didn't think he was good enough for her.
- On that count, they were right.

Melissa was convinced that her successful, materialistic parents were the enemy.

- Although he had initially agreed—enthusiastically, in fact—to accompany her to the West Coast, when it came time to leave he proved to be as spineless and undependable as her parents had predicted he would be.
- Only one semester short of graduation from the University of Wisconsin in engineering, he elected to finish school, vowing all the while to join her the minute he got his degree.
- Melissa had no—zero—interest in waiting for a guy who could not be spontaneous and free.
- So she took to the road traveling by thumb—catching rides when she could and walking when she couldn't.
- Melissa needed 13 days of hitchhiking to reach California, detouring at one point to New Mexico because the trucker was going that way, and then San Diego before reaching San Francisco.
- When she arrived, she was penniless, having given her money away to needy people along the way, and without a place to sleep.
- At the time, Melissa arrived in San Francisco's Haight-Ashbury district—Ground Zero for hippie culture—the Grateful Dead were a local phenomenon referenced often by TV commentators and bus operators ferrying middle-class tourists through Hippie City.
- The hippie hop tour through Haight-Ashbury was advertised as "The only foreign tour within the continental limits of the United States."
- The band was even photographed on their front porch for *Time* magazine's "Summer of Love" issue, making their abode a hippie White House of sorts.
- Melissa was quickly welcomed into a commune housed in a shabby chic Victorian that was exploring the emerging concepts of blending free love and free-form music.

Life on the Road

- To Melissa Goldberg, the Summer of Love in 1967 seemed to be one endless party.
- Everyone was either high on mescaline, grass or LSD; friends were living in tepees along the Big Sur, high school runaways were flocking to big harvest pot parties while she played bongos and drank red Mountain wine at all-night parties.
- As Melissa told friends back home, "it was the undressed rehearsal" for a changed world.
- When a British film crew from the BBC attempted to capture the essence of a "hippie party," they had to stop filming because there were too many naked party people.
- The footage was too risqué to be broadcast.
- Melissa had originally gone to the Monterey Pop Festival because the Jefferson Airplane and the Mamas & the Papas where there, but left in love with the Grateful Dead.
- The Grateful Dead, melded together in 1965, pioneered an eclectic style that fused elements of rock, folk, bluegrass, blues, reggae, country, jazz, psychedelia, and space rock.
- The Dead started their career as the Warlocks, a group formed in early 1965 from the remnants of a Palo Alto jug band called Mother McCree's Uptown Jug Champions.
- The first show under the new name Grateful Dead was in San Jose, California, in December 1965, at one of Ken Kesey's Acid Tests.

San Francisco's Haight-Ashbury district was Ground Zero for hippie culture.

- In January, the Dead appeared at the Fillmore Auditorium in San Francisco and played at the Trips Festival, an early psychedelic rock show.
- Charter members of the Grateful Dead were: banjo and guitar player Jerry Garcia, guitarist Bob Weir, blues organist Ron "Pigpen" McKernan, the classically trained bassist Phil Lesh, and drummer Bill Kreutzmann.
- The name "Grateful Dead" was chosen from an old dictionary, which defined "Grateful Dead" as "the soul of a dead person, or his angel, showing gratitude to someone who, as an act of charity, arranged his burial."
- The band's first LP, *The Grateful Dead*, was released on Warner Brothers Records in 1967.
- But their first live performance at the Monterey Pop Festival was unscheduled.
- Melissa awoke from sleep after midnight to discover an impromptu concert underway with Eric Burdon of the Animals singing "House of the Rising Sun" with Pete Townshend of The Who playing lead guitar.
- This was followed by jam sessions combining the talents of The Grateful Dead's Jerry Garcia, The Byrds, Jimi Hendrix, David Crosby, and the Jefferson Airplane.
- Once the official festival began, Melissa got to hear Country Joe and the Fish sing antiwar ballads, Otis Redding mesmerizing with his energy, and Jimi Hendrix playing his Stratocaster with his teeth and then setting the guitar on fire.
- But Melissa's personal showstopper was Jerry Garcia and the Grateful Dead.
- Live performances featured long musical improvisations that made every concert unique; "Their music," wrote Lenny Kaye, "touches on ground that most other groups don't even know exists."
- She especially appreciated the Dead's decision to "borrow" nearly one million dollars' worth of Fender audio equipment to perform another free concert, this time in San Francisco.
- Even after the equipment was returned, the authorities failed to see the humor in the situation.

- Melissa desperately wanted be part of this world, where people threw off theories concerning music just as casually as her mother discussed Jewish holiday recipes.
- The idea of the moment was three-dimensional sound; the goal was for every instrument to be in stereo by fashioning every guitar and every drum set to have a right and left channel, so the audience could hear everything.
- Most bands thought this concept was technologically impossible.
- Melissa's chance to meet Jerry Garcia came because of a water balloon fight among several members of the band.
- Melissa took half a dozen blows—soaking her from head to toe—when Garcia rescued her and they started to hang out, even after the Dead were busted for pot possession and harder drugs began to circulate.

After meeting Jerry Garcia, Melissa was ready to join the band's tour.

- And Melissa was unquestionably ready to join the caravan of fans when the Quick and the Dead Tour started in January 1968; the concept of the Dead spreading their vibe to the whole country was simply awesome.
- Melissa figured she was attached to the greatest show on Earth: a hippie Buffalo Bill show jammed with young, freaked-out American rock 'n' roll music.
- They took a song and turned it into a sound journey—one that sometimes had to be altered on the band's albums.
- The Grateful Dead's almost seamless, continuous soundtrack had to be cut into pieces because record companies paid royalties based on the number of tracks on an album, not the number of minutes recorded.
- Melissa trailed the Dead every step of the way; if they were playing, she was in the audience.
- She wasn't alone: One of the more unique customs of the Deadhead community was to go on tour with the band.
- Deadheads typically quit their jobs and left everything behind to follow the band from venue to venue, seeing as many shows as possible.
- The parking lot scene before and after a show resembled a street fair, complete with the sounds and smells one might expect.

The Grateful Dead held a news conference after their drug bust.

- It was the "show before the show" and where friends met afterwards to exchange thoughts on the night's experience and to make plans to meet later on in the tour.
- Deadheads from around the country converged on what was known as "Shakedown Street," the main row of venders (Deadheads with goods to sell or barter with), which over the years reached mythical proportions.
- Melissa bought and sold homemade tie-dyed clothing and hemp jewelry.
- All the while, Deadheads sat around playing acoustic guitars, banging out deafening rhythms in drum circles, throwing Frisbees, or sleeping to recoup energy for that night's show.
- Different songs filled the air; once the gates opened, the experience simply moved inside.
- To keep track of her travels, Melissa kept a journal of the shows she attended, decorated with ticket stubs, pictures of friends at the shows, hand-drawn pictures, and most importantly, setlists!
- Melissa became fanatical about the setlist as a written record of the songs played (in order) during a show.
- Some Deadheads scribbled them on ticket stubs, matchboxes, or envelopes—usually in the dark—during the show.
- But Melissa was meticulous.
- She knew her setlists were part of the living legacy of the Grateful Dead and the Deadhead community.
- It wasn't always easy: Unlike most bands, the Dead didn't always end their songs.
- Often, she found, they simply segued into another song.
- Several times an entire set was nothing more than several songs played continuously.
- These song pairings encouraged a setlist shorthand that joined songs with an arrow.
- For this reason, some familiar song pairings were condensed: "China Cat Sunflower" followed by "I Know You Rider" would be written as "China/Rider," while "Scarlet Begonias" followed by "Fire on the Mountain" was recorded as "Scarlet/Fire."
- When she lost the bound notebook in a police raid, she took it as a sign that it was time to return home.
- Besides, the health of original band member Pigpen had deteriorated to the point that he could no longer tour with the band; his final concert appearance was June 17, 1972, at the Hollywood Bowl.
- On June 18, 1972, Melissa made a long-distance phone call; she had not seen her parents in five years.

Life in the Community: San Francisco, California

- The flower child or hippie movement started around 1965 in San Francisco and spread across the United States, Canada, and parts of Europe.
- Inspired by the Beats of the fifties, who declared themselves independent from the "authoritarian order" of America, the Haight-Ashbury "anti-community" rested on a rejection of American commercialism.
- Haight residents eschewed the material benefits of modern life, encouraged by the distribution of free food and organized shelter by the Diggers, and the creation of institutions such as the Free Clinic for medical treatment.
- Psychedelic drug use became but one means to find a "new reality."
- According to Grateful Dead guitarist Bob Weir, "Haight-Ashbury was a ghetto of bohemians who wanted to do anything—and we did—but I don't think it has happened since. Yes, there was LSD. But Haight-Ashbury was not about drugs. It was about exploration, finding new ways of expression, being aware of one's existence."
- An all-volunteer army of hippies flocked to San Francisco, congregating near the corner of Haight Street and Ashbury Street, where the world got its first view of this unique group.
- The place came to be known as the Haight-Ashbury district, where average Americans took bus tours to view the flower child phenomenon.
- Average Americans were shocked by their hair, clothing, drug experimentation and alternative lifestyles, even though most hippies were young people from prosperous middle-class homes.
- The Haight-Ashbury district was in the very center of San Francisco and incorporated Golden Gate Park.
- Musicians in the Jefferson Airplane, the Grateful Dead, and Janis Joplin's band Big Brother and the Holding Company all lived a short distance from the famous intersection.
- The prelude to the Summer of Love was the Human Be-In at Golden Gate Park on January 14, 1967, billed as a "gathering of tribes."

- Haight-Ashbury's own psychedelic newspaper, the *San Francisco Oracle*, commented: "A new concept of celebrations beneath the human underground must emerge, become conscious, and be shared, so a revolution can be formed with a renaissance of compassion, awareness, and love, and the revelation of unity for all mankind."
- The gathering of approximately 30,000 like-minded people made the Human Be-In the first event that confirmed there was a viable hippie scene.
- This was followed by the term "Summer of Love," when thousands of hippies gathered there, popularized by hit songs such as "San Francisco (Be Sure to Wear Some Flowers in Your Hair)" by Scott McKenzie.
- A July 7, 1967, *Time* magazine cover story on "The Hippies: Philosophy of a Subculture," and an August CBS News television report on "The Hippie Temptation" exposed the hippie subculture to national attention and popularized the Flower Power movement across the country and around the world.
- The ever-increasing numbers of youth making a pilgrimage to the Haight-Ashbury district overwhelmed and alarmed the San Francisco authorities, whose public stance was that they would keep the hippies away.
- The mainstream media's coverage of hippie life in the Haight-Ashbury district drew youth from all over America, especially after writer Hunter S. Thompson labeled the district "Hashbury" in *The New York Times Magazine*.

During the Summer of Love, hippies flocked to Haight-Ashbury.

HISTORICAL SNAPSHOT
1972

- President Richard Nixon ordered the development of a Space Shuttle program
- World War II Japanese soldier Shoichi Yokoi was discovered in Guam, where he had spent 28 years in the jungle
- Shirley Chisholm, the first African-American congresswoman, announced her candidacy for president
- The HP-35, the first scientific handheld calculator, was introduced with a price of $395
- *Mariner 9* transmitted pictures from Mars
- U.S. airlines began mandatory inspections of passengers and baggage
- Phonorecords were granted U.S. federal copyright protection for the first time
- The Soviet unmanned spaceship *Luna 20* landed on the moon and returned to Earth with 1.94 ounces of lunar soil
- President Nixon made an unprecedented eight-day visit to the People's Republic of China and met with Mao Zedong
- North Vietnamese negotiators walked out of the Paris Peace Talks to protest U.S. air raids
- The *Pioneer 10* spacecraft became the first artificial satellite to leave the solar system
- The 92nd U.S. Congress sent the proposed Equal Rights Amendment to the states for ratification
- *The Godfather* was released in cinemas in the U.S.
- The United States and the Soviet Union joined some 70 nations in signing the Biological Weapons Convention, an agreement to ban biological warfare
- The Boston Marathon officially allowed women to compete for the first time
- The fourth anniversary of the Broadway musical *Hair* was celebrated with a free concert in Central Park
- Nixon ordered the mining of Haiphong Harbor in Vietnam
- The first financial derivatives exchange, the International Monetary Market (IMM), opened on the Chicago Mercantile Exchange
- Wernher von Braun retired from NASA, frustrated by the agency's unwillingness to pursue a manned trans-orbital space program
- Five White House operatives were arrested for burglarizing the offices of the Democratic National Committee in the Watergate Complex in Washington, DC
- Jane Fonda toured North Vietnam, during which she was photographed sitting on a North Vietnamese anti-aircraft gun
- Comedian George Carlin was arrested by Milwaukee police for public obscenity, for reciting his "Seven Words You Can Never Say on Television" at Summerfest
- The United States launched *Landsat 1*, the first Earth-resources satellite
- U.S. health officials admitted that African-Americans were used as guinea pigs in the Tuskegee Study, "Untreated Syphilis in the Negro Male"
- Eleven Israeli athletes at the 1972 Summer Olympics in Munich were murdered after eight members of the Arab terrorist group Black September invaded the Olympic Village; five guerillas and one policeman were also killed in a failed hostage rescue
- During a scientific meeting in Honolulu, Herbert Boyer and Stanley N. Cohen conceived the concept of recombinant DNA, which opened the door to genetically modified organisms
- The Dow Jones Industrial Average closed above 1,000 (1,003.16) for the first time
- Atari kicked off the first generation of video games with the release of their seminal arcade version of Pong, the first video game to achieve commercial success
- *Apollo 17* landed on the moon, and Eugene Cernan became the last person to walk on the moon, after he and Harrison Schmitt completed the third and final extravehicular activity
- The U.S. ban on the pesticide DDT took effect

Selected Prices

Bathroom Scale	$17.99
Food Processor	$39.99
Hair Dryer	$3.88
Home, Six Rooms, Flushing, NY	$48,500
Ice Bucket	$80.00
Maternity Top	$8.00
Radio, AM	$6.99
Stereo Cassette System	$400.00
Watch, Woman's Movado	$925.00
Woman's Jumpsuit	$32.00

The Touchhead's Guide to the Grateful Dead:

The language of the Deadhead community is sometimes confusing and incomprehensible to the outsider or newbie (a Deadhead who has just "gotten on the bus"). Some language has evolved over the years through the use of mind-altering chemicals, through endless hours of conversations with other Deadheads in the parking lot before shows, and in the venues themselves. Some of the language has come about due to necessity, such as the need to alert others to the sudden appearance of law enforcement. Some of the more colorful dialect that is heard among Deadheads, especially at shows, includes:

- tripping on DNA: Going to a show with a member of your family.
- tour rats: Hardcore Deadheads who travel from show to show, live in the parking lot during a tour, earn money by selling homemade goods, or wait for a miracle ticket.
- miracle ticket: An extra ticket given to another Deadhead without a ticket free of charge.
- wooks: Hardcore backwoods hippies who attend shows wearing nothing but a pair of dirty shorts.
- ick: Tour slang to describe the common bacterial or viral infections resulting from undernourishment and overexposure while on tour.
- spin: To copy a tape.
- puddle: A larger-than-average-size dose of LSD.
- noodling: The description of the band's searching excursions during jams and solos.
- benji: A hundred-dollar bill used in case of emergencies. I think these exist in folklore alone.
- bugment: The music being so intense it makes your eyes bug out.
- crisp: A soundboard tape that has no saturation or hiss.
- the Pepto pink: Bob Weir's painfully pink guitar.
- teef: To steal something small and of no significance.
- de-reek: Getting rid of "truck mouth" with mouthwash or a breath mint.
- puppied: Being so relaxed that you want to snuggle with somebody.
- spinning madly: The copying of several tapes.
- biscuit shows: Good shows in out-of-the-way venues only the most hardcore Deadheads attend.
- family: Friends that are Deadheads.
- get on the bus: The moment people realize they are Grateful Dead fans.

As stated previously, Deadheads can often be found frantically writing down names of the songs during shows. Many years ago, Deadheads started using setlist shorthand in their setlists. Some examples of this setlist shorthand are found throughout the Deadhead community:

- BIODTL: Beat It On Down the Line
- FOTD: Friend of the Devil
- GDTRFB: Goin' Down the Road Feelin' Bad
- GDTS: Grateful Dead Ticket Sales
- NFA: Not Fade Away
- NSB: New Speedway Boogie
- TLEO: They Love Each Other
- WALSTIB: What a Long Strange Trip It's Been
- PITB: Playing in the Band

Line Donkeys, Deadheads that enter the venue with a backpack filled with food, books, clothing, etc., are a source of irritation at shows. Line Donkeys hold up the line, as all bags and purses are emptied, checked, and repacked before being admitted through the gates. Line Donkeys can easily add an extra 20 minutes to the entrance process if more than one are in line. Wedgers, the adult version of "budgers" found in elementary school, are also held in low regard. Lines will explode in choruses of displeasure when wedgers try and slime into the line.

"Letter to the Editor: Back in His Room," *Berkeley Barb*, March 28, 1969:

An open letter from Rocky Raccoon concerning Caravan North '69:

Dear Friends,

Hundreds of letters and phone calls have come into the BARB office since an article explaining tentative plans for "Caravan North '69" first appeared several weeks ago.

The enthusiastic letters of inquiry came from all over the nation. I was able to answer only a handful of them personally. The BARB has given me space to answer the rest of you in this fashion.

The original plan called for a caravan of roughly 300 cars and 1,000 hip people to leave Seattle June 1 to settle in Alaska. The Caravan would travel over 1,523 miles of gravel road to the destination. Other turndown pioneers would join the group at a staging area in the Fairbanks vicinity before heading for the wilds of interior Alaska to establish a community from scratch.

As the time draws near, planners have been overwhelmed with details of such a giant undertaking. First, we've been unable to get title to adequate land. Second, in order to feed, house and care for 1,000 people, a smooth organization has to be set up in Fairbanks.

The BARB article got some mileage in Alaska, too, when a Fairbanks radio station picked it up and based a news story on it. The reaction there was not entirely friendly.

A lot of good work has been started. But not enough has been done, in my opinion, to pull the thing off successfully this summer.

I have decided not to return to Alaska during 1969. Probably by next summer, the plan could be carried out properly. But my decision need not put a damper on Caravan North '69 if there are still a number of people who want to go as a group, and if there is someone willing to get behind it as a driving force.

After eight years in Alaska and now several months in San Francisco, several factors make me think it is best for me to stay on this side of Canada this summer.

1. So much is happening here that is exciting. Farm communes in New Mexico, Colorado, and other rural areas with plenty of room and a climate less harsh than Alaska's are tremendously appealing.

2. Obtaining title to adequate land in Alaska can best be done from that end. That is why a small group (hopefully with a little bread and not too many children to feed the first winter) could accomplish this for a larger body to follow.

3.   Many of those who have written for information indicate they have no money, no craft (with which to earn a living), and only a foggy idea of what Alaska is really like. It takes $200 a person to cross the border from the U.S. and Canada. Jobs are sometimes scarce. People can sometimes be uptight.

In short, I don't want to be responsible for a possible fiasco, and I believe the idea needs more work on both ends: San Francisco and Fairbanks. I will help to work this end, but looking ahead to the summer of 1970.

If someone feels like being Brigham Young and wants to lead the children forth into the wilderness this summer, then I would like to speak to this brother. Meanwhile, I am checking out communes in New Mexico and California for myself.

If you want to go to Alaska, you're on your own unless you hear from Brigham.

Love and peace,

Rocky Raccoon

"Poll Reveals Significant Marijuana Use at Tulane," *The Tulane Hullabaloo*, November 3, 1967:

Thirty-one percent of the 200 students answering a HULLABALOO poll report they've used marijuana at one time, although only seven percent say they use it frequently.

But there was little difference noted in the poll between the percentages of male and female students who have tried marijuana; the poll showed a regular increase of use with age in both sexes. One out of six freshmen, six out of 10 juniors, and over 70 percent of graduate students responding to the poll said they had used marijuana at least once.

These figures are significantly higher than the national percentage of marijuana use by college students reported in a Gallup poll published in the November Reader's Digest. That poll, which covered 426 American colleges, indicated that only six percent of the nation's college students have ever used marijuana.

Of the students answering the Gallup poll, 51 percent said they did not even know a single student who had tried marijuana, and estimated that only four percent of those on the campus and 13 percent of all college students have tried marijuana or LSD.

The Gallup poll also showed that the majority of American college students were "reluctant" to try drugs and generally disapprove of those students who use marijuana or LSD.

On the Tulane campus, however, 59 percent of those responding to the poll felt that the use of marijuana should be legalized.

"Pot, according to scientific evidence, is less harmful to the body than tobacco and nicotine. Banning it is as ridiculous as the Prohibition laws in the 1920s, because of the increase in use of the drug," commented one student.

"Advertisement: To Commemorate the New Grateful Dead Album, We Present Our Pigpen Look-Alike Contest (Part Two)," *Berkeley Barb*, May 30, 1969:

To be downright brutal about it, Part One of our Peter Pan look-alike contest that we laid on you a few weeks back is a bust. Not that there weren't plenty of entries. There've been plenty. But so far, no one has, via black-and-white color photograph, captured the panache, the bravado, the insouciance—the true and the utter raunch of Mr. Pen.

Just to have a mustache doesn't make it.

Just to have long hair doesn't make it.

Blondes don't make it.

Photos with no name and address don't make it.

And the pigmy from Venice (California) who wrote that "contests suck" doesn't make it.

Now, because (1) in our heart of hearts we know there is a Pigpen look-alike in this world of ours, (2) the Grateful Dead have a new album called *Aoxomoxoa*, and deserve an ad, and (3) we need all the diversion we can get here in Burbank, the Box Top and Party Games Department has voted to extend the current deadline for the Pigpen look-alike contest and make it easier to enter.

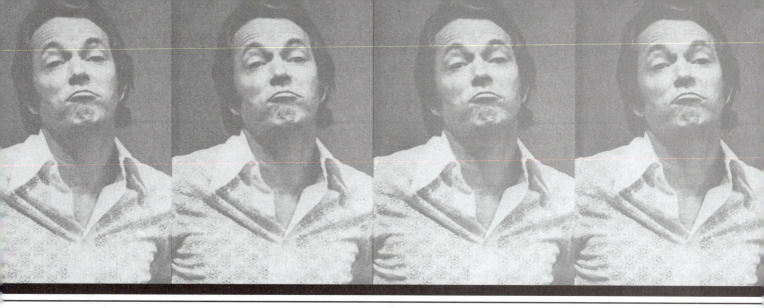

1973 News Feature

"The Sherrill Sound," *Time*, **October 22, 1973:**

The drugstore blonde with a guitar under her arm had been rebuffed by every other record company in Nashville. But when she appeared at the Columbia/Epic offices, Producer Billy Sherrill thought he heard something special—a tear in her voice. "Somethin' said, 'don't turn this chick down,'" Sherrill recalled later. Thus, it came about that he signed Tammy Wynette, supervised her first recording session, and even wrote a song for it: "Apartment Number Nine." The record reached the top 20 on the Billboard country charts. Tammy's next two, "Your Good Girl's Gonna Go Bad" and "D-I-V-O-R-C-E," also Sherrill songs, went all the way to number one—followed by 20 more, all Sherrill-written and produced. One of them, "Stand by Your Man," sold 1.5 million copies, became the second biggest-selling single by any woman in country music.

Billy Sherrill has performed the same kind of wonders for more than 30 country-styled singers, including such other stars as Johnny Duncan, Tanya Tucker, and Johnny Paycheck. In all, he has more than 50 No. 1 one hits to his credit. Nowadays, a week rarely passes without a couple of Sherrill-produced records among the top 10. Last week, for example, there were "The Midnight Oil" with Barbara Mandrell and "We're Gonna Hold On" with George Jones and Tammy Wynette. Little wonder, then, that many people who once spoke of the Nashville Sound have begun referring instead to the Sherrill Sound.

Sherrill has no formula for that sound but defines his stock and trade as feeling with a beat. "The song is so much more important than the artist, producer, studio or the record company," he says. He's one of the few record producers who tries to listen to every song submitted to him. After selecting the song, he relies on a series of instinctive, spontaneous choices in the studio, as a recent session with country star David Houston demonstrated. With Sherrill listening intently, Houston ran through "The Lady of the Night":

> "There's nothing a man can tell her
> She ain't done or seen,
> She'll hold any stranger tight for a drink,
> She's the lady of the night…."

"That's a mighty pretty song to be singing about a whore," Sherrill encouraged gently, "but say 'lady' a little faster, Dave; she's a fast lady." He turned to the band. "Don't get loud there at first when you go into the fifth chord, because he is whispering something filthy to her." The three guitarists, drummer and bass player nodded, jotting down numbers and symbols on scraps of paper to indicate chords and dynamics.

Cutting a record in Nashville is often a "head session" where musicians unable to read music learn the tune on the spot from the vocalist. "In New York, you start to change something, you tear up a $700,000 arrangement," Sherrill pointed out. "Here, we can make the lead sheet of a song in the time it takes to sing it." Not that Sherrill is easygoing. "All the guys I use are machines," he snaps. "They do exactly what I want 'em to—if the record doesn't hit, I go down in flames"….

The son of a Baptist evangelist from Alabama, Sherrill grew up touring the South with his parents, playing piano at the "tent meetings" and other functions where his father preached. He traces the beginning of his career as a professional musician to earning $10 for playing a funeral at age 10. Although he had no formal musical training, by his teens he could play half a dozen instruments. After finishing high school, he took up the life of an itinerant rock musician, playing mostly piano and saxophone with bands in Tennessee and Alabama and sleeping in his car or under bridges. In 1961, he and a musician friend set up their own small recording studio in Nashville. A year later, he joined Columbia/Epic, where he is now a vice president.

A slight man with reddish brown hair, Sherrill, at 36, has an old-young face lit with intelligence and sudden flashes of humor, but worn by the anxiety that comes with having to live by one's wits too early. He eschews the blaring Cowboy suits and diamond stick pins of Music City, lives quietly with his wife and 11-year-old daughter in a spacious, antique-furnished $100,000 house overlooking Nashville.

He holds to the fundamentalist faith of his father, but does not attend church because he cannot find one that teaches a literal enough interpretation of the Scriptures. His personal taste in music runs to classical. In fact, one of his early productions was a recording of Brahms' Lullaby that caused his daughter some confusion. When she heard the melody at school, she loyally insisted, despite her teacher's objection: "My daddy wrote that song, and we've got the record at home to prove it."

1976 PROFILE

Danny Goldberg started out as a low-paid writer at *Billboard*, but soon moved up to become a rock 'n' roll insider, hanging out with bands, writing, and critiquing the latest music.

Life at Home
- Danny Goldberg's entry into the music business was completely practical; he needed a job and wanted to get his own apartment.
- According to the newspaper advertisement, *Billboard* magazine had an opening and Danny certainly had a need.
- After graduating from high school, Danny had enrolled at the University of California at Berkeley where he saw Janis Joplin's band Big Brother and the Holding Company, was introduced to LSD and spent five days at the Alameda County Juvenile Hall.
- Raised in New York by well-heeled liberals, Danny began his career at *Billboard* in 1968, where, as an 18-year-old college dropout, he took a job compiling chart data.
- Initially, his job entailed calling dozens of record stores around the country and asking them what was selling, thus providing the raw data for the *Billboard* sales charts, which influenced radio station airplay, TV bookings and orders from retailers.
- "I was at *Billboard* a few months and a promo guy from Capitol gave everybody a copy of (The Beatles') the White Album the day it came out. That was one hell of a perk," Danny said.
- It dawned on Danny that he could be part of the music business without being a musician; "After that I did the best I could to climb whatever ladders were in front of me."
- One of his first major writing assignments for *Billboard* was to cover a weekend event upstate that none of the regulars had any interest in attending: the Woodstock Festival.

Danny Goldberg's job at Billboard *led to his status as a rock & roll insider.*

Danny's coverage of Woodstock led to his weekly column on rock music.

- For this special assignment he was paid $0.30 a published inch.
- Along with his press pass to Woodstock, Danny got to ride to the festival in a stretch limousine, heard Santana and Jimi Hendrix for the first time, slept in a clean hotel room and was mesmerized by the performances of Joan Baez, Johnny Winter, and Janis Joplin.
- His front-page rhapsodic review landed him a full-time writer's job with *Record World*, to include a weekly column on rock music.
- That entry point would lead to friendships with Patti Smith, Stevie Nicks, and image management of the 1970s British supergroup, Led Zeppelin.
- Music and the music business were undergoing change, and Danny was determined to be in the epicenter.
- Two rock magazines, *Crawdaddy* and *Rolling Stone*, were applying serious critical intelligence to writing about rock 'n' roll; *Esquire*, *The Village Voice*, *The New York Times*, *The New Yorker* and *The New Republic* all had assigned talented writers to the rock 'n' roll beat.
- Underground rock radio was emerging as a rebellious reaction to the highly repetitive play lists of Top 40 stations—allowing extended cuts from albums to be played and non-traditional groups to receive airplay.
- Even the way the records were put together had changed—moving from a collection of songs to a conceptual, interconnected collection of songs that visited a single theme.
- No longer was the goal to release a record as a vehicle to sell singles, which sold for a dollar, but to construct a coherent, unified body of work that incorporated an overall artistic concept.
- At the same time, Jimi Hendrix and Eric Clapton were eliminating the boundaries of what a rock guitarist could express, and the technology of sound was expanding bands' options.
- By 1969, Danny had become a fixture at the legendary artists' hangout Max's Kansas City, where he would "worm my way" into a clique of influential rock critics.

- There he met future rocker and poet Patti Smith; "Everything about her exuded creativity. Every sentence she uttered. She had an intensity that just came out of her."
- By the early 1970s, Danny was no longer simply a writer—an observer—to the music scene; he was an insider.
- "The truth was that I revered rock musicians and felt guilty when I criticized them," he said.

Life at Work

- Danny Goldberg's first few forays into music public relations were forgettable.
- But that was before he was asked to fly to London and meet the super hot, bad boy band Led Zeppelin—they had a PR problem: they hated the media.
- In the spring of 1973, Led Zeppelin was the biggest band on the planet: their previous album—their fourth—had already sold eight million copies and included the song "Stairway to Heaven," the most played song on the album rock radio stations that year.
- Sales of the first four Zeppelin albums were so consistent that they represented more than one-fourth of the annual sales for the entire Atlantic Records catalogue.
- Formed in 1968, the English rock band Led Zeppelin was known for its heavy, guitar-driven blues-rock sound, also known as heavy metal, and their bad boy antics.
- The American press and Led Zeppelin were uncomfortable in each other's company; even Led Zeppelin's mammoth American tour in 1972 had not eased the problem.
- They wanted to hire Danny as their press agent, but it would not be an easy task.
- Hypersensitive to early bad reviews, members of the band had long demonized journalists; plus, they developed a reputation for throwing television sets out of hotel rooms, driving Harley-Davidsons down hotel hallways, and mistreating young groupies.
- Some members of Led Zeppelin had simply stopped doing interviews or were rude when they did.
- Television performances were avoided because the band's big sound did not translate well in the little box—further limiting the media exposure available.
- Before meeting the band the first time, Danny had an audience with their legendary manager Peter Grant; who had "the ultimate chip on the ultimate shoulder."
- As one of the first managers to understand that the artists themselves had grown powerful enough to act independently, he had led Led Zeppelin away from the Premier Talent agency in 1971 and begun booking the band directly without an agent, thus saving 10 percent of the band's total cost, which did not endear him to the music establishment.
- Danny was 22, smart. innovative and possessed a long list of media contacts.
- Led Zeppelin, he was told, wanted the type of publicity that the Rolling Stones routinely received on tour; the former were selling out stadiums across the nation and felt they deserved better treatment from the press.

Touring bands were known for trashing the fancy hotels they stayed in.

- Danny began his assault by creating a press release that demonstrated that Led Zeppelin's sold-out show in Tampa Stadium, with 56,800 seats, was larger than the Beatles' Shea Stadium show in 1965.
- Led Zeppelin tickets cost $5.50 each; the Tampa concert grossed $312,400.
- Newspapers across the country carried headlines proclaiming that Led Zeppelin had "broken the Beatles' record" even though the relative size of Tampa Stadium to Shea Stadium was not a true measure of popularity.
- A second series of stories featured the band's leased private plane, called the *Starship*, which boasted the band's name on the side, velvet couches and rock-star grandiosity.
- The airplane also had a fur-covered bed that was often used, but rarely for sleeping.
- Danny's PR philosophy emphasized the band's popularity and emphasized its role as the people's band despite what some rock critics might think.
- These stories and the momentum they created attracted increased attention of the powerhouse *Rolling Stone* magazine, which promised a major feature; owner Jann Wenner even pledged that the band could pick the writer of the article.
- Danny pleaded, but the band said no.
- Led Zeppelin was accustomed to going their own way—although they would eventually say yes.
- When they were first formed, they rarely got radio play until Boston's WBCN featured "Whole Lotta Love."
- Boston had developed a reputation around the country of being reliable taste-makers, thanks to its concentration of trendsetting college students; Boston's acceptance of the band helped launch a national obsession.
- The band's first album and its blend of blues, folk and Eastern influences with distorted amplification made it one of the pivotal records in the creation of heavy metal music.
- In their first year, Led Zeppelin managed to complete four U.S. and four U.K. concert tours, and also released their second album, entitled *Led Zeppelin II*.
- Recorded almost entirely on the road at various North American recording studios, the second album was an even greater success and reached the number one chart position in the U.S. while establishing the blueprint for heavy metal bands that followed.
- Some early Led Zeppelin concerts lasted more than four hours, with expanded, improvised live versions of their songs.

- During this period of intensive concert touring, the band developed a reputation for off-stage excess.
- The group also increasingly resisted television appearances, enforcing their preference that their fans hear and see them in live concerts.
- Led Zeppelin were one of the most commercially successful and influential groups of the 1970s.
- By the mid-1970s, the symbols of success were everywhere: the band began to wear elaborate, flamboyant clothing, they traveled in a private jet airliner, rented out entire sections of hotels (including the Continental Hyatt House in Los Angeles, known colloquially as the "Riot House"), and became the subject of many of rock's most repeated stories of debauchery.
- Led Zeppelin's fourth album, released in November 1971, was a conspicuous display of fame: there was no indication of a title or a band name on the original cover.

- The cover displayed only symbols—no names or photographs—in response to being labeled as "hyped" and "overrated" by the music press.
- The band wanted to prove that the music could sell itself by giving no indication of who they were.
- Led Zeppelin IV, as it came to be called, was one of the bestselling albums in history, and its massive popularity cemented the band's superstardom in the 1970s.
- Zeppelin's next album, *Houses of the Holy*, was released in 1973. It featured further experimentation, with expanded use of synthesizers and mellotron orchestration.
- The orange album cover of *Houses of the Holy* depicted images of nude children climbing up the Giant's Causeway in Northern Ireland, causing controversy.
- In 1974, Led Zeppelin took a break from touring and launched their own record label, Swan Song, named after one of only five Led Zeppelin songs which the band never released commercially.
- In addition to using Swan Song as a vehicle to promote their own albums, the band expanded the label's roster, signing artists such as Bad Company, The Pretty Things, Maggie Bell, Detective, Dave Edmunds, Midnight Flyer, Sad Café and Wildlife.
- Led Zeppelin's double album, *Physical Graffiti*, was their first release on the Swan Song; a review in Rolling Stone referred to *Physical Graffiti* as Led Zeppelin's "bid for artistic respectability," adding that the only bands Led Zeppelin had to compete with for the title "The World's Best Rock Band" were The Rolling Stones and The Who.
- The album was a massive fiscal and critical success.

Led Zeppelin and other popular bands resisted appearing on TV, thinking it would diminish their fans' experience.

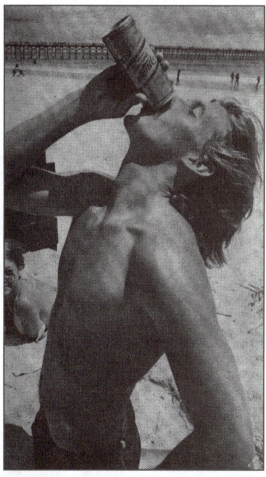

Drinking was part of a musician's life in the fast lane.

Life in the Community: Los Angeles, California

- Los Angeles, California, in the early 1960s was primed for a major musical innovation.
- With MGM musicals at their peak and film production a long-entrenched part of the scene, the city was filled with first-rate recording studios, orchestras, and session players.
- Initially, surf rock emerged as the southern California sound in the early 1960s, epitomized by the Beach Boys and their first single, "Surfin'," in 1961.
- By the middle of the decade, the tide had turned toward folk and psychedelic rock, and Hollywood clubs such as the Troubadour and the Whisky a Go Go propelled performers such as The Byrds, The Doors, Joni Mitchell, and Buffalo Springfield into the spotlight.
- Rock journalist Roy Trakin noted, "The summer of 1966 on L.A.'s Sunset Strip was a time when many young musicians thought anything was possible. A teenager from the San Fernando Valley might wind up jamming with Jimi Hendrix, while a 14-year-old hitchhiking on Sunset Boulevard could get picked up by Phil Spector's limousine."
- Folk and country rock dominated L.A.'s music scene in the early 1970s, best symbolized by the L.A.-based Eagles, whose *Hotel California* featured the Beverly Hills Hotel and Bungalows on the cover.
- The Rainbow Bar & Grill, which opened in 1972, emerged as a hot Sunset Strip hangout for rock stars.
- Los Angeles also enjoyed a very strong experimental rock scene in the early 1970s, centered around a club called the Rodney Bingenheimer's English Disco, run by Bingenheimer, who later, as a disc jockey for KROQ's "Rodney On The Roq," did much to promote L.A. punk bands.
- In the mid-1970s, California punk arrived on the Sunset Strip and especially at Whisky a Go Go, which regularly hosted homegrown punk bands such as X, The Runaways and The Germs.

Folk singers often performed in casual settings.

HISTORICAL SNAPSHOT
1976

- The Cray-1, the first commercially developed supercomputer, was released by Seymour Cray's Cray Research
- The United States vetoed a United Nations resolution that called for an independent Palestinian state
- *Live from Lincoln Center* debuted on PBS
- Clifford Alexander Jr. was confirmed as the first African-American Secretary of the United States Army
- Apple Computer Company was formed by Steve Jobs and Steve Wozniak
- The Jovian-Plutonian gravitational effect was first reported by astronomer Patrick Moore
- The United States Treasury Department reintroduced the two-dollar bill as a Federal Reserve Note on Thomas Jefferson's 233rd birthday as part of the Bicentennial celebration
- The punk rock group The Ramones released their first self-titled album
- The National Basketball Association and the American Basketball Association agreed on the ABA-NBA merger
- The Supreme Court ruled in *Gregg v. Georgia* that the death penalty was not inherently cruel or unusual, and was a constitutionally acceptable form of punishment
- The U.S. celebrated the 200th anniversary of the Declaration of Independence
- The first class of women was inducted at the United States Naval Academy in Annapolis, Maryland
- In New York City, "Son of Sam" killed one person and seriously wounded another in the first of a series of attacks that terrorized the city for the next year
- The first recognized outbreak of Legionnaires' disease killed 29 at the American Legion Convention in Philadelphia
- The *Viking 2* spacecraft landed at Utopia Planitia on Mars, taking the first close-up color photos of the planet's surface
- Chairman Mao Zedong of the People's Republic of China died
- The 100 Club Punk Festival ignited the careers of several influential punk and post-punk bands, sparking the Punk Movement's introduction into mainstream culture
- The Irish rock band U2 was formed after drummer Larry Mullen Jr. posted a note seeking members for a band on the notice board of his Dublin school
- The report, *Puerto Ricans in the Continental United States: An Uncertain Future*, documented that Puerto Ricans in the United States had a poverty rate of 33 percent in 1974, the highest of all major racial-ethnic groups in the country
- Ford Motors officially launched the production of its Fiesta
- The Copyright Act of 1976 extended copyright duration for an additional 20 years in the U.S.
- In the U.S. presidential election, Jimmy Carter defeated incumbent Gerald Ford, to become the first candidate from the Deep South to win since the Civil War
- In San Francisco, The Band held its farewell concert, *The Last Waltz*
- The Sex Pistols achieved public notoriety as they unleashed several four-letter words live on an early evening TV show
- Singer Bob Marley and his manager Don Taylor were shot in an assassination attempt in Kingston, Jamaica
- *Hotel California* by The Eagles was released
- The first laser printer was introduced by IBM (the IBM 3800)

Selected Prices

Baby Carrier	$14.00
Bean Bag Chair	$37.95
Beer, Stroh's Six-Pack	$1.49
Briefcase, Leather	$35.95
CB Radio	$39.88
Circular Saw	$22.88
Coffee Maker, Norelco	$23.88
Drive-in Movie Ticket, Carload	$4.00
Turntable	$199.95
Woman's Swimsuit, Bikini	$13.00

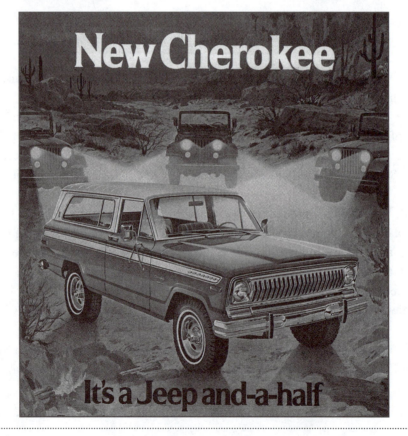

I was not a very good rock critic because I really just put musicians on a pedestal, and I had a couple of experiences where I wrote critical things about people and felt guilty about it. Being a super fan or cheerleader is very useful for a publicist, not so useful for a journalist.

—*Danny Goldberg interview*

I think that artists that I've met who have been successful all had some desire to be successful. Not that they would always do things the easiest way or most commercial way, but they had a focus that helped propel them. Like Stevie Nicks doing the songs with Tom Petty at a certain time or working with a producer that, at first blush, was not part of the community that she was into. Or Bruce Springsteen focusing on trying to get a pop radio hit. The music business is competitive, and having musical talent itself is not sufficient.

—*Danny Goldberg interview*

Catherine (all-girls Catholic) McCauley High School was 17 blocks from my house in Brooklyn, and I walked to and from. I enjoyed the walk and met up with various schoolmates along the way. School dances were especially fun to walk home from—it was dark and just a little spooky. My friends and I walked together in large groups, talked about boys, experimented with cigarettes, and felt very grown up.

My junior "prom," like all others, was held in the basement gym, accessed by a long, open staircase—a perfect spot for chaperones to keep track of the action on the dance floor. Nuns actually walked up to slow-dancing couples shouting "Fit the hand, fit the hand," (indicating that bodies were too close). I was so looking forward to this dance—until I learned that not only had my father volunteered to chaperone, but was planning to walk with "the group" to and from the dance! The only concession he would make was to walk a half block behind us. Our plan was to walk fast and lose him, which of course didn't work.

The band's last song was In-A-Gadda-Da-Vida by Iron Butterfly, which was released in 1968, but remained popular well past this 1972 dance. For my father, who patiently endured the 1970s rock and roll lyrics for the four-hour dance, this was the last straw. He just didn't understand "what it all meant" and was especially confused by this closing song. As we left the dance, he kept asking my friends "but what does it mean?," forcing us into a long conversation about the meaning of not only this song title, but rock music in general, which, of course, kept him close to us the whole walk home on the dark streets!

Persoanal Essay
Laura Mars

"The Truth Behind the Led Zeppelin Legend," *The Sunday Times*, London, U.K., November 1, 2008:

In the early 1970s, rock 'n' roll debauchery reached its peak. And no band scaled that peak as eagerly as Led Zeppelin. Mick Wall reveals the truth behind the legends and gossip.

If the first four years in the life of Led Zeppelin had been about empire-building, the next four (1972-75) would find them overseeing their kingdom with all the splendid pomp and inherent arrogance of pharaohs. Zep were now self-made millionaires so famous they hid behind armed guards, employed their own drug-dealers and flew by private jet. They were also at their creative zenith, taking their music far beyond the bounds of most other rock groups.

Indeed, only the Stones matched them at this time for musical promiscuousness, as both groups toyed, variously, with funk, reggae, country, West Coast…. Arguably, Zep went even further, allowing jazz, synthesizers, folk, doo-wop and Asian raga influences to seep into their signature sound. They went further in terms of on-the-road outrage, too.

Keith [Richards] may still have draped silk scarves over his bedside lamps, carried guns and knives and shot up heroin, while Mick [Jagger] certainly kept the ladeez busy, but no one was busting up rooms, cars and jaws like [John] "Bonzo" Bonham; nobody was a bigger babe-magnet than rocket-in-my-pocket [Robert] Plant; and not even Keef could keep up with nocturnal [Jimmy] Page's non-eating, non-sleeping regimen of smack, coke, Quaaludes, Jack Daniel's, cigarettes, weed, wine, whatever. Plus, Page was the only one using whips and magic wands on any sort of regular basis.

Still basking in the enormous success of the untitled fourth album, it was now in 1973 that the feeling of invincibility that their manager, Peter Grant, had helped foster really began to take hold of the band. Of course, this was also the rock-fabulous age of color TVs out of windows and white Rolls-Royces in swimming pools that bands like Zeppelin, the Stones and The Who came to embody. But no seventies guitar god represented the extreme Byronic sensibility in person quite like Jimmy Page. He may have begun cultivating this dark mystique as a way of concealing his, in reality, more introspective, quietly spoken, earnestly watching-from-a-distance nature, but by 1973, things had started to change….

Learning from the Stones—who had quickly shoehorned the new "glam" look of recent arrivals on the scene like Marc Bolan and David Bowie into the way they dressed on stage—the new Zeppelin show would be the first to feature a full-on professional lightshow, including lasers, mirror balls and dry ice, as well as a whole new set of stage costumes specially designed for each member—the most flamboyant being Page's now famous glittering moon-and-stars outfit, the button-less, wide-lapelled jacket flapping open, his flared trousers boasting three symbols down the side of the leg, the top symbol, like an ornate "7," representing Capricorn, his sun sign, a bastardized "M" representing Scorpio, his ascendant sign, and below that what looked like a "69" representing his moon sign.

Even the normally spotlight-avoiding John Paul Jones had his own specially designed suit, a commedia dell'arte-type jester's jacket with little red hearts hanging from the frockcoat sleeves, while Plant became bare-chested, the lion in spring, his "third leg" showing prominently through his ultra-tight jeans, his shoulders squeezed into a powder-blue puffed-sleeve blouse; even Bonzo was now done up in a black T-shirt with a big shiny star sequined upon it, the hair now very long indeed, hemmed in by a darkly sparkling headband.

"It's a work of art, that suit," Jimmy told me. "Originally, we saw the whole essence of our live performance as something that the audience listened to very carefully, picking up on what was going on, the spontaneity and musicianship. And you can't do that if you're running around the stage all night, or at least we couldn't back then." By 1973, however, "we were much more ambitious, in that respect. We really wanted to take the live performances as far as they could go."

They now traveled by private jet, hired at a cost of $30,000 per tour and christened *The Starship*– a Boeing 720B 40-seater owned by former singer Bobby Sherman, one of the creators of the Monkees.

When they picked it up at Chicago's O'Hare Airport, it was parked next to *Playboy* boss Hugh Hefner's plane, the words "Led Zeppelin" emblazoned down one side. Fitted with lounge-seats and dinner tables, a fully stocked bar and a TV lounge, there was also an electric Thomas organ which Jonesy would sometimes entertain the "guests" with, and, in a rear cabin, a double bed covered in shaggy white fur that became one of the most popular compartments on the plane—though few ever slept in it.

Back "home" in L.A. at the end of May, they had sold all 36,000 tickets for their two shows at the Forum within hours of the box office opening. The first show happened to coincide with Bonham's twenty-fifth birthday. His present from the band: a new top-of-the-range Harley-Davidson motorcycle. "He just tore up the hotel corridors and made an incredible mess, apparently," said his old pal Bev Bevan, who had left the Move and now joined ELO. "But he paid the bill the next day then told 'em—'Oh, and keep the bike.' Unbelievable, but that was John." The Forum audience had also given him a birthday cheer during his 20-minute rendition of "Moby Dick."

"Twenty-one today," Plant had announced from the stage, and "a bastard all his life." Afterwards there was a huge party thrown for him at the Laurel Canyon home of a local radio station owner. Guests included George and Patti Harrison, Roy Harper, B. P. Fallon, Phil Carson, and the usual gaggle of dealers, groupies and hangers-on.

Writer Charles Shaar Murray, who was also there, recalled "gallons of champagne, snowdrifts of cocaine, bayous full of unfeasibly large shrimp, legendary porn flick *Deep Throat* looping on a videotape player at a time when VCRs were hugely expensive items available only to the stupendously wealthy." George Harrison crowned Bonham with his own birthday cake. Bonzo threw the former Beatle and his wife into the pool fully clothed, followed by anybody he could lay his hands on.

Jimmy, meekly complaining he couldn't swim, was allowed to walk into the pool in his new white suit with the "ZoSo" symbol on the back. Harrison later claimed it was the most fun he'd had since the Beatles.

The L.A. music scene had moved on from the Laurel Canyon vibe the band had become so entranced by three years before. Just as in London and New York, the hip new sound of 1973 belonged to Bowie, T Rex, Mott the Hoople, Alice Cooper, and Roxy Music—glam rock.

The complete opposite of the bewhiskered, down-at-heel ambience of the nouveau pastoralists, suddenly artists like Rod Stewart and Elton John were shaving their stubble and donning pink satin pants, stack-heeled boots and spraying their hair with glitter. The new cool hangout was Rodney Bingenheimer's English Disco on Hollywood Boulevard.

Soon the walls of Rodney's office at the club were decorated in pictures of him not just with Bowie et al., but Phil Spector, Mick Jagger, John Lennon, and, eventually, Led Zeppelin, attracted to the club not for the music but because of the teenage girls that packed the place seven nights a week. Although the glam scene had a large gay following, you'd never have known it sitting at Rodney's table.

When Zeppelin hit L.A. now, they practically owned it. No longer content with booking the entire ninth floor at the Hyatt, they now took over the eleventh floor, too, just a few steps from the rooftop swimming pool. They had permanently reserved tables at all the best-known Hollywood rock dives, not just Rodney's, but at their other favorite new hangout, the Rainbow Bar & Grill, where they had their own special half-moon tables roped-off at the back. With a fleet of limos waiting curbside, they also attracted star-name hangers-on such as Iggy Pop, sitting cross-legged in the corner of Jimmy's suite, rolling joints as endless platoons of gorgeous girls wandered in and out, happy to trade "favors" in return for access to the Zeppelin magic kingdom.

Rejected by the Laurel Canyon sophisticates—much to Plant's chagrin—who were offended by Zeppelin's sleazy reputation, the band simply took over Rodney's or the Rainbow and treated the places as they did the Hyatt: to use and abuse at will. For many chroniclers of the L.A. music scene, this was the beginning of its bleakest period. Writer Nick Kent, another visitor to Rodney's, claims he'd "never seen anyone behave worse [there] in my life than John Bonham and [tour manager] Richard Cole.

"I saw them beat a guy senseless for no reason and then drop money on his face." Even Miss P (legendary groupie Pamela Des Barres)—still on the scene but now reconciled to a life without Jimmy after their brief affair, except for those occasions when he suddenly remembered her number—would later tell writer Barney Hoskyns: "As much as I really loved Zeppelin, they kind of f***ed things up in L.A. The magic really went out of rock 'n' roll."

1979 PROFILE

Just when Eduardo "Lalo" Guerrero, known as the "Father of Chicano Music," thought his glory days had passed, the Broadway play *Zoot Suit* employed four of Lalo's earliest Pachuco compositions.

Life at Home

- Billed as the "First Chicano Play on Broadway," *Zoot Suit* featured 1940s boogie woogie band music by Daniel Valdez and Eduardo "Lalo" Guerrero.
- The audiences loved the play and the music, breathing new life into Lalo's multi-decade career that encompassed 700 original songs, including "Canción Mexicana," the unofficial Mexican National Anthem.
- Fittingly, *Zoot Suit*, which hit Broadway in 1979, was a fictionalized version of the real-life Sleepy Lagoon murder trial, when a group of Chicano youths were charged with a murder that they did not commit, resulting in the Zoot Suit Riots.
- The play served as a modern-day symbol of the discrimination Chicanos often suffered in Anglo America, one of Lalo's many themes.
- During his career he recorded in virtually every genre of Latin music, including salsa, norteña, banda, ranchera, bolero, corrido, cumbia, mambo, cha cha cha, socially relevant songs, swing, rock 'n' roll and blues.
- He also created children's music, comedy songs and parodies; generations of children in Mexico and the U.S. grew up with his "Ardillitas" (squirrels), and his parodies such as, "Tacos for Two," "Pancho Claus," "Elvis Perez" and "There's No Tortillas."
- In his songs about Cesar Chavez and the farm workers, martyred journalist Ruben Salazar, and the plight of illegal aliens, Lalo chronicled Chicano history.

Lalo was known as the Father of Chicano Music.

- Lalo was born into a large family in Barrio Libre section of Tucson, Arizona, on Christmas Eve 1916, four years after his parents immigrated to the United States from Mexico.
- His father worked for the Southern Pacific Railroad as a boilermaker; Lalo gave credit for his musical skills to his mother and her philosophy of "embracing the spirit of being Chicano."
- At 17, and influenced by the dire conditions of the Great Depression, he dropped out of high school and took to the road without the benefit of musical training.
- In Los Angeles, he was introduced to the Latin nightlife of the Anglo nightclubs El Trocadero, the Mocamba, and the Coconut Grove, just as Latin music was beginning to invade the United States in the form of the conga, rumba and other African-Caribbean rhythms.
- Some nightclubs even adapted a Latin decor complete with palm trees, coconuts and flamingoes, which opened the door to Latin orchestras and Mexican trios.

- Eighteen-year-old Lalo was initiated into the world of Hollywood entertainment as a trio singer; when the headliner orchestra took a break, the trio sang Mexican songs such as "Amapola," Cuando Vuelva A Tu Lado," and "Munequita Linda," accompanied by three guitars.
- The story of Mexican-American music was indelibly written by wave after wave of immigrants who had spilled over the Mexican border throughout the twentieth century.
- When musicologist pioneer Charles Lummis went to California to record the fading remnants of the Spanish folk-song tradition in 1904, he had few hints that the popularity of Spanish-Mexican music was about to explode.
- Depressed conditions in Mexico in the first years of the century unleashed waves of opportunity-seeking immigrants into the Southwest.
- Many found middle-class prosperity by the 1940s, carving into society a gap between established Chicano families and impoverished newcomers; both groups thought about family, material wealth and music in different ways.

Life at Work

- Lalo Guerrero was performing on a Los Angeles street corner when producer Manuel Acuna heard him playing in 1939.
- He was in a recording studio the next day.
- Later that year, Lalo's first trio, Los Carlistas, represented Arizona at the 1939 New York World's Fair, and while in New York, they were invited to perform on *The Major Bowes Amateur Hour* on radio.
- A fixture on radio since 1934, *The Major Bowes Amateur Hour* used a loud gong to dispatch acts that did not meet Major Bowes's standards; Lalo survived his appearance without a bell or gong.

Lalo performed Chicano Boogie *on* The Major Bowes Amateur Hour.

- During the 1940s, Lalo would record 200 songs for Imperial Records, often under the Anglo name Don Edwards; the record company did not believe a singer with a Chicano name could sell records.
- He also appeared in several uncredited roles in movies, including *Boots and Saddles* and *His Kind of Woman*.
- During the Second World War, he held the only daytime job of his life, employed in an airline assembly line in San Diego where he also entertained at military camps and hospitals as part of a USO band.
- After the war ended, Lalo had returned to L.A. and was playing in a nightclub called "La Bamba," where the audience was largely Latin and he was forced to switch cultural gears; he was no longer performing to all-Anglo audiences.
- Mexican-Americans were emerging from their isolation, and Mexican nightclubs were proliferating.
- There, under the watchful attention of the audience, Lalo would compose and perform many of the songs that would be used in the Broadway play 30 years later.
- The rise of the Mexican-American middle class—and their appearance at his performances—encouraged him to focus more heavily on musical compositions for the Mexican market.
- Lalo quickly turned out hit after hit with Imperial Records, one of the most active labels on the West Coast; Lalo would compose the songs and Imperial's Acuna would write the arrangements.
- His first American hit was "Pancho López," a parody of the popular 1950s hit "The Ballad Of Davy Crockett."
- Lalo used the Davy Crockett melody and wrote his own lyrics, telling the story of a legendary Mexican character, winning acclaim in both the traditional American market and the Chicano world.
- Lalo went on to record several more parody songs, including "Pancho Claus," "Elvis Perez," "Tacos For Two" (to the tune of "Cocktails For Two"), and "There's No Tortillas" (to the tune of "O Sole Mio").
- Inspired by the success of Alvin and the Chipmunks, Lalo created a Latin chipmunk that became a child favorite and a magnet for lawsuits; Alvin creator David Seville sued for infringement, but the case was thrown out of court.
- Lalo used the profits from his novelty songs to buy a nightclub which he named Lalo.
- At the same time, Lalo understood the power his musical accomplishments allowed him to possess.
- So during the 1960s, he highlighted the discrimination suffered by the Chicano people and traveled to farming areas where he championed farm workers' causes, writing songs about Cesar Chavez and calling for the decent treatment of agricultural laborers.
- Then came the opportunities presented by the Broadway play *Zoot Suit*.
- The play was set in the barrios of Los Angeles, California, in the early 1940s against the backdrop of the Zoot Suit Riots and World War II.
- A Chicano, wearing his zoot suit on his last night of freedom before beginning his Naval service, was accused—along with his friends—of the murder of a rival "gangster" after a party.
- Unfairly prosecuted, the entire group was thrown in jail for a murder they did not commit.
- Narrated throughout, most of the songs were performed by El Pachuco, an idealized zoot-suiter.
- The Broadway production debuted at the Winter Garden Theater on March 25, 1979, and closed on April 29 after 41 performances.

The Palladium in Los Angeles in 1955.

Life in the Community: East Los Angeles, California

- Hispanic East L.A. began life as a Spanish settlement, parceled out among the Pueblo of Los Angeles, the Mission San Gabriel Arcángel, and several ranchos.
- Large-scale development commenced with the arrival of the Southern Pacific Railroad in 1875, and expanded by numerous electric streetcar lines laid over the following three decades to connect the area to fast-growing Downtown Los Angeles.
- Areas along the Arroyo Seco such as Montecito Heights and Mt. Washington were once among the wealthiest neighborhoods in the region, their winding streets lined with finely detailed Mediterranean villas and Craftsman frame houses and bungalows that enjoyed some of the finest views in Los Angeles.
- Meanwhile, Spanish Colonial bungalows and duplexes sprouted in working-class areas such as El Sereno and City Terrace.
- The East Los Angeles region had long had a very high concentration of Hispanic residents, primarily of Mexican descent.
- Since the early twentieth century, it had been the focus of the Hispanic population in Los Angeles County.
- And when the white population moved to segregated suburbs after World War II, Mexicans seized the opportunity to move into the region's housing at low prices.
- With the exception of a small but distinct Filipino population, the region was primarily Mexican-American by 1950.
- Many second- and third-generation Hispanics or Central Americans subsequently moved from East Los Angeles to other parts of southern California.
- From the 1970s onward, Orange County, the San Fernando Valley, the Inland Empire, and the Gateway Cities region of southeast Los Angeles County have also been major destinations for upwardly mobile Latino families.
- Meanwhile, recent immigrants from Mexico and Central America have continued to settle in the low-income parts of East Los Angeles where the parents of many U.S.-born Hispanics once lived.

A typical working class orchestra in 1915 East Los Angeles.

HISTORICAL SNAPSHOT
1979

- The State of Ohio agreed to pay $675,000 to families of the dead and injured in the Kent State shootings
- The Music for UNICEF Concert was held to promote the Year of the Child
- Former Attorney General John N. Mitchell was released on parole after 19 months at a federal prison in Alabama in connection with the Watergate scandal
- Following her 1972 sex reassignment surgery, musician Wendy Carlos legally changed her name from Walter
- The annual Mardi Gras celebration in New Orleans was canceled due to a strike called by the New Orleans Police Department
- *Voyager I* made its closest approach to Jupiter at 172,000 miles
- Philips demonstrated the compact disc publicly for the first time
- In a ceremony at the White House, President Anwar Sadat of Egypt and Prime Minister Menachem Begin of Israel signed a peace treaty
- The Pinwheel Network changed its name to Nickelodeon and began airing on various Warner Cable systems beginning in Buffalo, New York, expanding its audience reach
- Raymond Washington, cofounder of the Crips, one of the most notorious gangs in the United States, was killed in a drive-by shooting in Los Angeles
- Michael Jackson released his first breakthrough album *Off the Wall*, which sold seven million copies
- The Entertainment Sports Programming Network, known as ESPN, debuted
- The comic strip *For Better or For Worse* was launched
- The radio news program *Morning Edition* premiered on National Public Radio
- Senator Ted Kennedy announced that he would challenge President Jimmy Carter for the 1980 Democratic presidential nomination
- In response to the hostage crisis in Tehran, President Carter ordered a halt to all oil imports into the United States from Iran
- Eleven fans were killed during a crowd crush for unreserved seats before The Who concert at the Riverfront Coliseum in Cincinnati, Ohio
- The first experiments of Usenet, the precursor to Internet forums, were conducted by Tom Truscott and Jim Ellis of Duke University
- The Sony Walkman was first marketed
- McDonald's introduced the Happy Meal in June
- Chrysler received government loan guarantees upon the request of CEO Lee Iacocca

Selected Prices

Bicycle	$64.99
Cigarette Case	$34.95
Computer, Apple II	$1,300.00
Hotel Room, St. Moritz, New York	$31.00
Ice Cream Machine	$24.95
Massage Shower Head	$26.95
Microwave Oven	$168.00
Organic Roast Beef, per Half-Pound	$1.99
Stroller	$24.99
Theater Ticket, *A Chorus Line*, New York	$17.50

"The Mudd Club: Disco for Punks," Jim Farber, *Rolling Stone*, July 12, 1979:

It's a rainy night in Manhattan, but about 100 people are standing outside the disco, slowly getting drenched, desperately hoping they'll be let in. A woman dressed exclusively in Hefty trash bags is allowed in quickly, followed by a man who flashes the stub of his arm, which has been amputated at the elbow. When I asked the young woman what makes this place special, she replies tersely: "The door. I like the fact that some people are excluded."

The disco the woman is praising is not the famed Studio 54, but New York's trendiest punkatorium, the Mudd Club. While such a club may seem antithetical to punk's working-class base, in this post-Sid Vicious age, the Mudd Club's elitism could just be the newer wave. Clubs that play rock music to dance to instead of disco are on the upswing here, but the Mudd Club is the first to incorporate some of disco's more frivolous chichi pretentions.

"The fashion thing is very important," says Mudd Club owner Steve Mass, discussing his standards for admittance. "There's poor chic and rich chic. That Lower East Side funky dress is a fashion statement, and I give preference to those people."

Mass scoffs at any connection between the Mudd Club and Studio 54, claiming that his establishment does not sucker up to celebrities as does Steve Rubell's disco. "I actually instruct my doormen to make anyone who comes in a limo wait at least 10 minutes at the door," Mass announces proudly. "We don't want celebrities."

Musical Events of 1979

- Stephen Stills became the first major rock artist to record digitally, laying down four songs at The Record Plant in Los Angeles.
- Rod Stewart's "Do Ya Think I'm Sexy" hit #1 on the *Billboard* charts and stayed there for four weeks.
- Forty-three million viewers watched *Elvis!* on ABC, a made-for-TV movie starring Kurt Russell as Elvis.
- The Bee Gees collected four Grammys for *Saturday Night Fever*.
- B.B. King became the first blues artist to tour the Soviet Union, kicking off a one-month tour there.
- Soul singer James Brown performed at the Grand Ole Opry.
- The Pretenders signed a contract with Sire Records.
- Singer Donny Hathaway died after falling 15 stories from his hotel room in New York City.
- MCA Records purchased ABC Records for a reported $20 million.
- Sex Pistols bassist Sid Vicious was found dead from an overdose, a day after being released on bail from Rikers Island prison.
- The Clash kicked off their first concert on their first American tour at the Berkeley Community Theatre outside San Francisco, California, with the song "I'm So Bored with the U.S.A."

- Van Halen released their second album, *Van Halen II*.
- Eric Clapton married Patti Boyd, ex-wife of Clapton's friend George Harrison.
- Kate Bush became the first artist to use a wireless microphone, enabling her to sing and dance at the same time.
- One hundred ten thousand people attended the California Music Festival at the L.A. Memorial Coliseum, where the performers included Aerosmith, The Boomtown Rats, Cheap Trick, Ted Nugent, and Van Halen.
- Ozzy Osbourne was fired as lead singer of Black Sabbath.
- Iron Maiden, Samson, and Angel Witch shared a bill at the Music Machine in Camden, London; critic Geoff Barton coined the term "New Wave of British Heavy Metal" in a review of the show for *Sounds* magazine.
- Three of the ex-Beatles performed on the same stage, as Paul McCartney, George Harrison, and Ringo Starr jammed with Eric Clapton, Ginger Baker, Mick Jagger, and others at a wedding reception for Clapton at his home.
- Elton John played eight concerts in the Soviet Union.
- Alternative Tentacles record label was established by Dead Kennedys frontman Jello Biafra.
- Bill Haley made his final studio recordings at Muscle Shoals, Alabama.
- The Bee Gees played to a sold-out crowd at Los Angeles Dodger Stadium as part of their Spirits Having Flown tour.

- Aerosmith and Ted Nugent headlined the World Series of Rock at Municipal Stadium in Cleveland, Ohio.
- Two hundred fifty thousand turned out in Central Park for a free concert by James Taylor in a campaign to restore Sheep Meadow, a 15-acre preserve in New York.
- "My Sharona" by The Knack hit #1 on the Billboard charts—the first time in over a year that a #1 song was not either a disco song or a ballad.
- Musicians United for Safe Energy (MUSE) staged a series of five "No Nukes" concerts at Madison Square Garden; Jackson Browne; Crosby, Stills and Nash; Bruce Springsteen and the E Street Band; Bonnie Raitt; Tom Petty; James Taylor; and Carly Simon were among the participants.
- The single "Rapper's Delight" by The Sugarhill Gang marked the commercial emergence of hip hop music.
- Stevie Wonder used digital audio recording technology on his album *Journey through the Secret Life of Plants*

"High Hopes Held for *Zoot Suit*," Jay Sharbutt, *Winnipeg Free Press*, March 12, 1979:

It's an unlikely duo, the powerful Shubert Organization serving Broadway patrons and El Teatro Campesino, the "the peasant theater" originally formed in 1965 to serve striking farm workers in California.

But the two companies joined for *Zoot Suit*, a new play with music about pachucos, Mexican-American zoot-suiters in Los Angeles during the Second World War, bigotry, hysteria and injustice.

To premiere in New York March 25, it's by an American born 38 years ago in Delano, California, one of 10 children of a migrant farm worker.

Valdez and Shubert president Bernard Jacobs have great hopes for *Zoot Suit*.

For Valdez, it's that this play he wrote and directed will pave the way for other Hispanic works in mainstream theater. For Jacob, it's that *Zoot* will prove you can develop a theater audience from New York's large Hispanic community that's never really been tapped.

Jacobs, 62, likens it to efforts to attract black audiences. They didn't succeed on a large scale until the all-black *The Wiz* clicked on Broadway in 1976, followed by *Ain't Misbehaving* and *Eubie*. Now, he says, "we're interested in developing a Hispanic audience. We think the time has come, and that this has unusual qualities."

Valdez isn't new to the theater. He got hooked on it under the worst circumstances as a child of six, stranded with his family on a cotton camp in California.

"We got stuck there because our truck broke down," he said. "We just stayed there, no money, the cotton season was over."

His father, he said, fished a lot in the San Joaquin River, not for fun, but to feed the family. A school bus passed by and the Valdez children hopped aboard to spend some of their time in school.

"It was haphazard," Valdez says. "We kind of went because there was nothing else to do during the day. I couldn't speak English so much of the time, I didn't know what was happening."

Then he saw a teacher taking masks out of paper lunch bags. "It really fascinated me," he said. "Someone was communicating the idea there was a play to be put on and parts were available. I got very excited and got a part in the play."

But the play was produced without Luis Valdez. "Just before I went on, my dad got the truck fixed and we split. I never got to the show.

"But ever since then, I've staged my own shows. That one stop was the turning point."

"Lulacs Dance to Have Guerrero Music Friday," *Santa Fe New Mexican*, June 15, 1951:

Lalo Guerrero and his famed orchestra will play for a dance Friday night at Seth Hall under the sponsorship of the Lulacs.

Guerrero is the popular Latin-American singer, orchestra leader and prolific composer of Latin-American songs, as well as translator of American popular songs into Spanish. He is the composer of such songs as Prieta Linda, Tu Solo Tu, and wrote the Spanish lyrics to *Mule Train*. New releases such as "Dime Corazon" and "Lloro Por Te" are now being heard over the two local radio stations.

During the winter season, he plays in such nightspots as the Café Caliente, Olvera Street, Los Angeles, and the unique El Zarape nightclub in Hollywood. Most of his programs are televised nightly.

During the summer season, he tours the Southwestern states and sometimes travels down into Latin America.

"The Making of *Rock 'n' Roll High School*," Lloyd Sachs, *Rolling Stone*, July 12, 1979:

With competition like *Grease* and *FM*, it's not necessarily high praise to call New World Pictures' *Rock 'n Roll High School* best non-documentary rock film in years. But *High School*, which features the Ramones, exploding mice and white kids on punk who joyfully blow up their school, is indeed the real thing. It's a rowdy, exuberant, wonderfully sophomoric B-movie (it cost $300,000 to make) and puts its more expensive competition to shame.

High School has emerged as much more than the genre film executive producer Roger Corman thought he had, even though it took a while for the movie to find its audience. Corman, who hadn't heard of the Ramones before starting the film (he was more interested in producing a disco movie), first tried to sell *High School* to the 15- and 16-year-old crowd during the film's saturation run throughout the Southwest in April. The picture bombed, and in an effort to cut its losses, New World opened the film in San Francisco and Chicago with considerably less promotion.

But buoyed by the release of the soundtrack album on Sire, *High School* began attracting a mixed crowd of teens and older New Wave fans, and has done well enough to raise hopes that it still has a chance of becoming a hit, if not a regular attraction, than as a midnight feature.

"It's becoming a cult movie even before it's played everywhere," said Alan Arkush, the film's director. "It's playing with everything from *Grease* to *Dawn of the Dead*. What more can I ask for?"

High School's plot is certainly simple enough to appeal to the masses. In it, the power-obsessed, record-burning principal of Vince Lombardi High School, Ms. Togar (New World regular and former Warhol model Mary Woronov), is pitted against a vivacious blonde Ramones freak named Riff Randall (P.J. Soles, one of the girls in *Halloween*), who is determined to get the songs she has written to her idols when they arrive for a concert. Some difficulties arise, but Riff ends up ascending to Ramonehood, and Ms. Togar sees her school go up in smoke.

In capturing the rebellious adolescent spirit of rock 'n' roll, *High School* is downright masterful. It's an accomplishment that a director who is less passionate about rock 'n' roll could not have pulled off. The lanky, curly-haired 31-year-old who worked in New York's Fillmore East (he took tickets, a role he portrays in the film, and worked with Joe's Lights), Arkush said it was while he was a teen rock fiend in New Jersey that he first got the idea for the movie. Back then, he envisioned the Yardbirds in the starring role.

When he finally got the chance to make the film, after co-directing *Hollywood Boulevard* and *Death Sport* for Corman, Arkush's goal was to create a musical with a Hollywood feel and made a rock statement: something of a cross between *Bandwagon* and *A Hard Day's Night*. He said that Frank Tashlin's 1957 Jayne Mansfield romp, *The Girl Can't Help It*, is a major source of inspiration (it featured spot performances by Little Richard, Eddie Cochran, Gene Vincent, and others).

"I just love films in which groups suddenly appear," said Arkush, who studied under director Martin Scorsese at New York University, "but I was always dissatisfied with the way they were presented. The music never seemed to flow from the film. With *Rock 'n' Roll High School*, the shots are planned very carefully to correspond with what was going on with the song musically. I also tried to avoid talking down to the audience like some of those old films did."

Though Cheap Trick and Todd Rundgren were considered for *High School*, the Ramones were Arkush's first choice, not only because he was bowled over by their energy, but also because they seem to be "very present-day." But also because, unlike some groups, they were enthusiastic about making an unabashed B-movie.

"They were incredibly cooperative," said Arkush. "The concert sequence (filmed at the Roxy in Los Angeles) took 20 hours to shoot, but they never complained, even though they had to play the same six songs over and over again. The crew didn't know who the Ramones were when we started. But at the end, everybody was singing 'Pinhead.'"

Arkush stressed that *High School* was not intended as a new wave movie. "The idea was to make a movie that had the Ramones but didn't have the dominant sensibility of New York, of the Village," he explained. "The film is about high-school kids and how music lets them live out their fantasies, so the Ramones must appear to be fantasy figures."

That effect is felt most strongly in a scene where Riff smokes a joint and imagines the Ramones to be playing in her room and outside her house. At one point, she goes to take a shower, only to find Dee Dee playing bass under a steady stream of water. Dee Dee, a compulsive shower taker, came up with the idea himself, just as Joey devised the idea of having health-food stuffed into his mouth after the concert.

"There was a lot of give-and-take as to how the Ramones were going to be presented," said Arkush. "I was particularly concerned with whether they were going to be comfortable coming off as dumb as their songs imply they are. But they said that was okay with them."

The Ramones contributed seven songs to the soundtrack album, including two new ones: the title track and "I Want You Around." (The movie also features music by the Velvet Underground, Devo, Nick Lowe, Chuck Berry, Alice Cooper, Eno, the MC5 and others.) Joey, Dee Dee, Johnny and Marky also participated in the movie's graffiti spraying, trash flinging, window-shattering finale. It's a scene Arkush said had to be toned down a little. "We didn't want to make the kids look too mean."

Nevertheless, some theater chains have refused to show the film because of the ending, a stance that recalls the bad old days when some people perceived rock 'n' roll as dangerous. To add to the irony, Arkush said his cast and crew were shocked to discover on the first day of shooting that their main location, the defunct Mount Carmel High School in L.A., was once used to make another rock film: *Rock Around the Clock*.

"We couldn't believe it," said Arkush, laughing. "It was like some kind of omen. What a way to start! We just knew we were on the right track."

On each side of my parents' driveway are two deep gullies that are very easy to hit, if one is not being extremely careful. Somehow, I always manage to keep the car between the two and back out safely into the street. The closest I ever came to "ditching it" is one fall morning when I was leaving to go to class at our local community college. The year was 1971, I was 18 and the voice on the radio caught me by complete surprise. It was a voice like no other voice I had ever heard; a deep, manly voice, harsh and scratchy, and yet strangely beautiful. I could only describe it, at the time, as sounding something like "sandpaper dipped in honey." The song was "Wild World." The voice was Cat Stevens. I had no idea how that voice would follow me all through the years, or the impact his music would have on my life.

Young Steven Demetre Georgiou took his girlfriend's comment that he "had eyes like a cat" to heart and commonly became known as Cat Stevens, the perfect, catchy new name for a fast-budding, young pop star in the 1960s. This was his stage name from 1966 to 1980, when he shocked the world by suddenly ending his own career at its very peak, breaking my heart in doing so. For me, it was "the day the music died," as in comparison to Don McLean's "American Pie," and the reference to the death of Buddy Holly.

Cat Stevens burst on the scene at a critical point in my life. I did not know what I wanted to do, where I wanted to go, and had no plans or goals for my future. I had started hanging out with the proverbial wrong crowd, was listening to heavy metal and being pulled into a life of drugs. I had made a 180-degree turnaround and was unrecognizable even to myself. Cat Stevens' music brought me back to myself, with lyrics of love and peace and direct references to God and the beauty of his creation. He reminded me of the values I held dear, family, friends and God. Although he describes himself as being completely lost back in those days, it seemed to me that this guy knew exactly what he wanted, and how to get there.

My life took on meaning again. I decided on a major and went away to school that next fall. I felt like I had been "rescued" from certain death. Cat Stevens played a major role in that. He remains to this day, my hero.

Personal Essay
Suzi Kirby

1980–1989

The economic turbulence of the 1970s continued during the early years of the 1980s. Rates for both interest and inflation were at a staggering 1.8 percent. With the economy at a standstill, unemployment was rising. By 1981, America was in its deepest depression since the Great Depression of the 1930s. One in 10 Americans was out of work. Yet, by the end of the decade, thanks in part to the productivity gains provided by computers and new technology, more and more Americans were entering the ranks of the millionaire and feeling better off than they had in a decade.

Convinced that inflation was the primary enemy of long-term economic growth, the Federal Reserve Board brought the economy to a standstill in the early days of the decade. It was a shock treatment that worked. By 1984, the tight money policies of the government, stabilizing world oil prices, and labor's declining bargaining power brought inflation to four percent, the lowest level since 1967. Despite the pain it caused, the plan to strangle inflation succeeded; Americans not only prospered, but many believed it was their right to be successful. The decade came to be symbolized by self-indulgence.

At the same time, defense and deficit spending roared into high gear, the economy continued to grow, and the stock market rocketed to record levels (the Dow Jones Industrial Average tripled from 1,000 in 1980 to nearly 3,000 a decade later). In the center of recovery was Mr. Optimism, President Ronald Reagan. During his presidential campaign he promised a "morning in America" and during eight years, his good nature helped transform the national mood. The Reagan era, which spanned most of the 1980s, fostered a new conservative agenda of good feeling. During the presidential election against incumbent President Jimmy Carter, Reagan joked, "A recession is when your neighbor loses his job. A depression is when you lose yours. And recovery is when Jimmy Carter loses his."

The economic wave of the 1980s was also driven by globalization, improvements in technology, and willingness of consumers to assume higher and higher levels of personal debt. By the 1980s, the two-career family became the norm. Forty-two percent of all American workers were female, and more than half of all married women and 90 percent of female college graduates worked outside the home. Yet, their median wage was 60 percent of that of men. The rapid rise of women in the labor force, which had been accelerating since the 1960s, brought great social change, affecting married life, child rearing, family income, office culture, and the growth of rhe national economy.

The rising economy brought greater control of personal lives; homeownership accelerated, choices seemed limitless, debt grew, and divorce became commonplace. Two revolutionary changes on the music scene—the advent of MTV and the compact disc—began a technological and financial shift. Through MTV's around-the-clock broadcasts, the artist's image was elevated and sometimes overpowered the music. Music became more diverse, with new wave, heavy metal, rap, techno pop, and alternative rock all mixing with the "new" country sounds. Michael Jackson's *Thriller*, Bruce Springsteen's *Born in the USA* and Prince's *Purple Rain* all registered record sales during the decade. Also, music became a huge marketing tool as filmmakers, TV producers and manufacturers of everything from sneakers to soft drinks used hit songs to sell their products. The collapse of communism at the end of the 1980s brought an end to the old world order and set the stage for a realignment of power. America was regarded as the strongest nation in the world and the only real superpower, thanks to its economic strength. As democracy swept across Eastern Europe, the U.S. economy began to feel the impact of a "peace dividend" generated by a reduced military budget and a desire by corporations to participate in global markets—including Russia and China. Globalization was having another impact. At the end of World War II, the U.S. economy accounted for almost 50 percent of the global economic product; by 1987, the U.S. share was less than 25 percent as American companies moved plants offshore and countries such as Japan emerged as major competitors. This need for a global reach inspired several rounds of corporate mergers as companies searched for efficiency, market share, new products, or emerging technology to survive in the rapidly shifting business environment.

The 1980s were the age of the conservative yuppie. Business schools, investment banks, and Wall Street firms overflowed with eager baby boomers who placed gourmet cuisine, health clubs, supersneakers, suspenders, wine spritzers, high-performance autos, and sushi high on their agendas. Low-fat and fiber cereals and Jane Fonda workout books symbolized much of the decade. As self-indulgence rose, concerns about the environment, including nuclear waste, acid rain, and the greenhouse effect declined. Homelessness increased and racial tensions fostered a renewed call for a more caring government. During the decade, genetic engineering came of age, including early attempts at transplantation and gene mapping. Personal computers, which were transforming America, were still in their infancy.

The sexual revolution, undaunted by a conservative prescription of chastity, ran head-on into a powerful adversary during the 1980s with the discovery and spread of AIDS, a frequently fatal sexually transmitted disease. The right of women to have an abortion, confirmed by the Supreme Court in 1973, was hotly contested during the decade as politicians fought over both the actual moment of conception and the right of a woman to control her body. Cocaine also made its reappearance, bringing drug addiction and a rapid increase in violent crime. The Center on Addiction and Substance Abuse at Columbia University found alcohol and drug abuse implicated in three fourths of all murders, rapes, child molestations, and deaths of babies suffering from parental neglect.

For the first time in history, the Naval Academy's graduating class included women, digital clocks and cordless telephones appeared, and 24-hour-a-day news coverage captivated television viewers. Compact disks began replacing records, and Smurf and *E.T.* paraphernalia were everywhere, New York became the first state to require seat belts, Pillsbury introduced microwave pizza, and Playtex used live lingerie models in its ads for the "Cross Your Heart" bra. The Supreme Court ruled that states may require all-male private clubs to admit women, and 50,000 people gathered at Graceland in Memphis, Tennessee, on the tenth anniversary of Elvis Presley's death.

1981 NEWS FEATURE

"Purveying Hard-Core Funk," Robert Palmer, *The New York Times*, **February 15, 1981:**

NEW YORK—Funk permeates popular music. There's funk in hits by the Bee Gees and Barbra Streisand; there's funk in the glossy poprock of Steely Dan, the harder rock of the Rolling Stones, and the more experimental rock of the Talking Heads. There's funk in most varieties of black pop and disco. And there's a musical genre called funk which emphasizes whatever it is that makes music funky.

What is funk, anyway? The word was first applied to music in the early 1950s, when calling a player or a piece of music "funky" called attention to a certain gritty essence, a quality associated with black American "roots music" like gospel and blues. The association with grit and with roots music remains, but as black musicians and listeners have expanded their awareness of their own cultural backgrounds to include African traditions, funk's musical connotations have changed.

Nowadays, a piece of music is "funky" if it includes and emphasizes several distinct rhythmic elements—a stuttering bass, a backbeat from the drums, percussive guitar parts that cut across the fundamental beat, additional percussion parts that embroider the beat or tug against it. In other words, funk is a black American equivalent of the African tendency to combine layers of rhythms, and the more overtly rhythmic it is, the more authentically funky it's considered to be. The James Brown band of the mid-60s was a pioneer of funk in this modern sense, and, in fact, most influential present-day purveyors of what one might call hard-core funk (to distinguish it from slicker, sweeter pop-funk) are two former James Brown sidemen, George Clinton and Bootsy Collins.

Mr. Clinton makes records for several different companies, including his own, CBS-distributed Uncle Jam label, and he records under a variety of names. He sings and plays several instruments, but he is primarily a kind of director who comes up with an initial concept, assembles a cast, and then makes records rather than films. Recent albums by Parliament, Bootsy, and Philippe Wynne are all projects organized by Mr. Clinton, and he has also been responsible for recordings by Funkadelic, the Brides of Funkenstein, and other configurations of what is essentially the same pool of talented performers.

The most surprising of Mr. Clinton's recent recordings is *Wynne Jammin'* (Uncle Jam) by Philippe Wynne, formerly the lead vocalist with a very popular black sweet-harmony group, the Spinners. The album is aptly titled; the first selection, "Never Gonna Tell It," is a 12 1/2-minute funk jam that features extended gospel-like preaching from Mr. Wynne and some blazing electric guitar solos. The rest of the album strikes an interesting but somewhat uneasy balance between Mr. Clinton's fondness for eccentric vocal and instrumental effects and a more conventional pop-soul format.

Trombipulation (Casablanca), the new Parliament album, and *Ultra Wave* (Warner Brothers) by Bootsy Collins, are more typical of Mr. Clinton's brand of funk. Both albums overlay basic funk rhythms (the versatile Mr. Collins contributes bass, drums, and some guitar parts) with extravagant lyrics and special effects. Vocal choruses are filtered through electronic equipment until they sound like chanting robots, electronic keyboards chatter away at each other (some of them are manned by Bernie Worrell, who has recently been touring with the Talking Heads), and individual voices sing, moan, whoop, and indulge in fanciful recitations.

This is street music, laced with jive talk, as alive with sound and color as a busy Manhattan street corner during rush hour. It is frequently ingenious, but it's never very compelling emotionally. Mr. Clinton provides rhythms for dancing and sound tracks for living; his work with Philippe Wynne has its charms, but it's more a quirky hybrid than a successful fusion of emotive singing with Mr. Clinton's characteristic production techniques. And those techniques have been sounding more and more familiar since Mr. Clinton abandoned performing to devote himself exclusively to record production and began turning out one album after another.

Junie (Walter Morrison), who sometimes works with Mr. Clinton and is a former member of both Parliament-Funkadelic and the Ohio Players, has produced a more satisfying funk album, *Bread Alone* (Columbia). He is a multi-instrumentalist and singer who made every sound on the record except for some of the backup vocals, but he hasn't gone overboard. For the most part, the music is attractively, danceably functional; *Bread Alone* is special because Mr. Morrison is interested in communicating a range of emotions as well as in providing dance floor fodder, and he does so in songs that are distinctively personal. Unlike most one-man orchestras, he seems to be acutely aware of his limitations; the richness of the backup singing is a welcome reinforcement for his lead vocals, which are expressive but somewhat narrow in range.

Defunkt (Hannibal), by the New York-based group of the same name, harnesses the crisp polyrhythmic interplay of hard-core funk to a darker vision. Several of Defunkt's musicians have been associated with the New York jazz avant-garde, and almost all of them have played behind James Chance, whose punk/funk fusion has been one of the most intriguing musical developments of the past few years. Their credentials are definitely in order, but their first album plays it safe musically and spotlights lyrics that are fashionably decadent but rarely compelling. From time to time, a provocative solo break, an imaginative horn riff, or a piquant dissonance hints at Defunkt's potential, but that potential is only intermittently realized. Defunkt needs a producer who is capable of bringing out the musicians' special gifts without compromising the band's danceability. If George Clinton wasn't so busy, and if his work wasn't falling victim to an increasingly rigid formula, he might be an interesting choice.

1982 PROFILE

Brad Lawson, who loved music and understood the history of the television music show *Austin City Limits*, wanted a job assisting in sound production.

Life at Home

- Brad Lawson was a certified sound geek—not that anyone really wanted to certify such a thing.
- He was also least alone when nestled beneath a set of headphones listening to music, recordings of truck noise, birds chirping or the noise of city traffic.
- His life's work, as he saw it, was to isolate each sound into its component parts and worship the purity of each tone.
- His real job—the one that paid the rent and put gas in his four-year-old Honda—was working at Music World helping musical neophytes track down the newest album by Judas Priest, Eric Clapton, or U2.
- With an eagerness Brad almost found charming, customers invariably forgot the band's name and were therefore forced to describe, sing or hum the song they had heard and now wished to buy.
- Often he knew in a flash the recording they wanted, but waited patiently to see what the customer was willing to say or sing before Brad provided the solution.
- After work, Brad had begun slowly and meticulously combing through his taped recordings of the first six seasons of the weekly PBS breakout hit *Austin City Limits*, filmed just up the street at a University of Texas studio in his home town of Austin.
- Their sound, he believed, was better and he wanted to know why.
- Ever since Brad got tickets and attended his first show three years earlier at 16, he had been mesmerized by the possibility of accurately reproducing a band's sound for broadcast on television.
- Television's traditional inability to accurately capture the energy and intensity of a rock concert was traceable to TV's poor audio quality.

Brad Lawson's love of music led to a job on the TV music show, Austin City Limits.

- Programs were exclusively broadcast via single-channel monophonic transmission, and the speakers on most television sets—even the most expensive—were no larger than an automobile speaker.
- Brad was interested in inventing the perfect broadcast; he wanted to reinvent the personal experience of attending a rock concert while sitting at home.
- He knew his father would help him with the technical aspects—if he could get his father's attention.
- Four marriages, six children, two jobs and a new relationship with the mother of one of his high school friends—how embarrassing!—kept his father fairly busy.
- Brad's father shared his son's joy at listening to and accurately recording live music; the elder Lawson became a high school band director because he discovered an innate facility for talking to teenagers and he needed a job.

Brad wanted to bring the rock concert experience to the home viewer.

- Brad knew that to be effective, he had to get organized.
- He drew up a list of topics to discuss, including mixing techniques that added texture to the sound, microphone positioning to capture not just the sound, but also the magic that inhabited every well-performed song and the appropriate separation of instrumental tones.
- That's why he had turned his highly focused brain on the qualities of sound that made *Austin City Limits* different.
- He had also begun attending church so he could assist with recording and broadcasting services using the church's new sound equipment.
- That's also where he met a University of Texas sound technician who was often assigned to help out at *Austin City Limits* performances.
- It was Brad's first real chance to peek into the technical side of a commercial studio and explore the creation of *Austin City Limits*—a bold experiment in 1974 even for freethinking public television.
- Not only did the producers initiate the broadcast of long, uninterrupted musical acts before a live audience, but they audaciously booked promising performers who were not necessarily recognized stars.
- Historically, television had devoted relatively little time to live music beyond the lip-synched choreography of *American Bandstand*.
- To handle the sound quality limitations of television, many music programming efforts such as *The Midnight Special* emphasized quantity over quality and featured a parade of rotating acts who played two or three songs each.
- Further handicapping its appeal, *Austin City Limits* was not about the hottest music around; its focus was on the traditional R&B and country music favored in Central Texas.
- While the entire music industry was changing and embracing punk, *Austin City Limits* was looking back to its roots, critics charged.
- Austin resident Willie Nelson was the first featured artist on the pilot episode of *Austin City Limits* broadcast in 1975.

- At that time, Austin was not widely recognized for its musical heritage.
- In 1976, the original members of Bob Wills' Texas Playboys reunited for the first time in 30 years for their performance on *Austin City Limits*; three members of the band would pass away later in the year.
- *Austin City Limits'* theme song, "London Homesick Blues," which included the line "I wanna go home with the armadillo," became a regular feature of the show in 1977, the same year that Fleetwood Mac's album *Rumours* held the #1 spot on the *Billboard* 200 for 31 weeks, and performer Kenny Rogers re-emerged with his hit "Lucille."
- When the soundtrack to the movie *Saturday Night Fever* by the Bee Gees swept disco into dominance in 1978, *Austin City Limits* showcased Nashville country stars Chet Atkins and Merle Haggard.
- A new producer of *Austin City Limits* ushered in a more diverse lineup in 1979: Tom Waits, Taj Mahal, Lightnin' Hopkins, and the Neville Brothers, and in 1980 inaugurated the first "Songwriter's Special," including performances by Ray Charles, Jerry Jeff Walker, and Carl Perkins.
- The following year, when the 24-hour music video channel MTV debuted, *Austin City Limits* held an "Instrumental Showcase" featuring the mandolin playing Tiny Moore, Jethro Burns, Johnny Gimble and David Grisman.
- Then, in 1982 the skyline of Austin appeared as the show's painted backdrop, giving the image of the Texas capital an added boost and prompting viewers worldwide to fret about how possible rain showers would impact the show.

Lyle Lovett was a regular on Austin City Limits and very much appreciated the genuine quality of its music and musicians.

- Austin's skyline was modest in height and spread out to preserve the view of the Texas State Capitol Building from various locations around Austin, but it established a mood—a home—for the weekly performances.
- Since the show was taped six to nine months in advance of broadcast, the featured performers' tour schedule often dictated when the recording would be made.
- The free tickets were precious.
- Crowds lined up around the block for the limited seating; having Lone Star beer as a sponsor didn't hurt.
- At one point, University officialdom objected to free beer, but relented when it became clear that the audience was packed with music lovers, not party animals.

Bonnie Raitt performing on Austin City Limits.

Life at Work

- For Brad Lawson the news from *Austin City Limits* could not have been better; sound quality would be a high priority in the 1982 season, recorded in 1981.
- The nationwide success of *Austin City Limits* had made the booking of talent—Kris Kristofferson, Emmylou Harris, Crystal Gayle— much easier.
- Concurrently, sound technology as a craft was improving and was now a priority.
- As a first step, 40 stations, including those in the trendsetting markets of Los Angeles, Chicago, and Atlanta, would be broadcasting the show in stereo.
- Discussion was also underway concerning the purchase of an additional two-inch, 16-track mixer and the addition of high-caliber microphones that could more accurately capture the authentic sound.
- A mixer was designed to mesh an array of inputs into a few controllable outputs; Brad was overwhelmed by the oceans of knobs when he was allowed to attend his first *Austin City Limits* taping as an assistant's assistant with instructions to touch nothing.

The success of Austin City Limits made booking talent – like Emmylou Harris – easier.

- With a dozen microphones ringing the area, all the musicians were required to do was to play their best.
- One of the show's greatest assets was its four-story ceiling, which enhanced the sound.
- *Austin City Limits* had long distinguished itself with its emphasis on a limited number of acts who were privileged to play for one hour to 90 minutes before a receptive audience.
- The tape would then be edited and broadcast eight months to a year later—after sign-off from the artist.
- Band members always worked well below their usual scale: $500 per show, half that for sidemen; the famous and the obscure toiled for the same minimum wage.
- Thanks to the meticulous care and production quality, the show had earned its place on the TV schedule: 90 percent of all PBS stations carried the show, comprising over 260 stations and reaching 10 million viewers each week.
- In addition, an 11-part PBS series entitled *Southbound* had ignited considerable interest in Southern roots music featuring gospel music, Cajun, bluegrass, fiddling, Mex-Tex, ballad singing and mouth music.
- Brad soon learned that musicians loved the rhythms of *Austin City Limits* because they were asked to perform to an audience, not the red light on a bulky television camera.
- The show was about live music; even the long, lingering shots of the audience—featured in the early years—were shrunk to showcase the performance itself.
- Mishaps were inevitable: Following an afternoon of flawless rehearsals with singer/songwriter Kris Kristofferson, all the lights in the building went out.
- Trapped in the windowless building, the audience and performers alike had to feel their way to the exits in absolute darkness.
- The trouble had been caused by a rat eating through an electrical wire; the audience was readmitted the next night for the taping.
- As an assistant's assistant, Brad was earning more experience than money, and had to keep his sales job at Music World.
- But since the taping schedule ran from July to January, with most PBS stations broadcasting the shows in January through April, he could schedule paid work around heart work.

As an assistant's assistant, Brad was overwhelmed by the sound board on the set of the show.

Life in the Community: Austin, Texas

- Home of the University of Texas, the state legislature, and a more bohemian mindset than most of Texas, Austin became the center of the state's laissez-faire, go-with-the-flow artisans and musicians.
- Local historians trace Austin's musical heritage to the post-World War II decision by booking agent and band manager Johnny Holmes to open the Victory Grill on the city's East Side to showcase local and touring blues and R&B musicians.
- By the 1970s, Austin had room for the city's most psychedelic nightclub, the Vulcan Gas Company, and R&B clubs such as Ernie's Chicken Shack and Charlie's Playhouse.
- The city developed a gumbo-flavored musical palette, or as one tunes man described it, "freeform-country-folk-rock-science-fiction-gospel-gum-bluegrass-opera-cowjazz music."
- The official city slogan promoted Austin as "The Live Music Capital of the World" to honor the live music venues within the area and the long-running PBS TV concert series *Austin City Limits*.
- Many Austinites have also adopted the unofficial slogan "Keep Austin Weird" in defense of the proudly eclectic, liberal lifestyles of many Austin residents, plus a desire to protect small, unique, local businesses from being overrun by large corporations.
- The centrally located Austin was settled in the 1830s on the banks of the Colorado River by pioneers who named the village Waterloo.
- In 1839, Waterloo was chosen to become the capital of the newly independent Republic of Texas and was renamed for Stephen F. Austin, known as the father of Texas.
- Bitter Texas politics, Indian uprisings, Mexican army incursions and the wholesale movement of government documents repeatedly threatened the city's designation as the capital of Texas until 1846.
- In 1860, even though 38 percent of Travis County residents were slaves, voters in Austin and other Central Texas communities voted against secession at the outbreak of the Civil War.
- The opening of the Houston and Texas Central Railway (H&TC) in 1871 vaulted Austin into a major trading center for the region with the ability to transport both cotton and cattle.
- Austin was also the terminus of the southernmost leg of the Chisholm Trail and "drovers" pushed cattle north to the railroad.
- The University of Texas held its first classes in 1883, and the state capital building was completed in 1888.
- In the late nineteenth century, Austin expanded its city limits to more than three times its former area, and the first granite dam was built on the Colorado River to power a new streetcar line and the new "moon towers," which illuminated areas of the city at night.
- In the early twentieth century, the Texas Oil Boom took hold, creating tremendous economic opportunities in Southeast Texas and North Texas.
- The growth generated by this boom largely passed by Austin at first, with the city slipping from fourth largest to tenth largest in Texas between 1880 and 1920.
- Beginning in the 1920s and 1930s, Austin launched a series of civic development and beautification projects that created much of the city's infrastructure and parks.
- In addition, the state legislature established the Lower Colorado River Authority that, along with the City of Austin, created the system of dams along the Colorado River to form the Highland Lakes.
- These projects were enabled in large part because Austin received more Depression-era relief funds than any other Texas city.
- After the mid-twentieth century, Austin became established as one of Texas' major metropolitan centers, attracting companies focused on semiconductors and software.
- The 1970s also saw Austin's emergence in the national music scene, with artists such as Willie Nelson and venues such as the Armadillo World Headquarters.

HISTORICAL SNAPSHOT
1982

- The Commodore 64 8-bit home computer was introduced by Commodore International at the Winter Consumer Electronics Show

- The Fifty-fourth Academy Awards presented *Chariots of Fire* with Best Picture

- The Weather Channel aired on cable television for the first time

- A Unabomber bomb exploded in the computer science department at Vanderbilt University

- Spanish priest Juan María Fernández y Krohn tried to stab Pope John Paul II with a bayonet during a pilgrimage to the shrine at Fatima

- A rally against nuclear weapons drew 750,000 to New York City's Central Park Including Jackson Browne, James Taylor, Bruce Springsteen, and Linda Ronstadt

- The Equal Rights Amendment fell short of the 38 states needed to pass; Phyllis Schlafly and other leaders of the Christian right took credit for its defeat

- Italy beat West Germany 3–1 to win the 1982 FIFA World Cup in Spain

- Checker Motors Corporation ceased production of automobiles

- The Reverend Sun Myung Moon was sentenced to 18 months in prison and fined $25,000 for tax fraud and conspiracy to obstruct justice

- The International Whaling Commission voted to end commercial whaling by 1985–1986

- Ozzy Osbourne bit the head off a live bat thrown at him during a performance in Des Moines, Iowa

- Comedian and Blues Brother John Belushi was found dead of an apparent drug overdose in the Chateau Marmont Hotel in Los Angeles

- The most successful group of the 1970s, ABBA, released their final original single "Under Attack"

- The Dow Jones Industrial Average closed at 1,065.49, its first all-time high since January 11, 1973, when the average closed at 1,051.70

- The Vietnam Veterans Memorial was dedicated in Washington, D.C., after a march to its site by thousands of Vietnam War veterans

- Michael Jackson released "Thriller", the biggest selling album of all time

- Sixty-one-year-old retired dentist Barney Clark became the first person to receive a permanent artificial heart; he lived for 112 days with the device

- The first U.S. execution by lethal injection was carried out in Texas

- *Time Magazine*'s Man of the Year was given for the first time to a non-human—the computer

- In a Gallup Poll, 51 percent of Americans did not accept homosexuality as normal

Selected Prices

Air Conditioner	$299.00
Automobile, Honda	$7,132.00
Beef Jerky	$1.99
Briefcase	$89.99
Caftan	$22.00
Computer, IBM	$1,795.00
Fishing Tackle Box	$89.95
Game, Fisher Price	$9.97
Hunting Suit	$74.95
Video Game Home Arcade	$299.95

Many of my earliest memories are formed around times with music. When I was a preteen, I remember my parents visiting with their closest friends in Kenny Wilson's garage, which had been converted from an area to store cars to a bar with tables and an old jukebox. Generally there were no other children present, as I was the youngest child of the youngest couple. My parents' friends were other railroad employees, and they were generally older than my parents. Several of the men served during World War II, and the music on the jukebox was of the 30s and 40s. During this time I became a fan of the Ink Spots, and I remember my father pushing the big buttons on the jukebox to select "If I Didn't Care." He would sing along with the song while slow dancing with my mother. In the background the men would recount stories and experiences during the Big One or on the railroad. Even for a child, I got a feeling of nostalgia, given the mix of period music and lore. The evenings would go on well into the wee hours, and I would often fall asleep listening to all of this in the background.

I tried to play the cornet when I was in grade school, but my teeth were severely crossed before braces. We practiced in the basement of the school next to the cafeteria, and the practice room was very small, maybe 12' x 12' with a few folding chairs and a small table. I really wanted to play the cornet. I wanted to make music but those teeth made performing a bit difficult. The cornet never made a good tone in my hands.

But I loved listening to music. My best friend in high school, Greg Barker, worked his father's farm. He was paid pretty well for the work he did, and this allowed him to buy many record albums and high-tech stereo equipment. He managed to get all of this stuff into his small bedroom. When we wanted music, we just opened the windows and opened the door and played the music as loud as we could. Greg's mother would scream at us to turn it down, but we just laughed, because she would never really do anything to us. We listened to all the classic rock 'n' roll like Van Halen, AC/DC, Journey, Rush...it made life fun, because my parents would never let me play music as loud as we could at Greg's.

My first concert was in 1982, watching the Jefferson Starship perform in Rockford, Illinois, when I was about 14. I wasn't very familiar with the Jefferson Airplane before this show, but I instantly became infatuated with Grace Slick and the late 60s rock era. The music of The Doors, The Band, Jimmy Hendrix, and others became lifetime favorites.

My father could play the accordion, an instrument that he learned when he was a child. He told a story about being about nine or 10 years old when a traveling salesman came to his parents' home and offered to provide accordion lessons in the home once or twice a week. His parents agreed, and he played for several years during his preteen years. He gave up the instrument as he got older, but he always thought about playing. He picked up the accordion again late in life when I was in high school. He purchased a modern amplified version. Playing the accordion is quite difficult. One has to coordinate playing a keyboard with one hand, playing the bass buttons with the other hand, while squeezing the instrument in and out. On top of all that, with an electronic accordion, one has to work foot panels to modulate the tone and the amplification. Needless to say, my father's first attempts at playing the accordion after so many decades were pretty harsh. But in time, he was able to do a very nice job playing many of those same songs from the 30s and 40s that I listened to when I was very young. My father passed away over 12 years ago, but I still have several of the song sheets and playlists that he would work from during his accordion practice.

The musical talent has skipped a generation. Although I play a bit of electric bass guitar, my older son Aidan Batalia at 12 years old is a highly motivated percussionist. He has been playing the drums and other percussion instruments from the age of eight. Like many passing interests children have, my wife and I didn't think the drums were going to be anything but a passing fad. But six months of persistent nagging showed us his commitment to take music lessons seriously. After over four years of practice, Aidan has formed his own rock band, has several gigs planned for the fall of 2011, and has a short album produced and recorded.

Personal Essay
Michael Batalia

"The Austin Scene," *Austin City Limits: 25 Years of American Music*,
John T. Davis, 2000:

Austin was a smaller and saner place in the mid-70s, a different world in many respects....

George Strait used to play in the Broken Spoke for anyone with three bucks in his pocket. Stevie Ray Vaughan once struggled to draw a weekly crowd at the Rome Inn. Shawn Colvin came to town as part of a country rock band called the Dixie Diesels and gigged for whoever would have her. Nanci Griffith and Lyle Lovett used to share duet bills and happy hour gigs at Emmajoe's. There was no cover charge; Emmajoe's owners circulated a metal pitcher to solicit contributions for the future Grammy winners.

Then there was Willie Nelson, who came out of the Texas Hill Country like Moses. After his retreat from Nashville, Nelson came home, grew his hair, fired up a joint, and started a dance that featured a pas de deux between two improbable and seemingly irreconcilable figures, the redneck cowboy and the long-haired rocker. No one had ever seen anything quite like it.

"Country Balladeer to Give Acoustic Concert in SF," *Santa Fe New Mexican*, December 24, 1982:

Michael Murphey's Christmas gift to New Mexico will be a series of appearances in northern New Mexico over the next few weeks, including stops at the Kachina Lodge in Taos, Club West in Santa Fe, and the Golden Inn in Golden.

The progressive country-western performer recently had the hit song "What's Forever For." His 10th album, *Michael Martin Murphey*, which features the song, has remained in the top 100 albums on popular music charts since its release five months ago.

Murphey, who lives in Taos, has had several hit records over his 10-year career, including "Wildfire," "Geronimo's Cadillac," and "Cherokee Fiddle." He also was the musical supervisor, cowriter, and one of the actors in the film *Hard Country*....

Thursday night, Murphey will give an acoustic performance without his band at Club West. During a recent telephone interview, Murphey said he's really looking forward to the show.

"The acoustic shows are something I really enjoy doing. And Club West is one of the few places on earth that you can do that kind of thing and people really listen; it's really special for me," Murphey said

"It's something I get to do maybe just 20 times a year."

Murphey said he just recently was taped for an *Austin City Limits* television performance, which will probably air in February.

"When *Austin City Limits* asked me to play, I asked if it would be all right if I just came down there with my guitar and no band at all, not even a bass player, just play solo 40 minutes on TV with no commercial interruptions. It's a dream I've had my whole career to do one TV show that way. And they were very skeptical at first. They had only done one other acoustic show and it was with Chet Atkins. And no one doubts his ability to pull it off!" Murphey said with a laugh. "It worked out real well."

"There's a myth that sometimes stuck in people's minds that the fewer the instruments, the less the music, which really isn't true. There's a lot present in the guitar alone. People like Leo Kottke have proven it. Being friends with him is what inspired me to try it," Murphey said.

1983 PROFILE

Funk master George Clinton was known by a wide variety of names—The Prince of Funk, Dr. Funkenstein, the Prime Minister of Funk, and the Father of Funkadelic—but during his multi-decade career, mostly he was an innovator.

Life at Home

- Although George Clinton started his musical career playing doo-wop, his legacy was the transformation of black popular dance music using locomotive poly-rhythms, screaming guitars, R&B vocal harmonies and the down-home soul sounds of James Brown.
- Born July 22, 1941, in Kannapolis, North Carolina, George grew up in Plainfield, New Jersey, where his band the Parliaments first appeared on the music scene with its recording of "Sunday Kind of Love" in 1956.
- When the song was released, George was still attending junior high school and running a neighborhood barbershop where he cut and straightened hair.
- Two years later the band recorded and released "Poor Willie" and continued to play in the area, with its most regular gig coming from The Silk Palace, a barbershop, where they shared the spotlight with the Monotones and the Fiestas.
- Known in later years for his outlandish costumes and multicolored dreadlocks, George believed it was crooner Frankie Lymon and the Teenagers who originally inspired him to become a singer when, "Frankie Lymon's was the devil's music," he said.
- "Even 'bop-bap-ba-do-la-ba-bop-bam-boom' was considered to be bad. Then when the '60s came around, with Jimi Hendrix playing a loud guitar with all this feedback, then that was the devil's music. Now we got rappers, and *they're* the devil's music. So I never played what you could call safe music."

Music innovator George Clinton transformed black dance music with poly-rhythms and screaming guitars.

Rappers were considered the devil's musicians.

- "If you listen close you can hear Motown in what I do, and doo-wop evolved into Motown. Then funk became the DNA for hip-hop. Rock and roll, R&B, blues, gospel, you see them as different, but funk is the thread that goes through all of them."

- His first band may have started out as a doo-wop group, like the Temptations, who performed romantic ballads and four-part harmonies like "Goodnight, Sweetheart, It's Time to Go," but his musical statements had moved a long way by the time he recorded the raucous "Flashlight" and "The Atomic Dog" in the 1980s.

- Or, as George said, "In the beginning there was funk."

- Lured by the success of Motown in the 1960s, George sold the barbershop and drove to Detroit so the Parliaments could camp out on the steps of the Berry Gordy's hit machine.

- Once there, George became a staff songwriter for Motown and learned the entertainment craft, including the role of clichés, puns and hooks to boost a song's appeal.

- "I just went stupid with it. Instead of one or two hooks, we'd have 10 hooks in the same song. And puns that were so stupid that you could take it three or four different ways."

- He also recorded his first major hit single, "I Wanna Testify," in 1967, that scored on both the pop and soul charts for the Parliaments.

- While in Detroit, George also worked with Golden World where he co-produced Barbara Lewis's hit, "Hello Stranger," and Darrell Banks's "Open the Door to Your Heart."

- But when American cities began to go up in flames in the summer of 1968, George was inspired to produce music as fiery as the racial riots outside his door.

- Out went the perfectly matched tuxedos; in came psychedelic-influenced pink jackets, diapers made from hotel towels, outfits created from their suit bags—anything outrageous and over the top would do.

- Anything: rude carvings in his hair, language designed to shock, drugs.

- Their music also took on a new sound.

- One night after their equipment was late in arriving, they borrowed a double stack of Marshall amps, a triple stack of SVTs—high performance bass amps—and an oversized set of fiberglass drums from the front band Vanilla Fudge.

- After that, super loud and utterly outrageous were also part of their zany repertoire.

- At about the same time, due to trademark issues with Revilot Records, George changed the name of the Parliaments to Funkadelic and scored a hit with the song ""A New Day Begins."

- Same band—different name.

- Then in 1970, after George reclaimed the rights to the original name, he changed the group's name once again to simply Parliament and enjoyed a minor hit with "The Breakdown" and expanded his largely black, very loyal following.

- Over time, with the constant name and lineup changes, the group became known as simply P-Funk—short for Parliament-Funkadelic—and were discussed in the same breath as Jimi Hendrix, Sly and the Family Stone, Cream, and James Brown while exploring different sounds, technology, and lyrics.

Outrageous outfits replaced perfectly matched tuxedos.

- He mixed and matched musicians and singers into several groups, including the Parlettes, Parliament, Funkadelic, and P-Funk.
- Although essentially made up of the same personnel, the groups recorded in different styles, often on different labels.
- At one point, the same group formed Parliament on Casablanca Records, with a hot horn section and complicated vocal lines, while also being Funkadelic at Warner Brothers, a straight rock band with a blazing rhythm section.
- Detroit drummer Sam Dinkins explained, "By giving them different names, even though it was the same group, he was able to take one product and make it into several, if you would, but it was the same lineup."
- During their heyday in the mid- to late 1970s, following the success of their platinum-selling album, 1975's *Mothership Connection*, George and his band Parliament-Funkadelic engaged in a series of high-profile, no-expenses-spared stadium tours around the United States, culminating in the P-Funk Earth Tour.
- At these gigs, the much-referenced Mothership was seen to land on stage amongst the band before a baying and expectant crowd.
- At this point in the show, George would emerge from the Mothership in the form of Dr. Funkenstein, the "cool ghoul with the funk transplant," in order to better administer funk to the audience.
- During the 1970s, George and Parliament-Funkadelic produced over 40 R&B hit singles—including three number ones—and three platinum albums.

Life at Work

- The early 1980s were not kind to George Clinton.
- George went from the musical magician to industry pariah for three years, thanks to the same legal system that had tied his hands earlier in his career.
- As the decade opened, the 39-year-old showman/producer was the writer, producer and brains behind half a dozen different bands—each with their own sound.
- Some were described as Sly Stone Meets the Temptations, while others sounded like Stevie Wonder an acid, critics drooled.
- A night's entertainment with the Prince of Funk was designed to be an adventure; on stage "we were James Brown, the Temptations and the Three Stooges on acid," George himself claimed.
- On stage, George performed and preached his personal gospel of psychedelic funk, sexual liberation, ghetto realism, mind-expanding drugs, along with a God-given right to have a good time.

Bootsy of Funkadelic's Bootsy Rubber Band.

- Having sold 10 million albums within five years, George was the king of funk.
- That's when he challenged the musical establishment and filed three separate lawsuits for breach of contract, claiming a total of $100 million in damages against Warner Brothers, the label which had signed Funkadelic's Bootsy Rubber Band and Zapp.
- Warner Bros. then decided not to distribute George's Park Place label.
- Several other record producers followed suit, and George's wild, funkadelic world became tied up in the courts.
- So many deals fell through in such a short time that George was quickly broke.
- It was costing him more than $150,000 a week to keep his 88-man entourage of musicians, singers and crew on the road.

- Without new hits to keep the fans coming and his royalties tied up in courts, there was no money to pay his personnel, and his debts accumulated.
- George added free-base cocaine to his drug diet, which already included Quaaludes, acid, marijuana and cocaine.
- For several years he was locked out of recording studios because of unpaid bills.
- No major label would deal with him.
- Then Capitol Records signed on to a deal and advanced George $300,000 to relaunch.
- Despite his legal entanglements with Warner Bros., George was given an opportunity to make music again.

- Jettisoning both the Parliament and Funkadelic names (but not the musicians), George signed to Capitol both as a solo act and as the P-Funk All-Stars.
- His first solo album, 1982's *Computer Games*, contained the Top 20 R&B hit "Loopzilla."
- Several months later, the title track from George's *Atomic Dog* hit number one on the R&B charts and stayed at the top spot for four weeks.
- The funkmeister was back in all his outrageous glory.
- And once again, when the fans demanded an encore at the end of a concert, everyone knew that Dr. Funkenstein had one requirement—a rain shower of joints as a show of appreciation.

George Clinton, center right, performing in 1982.

Life in the Community: Detroit, Michigan

- Although the powerful music of Motown was indelibly linked to Detroit, the Motor City spent decades developing a distinct musical heritage.
- Even before Motown opened its doors, Detroit was already well on its way to being an R&B and soul hotbed.
- In 1955, the influential soul singer Little Willie John made his debut; then in 1956, the Detroit-based R&B label Fortune Records enjoyed success with Nolan Strong & The Diablos.
- In 1959, The Falcons, featuring Wilson Pickett and Eddie Floyd, released "You're So Fine," considered to be the first true soul record.

Detroit's musical heritage was R&B and soul.

- Also that year, Jackie Wilson had his first hit with "Reet Petite," which was co-written by a young Berry Gordy Jr.
- The Volumes had a hit single in 1962 for Chex Records with the single "I Love You," and singer/songwriter Barbara Lewis found success with the single "Hello Stranger."
- Digging back further, following the Roaring Twenties, Detroit's former "Black Bottom" area on the city's east side became nationally famous for its music; major blues singers, big bands, and jazz artists—such as Duke Ellington, Billy Eckstine, Pearl Bailey, Ella Fitzgerald, and Count Basie—regularly performed in the nightclubs of the Paradise Valley entertainment district.

- The Detroit blues scene in the 1940s and 1950s was centered around bars on Hastings Street and featured artists on the local JVB and Sensation labels such as Eddie "Guitar" Burns, John Lee Hooker, Bobo Jenkins, Boogie Woogie Red, Doctor Ross, Baby Boy Warren and Washboard Willie.
- Detroit also produced some excellent gospel singers.
- In the 1940s, Oliver Green had formed the popular gospel group The Detroiters, followed in the 1950s by Della Reese just launching her long career, while Mattie Moss Clark was pioneering three-part harmony into gospel choral music.
- In the 1960s, the Reverend C.L. Franklin found success with his recorded sermons on Chess Records' gospel label, and with an album of spirituals recorded at his New Bethel Baptist Church that included the debut of his young daughter, Aretha Franklin.
- In the 1980s, the Winans dynasty produced Grammy winners CeCe and BeBe Winans, as well as Bill Moss & The Celestials, and Fred Hammond.
- During the development of jazz, Detroit emerged as an important musical center, alongside New Orleans, Chicago, and St. Louis.
- Among the musicians who relocated to Detroit were drummer William McKinney, who formed the seminal big band McKinney's Cotton Pickers, with jazz great Don Redman.
- In the 1980s, pop icon Madonna—who was born and raised outside of Detroit—emerged.
- The star in Detroit's musical history was the success of Motown Records during the 1960s and early 1970s.
- Originally known as Tamla Records, Motown was founded by auto plant worker Berry Gordy and became home to some of the most popular recording acts in the world, including Marvin Gaye, the Temptations, Stevie Wonder, Diana Ross and the Supremes, Smokey Robinson and the Miracles, the Four Tops, Martha and the Vandellas, Edwin Starr, Little Willie John, the Contours, and the Spinners.
- In 1967, longtime backroom barbershop doo-wop group the Parliaments, featuring George Clinton, scored a hit with "I Wanna Testify" for Revilot Records, and marked the beginning of funk in mainstream R&B.
- In 1978, George Clinton's bass player Bootsy Collins had a top charting hit with Bootzilla.
- Then, in the late 1960s, Metro Detroit became the epicenter for high-energy rock music with the MC5 and Iggy and the Stooges, whose sound was equal parts anger, determination and attitude.
- This was followed by hardcore punk, which was louder, harder and more aggressive.

Madonna, born and raised in Detroit, emerged in the 80s.

HISTORICAL SNAPSHOT
1983

- Björn Borg retired from tennis after winning five consecutive Wimbledon championships
- Lotus 1-2-3 was released for IBM-PC-compatible computers
- The U.S. Environmental Protection Agency announced its intention to buy out and evacuate the dioxin-contaminated community of Times Beach, Missouri
- The final episode of M*A*S*H set records for the most watched episode in television history
- "Menudomania" arrived in New York as 3,500 screaming girls crowded Kennedy Airport to catch a glimpse of Puerto Rican boy band Menudo, who were playing six sold-out shows at the Felt Forum
- The Rolling Stones concert film *Let's Spend the Night Together* opened in New York
- Michael Jackson's *Thriller* album tracked 37 weeks as #1 on the U.S. charts
- Compact discs, which had first been released in Japan the previous October, went on sale in the U.S.
- Ellen Taaffe Zwilich became the first woman to win the Pulitzer Prize for Music
- Michael Jackson unveiled his version of the moonwalk during a performance of "Billie Jean" on the *Motown 25 Special* aired on NBC

A tale of two Michaels: A complex genius reigned as our King of Pop

- Johnny Ramone suffered a near-fatal head injury during a fight over a woman
- The members of Kiss showed their faces without their makeup for the first time on MTV
- Quiet Riot's *Metal Health* album became the first heavy metal album to hit #1 in America
- The Space Shuttle *Challenger* carried Guion S. Bluford, the first African-American astronaut, into space
- The Global Positioning System (GPS) became available for civilian use
- The Red Hot Chili Peppers launched their first, self-titled album
- Simultaneous suicide truck-bombings destroyed both the French and the U.S. Marine Corps barracks in Beirut, killing 241 U.S. servicemen, 58 French paratroopers and six Lebanese civilians
- Immunosuppressant cyclosporine was approved by the FDA, leading to a revolution in the field of transplantation
- *Flashdance* and *Star Wars Episode VI: Return of the Jedi* were box-office hits
- McDonalds introduced the McNugget

Selected Prices

Apple Macintosh Computer	$2,500.00
Butter, per Pound	$1.99
China, 10-Piece Tea Set	$69.00
Coffee, per Pound	$2.19
Gas Grill	$179.99
House, Four-Bedroom, New York	$156,000
Lawn Mower, Craftsman	$299.99
Screwdrivers, Stanley Set of Four	$26.95
Shotgun, Winchester 12-Gauge	$1,200.00
Woman's Leather Bag	$49.00

an Apple after school

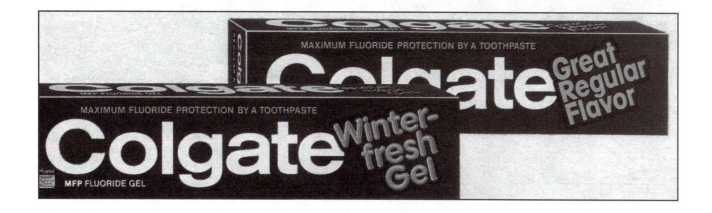

"What Is Funk?" *Funk, One Music, One People, and the Rhythm of the One,*
Ricky Vincent, 1996:

Funk is a many splendored thing. Funk is a nasty vibe, and a sweet sexy feeling. Funk is funkiness, a natural release of the essence within. Funk is a high, but it is also down at the bottom, the lowdown earthy essence, the bass elements. Funk is at the extremes of everything. Funk can be hot, but funk can be cool. Funk is primitive, yet funk can be sophisticated. Funk is a way out, and a way in. Funk is all over the place. Funk is a means of reference that cannot be denied.

Trying to put the thang called Funk into words is like trying to write down your orgasm. Both thrive in that gap in time when words fall away, leaving nothing but sensation.

—Barry Walters, *The Village Voice*

"The Serious Metafoolishness of Father Funkadelic George Clinton," Chip Stern, *Musician*, 1979:

Dr. Funkenstein may be crazy, but he is not insane. He has, in effect, got four or five different record companies putting out albums by the same basic group, so that all of them have an interest in promoting whoever's on tour. He gives $0.25 of every ticket sold at the Parliament/Funkadelic concerts to the United Negro College Fund. He comes up with so many slants on the same stroke that his fans have come to expect no surprises....

"You have a lot of choices of what to do with your music. You can dance to it or listen to it, but you don't have to get real serious with it. It can be funny. 'Cause to me it's just funny that it can be all these different things, and we don't have to feel seriously life-and-death about any portion of it."

"George Clinton Returns to the Limelight," *Lubbock Evening Journal*, (Texas), June 24, 1983:

Heads turn when George Clinton enters a room. Any room.

At the moment, the people in the lobby of the Beverly Hills Hotel are staring at him. It is a lobby designed for legendary movie stars; there is nothing funky about it. Except for George Clinton.

The 41-year-old mastermind behind Funkadelic, Parliament, Bootsy's Rubber Band, Zapp, the P-Funk All-Stars and so many other acts is wearing blue jeans, Nike running shoes, a black leather jacket and a gray sweatshirt. He is taking gulps from a bottle of Beck's and giggling. It is the giggle of a man who is stoned: stoned on life, stoned on drugs. A religious man, if you will. And right there, on the front of the sweatshirt printed in black, six-inch letters is the gospel of George Clinton: FUNK!

Here in the lobby, most people have not noticed the bottle of beer. They are too busy eyeing the hair. The two-inch wide Mohawk. The luminous purple Mohawk. And the rows of luminous purple cornrow braids. But George Clinton doesn't worry about what these people think of him. "Too many beautiful people in Los Angeles," he says. "That's why I can't stay in LA." He laughs again. "'Cause everyone comes here to be a star, and so everybody looks especially good. Too much of a good thing in LA. So I had to move."

That may be why, when he is not on the road or in the recording studio or taking care of business, Clinton leads a reclusive life with his wife Stephanie on a farm outside Detroit that has no phone. There he hunts and fishes and plays video games and reads science fiction novels and meditates and practices yoga and dreams up the strange concepts for his albums.

Clinton leaves the lobby and walks to his limo. A movie producer is getting out of a car parked directly in front of Clinton. He stares at Clinton, shakes his head, smiles.

"You laugh," someone says to the movie producer. "But at the moment, he's got a number one record."

Inside the limo, Clinton is laughing, too. He takes a sip of the Beck's and stretches out his legs. How does it feel to be back? he is asked. "I don't even know yet," he says with a grin.

Ah, but he knows. And it feels good, mighty good, to be back, to be out on the road again, playing to crowds of up to 20,000 fans, six nights a week. It feels fine to be back on the charts with a hit single, "Atomic Dog," and a hit album *Computer Games*.

1985 Profile

Carleen Cahill's classical music career began by "playing" a stringless violin, and progressed to successful New York City opera singer before transitioning into voice teacher/performer in a small upstate New York community.

Life at Home

- Carleen Rose Cahill was born in Detroit, Michigan, in 1951.
- She was first exposed to music through her parents, who would play 78 rpm records of swing and big band music.
- Her family would often dance and sing along to the music of Benny Goodman and Glen Miller, and Carleen actually sang before she spoke.
- Carleen sang in the school chorus as early as she could remember, and had her first solo—the third verse of "The Battle Hymn of the Republic"—in the fourth grade.
- Carleen's first instrument was the violin, which she started playing in fifth grade, after seeing her school's orchestra play *The Nutcracker Suite*.
- Carleen used a family violin that belonged to her grandmother, but it did not have any strings.
- She practiced finger positions and "played" on that stringless instrument for almost a year.
- When her teacher saw Carleen practicing finger positions on the edge of her desk, she encouraged Carleen's mother to put strings on her violin.
- As she got older, Carleen became increasingly interested in the rock music of the 1960s—including the Beatles, Chuck Berry, and the Rolling Stones—becoming a lifelong Beatles fan.
- Carleen's brother bought her a guitar for her sixteenth birthday, which she played in local bands, especially Joni Mitchell songs.

Classically trained singer Carleen Cahill thrived in New York City's opera scene.

- Although she continued to play guitar and violin throughout high school, she discovered that singing brought her the most pleasure.
- Singing had always felt very natural to her, and she sang it all while growing up—pop, rock, church, classic and folk, but not opera.
- In fact, she did not enjoy opera at all during high school.
- After high school, Carleen worked in an insurance company as a secretary.
- She also sang in a folk trio after work, performing at coffeehouses and making very little money.
- Her sister persuaded her to go to college to pursue a music career.
- Carleen got her Bachelor's of Music in Voice Performance at Western Michigan University in Kalamazoo, several hours west of Detroit—close enough to her family, but far enough to be on her own.

Make-up was important in transforming performers into many operatic roles.

- Studying music in college in the early 1970s was not terribly common.
- There were fewer career resources, and students had to figure out—by themselves—the practical aspects of how to become professional musicians.
- In college, Carleen discovered her love of opera and her ability to perform.
- Her music department put on three full-scale opera performances per year—a lot for a school of its size—giving Carleen the opportunity to experience a variety of musical styles, and to discover how much she enjoyed working as part of a team with the other cast and crew members.
- She found that she never got nervous when singing with other people in an opera production.
- As a voice performance music major, she was also required to study four languages: Spanish, French, Italian and German.
- During her college years, she sang with the Muskegon Symphony for $200, and with the Detroit Symphony for the experience.
- Upon graduating college, her goal was clear—to train as a classical singer.
- Carleen took the next step and got her Master's of Music in Voice Performance from the University of Michigan in Ann Arbor.
- In graduate school, Carleen performed six full-scale operas, which she added to her professional repertoire, as: the mother in E. Humperdinck's *Hansel and Gretel*; Donna Elvira and Donna Anna in Mozart's *Don Giovanni*; the widow in F. Lehar's *The Merry Widow*; Rosalinda in J. Strauss' *Die Fledermaus*; and Musetta in Puccini's *La Bohème*.
- Opera required much more than just singing; the best performers needed to act, be physically fit, have a good sense of timing, and the ability to work well with a cast and crew.
- Carleen paid her way through graduate school by singing at local church ceremonies for $50 per event, and by her permanent position as the church soloist.

In college, Carleen performed the leading role in Falstaff *by Verdi.*

Life at Work

- Armed with her Master's of Music in Voice Performance, Carleen Cahill moved to New York City in 1975 to pursue a classical singing career—a necessary career move for a classical singer.

- Upon arriving in New York, Carleen waitressed to support herself and her continued studies with a professional voice teacher—another necessary career decision that cost $50 per lesson.

- Professional voice teachers in New York required students to audition before being accepted to study in their studios.

- Carleen auditioned and was accepted into the studio of a teacher who was recommended by her professors in graduate school.

- The teacher was very strict, and would not let Carleen audition for anything for a year and a half.

- Once Carleen began auditioning for parts, however, she had great success and began performing often in and around New York.

Carleen with her sister, mother and brother after a graduate school performance.

- Her work at this time included three different roles with the Bronx Opera (Donna Anna in Mozart's *Don Giovanni*, Susannah in Carlyle Floyd's *Susannah*, and Violetta in Giuseppe Verdi's *La Traviata*).

- She also sang as the soprano soloist in Handel's *Judas Maccabeus* in the New York City's Choral Festival, and was engaged by Boris Goldovsky to sing for several of his numerous lectures at the Metropolitan Museum of Art lecture series on opera.

- Three years after arriving in New York, Carleen took her career to the next level by engaging a professional management company.

- The management company helped Carleen get high-level performing jobs, such as the soprano soloist in Beethoven's *Ninth Symphony* at the Saratoga Arts Festival, Musetta in Puccini's *La Bohème* with the Houston Grand Opera Festival, and Nedda in Ruggiero Leoncavallo's *I Pagliacci* with the New York City Opera Touring Company.

Conductor Boris Goldovsky engaged Carleen to sing at his opera lecture series at the Metropolitan Museum of Art

- Once professionally managed, Carleen was able to support herself exclusively with music, even though the management company typically took 15 percent of her paycheck for opera roles and 20 percent for oratorio and orchestral work.

- Carleen often got jobs through the international opera circuit that regularly traveled to New York to hold auditions for shows in other cities.

- The representatives of the opera companies in this circuit often cast performers based on very specific—and sometimes non-talent-related—criteria.

- For example, if a company had already found an especially tall woman to play the female lead, they would open auditions for the male lead to only tall men.

- Carleen's management company arranged for her to audition for suitable parts, one of her favorite being Violetta in Verdi's *La Traviata*.

- Once she got a role, Carleen would travel to the city of the performance for one to two months of rehearsals and shows.

- This gave her an opportunity to travel around the world and make many new friends and colleagues.
- The opera circuit was also a steady source of income, and compensation per show was $2,000-$8,000, depending on the size of the company.
- Carleen performed all over the country and abroad, including with opera companies in San Francisco, New Orleans, Austin, Phoenix, Seattle, Geneva, and Buenos Aires.
- Her favorite performance was as Mimi in Puccini's *La Bohème*, performed in Maracaibo, Venezuela; the audience sat in the aisles and sang along to all of the opera choruses.
- She also accepted roles with smaller opera companies, depite less pay; this was a way to try out new roles in a smaller and often more forgiving arena before performing them in a larger city.
- It was just such a role that led her to upstate New York, where she fell in love with the area's natural beauty and relaxed pace.
- In 1980, she bought a house in Hillsdale, New York, and began splitting her time between city and country.

Playing Mimi in La Boheme, *in Venezuela, was one of Carleen's most memorable performances.*

Life in the Community: Hillsdale, New York

- While Carleen enjoyed living in New York City and traveling around the world to perform, this lifestyle prevented her from putting down roots.
- In 1980, The Columbia County Opera Company was founded by a wealthy opera lover from New York looking to recreate the country opera experience that was popular in his native England.
- The small opera company offered an intimate performance environment, and produced a series of outdoor concerts set against the scenic backdrop of beautiful upstate New York.
- While the year-round population of the area was small, the community's proximity to the city made it a popular tourist destination, and the Columbia County Opera's audience was accustomed to top-rate performances.
- Despite its beautiful location and proximity to New York City, however, it was difficult for the opera company to attract top-rate performers, mostly because they couldn't meet big city salaries, which could be as much as $2,000-$5,000 higher per show.
- Despite less money, the Columbia County Opera Company was exactly what Carleen was looking for—more time in the country combined with her passion for music.
- In 1981, she performed in their second season, and again in 1982, in Mozart's *L'oca del Cairo* and *La Finta Giardiniera*.
- In 1983, Carleen married Joseph, the Italian repairman who often came to fix her less-than-dependable country phone service, ending her city/country lifestyle.
- In Hillsdale full-time, Carleen had fewer musical opportunities than in New York, but she enjoyed living in one place and being involved in the community.
- She began teaching voice at the local music school.
- She also became an adjunct music professor at a nearby college.
- Some of her students were involved in school plays for which Carleen enjoyed helping them rehearse, and was often in the front row on opening night.

Carleen as Rosalinda in J. Strauss' Die Fledermaus.

Carleen and husband Joseph.

HISTORICAL SNAPSHOT
1985

- In Hollywood, the charity single "We Are the World" was recorded by USA for Africa
- Minolta released world's first autofocus single-lens reflex camera
- The Food and Drug Administration approved a blood test for AIDS, used to screen all blood donations in the United States
- *Amadeus* won Best Picture at the 57th Academy Awards
- WrestleMania debuted at Madison Square Garden
- Coca-Cola changed its formula and released New Coke, only to reverse itself in the face of an overwhelmingly negative response
- The FBI brought charges against the heads of five Mafia families in New York City
- Thomas Patrick Cavanaugh was sentenced to life in prison for attempting to sell stealth bomber secrets to the Soviet Union
- John Hendricks launched the Discovery Channel
- Route 66 was officially decommissioned
- *Back to the Future* opened in American theaters and became the highest grossing film of 1985
- The Greenpeace vessel *Rainbow Warrior* was bombed and sunk in Auckland Harbor by French Directorate-General for External Security (DGSE) agents
- Live Aid concerts in London and Philadelphia raised over £50 million for famine relief in Ethiopia
- Nintendo Entertainment System, including the Super Mario Bros. pack-in game, was released
- The comic strip *Calvin and Hobbes* debuted in 35 newspapers
- Microsoft Corporation released Windows 1.0
- President Ronald Reagan sold the rights to his autobiography to Random House for a record $3 million
- The Ford Taurus and Mercury Sable went on sale
- NeXT was founded by Steve Jobs after he resigned from Apple Computer
- The Tommy Hilfiger brand was established
- DNA was first used in a criminal case

Selected Prices

Bicycle, Aero Urban Cowboy	$600.00
Briefcase, Leather	$565.00
Camcorder	$994.00
Coca-Cola, Two-Liter	$1.00
Doll, Playskool	$24.97
Ice Cream, Dove Bar	$1.45
Martini for Two	$1.08
Modem	$119.95
Synthesizer, Yamaha	$188.88
Walkman, Sony	$19.95

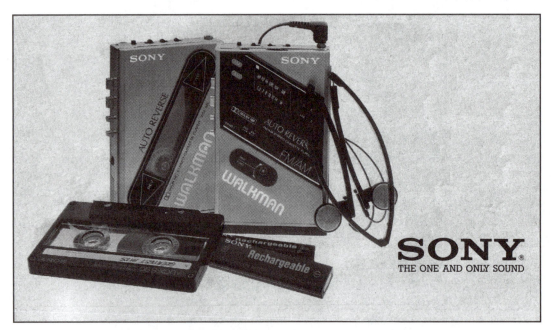

"Opera: Premiere of *Rinaldo* at Met," Donald Henahan, *The New York Times*, January 21, 1984:

It was a night of important debuts, some long delayed, at the Metropolitan Opera. The most important and most delayed was that of George Frideric Handel, none of whose more than 40 operas had ever been produced by the company before his 273-year-old *Rinaldo* found its way to the stage Thursday night. The production, borrowed almost intact from Canada's National Arts Center, might have astonished or perplexed him in some ways, but he probably would have found it as entertaining, ultimately, as most of the audience at this premiere obviously did.

Transporting a Handel opera from its Baroque setting to a modern house the size of the Met presents enormous problems, many of which this attractive production solves. The edition, edited by Martin Katz, was a conflation of Handel's several versions, expertly cut and trimmed to suit modern conditions.

Above all, however, the Handel opera demands important voices capable of handling the breathtaking coloratura and exhausting repetitions that figure so greatly in the opera seria genre. The Met had Samuel Ramey, for one, making his first appearance with the company as the Saracen warrior Argante. Mr. Ramey, who sang for years at the New York City Opera without attracting the Metropolitan's attention, went off to Europe several seasons ago and that apparently gave him the credentials necessary to impress the Met's casting department. At any rate, he made a tremendous impression with his powerful, pliable bass voice, particularly at his dazzling first entry in a wonderfully Baroque chariot. After throwing a big, steely tone out into the house in that aria, "Sibilar gli angui d'Aletto," he opened the following scene with a dulcet "Vieni, o cara, a consolarmi," demonstrating his great vocal as well as expressive range.

As brilliant a success in her own gentle way was Benita Valente as Almirena. Miss Valente actually drew one of the night's most sustained ovations with her plaintive and affecting aria rejecting the Saracen's advances, "Lascia ch'io pianga."

Marilyn Horne, in the title role, sounded a bit dry of throat and tired at first, but she warmed up for her vengeance aria to end Act I in a blaze of vocal pyrotechnics. On the whole, the evening did not find her in absolute top form, but Miss Horne's second best is anybody else's triumph. She ran out of breath at times in the final act's grand battle aria, which would have severely tested the powers of a steam boiler. Handel seldom wrote one note where 10 or 20 would do. She also contributed one of the premiere's more apparent flubs when she made a false start at one point in the finale. The house broke out in laughter and Miss Horne herself lost a desperate battle to keep a straight face.

Able, intermittently splendid performances also were turned in by Edda Moser (Armida), Dano Raffanti (Goffredo) and Diane Kesling (A Mermaid).

Along with technically polished singing, any Baroque opera needs spectacular stage effects if it is to come anywhere close to the spirit of that age of grand theatrical gestures. Mark Negin, making his debut as set and costume designer, provided a great deal of childish delight with a charming fire-breathing dragon, a waterfall of plastic ribbons, towers that opened out to become gardens—and the other way around—and scenes that magically transformed themselves in clouds of fog.

Frank Corsaro, in another of the evening's delayed debuts, directed the action with his usual ingenuity, but wisely stayed out of the way while sheer heroic vocalism was the point. Because of the rigidity of Baroque conventions, he was often hard put to find ways to keep things looking lively as singers spun out their florid repetitions and da capo arias. After Argante took a couple of turns around the stage in his chariot to fill up the time between verses, for instance, the novelty of that device wore out.

Two other welcome debuts added to the evening's satisfactions. Mario Bernardi, who early this season conducted the City Opera's beguiling *Cendrillon* (also a Canadian import, you remember), led this *Rinaldo* with great verve as well as sensitive concern for the singers.

Top Singles: 1985

1. "Careless Whisper," Wham!
2. "Say You, Say Me," Lionel Richie
3. "Separate Lives," Phil Collins and Marilyn Martin
4. "I Want to Know What Love Is," Foreigner
5. "Money for Nothing," Dire Straits
6. "We Are the World," USA for Africa
7. "Broken Wings," Mr. Mister
8. "Everybody Wants to Rule the World," Tears for Fears
9. "The Power of Love," Huey Lewis and the News
10. "We Built This City," Starship
11. "St. Elmo's Fire," John Parr
12. "Can't Fight This Feeling," REO Speedwagon
13. "Crazy for You," Madonna
14. "Easy Lover," Phillip Bailey and Phil Collins
15. "Everytime You Go Away," Paul Young
16. "Don't You (Forget About Me)," Simple Minds
17. "Take on Me," a-ha
18. "Party All the Time," Eddie Murphy
19. "Everything She Wants," Wham!
20. "Shout," Tears for Fears
21. "Alive and Kicking," Simple Minds
22. "I Miss You," Klymaxx
23. "Sea of Love," Honeydrippers
24. "Cool it Now," New Edition
25. "Part-Time Lover," Stevie Wonder
26. "Saving All My Love for You," Whitney Houston
27. "Sussudio," Phil Collins
28. "Oh Sheila," Ready for the World
29. "A View to a Kill," Duran Duran
30. "One More Night," Phil Collins
31. "Cherish," Kool & the Gang
32. "Heaven," Bryan Adams
33. "The Heat Is On," Glenn Frey
34. "Raspberry Beret," Prince and The Revolution
35. "You're the Inspiration," Chicago
36. "If You Love Somebody Set Them Free," Sting
37. "Miami Vice Theme," Jan Hammer
38. "Freeway of Love," Aretha Franklin
39. "Don't Lose My Number," Phil Collins
40. "Never," Heart
41. "Things Can Only Get Better," Howard Jones
42. "The Boys of Summer," Don Henley
43. "Rhythm of the Night," DeBarge
44. "We Don't Need Another Hero," Tina Turner
45. "We Belong," Pat Benatar
46. "Loverboy," Billy Ocean
47. "All I Need," Jack Wagner
48. "One Night In Bangkok," Murray Head
49. "Never Surrender," Corey Hart
50. "Lovergirl," Teena Marie

I've said that playing the blues is like having to be black twice. Stevie Ray Vaughan missed on both counts, but I never noticed.

Personal Essay
B.B. King

"Michael Jackson Inks Multimillion-Dollar Deal With Pepsi," *Rolling Stone*, June 19, 1986:

Whether or not it's the choice of a new generation, Pepsi's definitely generating a ton of money for Michael Jackson. Over the next three years, Jackson will make at least three commercials for Pepsi as part of the most lucrative advertising deal ever negotiated between a celebrity and a corporation: the singer will make $10 million.

Jackson and his brothers earned roughly $5.5 million when they appeared in two Pepsi commercials in 1984 and signed a tour-sponsorship deal with the soft drink company. In the new deal, Jackson is committed to producing two pieces of original music for the new ads. The singer's manager, Frank DiLeo, said that a song from Jackson's upcoming LP, due this fall, may also be used for one of the commercials. Jackson will film a minimum of two spots plus a Spanish-language ad. Pepsi plans to show the commercials worldwide and will premiere the first one in early 1987.

Under the terms of the deal, Jackson will be involved in writing the spots, choosing the directors, and designing the visuals. The contract also calls for Jackson to become a "creative consultant" for Pepsi in 1988, at which point he will direct a commercial itself. And while it is not definite Pepsi would be the sponsor of any forthcoming Jackson tour, Pepsi USA President Roger Enrico said that "whatever activities Michael does in support of his new album, we will be involved…."

Enrico estimates that the cost of the Jackson ad campaign, including production cost and airtime, "will be well in excess of $50 million." He has no doubt Michael is worth the price. The 1984 ads are credited with sharply boosting Pepsi sales. "My judgment is that these amounts of money, which seemed to be huge, do in fact payoff," Enrico said.

Jackson reportedly does not drink Pepsi himself and will not even hold the product in his hand for the ads, but, according to Pepsi spokesman, a truckload of the beverage is dropped off at his house every week.

"The Rod Stewart Concert Video, Video News," *Rolling Stone*, June 19, 1986:

Rod Stewart has one of the biggest egos in the music business, and every ounce of it is on display in the Rod Stewart Concert Video. There's not a moment when he's not swaggering, strutting and preening as he dominates the screen.

If he weren't having so much fun, this would be completely repellent. But Stewart seasons his posing with a sense of glee that, combined with the driving precision of his band, produces an unexpectedly entertaining show.

The cassette opens with an audio-visual bio that's just short enough to avoid being boring. Stewart begins the concert footage with a string of his hits starting with "Infatuation" and proceeding to "Tonight's the Night," "Young Turks," and "Passion." Between songs, he shows a reedy, easygoing magnetism that helps this tape escape the tedium that dogs most concert tapes.

"The New Lure of the Neighborhood," Nancy McKeon,
New York Magazine, June 17, 1985:

Only a few years ago, New York retailing mostly meant Saturday's Generation shopping in the Cellar while filling up the Gaps. But now, in the full bloom of the boutique age, with Benettons around every corner, shopping is becoming a neighborhood thing.

Outside of the city, discounters are nibbling at the bottom line of big stores. But in New York, where shoppers still trek regularly to Macy's, Bloomingdale's, and the other emporiums, it's the smaller retailers who are increasingly taking the initiative by creating "shopping centers" in residential neighborhoods, each with its own personality. There's the glossy Madison Avenue strip, now stretching into the Eighties, and raffish West Broadway in SoHo, the Fast Fashion of Columbus Avenue, and the energetic funk of NoHo. Chelsea's sprouting too: Gear, a home-fashion wholesaler, just opened on Seventh Avenue, and the neighborhood's major anchor, Barneys, will open its new women's store next winter, by which time Benetton's "superstore" will have opened down the block. The East Village has its own batch of offbeat boutiques and even lower Third and Fifth Avenues are bubbling over with new food and clothing shops.

The big stores are undeniably having their problems. April was the eleventh straight month of depressed sales—down 3.5 percent from April 1984, the largest monthly decline since August 1976, according to the monthly spot check of New York department stores by *The New York Times*.

New Yorkers have more opportunity to shop than ever before—retailing is increasingly a seven-day-a-week business. So the scramble for the customer's dollar has never been quite so intense. And when the target is the affluent consumer, the challenge to the retailer is novel. "Basically," says Ellen Fine, who owns the Fine Design store in the Flatiron district, "everybody has everything they need already," leaving the stores to compete for discretionary purchases.

Some of New York's big retailers have suggested that the younger consumers no longer think of the large stores as weekend entertainment. A cruise up Columbus or Madison or West Broadway certainly reinforces that impression: one big-store executive acknowledges that new shopping streets have siphoned off many of the recreational shoppers, and that the "intensity" of the weekend traffic isn't what it once was.

Meanwhile, the other major retailers are courting consumers by becoming "promotional," creating one-day sales and offering regular merchandise at short-term discount prices. The frequency of these price cuts, and the fact that regular prices are often pumped up so that items can be offered at significant reductions, has had negative results. The strategy has frequently led to sales increases in the short run but shrinking profits. In the longer term, it has trained customers to be cynical about the regular prices and to wait for sales.

These problems may be cyclical, of course, but the big stores are experiencing difficulties that just won't go away. Twenty years ago, says consultant Arlene Hirst, the innovative stores concentrated on developing private-label fashions, a fondly remembered example being the "Parisiennes" collection at Lord & Taylor, adapted from the Paris originals. Then came the designer era. Stores began promoting names that soon became international brands and, unfortunately for the stores that launched them, widely available. Now there's rekindled interest in private-label programs, with their potential for greater profits (items that are exclusive to one store can be comparison-shopped only in the most general way).

At the same time, the department stores are trying to produce excitement and increase store traffic by extending the designer-boutique formula to non-fashion areas, often asking manufacturers to share the expense of building discrete "environments." Ralph Lauren in domestic linens, Esprit in casual sportswear, Mikasa and Fitz & Floyd in china, even Macy's Metropolitan Museum of Art shop, are examples of the trend.

In big stores, manufacturers and importers are cooperating. But at street level, they're in hot competition. Many of the boutiques on Madison, Columbus, and West Broadway—Tahari, Laura Ashley, Hot House ceramics, Crabtree & Evelyn toiletries, MGA sportswear, and coming soon to Columbus, Murjani—are actually retail outlets owned, franchised, or licensed by manufacturers. They're joining the risky retail world in order to capture a bigger chunk of the dollar than plain old wholesalers get.

The feast-or-famine nature of retailing hasn't stopped developers from packing their projects with stores or from trying to mall the island of Manhattan. Like fast-food outlets, malls are essentially a suburban phenomenon that needs time to work its way into New Yorkers' daily routines.

Despite their problems, malls will continue to proliferate, mostly because builders want them. Still, there are growing pains. Trump Tower is the most successful, but it has had a couple of casualties, Fila and Loewe. Park Avenue Plaza's elegant specialty stores—like Chartwell Booksellers and Darabin Ltd., a haberdasher for executive women—remain semi-hidden treasures. Herald Center, trying hard to be uptown in the heart of Herald Square, is only a little more than half rented. And South Street Seaport's sales are only as good as the weather on any given weekend.

1990–1999

The 1990s, called the "Era of Possibilities" by *Fortune* magazine, were dominated by an economic expansion that became the longest in the nation's history. Characterized by steady growth, low inflation, low unemployment and dramatic gains in technology-based productivity, the expansion was particularly meaningful to computer companies and the emerging concept known as the Internet. Americans of all backgrounds invested in the soaring stock market and dreamed of capturing a dot-com fortune.

The decade opened in an economic recession, a ballooning national debt, and the economic hangover of the collapse of much of the savings and loan industry. The automobile industry produced record losses; household names like Bloomingdale's and Pan Am declared bankruptcy. Housing values plummeted and factory orders fell. Media headlines were dominated by issues such as rising drug use, crime in the cities, racial tensions, and the rise of personal bankruptcies. Family values ranked high on the conservative agenda, and despite efforts to limit Democrat Bill Clinton to one term as president, the strength of the economy played a critical role in his re-election in 1996.

Guided by Federal Reserve Chair Alan Greenspan's focus on inflation control and Clinton's early efforts to control the federal budget, the U.S. economy soared, producing its best economic indicators in three decades. By 1999, the stock market produced record returns, job creation was at a 10-year high, and the federal deficit was falling. Businesses nationwide hung "Help Wanted" signs outside their doors and even paid signing bonuses to acquire new workers. Crime rates, especially in urban areas, plummeted to levels unseen in three decades, illegitimacy rates fell, and every year business magazines marveled at the length of the recovery, asking, "Can it last another year?"

The stock market set a succession of records throughout the period, attracting thousands of investors to stocks for the first time, including the so-called glamour offerings of high-technology companies. From 1990 to the dawn of the twenty-first century, the

Dow Jones Industrial Average rose 318 percent. Growth stocks were the rage; of Standard and Poor's 500 tracked stocks, almost 100 did not pay dividends. This market boom eventually spawned unprecedented new wealth, encouraging early retirement to legions of aging baby boomers. The dramatic change in the cultural structure of corporations continued to threaten the job security of American workers, who had to be more willing to learn new skills, try new jobs, and move from project to project. Profit sharing, which allowed workers to benefit from increased productivity, become more common. Retirement programs and pension plans became more flexible and transferable, serving the needs of a highly mobile work force. The emerging gap of the 1990s was not always between the rich and the poor, but the computer literate and the technically deficient. To symbolize the changing role of women in the work force, cartoon character Blondie, wife of Dagwood Bumstead, opened her own catering business which, like so many small businesses in the 1990s, did extremely well. For the first time, a study of family household income concluded that 55 percent of women provided half or more of the household income.

In a media-obsessed decade, the star attraction was the long-running scandal of President Bill Clinton and his affair with a White House intern. At its climax, while American forces were attacking Iraq, the full House of Representatives voted to impeach the president. For only the second time in American history, the Senate conducted an impeachment hearing before voting to acquit the president of perjury and obstruction of justice.

In the music scene, a revival of the singer-songwriter movement of the 1970s, closely connected to the Lilith Fair, brought artists like Norah Jones and Sarah McLachlan to the fore. This movement was well represented by the multi-platinum *Jagged Little Pill* by Alanis Morissette. Grunge remained a local phenomenon until the breakthrough of Nirvana in 1991 with their album *Nevermind*, which also led to the widespread popularization of alternative rock in the 1990s. Nirvana's massive hit "Smells Like Teen Spirit" opened the way for alternative rock to enter the musical mainstream via groups like the Red Hot Chili Peppers with their album *Blood Sugar Sex Magik*. As the decade came to a close, teen pop singers and groups including Backstreet Boys, 'N Sync, 98 Degrees, Hanson, Christina Aguilera, Britney Spears, Jennifer Lopez, and Destiny's Child became popular, targeted at younger members of Generation Y. Mariah Carey's duet with Boyz II Men "One Sweet Day," recorded in 1995, spent 16 weeks atop the Hot 100 and was pronounced song of the decade.

During the decade, America debated limiting abortion, strengthening punishment for criminals, replacing welfare for work, ending Affirmative Action, dissolving bilingual education, elevating educational standards, curtailing the rights of legal immigrants, and imposing warnings on unsuitable material for children on the Internet. Nationwide, an estimated 15 million people, including smokers, cross-dressers, alcoholics, sexual compulsives, and gamblers, attended weekly self-help support groups; dieting became a $33 billion industry as Americans struggled with obesity.

The impact of the GI Bill's focus on education, rooted in the decade following World War II, flowered in the generation that followed. The number of adult Americans with a four-year college education rose from 6.2 percent in 1950 to 24 percent in 1997. Despite this impressive rise, the need for a more educated population, and the rapidly rising expectations of the technology sector, the century ended with a perception that the decline in public education was one of the most pressing problems of the decade. Throughout the decade, school violence escalated, capturing headlines year after year in widely dispersed locations across the nation.

The 1990s gave birth to $150 tennis shoes, condom boutiques, pre-ripped jeans, Motorola, 7.7-ounce cellular telephones, rollerblading, TV home shopping, the Java computer language, digital cameras, DVD players, and Internet shopping. And in fashion, a revival of the 1960s' style brought back miniskirts, pop art prints, pants suits, and the A-line. Black became a color worn at any time of day and for every purpose. The increasing role of consumer debt in driving the American economy also produced an increase in personal bankruptcy and a reduction in the overall savings rate. At the same time, mortgage interest rates hit 30-year lows during the decade, creating refinancing booms that pumped millions of dollars into the economy, further fueling a decade of consumerism.

1993 PROFILE

As a student at Howard University, Anwar X. Holliday noted that the student body included a large number of New Yorkers who missed the rap and hip hop performances so common in the city's parks and squares, so he decided to get into the promotion of music on campus.

Life at Home

- Anwar X. Holliday was born on a Monday in Queens, New York, October 16, 1971.
- His father John 23X Holliday immediately associated his son's Monday birth with the lead character in the 1970s blaxploitation film *Black Caesar*.
- *Black Caesar* starred ex-NFL player Fred "The Hammer" Williamson, who portrayed "Bumpy" Johnson's rise to the top of the Harlem numbers rackets.
- The theme song by soul singer James Brown began with the famous line "I was born in New York City on a Monday," hence, the connection between Anwar and his father's favorite song and favorite movie.
- "Blaxploitation" was a term used to describe the way in which Hollywood stereotyped blacks only as gangsters, pimps, hookers, dope dealers and addicts in movies of the era.
- While serving a short prison sentence involving a street-side Three-card Monte scam, John Holliday became involved with the Five Percenters, a Nation of Islam offshoot, and took the name of John 23X.
- The "X" represented the rejection of the "slave name" Holliday and signified that his true last name was unknown.
- Clarence 13X (Clarence Jowers Smith) founded the Five Percent Nation, which was based on Lost Found Muslim Lesson Number Two, written by Nation of Islam founder W.D. Fard in 1934.
- Fard wrote that 85 percent of the Earth's population were uncivilized people, 10 percent slavers, and the remaining five percent poor righteous teachers of the truths of Allah.
- Anwar's love of music came as a direct influence from his mother, Juanita, who had performed in several girl singing groups as a teen.

While still a student, Anwar X. Holliday promoted music on the campus of Howard University.

- She and several cousins had made the natural transition from church choir to performing covers of songs by popular girl groups of the 1960s, like the Supremes and Martha and the Vandellas at block parties and recreational halls around Queens.
- In 1969, Juanita and John Holliday met, and later that year the couple settled into a walk-up duplex in the Hollis section of Queens.
- When Anwar's grandparents migrated from the South in the 1950s, Queens was a magnet for blacks seeking upward mobility.
- Harlem had been the original black Mecca during the great South and North migration in the early part of the twentieth century.
- Due to deterioration and overcrowded conditions in Harlem, the focus shifted to Brooklyn during the 1930s and 1940s.
- By the 1950s, Queens had become home to jazz legends like Count Basie, Louis Armstrong, Ella Fitzgerald, and Dizzy Gillespie.
- By the 1960s, the tremendous influx of blacks and Latinos from the other boroughs triggered "white flight" from Queens to the more suburban Nassau and Suffolk County on Long Island.
- During the fall of 1978, eight-year-old Anwar started third grade at St. Pascal-Baylon Elementary School, a Catholic school that required its students to wear a blue and yellow uniform every day.
- While raising Anwar within the Five Percent Nation at home, his parents felt that a Catholic school would provide their son with a better education than the public school system.
- Anwar quickly learned to avoid the older bullies who waited outside the school each day to rob the younger kids of their possessions.
- At the same time, the hip hop culture was forming in New York City as block parties became increasingly numerous, especially when they incorporated DJs who played popular genres of music, especially funk and soul music.
- Soon DJs began isolating the percussion breaks of popular songs, a technique then common in Jamaican dub music, and developed turntable techniques, such as scratching, beat mixing/matching, and beat juggling that created a base that could be rapped over.
- Rapping was a vocal style in which the artist speaks lyrically, in rhyme and verse, generally to an instrumental or synthesized beat, which is almost always in 4/4 time.
- Anwar's father believed hip hop had emerged as a direct response to the watered-down, Europeanized disco music that permeated the airwaves.
- The first hip hop recording Anwar heard was The Sugarhill Gang's "Rapper's Delight," initially at home and then throughout the neighborhood.
- Hollis was a working middle-class neighborhood south of the Grand Central Parkway and east of 184th Street.
- Anwar grew into his teens in a neighborhood filled with private homes and busy main streets with stores and movie theaters.
- By the mid-1980s, a trend developed among black youngsters nationwide in which academic achievement lost its importance and was replaced by "street credibility," represented by various forms of thuggery in the pursuit of a cool image.
- Despite being from solid homes where good grades were expected, Anwar and his crew of friends shared many of the same ideas as their peers and allowed their grades to slip in solidarity.
- When the crew played basketball at 205th Street Park, they couldn't help noticing the drug dealers and other hustlers with their Mercedes and BMW cars, gold watch chains, and Movado watches.
- They also surrounded themselves with rap music.
- Anwar's infatuation with street life came to an abrupt end when his best friend's grandfather was abducted and shot in an attempted robbery and drug extortion scheme.
- In 1989, Anwar graduated from Harlem Brothers Rice Catholic High School with plans to attend Howard University in Washington, DC.

Anwar and his cousin Malik supported their way through Howard with a variety of entrepreneurial efforts.

Life at Work

- The fall of 1989 found Anwar X. Holliday as a member of the freshman class at Howard University in Washington, DC.
- Howard was founded in 1867 to educate freed slaves and their descendents.
- Anwar was joined at Howard by his cousin Malik, who, like Anwar, had chosen radio and television media studies as a major.
- Like most college students, Anwar and his cousin were plagued by cash flow shortages and were constantly brainstorming for a solution to this problem.
- They decided to be entrepreneurs, moving from project to project.
- Along with his brother Raymond, Malik's father had ridden the popularity wave of vinyl siding and window installation to achieve middle-class stability.
- So the two enterprising young men secured a $500 loan from their fathers to purchase the Supreme Bean Pies and Cookies concern from the Nation of Islam Bakery in Newark.
- They also arranged to distribute *The Final Call* newspaper, published by the Nation of Islam on campus.
- After that, the two young men roamed the campus selling pies, cookies and newspapers—it was a great education in business, human psychology and accounting.
- Not only did the venture provide snacks and much-needed income, but it gave the pair a high level of exposure and visibility.
- Then, when Anwar repaid the loan on time—with interest—he elicited a look of respect from his father that he had been seeking his entire life.

The cousins started a pie business with a loan from Anwar's father

- Being a New Yorker, Anwar noted that the Howard student body included a substantial percentage of New Yorkers who missed the rap and hip hop performances so common in the city's parks and squares.
- So Anwar decided on his summer break that he would get into the promotion of music on campus.
- In the fall, when the pair returned to Howard with the summer money they had earned working with their fathers, they began to stage special events on campus, especially parties at the fraternity houses.
- With his Five Percent connections, Anwar was able to bring the highly popular Big Daddy Kane to Howard for his football homecoming party.
- From that point on, their parties and events became the most popular on campus; Anwar quickly learned to balance the risks associated with an event, such as a concert, with the financial rewards it might bring.
- After two years of working in special events, Anwar knew he wanted a career in music.
- In 1991, he got his start as an assistant to Dante Ross, who was an artists and repertoire (A&R) man for a group called Brand Nubian, a Five Percent group that came to prominence in the 1980s.
- The Five Percent belief that white men were devils while black men were gods echoed loudly in hip hop lyrics.
- A white man, Dante Ross, seemed highly unlikely to sponsor and support groups that espoused such beliefs.
- However, Ross was a professional, and Anwar took note of his dedication to the groups under his care.
- More than just talent scouts, A&Rs were responsible for shaping the artists' sound, finding material to record, and generally nurturing an artist's career.
- They also attempted to predict musical trends, discover new artists, and then mold them into the image that maximized their talent.

Anwar and Malik worked distributing The Final Call *on campus.*

- At smaller labels, the job might consist of seeking out new talent the hard way: going to shows, scouring the Internet, sifting through endless demos, and then bringing the artists to the label, signing them, and bringing an album to fruition.
- Often, A&R professionals were a sort of liaison between the label and the artists.
- They oversaw most of the interaction between an artist's management and the label, lawyers, and publishing/distribution companies.
- It was the "Golden Age" in mainstream hip hop, characterized by its diversity, quality, innovation and influence.
- Its strong themes of Afrocentricity and political militancy blended well with music that was highly experimental and whose sampling was eclectic.
- "It seemed that every new single reinvented the genre," according to *Rolling Stone*.
- The artists most often associated with the period were Public Enemy, Boogie Down Productions, Eric B. & Rakim, De La Soul, A Tribe Called Quest, Gang Starr, Big Daddy Kane, and the Jungle Brothers.
- The freedom and creativity also spawned gangsta rap, a subgenre of hip hop that reflects the violent lifestyles of inner-city American black youths, best epitomized by rappers such as Schoolly D and Ice T.
- By the early 1990s, gangsta rap became the most commercially lucrative subgenre of hip hop.
- In 1992, Dr. Dre released *The Chronic*, an album that founded a style called G Funk, which was further developed and popularized by Snoop Dogg's 1993 album *Doggystyle*.
- The Wu-Tang Clan shot to fame around the same time and brought the East Coast back into the mainstream of rap, when the West Coast dominated.
- Another act Ross had worked with at Def Jam was 3rd Bass, one of the first successful interracial hip hop groups, featuring Michael Berrin, also known as MC Serch.
- Michael Berrin, who was raised in mostly black Far Rockaway, Queens, spent his teenage weekends facing initially hostile crowds at the Latin Quarter.
- Berrin continued getting to the mike and finally earned respect for his rhyme skills and give-no-quarter attitude.
- Through Dante Ross, Anwar met Michael Berrin.
- Ross, after his successful experience with 3rd Bass, had moved into management and production, while Anwar, following his internship under Ross of Def Jam, had moved into A&R with Sony.
- In his management and production capacity, Berrin came into contact with Nas, a young rapper with a reputation as one of the best lyricists ever.
- As Nas's manager, Berrin brought demos to Anwar's office.
- It was Anwar's first major signing.

The music of rapper Ice-T depicted the violent lifestyles of inner city youth.

Life in the Community: Queens, New York

- Hollis was a neighborhood within the southeastern section of the New York City borough of Queens.
- The boundaries of the predominantly African-American community were considered to be the Far Rockaway Branch of the Long Island Rail Road to the west, Hillside Avenue to the north, and Francis Lewis Boulevard to the east.
- The first European settlers were Dutch homesteaders in the seventeenth century.
- A century later, early in the American Revolutionary War, it was the site of part of the Battle of Long Island, a conflict in which the rebel Brigadier General Nathaniel Woodhull was captured at a tavern.
- The area remained rural until 1885, when developers built houses on 136 acres, and three years later it became a part of New York City with the rest of the borough of Queens.
- Since the end of the Korean War, the neighborhood had been settled primarily by African-American middle class families.
- Since the rise of hip hop, the neighborhood has been a hotbed of rap talent, sparked primarily by the fact that hip hop producer and icon Russell Simmons was from this community, as was his brother Joseph, who along with two other neighborhood residents, formed the rap group Run-D.M.C.
- Young MC—winner of the second and final Grammy Award for Best Rap Performance—Ja Rule, and DJ Hurricane were also from Hollis.
- LL Cool J was from nearby St. Albans.
- Anwar X. Holliday grew up in the Hollis community during a radical shift in the outlook of black youth.
- Although Hollis was a working middle-class neighborhood, its young people took on the attitudes of the more impoverished and crime-ridden areas like the Bronx.
- Hip hop's beginning flowed from the Bronx through people like Afrika Bambaataa a DJ known as the Amen Ra of Universal Hip Hop Culture as well as the Father of The Electro Funk Sound.
- Through his co-opting of the street gang the Black Spades into the music and culture-oriented Universal Zulu Nation, he was responsible for spreading hip hop culture.
- Zulu nation was a collective of DJs, break dancers and graffiti artists who filled the void once occupied by gang culture by de-emphasizing violence and crime in the mid-seventies.
- In the mid-1980s, when Anwar was in his teens, the crack cocaine epidemic emerged and changed the nation.
- Young men and women like Anwar were affected by the glamorization of the violent, cash-fueled cocaine culture glorified through hip hop music and images he saw on the streets of Hollis.
- The price of a kilo of cocaine dropped from $35,000 in 1982 to $12,000 in 1984, when it was estimated that 650,000 people were employed in New York City drug trade.
- In the fashion world, Run-D.M.C.'s My Adidas set the tone for a very high premium to be placed on the hippest sneakers and athletic wear.
- Michael Jordan was already on his way to revolutionizing sports apparel with his landmark Nike deal.
- By 1987, Run-D.M.C. had negotiated a $1.7 million sneaker deal with Adidas—the same shoes kids were fighting life-and-death battles over in the streets of Hollis.
- Many diverse influences affected the evolution of hip hop: cash, corporations, sampling, crime, violence, but none more important than the music video.
- As rap videos emerged as a viable business, two black-owned companies rose to prominence in New York: Atlantis and Classic Concept.
- *Yo! MTV Raps* debuted in September 1988 and scored the highest ratings of any show in MTV history.
- *Yo! MTV Raps* forced the more conservative Black Entertainment Television network to introduce *Rap City* a year later.
- Exposure and sales were increased dramatically by bringing the images of the clothes, cars, jewelry and attitudes into the average American home.

Fab 5 Freddy hosted the highest rated MTV show in its history, Yo!MTV Raps.

HISTORICAL SNAPSHOT
1993

- Cream reunited for a performance at their Rock and Roll Hall of Fame induction ceremony in Los Angeles; other inductees included Creedence Clearwater Revival, Ruth Brown, the Doors, Van Morrison, and Sly & the Family Stone

- In Super Bowl XXVII the Buffalo Bills became the first team to lose three consecutive Super Bowls when they were defeated by the Dallas Cowboys, 52–17

- Bobby Brown was arrested in Augusta, Georgia, for simulating a sex act onstage

- Oprah Winfrey interviewed Michael Jackson during a television prime time special; it was Jackson's first television appearance in 14 years

- A van bomb parked below the North Tower of the World Trade Center in New York City exploded, killing six and injuring over 1,000

- Whitney Houston's single "I Will Always Love You" became the longest-running number one single of all time

- Willie Nelson, John Cougar Mellencamp, Neil Young and more than 30 other artists performed at Farm Aid 6 in Ames, Iowa

- Janet Jackson's *Janet* debuted at #1—the first to do so by a female artist in the era of Nielsen SoundScan, an information and sales tracking system; the album included the single "That's the Way Love Goes"

- The Intel Corporation shipped the first P5 Pentium chips

- On his thirty-fifth birthday, Prince announced that he was changing his name to an unpronounceable symbol, which led to him being called The Artist Formerly Known as Prince

- Billy Joel released his final studio album before quitting music after 20 years

- Pearl Jam's second album *Vs.* sold 950 000 copies in one week to set a new record

- Wu-Tang Clan released *Enter the Wu-Tang (36 Chambers)*

- Bureau of Alcohol, Tobacco and Firearms agents raided the Branch Davidian compound in Waco, Texas, with a warrant to arrest leader David Koresh on federal firearms violations; four agents and 81 Davidians died

- *Unforgiven* won the Academy Award for Best Picture

- Andrew Wiles won worldwide fame after presenting his proof of Fermat's Last Theorem a problem that had been unsolved for more than three centuries

Selected Prices

Alarm Clock $9.99
Car Seat...$65.00
Christmas Tree, Artificial....................................$124.99
Comforter...$26.88
Lawn Mower...$289.00
Leggings $15.00
Light Bulb, Halogen $8.96
Microwave Oven..$99.00
Shower Curtain $19.77
Videotape, Three Blank $8.49

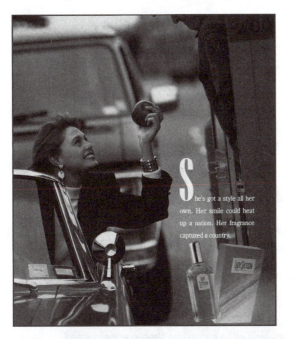

"Patents; The Jukebox Concept Applied to Music Video," Edmund L. Andrews, *The New York Times*, August 6, 1988:

WASHINGTON—"Everybody said I was an idiot," said Steven Peters, founder of Miami-based Video Jukebox Network. "But it works."

Mr. Peters' company received patent rights this week for an invention that lets television viewers select, by telephone, the music videos they want to hear a nearby station broadcast into their homes. The invention is already in operation at low-powered stations operated by the company in Florida, Texas and Maryland.

Mr. Peters explained: "Say you want to see Madonna sing 'Material Girl.' You pick up the phone in Jacksonville, dial 976-1010 and push 099." (The codes for each song are displayed regularly during the broadcast.) A computer at the station receives the call, logs the request and prepares the video for broadcast. Like a conventional jukebox, multiple requests are stacked up and played in turn.

As with other "976" numbers, the local telephone company bills the caller and splits receipts with the stations. A single music video costs $2.

"Nickelodeon to Offer Music Videos," *The New York Times*, March 12, 1991:

Nickelodeon, the cable channel for children, plans to begin a music video program aimed at creating a new marketplace for children's music.

Starting in July, the videos are to play as part of Nickelodeon's preschool programming, from 9 a.m. to 2 p.m., for ages 2 to 6. The programming is to include music of all types, from rock to rap to opera.

The idea was offered to Nickelodeon by the actress Shelley Duvall, who in recent years has become a successful producer of programs for children.

Ms. Duvall, who will be executive producer of the program, said yesterday that she expected to have eight videos ready to go on as a block of programming. "This is a groundbreaking idea," she said. "There has never been an outlet for children's music before. This will help children form their taste in music."

As is the case with the music videos on MTV and other channels, the children's videos will be supplied by record companies, which seek to recoup costs by selling albums. Ms. Duvall said she had received strong support from record company executives.

She said the videos would be chosen on the suitability of the lyrics and visuals for children. "They will be entertaining primarily," she said. "But I will also see that some are enlightening and educational."

"Pop View; Bobby Brown Brings a New Attitude to Pop," Peter Watrous," *The New York Times*, February 19, 1989:

Bobby Brown, short and thin and boyish, comes out in front of the sold-out Madison Square Garden audience wearing a bowler and smoking a cigar. The audience, which has been chanting "Bobby, Bobby" in anticipation, goes wild, screaming and rushing the stage. Mr. Brown breaks into his hit "Don't Be Cruel," his lithe, hard body moving almost impossibly fast, and, surrounded by his two male dancers (all three of them look too young to drink), he goes into a furious, intricate dance taken directly from a rap club, full of abrupt arm movements, hip gyrations and pumping knees.

For the next hour, he puts on a bravado performance that harks back to the glory days of the Apollo Theater, where soul acts used to tear up the place. He shows off dance steps, telling the audience that "this is my special walk," which drives them wild. He takes off his shirt, which drives them wild. He brings a girl up from the audience and demonstrates the proper seduction techniques. He sings, his hoarse, limited voice giving the sound of a man reduced to pleading. And he dances, and dances and dances.

The huge success of Mr. Brown, the 20-year-old performer who has sold 3.5 million records and whose album *Don't Be Cruel* has topped Billboard's pop chart for five weeks, is an indication that a new school of singers, who mix classic soul singing with the beats and attitude of rap, is on its way to becoming an integral part of mainstream music. Mr. Brown's concert audience, and those buying his records, are both black and white.

His success is a milestone for blacks in pop. The music he makes is the first to fully incorporate rap's beats, rhythms and hard street attitudes into a pop-music format. The mixture works, and, accompanied by Mr. Brown's rap-influenced dancing, and his rap attitude, it is startlingly new.

Mr. Brown has had the stage set for him by rap, which has reached a more limited but still sizable mainstream audience. Rap has introduced contemporary black musical culture to white America in a way that hasn't been done since the last golden age of black popular music in the 60s and early 70s, the time of Motown and Aretha Franklin. And rap, with its lack of sonic or political compromise, has changed the rules in popular music.

The history of black music and white audiences in America is largely the history of racial mediation, where a Benny Goodman translates the music of Fletcher Henderson for the benefit of a bigger audience, or the Beastie Boys use heavy metal and add a disarming cartoonishness to hip hop. By contrast, Mr. Brown doesn't offer a hint of compromise for a white audience.

A friend recently asked me, after I had seen Mr. Brown perform, whether he was as good as Michael Jackson. I was stumped by the question because they represent such radically different sensibilities, from such different traditions; they mean entirely different things.

Mr. Brown, from projects in the tough Roxbury section of Boston, presents himself as the kid next door—the black kid next door. Mr. Jackson is E.T., the creator of an otherworldly, more intricate set of images. And while some black artists—notably Prince and Mr. Jackson—have crossed over to reach a white audience, the references behind their ambiguous, eccentric facades are to Joni Mitchell and Gene Kelly.

continued

"Pop View; Bobby Brown Brings a New Attitude to Pop," Peter Watrous," *The New York Times*, February 19, 1989:

(continued)

Mr. Brown is from Roxbury; his context is the jazz-tinged black pop of Donny Hathaway and Stevie Wonder. Mr. Jackson is substantially more complex, in both the image he's built and in his showmanship. If you put him on stage next to Mr. Brown, he'd seem gifted, but from a different age. Mr. Jackson's image bank is Hollywood; Mr. Brown's is the black music of the last two decades.

Pop music always finds a way to combine styles that work, from country-rock to pop-jazz. In the combination of rap rhythm and pop melody, Mr. Brown covers the current marketplace. His songs, each armed with a solid melodic hook and a catchy title ("Don't Be Cruel," "My Prerogative") and thunderous rap beats, sound as much at home on a mainstream station as they do mixed into WBLS's *Rap Attack* radio show, surrounded by rap hits.

The music has all the necessary dance power, but it is pop in a more traditional sense as well—there are obvious melodies, it is sung not spoken (though he raps on one tune), and the music is played by instruments, not electronically sampled or taken from a record.

Beyond the music, Mr. Brown in concert is a wild, extroverted performer—so much so that in Columbia, Ga., which has a law forbidding lewdness on stage, he was arrested during a performance. Anybody watching his recent performance on *The Arsenio Hall Show*, where he turned the usually frigid television stage into a whirlwind of movement, climbing onto the drum risers, executing his athletically choreographed dances, would recognize a man made for the stage. Mr. Brown is the return of the classic soul man. His stamina is a teen echo of James Brown's energy.

Mr. Brown's success isn't a complete surprise. Twenty years after the soul man's commercial demise, the white world has absorbed the image thoroughly through bar bands, racist parodies (*The Blues Brothers*) and an appreciation of the music.

But five years ago, hip hop was considered a fad that only black audiences appreciated. The expanding popularity of rap (though it hasn't yet registered on the radio) and its uncompromised, tough rhythms and textures have paved the way for Mr. Brown's acceptance among white listeners. It has also changed the stakes in certain kinds of pop music.

Rap has brought far-reaching technological and esthetic changes to the sound and structure of popular music. There's a new vocabulary of electronic sounds that flaunt their artificiality and percussiveness, from sampled bits of older music to beefed-up machine-generated drumbeats. Just as important is the use of repetition, intercutting sounds and parts of songs that had their genesis in the manipulation of disk jockeys at rap dance clubs. More than any other form of popular music, rap has kept pace with the quick cuts and sudden juxtapositions of television.

1995 PROFILE

After years on the road riding in the back of an Econo-line van, the ultimate bar band—Hootie & the Blowfish—had become "an overnight success."

Life at Home

- The big break for Hootie & the Blowfish came in 1994 when David Letterman, the late night talk show host, heard one of their songs on New York radio station KNEW-FM and directed his producer to book the four musicians on his top-rated show.
- Then, following a set featuring songs from their self-penned album, the band heard Letterman say to the national audience, "If you don't have this album, there's something wrong with you," and sales tripled overnight.
- More Letterman invites were accepted; the next stop was the recording of the number one album in the nation in 1995.
- Their first album, *Cracked Rear View*, would sell 13 million copies and go platinum 16 times.
- Drummer and backup singer Jim "Soni" Sonefeld had fantasized that one day the band would be famous.
- But he did not wish to lose what they had.
- Soni enjoyed creating the exuberant, no-nonsense melodic sets that framed lead singer Darius Rucker's powerful rock/soul voice.
- The band had formed in 1986, originally with Brantley Smith as drummer; Soni took his place in 1989.
- Born October 20, 1964, Soni started his music career playing drums in the basement of his childhood home near Chicago, Illinois.
- His musical influences embraced classic rock and R&B bands that included Marvin Gaye; Blood, Sweat, and Tears; Led Zeppelin; and even Elton John.

Jim "Soni" Sonefeld of the overnight success band, Hootie & the Blowfish.

- He was a graduate of Naperville Central High School, one of the nation's top high schools, and then played soccer for the University of South Carolina in Columbia.
- Although intensely interested in music and drumming, Soni channeled his energy into sports, especially soccer, which kept him from playing in bands till he was well into college.
- At age 21, Soni joined his first band armed with his "flashy mullet and challenged fashion sense."
- He played in various bands in Columbia, South Carolina, from the mid- to late 1980s until he met and then joined a couple of college friends who had a cover band called Hootie & the Blowfish.
- The band had toured bars and frat houses in the South for many years before creating a self-financed, six-song EP *Kootchypop* in July 1993, and recorded with the help of R.E.M. producer Don Dixon.
- Atlantic Records A&R scout Tim Sommer, who was impressed with both their on-the-road reputation and the sounds they produced, struck a record deal in October 1994.
- Then came Letterman, endless play on radio, and the fame they sought.
- Hootie & the Blowfish was simply one more harebrained idea spawned in the freshman dormitory, where three-digit heat was both common and fully capable of frying a college student's brain.
- Mark Bryan was playing his guitar and reminiscing about high school when he heard Darius Rucker down the hall warbling along with the radio in his room.
- The two met and had visions of grandeur that would not remotely approach the phenomenal success of Hootie & the Blowfish.
- Within a month they did a gig at a chicken wing joint, calling themselves the Wolf Brothers.
- Their opening song that first night was "Take It Easy" by the Eagles, which foreshadowed their record-breaking style.

Hootie & the Blowfish.

- Soni joined Darius Rucker, Mark Bryan and Dean Felber in 1989, after they had adopted the Hootie & the Blowfish moniker borrowed from the nicknames of two college friends.
- It was a name that would delight and frustrate fans; they always wanted someone in the band to be named Hootie.
- By the time the four friends graduated, endless gigs at frat parties and local bars up and down the East Coast had created an enthusiastic following, so they started adding original material to their repertoire.
- When those songs went over well, the four decided to see if they could make a career out of it.
- "Even if we hadn't had a hit, I know we'd still be making music today, because it's exactly what we want to be doing," Mark Bryan said.
- The band's secret weapon, and the force that pulled all of its diverse influences together, was the voice of Darius Rucker, an expressive instrument brimming with gritty soul and subtle wit that connected with audiences on an almost spiritual level.
- Darius Rucker's voice allowed the band to experiment: funky, or rock, or bluegrass or a ballad, it didn't matter; the voice tied it all together.
- Their blend of pop, folk, blues, soul and rock made them hard to categorize, but it was easily accessible to anyone who loved good music.
- Atlantic Records, impressed by their regional draw, signed them and released *Cracked Rear View* in 1994.
- The album had been out for six months before the band played on the *Late Show with David Letterman*.
- The day after the show aired, sales went from four or five thousand a week to 17,000 a week, and eventually to number one on the Billboard charts the following spring.
- That's when the "blur" began for four guys living in two vans accompanied by a goofy name.

Life at Work

- Soni Sonefeld and his bandmates were in Omaha, Nebraska, of all places, when a young woman began screaming, repeatedly, "I want to have your children!" just as Hootie & the Blowfish were transitioning from an a cappella verse of "Motherless Child" before launching into "I'm Going Home."
- After the concert was over, Soni didn't remember the incident; it happened too often.
- Life had changed dramatically since *Cracked Rear View* had been issued, illustrated by photographs of their home base in Columbia, South Carolina, including a dilapidated "Heart of Columbia Hotel" sign and an intentionally out-of-focus picture of a statue of a wealthy owner of a plantation and slaves.
- Since the album had been launched, Soni found he didn't mind parking the old band bus to ride in custom rental coaches driven by someone else, complete with Sega video games and dressing rooms that didn't smell.
- It was quite a ride.
- Fans loved them, critics panned them, their album was selling 200,000 copies a week and they were on the road performing nightly.
- Steven Wine of the Associated Press carped, "Talk about your one-note Band. Hootie & the Blowfish appear to draw most of their inspirational materials from Kleenex."
- But while complaining about the album sporting too many crying songs, he added, "The South Carolina quartet with the silly name but serious musical talent sounds almost ready for the big time on its major label debut."
- Folk-rock had always spanned rock's generation gap: Counting Crows certified the neo-folk-rock boom with its 1993 debut album, *August and Everything After*, which sold five million copies.

Playing to sold out, screaming fans was a bit disconcerting to a band who was "afraid of being rock stars."

- The Gin Blossoms, Toad the Wet Sprocket, the Rembrandts, Deep Blue Something and a Hootie sound-alike, Dog's Eye View, had strummed their way onto the charts.
- In the new folk-rock, Baby Boomers heard pleasant echoes of past favorites from Bob Dylan to the Allman Brothers; younger listeners connected via R.E.M. and its collegiate-rock disciples.
- Folk-rock easily straddled the evolving world of radio formats from classic rock to modern rock.
- As one critic said: "Amid the distortion of grunge and the claustrophobic crunch of hip hop, Hootie's basic three-chord harmonies and steady-strummed guitars seem comforting, and they never attack. In the word most often used by Hootie's fans and detractors alike, the band sounds "normal."
- Soni saw the band as just a group of hardworking regular guys who loved football and golf, beer drinking, fast food eating and playing music.
- Guitarist Dean Felber, who majored in finance, set up the band as a corporate partnership, with tax withholding and health insurance like any other full-time job.
- "I guess we haven't let this thing sink in," Soni said, concerning the band's bestselling album, a hit song, the thrill of hearing their songs in constant radio rotation, and fans who could sing every word of every song.
- It was every bar band's dream and nightmare.
- "It's been this phantom thing that just caught up with us and we are still trying to figure out what it means," Soni said.
- "More than anything, we are afraid of being rock stars" Soni said.
- For years they had survived anonymity; the question now was, Could they survive fame?
- "We're breaking ground by being normal," Soni said. "In rock 'n' roll you got to do something whacked to be different. And now being ultra-normal is the most whacked thing of all."
- As one fan said after their show, "The music is happy, the songs make sense, you can understand the words."
- Even lead singer Darius Rucker's baseball cap and V-neck sweater communicated "normal," as did a clause in their contract that said the first 10 rows of any concert must be sold on a first come, first served basis to prevent institutional scalping of the best tickets.

- The "normal" band wanted "normal" people to get front-row tickets.
- Then they were paid the ultimate cultural compliment—next to being the answer to a Jeopardy question—when they were featured on the hit TV show *Friends*.
- During the episode, Monica, the character played by Courteney Cox, returned from a Hootie & the Blowfish concert with a hickey supposedly planted on her by a member of the band.
- What fun!
- When on the road touring, the band carried enough golf clubs to take impromptu trips to golf courses along the way or stop at the local YMCA to challenge all comers to a game of basketball.
- As the year ended, *Cracked Rear View* and the band won two Grammys—Best New Artist and Song of the Year by a duo or group for "Let Her Cry."
- They also took home an MTV Video Music Award for Best New Artist for "Hold My Hand"; also a Billboard Music Award for Album of the Year, a People's Choice Award for Album of the Year and a People's Choice Award for Best Selling Artist.

Monica, on the smash TV show Friends, spent an entire episode swooning over the Hootie & the Blowfish concert she went to.

Life in the Community: Columbia, South Carolina

- The main campus of the University of South Carolina, located in downtown Columbia, covers over 359 acres and accommodates approximately 26,000 students.
- Founded in 1801, USC offered 350 programs of study leading to bachelor's, master's, and doctoral degrees.
- Professional schools on the Columbia campus include business, engineering, law, medicine, and pharmacy.
- The University was founded as South Carolina College on December 19, 1801, by an act initiated by Governor Drayton in an effort to promote harmony between the affluent low country and the untamed backcountry.
- The park-like area known as the Horseshoe was listed on the National Register of Historic Places, and most of its buildings reflect the federal style of architecture in vogue in the early days of the nation, including the Caroliniana Library, the first freestanding academic library in the United States.
- The urban campus had exerted considerable influence on the music, pace and party atmosphere of Columbia—especially in a section of town known as Five Points.
- The best-known rock band to hail from South Carolina was Hootie & the Blowfish, but others came from there too—Marshall Tucker Band, the Swinging Medallions, Maurice Williams and the Zodiacs, and Crossfade.
- Native musicians, singers, and other artists born or raised in the state include James Brown, Dizzy Gillespie, Chubby Checker, Eartha Kitt, Peabo Bryson, Nick Ashford, Teddy Pendergrass, Josh Turner, Bill Anderson, Edwin McCain, Duncan Sheik, Rob Thomas, and John Phillips.
- The bluegrass scene has produced such bands as Hired Hands.
- South Carolina was known as the birthplace of three dances: the Shag; a product of early R&B and rock 'n' roll, the Charleston and the Big Apple, both popular in the Jazz Age.
- In the town of West Columbia, not far from the University of South Carolina, Bill Wells of the Blue Ridge Mountain Grass was the owner of a local music shop, next to which is held a weekly bluegrass show at the Pickin' Parlor.

Birds eye view of Columbia, South Carolina.

HISTORICAL SNAPSHOT
1995

- Rapper Tupac Shakur was serving one and a half to four and a half years in prison for a sexual abuse charge when *Me Against the World* became the number one album on the American Billboard 200 chart
- R.E.M. drummer Bill Berry left the stage during a concert in Switzerland after suffering a brain aneurysm; he underwent successful brain surgery two days later
- President Bill Clinton invoked emergency powers to extend a $20 billion loan to help Mexico avert financial collapse
- Astronaut Norman Thagard became the first American to ride into space aboard a Russian launch vehicle
- Mississippi ratified the Thirteenth Amendment, becoming the last state to approve the abolition of slavery
- Michael Jackson released his first double-album *HIStory*, which became the bestselling multiple album of all time, with 22 million copies sold worldwide
- Jerry Garcia died of a heart attack; the Grateful Dead disbanded soon after
- Rancid released their third studio album—*And Out Come the Wolves*—helping to revive mainstream interest in punk rock
- The Ramones released their final studio album, *Adios Amigos!*
- The Rock and Roll Hall of Fame opened in Cleveland, Ohio
- The Beatles released "Free as a Bird" as their first new single in over 20 years
- The Dow Jones Industrial Average closed above 4,000 and the NASDAQ Composite index closed above the 1,000 mark, both for the first time
- In Oklahoma City, 168 people, including eight Federal Marshals and 19 children, were killed at the Alfred P. Murrah Federal Building after Timothy McVeigh and one of his accomplices, Terry Nichols, set off a bomb
- Actor Christopher Reeve was paralyzed from the neck down after falling from his horse in a riding competition
- Hundreds gathered in Hiroshima, Nagasaki, Washington, DC, and Tokyo to mark the 50th anniversary of the dropping of the atomic bomb
- The DVD, an optical disc computer storage media format, was introduced
- eBay was founded
- *The Washington Post* and *The New York Times* published the Unabomber's manifesto, resulting in his arrest
- O.J. Simpson was found not guilty of double murder for the deaths of his former wife Nicole Brown Simpson and her friend Ronald Goldman
- The Million Man March was held in Washington, DC, conceived by Nation of Islam leader Louis Farrakhan
- The Dayton Agreement to end the Bosnian War was reached at Wright-Patterson Air Force Base near Dayton, Ohio
- *Toy Story*, the first-ever full-length computer animated feature film, was released by Pixar Animation Studios and Walt Disney Pictures

Selected Prices

Art Exhibit, New York	$8.00
Camcorder	$2,700.00
Cell Phone	$49.99
Chair, Walnut	$195.00
Low-Flush Toilet	$270.00
Roaster, Calphalon	$99.99
Rollerblades	$34.97
Shaving Cream	$0.99
Soccer Cleats	$129.95
Whirlpool Tub	$1,660.00

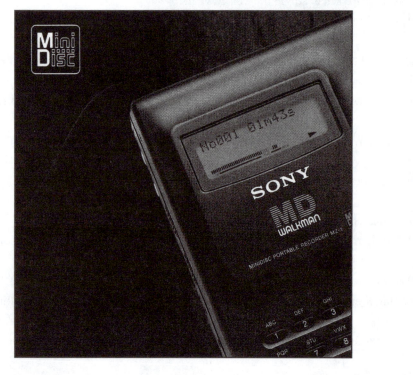

"They're Normal. And Rock Stars?" Neil Strauss, *The New York Times*, June 22, 1995:

WANTAGH, L.I., June 20—When Hootie & the Blowfish performed the second of two sold-out concerts at Jones Beach here on Tuesday night, there were no displays of angst, no cryptic lyrics, no resentment of its growing audience. There wasn't even a noisy guitar solo. There were just simple melodies, clean guitar lines and passionate vocals.

Hootie & the Blowfish are a slap in the face to alternative rock. The band's first album, *Cracked Rear View* (Atlantic), recently spent four weeks at No. 1 on the pop charts, breaking alternative rock's hegemony over successful young rock bands. Hootie & the Blowfish, a former bar band from Columbia, S.C., represents the return of the well-adjusted and the congenial to the rock world: it talks about sports onstage, dresses casually in T-shirts and seems to have neither a chip on its shoulder nor an ounce of artistic pretension. Its lyrics mime classic rock topics of love and betrayal by delivering strings of clichés as if they actually mean something again.

Here are a few of the clichés the band sang on Tuesday: "Tomorrow is just another day," "I'll take you to the promised land," "Nothing lasts forever" and "Don't look a gift horse in the mouth."

The band's vocalist and acoustic guitarist, whose name is Darius Rucker and not Hootie (as some fans yelling to him seemed to think), sang in a thick, expressive, well-trained baritone capable of a beautiful vibrato, hoarse emoting and descending melismas. Before "I'm Goin' Home," which Mr. Rucker wrote after his mother died two years ago, he sang a moving a cappella version of the blues song "Motherless Child" (which appears as a bonus track on *Cracked Rear View*).

Joined by Peter Holsapple of the Continental Drifters on keyboards, guitar and mandolin, Hootie & the Blowfish performed all 11 songs on *Cracked Rear View*. The band also trotted out an a cappella version of Barry Manilow's "Mandy" and two new mid-tempo rockers ("Tucker's Town" and "Fool"), which it said it wrote for its next album, to be released early next year.

Thanking its audience for its success profusely throughout the show, the band took sincerity to new heights. "You guys have made '95 the best year of my life," Mr. Rucker said to the crowd at one point during the show. "Thank you very much." There are few pop stars who admit to being grateful for the attention they receive, but Hootie & the Blowfish are not like other pop stars: they are the revenge of the normal.

Hootie & the Blowfish have just begun recording a follow-up to their year-and-a-half-old first album, *Cracked Rear View*, which after a slow start has sold 10 million copies to become the bestselling album of the year so far. The band recently entered a studio in San Rafael, Calif., to turn lyrics they wrote while in Bermuda this month into songs. They are working in anticipation of a summer release date.

continued

"They're Normal. And Rock Stars?" Neil Strauss, *The New York Times,* **June 22, 1995:**

(continued)

With the burdens of popularity knocking at its door, the band will not be holed up without respite. For New York fans with deep pockets or big hearts, Hootie & the Blowfish are to perform on Nov. 9 at Manhattan Center. The performance is to be part of a benefit for the New York Jets quarterback Boomer Esiason's Heroes Foundation. The foundation supports research on cystic fibrosis, which Mr. Esiason's four-year-old son, Gunnar, has. Tickets, which include dinner, are $750 (for one) to $12,500 (for what is called a platinum table). For information: (800) 789-4376.

The band is also to perform at Neil Young's annual benefit for his Bridge School at the Shoreline Amphitheater in the San Francisco area along with Mr. Young, Beck, the Pretenders and Emmylou Harris. The band's television appearances are to include a performance on Dec. 6 on Fox for the Billboard Music Awards and Dec. 12 on ABC for the special "Frank Sinatra: 80 Years My Way." On Nov. 21 on CBS, the band's singer, Darius Rucker, is to appear with his friend and fellow singer Edwyn McCain. The only major network the band is not planning to appear on happens to be NBC, though that does not mean that NBC has not got into the act.

Last week's episode of *Friends* centered on a Hootie & the Blowfish concert, from which the character played by Courteney Cox returns with a hickey supposedly planted on her by a member of the band. A spokesman for Hootie & the Blowfish said the band denied responsibility. The group, he said, was in the studio in San Rafael at the time.

I felt what it meant to have soul the day I picked up the cello at the tender age of nine. I experienced the raw beauty of music with the first stroke of the bow and the vibrato on my fingers. I learned about sorrow and joy and the swaying of the emotions with the plucking of those strings. But I grasped pure power when I went to a cello workshop comprising 180 cellos led by Yo Yo Ma on that September day back in 1997.

The workshop began at eight in the morning, and all 180 cellos were divided into 10 groups based on skill level. It did not bother me in the least to be in the second to lowest group. I was, after all, closer to the stage since the lowest and highest were positioned on the flat part of the half-circle on stage. If only I had sandbagged my audition a little more, I could have been even closer to the front.

The day was spent breaking down the songs that we were set to perform with each section working on their respective parts. For the first time in my short orchestra life, I could look over and not have to see the first violins always having the melody. They always looked so smug, knowing that they got to play the fun part. I, in the cello section, typically had some variation of the bass and beat. And when the song did allow us the rare opportunity of melody, you better believe we played our fingers off as loud as possible. This day was different. The best cellists got the reward of the melody and this time, I did not mind. I was proud to even be included with them.

As the day wore on, I started to lose sight of the end product. An 11-year-old has only so much capacity to push through the repetitiveness required to give a performance after only nine hours of rehearsal. Ultimately though, my patience paid off.

The curtain rose, the crowd applauded, and we began to play the theme from *2001: A Space Odyssey*. I froze momentarily. As the notes ascended, growing louder and louder, my knees shook with the weight of the sound of 180 cellos playing as loudly and as powerfully as the roaring waves of the ocean. The actual piece has a combination of brass, drums, and all variety of instruments, but on that evening, we were an army of cellos that declared that other instruments were not needed.

And I felt that moment of pride, that rush of power. I was not daunted by the humbling sound. I felt infused with energy as if I were standing on the edge of a great mountain with the ability to see far and know that my future was bright and full of confidence.

Personal Essay
Lucia Derks

Still, the pandemonium Hootie & the Blowfish elicits is a little surprising if you accept the judgment from certain quarters of the rock press that the band is "dull" and "conservative." Granted, the mates are not capering around the stage like shirtless punks, precipitating a Green Day-at-Woodstock mudslinging, nor are they inciting to riot, all off some of that choice or gangster backs. There's no hair show, no flash pots, no video screens, no Bee Girl. They're simply standing up there singing their well-liked songs, and a youngish high school to college age crowd is reacting fervently to them. Without smoke or mirrors, Hootie's solid, unpretentious pop evokes a surprisingly visceral reaction.

—Parke Puterbaughl, *Rolling Stone*, 1995

"What Makes Hootie Swim?"
Syracuse Herald Journal, May 10, 1996:

This is the central mystery of pop music: why Hootie & the Blowfish?

If anyone really knew, of course, there'd be a lot more Hooties on the horizon.

Atlantic records head Val Azzoli gave it a shot recently, describing the band's appeal as being based on "positive song-driven music in a world of angst-rock."

Azzoli's clearly a big fan, humming music to the positive tune of almost $100,000,000, which is how much the band has brought to Atlantic in selling an unbelievable 13 million copies of *Cracked Rear View*.

Two years after its release, Hootie & the Blowfish's major-label debut is still selling 200,000 copies a month. At that rate it's likely to pass Boston's 20-year record to become the top-selling debut of all time, even with competition from the Hooties' new *Fairweather Johnson*. That album, not incidentally, was snatched up by 411,000 fans during its first weekend.

In truth, neither Azzoli nor Atlantic—nor the band, come to think of it—had any idea of the potential booty in Hootie. Then the following happened and made all the difference:

In October 1994, video network VH-1 was getting rid of its hyphen and trying to overcome its reputation as MTV's ugly older sister. VH-1 was the graying end of the MTV Experience when it decided to "re-position" through an image makeover…. Once the province of veteran acts, VH1 became home to up-and-coming acts that stayed safely away from the edge.

And who better fit that category than Hootie & the Blowfish, a seemingly new band from a decidedly older sound rooted in familiar classic-rock and country-rock forms? Actually, the Hooties had been together almost a decade and had released three independent albums before Atlantic noticed they were selling pretty well in the South.

In February 1995, David Letterman, hardly known for musical hipness for some reason, anointed Hootie & the Blowfish as his "favorite band" and booked them almost as frequently as he did diet clown Richard Simmons….

The "runaway train" factor of popular culture took over from there.

But is it a fluke or a phenomenon?

Critics look at the songs and suggest a slick betrayal of pop craft.

Critics, it should be noted, had nothing to do with the success of Hootie & the Blowfish.

It's easy for them to slam the unbearable lightness of being Hootie. The music is often a bit sluggish, mostly medium tempo, mellow folk rock of no particular distinction. At worst: it's harmless.

1996 NEWS FEATURE

"NEW MUSIC: You've Heard This Rage Before: Hootie, Ritchie also Release New CDs," *Syracuse Herald American*, **April 28, 1996:**

RAGE AGAINST THE MACHINE
Evil Empire, Epic

On its long-awaited second effort, Rage Against the Machine is still mixing hard guitars with street beats, and still on the stump for revolution. The disc's liner notes provide contacts for the National Commission for Democracy in Mexico and a group in support of death row inmate Mumia Abu-Jamal.

But unlike Rage's genre-smashing 1992 debut—which contained perceptive, ultra liberal lyrics and equally acute musical provocations—this collection is organized around repetitive three- and four-note guitar riffs borrowed from bands like Blue Oyster Cult.

It's music you've heard before, pumped up with strident, fists-clinched slogans. Lead voice Jack de la Rocha may have lots to say about the impact of NAFTA and the hypocrisy of the gun-toting, right wing mindset ("Bulls on Paradise") but he rarely gets the chance to convey this point melodically.

The music is one long, unrelieved roar, punctuated by slapping funk backbeats and occasional tension-building interludes. As a result, even perceptive lines, such as a rant from "Wind Below," which criticizes the media for ignoring the plight of Mexican workers, are squandered.—Tom Moon, Knight Ridder

HOOTIE & THE BLOWFISH
Fairweather Johnson, Atlantic

Well-crafted, well-played, easy on the ear, vaguely familiar but resolutely nondescript, *Fairweather Johnson* is a fine effort for a band that has made being ordinary a badge of honor. It is also an apt follow-up to the stunningly successful, 13 million-selling, major-label debut, *Cracked Rear View*.
In *Fairweather Johnson*, the Hoosters revisited what is for them tried-and-true territory—a blend of mellow folk rock singer Darius Rucker's sweet-and-gruff baritone providing a rhythm and blues tinge. And they go at it with newfound confidence and flair.

There is a hint of updated Byrds ("Sad Caper") earnest Band-style country soul ("So Strange"), early Beatles-style sha-la-la harmonies ("Silly Little Pop Song"), catchy hooks ("She Crawls Away") and a touch of reflection ("Tootie").

Those who begrudge Hootie's success miss the point. Pop music might celebrate daring and change, but it has always rewarded conformity.—Fernando Gomez, Knight Ridder

BROOKS & DUNN
"Borderline"

Brooks & Dunn may be country's most successful duo ever, but you know you're in trouble artistically when the first single and lead track on their fourth album is a limp remake of the 70s pop hit "My Maria." It's no surprise: Kix Brooks and Ronnie Dunn's act was going stale even before 1994's dismal "Waiting on Sundown." "Borderline" does little to make it fresh again.

After "My Maria," you have to wade through some uninspired ballots, a couple of dimwitted rockers, and a bad Jimmy Buffet imitation ("More Than a Margarita") before you get to anything worthwhile. Buddy and Julie Miller's "My Love Will Follow You" is the album's best song, a simple declaration of devotion that benefits from Brooks & Dunn's nicely measured performance,

"Tequila Town" is a decent , Spanish flavored weeper, while performances of the freewheeling "One Heart ache at a Time" and "White Line Casanova" exude the charm in energy that once made these guys serving of their success. Here, however, it's too little too late.—Nick Cristiano, Knight Ridder

LIONEL RITCHIE
Louder Than Words, Mercury

Everyone has a comfy old pair of shoes. And fashion be damned, that sense of familiarity feels good!

Lionel Ritchie is like that old pair of shoes.

We haven't heard a whole new album from our pal Lionel in 10 years. From the sound of *Louder Man Words*, it's like he never left. Those looking for revelation or fresh insights are advised to move on. "Can't Get Over You," "Still in Love," and "Paradise" are amiable R&B ballads cut from the same cloth as "Hello," "Penny Lover," and "Love Will Conquer All."

What's missing here is a surefire smash hit such as 1983's "All Night Long (All Night)." But, that said, the concluding "Climbing" may be the finest music Ritchie has ever composed. An ambitious panorama of a song, it switches from soft balladry to pop/rock to lush classical orchestration and back again. "Climbing's" rah-rah arousing orchestration evokes the spirit of athleticism and would have made it a more suitable Summer Olympics theme song instead of the lifeless selection, Gloria Estefan's "Reach."—Howard Cohen, Knight Ridder

JACQUELINE DU PRE
Richard Strauss' Don Quixote and Edouard Lalo's Cello Concert in D Minor

A previously unpublished recording by Jacqueline du Pre is always big news.

After her meteoric rise, the popular cellist's career was cut short by multiple sclerosis, but, even now, nearly a decade after death, interest in her hasn't waned.

The Strauss piece was recorded live during concerts at Cleveland's Severance Hall in 1973, the year of her early retirement, and the Lalo in 1968, in London. The sound on this recording is not the clearest, and du Pre falters in spots. But, for the most part, the cellist who comes through is the same confident personality who made a big splash in 1965 with a recording of the Elgar Cello Concerto.—Peter Debris, Knight Ridder

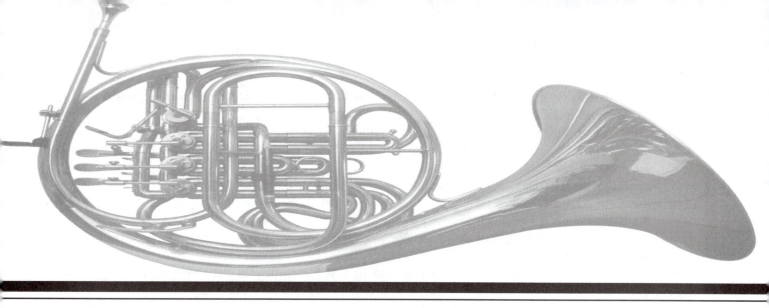

1998 PROFILE

Zachary Alexander's French horn earned him a partial college scholarship, a fellowship to Europe, and his first job—not bad for a brass instrument consisting of about 12-13 feet of tubing wrapped into a coil with a flared bell.

Life at Home

- Zachary Alexander used to describe himself as a musician who played the French horn in a symphony orchestra.
- But now that the International Horn Society had recommended that the German-made horn no longer be attributed to the French, Zachary tells people that he is a hornist—a word that's sometimes misunderstood.
- And now that he was spending more time teaching children to love music of all kinds than he was playing his horn, he liked to consider himself a musical mentor.
- All he knew was that he loved his life; he was living the dream.
- Born in Belleville, Illinois, in August 1968, Zachary moved with his family a dozen times before he graduated from high school in Bloomington, Indiana.
- Every move was more difficult than the last, especially as the potential friends got older and their social engagements more complex.
- Outgoing and eager to have friends, Zachery relied on his sense of humor and his French horn.
- He learned early that one short tune with the French horn would transform him from the dorky new kid to the interesting horn player; he was never the most popular, but the French horn allowed him to develop solid friendships wherever he went.
- Of all the instruments, the French horn boasts a certain glamour that goes beyond the mystique of its rich tone, developed through its unusual length.
- The second-highest sounding instrument group in the brass family, French horns had a difficult mouthpiece that supported a wide usable range—approximately four octaves—depending on the ability of the player.
- To produce different notes on the horn, Zachary had to press the valves and hold the appropriate amount of lip tension while blowing air into the instrument and placing his hand in the bell.

Zachary Alexander remained outgoing – and true to his French horn – during his dozen or so family moves.

- It wasn't for everyone.
- More lip tension and faster air produced higher notes; the right hand, cupped at a "three o-clock" position in the bell, could lower the pitch.
- The limitations on the range of the instrument are primarily governed by the available valve combinations for the first four octaves of the overtone series, and after that by the ability of players to control the pitch through their air supply and embouchure.
- Many pieces from the Baroque to Romantic periods are written in keys other than F.
- Early horns were originally played on a hunt, often while mounted, and the sound they produced was called a recheat; the change of pitch was effected entirely by the lips.
- Around 1815, the use of valves opened up a great deal more flexibility for playing in different keys; in effect, the horn became an entirely different instrument—fully chromatic for the first time.
- Zachary's first love was the trumpet, which he played until he was seven when his older brother told him he wasn't any good at it and then proceeded to demonstrate the musical holes in Zachary's education.
- Zachary found his father's French horn in the back corner of his closet a few days later, and the boy and the instrument became inseparable.
- Following college graduation and a fellowship in Barcelona, Spain, Zachary was named to the position of Third Horn with the Oklahoma Symphony Orchestra, where he spent five years struggling to learn the music of the Masters and how to interpret the tonal shifts of modern composers.
- But it was in his next position as Principal Horn with the Savannah Symphony Orchestra, where he helped create a youth program, that he understood how to blend his musical side with his gregarious teaching side.
- The youth program was designed to make classical music fun.
- Zachary wanted to mold the musically intelligent audience of the future.

Life at Work

- Zachary Alexander understood that the field of music was competitive; only a tiny percentage of those who trained as musicians actually became employed as performers.
- Yet everyone had been issued two ears and the intellect—with a little training—to appreciate the sounds made by a well-coordinated orchestra.
- So when he left Savannah for the Pittsburgh Symphony Orchestra two years later, his goal was to divide his time equally between musician and educator.
- Zachary liked to think that every musician who had breathed through its brass was a genial soul.
- He also learned the amazing variety of questions children invariably asked: "They want to know what I do with my lips, why I put my hand in the bell, and how my horn works. I have even been asked why my eyebrows go up and down when I play," he said.
- Those were just the kind of conversations he liked to have with curious kids; as for the twitching of his eyebrows: "I have no idea. It just happens."
- Now, prior to designated concerts, families had an opportunity to meet guest artists and learn more about the instrument and the music the musicians would be playing.
- "As musicians, we deal with communication through music," Zachary said. "This is an opportunity to use our mouths to explain how we make sounds come out of our instruments."
- The Family Night Backstage series was designed to introduce children of all ages to classical music and orchestral concerts in a non-threatening atmosphere.

Zachary developed and taught a youth program for young musicians.

- "It's good to have a little taste of the music beforehand; they should also know something about the instruments they will be seeing."
- Family Night parties, however, were not designed to be hands-on experience for children.
- Professional musicians are understandably squeamish about anyone else touching the instruments with which they make their living, Zackary said
- "Little kids are wide open for the experience," he said. "More and more, we see families there with little kids wearing jackets and ties. For busy families seeking ways to spend quality time with the children, the Symphony Orchestra has many pluses.
- "This is more than a visit to the McDonald's Playground—we are looking for something that is a real growing experience for the child. There's nothing like going to a live concert, and that goes for any age."
- Zachary said it doesn't bother him when a youngster stands up in the middle of a symphony concert and announces, "Look at that cool horn!"
- "If I were playing the Brandenburg Concertos, it might be disruptive," he said. "But at the family concert, it's not out of place. Nothing delights me more."
- The modern orchestra has its historical roots in ancient Egypt, where the first orchestras were composed of small groups of musicians who gathered for festivals, holidays or funerals.
- True modern orchestras started in the late sixteenth century when composers started writing music for instrumental groups.
- In the sixteenth century, wealthy Italian households had musicians to provide music for dancing and the court, as well as the theater, particularly opera.
- In the seventeenth century and early eighteenth century, instrumental groups were recruited from the best available talent.
- As nobility began to build retreats away from towns, they hired musicians to form permanent ensembles.
- Composers such as the young Joseph Haydn would then have a fixed body of instrumentalists to work with, while traveling virtuoso performers such as the young Wolfgang Amadeus Mozart would write concerti that showed off their skills, and they would travel from town to town arranging concerts along the way.

Family Night Backstage introduced children of all ages to classical concerts – above are the Pittsburgh Symphony Horns.

- Gradually, the financial sponsorship of the symphony shifted from private patrons to a civic enterprise; this change placed a premium on music that was easy to learn, often with little or no rehearsal.
- In 1781, the Leipzig Gewandhaus Orchestra was organized from the Merchants Concert Society, and it began a trend towards the formation of civic orchestras that would accelerate into the nineteenth century.
- In 1815, Boston's Handel and Haydn Society was founded, and in 1842, the New York Philharmonic.
- The invention of the piston and rotary valve in 1815 was the first in a series of innovations, including the development of modern keywork for the flute and the innovations of Adolphe Sax in the woodwinds.
- These advances would lead Hector Berlioz to write a landmark book on instrumentation, which was the first systematic treatise on the use of instrumental sound as an expressive element of music.
- As the twentieth century dawned, symphony orchestras were larger, better funded, and better trained than ever before; consequently, composers could write larger and more ambitious works.
- With the beginning of the recording era, the standard of performance changed from simply "getting through" the music to a higher level of performances—now that a recording could be played repeatedly.

- As sound was added to silent films, the virtuoso orchestra became critical to the establishment of motion pictures as mass-market entertainment.
- By the late twentieth century, dozens of public/private partnerships experienced a crisis of funding and support for orchestras.
- The size and cost of a symphony orchestra, compared to the size of the base of supporters, became an issue in city after city—encouraging symphonies of all sizes to rebuild their bases through educational programs.

Life in the Community: Pittsburgh, Pennsylvania

- Pittsburgh, the second-largest city in Pennsylvania, with a seven-county metropolitan area with a population of more than two million, was shaped by the confluence of the Allegheny and Monongahela rivers, which form the Ohio River.
- Known as "The Steel City" for its history of steel manufacturing, its economy had shifted to healthcare, education, technology, robotics, and financial services.
- No steel mills remained within the city of Pittsburgh, and only two mills remained in the county, while supporting 1,600 technology companies.
- In 1895, the Pittsburgh Symphony Orchestra was founded by the Pittsburgh Arts Society with conductor Frederic Archer, who brought with him a number of musicians from the Boston Symphony Orchestra.
- Archer was replaced by Victor Herbert, who took the orchestra on several tours and greatly increased its presence.

Pittsburgh steel mill, circa 1905.

- A number of prominent guest conductors were lured to Pittsburgh during these early years, including Edward Elgar and Richard Strauss, but the orchestra was dissolved in 1910 because of financial difficulties.
- In 1926, the orchestra was resurrected, with its members rehearsing for no fee and contributing money to make possible a new season the following year.
- In 1930, Antonio Modarelli was brought in as conductor, followed in 1937 by Otto Klemperer, who raised the orchestra to an international level.
- Since then, the orchestra has experienced ongoing growth and development, including building a substantial endowment fund.
- Fritz Reiner led the orchestra as Music Director for a decade (1938–1948), imposing his precise technical demands.
- He also made a number of recordings of a wide range of repertory, including music by Mozart, Richard Strauss, and Bela Bartók.
- From 1948-1952, a series of guest conductors led the orchestra, including Leonard Bernstein and Leopold Stokowski.
- André Previn (1976–1984) brought the Pittsburgh Symphony Orchestra to a national audience with a PBS television series, *Previn and the Pittsburgh*.
- Lorin Maazel, a Pittsburgh native, served as Music Consultant to the orchestra from 1984–1988, and Music Director from 1988-1996, followed by Mariss Jansons.

HISTORICAL SNAPSHOT
1998

- President Bill Clinton's sexual activities with a White House intern became a national obsession

- Sir Edward Elgar's unfinished third symphony was completed by Anthony Payne and performed for the first time at the Royal Festival Hall, London

- Unemployment, interest rates, murders, juvenile arrests, births to unwed mothers and infant mortality fell to 25-year lows

- The Stray Cats reunited for a benefit show for the Carl Perkins Foundation at the House of Blues in Los Angeles

- Stevie Wonder was honored as the 1999 MusiCares Person of the Year

- The Modern Library's "100 Best Novels of the Century" listed *Ulysses, To the Lighthouse, A Portrait of the Artist as a Young Man, The Age of Innocence, Brave New World, The Sound and the Fury,* and *The Death of the Heart*

- The Smashing Pumpkins filed a $1 million lawsuit against U.K.-based Sound And Media Ltd., alleging that the company released a book and CD about the band without proper clearances

- The CD *Van Halen III* was released—the first to feature Gary Cherone on vocals

- The second Terrastock Festival took place in San Francisco

- Steven Tyler broke his knee at a concert in Anchorage, Alaska, delaying Aerosmith's Nine Lives Tour

- Britney Spears' debut single "Baby One More Time" sold over six million copies worldwide

- Singers Brandy and Monica dominated the Billboard charts with the duet, "The Boy Is Mine," holding the Billboard Hot 100 #1 spot for 13 weeks

- Congress passed the Sonny Bono Copyright Term Extension Act, which gave the entertainment industry 20 more years of exclusive rights to all works created since 1923

- The Goo Goo Dolls single "Iris" set a new Billboard Hot 100 airplay record in the U.S. by achieving 18 weeks at number one

- Ramzi Yousef was sentenced to life in prison for planning the first World Trade Center bombing

- Suspected "Unabomber" Theodore Kaczynski pleaded guilty and accepted a sentence of life without the possibility of parole

- Data sent from the *Galileo* probe indicated that Jupiter's moon Europa had a liquid ocean under a thick crust of ice

- NASA announced that the *Clementine* probe orbiting Earth's moon had found enough water in polar craters to support a human colony and a rocket fueling station

Selected Prices

Automobile, Volvo Sedan $26,895
Bath Towel $24.00
Breadmaker $129.99
Cell Phone...$49.99
Computer, Apple MAC Performa $2,699.00
Digital Camera...$800.00
Man's Belt, Italian Leather $42.00
Palm Pilot..$369.00
Wine Bottle Holder $150.00
Woman's Purse, Kenneth Cole $148.50

"She Traded Cows for French Horn," David Abrams, *The Syracuse Post-Standard*, March 13, 1997:

When you think of it, the French horn is a mighty piece of architecture: a long, sprawling brass highway that starts modestly at one end, then twists and turns its way until it flares into a glorious musical cornucopia.

Which, coincidentally, describes the career path taken by hornist Gail Williams.

The Western New York-bred and central New York-educated Williams is Associate Principal Horn with the renowned Chicago Symphony Orchestra. She comes to town this weekend as soloist in the Syracuse Symphony Orchestra's set of Classics Series concerts.

Surprisingly, her journey to orchestral stardom began rather modestly, without fanfare. She was the typical "farmer's daughter," raised on the family farm near Rushford.

"I spent half of my youth, summer after summer, showing cows at the state fair (in Syracuse)," Williams recalled during a recent phone interview from her home in Chicago. After bovines, the country girl preferred sports. The French horn, which she began playing in fifth grade, was a distant third.

"I just didn't have any interests," she recalled. While many young instrumentalists at her school took private music instruction to improve their playing skills, Williams refused, despite her mother's urging, and her mom was the school music teacher!

By the time she entered Ithaca College, Williams, strong like a bull from milking cows every day, was in great shape, excelling in basketball, track, gymnastics and soccer. She decided to major in physical education.

That is, until she bumped into Walter Beeler—the formidable former director of bands at the IC School of Music—who at the time was the school's assistant Dean.

Beeler, who taught Williams' mother during her school days at IC, learned that the young hornist had been accepted into the prestigious All-Eastern Band while in high school. He insisted the young woman forget soccer and basketball and major in music.

Williams studied with John Covert, the school's horn teacher, until his retirement in 1995.

She never expected to play professionally in pursuit of degree in music education, following in the footsteps of her mother. In 1972 she fulfilled her student teaching requirement at West Genesee High School in Camillus. It proved to be the turning point in her career.

"The experience suggested to me that I didn't really have the patience necessary for teaching," she recalled. "Besides, right around that time I began to get the bug to play. The "bug" grew into a full-fledged virus, thanks to a summer at the famous Tanglewood Institute in Massachusetts.

Williams began to fine-tune her skills on the horn at Northwestern University and landed a job at the Chicago Lyric Opera. The experience proved invaluable in preparing her for what was to be the biggest, most competitive audition of her life: the Chicago Symphony Orchestra, under Sir Georg Solti. When the smoke had cleared, she found herself the newest member of what is arguably the finest horn section of any orchestra in the world.

After Solti appointed Williams in 1984 to the position of Associate Principal alongside the legendary horn virtuoso Dale Clevenger, Williams' career began to take off.

Yet while her performances took her all around the world, Williams always managed to stay close to Ithaca College.

She continues to participate in a variety of IC-sponsored events, and still uses as her accompanist Mary Ann Covert, Ithaca College professor of piano.

"Musician Credits Sibling Rivalry With Instrument Choice,"
Kerrville Daily Times (Texas), January 6, 1999:

Sibling rivalry played an important role in the life of a French horn player with Kerrville ties.

"It's the only instrument I've ever played," said Jane Lehman, with a slight German accent.

Jane is the daughter of Kerrville's Ray and Mary Louise Lehman, who moved to Kerr County more than 20 years ago.

Jane began playing French horn at 13 while attending school in Florida.

"My sister played the flute, and she didn't want me playing her instrument," she said.

Using a little psychology, "she told me it looked like Christmas," and sister JoAnne convinced Jane to take up the French horn.

And although the instrument was challenging, "I never wanted to put it down.

"I started taking lessons and it was so interesting I did not notice that it was difficult," she said.

After graduating from Florida State University and the Curtis Institute of Music in Pennsylvania, she landed a job with the Savannah Symphony in Georgia. There she quickly learned that she would be hard-pressed to make a decent living playing the French horn.

So she set off for Cologne, Germany, to take French horn lessons.

"I started taking auditions and got a job real quick substituting in an orchestra," she said.

A short time later, she landed a full-time position with the Radio Symphony Orchestra of Saarbrucken, a city of approximately 300,000 located near the German-French border. The town has two full-time orchestras and the job pays quite well.

"It's like living in Kerrville, but you're taken care of as a musician, well taken care of," she said.

"If you're going to make that kind of money playing in the States, you have to be in big-city Boston, Dallas. I prefer living out in the country," she said.

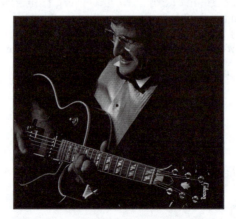

Top Songs: 1998

1. "I Don't Want To Miss a Thing," Aerosmith

2. "Everybody (Backstreet's Back)," Backstreet Boys

3. "Jump Jive An' Wail," Brian Setzer Orchestra

4. "I Want You Back," N*Sync

5. "The Cup of Life," Ricky Martin

6. "Too Close," Next

7. "Good Riddance (Time Of Your Life)," Green Day

8. "From This Moment On," Shania Twain

9. "My Heart Will Go On," Celine Dion

10. "Suavemente," Elvis Crespo

11. "Nice & Slow," Usher

12. "Tearin' Up My Heart," *NSYNC

13. "A Song For Mama," Boyz II Men

14. "The Boy Is Mine," Brandy & Monica

15. "Ghetto Supastar (That Is What You Are)," Pras Michel

16. "Intergalactic," Beastie Boys

17. "Stay (Wasting Time)," Dave Matthews Band

18. "No, No, No part 2," Destiny's Child

19. "This Is How We Party," S.O.A.P.

20. "I'll Be," Edwin McCain

21. "Just The Two of Us," Will Smith

22. "Cruel Summer," Ace of Base

23. "Gettin' Jiggy Wit It," Will Smith

24. "Zoot Suit Riot," Cherry Poppin' Daddies

25. "Landslide," Fleetwood Mac

"Hello Fender, Hello Gibson; Out of the Garage and Into Rock-and-Roll Day Camp," Andrew C. Revkin, *The New York Times*, July 7, 1999:

WHITE PLAINS, July 6—There is a rhythm to day camps, whether they are focused on soccer, computers or just enduring summer days while parents work. The cars line up, the children, at first a bit unsure, emerge, the counselors greet them, and off they go.

That familiar cycle was evident at a new camp at a private school here last week, but quickly a different rhythm dominated: the boom-tch, boom-boom-tch of rock-and-roll. Instead of carrying balls, rackets or gym bags, the arriving children, from 10 to 15 years old, held electric guitars, drumsticks and keyboards. Conrad Capalbo, 10, had blue spiked hair. Erik Peterson, 14, had glossy red fingernails.

Several moms served as roadies, lugging heavy amplifiers down the hallways of Archbishop Stepinac High School, past framed pictures of Pope John Paul II and Cardinal O'Connor.

The weeklong sessions of the camp, called Day Jams, offer children a chance to learn basic music theory, form rock bands, write songs, design album-cover art and perform a Friday-night concert that is recorded on a CD. In its first year, the camp is taking place here and at private schools in Ann Arbor, Mich., Towson, Md., and Alexandria, Va.

After the first music-filled day, Ronald Gerard, a computer programmer from Dobbs Ferry, N.Y., asked his grinning son, Timothy, a shy 10-year-old keyboard player, what he liked best about the camp so far.

"It's loud," Timothy said.

Day Jams was created by David Smolover, 49, a guitar teacher from Lakeside, Conn., who also has a 16-year-old business running one- to four-week guitar workshops for adults and teenagers around the country and in Germany. From the reactions of the 29 children who enrolled in the first session in White Plains last week, rock camps for children will be around for a long time. Another weeklong session, costing $375, ends on Friday.

An indirect gauge of the students' enthusiasm was the failure of one part of the curriculum: recreation. Originally, the schedule included daily breaks for sports. "We bought soccer balls," Mr. Smolover said. "But no one's used them."

Even in snippets of free time, the children focused largely on making music. Their tastes ranged from hip-hop to heavy metal, from the Spice Girls to punk ska bands like Blink 182 and Reel Big Fish. A few were not afraid to play tunes they learned from their parents' album collections: "Sunshine of Your Love," "Stairway to Heaven."

Some, like Erik, the red-nailed bass player, and Conrad, the blue-haired guitarist, had already cut their teeth in garage bands. But most, like Timothy Gerard, said that they had never performed with other children. Music, so far, had been a solitary activity, picking out piano scales or aping guitar chords from a favorite CD in their bedrooms.

That was all about to change.

continued

**"Hello Fender, Hello Gibson; Out of the Garage and Into Rock-and-Roll Day Camp,"
Andrew C. Revkin, *The New York Times*, July 7, 1999:**

(continued)

Despite the mix of skills and tastes, over the course of the week the corridor echoes evolved from an ear-numbing cacophony of clacking drumsticks, synthesizer notes and distorted guitar into original songs penned by the children, backed by sturdy drum beats and throbbing bass lines.

On Monday morning, June 28, the arriving students sank into velvet-covered seats in a cavernous, 1,000-seat auditorium at the school. On stage, their teachers, from Westchester County and New York City, formed a band and began slamming through several rock and blues tunes, laced with acrobatic guitar solos, one of which evoked a smile from Jonathan Gerundo, 12, of White Plains, who began strumming his unplugged black Fender Squire guitar in synchrony.

Jonathan said his main influences were Pantera, Metallica and "all the hair bands," a galaxy of heavy metal acts known for their fluffed manes.

The budding musicians then headed down the hallways to separate classrooms for different specialties: drums in room 102, guitars in 104 and 105, keyboard and bass players in 107, and singers in 108.

Several guitar players began setting up for David Moreno, a music teacher from the East Village who had the glazed, scruffy look of someone who had awakened long before his normal sleep cycle had ended.

Soon, the room began to vibrate as Jonathan Gerundo did his best Black Sabbath imitation, followed by Jonathan Vingiano, 12, from Hastings-on-Hudson, who chopped out syncopated ska chords in the style of the Police. The two Jonathans spent the rest of the week trading lead riffs and becoming friends.

Down the hall, the voice teacher, Leslie Barlow Mostyn, asked her pupils to sing a few lines so she could gauge the work ahead of her. Junki Sugiyama, a 12-year-old vocalist from Rye, stood straight as a stick and proudly sang the Japanese national anthem.

By the end of the first day, the children had been formed into three sprawling Grateful Dead-size bands, each with a bass player, two drummers, several singers, a keyboard player and an abundance of guitarists. They voted for names: New Generationzzz, 103 (the classroom number), and Zero.

On June 29, the bands began to create the foundations for songs, working out melodies and parts. By Wednesday, lyric writing was in full swing. Junki and Michael Marell, 14, from White Plains, were the vocalists and lyricists for the band called 103.

Junki had come a long way from his stiff debut and now belted out a blues-style beat poem, "Sacrifice," like a veteran punk rocker, leaning into the microphone and tripping over the tangle of cords and cables.

"I need something better to do," he sang. "It looks like tasty music."

Michael took his turn as the band's front man, holding his lyric sheet for "Thunder" high as he quietly sang: "I don't know what I'm singing. I don't know the words. It doesn't need a melody or even a single chord. It just needs some beat, rhythm, and a style. When it all comes together you get music with a smile."

continued

"Hello Fender, Hello Gibson; Out of the Garage and Into Rock-and-Roll Day Camp," Andrew C. Revkin, *The New York Times*, July 7, 1999:

(continued)

During a brief break, Mr. Moreno and Adam Issadore, the drum teacher, conferred about how to make the bands coalesce. Even though both had taught music for many years and played in bands themselves, neither had taught kids how to become a band, certainly not how to do it in the space of a week.

Late on June 30, the pupils were clearly drifting in the building summer heat and humidity. Waves of chatter and stray notes built to a crescendo before Jonathan Rubin, one of the guitar teachers, called for silence. Miraculously, silence descended.

He smiled. "You hear that?" Mr. Rubin said, describing the momentary quiet. "On every CD you own, just before the song starts, you hear that sound."

Then he warned them that the clock was ticking toward their stage debut. "Here's the deal," he said. "We're halfway through the week and we've got a gig in 48 hours."

Friday morning, the campers arrived nervous but well coiffed, girded for their culminating stage performance. Erik Peterson showed up with freshly dyed Day-Glo pink hair.

Samantha Green, 11, from Dobbs Ferry, was primed for her role as part of a reincarnated Spice Girls ensemble, but also provided makeup assistance for several newfound friends. Using a mascara brush, she added sparkling purple highlights to the dark forelocks of Ryan Clark, a 12-year-old bass player from White Plains.

Finally, the auditorium began to fill with parents and siblings brandishing an array of camcorders and cameras.

Bill and Janet Vingiano, whose son was the Jamaican-influenced guitarist, smiled broadly as the concert got under way. "When you see kids this motivated to learn music, it's pretty wonderful," Mr. Vingiano said.

The first band, 103, took the stage, and Junki, despite shining loafers and pressed khakis, did his best Jim Morrison imitation, smoothly delivering his memorized meandering poetry over the steady hiss of cymbal strokes. Behind the curtains to each side, the teachers dripped sweat in the stuffy air as they waved their arms and counted out beats.

Zero, comprising the most experienced students, sandwiched its original song between two Jimi Hendrix classics, with Ryan Clark, the sparkle-haired bassist, falling to his knees on stage as he slammed out the closing notes. As Zero left the stage, Ryan high-fived his band's Hendrix-playing guitarist, Alex Gordon, and even though they lived miles apart in White Plains and Hastings-on-Hudson, respectively, they vowed to start a band together.

Young Generationzzz played an artfully arranged pop tune punctuated with cymbal crashes and clavier chords that built to a punchy finale, with blue-haired Conrad and his cousin, Arden Rosenblatt, 10, slashing closing windmilling guitar chords, in the best Judas Priest tradition, then tossing their plastic picks into the audience.

All of the children and teachers took the stage for a final bow, bathed in applause. Then the campers rushed the exits, ready for the rest of summer.

2000–2011

No industry was rocked more by the Internet than the music industry. The online music decade started with Napster, a free music file-sharing service that eventually morphed into Apple's iTunes, which offered songs for $0.99. MySpace and Facebook became popular hangouts for local bands, especially indie rockers. Bloggers pushed their way to the front with the unsanctioned message: the music industry heads were no longer in control of the manufacturing or distribution of music. Nearly 20 years after record stores dumped their records and replaced them with the bright, shiny compact discs, the CD itself was replaced digital music. Fans could virtually make their own albums. The TV show *American Idol* turned the nation into talent scouts and music judges producing pop culture phenomena Kelly Clarkson, country heavyweight Carrie Underwood, rocker Chris Daughtry and fan favorite Clay Aiken. The decade was extraordinarily rough on soap operas. *As the World Turns* and *The Guiding Light* both ended half-century runs as the number of entertainment devices, cable channels and DVRs exploded.

History will record that the new century began in the United States on September, 11, 2001, when four American commercial airliners were hijacked and used as weapons of terror. After the tragedies at the World Trade Center in New York; Shanksville, Pennsylvania; and the Pentagon in Washington, DC, Americans felt vulnerable to a foreign invasion for the first time in decades. America's response to the attacks was to dispatch U.S. forces around the world in a "War on Terror." The first stop was Afghanistan, where a new brand of terrorist group known as al-Qaeda leader Osama bin Laden and stabilizing a new government proved more vexing. With the shell-shocked economy in overall decline and the national debt increasing at a record pace, the United States rapidly shifted from Afghanistan to Iraq. Despite vocal opposition from traditional allies such as Germany and France, President George W. Bush launched Operation Iraqi Freedom with the goal of eliminating the regime of Saddam Hussein and his cache of weapons and mass destruction. The invasion resulted in worldwide demonstrations, including some of America's largest protest marches since the Vietnam War. As in the invasion of Afghanistan, the U.S. achieved a rapid military victory, but struggled to secure the peace. When no weapons of mass destruction were found, soldiers continued fighting while an internal, religious civil war erupted; support for the war waned and vocal protest increased.

Despite the cost of the war, the falling value of the dollar and record high oil prices the American economy began to recover by 2004. Unemployment declined, new home purchases continued to surge, and the full potential of previous computer innovation and investment impacted businesses large and small. Men and women of all ages began to buy and sell their products on the Internet. eBay created the world's largest yard sale; Amazon demonstrated, despite sneering critics, that it could be the bookstore to the world, and we all learned to Google, whether to find the exact wording of a Shakespearian sonnet or the menu at Sarah's Pizza Parlor two blocks away. At the same time, globalization took on a new meaning and political importance as jobs, thanks to computerization, moved to India, China or the Philippines, where college-educated workers were both cheap and eager. American manufacturing companies that once were the centerpiece of their community's economy closed their U.S. factories to become distributors of furniture made in China, lawn mowers made in Mexico or skins from Peru. The resulting structural change that pitted global profits and innovation against aging textile workers unable to support their families resulted in a renewed emphasis in America on education and innovation. If the U.S. was to maintain its economic dominance, the pundits said, innovative ideas and research would lead the way.

As the decade drew to a close, after eight years of the presidency of George W. Bush, America's economy was in recession—the victim of its own excesses: too much consumer borrowing, extensive speculation in the housing market and widespread use of "exotic" financial instruments that failed to reduce risk. In the wake of the economic crash, some of the most respected firms on Wall Street disappeared through mergers or collapse, unemployment topped 10 percent and consumer confidence plummeted. When newly elected President Barack Obama took office in 2009, America was at war in Iraq and Afghanistan, the federal government was spending billions of dollars to save the banking system and the price of oil was on the rise. President Obama made universal health care a key element of his first year in office, igniting controversy and exposing the deep divisions that existed nationwide.

Sports during the first decade of the twenty-first century became a 24/7 obsession for many. With the dramatic expansion of the Internet, cell phones, the addition of new cable channels and a plethora of new sporting events, America was clearly addicted to sports, including many whose lure was tinged with danger. NASCAR expanded its geographic reach and began challenging football for most viewers, the Williams sisters brought new life to professional tennis and Tiger Woods continued his winning ways on the golf course. Despite a decade of falling television ratings, NBC paid an astonishing $2.3 billion for the combined rights to the 2004 and 2008 Summer Games and the 2006 Winter Games.

Cyclist Lance Armstrong captivated racing and non-racing fans alike as he won the Tour de France an unprecedented seven consecutive times. Baseball's Boston Red Sox finally shook the "Curse of the Bambino" to win a World Series, and Barry Bonds slugged 73 home runs for the San Francisco Giants in 2003, only to be accused of improper drug use as the decade came to an end.

Professional women, who for decades had struggled to rise past the glass ceiling in their companies, began to find bigger opportunities in the 2000s. Significantly, the promotion of a woman to a top slot in a Fortune 500 company ceased to make headlines. Some top female CEOs even began to boldly discuss the need for more balance in the workplace. Yet surveys done at mid-decade showed that more Americans were working longer hours than ever before to satisfy the increasing demands of the marketplace and their own desire for more plentiful material goods. In some urban markets the average home price passed $400,000; average credit card debt continued to rise and the price an average new car, with typical extras, passed $20,000.

2006 PROFILE

William Bartlett Barrett IV was 58 and married with three children when he discovered the tangled web of music law, thanks to his oldest daughter's boyfriend, a bass guitarist in a cover band concerned about the upcoming release of their first CD.

Life at Home

- William Bartlett Barrett IV was an attorney just like his father, grandfather, great-grandfather and great-great-grandfather.
- Until he discovered the complexity of music copyright law was exposed by the rapid rise in technology, he hated being a lawyer.
- For Bill, the challenges of commercial law were financially rewarding, occasionally stimulating and perennially soul-sucking.
- For the past decade he had been attempting to negotiate the slow-moving field of copyright law vis à vis the lightning quick evolution of music technology.
- The Barrett dynasty, as Bill's father liked to say, was planted in Yuma, Arizona, more than 150 years earlier when settlers began wrestling fruits and vegetables from the parched ground.
- William Bartlett Barrett II had gone West from Oklahoma City to chase the sun, escape an arranged marriage, and hide from his father.
- As the eldest son of an ex-Confederate soldier who had moved West after the war, the expectations were high for William II.
- Since he was a baby, William II had repeatedly been told what his future was to be—as envisioned and constructed by his father.
- Working beside his father, he wrestled crops from the ground, fought over water rights and learned the law well enough to acquire an expansive track of farm land.
- By the turn of the twentieth century, the evolving legal issues of land ownership and future rights infringements dominated his time.

Attorney William Barrett discovered the complexity of music copyright law.

- By the turn the twenty-first century, his great-grandson found himself knee-deep in ownership questions over music, questions about the future remuneration of artists, and deeply caught up in infringement cases that were robbing his clients of revenues.
- What was clear was that in the midst of technological change, the financial side of the music business was broken; digital technology had fundamentally changed the operating model as dramatically as electricity had altered American industry.
- The Internet had made many traditional corporate music jobs obsolete, while simultaneously broadening the reach of recorded music.
- Peer-to-peer file sharing had turned consumers into distributors; CD burners made everyone a potential manufacturer.
- The only job left exclusive to the music industry was as policeman—the enforcer of the copyright laws and stopper of progress.
- But to Bill's way of thinking, the financial train wreck had been inevitable; when only 5 percent of the musical artists were making 95 percent of the revenues, revolution was already in the air.
- The record industry was seen as greedy by consumers and artists alike so when technology stormed the gates of the giant companies' castle, there were few soldiers to defend them.
- Now, as Bill saw it, his job was to make sense of the mess.
- His daughter's boyfriend had come to him with a legitimate concern: how to protect his intellectual property from theft by other bands, powerful music companies or foreign distributors beyond the reach of U.S. law.
- The boyfriend and his band disappeared from his daughter's life only a few months later, leaving behind a reinvigorated commercial attorney with a curious mind.
- The music industry in the twenty-first century had become a brave new world; a virtual Wild West where the old rules no longer applied.
- After all, the entire power structure had been up-ended by technological change the courts were powerless to stop.
- In less than a decade, a new Internet-savvy music hierarchy had been created by artists themselves without asking permission from the reigning power structure: commercial radio, MTV, retail stores and record companies.
- At the same time, the once-passive music-listening crowd had become music programmers fully capable of mixing together their own new musical ideas and communicating them via message boards, Web pages, e-zines and MP3s.
- Suddenly, the American music market had morphed into a gaggle of niche markets no longer focused on the mass market potential of a song or band; power had shifted from the highly paid corporate executives in suits to a 15-year-old girl relaxing in her bedroom with a brand-new laptop.
- It was a rude awakening for the record industry, which had spent decades consolidating its power; as the new millennium began, the industry had been reduced to only six multinational record labels and one corporation that dominated the concert and commercial radio business.
- They assumed the artists themselves would be up in arms over the piracy and the potential loss of revenues facilitated by technological innovations such as the file-sharing Napster.

Technology turned music listeners into music programmers.

- Instead, groups like the Beastie Boys and then Tom Petty and the Heartbreakers joined the insurrection; in March 1999, Tom Petty uploaded a free version of the garage-rock single "Free Girl Now."
- More than 150,000 fans downloaded the song in 56 hours before Warner Brothers shut down the giveaway.
- Where Warner Brothers saw no revenues from lost record sales, Tom Petty saw the acquisition of 150,000 e-mail addresses that could be used to promote his upcoming summer tour.
- Even with ticket prices at under $40 each, the concert—thanks to the e-mail promotion—grossed $27 million, legitimizing the concept; the rebellion was underway.

Life at Work

- The first concept that Bill Barrett grasped was how unprepared the music industry was for change.
- They liked being in charge of what CDs were made, when they were distributed and how the revenues were divided.
- For decades artists had carped about the size of the industry's take from every record; by 2000 they had institutionalized the process with lawyers, accountants and contracts that resulted in company expenses and promotions absorbing virtually all the revenues from a hit record—fueling excellent industry profits.
- The Internet simply looked like a menace.
- It was a familiar pattern: phonograph machines were seen as a threat to live music in 1900; radio was attacked as a threat to the phonograph machine in the late 1920s; home taping was seen as the enemy of music makers in the 1980s, and Napster was decried as potentially a fatal blow.
- Bill knew through his children that the head-banger band Metallica had gained a wide following thanks to home taping of their first cassette, *Life 'til Leather*; obviously, the record companies were no longer in control of the music scene.

- Then Napster's simple-to-use file-sharing service ignited panic.
- The music industry moved quickly to shut down Napster, hardly recognizing that the tiny upstart was the beginning, not the end, of their problems.
- By the end of 2001, the number of homemade burned CDs topped 2.5 billion—the same number of CDs sold in retail stores; in 2002, industry revenues fell from $12.6 billion from their 1999 peak of $14.6 billion—a 13.7 percent decline.
- Even worse, the industry discovered that, unlike Napster, which required users to connect to its servers to download files, the emerging file-sharing companies only created software that had no control over user activity.
- Instead of neutralizing the problem, the industry opened the way for decentralized software that only made music file sharing far more efficient.
- The industry decided to fight back by suing file-sharing music lovers, who used to be their customers.
- They likened their action to a retailer prosecuting a shoplifter; most media stories betrayed the industry as giant bullies eager to intimidate 12-year-olds who had downloaded the music they loved.
- In September 2003, when the music industry filed its first major round of lawsuits, naming 261 consumers who had shared more than 1,000 songs each from music-swapping websites, Bill became much more visibly involved with the controversy.
- At the time, the average price of a compact disc was $18.98, of which 29 percent went to the label, 29 percent to retailers, 15 percent for marketing and promotion, 6 percent to the distributor, 5 percent for publishing royalties, 5 percent for packaging, 1 percent to the musicians' union, and 10 percent to the artist, minus recording expenses and other costs.

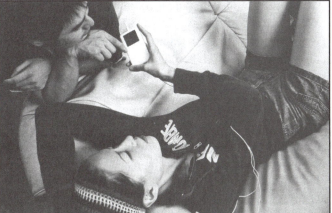

Sharing music was easy between users and hard for the industry to control.

- Consumers thought CD prices were too high; the musicians thought they were being ripped off, colleges threatened their students with expulsion for file sharing, and a new concept known as iTunes attracted a million sales in a week by offering downloads at $0.99.
- The industry filed a slew of suits, Bill took the side of the consumer, and newly created file-sharing companies such as Grokster and BearShare were taken to court.
- Industry experts estimated that while iTunes stores produced $1 billion in sales, more than 20 billion songs were downloaded "illegally."
- Bill maintained that for distribution to take place, a physical copy had to change hands; peer-to-peer file sharing was no more a violation of the copyright than playing a CD for 20 people at a party at your home.
- In defense of college students sued by the industry, Bill argued that, even though the copyright laws were written in the days when mimeograph machines and vinyl records were king, it was the burden of the music industry to show that theft had occurred.
- He quoted Ken Waagner, a digital guru for Wilcox, who said, "the record industry suing the sharers is like the railroad industry trying to shoot down airplanes."
- And he refused to settle the suits, as many did for $3,000.
- Fundamental changes in the way music was made and sold were coming; the artists were gaining more control over their music and technology was their friend.
- By the end of 2006, the ratio of free downloads to paid downloads was 40 to one.
- The industry filed more lawsuits.

Life in the Community: Yuma, Arizona

- Residents of Yuma like to say that its geography shaped the Southwest.
- Because Yuma was the safest spot to cross the Colorado River, all roads led to Yuma for travelers from Spanish explorers to Okies fleeing the Dust Bowl.
- As a result, Yuma became a vibrant, multicultural community with a rich heritage, defined geographically by wide-open spaces and pristine desert scenery—all with a river running through it.
- Yuma featured a desert climate, with extremely hot summers and warm winters.
- According to *The Guinness Book of World Records*, Yuma was the sunniest place on earth; on average, Yuma received about three inches of rain annually.
- The year-round near-perfect flying weather attracted military interest in training its pilots.
- Yuma's estimated population was nearly 200,000 with approximately 85,000 retirees making Yuma their winter residence.

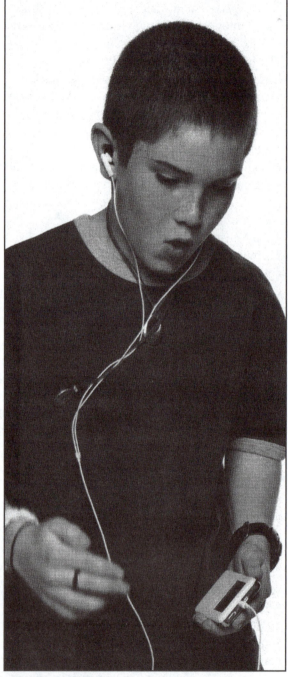

Music lovers continued to download favorite songs despite the many lawsuits filed by the music industry.

HISTORICAL SNAPSHOT
2006

- MahlerFest XIX, honoring Austrian composer Gustav Mahler, was held in Boulder, Colorado
- U2 won five awards at the 48th Annual Grammy Awards, Mariah Carey won three, and Kelly Clarkson became the first *American Idol* contestant ever to win a Grammy
- The Rolling Stones gave a free concert to two million people in Rio de Janeiro, Brazil
- The International Astronomical Union defined "planet" at its 26th General Assembly, demoting Pluto to the status of "dwarf planet" more than 70 years after its discovery
- *No. 5, 1948* by Jackson Pollock was sold privately for $140 million
- The one-billionth song was downloaded on iTunes; the song was "Speed of Sound" by Coldplay
- At the fourth annual Total Request Live Awards, Madonna won the Lifetime Achievement Award and Bono captured the Most Inspired Artist/Humanitarian Award
- Bon Jovi's second single, "Who Says You Can't Go Home" from the album *Have a Nice Day* went to number one in the U.S. Hot Country Charts
- Rapper Proof was shot and killed by a nightclub bouncer in Detroit, Michigan
- NASA's *Stardust* mission successfully ended, the first to return dust from a comet
- Mary J. Blige's single "Be Without You" was number one on the U.S. Billboard R&B chart for 15 weeks
- Tickets for Madonna's Confessions Tour in North America, Europe, and Asia sold out in minutes; the tour grossed more than $260 million
- Taylor Hicks won the U.S. television talent contest, *American Idol, Season 5*; Katharine McPhee was the runner-up
- Shakira's single "Hips Don't Lie" sold 266,500 downloads in its first week of availability, overtaking D4L's record of 175,000
- The Bonnaroo Music Festival in Manchester, Tennessee, featured Radiohead, Tom Petty, Phil Lesh and Friends, Beck, and Sasha
- Chicago rock band OK Go's video for their single "Here It Goes Again" became an Internet phenomenon on YouTube
- MTV celebrated its 25th anniversary
- Rock group Panic! At the Disco won the MTV Video of the Year award for their hit single "I Write Sins Not Tragedies"
- Beyoncé Knowles released her second consecutive number one solo album *B'Day*, which sold 541,000 copies in its first week
- Justin Timberlake released his sophomore album *FutureSex/LoveSounds*
- Celebrations were held worldwide for the 250th anniversary of the birth of Wolfgang Amadeus Mozart
- The Human Genome Project published the last chromosome sequence in *Nature*

Selected Prices

Bathroom Scale, Digital $49.99
BlackBerry Phone...$649.99
Bluetooth Headset..$99.99
Computer, Toshiba Laptop.....................................$499.99
GPS Navigator, Garmin...$219.99
La-Z-Boy Recliner...$499.99
Pampers, 176 Count...$48.99
Refrigerator/Freezer, Whirlpool $471.72
Sole F80 Treadmill $1,999.99
Vacuum, Hoover WindTunnel................................$129.99

How well you'll see in the future depends on the lenses you wear today.

TRANSITIONS® LENSES -

BlackBerry® 8703e™

It stays connected all over the world so you can, too.

Piracy? The biggest Pirates have been the record companies. The people running the record labels own lawyers and accountants, and they could be selling Brillo pads for all they care. It's not about the art at all. What has that got to do with music? So when people download a song, if it's a good song, people want the artist. People worship Eric Clapton or Ray Charles. What they do is bigger than any song. Downloading music gives people a chance to be exposed to an artist, not just a Brillo pad manufacturer.

—*Chuck D, Public Enemy*

"The Pop Life; 2 Big Forces Converging to Change the Sale of Music," Neil Strauss, *The New York Times*, December 10, 1998:

This winter is quickly shaping up as one that will affect the music business and market for years to come. Two enormous changes have been taking place, utterly separate yet inextricably interlinked.

The first is that on Thursday, Seagram is expected to close its deal to buy Polygram Records from Philips. Over the next month, beginning with a meeting on Friday morning with Polygram employees at the Hudson Guild Theater in midtown Manhattan, the beverage and entertainment corporation will begin merging Polygram with the Universal Music Group, which it already owns.

This will be the country's biggest record company, reducing the number of major labels from six to five and accounting for nearly a quarter of the music market. As a side effect, over the next month, as many as 3,000 employees are expected to lose their jobs, important record labels will disappear, and executives at the labels estimate that anywhere from dozens to 200 bands will be released from their labels.

The second change is that a war of sorts has been taking place between online entrepreneurs and the music establishment. The battlefield is the Internet, where in the last year some 150,000 songs, according to the research company Forrester Research in Cambridge, Mass., have become available as computer files in a format called MP3, which compresses songs into easy-to-transfer bundles of CD-quality information.

Some of these songs are on the Internet legally, with the permission of the band or record label that holds the copyright; others are bootlegged. Producers and consumers of MP3 music have accused the record industry of trying to suppress the spread of the format under the guise of stamping out piracy. But already there have been an estimated five million downloads of Winamp, which is just one of many software packages created to play MP3 files. And Internet sites like www.MP3.com, a gateway to thousands of free and cheap songs and albums, reports some 150,000 visitors a day. Recently, Chuck D of the rap group Public Enemy became the first mainstream musician to take an adversarial stand on the matter, striking out against his label, Polygram-owned Def Jam, after he uploaded a new song, "Bring the Noise 2000," onto his Web site for fans.

"Today Polygram/Universal or whatever they're now called forced us to remove the MP3 version of 'Bring the Noise 2000,'" he complained on the Web site. "The execs, lawyers and accountants who lately have made most of the money in the music biz are now running scared from the technology that evens out the creative field." Executives at Def Jam and Polygram declined to comment on the matter.

Clearly what is happening on the Internet is diametrically opposed to what is happening at record companies: as major labels are consolidating and tightening, the music world on the Internet is expanding and opening. In the process, Seagram is finding an artist rebelling; other record labels are finding that some acts want to make deals only if they are allowed to distribute or even sell some of their own music on the Internet, and still other acts, like the Beastie Boys, are uploading live songs on the Internet as MP3 files instead of giving them to their record company to use for their own promotional purposes. And the band Less Than Jake found itself in trouble when it posted songs owned by its label, Capitol, without permission.

"When you become very big, it becomes very hard to turn around," said Dave Turin, a producer who runs People Tree, an Internet label and music store for releasing less commercial side projects by well-known musicians, including members of Porno for Pyros and the Dust Brothers. "I see major labels as a huge Michelin man made of cement, trying to turn around to see what's behind him but crumbling into pieces in the process."

Even some major labels agree with Mr. Turin's assessment. "Labels are going to wait to see what happens and then plug into it," said the top executive at one label, speaking on condition of anonymity about his label's lack of a plan for distributing music on the Internet. "They have to deal in the here and now. The economics and expectations of corporate owners is to make short-term financial results, not to be pioneers of the future."

Perhaps a perfect David and Goliath Internet story is the controversy over Diamond Multimedia's Rio device, the first portable MP3 player (able to store songs from the computer on a flash card, or memory chip, in a Walkman-like device the size of a deck of cards). Instead of trying to reissue records, create compilations and release live recordings on flash cards for the Rio, critics say, record labels have been trying to wipe it out.

"Devices like the Rio are troubling because they encourage consumers to download illegal copies of our recordings," explained Kevin Conroy, the senior vice president for worldwide marketing at BMG Entertainment. He added that "the proliferation of illegal MP3 recording devices will undermine and possibly destroy the legitimate commercial market for digitally delivered music before it even has a chance to develop."

Last month, the Recording Industry Association of America obtained a temporary restraining order to keep Diamond from shipping its Rio player. But the order was overturned by a federal judge, and the Rio is now available for $199. The R.I.A.A. appealed the decision, and last week Diamond Rio countersued, accusing the association of engaging in anti-competitive business practices.

Ken Wirt, Diamond's vice president for corporate marketing, said the Rio was not intended to encourage piracy, which, he said, could be found and stamped out much more easily on the Internet than in the flea markets and street stalls where bootlegged CDs are available. "It's the right of major labels to encrypt their music," he said, referring to the ability to make Internet music files difficult to copy. "But it's not their right to tell the thousands and thousands of independent musicians who use the MP3 market as their lifeline to distribute and sell their music that they can't do anything until the major labels get their voice in there. The R.I.A.A. wants to delay everything as long as possible, discouraging the production of MP3 among their members and discouraging the market for the players."

Hillary Rosen, the president of the association, disputed Diamond's claims. Rather than suppressing technology, she said, the association is concerned about upholding copyright law. It cannot support devices like the Rio until there are effective security measures in place, she said. A record-business policy on the subject could emerge as early as next month, executives said.

"I know there's a lot of frustration with the slow pace of the majors in approaching these issues," Ms. Rosen said. "But there's a lot at stake. When there's a major release," costing "$2 or $3 million in the making, the idea of putting it up for free in an MP3 format is not your first priority, by nature."

For many keeping tabs on the battle, the issue seems like a rerun of the music industry's offensive against the spread of cassette decks, which saw the rise of skull-and-crossbones stickers that read "Home Taping Is Killing Music." It didn't.

Already, technology may be moving beyond MP3 (short for MPEG-1, layer 3) and into MPEG-4, which compresses the data even more and is more adaptable to multimedia files. Companies like Sony and Creative Labs are working on portable devices that will play these files and prevent them from being easily copied.

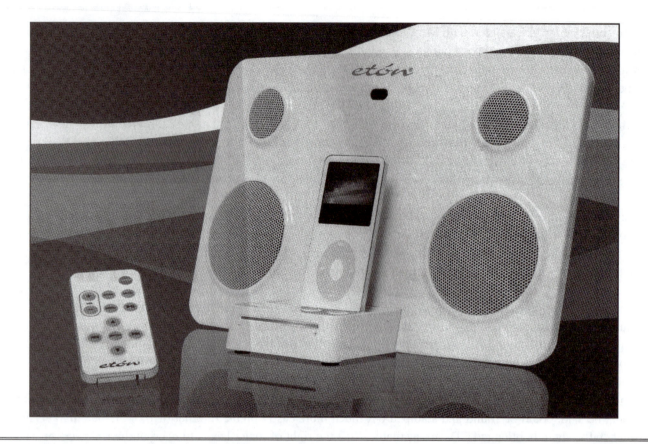

"E-Commerce Report: Services for Downloading Music legally and With Making a Profit in Mind Are Gaining Momentum," Bob Tedeschi, *The New York Times*, July 28, 2003:

The dot-com frenzy has returned at least in one category.

The introduction last Tuesday of BuyMusic.com, an online music download store meant for consumers who eschew music piracy, was promoted by its owner as the first of many new single-song download services expected from online media sites and retailers.

The iTunes service from Apple Computer was there first, having demonstrated since April the demand for such services. But iTunes works with only Apple Macintosh computers, while BuyMusic.com is aimed at the far larger universe of PCs using the Microsoft Windows operating system.

BuyMusic.com's debut evoked memories of the Internet boom years for reasons that go beyond the company's news conference in Times Square and the coverage it generated. The founder is Scott Blum, one of a handful of dot-com entrepreneurs who got out of the market with his shirt still on his back. He earned $125 million or so from Buy.com stock before those shares, and the market that lifted them, lost nearly all their value.

Mr. Blum bought back the company for about $23 million in late 2001. He took it private and, he says, has nursed it to profitability through its sales of electronics, books and other items.

Other services, like AOL Time Warner's America Online and Listen.com's Rhapsody, have enabled Windows users to download single songs, but only as subscribers to a monthly service. BuyMusic.com is the first Windows-based service to enable customers to buy songs à la carte à la Apple.

Mr. Blum, 39, says he sees a chance to gain an edge over Internet companies like Amazon.com that beat him to the market the first time around. Though it is true that many online merchants with the vaunted "first mover advantage" died after seeding the market for traditional retailers, eBay and Amazon are two first-mover notables that became market leaders in their own right.

"When I showed up on the Internet, I was a distant second to Amazon and I never made it up," Mr. Blum said. In his 20 years of being involved in entrepreneurial ventures, he said, "I haven't had this window ever in my life, so we're just going for it."

The BuyMusic.com service, which is not affiliated with Buy.com and is being financed entirely by Mr. Blum, is similar to iTunes, which has sold more than 6.5 million songs in about three months. BuyMusic.com shoppers can browse through more than 325,000 songs, which sell for $0.79 to $1.29. Full albums sell for $8 to $12.

BuyMusic.com customers retain different rights to the songs, depending on the artist's record label. Some titles, for example, can be downloaded and copied an unlimited number of times, though the technology is intended to prevent the sharing of them on music file-swapping services, while others can be copied just three times.

Mr. Blum said he expected his service to have a head start of perhaps three months before competitors appeared. He has begun a multimillion-dollar television advertising campaign in hopes of generating a loyal following before that happens.

When competition comes, it will take many forms, said Josh Bernoff, who covers online music for Forrester Research, a technology consulting firm. "There's a very long list of competitors," he said. "But that's good news, because it means someone will get it right."

Mr. Bernoff said that, besides BuyMusic.com, consumers could expect the rollout of online stores selling individual songs and subscriptions from online giants like Amazon, Microsoft and others. America Online, which began a music subscription service in February, plans to introduce an à la carte version later this year.

Other online companies are also lining up to sell digitized single songs without requiring subscriptions, Mr. Bernoff said, including RealNetworks, MusicMatch, and Roxio, which intends to revive the Napster brand it acquired for $5 million in November.

Roxio is set to unveil plans today for the new Napster service, which it will call Napster 2.0, Chris Gorog, Roxio's chief executive, said. The service will debut by Christmas and will include both subscriptions and à la carte downloads. Napster's technology will rely on the Pressplay music service it bought from Sony and Universal in May for close to $40 million in cash and stock.

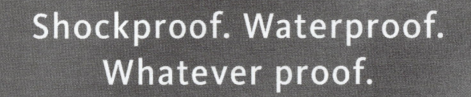

2007 PROFILE

Jazz saxophonist and recording engineer Ryland Edwards moved from California to New York City, where he plays in jazz and R&B bands to feed his passion, does music recording and production to pay some of his bills, and works in a restaurant to make it all work.

Life at Home

- Ryland Edwards was born in Berkeley, California, in 1982 and started playing alto saxophone in school when he was nine.
- His interest in machines and technology drew him to the saxophone because it had so many parts, and because his father had played saxophone as a young man.
- Ryland often could be found in his father's workshop adjusting the keys of his instrument with small screwdrivers to make his sax not only sound better, but play faster.
- Ryland found that the closer the keys were to the body of the instrument, the faster he could play.
- He wanted to play as fast as his hero, bebop saxophonist Charlie Parker, whose speed was legendary.
- Even as a teenager, Ryland was very disciplined, and practiced every day for three or four hours, which helped him strengthen the muscles in his lips and mouth.
- He also used a lot of reeds—which had to be soaked and properly filed down before they could be used.
- His parents were very supportive, and secretly happy he didn't play the drums.
- They gladly paid for the performing arts summer camp in the hills north of San Francisco.
- There he met musicians from many different walks of life who were all interested in different styles of music.

Ryland Edwards earns a living in New York City playing and recording the music that he loves -- and waiting tables.

- The highlight of his time at camp was when the blues legend Taj Mahal came to see his daughter, who was a camper, play in the final concert.
- One year, on the flight home from camp, Ryland nearly grounded the plane by insisting that he be allowed to carry on his instrument.
- In addition to playing music, Ryland discovered his talent for recording.
- Using a borrowed four-track tape recorder and a microphone, Ryland recorded himself playing four different parts on his saxophone and then layered them together into unique compositions.
- He even borrowed a baritone sax from his school to record bass parts in his harmonies.
- He and his friend Ben, who played the trumpet, practiced playing harmonies and backup parts in the style of Motown and soul records.
- Their favorite artists were Otis Redding, the Jackson 5, and Sam and Dave.
- In high school, the two friends joined a funk band together called The Confusion.
- The Confusion played cover songs by Stevie Wonder and Herbie Hancock, and got gigs at school dances, talent shows, and fundraisers.

Ryland was very dedicated to his music, from practice to performances.

- He loved the attention, but the money was terrible and they often played for free.
- Ryland recorded a five-song demo tape for the band, and enjoyed the challenge of figuring out the best way to record each instrument.
- Drums were hard to record because they required multiple microphones.
- The saxophone was also difficult because the sound came from different parts of the instrument.
- In addition to playing in the band, Ryland also played with the locally popular Berkeley High School Jazz Ensemble.
- When he joined the ensemble, there were no positions for alto saxophone players, so Ryland switched to tenor, and used his father's old tenor saxophone.

Berkeley High School Jazz Ensemble helped Ryland develop his style.

- Ryland was inspired by a Korean exchange student, Mika, who played first chair saxophone in the ensemble and encouraged him to pursue music in college—something he hadn't seriously considered before.
- When Mika left, he took her place as first chair in the jazz band and became a popular draw at school performances.
- His father was very proud of Ryland and recorded all his school performances, giving him a tape that spliced together all of his solos when he graduated.
- Ryland worked as much as he could to save money for college—as a sandwich maker at a bagel shop, a waiter at a Mexican restaurant, and a line cook at a gourmet pizza restaurant—making at most $10 an hour.
- It was at the pizza restaurant where he discovered that he liked to cook and experiment with different ingredients—not a bad Plan B if music didn't work out.
- Ryland took private saxophone lessons at $35 per hour and also gave lessons to elementary and middle school students, charging $20 per hour.
- One of his students went on to study saxophone in Chicago and, years later, Ryland took pride in seeing him perform.
- Ryland got his first professional performing experience while still in high school, playing sax in a jazz trio at the wedding of the daughter of one of his teachers.
- They played jazz and bossa nova during dinner and got paid $150 for the gig—his share was $50.
- While Ryland was happy to be making money, he realized that he would need other ways to support himself—especially if he got into one of the New York City College music programs.
- Because he lived in a culturally rich area, there were many musicians at all stages of their careers.
- It wasn't unusual for Ryland to be watching a band at a restaurant in his hometown and be asked to play something with them; he learned to always carry his saxophone!
- To take advantage of the area and his passion for music, Ryland bought a digital multi-track recorder and began reading books on recording, mixing, and engineering.
- He was able to earn $25 per song by producing demo recordings for local bands before he left for college.

Fellow saxophonist Mika encouraged Ryland to study music in college.

Ryland's first paying gig was at his teacher's daughter's wedding.

Life at School and Work

- Many non-classical college music programs were focused strictly on jazz, but Ryland wanted a program that would allow him to study R&B, hip hop, and funk—as well as recording.
- He applied to several schools, but his first choice was the New School for Jazz and Contemporary Music in New York City, with a tuition of $21,000 per year.
- Since he had never been to New York, he was nervous.
- He lived in the school dorms during his first year, then found an apartment with friends in the basement of a Brooklyn brownstone.
- Being in the basement allowed Ryland to build a very small recording studio.
- Living in Brooklyn was less expensive than living in Manhattan where his school was located, and he saved even more by cooking many of his own meals.
- When he first moved to New York, he got a part-time job at a coffee shop, making $11.00 per hour plus tips.
- He then got hooked up with a local jazz club and played every Monday night, where he earned $25 plus dinner.
- This night job was a good fit with his school and music schedules because he had class in the afternoons and worked mornings at the coffee shop.
- At school, he met musicians who played a range of musical styles.
- The diversity of the people he met, and the energy of New York in general, provided him with a wide variety of freelance opportunities.
- He started playing dinner parties with a jazz trio; bars and nightclubs with a 10-piece funk band; church ceremonies with a saxophone quartet; and weddings with a 1980s cover band.
- Most gigs paid between $50 and $200 per person.
- He also played background on a variety of side projects, including for hip hop tracks and film scores, the most famous of these being a background track for Talib Kweli.

Life in the Community: New York City

- Upon graduating, Ryland was intent on continuing his musician's lifestyle, and knew that he could make more money recording and engineering than by playing his sax.
- He was determined to meet as many musicians as possible—each one a potential recording and/or engineering job and easy to find in New York City.
- He charged $100 per song to record and mix a demo tape.
- The problem with this, however, was Ryland's friendly personality—because his friends and clients were the same, he often gave them a deal or worked for free.
- Living in the city was very expensive, and his share of the rent was $850 per month.
- The equipment that he needed to do professional recording and engineering work was also very expensive, with a microphone typically costing between $200 and $800.
- Also, to be able to compete with professional saxophone players, he needed a professional sax, which cost between $2,500 and $6,000.
- Needing to make more money, he got a job in a high-priced New York City restaurant where he could make up to $300 on a good night, and found it a good place to network.

- Actor Robert De Niro owned the restaurant and often ate there, along with actor Adrien Brody and singer John Mayer.
- Ryland loved to be able to get his friends hard-to-get reservations.
- While this cut into his time for performing, he hoped it wouldn't be long before he got his big break.
- It was during this time that he met up with his old roommate from camp, who was a blues guitar player.
- They played a few gigs together and introduced each other to their circles of friends and bandmates.
- Networking was very important for musicians in the city.
- It was not uncommon for musicians to play gigs for free if it helped them improve their reputations.
- Ryland met a young soul singer named Arielle through a friend of a coworker, and began playing backup in her horn section, making $75 per show.
- As they got to know each other better, they began writing songs together.
- Arielle was very talented, but, having recently moved from Austin, Texas, didn't know many people.
- Ryland helped her record and mix a demo CD so she could get gigs at clubs and gain more exposure.
- He hoped that if she made it big, it just might be his big break.

John Mayer was co-owner of the restaurant where Ryland worked.

HISTORICAL SNAPSHOT
2007

- The Police reunited for a tour after 23 years to mark the thirtieth anniversary of the release of "Roxanne" and subsequently announce The Police Reunion Tour
- Chris Cornell left Audioslave because of "musical differences"
- Christina Aguilera's Back to Basics Tour was the highest grossing tour for a female artist in 2007
- Angela Hacker was voted the 2007 champion of the televised singing competition *Nashville Star*, earning her a record contract with Warner Bros. Records
- Grandmaster Flash and the Furious Five, R.E.M., The Ronettes, Patti Smith, and Van Halen were all inducted into Rock and Roll Hall of Fame
- Elton John played Madison Square Garden for the sixtieth time to celebrate his sixtieth birthday; he was joined by Whoopi Goldberg, Robin Williams, and former President Bill Clinton
- *Minutes to Midnight* by Linkin Park sold more than 600,000 copies in the U.S. and more than one million worldwide in the first week
- Jordin Sparks of Arizona won Season 6 of *American Idol*
- The Spice Girls announced their reunion at the O2 in London in a press conference televised worldwide
- Live Earth, a worldwide series of concerts to initiate action against global warming, took place
- "Gimme More," Britney Spears' comeback single, sold one million copies shortly after its release
- Fred Mascherino announced his departure from Taking Back Sunday to pursue his solo career called The Color Fred
- Led Zeppelin reunited for their first show in 25 years
- Celine Dion made the final performance of her five-year engagement at Caesars Palace in Las Vegas
- The International Red Cross and Red Crescent Movement adopted the Red Crystal as a non-religious emblem for use in its overseas operations
- A 2,100-year-old melon was discovered by archaeologists in western Japan
- The final book of the Harry Potter series, *Harry Potter and the Deathly Hallows*, was released and sold over 11 million copies in the first 24 hours, becoming the fastest-selling book in history
- Track and field star Marion Jones surrendered the five Olympic medals she won in the 2000 Sydney Games after admitting to doping
- Hilary Duff released *Dignity*, her first album in three years
- Beyoncé launched The Beyoncé Experience in Tokyo, Japan
- Russian President Vladimir Putin was announced as *Time* magazine's 2007 Person of the Year
- The Picasso painting *Portrait of Suzanne Bloch*, and Candido Portinari's *O Lavrador de Café* were stolen from the São Paulo Museum of Art

Selected Prices

Backup Hard Drive $44.71
Book, Paperback $10.20
Business Cards, 250 Count $19.99
Coffeemaker, Krups $90.00
Combination Router/Modem $160.00
Phone Service, Land Line, Monthly $70.00
Printer Ink, Three-Pack..$71.00
Surfboard $735.00
Toaster, Krups $90.96
Trimline Corded Telephone $14.72

Introducing the Dell DJ for just $249.

Loaded with All the Right Stuff

Why my TV is way better than yours.

DIRECTV° DVR with TiVo°

"Remember the Alamo—in Music," *Orlando Sentinel*, April 8, 2004:

San Antonio—When he heard there was a new movie being made about the Battle of the Alamo, Asleep at the Wheel's Ray Benson figured there would be a CD featuring music from the film.

Then the Alamo co-star Billy Bob Thornton told him there wasn't any such album in the works.

"I said, 'Shoot, now there's an opportunity I can't resist,'" says the lead singer of the Western swing group.

Asleep at the Wheel Remembers the Alamo features a wide range of songs—from the melancholy trumpet standard "El Degüello" played by the Mexican army while it surrounded the Alamo in 1836, to a humorous ditty about the 1982 night Ozzy Osbourne was arrested for relieving himself in front of the shrine.

Benson had a lot of songs to choose from that focused on the battle—or merely mentioned the Alamo—between the Texans in Santa Anna's troops.

"We just wanted to show how it permeates our culture," he says.

There are 10 verses of "The Ballad of Davy Crockett," made famous in the 1950s Disney classic *Davy Crockett, King of the Wild Frontier* that set off a coonskin cap craze among American boys.

Benson said the Crockett song has 31 verses in all, and that he took out as many of them as he could without shortchanging the frontiersman, who was among those who died at the Alamo.

"What Music Is to Me," J'Vontea Perminter, Age 16:

What's music to me? It's more than an individual singing words. For me, it's an emotional stimulator. People like myself would listen to music all day. It helps to pass the time for a long day at work. Or it can even be something soothing to sleep to on restless nights.

For most people music is a form of entertainment. You can dance, sing along, it's even used to set the mood in movies. All songs have, as I like to think, a purpose. To understand that meaning, I just don't listen to the song; I try to interpret what the artist is saying. For example, classical music doesn't have very many words incorporated in it, but that's the gateway for your mind to explore and imagine anything you want.

Furthermore, hip hop music wasn't very popular among the majority. Hip hop to older audiences might just be artists cursing and being disrespectful. But to audiences of the ages between 13 and 30, it's the music of their era. Not saying that R&B or gospel doesn't have a place; just younger age groups can relate more to younger artists. It's not so much that we love to listen to them be disrespectful; its more when you experience or witness some of the things that they say, you become accustomed to hearing that artist.

In conclusion, hip hop, R&B, gospel, etc., all have their own style, but like fashion, style can become "outdated" as we say; so do music styles. If everyone listened to the same music with the same artist, what's going to happen when he or she becomes "outdated"?

MUSIC

POWER COUPLE:
Beyoncé and
Jay-Z duet again
on her new album

"JAZZ REVIEW; Saxophone, Bass and Drums, With an Equal Role for Everyone," Nate Chinen, *The New York Times*, May 13, 2006:

The Village Vanguard has a history of spotlighting tenor saxophonists in trio settings, backed only by bass and drums. Sonny Rollins was the first prominent example, nearly 50 years ago; Joe Henderson memorably took up the challenge in the 1980s. (Both instances were documented on excellent live recordings.) What's attractive about the format, for such improvisers, is a precarious kind of freedom: few harmonic constrictions, but no safety net either. It's something like a Spartan endurance test for the thinking man.

This week the tenor saxophonist Mark Turner was playing at the Vanguard with a bassist, Larry Grenadier, and a drummer, Jeff Ballard, and some of the old challenges are still relevant. But the band, which calls itself Fly, doesn't heed the usual hierarchies of the saxophone trio, which cast the rhythm section in a supporting role. Instead, it proposes a collective model, in which all parts carry equal weight, and none necessarily takes the lead.

On Wednesday night that ideal was put to the test within the first few measures of "Fly Mr. Freakjar," a composition credited to all three musicians. (Fittingly, if awkwardly, the title is an anagram of their first names.) It began in quintuple meter, outfitted with complex rhythmic scaffolding by Mr. Ballard. Then Mr. Turner and Mr. Grenadier both entered, playing separate strands of a loosely braided melody. When, after several shifts in tempo, Mr. Turner ventured a solo, it was inextricable from his partners' commentary.

That's not to say that Mr. Turner's efforts were insufficiently heroic. Though disconcertingly egoless as a soloist—sometimes to the point of self-effacement—he left no doubt as to his command. Starting out with terse, scrappy phrases, he patiently developed a motif; gradually, he grew more emphatic, until he was unfurling eighth-note patterns in a billowing stream.

What apparently keeps Fly aloft is a modular sort of ensemble interaction, a flexible determination of roles. Mr. Turner's saxophone was often deployed as a rhythmic or harmonic tool, spelling out chords in shapely arpeggios. The most prominent feature of a funk number called "JJ" was Mr. Grenadier's strutting bass line; he also took the first solo on the tune. Another piece, the appropriately titled "Stark," suspended all three instrumental parts in a delicate equipoise, even during Mr. Ballard's feverish double time.

The sound of the band in the Vanguard was just as exquisitely balanced: Mr. Grenadier's resonant tone filled the space, and Mr. Ballard kept his polyrhythmic energies at a quiet roar. They both laid back considerably in one exceptional moment that seemed to acknowledge the lineage of the room: an austere arrangement of the standard "I Fall in Love Too Easily," complete with leading-man essay on tenor saxophone.

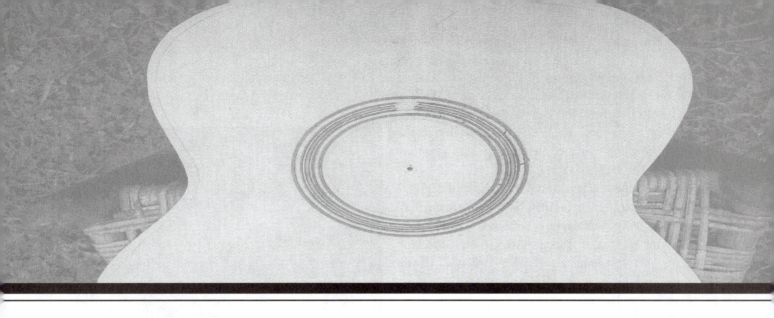

2011 PROFILE

To many, especially those who read his biography, Wayne C. Henderson was the man who made Eric Clapton wait a decade for the guitar he had ordered.

Life at Home

- For those along the Crooked Road in southwest Virginia, Wayne C. Henderson was the son of an old-time fiddler who developed into a superb guitar picker, fully capable of keeping up with the legendary Doc Watson.
- Then there's the nationwide fan base who dream of being able to acquire one of the 30 guitars he custom-made each year—considered by many to be the finest acoustic guitars made today.
- Born May 3, 1947, Wayne grew up in a family in love with old-time music in a town that boasted less than a dozen people.
- His grandfather gave him his first guitar, a plastic toy model, when Wayne was three, and the future aficionado started playing a real guitar—his brother's Gibson—when he was five.
- At 10 years old, he made his first attempt to build a guitar of his own using a cardboard box with a whittled-down two-by-four for the neck; fishing line became the strings
- His next attempt, employing wood veneer and weather stripping glue, was slightly more successful, but over time the glue melted and the guitar came apart.
- About 1960, when Wayne was 13, his father introduced him to Albert Hash, a local luthier, who taught the eager young man many of his guitar-making tricks—some as old as the country songs embedded in the hills of this neglected corner in southwestern Virginia.

Wayne Henderson built guitars, and it took more than money   even for Eric Clapton -- to get one.

479

- By the time the Wayne turned 17, he had constructed seven complete guitars, the last of which sold for $500 and convinced him that there was money to be made in music.
- His first job as a musician came in 1964 on a Saturday morning radio show on WKSK in West Jefferson, North Carolina, as the member of the Virginia-Carolina Boys.
- The music they played traced its roots to the 1740s when the Scots-Irish brought fiddling, dancing and drinking to the backwoods of America.
- Many of the tunes had survived under different names; the instrumental "Leather Britches" began its musical life as "Lord McDonald's Reel" and later "Four Nights Drunk."
- By the 1780s, the banjo was married to the fiddle tunes; guitars were not invited to the party until much later.
- Old-time music was resistant to change and evolved slowly in the secluded enclaves of Appalachia, retaining its insistent drive essential to dance music.
- And where Wayne came from, local dancing equated to a style known as flatfooting—a high-energy, dance-till-you-drop locomotion developed around live music before phonographs and radios were invented.
- By the turn of the twentieth century, the widespread availability of Sears and Roebuck Catalogs made a plethora of new products available in the rural areas, including a wide range of musical instruments.
- The 1902 Sears Catalog listed Acme brand guitars for $6.95 and Edgemore banjos for $3.95.

Wayne, at 17, was paid $500 for this guitar, the seventh he had built so far.

- In the mid-1960s, Wayne Henderson left Virginia for Nashville where he repaired and made vintage instruments.
- From 1968 to 1973, Wayne examined how well certain glues had held through the ages, the type of interior braces that produced a warm tone, and the care taken with inlaying delicate purfling or a complex mother-of-pearl design.
- A four-year master course in antique instruments gave Wayne an insight into the inner workings of the world's great and not so great instruments.
- In the process, he became a walking encyclopedia of knowledge concerning American acoustical guitars, especially those made by C.F. Martin & Company.
- Even from a distance, he could tell the difference in a 1946 and 1947 Martin D-18 based on the pick guard and the wood selection.
- All the while, Wayne continued to play in bands, including one with his wife, using a unique pinch picking technique he learned as a child.
- Instead of a customary flat pick, Wayne exclusively used fingerpicks, alternating his thumb and forefinger to play the single-note lines of old-time songs.
- By 1985, Wayne put his picking power to work with the High Country Ramblers before evolving to a pattern of playing with an ever-changing cast of musicians as he traveled the world entertaining.

Life at Work

- It was not unusual to find Wayne Henderson building a guitar in his cluttered woodworking shop at 2 a.m.
- For several days he had been touring with his girlfriend Helen White and piano aficionado Jeff Little, and as usual he was behind.
- Most of the time, that meant that his legion of admirers would simply have to wait a few more weeks—on top of years—for the delivery of their custom-made instrument.
- But now Wayne had a deadline he couldn't escape—he needed to complete the grand prize guitar he built and awarded annually to the winner of the Wayne C. Henderson Music Festival.
- Scattered throughout the shop were the sides and back to a guitar destined for a medical doctor who had supplied a truckload of 60-year-old mahogany that Wayne needed: a complete guitar—except for the inlay—for a woman in New York who had waited 22 years.
- But the issue at hand was completion of a Brazilian rosewood-sided instrument perfect enough to give away.
- That weekend, as usual, thousands would gather for the annual Wayne C. Henderson Music Festival, held at Grayson Highlands State Park, close enough to be visible from Wayne's Guitar Shop.
- Since 1995, the country's best guitar pickers had journeyed to this obscure mountain vista for the opportunity to win a Wayne Henderson guitar given to the event's best performer—and of course, bragging rights that no one could take away.

Wayne built his guitars in this cluttered workshop.

Wayne played with an ever-changing cast of musicians all over the world.

- The 20 contestants were allowed to use any style; Wayne was once barred from competing in the National Flatpicking Championships in Winfield, Kansas, because he played with a thumbpick and fingerpicks, and he wanted all comers.
- The judges, who were secluded where they couldn't see the identity or expressions of the contestants, picked five finalists.
- The talented five then played two tunes each before a large and musically sophisticated audience; a single flaw might separate the winner from the rest.
- Following the decision, announcement and presentation, the champion often cradled his or her new Henderson-made guitar with both hands as gently as one might handle a newborn baby.
- Then, while the adrenaline rush of winning was still fresh, the nervous winner was expected to christen the new guitar on stage while standing next to the master himself.

- Contestants joked that it took either five minutes or 10 years to get a Henderson guitar—depending on whether you won first place in the festival or simply got on the list for the honor of buying musical gold.
- Even getting on the list could be difficult.
- The constantly ringing phone could bring five at least 10 orders a day, which Wayne politely deflected.
- It took more than money to get a Henderson guitar.
- Prospective clients had sent cakes, weekly postcard reminders, videos and even souvenir car parts in blatant attempts to bribe Wayne so that their names would go higher on the list.
- For some, the acquisition of a Henderson guitar was a courting process more complex than their engagement and wedding.
- But his customers were not the only ones who lusted for the perfect guitar; Wayne was a collector himself—mostly Martins—to include a 1942 D-45 valued at more than most houses.
- Henderson-made guitars had sold for $25,000 and more on Ebay on those rare occasions when death, divorce or drugs have separated the guitar picker from the guitar he or she loved most.
- Wayne's price was considerably less.
- But he had one strict rule—only one guitar per customer; Henderson guitars were all numbered and, like orphan babies, were intended for only one home.

Life in the Community: Rugby, Virgina

- Tiny Rugby, Virginia, was part of the state designated Crooked Road, Virginia's heritage musical trail that winds some 300 miles through the southwest corner of the state from the Blue Ridge into deeper Appalachia.
- The original pathway was forged first by woodland buffalo and the Indians who hunted them, followed by early white settlers.
- Some of the road curves so dramatically that locals joke that you can see your own taillights as you drive around the bends.
- The Crooked Road cuts through pastures dotted with cows and horses and weather-beaten barns, some abandoned and left to splinter, as well as acre after acre of Christmas trees, a boom industry that changed the landscape.
- But what binds the twisting roads is music.
- Every night, pick-up jams ring out from front porches, theaters and storefronts, old courthouses, and even a Dairy Queen or two.
- In summer the area is awash in festivals, from Dr. Ralph Stanley's Memorial Day Bluegrass Festival in the mountains of Coeburn, Virginia, to the venerable Old Fiddlers Convention held every August in Galax.
- Starting in 1934, the first old fiddlers convention set the standard for most of Appalachia; by 1960 the festival was expanded to include a guitar contest.

Guitar maestro Wayne Henderson himself won first place at Galax more than a dozen times; in 1995, the National Endowment for the Arts awarded Wayne a National Heritage Fellowship.

Jam sessions commonly cropped up anywhere from front porches to storerooms.

HISTORICAL SNAPSHOT
2011

- An estimated two billion people watched the wedding of Prince William, Duke of Cambridge, and Catherine Middleton at Westminster Abbey in London
- A 9.1-magnitude earthquake and subsequent tsunami hit the east of Japan, killing over 15,000 and leaving another 8,000 missing; four nuclear power plants were seriously affected by the quake
- Long-simmering resentments produced the Arab Spring, in which governments were toppled in Egypt, Tunisia, and Libya, and citizen-led riots erupted in a half dozen more places
- President Barack Obama announced that Osama bin Laden, the founder and leader of the militant group Al-Qaeda, had been killed during an American military operation in Pakistan

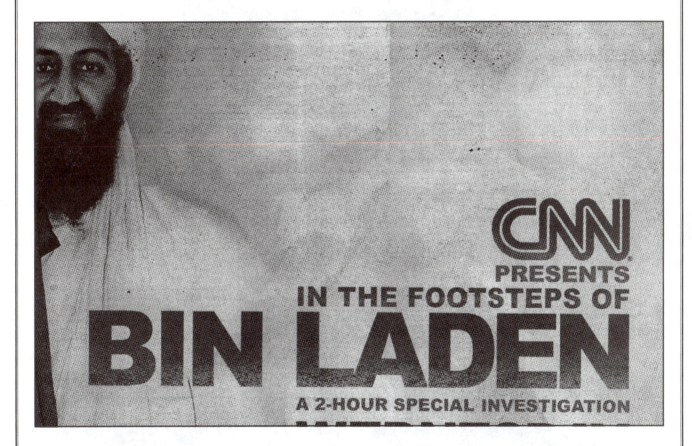

- The world's first artificial organ transplant was achieved using an artificial windpipe coated with stem cells
- South Sudan seceded from Sudan—the result of the independence referendum held in January, following a civil war that lasted for nearly a quarter of a century
- Space Shuttle *Atlantis* landed successfully at Kennedy Space Center after completing STS-135, concluding NASA's space shuttle program
- NASA announced that its Mars Reconnaissance Orbiter captured photographic evidence of possible liquid water on Mars during warm seasons

Selected Prices

Bookcase	$119.00
Bottled Water	$1.50
Coffee Grinder	$60.53
Concert Ticket, Allman Brothers	$159.00
Digital Cordless Phone	$119.99
Kindle, 3G + Wi-Fi	$189.00
Phone, Camera Flip Phone	$99.00
Printer, HP All-in-One	$548.88
Sofa	$899.00
Toolset, 137 Pieces	$99.99

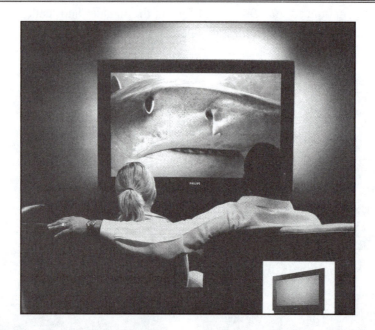

"Sounds Like America," Lawrence Downes, *The New York Times*, February 14, 2011:

Berkeley, Calif.—The party space wasn't perfect. There were no wandering dogs or children, no grass or worn linoleum underfoot. Nobody had pushed benches to the walls to make room for dancing. Nobody was shoeless, shirtless or visibly intoxicated, though the man of honor did seem drunk with delight.

It should have been a backyard in the bayou or barrio. But a cozy theater was still a fine place to celebrate the last 50 years of Chris Strachwitz's life.

Mr. Strachwitz is the founder of Arhoolie Records, a little label in El Cerrito, just north of Berkeley, dedicated to America's roots: blues, bluegrass, Mexican, Tex-Mex, country, Cajun, zydeco, Hawaiian, gospel. If it was homegrown and honest, Mr. Strachwitz found it, captured it and shared it.

Mr. Strachwitz, 79, left Germany at 13 and has been discovering America ever since. Arhoolie's 50th anniversary celebration this month went three nights, each one a tribute to his life's work, but also to the geniuses who made America an immigration nation.

The lineup told the story:

There was a Mexican-American from San Antonio, singing in Spanish with a squeezebox, an instrument brought by Germans and Poles to the Rio Grande borderlands and adapted by Mexicans there with wild abandon. And a white guitarist from Santa Monica who grew up idolizing old black bluesmen, playing a song about bagels, and also "Wooly Bully," accompanied by a thumping sousaphone and young Mexican-American women stomping out the beat on a wooden box.

A Mexican-roots band played in the son jarocho style, to the clacking rhythm of a quijada, a donkey's jawbone. A bluegrass musician channeled Bill Monroe. A Cajun guitarist did a riff on Hawaiian slack-key. An all-women's string band led the folkie-dokie singalong "Goodnight Irene," and ended everything with "I Bid You Goodnight," a lullaby from the guitarist Joseph Spence, of the Bahamas.

That was just the first night. Still to come were the jazz combo, the New Orleans brass band, the blues chanteuse and the long unanticipated reunion of The Goodtime Washboard 3.

Each night had a melancholy undercurrent. Roots music, uprooted, loses its essence. American regionalism has died out as strip malls have buried farms, ranches and dance halls. The fear that the people's music is doomed to end life as a PBS special looped over and over, was the joke behind "A Mighty Wind"—a good one, because it's mostly true.

But not completely. Barbara Dane, a Bay Area blues singer since the early '60s, still has pipes of polished brass. Ry Cooder sang a new song about evil bankers and combined two old ones—"Vigilante Man" by Woody Guthrie and "Across the Borderline"—adding spy planes and Dodge Ram trucks, for a fresh commentary on today's immigration lunacy.

Mr. Strachwitz, who was due for hip replacement the minute the anniversary folderol was over, beamed from the edge of the stage, dancing, waving his cane and giving out hugs. He doesn't record anymore, but he's busy: he has the largest collection of Mexican-American border recordings anywhere, and is digitizing them all. The concerts were a fund-raiser to finish the project.

And there's still tomorrow to look to, thanks, as always, to new immigrants. It was the Mexicans—the people of the future, Mr. Cooder calls them—who supplied the most potent doses of immediacy and urgency. The youngest act by decades, Los Cenzontles, is based in an arts center in a strip mall in San Pablo, a gritty Bay Area town troubled by gangs and poverty but also energized by newcomers: Filipinos, Southeast Asians, Chinese.

The group's founder, Eugene Rodriguez, invited the audience to come up from Berkeley to visit, to discover an America still being reborn.

"Rockabilly Queen Prolongs Her Party," Melena Ryzik, *The New York Times*, January 21, 2011:

The crowd was rockabilly through and through: girls in pegged jeans and crimson lipstick, boys in flattops and pompadours, shrunken leather jackets. When Wanda Jackson, 73, took the stage with her guitar for a sold-out show at the Knitting Factory in Brooklyn recently, it was all cat growls, howls and hip swivels—and that was from Ms. Jackson herself. The audience followed suit, with a chorus of fans joining in on her song "I Gotta Know." She first recorded it in 1956, not long after she met and began dating Elvis Presley.

"Now girls, don't get ahead of me here," Ms. Jackson said, telling the story from the stage as the crowd hooted. "It was 1955. My daddy traveled with me and kept my reputation intact."

Elvis, though, changed her life. In 1958 Ms. Jackson recorded "Let's Have a Party," which he originally performed (as "Party" in the 1957 movie *Lovin' You*). Released as a single two years later, her version became a hit on the pop charts—cementing her place in music history as the first woman to record a rock song. In the years since, she has swung from rock to country to gospel, earning a cult following as the Queen of Rockabilly. Now, like Johnny Cash, Loretta Lynn and Mavis Staples before her, she is the latest veteran artist to work with a devoted younger producer, in the hopes of a third-act career shift.

On Tuesday, Third Man and Nonesuch Records will release "The Party Ain't Over," Ms. Jackson's first studio album in eight years and the first produced by a paragon of contemporary rock: Jack White. The collaboration, with Mr. White playing guitar, is largely retro, a collection of covers recorded live with a 12-piece band. But everyone involved hopes it will introduce Ms. Jackson to a new audience, affording her a level of attention that's closer to her more famous contemporaries like Buddy Holly, Jerry Lee Lewis, Carl Perkins and Johnny Cash, all of whom she performed with. "She's influential to every modern female singer, whether they know about her or not," Mr. White said. "She broke down those walls in the beginning, when it was the hardest to do."

Since she was discovered at 15 in Oklahoma City, Ms. Jackson's career has been etched by men: Hank Thompson, the country star who got her signed after hearing her on local radio; Elvis, who encouraged her to wield her singular voice—a graveled purr—in rock instead of country; Wendell Goodman, her husband of 50 years, her tour manager and constant companion; and now Mr. White. But through it all she has become a shimmying emblem of female independence in a male-dominated industry, testing boundaries with her forward style and lyrics about mean men and hard-headed women (and those are the love songs). As she allowed, winkingly, at the Knitting Factory show, "No wonder I have a bad-girl reputation."

Terry Stewart, the president and chief executive of the Rock and Roll Hall of Fame, said, "She's still working sort of a wildcat sound, and she had it as a young lady, which was pretty much unheard of at the time." Vouched for by the likes of Elvis Costello and Bruce Springsteen, Ms. Jackson was inducted in 2009 as an early influencer, and she will be a spokeswoman for the museum's "Women in Rock" exhibition, opening in May. And she continues to tour, as many as 120 dates a year in the United States and abroad. (Mr. White will join her for a few concerts this year; she plays the Bowery Ballroom in New York on Feb. 24.) "They all point to her as the source of the Nile on this stuff," Mr. Stewart said of early rock fans."

For Ms. Jackson, the album with Mr. White is the latest surprise in a career full of them. "You can't hardly name anything that I haven't experienced somewhere along the way," she said in a recent interview in a quiet Midtown hotel. Her husband sat nearby, typing on a computer, pausing to offer a cough drop. Ms. Jackson wore gray slacks, a gray cardigan, and a gray sequined top—she favors sparkly—and her blue eyes were sharp. "I always liked fishnets," she said, complimenting a reporter's. Her taste can be grandma-sweet, too; she called Mr. White "so cute."

"He's not one of these sloppy dressers," she explained. "I said, I'd like to just take you home, Jack, and set you up on the mantel on my fireplace and just get to see you when I walk by."

She knew his name mostly from a 2004 record he produced for Ms. Lynn, *Van Lear Rose*, which was well received and earned two Grammys. But she was not a fan of the White Stripes. "I told Jack, too, I love him, but that type of music, I just don't relate to it," Ms. Jackson said. "It kind of goes over my head."

Initially, Ms. Jackson and her husband hoped to make a Sinatra-and-friends-style duet record. "I think those kind of albums should be made illegal, they are such a bad idea," Mr. White wrote in an e-mail. Instead, he preferred to get Ms. Jackson in the studio at his home in Nashville, recording an album of her own.

She was reluctant at first. "I was nervous about it because I didn't know what he was going to expect," she said. And she worried that her rockabilly fans would rebel at more contemporary stuff. "Wendell kind of had to drag me into the studio kicking and screaming," she added.

Mr. White, who first heard "Let's Have a Party" as a teenager in a cover by the 5678s, an all-girl Japanese garage-rock group, put her at ease quickly, helped by the familiar songs he selected: the Andrews Sisters' "Rum and Coca-Cola," Bob Dylan's "Thunder on the Mountain" and the country staple "Dust on the Bible." Ms. Jackson suggested an Elvis tune, "Like a Baby," and they both loved "Teach Me Tonight," recorded by the Cuban-born De Castro Sisters.

One song that Mr. White offered made his singer balk—Amy Winehouse's "You Know That I'm No Good." Some of the raunchy lyrics were too much for Ms. Jackson, a born-again Christian since 1971. So Mr. White rewrote them. "He sang in my headphones with me to teach me the melody," Ms. Jackson said, "and then once I got it I said, 'Oh yeah, this is a great song.'"

But he was a demanding producer. "I'm not really used to that," she said.

In the studio, Ms. Jackson likened his approach to a "velvet brick," which he said was one of the best compliments he's ever received. ("It's got me wondering about coating my tombstone in red velvet flocking," Mr. White said. "I'm looking into that.")

They played with the song selection to achieve the right mix of inspiration and believability. "Making an album of rockabilly covers would've been too easy and boring," he said. "The idea was this woman has an attitude in her that can work in calypso, funk and yodeling, just like it can in rockabilly. Wanda and I wanted to get someplace further out there and see what she could pull off at this stage in her career."

2011 NEWS FEATURE

"Me and Brian McGee, Leaving His Roots Behind," Robin Tolleson, *Bold Life*, August 2011:

"Any farewell show feels a little bittersweet. I've been through two or three of those," says Brian McGee. McGee has lived in North Carolina for the last decade, establishing himself in the local singer/songwriter scene and releasing two albums, including last year's *The Taking or the Leaving*.

McGee and his wife are moving to New Jersey on August 21, the day after the singer performs a farewell show at The Grey Eagle in Nashville. She will be attending graduate school at Rutgers, he will be reuniting with his punk rock group Plow United to headline the Riot Fest East in Philadelphia on September 24.

"I'm looking forward to the change," he says. "I've been in North Carolina for 11 years, it's been great. I think I'm ready for something else, something new, something to take me out of my comfort zone and shake things up a little bit."

McGee, like fellow singer Pierce Edens, was influenced strongly by Nirvana and the Seattle grunge scene. "From playing in punk bands, I definitely was not the quintessential, clean country bluegrass singer or writer. So I have naturally more not-so-smooth edges. I think of Pierce kind of the same way. He definitely has that guttural, grungy kind of thing."

McGee's first album, *Brian McGee & The Hollow Speed*, reflects the strong interest he had in old-time country music. "I wanted my songs to have that flavor, with banjos and fiddles on them."

His new album, *The Taking or the Leaving*, is a point of departure from that roots music sound. "I walked away from that because, to be honest, I don't think clean Americana stuff is where I thrive.

"I came from loud punk rock, so playing rock 'n' roll with electric guitars is much more natural to me, and a lot of that comes through," he says. "I was listening to the Rolling Stones and the Replacements, which I've always loved. It was more where my writing was going, to a rock 'n' roll vibe."

McGee feels he learned how to sing while living in Asheville. "To be honest, a lot of what I did in Plow United was yelling. I did what I needed to for those tunes, and that's just what I learned first. When I lived in Pennsylvania I was getting into folk music, Woody Guthrie and Bob Dylan. It took a long time to wrestle my voice into being confident with singing instead of yelling. Through going to see old-time bands and country bands and rock 'n' roll bands around Asheville, I feel like I've really learned to sing.

"I got a big lesson in the traditional music of the area, and learned to appreciate and respect it and see where it came from and who's taking the traditions and building off of them. It was definitely a huge lesson in American roots music."

The *Taking or the Leaving* was recorded over three days at the Echo Mountain Studios in Asheville. "It was intense. We worked nonstop for 12 to 14 hours a day. It was a much more live record than going into the studio and experimenting. Pete James (The Honeycutters) and I did a lot of preproduction, deciding what songs would be picked, and what overdubs, like keys or pedal steel to use. We did a lot of the figuring before we set foot in the studio.

"The album shows a real growth in playing. I was playing with those guys for a couple of years, so it shows a tighter group, and that's one growing part of it. Another part is, I think the songs are stronger. I feel a lot more confident about the writing. Between the two records I played a lot of shows, a lot of guitar, and that comes through on the record as well."

Sources

We thank the following publications for permission to use material
that appears throughout this volume.

Bold Life, 489
Columbus Daily Telegraph, 320
DownBeat Magazine, 268
Frederick Post (Maryland), 242
Hit Parader, 295, 321
Kerrville Daily Times (Texas), 448
Long Beach Independent, 259, 279
Lubbock Evening Journal, 400
Muscatine Journal and News-Tribune, (Iowa), 231
New York Magazine, 412
Oakland Tribune, 244, 268
Oelwein Daily Register (Iowa), 269
Orlando Sentinel, 476
Portsmouth Times (Ohio), 243
Reminisce, 221
Rock Hill Evening Herald, 317
Rolling Stone, 365, 370, 410-411
Santa Fe New Mexican, 369, 388
Syracuse Herald American, 439
Syracuse Herald Journal, 438
The New York Times,
319, 377, 407, 424-426, 435, 450, 464, 466, 477, 485-486
The Sunday Times, (London, U.K), 355
The Syracuse Post-Standard, 447
The Tulane Hullabaloo, 338
Time, 343
Winnipeg Free Press, 368

INDEX

A

Italic page numbers indicate images. **Bold** page numbers indicate profile subjects

---

Italic page numbers indicate images. **Bold** page numbers indicate profile subjects

Bell, Maggie, 349
Bellamy, Edward, 11
Belushi, John, 384
Ben-Hur, 277
Benny, Jack, 239
Benny Goodman Orchestra broadcasts, 301
"Beri-Beri," 22
Berkeley Barb, 337, 339
Berkeley Tribe, masthead, 336
Berklee College of Music, 228
Berlin, Irving, 110, 142, 188, 256
Berlin Hopfer, 96
Berliner, Emile, 126
Berlioz, Hector, 111
Bernstein, Artie, 215
Bernstein, Leonard, 252–253, 282
Berry, Bill, 433
Berry, Chuck, 401
Beruit, Lebanon, U. S. troops bombed in, 396
"Best Things In Life Are Free, The," 145
Beveridge, Albert J., 73
Beyoncé, 461, 474, 478
Biblical allusions, 85
bicycle costume (prices), 9
bicycles
    developments in, 8
    racing, 29
Bierce, Ambrose, 8
Big Band blues, 292
Big Band era, 187, 203, 263–264, 272
Big Band jazz, 301
Big Bang theory, 240
Big Brother and the Holding Company, 331, 345
Bill Moss & The Celestials, 395
Billboard magazine, 216, 237, 293, 318, 345, 381, 430, 445, 461
"Billie Jean," 396
bin Laden, Osama, 483
Binet, Alfred, 58
Bingenheimer, Rodney, 350
Biograph Theater, 178
Biological Weapons Convention, 333
birds, regulating shooting of migratory, 89
birth control controversy, 314
Birth of Cool, The, 261, 264
Bissell Carpet Sweeper (advertisement), 73
Bizet, Georges, 98
Black, Bill, 292
Black, Harold Stephen, 145
Black Caesar, 417
Black churches, 85–87

black colleges, in Nashville, 275
black Gospel music, 292
Black Panther Party, 302
Black Power salute, 314
Black September, 333
Black Swan Records, 140
BlackBerry (advertisement), 462
Blacks, ability to vote, 56
Blake, Eubie, 141
Blaze magazine (cover art), 428
BLIMPIE restaurants, 293
Block, Martin, **235–238**
Blonde on Blonde, 302, 310
Blood, Sweat, and Tears, 429
blood transfusion, first successful, 100
Blue Amberol Record, 126
Blue Note, The Album Cover Art, 308
Blue Note look, 300
Blue Note Records, 299
    history of, 304
Blue Ridge Mountain Grass, 432
blues, classic, 292
Blues Brothers, The, 384
Bluford, Guion S., 396
Boehm, Theobald, 32
Boeing, William, 100
Boggs, Moran Lee "Dock," **155–159**
bohemians, 331
Bold Life, 489
Boleyn, Anne, 22
Bollingen Prize, 240
Bon Jovi, 461
Bond, The, 174
Bonnaroo Music Festival, 461
boo-boo-booing (singing style), 176
boogie-woogie, 202
Boogie Woogie Red, 395
Booker T and the MGs, 287, 292
"Boomers" (Oklahoma pioneers), 216
Bootsy Rubber Band, 393
"bop" (musical style), 216
Borden's Cheddar Cheese (advertisement), 278
Bordoni, Irene, 142
Borg, Björn, 396
Borowitz, Marshall, **309–312**
Borsch Capades, 252
Bosnian War, 433
Boston, Massachusetts, 18–19
    the Athens of America, 15
    immigration into, 19
Boston Common, 18
Boston Daily Globe, The, 64

Boston Gazette, 15
Boston Latin School, 18
Boston Marathon, 58, 72, 333
Boston Massacre, 18
Boston Music Hall program, 16
Boston Red Sox, 112
Boston Sunday Globe, The, 52
Boston Symphony Hall, 19
Boston Symphony Orchestra, 15, 17, 66, 112, 444
Boston Tea Party, 18
Bourbon Street, 57
Bowly, Al, 175
Boy Scouts of America, 100
Boyer, Herbert, 333
Bradham, Caleb, 20
Bradley, Owen, 276
Bragg, Johnny, **271–275**
Branch Davidian compound, raided in Waco, Texas, 422
Brand Nubian, 419
brass bands, 56
Braun, Eva, 228
"Brave Little Japs, Many of Those Who Come to New York Are Bitterly Poor," 52
"Bread is the Staff of Life" (postcard), 128
Brearley, Harry, 89
Breaux, Zelia, 213
brewery business, 7
Brice, Fanny, 255
"Bride of the Waves" (Clarke), 28
Bridge on the River Kwai, The, 257
Bridges, Henry, 217
Brigadoon, 302
Briggs' Mentholated Hoarhound Cough Drops (advertisement), 101
"British Invasion," 293
British rule, in India, 204
Broadcast Music Inc. (BMI), 237, 274
Broadway-style music, 188, 265
Broadway theater, 99, 141–142, 161, 228, 240, 252
    Golden Age of, 256
Brody, Adrien, 473
bromine, electrolytic production of, 8
Bronx Opera, 403
Bronx Zoo, 29
Brooklyn Dodgers, move to Los Angeles, 257
Brooklyn Eagle, 17
Brooklyn Public Library, 58
Brown, Bobby, 422
Brown, James, 144, 312, 392–393

D

Italic page numbers indicate images. **Bold** page numbers indicate profile subjects

H

Italic page numbers indicate images. **Bold** page numbers indicate profile subjects

Italic page numbers indicate images. **Bold** page numbers indicate profile subjects

Italic page numbers indicate images. **Bold** page numbers indicate profile subjects

Italic page numbers indicate images. **Bold** page numbers indicate profile subjects

Italic page numbers indicate images. **Bold** page numbers indicate profile subjects

Italic page numbers indicate images. **Bold** page numbers indicate profile subjects

Italic page numbers indicate images. **Bold** page numbers indicate profile subjects

Italic page numbers indicate images. **Bold** page numbers indicate profile subjects

Italic page numbers indicate images. **Bold** page numbers indicate profile subjects

Italic page numbers indicate images. **Bold** page numbers indicate profile subjects

Italic page numbers indicate images. **Bold** page numbers indicate profile subjects

Italic page numbers indicate images. **Bold** page numbers indicate profile subjects

Italic page numbers indicate images. **Bold** page numbers indicate profile subjects